PLAY:
DRAMATURGIES OF PARTICIPATION

JENN STEPHENSON AND MARIAH HORNER

ILLUSTRATIONS BY JEFF McGILTON

PLAYWRIGHTS CANADA PRESS
TORONTO

PLAY: *Dramaturgies of Participation* © 2024 by Jenn Stephenson and Mariah Horner
Illustrations © 2024 by Jeff McGilton
First edition: June 2024
Printed and bound in Canada by Imprimerie Gauvin, Gatineau

Jacket design by Jeff McGilton
Author photos © Cameron Nelles

Playwrights Canada Press
202-269 Richmond St. w., Toronto, ON M5V 1X1
416.703.0013 | info@playwrightscanada.com | www.playwrightscanada.com

LIBRARY AND ARCHIVES CANADA CATALOGUING IN PUBLICATION
Title: Play : dramaturgies of participation / Jenn Stephenson and Mariah Horner ;
    illustrations by Jeff McGilton.
Names: Stephenson, Jenn, 1971- author. | Horner, Mariah, author. | McGilton, Jeff, illustrator.
Description: First edition. | Includes bibliographical references and index.
Identifiers: Canadiana (print) 20240375211 | Canadiana (ebook) 20240376439
  | ISBN 9780369105042 (softcover) | ISBN 9780369105066 (EPUB) | ISBN 9780369105059 (PDF)
Subjects: LCSH: Participatory theater—History and criticism.
  | LCSH: Participatory theater—Social aspects. | LCSH: Theater audiences. | LCGFT: Essays.
Classification: LCC PN2049 .S84 2024 | DDC 792—dc23

Playwrights Canada Press staff work across Turtle Island, on Treaty 7, Treaty 13, and Treaty
20 territories, which are the current and ancestral homes of the Anishinaabe Nations (Ojibwe
/ Chippewa, Odawa, Potawatomi, Algonquin, Saulteaux, Nipissing, and Mississauga / Michi
Saagiig), the Blackfoot Confederacy (Kainai, Piikani, and Siksika), néhiyaw, Sioux, Stoney
Nakoda, Tsuut'ina, Wendat, and members of the Haudenosaunee Confederacy (Mohawk,
Oneida, Onondaga, Cayuga, Seneca, and Tuscarora), as well as Métis and Inuit peoples. It
always was and always will be Indigenous land.

We acknowledge the financial support of the Canada Council for the Arts, the Ontario Arts
Council (OAC), Ontario Creates, the Government of Ontario, and the Government of Canada
for our publishing activities.

ACKNOWLEDGEMENTS

First, gratitude beyond words goes to all the artist-creators who so generously (and bravely) shared their time with us. The relationship between artists and those of us who write about the art can sometimes be fraught. There is a lot of vulnerability needed to have these conversations and allow scholars like us to poke our curious fingers into the work. Artist-creators met with us in person over coffee and avocado toast (You know who you are!) and they talked to us while they reset for the next show. They allowed us to peek backstage and they allowed us to play again. So many Zoom calls! Often we began as perfect strangers. (Speaking of vulnerable and generous, I interviewed Shira Leuchter, creator of *Lost Together*, whom I had never met before, in her living room while she nursed her new baby daughter.) The artists shared with us their unpublished scripts and their private archival videos. (Alex McLean unlocked *The Archive of Missing Things* just for us, so we could explore at our leisure.) We often had the privilege of seeing a show in several developmental iterations and were invited to be beta testers. (The second time I saw *Foreign Radical* I was coached by Tim Carlson on what to say so that I would be diverted into a new and different track of the show.) We are incredibly appreciative because without this kind of access, we could not begin to think these thoughts, and this book could not exist. A full list of names would stretch to several pages. You will find these artists in the Selected Production Index at the back of the book.

It would be impossible to write a book about participation without ourselves being participators. And so we saw and did lots and lots of participatory theatre things. But we are only two people and Vancouver is very far away from Kingston. Another debt of gratitude goes to our surrogate audience members, who went to see shows that we couldn't and reported back to us what they saw. At several points in the book, our documented observations are in fact theirs. Thank you to Hannah Komlodi, Salen Currie, Maddie Scovil, Ashley Williamson, Lisa Aikman, Charlotte Dorey, and Derek Manderson who were our eyes, and ears, and hands, and feet.

This project also benefited from having a team of co-thinkers. Supported by Queen's University, we were able to hire a rotating series of research assistants. While developing and pursuing their own related research questions, they participated in shows, gathered production

ACKNOWLEDGEMENTS

histories, wrote summaries, checked quotations for errors, and managed our filing systems. They helped to organize the Dramaturgies of Participation online summit in April 2022 and edited archival video from those panel discussions. This group is also responsible for the creation and maintenance of our online gallery of contemporary Canadian participatory performances, which now extends to more than one hundred examples. They are Derek Manderson, Jacob Pittini, Dylan Chenier, Hailey Scott, Charlotte Dorey, Christina Naumovski, Hamish Hutchison-Poyntz, Mary Tooley, and Benjamin Ma. Each one who began with us as an undergraduate student has gone on to further research and graduate studies. The future is bright! Thank you very much for your energy, your commitment, and your curiosity.

Another group of co-thinkers are our academic colleagues. Thank you to Stephanie Lind, Grahame Renyk, Colleen Renihan, Margaret Walker, and Kelsey Jacobson for all the hallway conversations. Thank you to them for the times that they popped into the office and allowed us to regale them with a tour of the giant bulletin board of myriad Post-it Notes that constituted the map of the book in progress. Thank you to them also for their questions and insights. Kelsey also deserves an extra shout out as the organizer and host of the DAN School "snack writing group." The meetings of this group of drama and music colleagues have been an oasis of silent sociability as we wrote separately together. Another person who dropped in and stayed to chat was Barbara Crow who helped us to see an important angle from a non-expert perspective. And we now refer to a certain kind of participatory dramaturgy as "another Barbara example!" Marlis Schweitzer was a reader of some early draft material and was the one who pointed out that probably the book would benefit from some kind of introduction; we think the idea for a pre-show email is hers. Likewise, she also was inescapably immersed in the book during our wrapping-this-up writing retreat and suggested that a concluding entry was also in order. Blake Sproule acted as our "book dramaturge" and helped us to understand how all the separate pieces worked together as a whole. He encouraged us to be bold and explore the book's interactive potential. Signy Lynch offered invaluable insights in the last leg of the writing process. Her rigorous reading made this a better book. Many, many thanks to you all for your provocations and reassurances, for your intellectual support and encouragement.

Jeff McGilton is the creative genius behind the illustrations and puzzle games throughout. He embraced the challenge to make a book about audience participation truly participatory, and we are endlessly grateful. (Also we could never have done this on our own in a zillion years.) It was Annie Gibson at Playwrights Canada Press who green-lit this book and slotted it into her publishing schedule on the very scantest proposal and gifted us with her confidence that it would all work out in the end. In additional to being our book dramaturge, Blake Sproule kept us on track. He struck a balance between correcting all our errors of spelling and style while at the same time being totally on board as we coined new words and usages. Many thanks to the team at Playwrights Canada!

Mariah says: I am endlessly grateful to my love, Cameron, for participating too, offering many brilliant thoughts on the book as it progressed, and softly encouraging me every step of the way. Jenn says: Thank you to my family—John, Jess, Ben, and Sarah—for your participation in the creation of this book. Your support, whether I was far away travelling or doing weird participatory things in the living room, means a lot to me.

ACKNOWLEDGEMENTS

WRITE YOUR NAME: _____

WRITE YOUR NAME IN FANCY LETTERS: _____

WRITE TODAY'S DATE: _____

HOW TO PARTICIPATE

From: Jenn Stephenson & Mariah Horner <dramaturgiesofparticipation@gmail.com>
Date: Tuesday, May 14, 2024 at 9:25 PM
To: You, the audience-participant-reader <playerone@emailbox.com>
Subject: How to participate

Welcome to PLAY: Dramaturgies of Participation! *Thanks for being here. We're thrilled you're joining us for this interactive adventure. Get ready to become the protagonist of your own narrative. Be bold. Your experience is what you make of it. To ensure the best possible experience, please see below for some important information.*

This book, PLAY: *Dramaturgies of Participation*, collects, describes, and analyzes live performances in which the audience become participants. For work in this genre, the participation of audience-players is absolutely central to the performance such that the performance cannot exist without an active, co-creative audience. Our specific focus is on audience play in a dominantly theatrical context, but we are seeing echoes of this same interactive phenomenon in contemporary culture where passive consumption is being replaced by engaged contribution in everything from escape rooms to crowdsourced recommender apps like Yelp to the popular DIY performance channel TikTok.

What you need: Carry a fully charged cellphone. Wear shoes suitable for walking on uneven terrain or for salsa dancing. Apply insect repellent spray. Ensure a stable Internet connection. Find a private quiet place in your own home. Brew a cup of tea. Bring reading glasses if you need them. Reserve thirty or sixty or ninety minutes of uninterrupted time. Pick your favourite karaoke song. Leave coats and bags at home if possible. Prepare for inclement weather. Headphones are preferred. Sign this waiver. Assemble a team of four. Think about a thing you have lost.[1]

---

[1]   Each of these instructions in the italic sections of this introduction are not things we just made up. These are all actual instructions from actual participatory performances that we have seen and will discuss in the book as case studies.

Why participation now? The contemporary desire for experiences that are "by me," "for me," and "about me" arises out of a confluence of disparate paradigm shifts. First, we might look to the advent of Web 2.0 circa 2004.[2] This is when the Internet becomes interactive, (Facebook was launched in 2004, YouTube in 2005, Twitter in 2006, and Instagram in 2010) hosting for the first time "websites that emphasize user-generated content, ease of use, participatory culture and interoperability." Internet pioneer Tim O'Reilly calls this an "architecture of participation."[3] In his book *The World is Flat*, Thomas L. Friedman identifies "uploading" as one of the key "flatteners." Uploading speaks to how the "newfound power of individuals and communities to send up, out, and around their own products and ideas, often for free, rather than just passively downloading them from commercial enterprises, or traditional hierarchies, is fundamentally reshaping the flow of creativity, innovation, political mobilization, and information gathering and dissemination."[4] The ability to upload gave everyone with Internet access their own printing press and broadcast channel. We all became content creators, while simultaneously becoming the audience for each other's content. And having been introduced to publishing our thoughts and feelings, our art, our music, our photographs, our ideas and innovations, we are not only accustomed to it, but we also expect it in all areas of our lives.

Another (perhaps unexpected) parallel manifestation of the rise of meaningful play is in thinking about geological time. We now live in what has been called the Anthropocene Epoch. This is defined as the era in which humans and our society are the dominant geophysical force impacting our planet, impacting the Earth's systems more than all other natural processes combined. Nobel Laureate Paul J. Crutzen, who popularized the term starting around 2000, locates the boundary of the Anthropocene at the end of the eighteenth century with the invention of the steam engine and the exponential increase in atmospheric CO_2 levels. This phenomenon, which recognizes the centrality of human action on the environment on an unprecedented global scale, finds a parallel in artworks that also privilege human agency (specifically that of the audience) on the generation of artistic experience and meaning. We recognize that our actions (and inactions) have consequences, in

---

2   "Web 2.0," *Wikipedia*, en.wikipedia.org/wiki/Web_2.0.

3   Tim O'Reilly, "What is Web 2.0: Design Patterns and Business Models for the Next Generation of Software," *O'Reilly*, 30 September 2005, oreilly.com/pub/a //web2/archive/what-is-web-20.html.

4   Thomas L. Friedman, *The World is Flat: A Brief History of the Twenty-First Century* (Picador, 2007), 95.

both the realm of the changing climate and in live performance with a porous space between art and audience. Examining participatory art allows us to notice and critique the other ways we are participating in world-building (or world-destroying) on planet Earth.

Arguably, this is the moment when we all become players; the moment when the principal value marker is meaningful impact, when my actions have effects. PLAY: *Dramaturgies of Participation* looks at how theatre-makers are responding to this audience impulse. The first title keyword "play" is central. Drama has long been connected to play. English medieval/Renaissance actors are called players, from the Latin verb "ludo," meaning "to play." Players of plays. Audiences in a conventional bourgeois context, influenced by European tradition, are not players. They are listeners and watchers, but not players. In the context of this book, where audience members become active co-creators, audiences become player-participants. Additionally, the word "play" speaks to another productive perspective for this research, which has been to think of these newly interactive dramas as games. Within game studies, there is a small segment of that discipline where games blend with theatre. Performative play-games include "pervasive games,"[5] Nordic larp (a strongly collaborative style of live-action role-play concentrated in Scandinavia), tabletop role-play games (TTRPG), long-form narrative video games, and "art games."[6] Although PLAY: *Dramaturgies of Participation* draws on game concepts to generate a productive framework for new dramaturgies, we are pulling these terms through the sieve of performance, focusing on how drama is game-like rather than the opposite—how games are dramatic. (This is an important distinction.) Here, audience players are "gamers."

Eric Zimmerman argues that, whereas the primary cultural vehicle of the twentieth century was "moving pictures"—film and television—the twenty-first century will be similarly dominated by video games. Zimmerman names the current era the "Ludic Century," or the Age of Play. In his "Manifesto for a Ludic Century," he writes, "Media and culture in the Ludic Century is increasingly systemic, modular, customizable, and participatory. Games embody all these characteristics in a very direct sense."[7] Play and games are everywhere. We get loyalty points

---

5   Pervasive games are games where the boundaries between fictive and real worlds are intentionally blurred.

6   Artworks, usually found in galleries or visual art exhibits, that take the form of games.

7   Eric Zimmerman, "Manifesto for a Ludic Century," *Kotaku*, 9 September 2013, kotaku.com/manifesto-the-21st-century-will-be-defined-by-games-1275355204.

from retailers, digital confetti for achieving our daily ten thousand steps, app badges for language learning milestones. My email system shows me a colorful hot-air balloon when I reach the so-rare status of "inbox zero." One of the drivers of this ludism is pervasive access to computers, which offer accessible gateways to an unprecedented amount of information, especially personal data. Zimmerman glibly points out that "computers didn't create games; games created computers."[8] Another driver of gamification is the blurring of the boundary between leisure and work, "with your work designed to look more fun, and your entertainment looking more like work."[9] Game structures are not just pleasurable, but they help us to manage a vast flow of information. Through games we can engage emotionally and not just survive but thrive in an increasingly complicated and entangled world. We are inundated by wicked problems that "force us to understand how the parts of a system fit together to create a complex whole with emergent effects. They require playful, innovative, transdisciplinary thinking in which systems can be analyzed, redesigned, and transformed into something new."[10]

The second title keyword is "dramaturgy." When we are talking about dramaturgy we mean play-making techniques. Again, leaning on the Latin etymological root, the stem "-urgy" means work technique. (Think metallurgy.) This is the "how to." The arguments presented here pair dramaturgy with participation in two directions. In one direction, the question "What are the dramaturgies of participation?" means "What are the different techniques of participation?" What are its parameters? How is it engendered, manipulated, or contained. What is the work that we are asked to undertake? How do we understand those expectations? How are audiences kept safe (or not)? How expansive is our capacity for participation in a given context? Are we free (or not)? In the other direction, when we ask, "What are the dramaturgies of participation?" we are asking, "How does participation create meaning?" In the play-game hybrids presented here, participation is more than just a fun gimmick. It is doing something particular. What is that? How does participation mean in relation to a specific performance work? And beyond that, how does participation mean in general as a set of patterns? Are there certain understandings or experiences that lend themselves to participatory engagement?

8   Zimmerman, "Manifesto for a Ludic Century."
9   Miguel Sicart, "How the 21st Century Will be Defined by Games," WIRED Magazine, 2 April 2015, wired.co.uk/article/ludic-century.
10   Zimmerman, "Manifesto for a Ludic Century."

Participatory behaviour is pervasive in all aspects of life. The word "dramaturgy" also serves to keep us grounded in dramatic performance and to establish some boundaries to our investigations. Works examined here all have roots in theatre performance. Some feature actors in character roles. Some feature mimetic fictional worlds. Some are produced by theatre companies and presented in the context of theatre festivals. One critical feature is that the audience begins as audience. The audience-players do not arrive already inside the game. Within the performance, there is a necessary invitation and transition to become a participant. This requirement serves to exclude from our consideration the vast fields of applied theatre and community-engaged performance where amateurs take the stage. Likewise, this also excludes quotidian social participations like playing sports, attending a political demonstration, or flash mobs. These adjacent social phenomena are discussed as fringe examples, but we set them apart from narrowly defined participatory performance. On the other hand, it is not uncommon in our dramatic examples for a basketball game to break out between monologues or for you to be sent on a city-wide scavenger hunt seeking the next scene.

What you do: Place a lemon in an urban laneway. Paddle a canoe with twenty other people to an island where there will be a party. Play basketball. Confess your worries. Confess illegal smuggling or border crossing. Fail to solve the puzzle and die in a German air raid. Play with one thousand dollars cash. Carry a meaningful stone and return it to the land. Dance. Navigate a (virtual) museum maze. Look with purpose. Attend a concert in your imagination. Give a gift to a friend. Celebrate your birthday. Build a barricade and throw bricks at riot police. Sing. Exchange text messages with a stranger on the other side of the country. Be brave. Explore. Make choices.

PLAY: *Dramaturgies of Participation* is arranged as an alphabetical list of keywords. It is inspired by other volumes of keywords, notably Raymond Williams's *Keywords: A Vocabulary of Culture and Society*, Ambrose Bierce's *Devil's Dictionary*, Daniel Sack's edited collection *Imagined Theatres: Writing for a Theoretical Stage*, and John Ralston Saul's *The Doubter's Companion: A Dictionary of Aggressive Common Sense*. Each entry is a self-contained mini-essay tackling a particular key concept or performance event. More extended arguments emerge in aggregate, stitched together in the juxtapositions of clusters of entries. The relatively short entries attempt to capture the contemporary aesthetic of a blog post or an Instagram story; audience-players of participatory theatre tend to skew young, catering more to the bar-hopping concert crowd than typical septuagenarian theatre subscribers. (Jenn says: Apologies for invoking these stereotypes. But I can attest that I am, at fifty, almost invariably the oldest person in attendance at the performances we discuss here. This is not my parents' theatre.) We imagine you the reader as an audience-player, a gamer, an arts student, a participatory theatre-maker, a critical devotee of the genre. Or, all of the above. From those inspirational keyword collections, in addition to borrowing the organizational structure, we also attempted to mimic their brisk style, mixing serious rigorous scholarly analysis with warm personal anecdote, and a healthy measure of sass. Following Bierce's declaration in his Author's Preface, we too hope "to be held guiltless by those to whom the work is addressed—enlightened souls who prefer dry wines to sweet, sense to sentiment, wit to humour and clean English to slang."[11]

Another source of inspiration that informed this book's format is the *Wreck This Journal* phenomenon, created by "guerrilla artist" Keri Smith. If you've never seen one, these are a series of paperback journals that purport to stimulate creativity by offering page-by-page prompts to engage in destructive acts like aesthetically ripping the pages, running the book through the washing machine, taping in family photos and scribbling on them, planting the book in the garden for a few weeks, painting with coffee, and so on. In a very early discussion about this project, participatory theatre-maker Adrienne Wong challenged us to make form match content and to create a participatory artifact. This is easier said than done. (Thanks a lot, Adrienne!) She directed us to *Press Here* by Hervé Tullet, an interactive book for toddlers. The first page displays a large yellow dot with the instruction: Press here and turn the page. The child touches the dot, turns the page, and voila! There are now two yellow dots! Amazing. Another press and another page flip, and the dots change colour, turning red or blue. Tilt the book and they all slide to the edge. To that end, we have partnered with illustrator Jeff McGilton, who has designed a paper-and-pencil "escape room" for this book. Scattered throughout are a series of puzzle activities with clues that accumulate to unlock a final door at the end of the book. There are also meaningful invitations for you to take up if you choose to do so: make a cup of tea, make a paper airplane. Encouraging a reader to actually deface a book is a pretty heavy lift, so you may not get there; but hopefully there is some participatory magic here for you. Our goal is to evoke, in some small way, the phenomenological frisson, that sensory

---

11 Ambrose Bierce, Author's Preface, in *The Devil's Dictionary* (1906), *Wikisource*, en.wikisource.org/wiki/The_Devil%27s_Dictionary.

thrill, activated by the uncertain potential of your personal action, which is common to many of these participatory works.

You could read this book straight through end to end. You can choose your own path. You can open the book and fan all the pages, open to something random and begin in the middle. At multiple points in the book experience, you will be given the choice of which thought to follow. When these points occur, you will see certain words in all caps; these indicate lo-fi hyperlinks. Pick one and flip to that page. Or you could choose a play from the Selected Production Index at the back and track it through the book, reading entries where that play pops up. Or not. If you don't want to jump around, you can simply continue your linear reading. Taking inspiration from Daniel Sack's alphabetical "paper theatre," this book "works in fragments, only suggesting the outline of a shape and leaving the reader to fill out the volume. For the imagination, it flits and falters; it does not finish a form or stick to its intentions; it fragments attention."[12] For the best experience, we recommend using headphones/earbuds and bringing along something to eat.

The working thesis of PLAY is that participation is always about participation. The performance-game hybrids that are collected and parsed here offer perspectives on how we participate in the world. They are rehearsals for "taking part." Some offer commentary on the values that underpin democracy. Some speak to the responsibility we bear when our exercise of agency has moral consequences ranging from complicity with genocide to the causes of climate change. From some other performances we experience the effects of seeing the world afresh through our active engagement in it. Still other performances challenge us to be brave, to confront fear, and to offer and receive care and love. In all these realms, participation changes the stakes. This diversity of applications has led us to also draw on a diversity of theories. We are critical magpies. We range across geography and time, citing thinkers from theories of performance and art-making, game studies, cultural studies, ideas about everyday design and user experience, frameworks for how we process information, and political, economic, ethical, epistemological, and aesthetic theories.

Where: On the day and time indicated on your ticket, travel to Cherry Beach, wait at TTC stop 39872. You will be approached by one of the actors and addressed by name. This is the beginning of your experience. Board the yellow school bus for a short journey to the high school reunion. Board the yellow school bus for a short

---

12   Daniel Sack, "Introduction," in *Imagined Theatres: Writing for a Theoretical Stage* (Routledge, 2017), 1.

journey to the wilderness park site. Meet at the storefront of the former Queen Street Video. Meet at the Harbourfront Canoe and Kayak Centre near Queen's Quay. Meet on the steps of Mackintosh-Corry Hall on Queen's University campus. Meet at a secret location to be revealed on the morning of the performance. Here is a link to the Zoom; please ensure you're muted. Have your phone with you and expect a call. Climb into your bathtub and bring a cup of tea.

All of the shows that are included in the *Dramaturgies of Participation* project are from the geographical zone so-called Canada, witnessed in festivals or created by artists who call this land home. Because participatory work involves an extremely intimate relationship between audience and artists, (Think: "I guess you had to be there.") the scope of this book is intensely local. We write about things that we could actually see (and do). Even though Canada is a very large country, the theatrical ecology tends to flow north, east, and west within those borders. We saw artists from Montréal in Banff, artists from Calgary in Kingston, and artists from Ottawa in Whitehorse. The pandemic, of course, pushed performance into virtual non-locations. For a time, it was nothing to attend a Vancouver theatre festival, thousands of kilometres away, for the afternoon. In those cases, however, you needed to carefully mind the time zones. (I am still grumpy about the show I missed at 4:30 a.m.)

In addition to national geography as a shaping influence, this corpus of shows featured in PLAY: *Dramaturgies of Participation* mostly took place in purpose-built theatres or were programmed as part of theatre festivals. Not exclusively, but mostly. This physical context instigated fruitful tensions between traditional playgoing attitudes and the participatory beckoning of the works. Finally, thinking about space and where we are embodied, it is worth noting that sometimes, we sent two or three members of our research team to see the same shows, recognizing that each participatory performance is entirely unique to the position and engagement of the participant.

When: The actors will ring your doorbell at the appointed time. Show time is 8 p.m. EST/GMT -5. We encourage you to log in with this link fifteen minutes before show time. Be prepared to answer your phone when it rings at noon each day next week. At midnight, text "I want to escape" to the number below. When you receive your package in the mail, don't open or unwrap it until instructed to do so. Double-check your time zone. You have sixty minutes to solve the clues and unlock the door. This play is a twenty-one day guided journey through the afterlife. You have an hour and a half to successfully design a utopia.

The particular participatory era under consideration here begins in Canada around ten years ago, give or take. The three main drivers of contemporary participation—the democratic flattener of socialized media, the intensification of mainstream awareness of climate change as a crisis, and the playful gamification of everything—locate this phenomenon in the second decade of the twenty-first century. Most of the shows featured here date from 2016 or later. The marker of the COVID-19 pandemic and its profound social effects crystallize this work even more narrowly. The pandemic and the resulting cancellation of live art events put a sudden halt in March 2020 to the creation of participatory theatre in its then dominant in-person mode. In addition, these same novel conditions have been significant to this project in two ways. First, the same artists who were focused on creating participatory work sprang to the forefront of embracing new ways of bringing audiences together, innovating alternate dramaturgies of participation that foster meaningful connection and engender proximity in a time marked by isolation and distance. After all, distance is just another kind of proximity. Second, social distancing spawned an unprecedented outpouring of spontaneous acts of collective participation that are both global and local, from balcony choirs to courtyard bingo to honking and clapping at set times of day in support of healthcare workers. By staying at home and performing rituals of social distancing, more than a billion people engaged in acts of self-conscious participation on an immense scale. PLAY: *Dramaturgies of Participation* eagerly embraces participatory performance in the time of the pandemic, in the time "before," and anticipates what is to come.

After unpacking the why, what, where, and when of this book, perhaps we should say something about the who. This book has two principal authors, Mariah Horner and Jenn Stephenson. Jenn and Mariah met on the first day of class in September 2011. We have been talking about theatre together pretty much non-stop ever since. Our distinct perspectives are marked by a two-decade difference in our ages. An artist and an emerging academic, Mariah (or Mo) is a white and able-bodied queer woman who grew up middle class in the Greater Toronto Area. I was introduced to radical change by grassroots artists and activists in Kingston during the pandemic and, while co-writing this book, I've been working on a Ph.D. dissertation about abolitionist dramaturgies, analyzing how theatre can help us materialize a world that doesn't rely on carceral logic to address harm. Jenn is a middle-aged person with pale skin and frizzy hair. She is the author of two books and the mother of three almost-adult children. I am a full-time academic and the child of immigrant parents who attained university degrees. I try to be aware of my privileged position. I am a worrier by nature. I have never been a performer and paradoxically, given the focus of this book, am terrified of being asked to participate. Out of these self-descriptions, it should be noted that we are only two people, and we do not contain multitudes. Our impressions are necessarily limited by our identity positions, our life experiences, and all the other things that make us unique humans.

Positionality has a unique effect on participation broadly. For participating audiences, the personal is inescapable. Many participatory performances are physically inaccessible. Who we are greatly affects how we participate and we acknowledge the limitations that may accompany our positionalities in the participatory context. In the introduction to her book, *Theatre of Good Intentions: Challenges and Hopes for Theatre and Social Change*, Dani Snyder-Young brilliantly addresses positionality and its relationship to research in a section she titles "Limitations." "I am far from neutral," she says. Us too. We've never thrown bricks at police, never been under surveillance by our own government, never had a Turkish coffee in Sarajevo, or never experienced the grief of losing a parent. The book has an "I" voice, which could be that of either Mariah or Jenn or occasionally neither one in particular. Because participation is intensely personal, we recognize our need to speak through lived experience while also noticing patterns and making wider dramaturgical observations. We deliberately decided not to overtly flag which of us is the author of each entry. But likewise, we have not attempted to efface our own distinct voices. Often the work is dialogic as we record our conversations, our disagreements, and our individual participatory experiences.

This is perhaps assumed but in order to write about participation we needed to participate. We are the audience-player-participants of the performances described here. We have walked (and walked) and danced and eaten food and told secrets and solved puzzles and read aloud and played blindfolded hide-and-seek and walked on beaches in the dark and gazed at the clouds and and and and . . . But we also must confess that we ourselves didn't do all of the things. Canada is a big country and life is a busy life and so we often invited what we call "surrogate audience-players" to attend performances on our behalf and then report back to us what they had experienced. Another part of our methodology also featured a kind of multiplicity. Because participation is so personal and asymmetrical, it was useful to collect a set of perspectives and so, on occasion, we participated as groups or went separately to different iterations of the same show. Beyond Jenn and Mariah, this group of dedicated participators includes our rotating research team of Derek Manderson, Jacob Pittini, Hailey Scott, Hamish Hutchison-Poyntz, Mary Tooley, and Charlotte Dorey. Thanks to this group for their bravery and generosity.

Informed consent: I have read and understand the information regarding this event and understand that I participate in this event at my own risk. I hereby attest and verify that my physical condition will allow me to participate in this event. I agree to comply with the rules and directions of event officials and their personnel. You may stop participating at any time. You may decline to answer questions or take directives. If you feel the need to pause the experience and step away, you can find a safe space in our quiet room.

"The pace of this piece is slow and steady—don't panic if things unfold slowly. You're right where you should be." (*Good Things To Do*)

Sincerely,
Mariah and Jenn

P.S. *If you experience technical difficulties during the performance, let us know and we will gladly rebook you for another performance.*

DEAR AUDIENCE-PARTICIPANT-READER,

AS YOU MAKE YOUR WAY THROUGH THIS BOOK, YOU MAY NOTICE SOME UNUSUAL THINGS. IN ADDITION TO ALL THE LEMONS, TRAVELLING SHEEP, AND A CHEESE-SANDWICH-EATING ALIEN, THE TEXT IS FILLED WITH IMAGES, ACTIVITIES, AND PUZZLES. AFTER ALL, WHAT IS A BOOK ON PARTICIPATORY THEATRE WITHOUT A LITTLE PARTICIPATION? WHILE READING, PLEASE FEEL FREE TO FOLLOW A PROMPT, COMPLETE A TASK, COLOUR IN A DOODLE, OR CREATE A DOODLE YOURSELF. WHAT YOU MAKE OF THE BOOK IS UP TO YOU; DON'T BE AFRAID TO PLAY!

THERE ARE SIXTEEN PUZZLES IN THIS BOOK, LEADING TO A FINAL PUZZLE AT THE END. YOU WILL KNOW WHAT YOU'RE SEEING IS A PUZZLE WHEN THIS SYMBOL APPEARS IN THE TOP CORNER. EACH PUZZLE WILL GIVE YOU EITHER A NUMBER OR LETTER ANSWER. KEEP TRACK OF THESE ANSWERS, AS YOU WILL NEED THEM TO SOLVE THE FINAL PUZZLE. IF YOU FIND YOURSELF STUCK, TRY COLLABORATING WITH A FRIEND, SEARCHING THE WEB, OR TAKING A BREAK AND COMING BACK TO IT LATER. IF NONE OF THESE WORK, YOU CAN ALSO OF COURSE CHECK THE ANSWER KEY AT THE BACK OF THE BOOK!

I HOPE THAT THESE ILLUSTRATIONS PROVIDE NEW AVENUES FOR ENGAGEMENT, CREATIVE EXPLORATION, AND INSPIRE A FEW GIGGLES ALONG THE WAY. THE BOOK (OR E-BOOK) THAT YOU NOW HOLD IS YOURS TO EXPLORE.

ENJOY THE JOURNEY!
-JEFF

A AND B

Neither Antonin Artaud nor Bertolt Brecht are advocates for a participatory audience in the way that we are sketching here, where audiences are players, active co-creators of the work, engaged with a responsive and iterative performance. Nevertheless, both writers occupy important territory as theorists of a novel audience, both imagine alternate audience behaviours and audience situations that stand as critique to the typical behaviour and situation of their day. Writing at the mid-twentieth century, some of their ideas tap into some protoparticipatory ideas. They both want the audience to do more or have more done to them.[1] They both then propose new theatrical forms, Theatre of Cruelty and Epic Theatre respectively, that (they imagine) will make those things happen. (I'm now doubting the wisdom of summarizing how the audiences imagined by Artaud and Brecht are pushed out of a perceived passivity, moved to a more central position in relation to the artwork, but are still not quite participatory in 250 words or less, but here goes ...)

Brecht believes the audience of his day to be "a passive (suffering) part of the total work of art." He calls this out, with some colourful posturing, arguing that "witchcraft of this sort must of course be fought against. Whatever is intended to produce hypnosis, is likely to produce sordid intoxication, or creates fog, has got to be given up."[2] To wake the audience from this stupor, Brecht's model of Epic Theatre is positioned in contrast to "dramatic theatre." Epic Theatre is not "epic" in the sense of being gigantic or overwhelming. It is intended as a set of techniques that keep the audience slightly at a perceptual distance so that they retain a critical distance from the narrative. The audience of Epic Theatre is turned from a "spectator into an observer." The work "arouses his capacity for action [and] forces him to take decisions." Significantly in contrast to the participatory audience-player, Brecht's Epic audience engages in this action

---

1   James Frieze, in the first sentence of his 2013 article about participation in Ontroerend Goed's production of *All That is Wrong*, asserts boldly that "the idea that performance should liberate the spectator from a state of inertia informs all radical theatre practice" ("A Game of Two Halves: Participation, Performance and All That is Wrong," *Studies in Theatre and Performance* 33, no. 3 (2013): 321).

2   Bertolt Brecht, "The Modern Theatre is the Epic Theatre," in *Brecht On Theatre: The Development of an Aesthetic*, edited and translated by John Willett (Methuen, 1978), 38.

and takes decisions outside the theatre, after the performance is over. During the performance, the lauded stance of the Epic audience member is studiously detached; they are "made to face something," to "stand outside" and assess with reason rather than feeling. Cultivated distance is for Brecht a key driver in the political awareness of the audience that there is a capacity for change. Social conditions are not unalterable. He sees "man as a process." It is through newly alert studious watching (simulated by deliberate alienation effects) that the audience-observer gains the capacity to become active (but later, afterwards).[3]

Artaud, likewise, depicts audience members as needing to be shaken from a slumbering passivity. He writes, "It is certain that we need above all a theater that wakes us up: nerves and heart."[4] And like Brecht, Artaud locates the source of this laxity in merely watching, he calls the audience "Peeping Toms" and lays blame on "the misdeeds of psychological theater [which has] unaccustomed us to that immediate and violent action which the theater should possess."[5] But whereas Brecht projects the activation of the audience in intense thoughtful and analytical observation, Artaud's Theatre of Cruelty seeks to stimulate the senses, looking for a theatre experience that "inspires us with the fiery magnetism of its images and acts upon us like a spiritual therapeutics whose touch can never be forgotten. Everything that acts is a cruelty. It is upon this idea of extreme action, pushed beyond all limits that theatre must be rebuilt . . . The theater must give us everything that is in crime, love, war, or madness, if it is to recover its necessity."[6] Like Brecht, Artaud's strategy is to effect radical change in theatre praxis in order to move the audience to think and feel differently.

French philosopher Jacques Rancière (whose name begins with neither A nor B) also does not push for audience participation. He does not call for running, dancing, or eating. This is the performance of what he dismissively calls the "hyper-theatre that wants to transform representation into presence and passivity into activity."[7] It is easy to fall in love with participation. There is, out there, a tendency to the apotheosis of the newly activated audience-doer—who runs and dances and eats, who becomes a character, and in generating content for the art, becomes (almost) an

3   Brecht, "Modern Theatre," 37.

4   Antonin Artaud, "The Theatre and Cruelty," in *The Theater and Its Double*, translated by Mary Caroline Richards (Grove, 1958), 84.

5   Artaud, "Theatre and Cruelty," 84.

6   Artaud, "Theatre and Cruelty," 84–85.

7   Jacques Rancière, *The Emancipated Spectator*, translated by Gregory Elliot (Verso, 2009), 22.

artist herself—over the traditional, staid and pallid audience-watcher who sat in silence, immobile in the darkness. Of course, this oppositional pairing is too simplistic. Rancière fiercely, sometimes caustically, defends the essential role of theatre spectatorship, and more than this, redefines that contribution to restore the spectator to her proper place.

In "The Emancipated Spectator," he urges us "to dismiss the fantasies of the word made flesh and the spectator rendered active, to know that words are merely words and spectacles merely spectacles."[8] Rancière's concept of the SPECTATOR as "emancipated" performs a critique of the ostensibly improved and activated audiences of Artaud and Brecht. Whereas Artaud and Brecht perceive the need for immediate radical change in audience behaviour and in the practice of theatre that is being offered to that audience, Rancière questions the foundational assumptions that locate the source of Artaud's and Brecht's disaffection in the audience. Rancière summarizes their argument thusly: "The spectator must be removed from the position of observer calmly examining the spectacle offered to her. She must be dispossessed of this illusory mastery, drawn into the MAGIC CIRCLE of theatrical action where she will exchange the privilege of rational observer for that of being in possession of all her vital energies."[9] He concludes, "Such are the basic attitudes encapsulated in Brecht's epic theatre and Artaud's theatre of cruelty. For one, the spectator must be allowed some distance; for the other he must forego any distance. For one, he must refine his gaze, while for the other, he must abdicate the very position of the viewer."[10] Basically, Rancière says both the theatre and the audience are actually okay. Leave them alone. They are not in need of changing, rather we need to change our value system to recognize that "being a spectator is not some passive condition that we should transform into activity. It is our normal situation . . . We do not have to transform spectators into actors . . . Every spectator is already an actor in her own story."[11] What those audiences are doing (are always already doing) is just fine. Same as they ever were. The audience of BOURGEOIS THEATRE formed in the late-nineteenth century persists.

See INTERPRETATION

---

8   Rancière, *The Emancipated Spectator*, 23.
9   Rancière, *The Emancipated Spectator*, 4.
10   Rancière, *The Emancipated Spectator*, 4–5.
11   Rancière, *The Emancipated Spectator*, 17.

ABYDOS

It is possible that the earliest documented commemorative re-enact-ment "sim" was recorded on a stone stela, or slab, in the first person by Ikhernofret, a senior court official (possibly treasurer) to Senusret III, a king of the Egyptian twelfth dynasty.[1] Known as the Ikhernofret stela, this carved text provides an account of Ikhernofret's participation in what seems to be a dramatic performance of key events in the life of Osiris (or possibly a performed ritual funeral).[2] Theatre history schol-ars sometimes refer to this as the Abydos "Passion Play," making an overt (and chauvinistically Eurocentric) link to parallel popular mythical Christian biblical dramas of medieval Europe.[3] The event seems to have entailed the procession of a barque carrying Osiris along the Nile from the god's temple to the desert site of his tomb and back again.[4] What is riveting about the text of the stela is that, on the one hand, Ikhernofret seems to describe his involvement as an organizer of the performance event: "I caused the lay priests to [know how] to do their duties . . . I superintended the work on the sacred barque. I fashioned [its] chapel. I decked the body of the lord of Abydos with lazuli and malachite, elec-trum, and every costly stone, among the ornaments of the limbs of a god. I dressed the god in his regalia by virtue of my office as master of secret things."[5] On the other hand, he also describes what seem to be mimetic actions in replication of past mythic/historical events, assuming a fictional role: "I acted as 'Son, Whom He Loves,' for Osiris . . . I repelled the foe from the sacred barque. I overthrew the enemies of Osiris . . . I championed Wennofer at 'That Day of the Great Conflict;' I slew all the enemies upon the [flats] of Nedyt."[6] Tantalizingly, still other statements are ambiguous as to their ontology; these actions could be "real-world,"

---

1   "Ikhernofret," *Wikipedia*, en.wikipedia.org/wiki/Ikhernofret.

2   Senusret ruled from 1870 BCE to 1831 BCE (Phillip B. Zarrilli, Bruce McConachie, Gary Jay Williams, and Carol Fisher Sorgenfrei, *Theatre Histories: An Introduction*, 2nd edition (Routledge, 2010), 56).

3   Oscar G. Brockett and Frank J. Hildy, *History of the Theatre*, 8th edition (Allyn and Bacon, 1999), 8–9; Alan Sikes, "Theatre History, Theatrical Mimesis, and the Myth of the Abydos Passion Play," *Theatre History Studies* 34, no. 1 (2015): 3–18.

4   Zarrilli et al., *Theatre Histories*, 57.

5   James Henry Breasted, *Ancient Records of Egypt: Historical Documents*, vol. 1 (U of Chicago P, 1906), 299.

6   Breasted, *Ancient Records of Egypt*, 300.

annually-repeated, ritual tasks for the god as effigy, or representational acts in role, fictionally framed as if this is the first time and the god just now deceased: "I celebrated the 'Great-Going-Forth,' following the god at his going . . . I led the way of the god to his tomb before Peker."[7] In addition to Ikhernofret and other religious leaders, other performers also included thousands of supernumeraries "who constituted the warring factions of Seth and Horus/Osiris."[8]

As defined by Scott Magelssen in his book *Simming: Participatory Performance and the Making of Meaning*, a "sim" is a "simulated, immersive, performative environment."[9] A SIM provides an opportunity to explore alternate scenarios, specifically with an eye to producing understanding of that other situation. It is worth underlining here that sims are things done by participants who occupy a similar status to audience-players. Benefit accrues to them directly as their performative actions stimulate their own experience through the doubled channels of embodiment combined with self-witnessing; they are not a spectacle for others. (see FIRST-PERSON SHOOTER) Simming "promises . . . a different kind of efficacy and social change . . . through affective embodied practice."[10] Magelssen notes with some deprecating humour that he is "by no means the first to suggest that embodiment is a powerful modality for acquiring and producing knowledge."[11] While "sandbox" sims, which activate curiosity in somewhat unstructured environments to investigate future-oriented "what ifs," are fairly common in audience-player performance-game hybrids, historical sims, which combine features of "time-travel" sims with "effigy" sims, are more rare. EMBODIED re-enactment is a staple of educational tourism programs at museums and other historical sites. Outside the institutional context, there are vibrant communities of devoted history buffs who not only enact amateur reanimations but also research and assemble their own costumes and props with obsessive authenticity.[12] Even though these re-enactors

---

7 Breasted, *Ancient Records of Egypt*, 300.

8 Zarrilli et al., *Theatre Histories*, 57.

9 Scott Magelssen, *Simming: Participatory Performance and the Making of Meaning* (U of Michigan P, 2014), 3.

10 Magelssen, *Simming*, 3.

11 Magelssen, *Simming*, 7.

12 Katherine Johnson, "Performing Pasts for Present Purposes: Re-enactment as Embodied, Performative History," *History, Memory, Performance*, edited by David Dean, Yana Meerzon, and Kathryn Prince (Palgrave Macmillan, 2015), 36–52; Ian McCalman and Paul Pickering, editors, *Historical Reenactment: From Realism to the Affective Turn* (Palgrave Macmillan, 2010).

are often strongly resistant to their endeavours being contaminated with theatrical thinking (they are doing history not drama), crossover applications can be fruitful. Originating in Toronto, but touring to the Edinburgh Festival in 2016, *Counting Sheep*, created by Mark and Marichka Marczyk and performed with the "Balkan-Klezmer-Gypsy-Party-Punk-Super band" Lemon Bucket Orkestra, is one such example. In this theatre-embedded sim, audience-participants are invited to collectively re-perform episodes from the pro-EU, anti-government demonstrations that occupied Maidan Square in Kyiv in the winter of 2014. The show fills both of these functions, commemorating those events for the Ukrainian community in diaspora while also serving to inform less knowledgeable non-Ukrainian audience members. (see SHEEP)

Draw Me Close by Jordan Tannahill is also arguably a historical re-enactment sim, but the events contract from the global stage to the living room of Jordan's childhood home. Produced by National Theatre's Immersive Storytelling Studio (London, UK) in conjunction with the National Film Board of Canada, *Draw Me Close* uses virtual reality technology to create the immersive environment. The visual virtual world that is rendered as animated line drawings is augmented with a tactile physical world set, including a working door that opens a window sash that you can raise, and Jordan's mother, performed by an actress in a motion capture suit.[13] "JORDAN *begins to speak in the headphones.* I walk up to the front door / grab the knob, turn it, and walk in. / Go on. / And close the door behind you." And just like that we are in role as five-year-old Jordan. (Like Ikhernofret at Abydos, we are also a beloved son, enacting mourning.)

The title of the work elegantly captures the twined core images of the play—literal drawing and hugging (draw me close to you). In the first episode, Jordan (you) and his (your) mother get down on the floor to draw with markers on a large piece of paper. Distressingly, the markers accidentally bleed through the paper, staining the carpet. Even after frantic cleaning, the colours persist, still visible as a pale remnant. The hug is the same. The mother hugs you, aged five; then twenty years later, absorbing the news of her terminal cancer diagnosis, you hug her. "JORDAN: I held her / I held her that winter / And into that spring / . . . Until, early in the morning in March / just as the last snow was beginning to melt / she disappeared altogether / I swear I could actually

---

13   Watch the trailer at drawmeclo.se/ to get a sense of the animation. This video posted by National Theatre gives a behind-the-scenes perspective showing the VR set up: youtube.com/watch?v=mqCcFRuwRdl.

feel the moment she departed / The moment she left me / The world / The sense memory I have of hugging her is still so strong / it feels sometimes like I've just done it a few seconds ago / As if I could still feel her warmth on my arms." The sensory ghosts of the bright marker colours and the heat of bodily closeness evoke a potent melancholy sketching the fading losses of time.

Jordan says it feels like the hug was just a few seconds ago; and for the audience-participant in the sim it really just was. This is how the formal elements of the embodied sim work to heighten our emotional attunement to this experience. In *Performing Remains*, Rebecca Schneider writes regarding historical re-enactment that "[she is] interested in the attempt to literally touch time through the residue of the gesture or the cross-temporality of the pose."[14] Veiled in the I of VR, we do touch time. The residue of the hug, of a mother's love for her son and a son's love for his mother, is carried into the here and now by the sim. Experienced through my material body, love manifests as I feel the pleasure of its colour and its heat and am saddened by its cooling fade.

---

14   Rebecca Schneider, *Performing Remains: Art and War in Times of Theatrical Reenactment* (Routledge, 2011), 2.

ACTING

When I cross into the fiction to become a character, I am desperate for clues that will help me know who I am. It is the classic actor's nightmare; I am clearly someone in this world, but I've missed all the rehearsals. In this case, for the participatory audience-player, of course, there were no REHEARSALS. I rely on how others address me. Got it. I must be "Jordan" and I'm five years old (*Draw Me Close*), or I'm "Alice" who has fallen down the rabbit hole into Wonderland (*Saving Wonderland*). I rely on my physical environment and props and costumes if provided. I'm on a yellow school bus and this building is a high school, probably I'm a student (*Brantwood*). I rely on what other people say about me or to me to glean my situation. It's my birthday (*To You*). Okay. Or, I'm dead and this is the afterlife (*TBD*). Also okay, I guess. It is a common trope of participatory performance that the nature of my participation is that I become a character (i.e., Jordan, Alice, high school student). Sometimes this character is basically me, but in an alternate context. (Still Jenn but it's my birthday; still Jenn but I'm dead.) To supplement the specific information that I receive about my character, I also depend on more generic "activity" scripts that I transfer from my actual-world experience. For example, I have knowledge of patterns of behaviour that help me to be a five-year-old, Alice in Wonderland, a high school student, or the birthday girl. (see THE MATRIX)

Or then it happens that I am handed an actual script. In addition to being a character, I also become an actor. "Actor" is another layered role or function that I am asked to fulfill. Parallel to the known activity-frame of being Alice, being an actor is also a somewhat familiar frame. With a script in hand, I know what to do. Read. I know to read only my lines (and not the stage directions) and to take turns, waiting for the other actors to read their lines before continuing. I comprehend that my lines are the words spoken by the character whom I am representing. Admittedly, this is a somewhat specialized knowledge in decoding the textual layout and the conventions of reader's theatre. But, for those who do possess this knowledge, scripts are TEACUPS; they have affordances, and we understand what to do from these structures.[1]

---

1   Scripts can also be comfort objects. A script is a document that contains a whole conversation beginning to end. I could read ahead and know what will happen next. Unlike the spontaneous life they seek to replicate, scripts are not "live" and so anxiety

Presented in April and May 2020, *The Corona Variations* by Julie Tepperman (Convergence Theatre) is an eclectic variety show of scenes that come to me by PHONE. Every half-hour my phone rings and a new audio play awaits. One of the six playlets comes with a script and begins with stage direction: *"Your phone rings. You answer it. You are the first person to speak."* I'm holding two pages of sides. My character is "Therapist" and the other character—the voice on the phone—is "Jean." Therapist listens. Therapist asks some gently nudging questions: "Do you live on your own, Jean?" "Do you have anyone checking in on you?" Because I am reading from a script, there is not only no pressure to improvise, but there is also no pressure to think of how to help Jean.[2] The answer is on the page. Speaking the words to Jean feels like an affirmation. I say, "Ninety per cent of the people who call this hotline have expressed similar feelings ... There are people all over the world right now experiencing this 'collective grief.' People everywhere are grappling with some sort of loss—be it the untimely loss of loved ones, or the loss of simple everyday freedoms, the loss of a feeling of safety, the loss of normalcy, and the idea that life as we know it will never again be the same."

I say these words that aren't mine. I kind of say them to myself and in the voicing of the sentences, I get the message. It's a bit like reciting RITUAL passages or prayers. (see CEREMONY) There is also a nice little self-reflexive moment in one of my speeches to Jean where I say, "What I'm trying to say is that these feelings you're experiencing—this amplified sense of not knowing what's going to happen and anticipating the worst—can cause a great deal of anxiety." I'm comforting Jean and I'm comforting myself. For the next few minutes, I've got a script. I do know what's going to happen, it's right here on the page. That said, there is some anxiety. I only have my half of the conversation and I don't know what Jean will say or where this is going overall. There is also some literal performance anxiety as I don't want to stumble over my words. I want to be at minimum an acceptably competent performer. But of course, even though this show has a script, life doesn't.

If we take this idea that audience-participants become actors to its logical extreme, then who needs actors? Without access to actors in

---

about the future might be allayed temporarily. I think it is not coincidental that a show about resilience in the face of uncertainty like *This is the Story of the Child Ruled by Fear* is a cooperative script reading. (see CONSENT)

2   In this relationship between a therapist and a phone-in client, casting me as the therapist puts me in a position of relatively more power to the client. This nicely offsets the opposite power dynamic where the actor portraying the client knows how this scenario ends, but as an untutored new arrival, I do not. (see OPT OUT)

purpose-built theatres during phases of pandemic lockdowns, Sherry J. Yoon and Jay Dodge of Boca del Lupo proposed an innovative live theatre alternative. *Plays2Perform@Home* is a box set of short scripts, commissioned specifically to be read in the company of close friends and loved ones, whoever happens to be in your socially isolated COVID "bubble."[3] Each box arrives in the mail and contains four different scripts; there are matching numbers of copies of each script for the number of characters needed. Requiring between two and four actors, the plays need little else. The setting is wherever you happen to be—around the dining table or a campfire—and the props are whatever easily comes to hand. (see NEGOTIATION)

Digression: There is much hilarity to be found in the specifically "at-home" dramaturgy of using of domestic ad hoc props. *The Impossible* by Joseph Aragon is set in a museum and is a 1930s camp detective noir with an occult twist. Think *Indiana Jones* meets Charles Ludlam's *The Mystery of Irma Vep*. At four or five key points, the script calls for an object to be grabbed or quickly brandished. The substitution of a mundane household thing, say a spatula or a box of tissues, which is then flourished and described by one of the characters as "one of the most singular objects in the world, older than the pyramids, Stonehenge or the Skara Brae" is pure comedy.

It's Like a Highlight Reel by Jena McLean, from the 2021 *Plays2Perform@ Home* Eastern box, employs a similar dramaturgy to *The Corona Variations* tele-therapy scene, inviting readers to read aloud a verbatim assemblage of other people's memories of joy, anecdotes about the "best day of my life." Then after about a dozen mini-stories, there is a stage direction that says, "*It's your turn now.*"

    A. Think about the best day of your life.
    B. Try your best to remember it.
    A. What do you remember about it?
    B. Was it a party?
    A. A birth?
    B. A date?
    A. A trip?

---

3   The original box set from summer 2020 featured plays from Western Canada by Karen Hines, Jovanni Sy, Tara Beagan, and Hiro Kanagawa. In the summer of 2021, a second set of four boxes was produced featuring playwrights from the Prairies, Ontario, Quebec, and Eastern Canada. See Signy Lynch, "Performing at Home in the Pandemic: Boca del Lupo's *Plays2Perform@Home* Collection," *Canadian Theatre Review* 191 (Summer 2022): 82–86.

B. A goodbye?

A. A hello?

[. . .]

A. Can you hear it?

B. Was there music?

A. Do you still know the words?

B. Or was it silent?

A. Peaceful?

B. A turning point?

A. A day where everything was the same?

B. What made it the best day?

A and B prepare to tell each other the stories of their best days. A and B take three breaths together. They set down the play and share with each other.

Another of the *P2P@H* plays (*Negotiations* by Hiro Kanagawa) is explicitly about the polite convolutions we all undertook to avoid contagion while simultaneously maintaining social niceties. *The Fifth Setting* by Yvette Nolan takes place at your dining table as "four members of a household prepare dinner for a mystery guest." As they wait and worry, they consider what it means to be hospitable in their sharing and conversely to be grateful for what they have. *Our Tree* by Lior Maharjan is almost musical. The four participant-actors take the roles of the Leaves, the Bark, the Roots, and the Water to make an overlapping collaborative soundscape of being a tree. ("We are the tree on the top of the hill.") Both explicitly in their content (sometimes) and implicitly in their form (always), these "takeout plays" or "mail order plays" crafted for domestic players create situations for us to model cooperation. We have to figure out how to do the thing together—What parts will each person play? When do we begin? Are we really even gonna do this? And then we have to do the thing together—Take turns. Be patient. Be encouraging. Do your share. We are actors, but critically, we are actors together. Either by consciously alternating or aesthetically arranged in synchrony, being together is the focal point of these experiences.[4]

See FIRST-PERSON SHOOTER and US

---

4   Drop-in choir performances like Nightswimming's *Why We Are Here!* and Daveed Goldman and Nobu Adilman's *Choir! Choir! Choir!* rely on a similar skill-frame prompt for audience action, except we sing our given text instead of reading it.

AGENCY

See PHONY MULTIPLICITY

ALEA

Roger Caillois (*Man, Play and Games*) identifies the randomness of chance or what he calls "alea" as one of four core categories of games.[1] In opposition to "agôn," or games of skill, that engage players in direct competition, alea involves no skill at all. Both agôn and alea are premised on equality; but whereas equality in agonistic competition is about fairness in the rules so that either player has the same chance of winning, equality in alea manifests in contingency, putting the players in the hands of fate or the universe. The player in a game of chance is entirely passive and whatever happens happens. The only determinate action the audience-player makes is the decision to begin to play and then subsequently to end play. (see YES, LET'S!) In between, active choice is from among random, superficially identical options—Do you go through the door on the left or on the right?—or the choice is to activate the randomizing mechanism, rolling the dice, flipping a coin. The choice is heartless. As Caillois writes, "It grants the lucky player infinitely more than he could procure by a lifetime of labor, discipline, and fatigue. It seems an insolent and sovereign insult to merit."[2] Either the audience-player chooses directly in this kind of desultory fashion or defers choice to a nonhuman participant. (see THINGS)

The morality of gambling as an affront to the Protestant work ethic and possible social damage of addiction aside, it is worth thinking about how choices with unpredictable, seemingly random outcomes generate aesthetic understanding, since this is a common dramaturgical strategy for shaping participation. How does alea mean? The audience plays the game, but we are merely the conduit of fate. We spin the wheel, but choice is external; the mechanism is the dominant driver rather than the player. The universe is the playwright. This feeling of passively "letting it ride" can be pleasurable if the stakes are low and the attitude not too existential. Sometimes the effect is a hopeful sense of being safe in the hands of providence, that things are as they should be. Sometimes, by contrast, being subject to randomness is a desolate peek into the abyss; we are adrift in an uncaring universe. Nothing matters.

---

1   Roger Caillois, *Man, Play and Games*, translated by Meyer Barash (U of Illinois P, 1961), 17.

2   Caillois, *Man, Play and Games*, 17.

In the *Dungeons & Dragons* themed, live-action participatory show *Roll Models*, randomness manifests in the repeated rolling of the dice. Four selected PROXY audience-players are paired with four actor-avatars. Just as in the tabletop role-playing version of the game, the dice determine the outcome of a player's asserted prospective action. In an improvised response to a narrative obstacle, the player might declare, "I will cast a spell to throw a magic net on the dragon." Roll an 8 and you are successful. Roll an 18 and perhaps you not only avert the danger, but you may also be rewarded when the dragon becomes a friend and ally. Roll a 4 however and you might find yourself in the net instead. Part of the superlative improvisatory story-weaving skill of the performer who acts as the *Roll Models* "Dungeon Master" host character is to interpret the raw number generated by the dice, translating that information into context-specific (usually absurd and hilarious) dramatic exposition. The resulting action (also absurd and hilarious) is then acted out by the avatars.

Greg Costikyan, in his book *Uncertainty in Games*, notes that among the sources of uncertainty (performative uncertainty of player skill, puzzle solver's uncertainty, hidden information, and so on), randomness, which many players despise, has some particular strengths, notably "it adds drama, it breaks symmetry, it provides simulation value, and it can be used to foster strategy through statistical analysis."[3] Actually, the dice are a pretty good substitute playwright. Perhaps the possible message here is simply a reminder of the unpredictability of the universe. It is a truism that even the best plans, enacted by highly skilled characters, might fail or, conversely, the unconsidered shot in the dark by an unprepared novice might succeed.

Humans also introduce randomness into participatory performances. Another way that contingency appears is as a branched narrative or experience. For example, *Monday Nights* is actually four plays in one. The performance is divided into four strands from the very outset when the first task of each audience member is to inspect the contents of four gym bags. From these autobiographical assemblages, I pick whose team I want to be on. In the moment of choosing, the other three branches vanish. Others will follow those paths, but they are closed to me. I can see the other teams across the court, but I watch from the outside and cannot access their experience. This melancholic regret of the path not taken (Think FOMO) is always embedded in any CHOOSE YOUR OWN ADVENTURE schema. In *Monday Nights*, the dominant feeling is a sense of belonging, attachment to my captain and the other audience-players

3   Greg Costikyan, *Uncertainty in Games* (MIT P, 2013), 86.

who made the same choice. I am on the red team. Do I wonder what it is like to be on the blue team? Perhaps a little.

By contrast, the regretful wonder of what might have been is the principal theme of Outside the March's play *Love Without Late Fees*. The central conceit is that the immersed audience is running a video-store dating service called "Six Tapes to Find the One." A series of escape-room-style puzzles activates the branching mechanism. Successfully solve the puzzle and our couple, Matt and Sarah, do one thing. Fail to solve the puzzle and Matt and Sarah's relationship takes a different track. The effect here of alea in the creation of thirty-two unique endings is to remind us that the journey of a love relationship can indeed feel like an exercise in serendipity. If this or that hadn't happened we wouldn't have met. Randomness is a life quality that we recognize. And so, the flip-a-coin branches replicate a real-world situation. The audience then plays the role of "the universe"; our puzzle games are part of a superior ontological realm that somehow determines the romantic fate of the would-be lovers. This game mechanism stands in as a simplified parallel for the impossible-to-comprehend complexity of the world.

That impossible-to-comprehend logic of the universe made manifest in games of alea is adapted in *Foreign Radical* to comment on the Kafka-esque arbitrariness of bureaucracy, specifically the all-powerful surveillance of border control. Badgered by a maniacal game show host, the audience-players are compelled to answer revealing questions with public actions, dividing ourselves into four corners of the room based on yes or no responses. "Have you signed a petition critical of the government?" "Do you use encryption to mask your Internet use?" "Do you own a pressure cooker?" The answers to the questions are not random; they are autobiographical confessions. But the consequences of the answers are random. Based on their answers, certain members are banished out of the room. Is this a reward or a punishment? Do I want to go there or stay here? The underlying value system is purposely opaque. We are at the mercy of a game we cannot comprehend, unsure if we are WINNING or losing.

Beyond game structures that mimic the contingency of choosing this or that to create meaning, audience participation itself is a prime source of randomness. In her list of reasons that drive participatory art, CLAIRE BISHOP notes that not only does participation create a more egalitarian or democratic base for creative engagement, but also it offers an aesthetic benefit in the greater unpredictability of input via audience contributions.[4] The benefits from greater diversity of randomness as well as the pleasures

---

4   Claire Bishop, "Introduction: Viewers as Producers," in *Participation: Documents of Contemporary Art* (MIT P, 2006), 12.

of surprise and serendipity are held in balance with reduced coherence resulting from less artistic control. Participatory works, built as a series of one-way gates or that are "on rails," manifest relatively low randomness and relatively high control. Works that incorporate improvisation, by contrast, feature high randomness and low control.

Dice are not the only source of alea in *Roll Models*. Although there is a traditional audience, four audience members are invited to become role players. Each one creates a fantasy-adventure-style character; they are paired with an actor who plays that character and who is effectively their live avatar. (see REMOTE CONTROL) Through their role-play quest, the players make choices and declare their intentions (with success or failure determined by the dice), and the actor-avatars are challenged to realize those actions. In this way, *Roll Models* centrally locates the randomness of audience input as the catalyst for its core understanding. Costikyan notes that not only are endings uncertain in games (unlike in drama), but the journey to that ending is also uncertain. "The uncertainty is in the path the game follows, in how players manage problems, in the surprises they hold."[5] It is precisely this grappling with uncertainty that is the source of pleasure in *Roll Models*. The audience-players are randomness generators; they are part of the game mechanic generating "friction" for the actors. They are basically more sophisticated dice in human form. The appeal of the show then, and indeed its raison d'être, is to generate JOYFUL laughter not only at the absurdity of the ad hoc plots but also in the virtuosity of the actors as they frolic in unpredictability. In the secondary audience, we thrill to the successful struggle in their performative acrobatics to respond to the unexpected twists of the plot and to bring it all together (somehow) in the end. Their victory over the obstacles of alea is our delight.

See GAME OVER. PLAY AGAIN?

FLIP A COIN! IF IT COMES UP HEADS, CALL THE LAST PERSON YOU TEXTED RIGHT NOW AND ASK ABOUT THEIR DAY. IF IT COMES UP TAILS, GO AND MAKE YOURSELF A CUP OF TEA.

5   Costikyan, *Uncertainty in Games*, 13.

ANTS

In April 2022, *Reddit* launched another iteration of r/place. Over the course of four days, redditors participated in collaborative art-making by choosing from a palette of thirty-two different colours and placing one coloured pixel tile at a time on a field of four million pixels.[1] In order to paint another pixel, redditors had to wait five minutes. On the subreddit, r/place is described as "a place where togetherness created more. / Now in numbers far greater, taking more space."[2] The subreddit's description ends with a familiar call towards collective UTOPIA-building. "It falls upon you to create a better place." While the space was live, redditors worked together to make flags and portraits and memes.[3] Lightning McQueen from the movie *Cars* sits nestled between a portrait of Nelson Mandela and a copy of da Vinci's *The Last Supper*. Cannabis leaves and Pokémon characters are hidden in the trans flag. An unimaginable number of references to anime shows and cult characters dot the screen and boldly featured in the middle of the canvas is a link to another subreddit, r/fuckcars.

Nearly every time I returned to r/place during the four-day sprint, the canvas looked different. Because pixels could be repainted over and over again, tiles were immediately overwritten. This built-in impermanence of any painting made r/place an unstable and highly fluid form. By the end of the event, there had been 160 million pixel changes made by more than 10.5 million redditors.[4] (On the final day, redditors were restricted to only placing white tiles and the entire canvas returned to a blank page.) In an *Esquire* piece on the art experiment, Cameron Sherrill writes, "Each pixel has its own timer, meaning no individual or group can endlessly spam their shapes, which forces either coordination between users (if you want beauty), or absolute chaos, if that's what you're into. r/place mixes art, teamwork, and sheer randomness into an awe-inspiring tapestry that the designer in me finds truly beautiful."[5] A redditor can't dominate a section

---

1   "r/place," *Wikipedia*, en.wikipedia.org/wiki/R/place.

2   "Place," *Reddit*, reddit.com/r/place.

3   There is a corner dedicated to the province of Quebec that features a pile of fleurs de lis, Le Bonhomme Carnaval, the word "TABARNAK," a can of maple syrup, and the McGill and Concordia University crests.

4   "r/place," *Wikipedia*.

5   Cameron Sherrill, "What is r/Place? The Life and Death of r/Place, Home to the Internet's Greatest Art War," *Esquire*, 6 April 2022, esquire.com/lifestyle/a39636815/what-is-r-place-explained/.

alone; in order to create something coherent there must be collaboration. One red pixel doesn't make a Canadian flag, but if enough redditors recognize the beginning of the red and white, they can follow the familiar blueprint for an eleven-point maple leaf. SNEAKY NINJAS could work together to hide *Among Us* characters in every corner. The usefulness of a GUIDE to shape a leaderless collective action might explain the prevalence of flags, brands, and other images of popular culture.

A symptom of Web 2.0, this principle of collective and participatory world-building is taken up in transformative justice practices too. In her book *Emergent Strategy*, American activist, writer, and facilitator adrienne maree brown draws on the concept of biomimicry to communicate how these small patterns of transformation are recognized in the plant and animal world. She links the evocative image of fractals,[6] which are mathematical visualizations that replicate the same patterns no matter how far you zoom in, to the work of the noble ant. For brown, "Ant societies function through individual ants acting collectively in accord with simple, local information to carry on all of their survival activities. Every ant relies on the work of others in producing their own work."[7] This kind of faith in collective meaning-making allows for a manageable approach to change—change that is local in a way that we can see its effects for ourselves. (see WITNESS) Where Nicolas Bourriaud (*Relational Aesthetics*) believes participatory and relational work at the level of micro-utopia creates an "extraordinary upsurge of social exchanges,"[8] r/place and adrienne maree brown are interested in what can come from the increase of those mundane miniature social ENCOUNTERS. When tiny ants work together, they can lift a banana! When redditors work together, they can create a detailed recreation of a poster from the *Star Wars* franchise!

This work is different from the crowdsourced process of BETA testing as a creation and rehearsal tool for participatory theatre. In these ant-colony-as-artist examples, crowdsourcing isn't a kind of data collection to determine the best solution to a problem, but rather it is itself the site and source for meaning-making. The work is a composite or a collage of our collective action. There is no meaning in only one pixel. Meaning arises only out of the responsive combination of many, many, many (perhaps thousands or millions) of tiny contributions.

---

6   adrienne maree brown, "Fractals: The Relationship Between Small and Large," in *Emergent Strategy: Shaping Change, Changing Worlds* (AK, 2017), 51–66.

7   brown, "Fractals," 45.

8   Nicolas Bourriaud, *Relational Aesthetics*, translated by Simon Pleasance and Fronza Woods (Les presses du réel, 2002), 14.

Other kinds of place-making shows do similar work in the name of celebrating the power of collective participation. In Daveed Goldman and Nobu Adilman's *Choir! Choir! Choir!*, dozens or even hundreds of assembled audience members are taught a choral arrangement of a well-known pop song. Like the flags and memes in r/place, the familiarity of pop songs function as a clear guide to follow. In one evening, participants learn the parts and then perform the song together. Like many community choirs, singing perfectly isn't the point, but rather the point lies with the collective JOY of singing with others. In 2018, the Festival of Live Digital Art (FOLDA) helped incubate a digital experiment with the *Choir! Choir! Choir!* artists where participants in three different cities—Montréal, Toronto, and Vancouver—learned the lyrics in multi-part harmonies to Leonard Cohen's "Hallelujah" and then sang together over (a delightfully glitchy) livestream. I was there, singing along. Like r/place, singers can't sing in harmony alone, it requires the coordinated action of a group of voices rising. A collage of individual voices, (each one like a coloured pixel) spread across a country to make a choir.

In Michael Rubenfeld and Clayton Lee's *Ways of Being*, two participating audiences, one in Kingston, Ontario, and one in Krakow, Poland, collaborated in a series of encounters to materialize the possibility of pandemic connection across the globe. Most of these encounters had relatively low stakes. Prompted with questions from Michael and Clayton, Polish and Canadian participants talked to each other through Zoom. A participator in Kingston asked someone in Poland about their first pet. Audiences in each city answered questions about their hopes and worries in a shared Google doc. At one point, audience members in each city danced "together" via live projection feeds. In the last moments of the show, a dynamic collage of this video footage replayed live in front of us, projected on the walls of the theatre. We saw a montage of participators in both cities dancing, overlaid with a few sentences from our cooperative Google doc. Remarkably, this montage wasn't just a record of our *specific* performance, but rather an aggregate collection of encounters between other audiences in Kingston and Poland from earlier in the show's run. We saw ourselves, our partners in Poland, and other Polish/Canadian audiences from previous shows. Like a long FRIENDSHIP bracelet made of a series of artful knots, this live-rendered composite of the show's actions was a retrospective series of recorded encounters. The collage looked like a short film of two cities in conversation on either side of the planet, offering a beautiful glimpse at complex webs of relationality that extended in both time and space. Despite the global shutdown on travel, we were collaborative ants on either side of the ocean, dancing and singing.

In these examples, participants (actual ants or metaphorical ants in the form of choir singers or redditors, take your pick) are producing phase change through the power of large-scale, responsive iterations. EMERGENCE is possible, but only if we are not acting alone.

See MOB and TYRANNY

COMPLETE THIS PUZZLE BY COLOURING IN EACH SQUARE OF THE GRID. CHOOSE A CORRESPONDING COLOUR FOR EACH FIGURE (EG. 🐜 = BLUE, 2 = YELLOW, 3 = GREEN) AND COLOUR UNTIL YOU SEE AN ANSWER.

🐜 =   2 =   3 =

🐜	3	🐜	2	2	2	1	🐜	3	🐜
3	🐜	2	2	2	2	2	2	2	3
3	2	2	2	🐜	🐜	3	2	2	🐜
🐜	2	2	3	🐜	3	🐜	🐜	🐜	3
3	2	2	3	3	🐜	3	🐜	3	🐜
🐜	2	2	🐜	3	🐜	🐜	3	🐜	3
3	2	2	3	3	🐜	3	2	2	3
🐜	2	2	2	🐜	3	3	2	2	🐜
3	🐜	2	2	2	2	2	2	3	3
3	🐜	🐜	2	2	2	2	🐜	3	🐜

AROUSAL

The question that I always get asked by non-participators about partic-ipatory performance: "Why would anyone do *that*?" (Invitations to join me have been turned down numerous times by prospective participatory audience companions. I'm not taking it personally. You know who you are.) Michael J. Apter's book *Danger: Our Quest for Excitement* offers a fruitful model for thinking about the psychology of participatory risk-taking. One driver is the desire for authenticity, for the do-it-yourself, custom-ized, AUTOBIOGRAPHICAL narcissism of art that is by me, for me, and about me. (see MEEPLES) But another driver is the thrill of it all. The thrill of being looked at, of being the centre of attention, and the pressure cooker of being responsible for what happens next. But also, the thrill that comes from the uncertainty of the situation. In collabora-tive participation, what happens next is unpredictable. And more than unpredictable, it might be downright dangerous, which is thrilling, until it isn't. This is when thrill turns to panic.

Apter recognizes that the excitement of thrill and the anxiety of panic are two opposing manifestations of the same state of physiological arousal, experienced as accelerated heartbeat, perspiration, queasiness, elevated adrenaline, accompanied by a sense of becoming more men-tally alert.[1] The key difference in these two high arousal states is that excitement is pleasant, and anxiety is unpleasant. And the determin-ing factor, according to Apter, as to whether we experience arousal as excitement or anxiety depends on our perception of the existence of a protective frame.[2] The example he gives is of being submerged in a cage into shark-infested waters. The cage allows us to be close to the source of the danger, to skirt along the dangerous edge, without crossing over into what he calls the "trauma zone" where actual harm awaits. It is in this liminal danger zone that I can access the adrenaline rush of proximity to a carnivorous predator who thinks I might be lunch, while remaining safe from its actual teeth.

In participatory theatre, the risks are (usually) not physical. The trauma that stalks audiences on the other side of the dangerous edge does not involve bodily harm. Yes, accidents are possible in this kind of work, especially if we are being challenged to move around in unfamiliar

---

1   Michael J. Apter, *Danger: Our Quest for Excitement* (OneWorld, 2007), 14–15.
2   Apter, *Danger*, 30.

or atypical environments. But this is not the thrill that I am here for. The excitement of participatory theatre does not hinge on the risk that my parachute might not open. In some cases, excitement is stimulated by EMBODIMENT, by the exertion of running or dancing or throwing (foam) bricks at riot police. (see SHEEP) But here again, the thrill of the work is not dependent on the potential for a sprained ankle.

More commonly, arousal in participatory theatre arises out of the uncertainty mentioned above. Being outside not only traditional theatre spaces, but also traditional audience behaviours (see INTERPRETATION) increases this insecurity exponentially. Something is being asked of us as participants, but what? Danger, then in this context, is aligned with the potential for BEING LOST, for making a mistake, for looking foolish, for oversharing. These are social risks. And these are the thrills that I am here for. Getting outside my comfort zone. Temporarily being a little more brave, a little more engaged, taking a little more responsibility in the outcome. All these characteristics of you yourself taking part in something opens the risk of giving away too much of yourself.

Instead of the literal protective frame of the sharkproof cage, participatory theatre taps into two layers of frames. The first is that of the MAGIC CIRCLE of game playing. Inside the circle, we are safe. The sharks of the real world cannot touch us here. What we say and do doesn't "count." As Gregory Bateson asserts in his influential essay, "A Theory of Play and Fantasy," "These actions, in which we now engage do not denote what those actions for which they stand would denote."[3] He calls this a peculiarity of play, and recognizes that the frame that declares that "this is play" is not entirely secure: "This example [of cats play fighting] however also illustrates the labile nature of the frame ... The discrimination between map and territory is always liable to break down, and the ritual blows of peace-making are always liable to be mistaken for the 'real' blows of combat."[4] And you still might end up with a scratch. It is in this liability of breakdown that we might experience some excitement. What is happening is not real, ... probably. The other protective frame is constituted of various cues and supports specific to each performance that help us figure out what to do or not do. Lacking the expected behavioural conventions of BOURGEOIS THEATRE, we need GUIDES. In creating a new horizon of expectations,

---

3   Gregory Bateson, "A Theory of Play and Fantasy," in *Steps to an Ecology of Mind: Collected Essays in Anthropology, Psychiatry, Evolution, and Epistemology* (U of Chicago P, 1972), 180.

4   Bateson, "A Theory of Play and Fantasy," 182.

the creators of participatory theatre games want to encourage me to be excited or anxious about the right things, in ways that are aligned with the intended experience. (see THE MATRIX)

In terms of the dramaturgies of arousal, simply being outside of traditional theatre practices is stimulating. Beyond that, being alone creates arousal. Solo audiencing separates me from the security of herd invisibility. (see MOB) Now not only am I visible, and the performers are looking at me, being just one person, I bear increased responsibility for the art experience we are co-creating. I need to be "good." Sense deprivation, especially darkness, is another technique for stimulating arousal through uncertainty. An immersive production of the medieval mystery play *Everyman*, which casts the audience-participant in the title role, is perhaps one of the highest arousal performances I have participated in. The work generates serious anxiety, combining the dramaturgies of the high execution pressures of being alone with darkness, in support of the show's central understanding. In your journey as Everyman, you are commanded by Death to make a final existential reckoning before God. You are abandoned by personifications of Fellowship, Kindred and Cousin, Goods, Strength, Beauty, Discretion and your Five-Wits, before being placed in your grave. When facing the moral implications of your ultimate end, fear is definitely the point.[5]

The Stranger 2.0: Above, created by DLT, counteracts the anxiety of being alone by allowing audiences to participate in pairs. Here the dominant dramaturgies of arousal in play reside in the performative invitation to be a co-creator, to answer questions, paint, and play hide-and-seek combined with the permeability of the magic circle where we do these things in public, flapping our arms like birds and dancing down the sidewalk like SECRET WEIRDOS while being honked at by passing cars. It is indeed thrilling. And this bodily excitement translates into a heightened awareness not just of my blood pumping in my veins and my blush of joyful silliness. Through this liberation, I am opened to grateful appreciation of the world and of my companion-FRIEND.[6]

When a high arousal state is not the goal of the work, dramaturgies of mitigation come into play to defuse anxiety and bring the

---

5   Jenn Stephenson, "Real Bodies Part 2: Narcissistic Spectatorship in Theatrical 'Haunted Houses' of Solo Immersive Performance—*Everyman*," in *Insecurity: Perils and Products of Theatres of the Real* (U of Toronto P, 2019), 210–25.

6   During an introspective moment in the show (immediately prior to the flapping dancing) where my friend Kim and I were "parked" at a bus shelter, waiting for the next performer interaction, we realized that this was in fact exactly the twentieth anniversary of our friendship.

audience-player back into the safety zone. Pre-show emails or announcements telling me what to expect, where we are going, and what I will or will not be doing, provide contextual information and sketch the boundaries of my experiential frame. (see CONSENT) For example, the show *Good Things To Do* strives to create a calm, almost meditative state, for the participants. When I am told directly that no one will see me or interrupt my solitude for the duration of the performance, I am reassured that I can relax in security. OPTING OUT is another strategy to shore up the protective frame. Just knowing I could step out is helpful in reducing anxiety because it gives me control over the experience. I know in advance that I am not stuck.

SENSORY EXPLORATION! IDENTIFY:

- 👁 • 5 THINGS THAT YOU CAN SEE
- ✋ • 4 THINGS THAT YOU CAN FEEL
- 👂 • 3 THINGS THAT YOU CAN HEAR
- 👃 • 2 THINGS THAT YOU CAN SMELL
- 👅 • 1 THING THAT YOU CAN TASTE

ASYMMETRY

Participatory dance artist Jacob Niedzwiecki defines asymmetry as an awareness of the multiple audience-player perspectives that feature in his site-specific work. In a very ordinary but important way, asymmetry describes how each member of the audience is standing somewhere different, viewing the work through their own embodied lens. Asymmetry is a useful idea in the "post-proscenium era," an abandonment of the notion that "the whole creative team is working to bring everyone in the house the same experience of the show—the same information."[1] (see NOISE) The conventional proscenium, originating in fifteenth-century Italy, uses perspective illusion, built around a vanishing point and contained by a frame to privilege a single ideal view.[2] For a mobile audience, however, dispersed on and in a performance site, there are necessarily a multiplicity of views.

There is a spectrum of asymmetrical experiences.[3] Asymmetrical difference could be spatial, that is, I could literally be standing somewhere different and unique. The neoclassical stage with its picture frame proscenium privileges that one perfect viewpoint, whereas environmental theatre is a free-for-all. Or asymmetrical difference could be informational. In talking about informational asymmetry, Niedzwiecki likens proscenium theatre to chess, where all aspects are visible and known to participants. We are all looking at the same board. Compared to chess, poker players only know the information of the cards in their own hand. The strategy of poker manifests in trying to crack through the informational asymmetry, making guesses at the cards hidden from you in your opponent's hand or remaining in the deck.

In Adrienne Wong and Dustin Harvey's *Landline*, audience-players in two separate cities are paired for a reflexive audiowalk through an urban

---

1   Jacob Niedzwiecki, "Jacqueries: Mind Games, Street Action, and the Art of the Heist," *Canadian Theatre Review* 178 (Spring 2019): 30.
2   The earliest surviving proscenium, the Teatro Farnese, dates from 1618 and is in Parma, Italy (Edwin Wilson and Alvin Goldfarb, *The Living Theatre: History of Theatre*, 6th edition (McGraw-Hill, 2012), 142–44).
3   Asymmetry can refer to physical point of view, the outcomes of choices made, and gates locked, but can also refer to the varying levels of participation, current and previous experience, positionality, and power differences and adoption of AGENCY. It speaks to the different roles we assume, our different engagement with "the rules," and a phenomenological meta-awareness of asymmetrical reception itself. We don't all know (or see) the same things, and that is okay.

ASYMMETRY

landscape. Exchanging cellphone numbers, these pairs respond to prompts through TEXT MESSAGES while they wander around their respective locations. The paired cities are often far away from one another and sometimes quite different in their urban geography or climate. Kitchener is linked to Vancouver, Edinburgh to Reykjavik, Calgary to St. John's. When I first participated in *Landline*, I was in Whitehorse, Yukon, while my scene partner was in Ottawa, Ontario. While I DRIFTED around the city of Whitehorse, the ambient soundtrack playing in my headphones had been recorded in Ottawa. While I looked at the relatively quiet streets of Whitehorse, I heard cars whizzing by and honking horns from the streets of Ottawa. With a three-hour difference in time zone, I walked Whitehorse long before the sun went down, and my partner roamed Ottawa in the dark. (I was living in Ottawa at the time and had flown to Whitehorse to attend the show at the Magnetic North Theatre Festival. Funnily enough, my texting partner in Ottawa was *not* local and got very lost during the wandering performance. I had to direct him out of the labyrinth around the Rideau Centre from the quiet streets of Whitehorse.) When the prompt in my headphones asks us to lean on a tree, my partner and I are obviously supported by trees that are not the same. Our bodies stage the site of asymmetry; our eyes are in one city and our ears in another. The unlikely meeting of this asymmetrical pair is a core dramaturgy of *Landline*.[4]

Asymmetry can also be thematized as a result of divergent consequences in theatre-game hybrids when player choices affect the outcome of the story, like doors closing (and locking) on branching narrative paths. In escape rooms, some teams solve the puzzle and others do not. Some WIN the game and others lose. In Sébastien Heins's *The Itinerary: Playtest*, four audience members take turns prescribing tasks to Calvin (played by Heins) on the last night of his life. These four players literally operate his actor body with a REMOTE CONTROL. Brush teeth. Eat breakfast. Meditate. Write a song. Pray aloud. Play "trashketball." Attempt escape. Call for help. Psych yourself up. Promise organs. Sleep.[5] If Calvin sleeps, Calvin dreams and a series of five participatory games begin,[6] with each game reanimating a specific memory in Calvin's life prior to his time in the room. Again taking turns with the controller, players are invited to play these games, each one modelled after a classic genre of tabletop or video game (jigsaw

---

4   Jenn Stephenson, "Real Space: *Garden//Suburbia* and *Landline*," in *Insecurity: Perils and Products of Theatres of the Real* (U of Toronto P, 2019), 130–168.

5   Sébastien Heins, "*The Itinerary: Playtest*," *Canadian Theatre Review* 188 (Fall 2021): 70.

6   Heins, "*The Itinerary: Playtest*," 70.

puzzles, a journey on a map, role-playing games, an avatar creator, and a rhythm game). We are reliving his life in his final moments. We play his first day of school and his first job interview. One player toggles a set of hands to move a figurine through a cardboard map. Another player selects outfits for Calvin in a mirror like we're dressing a SIM.

If Calvin doesn't sleep, Calvin doesn't dream and he isn't afforded the opportunity to re-experience his memories on the final night of his life. Beyond the fiction, audience-players face actual consequences. In a performance of the show at the 2020 Kick and Push Festival, when players were invited to let Calvin sleep and ultimately dream, no players selected that option. Players continued to "play" his life, selecting more options like "do push-ups" or "write a song." Calvin never slept and Calvin never dreamed, so Calvin (and the players) stayed in his room. Calvin and the four players never played the memory games. As a result, they lost about a third of the show. Although players can't "win" *The Itinerary: Playtest*, they can certainly lose. In this case, the asymmetry of the experience is not among players inside one performance but from performance to performance. By not selecting "sleep," players experienced the asymmetrical consequences of participatory choices they made.[7]

Where traditional fourth-wall theatre privileges reproducibility, Niedzwiecki says that asymmetry privileges "replayability" as people will keep coming back for another perspective.[8] (see GAME OVER. PLAY AGAIN?) Because audience members are often in motion and their trajectories are unpredictable, the creator of participatory work likewise has to be flexible as the fixity of a single meaning can't be achieved. Some predictability or insight into a range of possibilities might be revealed through BETA testing in rehearsal. This increased mobility, which generates the potential for a multiplicity of personally variable INTERPRETATIONS, connects to Jacques Rancière's notion of emancipation. By embracing the randomness of meaning introduced by a contingent audience, participatory artists make space for the audience to be legitimate co-creators. Niedzwiecki says that "working asymmetrically is about balancing all these choices and giving some of them to the audience."[9]

---

7 Something similar happens in *asses.masses*. In Episode 5, audience-players are given a choice between going to the "Circus" or the "Zoo." Depending on which one we choose, we will not have access to some part of the story; a whole chunk of the game narrative is simply inaccessible.
8 Niedzwiecki, "Jacqueries," 31.
9 Niedzwiecki, "Jacqueries," 31.

AUTOBIOGRAPHY

Participatory theatre invites audience-participants to become autobiographers.[1] Being a participant means not only that we do something (see OR ELSE), exercising what Shannon Steen calls "verbiness,"[2] but as part of that doing, we are also often giving, making contributions to the work. And what we have to contribute is ourselves, because, hey, we didn't bring anything else with us. Whether we are doing heavy lifting by building barricades in *Counting Sheep* or manipulating tiny objects by planting seeds in *Remixed*, we contribute physical LABOUR. Even walking in environmental performance works—so much walking!—is also a manifestation of our physical labour. Beyond the physical, we also contribute what Michael Hardt calls affective labour.[3] I am contributing my thoughts, my emotions, and my creative inputs when I make choices to CHOOSE MY OWN ADVENTURE or to fill in the blanks. (see MAD LIBS) Sometimes these inputs are just the everyday ideas floating around in my brain, but sometimes they are more intimately "of me"; that is, the stories I tell are bits and pieces of my own autobiography.

This might start with just my name. "I'm Jenn," I say. Or the artists might lift my name from the ticket purchase list. (It is sometimes quite a short list after all.) "Hello, Jenn," they say. The centrality of me-qua-me is a core characteristic of participatory theatre under neoliberal capitalism. By putting individualism and self-sufficiency at the heart of neoliberalism, this ethos fosters a pleasure-pride in being able to do it myself and encourages an entrepreneurial drive to seek out not only the "best" experiences, but also those that are exclusive and singular.[4] (see SHOPPING) This desire for singularity turns on itself, manifesting as customization and experiences that focus on my specialness. The empowerment of "by me" curdles into the narcissism of "for me" and "about me."

---

1   Jenn Stephenson, "Autobiography in the Audience: Emergent Dramaturgies of Loss in *Lost Together* and *Foreign Radical*," *Theatre Research in Canada* 43, no. 1 (2022): 81–95.

2   Shannon Steen, "Neoliberal Scandals: Foxconn, Mike Daisey, and the Turn Toward Nonfiction Drama," *Theatre Journal* 66, no. 1 (March 2014): 1–18.

3   Michael Hardt, "Affective Labour," *boundary 2* 26, no. 2 (Summer 1999): 89–100.

4   Keren Zaiontz, "Narcissistic Spectatorship in Immersive and One-on-One Performance," *Theatre Journal* 66, no. 3 (October 2014): 405–25.

Leaning into this baked-in dramaturgical inclination for person-alization, the confessional performance is a common subgenre of participatory experiences. Different shows elicit autobiographical infor-mation with differing moods of the request and employ that information for different meaningful ends. *Foreign Radical* roughly demands that we answer personal questions to expose our hypocrisy about how we conceptualize safety and security in the tension between freedom and surveillance. (see COMPLICITY) Other shows like *Lost Together* that invite the sharing of a personal story gently transform that story before returning it to me. To my comfort, my reconfigured story is knit into a continuum of other stories. (see SURROGATION) Sometimes there is no one to listen to my story; the performance experience provides the prompts, but the material remains mine. Although my autobiography is made particularly visible to me through the performance structures, in the end, it remains private.[5]

Sometimes, I simply don't want to play the autobiographical game today. Sometimes the questions are just too hard to grab onto. The ask is too much—out of proportion with my trust. I have not been adequately prepared (softened?) into the requested level of openness. That might not happen today—or ever. *Ça a l'air synthétique bonjour hi* mocks this kind of excessive personal sharing when in the second act, one of the actors interviews a shrub. (see STRUMPET) On the other hand, the desire to be a good sport, to get the most out of the experience that I have paid for, and also the vanity of wanting to be seen can get the better of me and I find myself eagerly (undoubtedly too eagerly) confiding my innermost thoughts to an actor-performer who is a complete stranger.

And that brings me to *Worry Warts*. Conceived by Julie Tepperman under the banner of Convergence Theatre, this is a play about anxiety. "Anxiety is at an all-time high," says the promotional blurb. "And we want to know what keeps you up at night." Seated on a bouncy brightly coloured yoga ball, I face my personal "Keeper," Colin, across a tiny child-sized table. The entire space of *Worry Warts* reminds me of a kindergarten classroom. At other tables around the room, there are about six other pairs of audience-participants

---

5   *The Candlemaker's Game* works this way. I am prompted to write my thoughts in a notebook but I know this notebook won't be shared. After the show, I'm invited to take the book home with me or ceremonially dunk the notebook in the water to obscure my scribbles. Creator Richard Lam tells me they have been looking for a performance venue that will allow participants to burn the books, but no luck yet. For *It Comes in Waves*, we are also given "field guides" in which to record our thoughts, and at the end, before we depart the island, we toss the booklets into a fire barrel.

and Keepers. Streamers in red, blue, yellow, and white are hung from the ceiling. Giant hand-drawn posters cover the walls. Around the perimeter, there are what look like CRAFT stations with neon rainbow Post-it Notes, construction paper chains. One table has bowls of candies and children's picture books about having worries. The tablecloth looks like the mat from a game of Twister with large primary-coloured circles.

The first part of the performance is an interview between me and my Keeper. Honestly, I cannot remember the exact questions now; but I have very clear memories of my answers. I am a person with worries. Looking back, I am aware that being worried was a dominant register of my childhood. Now, truly, I had no real cause to be worried—I was secure and fortunate in so many ways. And yet, I felt continually anxious, never quite 100 per cent confident that the grown-ups who were in charge actually had it all under control. So, when I am asked by Keeper Colin if I have worries, the answer is most certainly yes. (Oh yes.) I find myself explaining that I don't drive. I could drive a car and I know how, but I don't anymore. And we talk about why not. (Several years ago, I was driving too fast on a highway in a bad rainstorm, and I lost control of the car. It hydroplaned across all the lanes of the highway, and we barely avoided landing in the ditch or being hit by another vehicle. The car was carrying not just one of my children but several others for whom I was responsible. It was fine and we got home. Everyone survived.) Basically, I don't drive because I would rather not. And as I get older there are more and more things that I would just rather not. No biggie. I actually find this empowering. I get to choose to say no to things. What rattles me, reflecting afterwards about *Worry Warts*, is what happened next. I found myself still talking and responding to Keeper Colin's empathetic and concerned expression by revealing my real worry, the meta-worry. What happens when the list of things that I would rather not becomes too long? What happens when my world gets really small? It occurs to me (and perhaps also to Colin) that this has now shaded from "some worries" into what might be considered clinical anxiety. I have overstepped some line somewhere. And now we are just looking at each other. He says something kind to me, and I proceed to the next phase of the performance where I am encouraged to independently explore the various play stations around the room to express my worries through artistic and tactile activities.[6]

---

6   For example, we were asked to choose different-coloured slips of paper representing the source of our worries (health, money, relationships, etc.) and to make connected paper chains that we attached to a hanging structure. A brown craft-paper

Nothing about what happened or how I felt about it is the fault of the show. It was (and is) my responsibility as an audience-participant to maintain my boundaries as needed. CARE in these EXCHANGES must be not only reciprocal, but also self-reflexive.[7] The performance cares for me. I express care for the performers. But I also need to care for myself. As I was reminded in a conversation with theatre artist and noted memoirist Tanya Marquardt, we are not just one singular self in this situation.[8] Even without lying, I don't have to offer an unvarnished version of myself. Ever. We are all always performers. This is especially worthy of consideration as a tactic when the site of ENCOUNTER is in a theatre, for goodness sakes. The person that I am talking to is not themselves.[9] They are encompassed (as I am) by the theatrical frame; and even under their own names, they are a character. I can (and should) adopt a protective character persona too. And of course, I know this. I do. My naïveté on this matter is ridiculous and rather embarrassing, given that I am a very experienced theatregoer. Moreover, I am an expert on autobiographical performance and have thought about this exact question of the ontology of the autobiographer in some depth. (I did, after all, once write a book on this subject.) And yet, I am fascinated by how the constellation of dramaturgical qualities of participatory performance sets the stage for shows that ask these kinds of questions, and audience-participants (like me) who, with wholehearted innocence, answer them.

---

poster with a life-size human body outline invited us to place Post-it Notes on the body form to indicate where we feel our anxiety.

7   Sarah Conn, "Experiments in Care as a Reciprocal Act," *Canadian Theatre Review* 197 (Winter 2024): 64–70.

8   Tanya Marquardt and Jenn Stephenson, "Some Must Watch While Some Must Sleep: An Impromptu Text Thread," *Canadian Theatre Review* 197 (Winter 2024): 56–59.

9   Keeper Colin in my performance of *Worry Warts* is actor Colin Doyle. Doyle was also my Inspector in the one-on-one *Ministry of Mundane Mysteries*. I have wondered a few times since this experience what he must think of me.

PRESS THIS BUTTON FOR A JOLT OF ELECTRICITY

PRESS THIS BUTTON TO HEAR WATER

PRESS THIS BUTTON TO CLEAR YOUR MIND

PRESS THIS BUTTON TO TASTE CITRUS

PRESS THIS BUTTON TO UNLOCK A MEMORY

PRESS THIS BUTTON TO _____

AUTOPOIESIS

Etymologically *auto* "self" plus *poiesis* "creation."[1] Coined by Chilean biologists Humberto Maturana and Franciso Varela, the term autopoiesis describes any self-contained, autonomous system, a system that is both process and product. Erika Fischer-Lichte (*The Transformative Power of Performance*) transposes the term from biological systems to aesthetic systems, using it to identify a particular emergent trend in contemporary performance. "Self-generation requires the participation of everyone, yet without any single participant being able to plan, control, or produce it alone. It thus becomes difficult to speak of producers and recipients . . . through their actions and behaviour, the actors and spectators constitute the elements of the feedback loop, which in turn generates the performance itself."[2]

Reconfiguring the usual relationship between performer and spectator, these works insist that the normally reluctant audience step up and insert themselves into the event. Without our action, the work cannot go forward. In her first chapter, Fischer-Lichte gives the example of Marina Abramović's *Lips of Thomas* where, after consuming a litre of wine and a kilo of honey, the performer then carved her skin with a razor blade and laid herself down on a cross of ice. Unable to continue as WITNESSES to this self-torture, audience members intervened to move the performer to safety and effectively ended the event. In that moment of radical contingency, anything can happen and the work swings around the U-turn of the closed system loop. The intervention is part of the performance. Respecting the spontaneity of this EMERGENT process, autopoiesis shifts focus to theatrical performance as a communal durational event rather than an autonomous artistic object. (see STRUMPET) "[Performance] is made up of the continuous becoming and passing of the autopoietic feedback loop."[3]

Although she recognizes autopoiesis as an aesthetic feature of all live performance events, one of the key ways that autopoiesis manifests mostly strongly in practice, according to Fischer-Lichte, is through role-reversal,

1   "Autopoiesis," *Wikipedia*, en.wikipedia.org/wiki/Autopoiesis.
2   Erika Fischer-Lichte, *The Transformative Power of Performance*, translated by Saskya Iris Jain (Routledge, 2008), 50.
3   Fischer-Lichte, *The Transformative Power of Performance*, 75.

where audience members become interactive actors.[4] And what Fischer-Lichte calls role-reversal aligns with the case studies that we are collecting under the umbrella of participation. Work in this mode needs the audience to do something or at the minimum become culpable in the making of meaning by our inaction. In participatory performance, the typical passive audience attitude is not a neutral stance. (see REFUSAL)

Meaning in participatory performance cannot be planned in advance because what might happen is contingent on audience involvement, on our choices to act (or not act). Audience input generates an aesthetically beneficial randomness. (see ALEA) Fischer-Lichte argues that the audience function of autopoietic art then is not INTERPRETIVE, but rather is experiential. (Or at least not as dominantly interpretive as BOURGEOIS THEATRE tends to be.) It does not live in a text but in the immediate time-space of co-presence. Audiences enter as audiences, and become actors through performance; nevertheless, we do not entirely shed our spectatorial awareness: "[It is] the experience of liminality that generates transformation. This liminal state results from the ostensible contradiction between actively participating in a performance . . . while experiencing the elusiveness of the entire event. The spectators remain on the threshold for the duration of the performance. Their position is never fixed; they do not control the performance, but their influence can be felt nonetheless. The audience constantly oscillates between these various states, ultimately enabled, defined, and triggered by the bodily co-presence of actors and spectators."[5]

Autopoiesis drives my experience of *Lost Together*. The performance for solo audience member, created by Shira Leuchter and performed by Leuchter with Michaela Washburn, is structured as an EXCHANGE. The first section of the play is an interview as I am asked by the pair to share a story about something that I have lost. Their questions encourage me to provide more details, to delve into both the memory and my current feelings, and to consider my account from different angles. This dialogic structure establishes an autopoietic feedback loop. This looping pattern generates EMERGENCE as subsequent "scenes" are deeply collaborative and unpredictable in their cooperative contingency. There is a framework for our interaction. A framework that is repeated for each singular audience-participant and yet how that frame is filled is almost infinitely variable. Likewise, what they ask is also variably dependent on what I have already said. Back and forth. Embroidering as we go. Anything could happen.

---

4   Fischer-Lichte, *The Transformative Power of Performance*, 40.

    5   Fischer-Lichte, *The Transformative Power of Performance*, 67.

In the second section of the play, Leuchter and Washburn create a CRAFT, an approximately palm-sized sculpture of my loss. It is ambivalently a representation of my experience of loss—how it feels to them—and also the thing itself now "found" and returned to me in this alternate expressionistic form. Autopoiesis creates transformation. It is Fischer-Lichte who proposes this connection: "[Autopoietic performance] aims at the involvement of all participants, in order to create a reciprocal relationship of influence. The feedback loop thus identifies transformation as a fundamental category of an aesthetics of the performative," she writes.[6] Transformation through performance is key to the understanding of what the play is doing with losses. My lived historical loss becomes a story via their questions. Then my story becomes a material THING. Then this thing as presented to me becomes the feeling of the original loss that has been "found," re-actualized as representation for me in this moment. The journey of this autopoietic loop changes my experience of loss.[7]

See SURROGATION

DRAW HERE SOMETHING THAT YOU HAVE LOST

---

6   Fischer-Lichte, *The Transformative Power of Performance*, 50.

7   Jenn Stephenson, "Autobiography in the Audience: Emergent Dramaturgies of Loss in *Lost Together* and *Foreign Radical*," *Theatre Research in Canada* 43, no. 1 (2022): 81–95.

BAD FAITH

When I attend a participatory performance and take up the INVITATION to participate, I am, in essence, adding "player" to my pre-existing role as "audience." This is an important qualification. Audience-players are different from ORDINARY PEOPLE who are recruited into the performance ahead of time. In *100% Vancouver*, one hundred ordinary Vancouverites were identified and selected. Their onstage performance was premised on their ordinariness, on their being just themselves. Their self-ness was the focus of their staging. (see PAINT) In the event, they crossed over fully to being "players," performing for a separate traditionally seated and traditionally spectatorial theatre audience. This has been, for us, a critical distinction towards delineating some boundaries for what constitutes participatory theatre. The participants must begin as audience, arriving at the event as such, with their primary goal being spectators to a work of theatrical art. (I am hesitant to use the word "consumer." But if the shoe fits . . .) Then after arrival, the audience retains their spectatorial role (see FIRST-PERSON SHOOTER) but also enters into a new and different kind of relation to the theatre work as a performer. (see ACTING)

Metatheatre theorist Sławomir Świontek describes the basic arrangement of theatrical enunciation as following two perpendicular vectors; dialogue is both communication *to* someone and communication *for* someone. On the stage-stage vector, characters speak to each other in a replication of ordinary dialogue. On the stage-house vector, enunciation is for the audience, communicating needed expository information to the audience eavesdroppers. We need to know things that the characters already know.[1] This is what Świontek calls its "meta-enunciative

---

1   The first few lines of *Hamlet* are a perfect example of telling the audience who these characters are and the setting of the scene (especially important in the original context of an outdoor, daytime performance in presumably mild weather). The characters already know who they are and what time it is, but we don't:

BERNARDO: Who's there?

FRANCISCO: Nay, answer me. Stand and unfold yourself.

BERNARDO: Long live the king!

FRANCISCO: Bernardo?

BERNARDO: He.

FRANCISCO: You come most carefully upon your hour.

BERNARDO: 'Tis now struck twelve. Get thee to bed, Francisco.

aspect."[2] Metatheatricality, which reveals the workings of theatre as theatre, arises from the revelation and/or thematization of this secondary vector that is outside the fictional situation.[3] Setting metatheatre aside, what is useful about Świontek's model is its acknowledgement that fictional dialogue is always looking sideways, over its shoulder, as it were, to provide key exposition knowledge to audience members who are newly arrived in this incipient fictional world. (see THE MATRIX) This model is also productively applicable to participatory audience-players who often become characters, while remaining spectators, and so need to send and receive information on both vector channels, which align respectively with their two roles. From this doubled ontology, we now have not only a doubled perspective (see ONTOLOGICAL DUALITY) but also a doubled obligation.

In his writing about participatory art, Alexander García Düttman recognizes the dual commitment of the audience-player to the sustainment of both the fictional world and the performance as event, to both the content and the form. "Bad faith" is a term Düttman uses to talk about how we are committed to supporting and realizing the form as well as the content; we want to participate, and we don't, simultaneously. He suggests "such art demands a moment of immediate belief in the world opened up by it as much as it demands an attentiveness to the mediated quality of art that breaks down this belief."[4] The work of art then manifests in the tension between these two perceptual positions. "From this perspective, participation in art has a 'dual character,' according to which neither of its poles, neither that of the side of content nor that of the side of form, can be resolved without at the same time ending the aesthetic experience through this resolution."[5] Then as Juliane Rebentisch points out in her discussion of Düttman's ideas, this renders the nature of participation itself as thematic. "Precisely because

---

FRANCISCO: For this relief much thanks. 'Tis bitter cold, / And I am sick at heart. (*Hamlet* 1.1.1–9)

2   Sławomir Świontek, "Le dialogue dramatique et le metathéâtre," *Zagadnienia Rodzajów Literackich* 36, no. 1–2 (1993): 30. Jenn Stephenson's English translation of excerpts from this article was published in *Journal of Dramatic Theory and Criticism* 21, no. 1 (Fall 2006): 129–44.

3   Jenn Stephenson, "Meta-enunciative Properties of Dramatic Dialogue: A New View of Metatheatre and the Work of Sławomir Świontek," *Journal of Dramatic Theory and Criticism* 21, no. 1 (Fall 2006): 117.

4   Juliane Rebentisch, "Forms of Participation in Art," translated by Daniel Hendrickson, *Qui Parle: Critical Humanities and Social Sciences* 23, no. 2 (Spring/Summer 2015): 46.

5   Rebentisch, 46.

even those works that emphasize a real always at the same time harbor a moment of semblance, those who participate in them are rebuffed back to themselves, to their behavior, their perception, as well as the social schemes of interpretation at their base. Our participation is reflected in art as a question."[6] In other words, in parallel with our participation in the fictional worlds represented, we begin to examine our participation in the real-world enactment of the event itself and in our lives at large. Participation is always about participation.

In certain cases, beyond the thematization of participation, even my fraught enactment of bad faith is thematized. This happens when the tension between my two potentially incompatible modes of participation is raised to awareness. Sometimes this is done deliberately as part of the baked-in dramaturgy of the performance text. Sometimes this arises spontaneously, catalyzed by particular performance conditions.

When participating as part of a four-person team in an escape room called *Yesterday's Heroes*, my random teammates were a family of three—a dad and two preteen children, all strangers to me. The imbalance of knowledge and skill between me and the preteens, between my decades and theirs, opened a schism between my dichotomous audience-player obligations. The fictional content goal of "escape from the room" came into collision with the formal play goal of "participate in an escape room," that is, contribute to an enjoyable collaborative event experience. I quickly realized (because I am not a monster) that I needed to hold space (a lot of space) for the two children. Even though I might know "the answer," I stayed silent or, at most, offered gentle clues. As a result, my dominant takeaways from that experience were a heightened awareness of our differential abilities, consideration of how to play productively (still superficially trying to win for the team) but equitably and respectfully within the space of that difference and trying to patiently remember that winning isn't everything. If I stretch, I can perhaps make a connection in my mind to the escape room itself. Part of the *Tape Escape* trilogy, *Yesterday's Heroes* was expressionistic and melancholy. Each of the puzzle clues and solutions involved vhs tapes of movies with various kinds of "heroes" (*The Wizard of Oz, Cool Runnings, Hamlet, Jaws*) and the dreamlike, time-travelling narrative took us back to August 1999 (twenty years before our game play) when the video store was destroyed in a fire that claimed the lives of five teenaged employees. (see GAME OVER. PLAY AGAIN?) In an escape room, where we (impossibly?) race

---

6   Rebentisch, 46–47.

to alter history and save the teens, I might ask as a player-teammate, what kind of hero am I? (see US)

This question—What kind of team player-hero am I?—is more directly and congruently thematized in the basketball show *Monday Nights*. Created by the 6th Man Collective and set on a basketball court inside a theatre, *Monday Nights* is hosted by a referee (the ubiquitous Colin Doyle) who introduces us to the Rules of the Court: "Be curious. Be brave. Be in the moment. Play." Good lessons for playing basketball; good lessons for participatory audience-players; good lessons for living. After dividing ourselves into four teams of approximately twenty players each—red, blue, green, and black—we sit with our teammates on bleachers facing the court-stage. Interspersed with watching and cheering the actors who are our team captains enact various skills drills and two-on-two mini-games, we listen to private audio monologues. Through our headsets, we are privy to our team captain's self-talk, their worries, and their aspirations. Each of the four men, in these intimate portraits, work through what it means for them to be variously a father, a husband, a friend, to have professional success, to have personal struggles, to play the game as a man who is no longer "young." Each speech circles around a common message, asserting that who you are is how you play. Team Red captain Byron (Byron Abalos) says in his monologue, "The most important thing about basketball is that who you are on the court reflects who you are in life . . . Be a good person." Darrel (Darrel Gamotin) from Team Black exhorts us to take care of each other. In his confessional monologue, Richard (Richard Lee) (Team Blue) overextends himself, worried that he is not enough; his teammates remind him gently that he is "not Superman. Just do you." Team Green captain Jeff (Jeff Yung) cuts us all some slack, saying, "Sometimes who I am on the court isn't great, but it's okay, 'cause it's real."

After the opening game demonstrations, the audience-teams are invited to take the court for some group skills practice and volunteers are drafted to play for their colour team in relays and a little three-on-three with their captains. Through our participation, the play inverts its initial message to assert that conversely how you play is who you are. Although there are points awarded to the teams for "winning," there are also additional points for each new "volun-teammate" who joins the game. (When I played *Monday Nights*, I was volun-told to play in almost every round. I was the only player on my team who was wearing closed-toe basketball-appropriate shoes.) The ethos of "be curious; be brave," is rewarded and the dramaturgy of the piece maximizes the correspondence between commitment to participation in the event and WINNING in the game-fiction. The pinnacle of the performance is a high-energy three-on-three game that showcases two audience-players for each team as excellent good sports and also, as occasion permits, as heroes. In one version I saw, the game ended spectacularly with confetti and a triumphant blast of the Queen anthem "We Are the Champions" when a young girl scored a basket to put her team over the top. The post-show trickles out as anyone who wants to can stay behind on the court, queuing up to "shoot for the wishes." (Anonymous audience wishes were written out and collected at the beginning of the show.) As a wish is read aloud, the next person in line, including the actor-players and the audience-players, attempts to sink a basket. If they fail, the next person tries. This continues for each slip until all wishes are successfully "won." There is no "ending" and the show is over when the task is complete. And it takes as long as it takes. I am reminded watching this sequence that in basketball, everyone misses the net a lot. Even NBA players taking free throws miss. Somehow this game dynamic flattens the field, emphasizing the theme that just showing up, being brave and curious, and doing your best is valuable.

Monday Nights elegantly manifests the paired obligations described by Düttman to the content as well as to the form by displacing, or at least questioning, the perhaps assumed content goal of winning at basketball, and prioritizing the formal goal of being a good volun-teammate, which then becomes its own contribution to winning. In this arrangement, we can embrace both roles in good faith.

See COMPLICITY

BEING LOST

Janet H. Murray in her book *Hamlet on the Holodeck* offers a full and varied analysis of all the reasons why a participant might be fearful in an interactive immersive environment: "Suspense, fear of abandonment, fear of lurking attackers, and fear of loss of self in the undifferentiated mass are part of the emotional landscape of the shimmering web."[1] First, suspense. This is the fear related to ignorance. Readers, audience, and gamers invariably function in a perpetual state of not yet knowing. Moving forward in linear time (unless we are repeat readers, viewers, or players), we don't know what will happen next. More than just a mild tension of curiosity in turning pages, the stakes are heightened in immersive experiences since I am a live character in this plot. This suspense of unfolding action over time is a locus of pleasure as well as anxiety. (see AROUSAL) Yes. Life is like this too, unfolding in linear and unpredictable ways. But at least in my life I hopefully have a better understanding of the stakes and have some pre-existing knowledge and survival skills. Moreover, I'm not likely to be attacked by Murray's imagined digital goblins or orcs. There is another fear in ignorance related to worlding conventions and participant behaviour. Once we are asked to interact with a novel environment, with foreign laws and mores, uncertainty drives my concern about what I can do. What I am materially capable of? Can I fly? In VR, I might indeed be able to fly. Virtual environments open the possibility of alternate laws of physics and personal capabilities. Correspondingly, however, I also need to relearn very simple manipulations of my new virtual body like walking and using my hands. And what is permitted or appropriate within this world's interpersonal social, legal, or ethical parameters? (see THE MATRIX)

Yet another aspect of fear is located in the spatial quality of being immersed in a novel world, a kind of spatial ignorance if you will; we call this "getting lost." For the most part, immersive experiences don't want me to be lost. Not actually lost lost. And so, they provide various

---

[1] Janet H. Murray, *Hamlet on the Holodeck: The Future of Narrative in Cyberspace*, updated edition (MIT P, 2017), 168. It is worth noting that Murray is writing about digital environments, immersive video games, but also exploratory literary texts. In these online spaces, we are not physically embodied. Any risk accrues only to my virtual avatar and my pride. (see GAME OVER. PLAY AGAIN?)

signposting strategies. For example, in *The Stranger 2.0*, which involves roaming around both inside and outside an unfamiliar building in an unfamiliar neighbourhood, we are accompanied by a GUIDE.[2] Actors lead us—sometimes literally holding our HANDS—from one station to another. Occasionally there is a pause as we are "parked" somewhere to await our next navigator. In plays with an escape-room structure, the experience is "gated" or "on rails,"[3] that is, movement is restricted to one scene at a time. As the door in front of us unlocks, we move ahead and cannot circle back. The *Tape Escape* trilogy of plays by Outside the March works like this. So does Moment Factory's installation *Illuminations: Human/Nature* co-located in the Banff National Park and the Rouge National Urban Park. (see CREW) Some shows like *b side* just hand us a map. Of course, each of these specific dramaturgical choices that shape our independent movement patterns may contribute to generating show-specific meanings, but in general, structures like guides, gates and rails, or maps that keep us on track work to mitigate the innate navigational worries that are baked into the genre.[4] Feeling the disorientation of being lost is not the point, until it is.

Produced by bluemouth inc. from a script conceptualized by the company, written by Jordan Tannahill and directed by Jennifer Tarver, *It Comes in Waves* begins literally on the waves as me and my new twenty-plus best friends paddle a giant canoe from the shores of downtown Queen's Quay to Toronto Island. Thirty minutes later we land and disembark. (see SWEATING) There is rough scrub and some trees, a path and a nineteenth-century stone lighthouse. It is twilight. We are greeted by a man (actor Stephen O'Connell) and he is confused: "Let me start again" "Shit, how does it go again?" "A man wakes up on an island and

---

2   *The Stranger 2.0: Above* also asked us to walk blindfolded to a new location, which was then the starting point for a game of hide-and-seek, yet another kind of play-game about being lost (or found).

3   "An on-rails game behaves much like a train: while sometimes the player can choose which path is taken, they cannot deviate from it." Limiting players to a single, sequenced path allows game designers to control the visual experience. Games like this are also easier to develop as it makes the game less complex and cheaper to produce. "On-Rails: Concept," *Giant Bomb*, 20 June 2021, giantbomb.com /on-rails/3015-169/.

4   Murray writes that there can be an optimal balance: "Both the overdetermined form of the single-path maze adventure and the underdetermined form of rhizome fiction work against the interactor's pleasure in navigation. [The optimal form] would seem to lie somewhere between the two, in stories that are goal-driven enough to guide navigation but open-ended enough to allow free exploration and that display a satisfying dramatic structure no matter how the interactor chooses to traverse the space" (Murray, *Hamlet on the Holodeck*, 168).

finds himself in front of a crowd and he has no idea why he's here." Yup, I think. Me too. He says, "Thank you for being here with me." Yup. Wherever here is. We are given booklets that are referred to as "field guides," but they are blank. Despite its ostensible purpose of guiding lost souls, the darkened lighthouse is not much help either. I have very poor spatial skills even at the best of times, (I take comfort in telling myself that my talents are verbal, not spatial) but the collation of being lost with unhelpful navigation guides (both human and manmade) to establish a sense of disorientation strikes me as purposeful.

As we journey to various sites on the island, my perception of where I am in space is persistently eroded. In the fading light, the first scenes are hazy and distant and surreal. Stephen dashes across an open field, shedding his clothes as he runs away from us. Two musicians, playing a trumpet and an accordion, drift by in a canoe. In concert with these incongruous images, I have to watch my footing carefully, treading across the beach in thick sand. The beach is festooned with lanterns. One of the actors stands in the crashing waves up to his waist in water, a lit road flare clutched overhead. It is a striking image. We finally arrive at a rustic building (which I now know is Gibraltar Point Artscape) to find a campfire in progress. One of the final images of the show is Lucy (actor Lucy Simic), illuminated in the darkness, wearing a white dress, dancing at the end of a jetty, surrounded by the black water.

We aren't lost exactly. Since we aren't responsible for our own navigation, I'm not stressed or anxious. I just don't know where I am. The images and the locations don't fit together. From our wandering and backtracking, I don't have a sense of the map.[5] Stephen, the protagonist, is also disoriented. He says, "The path is not as clear as I thought / But I sense we're getting close / Follow me." He is not where he needs to be. What becomes clear as the play progresses is that Stephen has died in a car crash. He knows he should be home but is not there. The party we are planning for "Him" is in fact a wake for Stephen. Stephen, who doesn't know that the party is for him, that he has died in the car crash,

---

5   As I've noted elsewhere (see ELBOWS) with regard to other work by bluemouth inc., my EMBODIED experience is shaped by dramaturgies of form in correlation to the play's expressionistic content. Writing about the site-specific spatialized nature of their work, bluemouth inc. explicitly claims disorientation as one of their signature dramaturgies. See their manifesto, "Please Dress Warmly and Wear Sensible Shoes," published in *Canadian Theatre Review* 126 (Spring 2006), where they identify "Lost in Space" as one of their four recurring "issues." In her article "'This is not a conventional piece so all bets are off': Why the bluemouth inc. Collective Delights in our Disorientation," Keren Zaiontz treads similar territory (*Environmental and Site-Specific Theatre*, edited by Andy Houston (Playwrights Canada, 2007), 175–88).

worries, "I don't feel ready / I don't feel prepared at all / He's going to be here any minute." As he is driving, his mind wanders and he misreads a sign that says "right lane must exit" as "right lane must exist." Lucy explains, "For a second you think the sign is telling you that somewhere on this road there is the right lane to be in, the perfect lane / A right way to be in the world." What we learn about Stephen at the wake, however, is that he has not found the right way to be in the world. Both his sister Ciara and best friend Danny in their eulogies fault Stephen for not knowing where to be; how to be. Stephen concludes his own remembrances with his own eulogy: "The only truthful thing I can say about the dead is / They are not here / That's the only thing they will say about me with certainty: He is not here."

In this liminoid,[6] almost purgatorial space, of the darkened island, I am not dead. I am probably not dead. I am, however, thinking deeply with my head, but also with my feet, about what it means to be here, 'cause I'm not at all sure where here is anyway. The word "lesson" might be too strong, too on-the-nose, for what I've experienced. But certainly, in a fuzzy way, through disorientation I have been given a prompt to think about how I am oriented to the world and to my loved ones in it. As we board water taxis, the lights of the city sparkle across the black water and I know where I am.

See SEEKING and DRIFT

---

6   Of course, theatre is, itself, in general, a kind of liminoid space. "As a public space, theatre functions as what the anthropologist Victor Turner calls the liminoid, a place set apart for the process of social or personal transformation, or what Foucault calls heterotopia, a quasi-public space which functions to reflect, expose, invert, support or compensate for the outside world" (Mark Fortier, *Theory/Theatre* (Routledge, 2002), 168).

MINI SHEEP IS LOOKING FORWARD TO THEIR TRAVELS, BUT WHEN THE BOARDING PASSES WERE PRINTED, ALL THE CITIES CAME OUT SCRAMBLED. IF YOU CAN UNSCRAMBLE THESE, THE RESULTING CIRCLED LETTERS WILL SPELL OUT AN ANSWER.

YOU MIGHT NEED TO "TRAVEL" AROUND FOR HINTS!

AVJOASER (hint: see ELBOWS) ◯ _ _ _ _ _ _ _

OTRLMEAN (hint: see DEMOCRACY) _ _ _ _ _ ◯ _ _

IXAAFLH (hint: see NOISE) _ _ _ _ _ _ _

IYVK (hint: see SHEEP) _ _ _ ◯ _

OONOTTR (hint: see BEING LOST) _ _ _ _ _ _ _

HWIOTEHSRE (hint: see DRIFT) _ _ _ _ _ ◯ _ _ _ _

ARADA (hint: see RECIPE) _ _ _ _ _

VRVENCUOA (hint: see SECRET WEIRDOS) _ _ ◯ _ _ _ _ _ _

ANSWER:

BETA

How do artists rehearse a participatory show, knowing the show in performance will change in myriad ways when it is populated by participants? If audience-participants are active co-creators of meaning, who arrive only at show time, how can artists prepare for their AGENCY and their variability? Audience-players are basically (and wonderfully) randomness generators. (see ALEA) In his book *Uncertainty in Games*, Greg Costikyan calls this variability in games, introduced through interaction, "performative uncertainty."[1] One way that this uncertainty can be managed "on-the-fly," during the experience in progress, is to build in SLACK, creating an elasticity in the journey of the participants, making it easier and harder as needed in relation to their skill level. But, what about before the audience-players even arrive? How can creators of participatory shows prepare in advance to accommodate the uncertainty introduced by an interactive audience?

Some artists turn to beta testing. Drawing inspiration from tech sector development models, beta testing asks for "feedback on design, functionality, and usability and this helps in assessing the quality of the product . . . [It works to provide] a complete overview of the true experience gained by the end users while experiencing the product."[2] Essentially beta testing is a kind of REHEARSAL. It is a purposeful kind of preview designed to collect user feedback, by providing practical immersion in the experience in a testing environment. Christina Bonnington, in a *WIRED Magazine* article about beta testing, points out that being in beta "used to mean that a product wasn't finished [but], now we know they never will be."[3] Many tech creators will keep certain software platforms in beta even after commercial release to gain even more data on user practice and apply those insights to continually iterate to improve their products.

BOURGEOIS THEATRE does make use of audience feedback in certain ways. Often there are invited dress rehearsals, previews, or, if you are a Broadway show, out of town tryouts in front of a presumably

---

1   Greg Costikyan, *Uncertainty in Games* (MIT P, 2013), 25.

2   "What Is Beta Testing? A Complete Guide," *Software Testing Help*, softwaretestinghelp.com/beta-testing/.

3   Christina Bonnington, "We Live in a Beta World," *WIRED Magazine*, 16 April 2013, wired.com/2013/04/beta/.

less-critical, non-New York audience, that bring in "test" audiences to gauge their reactions. But since the product is intended to be fixed, once it is set, the process is less responsively dynamic, and of shorter duration, ending on opening night. For participatory theatre, the work is less like fine tuning and more like trying to compensate for the fact that half your cast is missing while you rehearse. As James Long (Theatre Replacement) notes, "It really is guesswork. You become so deeply entrenched in your own process and your own impulses—making sense of all the 'wonderful brilliant' choices you have made—you might lose track of some simple practicalities or realities that come up."[4] Beta testing, then, is a way to blur boundaries between private rehearsal and public performance, bringing in audiences at selected critical stages of the development process. The annual Festival of Live Digital Art (FOLDA) has built this borrowed-from-the-tech-sector methodology explicitly into its operations, offering performances in differing stages of Alpha, Beta, and Go. It is not uncommon at FOLDA to see a show several years in a row as it moves through these evolutionary steps.[5]

In their participatory show *4inXchange*, performance and pop art duo xLq (Maddie Bautista and Jordan Campbell) invites four audience members at a time to talk about their relationship with money through a series of games played with $1,000 in actual cash dollars as the props. Inspired by Brandy Leery's Anandam Dancetheatre practice of Audiences in Residence (AIR), xLq invited an "Audience in Residence" into their rehearsal process. Anandam Dancetheatre describes AIR as a process that allows artists "the privilege of meeting the audience as WITNESS: seeing, listening, and making meaning with us in the moment, and in the collective remembrance of performance."[6] It is notable that xLq paid these participants as they would artists in the rehearsal hall.[7] Choosing to pay the AIR shifts the power dynamic in rehearsal infrastructure, reorganizing and crediting participants as "co-creators" explicitly in the piece, and for a show explicitly about money, this seems especially

---

4   James Long and Amy Amantea, quoted in "Volume 197 Online Feature," *Canadian Theatre Review* 197 (Winter 2024), https://ctr.utpjournals.press/ctr/197/online-feature

5   "Incubator," FOLDA (Festival of Live Digital Art), folda.ca/incubator/.

6   "Audience In Residence A-I-R," *Anandam Dancetheatre*, anandam.ca/a-i-r.

7   It's noteworthy that *4inXchange* also offers payment to the four participants in the actual show. At the end of the performance, xLq exits the performance space, leaving $1,000 in cash on the table, telling attendees that they can "pay themselves for their time" and LABOUR and take home the money. In the performance I attended, the participants divided the money among ourselves, giving the most to the fellow participant who really wanted to buy an expensive weighted blanket.

relevant. Campbell and Bautista note that when they were working alone in isolation, they "had no idea of how people would respond."[8] One of their insights from beta testing was that the initial version of *4inXchange* got, in their words, "too personal too fast," and so required adjustment to the pacing of audience revelations. The rehearsal process for this show took seven audience-in-residence trials to find the right balance between freedom and limits.[9]

Dustin Harvey of xoSecret Theatre describes his development process as "a cyclic dance of imagining, testing, and refining, deeply informed by a mixture of projected scenarios, surrogate audience feedback, and public preview responses."[10] Brian Postalian, reflecting on the development process of *New Societies* embraces a similar set of strategies. Describing his process, he outlines this action list of rehearsal activities, "Pretend to have audiences that are really slow at engaging, what happens? Pretend to have audiences that catch on really quick, what happens? Pretend to have audiences who don't listen, what happens? Change one thing at a time. Then test it . . . Plan a full 'What If . . . ' rehearsal. List out all of the possible scenarios of things that could happen. Talk through each one. Ninety per cent of them might have the same answer, but it's useful to articulate all those if-this-then-that situations."[11] James Long and Amy Amantea (*Through My Lens*) also lean into a methodology of pretending as they assume the roles of imagined audience-partners: "We spend a lot of time speculating. We put on personas. We took the liberty with our own identities. We laughed a lot."[12]

See CROWDSOURCE

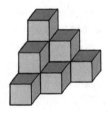

8   Maddie Bautista and Jordan Campbell, personal interview, 22 March 2019.

9   Aurélie Pedron and Kathy Casey, "Freedom in the Invitation: Lilith & Cie's *Invisible,*" *Canadian Theatre Review* 197 (Winter 2024): 82–89.

10   Dustin Harvey, quoted in "Volume 197 Online Feature," *Canadian Theatre Review* 197 (Winter 2024), https://ctr.utpjournals.press/ctr/197/online-feature.

11   Brian Postalian, quoted in "Volume 197 Online Feature," *Canadian Theatre Review* 197 (Winter 2024), https://ctr.utpjournals.press/ctr/197/online-feature.

12   James Long and Amy Amantea, quoted in "Volume 197 Online Feature," *Canadian Theatre Review* 197 (Winter 2024), https://ctr.utpjournals.press/ctr/197/online-feature.

BOUNDARY VIOLATIONS

How do we break the game? One way to break the game (or the play) is to REFUSE to play. We can walk out, walk away. No players, no game. No audience, no theatre. If we choose not to enter the MAGIC CIRCLE, then that special world of the game-fiction, separate from life, cannot come into existence. Another way that we break the game is for there to be breaches of that essential boundary dividing inside from outside that generates ONTOLOGICAL DUALITY. Roger Caillois (*Man, Play and Games*) frames the question this way: "What becomes of games when the sharp line dividing their ideal rules from the diffuse and insidious laws of daily life is blurred?"[1]

Taking it all too seriously is a breach where life—and all its priorities and values—becomes inappropriately mixed into the play-game. In the game context, this manifests as a determination to win at all costs. The "too serious" player forgets that an essential quality of play is that outside the circle it doesn't count. To this player, WINNING matters and is perhaps seen as having real world consequences. That need to win produces bad game behaviour that manifests as cheating, match fixing, or even violence.[2] Caillois devotes a chapter in his book to "The Corruption of Games" where he identifies this phenomenon as an excess of agôn ("the desire to win by one's merit in regulated competition"[3]). He writes, "A good player must be able to contemplate with objectivity, detachment, and at least an appearance of calm, the unlucky results of even the most sustained effort or the loss of large sums. The referee's decision is accepted in principle even if unjust. The corruption of agôn begins at the point where no referee or decision is recognized."[4]

That "contagion of reality"[5] that makes things too real also haunts theatrical performance. Samuel Taylor Coleridge's call for an ambivalent belief stance that positions theatrical worlds of fiction as provisional realities offers a perceptual model for managing participation across

---

1 Roger Caillois, *Man, Play and Games*, translated by Meyer Barash (U of Illinois P, 1961), 43.
2 Tom Brock, "Roger Caillois and E-Sports: On the Problem of Treating Play as Work," *Games and Culture* 12, no. 4 (2017): 321–39.
3 Caillois, *Man, Play and Games*, 44.
4 Caillois, *Man, Play and Games*, 46.
5 Caillois, *Man, Play and Games*, 45.

the precarious boundary. Famously, Coleridge asserts the necessity for a "willing suspension of disbelief."[6] However, contrary to the casual popular usage of this phrase, Coleridge is not asking for an easy unquestioning immersion into the fiction, where the audience takes the dramatic action as real. Not quite. Here is Coleridge: "The suspension of the act of comparison [to reality] . . . permits this sort of negative belief . . . The true stage-illusion in this and in all other things consists—not in the mind's judging to be a forest, but in its remission of the judgment that it is not a forest."[7] The key idea is that the audience remits judgment, we suspend not our belief but our disbelief. For the moment, engaged in the act of creating theatricality, we set aside the question entirely. Is it a forest or not? We are acutely aware both of what is accepted (the forest) and what is set aside (not a forest), as well as the boundary that separates these two states. Coleridge calls this "a sort of temporary half-faith, which the spectator encourages in himself and supports by a voluntary contribution on his own part, because he knows that it is at all times in his power to see the thing as it really is."[8] If this half-faith breaks down or becomes unbalanced, the fixity of the boundary itself is at risk. And so, playing the game with disproportionate intensity or giving oneself over to excessive belief in the dramatic fiction are the same kind of fault; both stances allow too much real-world stuff to leak into the protected circle. The game-play circle becomes contaminated by life.

A popular urban legend spins the tale of ignorant audience members who are either untutored in dramatic conventions or passionate audience members who are so emotionally moved by the action on the stage they forget that they are watching a fiction that they breach the theatrical frame to call a halt to the action. This doesn't actually happen—but we commonly believe that it does and fear that it might. In decades of writing about audience behaviour in relation to theatrical frames, I have found no documented cases of this kind of interruption, either historical or contemporary, stemming from a wrongly excessive belief in the reality of stage action. The persistent popular belief that such things happen is telling nevertheless.

In fact, it is the opposite behaviour that occurs. An accident happens on the stage and audiences are slow to respond to an endangered actor

---

6   Samuel Taylor Coleridge, "Biographia Literaria," in *The Complete Works of Samuel Taylor Coleridge*, edited by W.G.T. Shedd, vol. 3: Biographia Literaria (1884), 365.

7   Samuel Taylor Coleridge, "Progress of the Drama," in *The Complete Works of Samuel Taylor Coleridge*, edited by W.G.T. Shedd, vol. 4: Lectures Upon Shakespeare and Other Dramatists (1884), 37.

8   Coleridge, "Progress of the Drama," 37.

or other imminent catastrophe (like fire or collapsing scenery). We trust that the theatrical frame is strong and that the events that occur, no matter how alarming or seemingly risky, are safely contained in the fiction and thus require no real-world uptake. The opening moments of Cliff Cardinal's *Huff*, which urgently demand audience action as the protagonist risks suffocation from a plastic bag duct-taped over their head, apply this audience dramaturgy of tending to inaction as our moral failure. (see FUTILITY) This condemnation is premised on the built-in tension between Coleridge's appropriately distanced audience behaviour where, despite our being moved by the unfolding tragedy, we understand perfectly clearly that the protagonist does not need to be saved by a real-world bystander who really ought to call emergency services. It is a not uncommon dramaturgical strategy to purposely twist or blur the boundary so as to implicate the audience-participant who uncertainly straddles both positions. The landmark environmental work *Tamara* does this by laying down rules to strictly enforce non-engagement by the wandering audience and then suggests that by our silence we endorse FASCISM. Conversely, plays like *The Itinerary: Playtest* and *Foreign Radical* generate the same uncomfortable COMPLICITY by putting the participants into a situation where good and active game-playing conflicts with being a good and ethical person. (see BAD FAITH)

Caillois, interestingly, only considers excesses of game behaviours, not insufficiencies. The flip side of trying too hard, of believing too much, of being too "warm" as it were, is being too "cool." This stance is characterized by not trying hard enough, or having insufficient belief, to bring the fiction into full-blooded existence, being generally standoffish and disengaged in play-game. So rather than distorting play by being "serious," these participants resist play by being "unserious." This reluctance or resistance to participate in the fictional world of play might stem from lack of skill in precise opposition to being too serious. Lack of skill can also be caused by too much alcohol taken.[9] More than once I have witnessed drunk audience members attempt to participate in immersive participatory experiences. (I'm sure they think they are superstars. Not

9   Alcohol consumption, which lowers social inhibitions, increases our boldness and becomes (for better or worse) a lubricant to participate. Several participatory shows feature on-site bars, not just in the lobby but as part of the set or experience. Laura Levin comments on this phenomenon in her discussion of *Sleep No More* in *Performing Ground: Space, Camouflage and the Art of Blending In* (Palgrave Macmillan, 2014). In my experience of *A Grimm Night* (Transcen|Dance), not only was a custom cocktail included with my VIP ticket, during my one-on-one experience with *Sleeping Beauty's* Wicked Queen, I was "encouraged" to gulp down a goblet of a mysterious potion that tasted like a sweet red wine.

pleasant for the rest of us.) Or non-seriousness could come from simple disinterest in playing, shyness, fear of embarrassment, or indeed actual fear. Once while participating in a haunted-house-themed escape room, I was startled by one of the actor-characters hiding behind a door. After that point, I was so terrified of being again startled that I was unable to assist my fellow escapees in solving the puzzle. This tension between fear and winning is a staple of reality TV shows like *The Amazing Race* where successfully accomplishing game tasks typically involves bungee jumping, public speaking, scaling heights, and/or eating insects. (see AROUSAL)

Paradoxically, breaking the rules doesn't always break the game. Sometimes the game can be irredeemably broken by *not* following the rules. True. However, at heart, this kind of violation only becomes a problem in relation to the player attitude where rule breaking is the result of excessive or insufficient seriousness. But where there is a commitment to play and to the maintenance of the magic circle, the game might be sustained. An improvised change of rules, if agreed to and playfully absorbed, just means that we are all now playing some other new game.

See GOING ROGUE and KILLJOY

BOURGEOIS THEATRE

What about these other theatres that are not participatory? Can they be defined and given a convenient handle? Certainly, it would be useful for us in the analysis of dramaturgies of participatory theatre to also be able to speak to dramaturgies of theatre praxis that are not all that. Finding the right term, or at least a term that gestures in the right direction, has been a challenge. It is not a theatre of passivity in contrast to a theatre of activity. Audiences are by their nature active; however, their primary function in much traditional theatre is INTERPRETIVE. It is not a theatre of non-participation. Even in work that invites participation, there are productive dramaturgies of REFUSAL. How to describe the "other" kind of theatre, the "usual" kind of theatre, without being reductive?

The term that seems to come the closest, and that we have employed here, is bourgeois theatre. Emerging in parallel with the rise of a property-owning, mercantile, middle class in eighteenth-century Europe, the bourgeois theatre was a cultural phenomenon that placed this new social class firmly in its view.[1] Described by eighteenth-century theorists like Denis Diderot and Gotthold Ephraim Lessing, the bourgeois theatre features non-aristocratic protagonists, and eschews general or "stock" character types, looking instead at socially situated individuals. Typical narrative themes concern domestic misfortunes, the necessity of civic duty, and the promotion of virtuous behaviour. Aligned with its attention to the prosaic concerns of the middle class, bourgeois theatre also encourages a move towards a more mimetic or representational acting style, grounded in the observation of daily life, and speaking prose rather than poetry. George Lillo's *The London Merchant* (1731) is often cited as the quintessential exemplar of this genre.[2] In her book on the history of European theatre, Erika Fischer-Lichte connects the "bourgeois theatre of illusion" with the acting theory of Moscow Art Theatre director Konstantin Stanislavski, noting that these acting techniques were able to

---

1   Meg Mumford, "Bourgeois Theatre," in *Oxford Encyclopedia of Theatre and Performance*, edited by Dennis Kennedy (Oxford, 2005), 176–77.

2   Mumford, "Bourgeois Theatre," 176.

finally realize in performance the ideals of Diderot and Lessing, creating individual characters, located in specific circumstances.[3]

In recent times, as Meg Mumford notes in her entry for the *Oxford Encyclopedia of Theatre and Performance*, the label "'bourgeois theatre' has tended to refer more to theatre events dominated by [...] capitalist modes and relations of production ... institutions owned, controlled, and frequented by the bourgeoisie and those who have assimilated its codes and values."[4] This is the culinary theatre that Brecht (see A AND B) takes exception to, associating the genre with mass consumption and the facile reproduction of dominant ideology.[5] It is ironic that in its own time, the bourgeois theatre saw itself as oppositional, even revolutionary, and yet, as Patrice Pavis observes, the term is "used today in a pejorative sense in reference to boulevard theatre[6] and repertory, produced for maximum profits, its themes and values addressed to a '(petit-) bourgeois' audience who spend large amounts of money to consume an ideology and aesthetic already familiar to them."[7]

Setting the pejorative connotation aside, (we are not trying to pick a fight here) Pavis continues, saying that the bourgeois theatre is "identified in the minds of the public at large with quintessential theatre."[8] This is what we are trying to grab onto. And so, for us, "bourgeois theatre" is a convenient shorthand for the theatre that dominates the cultural landscape in North America and Europe. Although it is not entirely homogeneous in its aesthetic, this quintessential theatre is one that (for the most part) embraces mimetic realism, committed to what Hans-Thies Lehmann (*Postdramatic Theatre*) calls "a closed fictive cosmos, a 'diegetic universe' ... produced by means of mimesis."[9] (This is Lehmann's fancy way of saying that theatre creates representational

---

3 Erika Fischer-Lichte, *History of European Drama and Theatre*, translated by Jo Riley (Routledge, 2002), 282.

4 Mumford, "Bourgeois Theatre," 177.

5 Patrice Pavis, "Bourgeois Theatre," *Dictionary of the Theatre: Terms, Concepts, and Analysis*, translated by Christine Shantz (U of Toronto P, 1998), 38.

6 Pavis, in his entry on "Boulevard Theatre" (which conveniently for our purposes immediately precedes "Bourgeois Theatre" in his dictionary), defines this style as making use of a familiar and easily digestible, traditional aesthetic, featuring mainstream political views and aimed at middle-class audiences. These light comedies provided "an art of pure entertainment" (*Dictionary of the Theatre: Terms, Concepts, and Analysis*, translated by Christine Shantz (U of Toronto P, 1998), 36).

7 Pavis, "Bourgeois Theatre," 37.

8 Pavis, "Bourgeois Theatre," 38.

9 Hans-Thies Lehmann, *Postdramatic Theatre*, translated by Karen Jürs-Munby (Routledge, 2006), 99.

 worlds that pretend to be real. Like Elsinore in *Hamlet*.) **And in support of that requirement for maintaining a closed world, the behaviour of the audience is circumscribed by what we recognize as familiar conventions, penned on the far side of the fourth wall. The audience is (for the most part) static, invisible, and silent.**

Contemporary expressions of the participatory theatre dramaturgy aim to dislodge each of those behaviours, pressing the audience to cross that fourth-wall barrier. The audience is reconfigured as creative participants and so become mobile, visible, and talkative. And yet, as Pavis provocatively suggests, any contemporary theatre (even the participatory theatre that we pose as being in direct opposition to bourgeois theatre) cannot break free of the all-encompassing ethos of modern capitalism. As he writes, "One might well ask whether any theatre today can really escape being qualified as bourgeois, if we think of the term in the historical sense rather than as a slogan . . . Unless another kind of society should redistribute value with no debt to bourgeois taste and ideology, will theatre not necessarily remain tied to so-called bourgeois culture"?[10]

See INSTRUMENTALITY and SHOPPING

CARE

See SELF-CARE, REHEARSAL, and CONSENT

CEREMONY

In 2020, Tkarón:to-based performance circle manidoons collective, led by Yolanda Bonnell (Ojibwe-South Asian) and Cole Alvis (Métis), requested that only Indigenous people or people of colour review Bonnell's show *bug*.[1] In an official statement, Bonnell and Alvis insisted that in their process of "Indigenizing performance practices" for *bug*, there "is an aspect to cultural work—or in our case, artistic ceremony—which does not align with the white supremacy in colonial reviewing practices. In order to encourage a deeper discussion, our expectation of the media is that they will hire IBPOC reviewers to engage with our work."[2] This statement about the praxis of criticism in the Canadian theatre ecology is founded on the key declaration that *bug* is a work of ceremony and for manidoons, although *bug* was presented in a theatrical context, theatre and ceremony are not necessarily interchangeable frameworks. Or, specifically, theatre and its institutional structures in colonial Canada (or even more specifically in theatre criticism in Toronto) are not equipped or invited to comment on the work *as* ceremony.

In her book *Medicine Shows: Indigenous Performance Culture*, Algonquin-Irish theatre artist and scholar Yvette Nolan argues that for some Indigenous creators, every act of theatre is an "act of medicine" and artists like those in manidoons "make medicine by reconnecting through ceremony, through the act of remembering, through building community, and by negotiating solidarities across communities."[3] Nolan asserts that some Indigenous performance ceremony is medicine and, "like all medicine, ceremony is about reconnecting: reconnecting the artist to her ancestors, the viewer to lost histories, the actor to the audience."[4] Theorizing performance *as* ceremony is a fulcrum that can connect some Indigenous artists and their audiences to both the future

---

1   *bug* was created and performed by Yolanda Bonnell. It premiered at the Luminato Festival (Toronto, Ontario) in June 2018. The published play text was a finalist for the 2020 Governor General's Literary Award.

2   "manidoons collective Media Request," *manidoons*, manidoons.com; Yvette Nolan, "Why It Matters Who Reviews Indigenous Theatre," *CBC Arts*, 19 February 2020, cbc.ca/arts/why-it-matters-who-reviews-indigenous-theatre-1.5467785?s=09.

3   Yvette Nolan, *Medicine Shows: Indigenous Performance Culture* (Playwrights Canada, 2015), 3.

4   Nolan, *Medicine Shows*, 55.

and the past, the concrete to the cosmic. However, Nolan is wary of the implications of collapsing theatre and ceremony into one, despite some structural similarities. All Indigenous performance ceremony may be medicine, but not all Indigenous performance is innately ceremonial. Some Indigenous artists are doing other things with their work. On the other hand, although some Indigenous performance is both *capable of* and *comes from* ceremony, there are elements of contemporary performance that prevent the sacredness of ceremony from manifesting in a black box theatre. Nolan and Bonnell are specifically suspicious of the implications of *performing* ceremony within the capitalist context. In Nolan's chapter on ceremony she says, "On the one hand, ceremony is integral to our lives as Indigenous people; on the other, performing ceremony for a paying audience can feel like sacrilege."[5] Nolan thinks about the heterogeneity of her audience and wonders "how important is it that the audience understands the ceremony inherent in [works by Indigenous creators]? Is it at all important? For whom is the ceremony?"[6]

When I (a white settler of European descent) entered the theatre for Métis, French, and Finnish puppeteer and musician Jani Lauzon's performance-ceremony *Prophecy Fog*,[7] I felt a sense of reverence. The audience sat on chairs or on cushions on the floor, forming a nearly complete circle around Lauzon. Dressed all in white, she stood in the centre of a soft orange mat; yellow strings were arranged, radiating outwards from the orange circle—the sun. Moving silently and slowly, Lauzon reached one hand to the sky and the other to the ground. When the doors to the theatre closed, she began the show by putting her forehead to the ground and singing, shifting her orientation towards each of the four cardinal directions. As she continued to sing, she swept her hand around the edge of the sun-rug, pulling the rays in. Sunset. After these formal gestures, the play began.

Prophecy Fog takes us through a history of Lauzon's relationships with stones and their teachings, specifically sharing stories about her pilgrimage to the largest free-standing boulder in the world, "the Great Stone" in the Mojave Desert. At intervals throughout the show, Lauzon emptied about twenty large wooden bowls full of rocks onto the performance floor. She told us that ever since she was young, she would bring river

---

5   Nolan, *Medicine Shows*, 55.

6   Nolan, *Medicine Shows*, 60.

7   *Prophecy Fog* was created and performed by Jani Lauzon and directed by Franco Boni. Environmental design by Melissa Joakim and movement consultation by Julia Aplin. It was co-produced by the Theatre Centre and Paper Canoe Projects in association with Nightswimming and premiered in May 2019.

rocks inside her childhood home—and these were those rocks. When her family left the house behind, she left rocks in a circle around the house to protect it. After this story, she enclosed the audience inside a circle of stones around the perimeter of our seats. At the end of the show, she asked us to pause and refrain from leaving our seats until she retraced that circle, picking up the rocks. By encircling the audience, Lauzon establishes us as a kind of collective. Literally, we are now "in." We become participants in her ceremony. As participants, we sing together with Lauzon, humming together a single note, layering our breathing pauses, as she sings above and around us. (see JOY) In a lovely scenographic image, seven selected audience-congregants are asked to lift the stones they are holding in their hands over their heads, and the seven stones constellate the seven stars of Ursa Major. At the end of the show blackout, some of the stones glow and indeed become stars.

In all of our positionalities, heterogeneities, and intentions in attending the theatre on a given night, can we all really become *participants* in this ceremony? Can a theatre ticket buy a ceremony?

For Indigenous creators like Bonnell and Lauzon, the elements of ceremony are understandably to be protected[8] to preserve the sacredness of the medicine and the teachings. (see SCREENS and UNWELCOME) Although some Indigenous theatre-makers may utilize ceremonial structures, theatres in so-called Canada, with their donors and their boards[9] and their buildings on unceded LAND, may not be able to fully hold ceremony. In her writing about governance structures in the theatrical landscape, Yvette Nolan says that although "Indigenous theatres have created circles of elders and knowledge keepers in an effort to make their organisations reflect their realities; unfortunately, the circle keeps bumping up against the extant structure." That extant structure, the capitalist context of theatre is not equipped. In the talkback following the performance of *Prophecy Fog* in Kingston in February 2023, when asked about her thoughts on the connections between the performance and ceremony, Lauzon quoted artist Floyd Flavel who taught her that theatre is like "ceremony through a sieve." Audience-participants can

8   For more on this concept, read David Garneau's chapter, "Imaginary Spaces of Conciliation and Reconciliation; Art, Curation and Healing," in Keavy Martin and Dylan Robinson's *Arts of Engagement: Taking Aesthetic Action In and Beyond the Truth and Reconciliation Commission of Canada* (Wilfred Laurier UP, 2016), 21–42.

9   See Yvette Nolan, "Governance Structures For Theatres, By Theatres: What I Wish Existed," *Mass Culture/Mobilisation Culturelle*, 28 September 2020, massculture.ca /2020/09/governance-structures-for-theatres-by-theatres-by-yvette-nolan/.

act as WITNESS to a kind of ceremony with a set of maintained barriers to keep the teachings sacred.

In her master's thesis, "Defiance, Reclamation, and a Call to Mino Bimaadiziwin/The Good Life Through Ceremonial Performance Praxis," multidisciplinary artist and writer of Ojibwe/Swampy Cree and English/Irish descent Lisa Cooke Ravensbergen grapples with ceremony as a performance methodology. Ravensbergen says that "carrying ceremony and its embodiments into a theatre activates sacred space that already *is* a reuniting place, land, body, and memory in All Time for all bodies."[10] In addition to building this bridge, for Ravensbergen, Indigenous performance ceremony and its medicine has implications on and beyond the stage. In talking about her performance work she says, "To animate these artifacts one fuels the heart of ceremony that embodies ancestral memory inside the present and in today's theatres, implying futurities for Indigenous bodies that are on stage, unlearning colonial theatrical structures through resurgent acts of reclamation."[11] Although the transformative and meaningful effects of ceremony may be troubled within the contemporary capitalist theatre context, Ravensbergen asserts the reclamation and the power of "implying futurities for Indigenous bodies that are on stage" through performance ceremonies.

GO OUTSIDE AND FIND THREE LEAVES.
PRESS THEM INTO THIS BOOK.

---

10   Lisa Nadine Ravensbergen, "Defiance, Reclamation, and a Call to Mino Bimaadiziwin / The Good Life Through Ceremonial Performance Praxis" (ProQuest Dissertations Publishing, 2019), 11–12.

11   Ravensbergen, "Defiance, Reclamation," 10.

CHEATING

Thinking about participatory theatre through the lens of game studies is generally productive, generating fruitful connections, especially in terms of audience behaviours when we become players. (see ILINX, REMOTE CONTROL, and MAGIC CIRCLE) However, applying game thinking to theatre performance also exposes some intriguing contradictions when, for some terms, the two contexts don't easily or sensibly map onto each other. (see GAME OVER. PLAY AGAIN?) Winning is a prime example. You can win a game. In fact, the core purpose of most games is to "win." You can't win a drama. That doesn't make intuitive sense. Certainly, dramas have outcomes, for the characters, for the actors, and for the audience, but it would be strange to call any of those "winning." And what about cheating? The conditions that underpin winning—rules and outcomes—apply to cheating. Can you cheat in a participatory performance? And why would you want to?[1]

In *Rules of Play: Game Design Fundamentals*, Katie Salen and Eric Zimmerman argue that "generally speaking, looking across all phenomena of games, players do follow the rules."[2] Cheaters—players who purposefully break the rules of a game in order to win it—seem to be very much the exception. It is interesting to note that while a cheater will abandon their commitment to the lusory attitude,[3] which requires them to follow the entirely arbitrary and inefficient requirements of the game that make it fun to play, they still respect the authority of the game.[4] As Roger Caillois writes, "The cheat is still inside the universe of play. If he violates the rules of the game, he at least pretends to respect them . . . He is dishonest but hypocritical."[5] Winning matters to cheaters.

So why don't players who are also theatrical audience members cheat? One possible reason is, as mentioned above, there is no "win."

---

1   Major parts of this entry were originally conceptualized and written by Mary Tooley as part of her independent study project in fall 2021 under Jenn's supervision. This version is published here with her permission.

2   Katie Salen and Eric Zimmerman, *Rules of Play: Game Design Fundamentals* (MIT P, 2004), 269.

3   Bernard Suits, *The Grasshopper: Games, Life and Utopia* (U of Toronto P, 1978), 46.

4   Salen and Zimmerman, *Rules of Play*, 269; Johan Huizinga, *Homo Ludens: A Study of the Play-Element in Culture* (Routledge & Kegan Paul, 1955), 11.

5   Roger Caillois, *Man, Play and Games*, translated by Meyer Barash (U of Illinois P, 2001), 45.

In participatory theatre there are rarely what we might call outcome stakes. In some situations, you might try to "optimize" your experience; enacting what Keren Zaiontz calls "narcissistic spectatorship" or what Elinor Fuchs characterizes as SHOPPING.[6] But for the most part, there is nothing to gain by taking a shortcut. In fact, just the opposite; if you take a shortcut, you might miss something important—a pivotal plot point (see BEING LOST) or an emotional experience. (see AROUSAL) Having purchased a ticket and embarked on the show, I put myself metaphorically into the hands of the artist-creators. This is a game I want to play in full. Cheating would be antithetical to that. Now that said, if the play were not as expected, then I might attempt some remedial embroidery. Boredom or confusion might encourage GOING ROGUE or being a spoilsport. Feeling uncertainty, or even fear, I might OPT OUT or REFUSE; but I'm unlikely to cheat.

Although we have gathered no examples of cheating to "win" in participatory performance, we do know of an instance of intentionally not following the rules—do we call that cheating?—with the goal of creating a pleasurable and engaging experience for oneself, other audience members, and the actors—do we call that winning?[7] In a production of the live-action, improvisational, *Dungeons & Dragons* show, *Roll Models*, our research assistant Mary was one such "cheater." Mary, by her own admission, knows nothing about *Dungeons & Dragons*. Mary, also, I can attest, is a skilled actor and committed good sport. The show expects the audience-avatars to follow certain (admittedly arcane) rules that define your character's abilities in actions such as spellcasting or fighting. Mary says, "I got so nervous I could barely see the [character description] sheet. Instead of wasting time by searching for it anxiously, I would make up numbers instead, in order to maintain the pace and flow of

---

6   Elinor Fuchs, "Theater as Shopping," in *The Death of Character: Perspectives on Theater after Modernism* (Indiana UP, 1996), 128–43; Keren Zaiontz, "Narcissistic Spectatorship in Immersive and One-on-One Performance," *Theatre Journal* 66, no. 3 (2014): 405–25.

7   I remember intentionally not following the rules in Zuppa Theatre Co.'s *The Archive of Missing Things*. As we got closer to the end of the designated performance time, I was embarrassed to have failed on my mission to "get to the heart of the archive" through the interactive maze. I was shopping for the best experience and worried I would miss something, so I disregarded storytelling in favour of button-mashing my way to the heart. I would skim or barely read the text on the iPad, clicking buttons feverishly in hopes they would lead me in the right direction. This tension between winning and wandering, between game play and dramaturgical discovery, pushed me to disregard the rules of drama in favour of the rules of the game. Who cares how it happens as long as I find the prize, right? Wrong!

the performance. Sometimes, when asked to roll a die, and there are so many differently shaped and sided dice in this game, I couldn't find the right one to roll. So, I would either pretend to roll a die and then call out a random number, or I would roll the wrong die and call out the number on that specific die. These were my 'survival' tactics so that I would not get bogged down in the rules and in my inability to play correctly."

Mary rejected the rules not because she wanted to win the game, certainly there was no prize for the level, style, or impact of her participation, but because she did not fully comprehend the rules. Her goal was to play well, to maintain the spirit of the game, to avoid irritating the performer-GUIDES with frequent questions, and to make the experience of this performance an enjoyable one for everyone involved. (see JUICINESS) As she reports, "I allowed this newfound excited energy to inspire courageous acting choices and confident involvement in the game." I would argue that this creative chicanery not only surreptitiously smoothed over an obstacle in the gameplay, it actually enriched the game, allowing Mary to use her acting skills in lieu of following the formulae of the rules to produce better humorous effects. (see ALEA)

In *The Well-Played Game: A Player's Philosophy*, Bernard De Koven argues that the cheat is not necessarily always a negative force. Instead, sometimes a person alters the rules of a game with positive intent, because for some reason it doesn't "work" anymore or has ceased to be fun.[8] A player who cheats in this way gives themselves a "more than even chance to win" in order to change the atmosphere of the space for the better.[9] De Koven describes a scenario of musical chairs, a game commonly played by children that asks them to dance around a circle of chairs until a piece of music stops. They must then rush towards the chairs and capture one quickly because there is always one less chair than the number of children hoping to sit down. In his example, on one particular day, when the music pauses, instead of sitting down, a young boy picks up his chair. When the music begins again, he parades around the circle with it. He cannot fail, for he has physically secured his spot in the game. He now will always have a chair. He has become a cheater; he has broken the rules so that he cannot lose. And, interestingly enough, the other children begin cheering for him and applauding his clever action. (Okay. But sometimes we don't cheer the cheater. Some of us still wanted to play musical chairs.) His cheating enlivens the game and reveals that the children are bored of the rules as they exist. They are in need of alternative rules in order to improve their experience and make it more

8   Bernard De Koven, *The Well-Played Game: A Player's Philosophy* (MIT P, 2013), 26.

9   De Koven, *The Well-Played Game*, 24.

enjoyable. De Koven calls this the "well-timed cheat," as evidenced by his success with the crowd. Certainly, a key feature of his triumph stems from the performative, fearless, and public nature of his cheating.[10] He took a bold risk. He intended to break the game in order not only to win it, but also to make the experience more exciting for everyone. His self-centered goal is also somewhat generous in nature. When cheating is a SNEAKY and purely selfish act that deceives rule-abiding players, the response from others, when the cheater is exposed, is invariably frustration and contempt, as opposed to the celebratory reaction exemplified in the aforementioned experience.

I'm also wondering about lying as a kind of pseudo-cheating. In MAD LIBS-style, confessional performances, audience-players are asked to reveal personal details. There is an assumption, but no guarantee, that we will be honest. It seems evident that in order to get the optimal experience, to access that special feeling of being "seen," honesty would be the best policy. Lying undermines the point of this authentic sharing. And yet, there are occasions where, as an audience-AUTOBIOGRA-PHER, I concede that I have been less than candid. In my defence, in most cases, my prevarications have been triggered by a combination of a lack of trust with the performers and a shy hesitancy to share a truth that is unorthodox, too revealing, or just too complicated. The other reason that I have sometimes lied in the context of performance confessions is that as a theatre researcher I am sometimes "hiding in plain sight." Sometimes a slight bending of the truth has been necessary to obscure my involvement as a researcher with an autonomous agenda. Sometimes a different answer is required as a researcher so that I can access a different performance pathway that would otherwise be closed to the "true" Jenn. Lying can be a protective and convenient camouflage, a kind of soft REFUSAL.

See SCREENS

10   De Koven, *The Well-Played Game*, 27.

THIS CHART SHOWS MARY'S DICE ROLLS IN ORDER.
ADD UP EACH TOTAL BEFORE FOLLOWING ALONG ON THE BOARD.

⬡	◈	T
10	4	14
2	7	
8	3	
4	1	
3	3	
13	9	
6	8	
1	3	
7	5	
14	3	
5	2	
2	3	
1	2	

(see WINNING)

CHOOSE YOUR OWN ADVENTURE

If you offer the alien a cheese sandwich, turn to page 18. If you run back to your own spaceship, turn to page 22. (This is not really a direct quote from a Choose Your Own Adventure series book. I made this up based on my recollections of my ten-year old self circa 1982.) Staples of preteen reading in the 1980s, the genre of Choose Your Own Adventure book series provides a quick popular shorthand for the experience of a choice-based branching narrative. At regular points in the narrative, the reader, addressed in the second person, is invited to make a choice and turn to the appropriate page to discover the consequences of their decision. The reader becomes an active protagonist, shaping the experience of their avatar (see MEEPLES), and assumes some combinatory authorial powers, arranging the narrative from predetermined possible pathways.

Writing about dynamic, user-driven, multipath narratives, Espen J. Aarseth collects games, puzzles, poems, and novels (both print and virtual) under the umbrella genre of "cybertexts."[1] Aarseth is primarily concerned with the 1980s and 1990s flourishing of interactive fictions like Michael Joyce's foundational hypertext novel *afternoon: a story* and player-centric narratives in digital adventure games like MUDs (or multi-user dungeons). The earliest example Aarseth documents is a game called alternately *Adventure* or *Colossal Cave Adventure* (circa 1976) inspired by the tabletop role-playing game *Dungeons & Dragons* and coded by William Crowther and Don Woods.[2] Cybertexts are not limited to works facilitated by digital technology, but rather are an alternate name for what Aarseth calls "ergodic literature." The word "ergodic" is a neologism assembled from *ergon* meaning "work" and *hodos* meaning "path."[3]

In Aarseth's model of four user functions, that is, different types of labour undertaken by readers (also audiences), the choose-your-own-adventure model is "explorative, . . . in which the user must decide

---

1   Espen J. Aarseth, *Cybertext: Perspectives on Ergodic Literature* (Johns Hopkins UP, 1997), 1–17.

2   Aarseth, *Cybertext*, 98–100.

3   Aarseth, *Cybertext*, 1.

which path to take."[4] The explorative mode is driven by intrigue and extends not just to the flipping of pages; walking around an environment and choosing where to walk and what to look at manifests the same quality. Instead of navigating a fixed set of textual chunks that comprise the whole book (what Aarseth calls "textons") from which a reading path is chosen (what Aarseth calls "scriptons"),[5] a mobile audience physically explores an immersive environment. What you experience as a string of meaning is dependent on where you walk and what you look at, shaping which elements of the mise en scène and live performance you will witness. Writing about immersive participatory performance, Elizabeth Swift draws on possible-worlds theory, specifically the writing of Raine Koskimaa, to argue that audiences who combine visual or aural perception with movement to act as both a kind of cinematographer and editor of their own "film" are "actively creating an individual route through the text."[6] More than just an individual interpretation, this is arguably an actual new text. "This process constitutes what the work is because 'any single reading *is* just one possible actualization.'"[7] Thus, "'hypertextual' reading operates as an actualisation of a world-creating process."[8] As Swift notes, the high-degree of flexibility of work in this mode characterized by significant indeterminacy and plurality is offset by its structural limitations.[9] Even with myriad choices, because the basic set of choices is prescribed, the potential resulting world-texts are not infinite; they are bounded both in number and also in narrative possibility. The creative play of the audience is literally that of explorers; our work is to seek, to discover, and to reveal pre-existing territory. We choose our routes, but the environment does not respond. I can flip the pages to make new assemblages, but I have not been invited to write new entirely new scenarios. (see MAD LIBS)

In a number of cases, this experiential quality of being an explorer is tied thematically to the story of the performance as the form influences understanding. For Zuppa Theatre Co.'s *The Archive of Missing Things*,

---

4 Aarseth, *Cybertext*, 64.

5 Aarseth, *Cybertext*, 62.

6 Elizabeth Swift, "Negotiating the Possible Worlds of Uninvited Guests' *Make Better Please*: A Hypertextual Experience," in *Reframing Immersive Theatre: The Politics and Pragmatics of Participatory Performance*, edited by James Frieze (Palgrave Macmillan, 2016), 105.

7 Swift here cites Koskimaa's "Reading Victory Garden–Competing Interpretations and Loose Ends" ("Negotiating," 106).

8 Swift, "Negotiating," 105.

9 Swift, "Negotiating," 108.

set in a public library, we are SEEKERS, trying to find the "heart" of the archive. Audience explorers are given iPads and tasked with being "finders" as well as seekers, as the work combines choose-your-own-adventure with associative puzzle-solving. Through our headsets, we are told quite explicitly "there is much to uncover;" "get as deep as possible;" "see how much you can discover before the clock runs out." Presented with the choice of several virtual museum galleries, the archive is spatialized; we are told that we need to find the correct "door" that leads to the next level. Initially, the options at each junction of the forked narrative appear to be indifferently indistinguishable from one another, and the outcomes not linked in obvious or rational ways to the choices we make. However, as we comb through the digital hypertextual archive of *The Archive*, making navigational selections, (if we are paying close attention) we come to realize our determinations are not subject to the random coin toss of ALEA. There are "right" answers. Given a choice between "Clothespins," "Lace Curtains," and "Safe Key," I know I should choose the lace curtains, because one of the actors in their guise as a random library patron is wearing a lace dress. Following a successful series of choices, I am informed that I have found the staircase and I descend to the next level. *The Archive* talks back to me, reflecting on my experience as an adventurer and offering subtle reassurance. "Consider the impact of a milestone on an unexpected journey." Later, I encounter an exhibit in the archive that is an actual milestone: "This milestone is part of a sub-exhibit dedicated to things that are obsolete," I am told.

Speaking of things that are obsolete. A decommissioned school provides the built environment for the musical *Brantwood*; here the rooms and staircases that the adventuring audience traverses are not virtual, but actual. Set in a high school on the eve of graduation, *Brantwood* also incorporates the exploratory function of a site-immersed audience as a central theme. This idea is introduced in the opening song, known to the creators as the "Audience Incantation." Sung by a chorus of high school students in uniforms spanning a century of decades, the song speaks both to what it means to be a student on the brink of graduation, ready to embark on their life's journey, and simultaneously prepares the audience for our own incipient theatrical journey. "I think I'm getting closer. I'm just around the corner. Won't you hear me. Won't you see me." "Coming back, I don't know what I will find." "Where am I going?" "Where will the hallway lead me? So many doors to open . . . No one knows the way to go." "All these choices, never clear, and all these voices." "Standing on the edge. I look to the horizon." Here, the dramaturgy of the mobile audience is not framed as an active seeker. We are not given a goal or thing to find. Rather, we are curious wanderers. Cruising the hallways, we peruse the stories of the decades. We bear witness as GHOSTS, not only to the narratives of past teens, but also to reflexive contemplation of our own teenage pasts.

In participatory events with an even weaker narrative teleology, the main audience action is DRIFT. It is perhaps a stretch to characterize these as performances as they are more like experiential spaces. I'm thinking of mirror mazes,[10] funhouses,[11] or PLAYGROUNDS. Take for example the "Playing In Public" installation at the Bentway in Toronto during the summer of 2021.[12] One of the interactive works, created by Montréal's Daily tous les jours, called *Walk Walk Dance*, featured what looks like a long teal carpet with orange stripes. Contact with the stripes generated musical noises. Players strolled, jumped, skipped, and wheeled along the path. Each individual action or combination of simultaneous group actions contributed to the sonic score. The experiential scope in works like this is almost entirely sensory and existential. Through our adventurous engagement, these configured spaces invite MINDFULNESS, to see the world afresh, to ask, "What is it like to be in the world?" And of course, take a selfie.

See SHOPPING

---

10   *House of Mirrors*, created by Christian Wagstaff and Keith Courtney (Australia), made its Canadian premiere at Luminato Festival, Toronto, in June 2019. The installation is described as "basically a giant kaleidoscope you can get lost in" (Tanya Mok, "Toronto is Getting a Massive Mirror Maze," *blogTO*, 13 June 2019, blogto.com /arts/2019/03/luminato-2019-toronto-mirror-maze/).

11   *The Funhouse* created by art collective Mondo Forma ran intermittently in Toronto from June to December 2019. The advertising blurb proclaims, "Step into another world: *The Funhouse* is an immersive experience brought to life by visual artists from across Toronto, with featured environments inspired by local musical artists. The adventure begins in a 1920s inter-dimensional hotel. As you descend down the rabbit hole, discover an alternate universe of art, interactive tech and music" ("*The Funhouse* Toronto," *Showclix*, showclix.com/event /the-funhouse-toronto).

12   "*Playing in Public* is a neighbourhood exhibition that explores the history and future of play, and its role in shaping decisions about public space. A wide variety of artists, educators, technologists, planners, and community organizers have created works that address questions like: How does space shape the rules of play, and how can non-traditional spaces teach us to play differently? How does play influence our interactions in public space? How has the nature of play changed in a mid/ post-COVID city?" ("*Playing in Public*," The Bentway, play.thebentway.ca/).

GADZOOKS! YOU HAVE COME ACROSS A SLEEPING ALIEN.
BESIDE THE ALIEN SITS AN EXTRATERRESTRIAL CHEESE
SANDWICH, COOKING ON A PANINI GRILL. IF IT COOKS FOR
MUCH LONGER, IT'LL LIKELY BURN. TO WAKE THE ALIEN AND
WARN THEM, TURN TO PAGE 166. TO TAKE THE SANDWICH AND
RUN, TURN TO PAGE 93.

CLAIRE BISHOP

In her landmark book (with the best title ever) *Artificial Hells: Participatory Art and the Politics of Spectatorship*, Claire Bishop provocatively asks how we are able to assess the value of participatory art. Before one can ask if it's "good," we have to ask, "Good at what?" From her position, writing about participatory art—visual art and installation art, not theatre or performance, mind you—under the neoliberal regime of mid-1990s "New" Labour governments in the UK, Bishop is concerned about the INSTRUMENTALIZATION of participation as a kind of soft social engineering.[1] And you can see how this happens. It is Nicolas Bourriaud (*Relational Aesthetics*) who proposes a real-world social effect of the interpersonal ENCOUNTER. Participation, according to Guy Debord (*Society of the Spectacle*), "rehumanises a society rendered numb and fragmented by the repressive instrumentality of capitalist production."[2] To heal a broken society, art is the answer. Of course, this is in no way a new formulation. Art is frequently recruited to real-world ends. Theorists looking to art as a vehicle for real-world social or political benefits will be in good company going back millennia to Roman writer and benevolent mentor Horace in the first century of the Common Era, who famously advises his young playwright-wannabe friends that the purpose of drama is to entertain and to instruct.[3]

---

1   I don't think this phenomenon comes to Canada in quite this same way. (Some neoliberal policies were enacted under Ontario Premier Mike Harris and Conservative Prime Minister Stephen Harper.) See *Neoliberalism and Everyday Life*, edited by Susan Braedley and Meg Luxton (McGill-Queen's UP, 2010). Although that said, I did find a report by the Canada Council from 2021 titled *Canadians' Arts Participation, Health and Well Being*, authored by Hill Strategies Research, that proposes a meaningful correlation between "cultural participation" (meaning attendance at arts events and museums and galleries) and self-reported positive feelings of physical and mental health. Another study by the Ontario Arts Council, *Impressions of the Impact of the Arts on Quality of Life and Well Being in Ontario* (2017), reports, for example, that "88 per cent of Ontarians agree that participation in arts activities builds a shared sense of community."

2   Claire Bishop, *Artificial Hells: Participatory Art and the Politics of Spectatorship* (Verso, 2012), 11.

3   Horace, "Ars Poetica," *Poetry Foundation*, poetryfoundation.org/articles/69381 /ars-poetica. "He who joins the instructive with the agreeable, carries off every vote, by delighting and at the same time admonishing the reader."

Francois Matarosso is the author of a 1997 study titled *Use or Ornament?: The Social Impact of Participation in the Arts*, which examines the engagement of ORDINARY PEOPLE in local arts projects across the UK "to recognize the social and cultural value of community arts." From survey data, the study presented such statistics as "91 per cent of participants made new friends," "37 per cent have decided to take up training or a course," "21 per cent have a new sense of their rights," and "73 per cent have been happier since being involved." Ultimately, the study concludes that "participation in the arts is an effective route for personal growth, leading to enhanced confidence, skill-building and educational developments which can improve people's social contacts and employability."[4] Personally, I find this kind of blunt instrumentalization of art patronizing. It seems like wallpapering over basic problems, ignoring systemic barriers that perpetuate exclusion and oppression, and instead is oriented towards making people content and passive within existing systems.[5] Cynically, I note that this is the kind of thing that looks really good on grant applications seeking funding from government-sponsored arts councils. Participation invites a kind of super engagement and granting bodies love engagement. (More than once, I have attended a performance billed as participatory, only to find that the promotional blurb or genre tag did not match the reality.) Bishop similarly takes exception to this narrative that places the primary benefit of participatory art to be a panacea for poverty, unemployability, crime, and social exclusion. She writes, "Participation became an important buzzword in the social inclusion discourse . . . [meaning] to conform to full employment, have a disposable income and be self-sufficient . . . [To this view] the social inclusion agenda is therefore less about repairing the social bond than a mission to enable all members of society to be self-administering, fully functioning consumers who do not rely on the welfare state and who can cope with a deregulated, privatized world."[6]

The value, then, of a participatory artwork is measured by how much participation is generated, and the artwork is relegated to secondary status, a vehicle for generating that participation. It is no different, say, from an amateur sporting event or community gardening project. Bishop points out the corollary impact of this perspective on art criticism: "the

---

4   Francois Matarosso, *Use or Ornament?: The Social Impact of Participation in the Arts* (Commedia, 1997), 6.

5   For further discussion of this perspective, see Paola Merli, "Evaluating the Social Impact of Participation in Arts Activities," *International Journal of Cultural Policy* 8, no. 1 (2002): 107–18.

6   Bishop, *Artificial Hells*, 13–14.

urgency of this *social* task has led to a situation in which socially collaborative practices are all perceived to be equally important *artistic* gestures of resistance: there can be no failed, unsuccessful, unresolved or boring works of participatory art, because all are equally essential to the task of repairing the social bond."[7] Beyond assessing participatory art according to the nature of its participation measured by quantity, I want to suggest that we reverse that equation. Participatory art is, in the first place, art. So rather than thinking about art in service of generating opportunities for participation, this book flips that script, positioning participation as an artistic technique used in service of whatever art is good for. Of course, there are failed, unsuccessful, unresolved, or boring works of participatory art. Just as there are failed, unsuccessful, unresolved, or boring works of every other kind of art. Taking Bishop's question as inspiration, I argue that we need to care about this. Participatory art is not excused from critical engagement and assessment.

Using this formulation, we ask here how dramaturgies of participation contribute meaningfully to the artwork's central audience understanding or experience. This approach sets aside as uninteresting instances where participation is merely a random gimmick unconnected with other elements of the work. It also sets up an expectation that participation is a dramaturgical choice—no different from other strategies like direct address or writing in verse. Participation is doing something meaningful. With respect to Goethe's Three Questions of arts criticism, we are asking our own three questions: What is participation doing as a dramaturgical technique? How does a particular application or instance of participation create meaning or shape our experience? And why is that important? This book provides a long answer to these questions. Our short answer is that participation is always about participation. Participation in art, in all the works discussed here, functions to shed light on the nature of participation in the world.

See PAINT and STRUMPET

---

7 Bishop, *Artificial Hells*, 13.

COMPLICITY

"Let's play the game! We're going to fucking play a fucking game! Goddamn play the goddamn game! Who wants to bag some tourists . . . I mean terrorists? Right on—okay! Thank you very much for agreeing to participate."[1] Addressed to a theatre audience of about twenty, standing in a loose circle, in a black box studio, this is how we meet our Host. Manic and not a little threatening, dressed in a white tuxedo and pink bowtie, the Host subjects us to relentless questioning about our habits and beliefs: "Who purchased something online using their credit card in the past week?" "Who here has looked at online pornography, sometime in the past 24 hours?" "Who here has used encryption in their messaging apps or email?" Everyone is compelled to declare themselves and there is no OPTING OUT. Interspersed with this surreal and hostile quiz game are dramatic monologues from the character Hesam, an Iranian-Canadian student at Laval University who has been detained as a possible homegrown terrorist. In the course of *Foreign Radical*, these two worlds merge, and not only are we subject to bureaucratic interrogation and profiling, but we are also, in other scenes, empowered by game tasks to make decisions about Hesam. We search his suitcase, we read his private papers. Is he a terrorist threat? Should he be added to the "no-fly" list? How do we decide?

Foreign Radical problematizes borders—the border of the MAGIC CIRCLE, inscribing the distinction between game and not game, but also that between dramatic fiction and the actual world—in order to make us think about national borders and who is allowed to cross and who is not. (see BOUNDARY VIOLATIONS) These permeable and uncertain borders between fiction and reality, between game and not-game, create an ethical conundrum where, by being a good player and following the rules of the game, I am compromised in the real world.[2] The embodied actions of the audience-players have unpleasant consequences. And throughout this play-game hybrid we are confronted by

---

1   Tim Carlson, Jeremy Waller, David Mesiha, Kathleen Flaherty, Milton Lim, Aryo Khakpour, Florence Barrett, and Cande Andrade, *Foreign Radical*, *Canadian Theatre Review* 175 (Summer 2018): 61.

2   Jenn Stephenson, "Real Bodies Part 1: The Traumatic Real in Immersive Performances of Political Crisis and Insecurity—*Counting Sheep* and *Foreign Radical*," in *Insecurity: Perils and Products of Theatres of the Real* (U of Toronto P, 2019), 169–209.

COMPLICITY

questions of what we are willing to do or to sacrifice, calling out the balance of security and the freedom to travel. (see BAD FAITH)

The suitcase-searching task/mini-game is a pivotal example of how we are accused by our own ONTOLOGICAL DUALITY. The Host instructs selected audience-players to conduct a thorough search of the suitcase belonging to Hesam. And we do. Some audience members embraced the task with determination. Clothes were rummaged. Books and papers flipped through. I myself witnessed a gift being unwrapped. I heard tell from another performance of an entire tube of toothpaste being squeezed out. In the end, the suitcase was an irreparable mess, our invasive actions impossible to undo or to hide. On the one hand, we were asked to do this as part of the game of *Foreign Radical*. The suitcase belongs to a fictional character, and we have been deputized in the fictional world to conduct a judicial investigation. On the other hand, in a subsequent scene, Hesam reappears standing on a table, his disarrayed belongings around his feet. Stepping off the table, he takes a seat facing a selected audience-player who is also seated. He then asks them a series of serious personal questions. His demeanor is quiet and composed but decidedly unfriendly. We are being accused. "Why do you want to travel?" "Is life a game?" "I have known someone who could be associated with a terrorist group. Do you know anyone like that?"[3] We are asked to say why we would choose freedom of association over freedom to travel. The tables have been turned and the switch from being investigators to being the subjects of interrogation is potent enough to make one a bit nauseous. Hesam has stepped through the frame and the context of our playful game action is rendered unstable.

The nature of participatory choice (or the lack of it) is a powerful dramaturgical tool in shaping the ethical and political context of action. In *Tamara*, set in 1927 Italy in the home of Gabriele d'Annunzio, we are free to roam and watch any scene, but our AGENCY is significantly restricted. Our compelled passivity as observers speaks to an understanding of the implications of being neutral under FASCISM. In *Foreign Radical* we are under compulsion like *Tamara*, but instead of being forced to silently obey, we are forced to speak, to reveal ourselves. Under interrogation and surveillance—step forward if you did this, raise your hand to vote for your preference, clap if you agree that this is true—we reveal ourselves, exposing intimate foibles and private opinions on charged issues. *Foreign Radical* is not so much a CHOOSE YOUR OWN ADVENTURE, but rather your adventure is chosen for

3   Carlson et al., *Foreign Radical*, 70.

you. The two plays take parallel paths on the tension in audience participation between being a good audience-player (Don't break the show by your refusal of the game!) and being a good human being (Doing things that we think are inappropriate or unethical). *Tamara* commands us to be silent and meek and then holds us responsible for that behaviour. *Foreign Radical* does the same. We are commanded to participate to play the "fucking game." And then we are made to regret what we have done.

In both cases, we are good audiences. In the actual world, we are engaged in the preservation of the performance event out of respect for the work of art and the artists. In both cases, this gets us into trouble since the fictional world wants something else from us. We play these games according to their rules, but *Tamara* and *Foreign Radical* provoke us to think differently about the participation that is offered. Impossibly, they want us to REFUSE their game.

See TYRANNY

THE ALIEN DOESN'T WAKE AS YOU GRAB THEIR SANDWICH AND HIGHTAIL IT OUT OF THERE. WHEN YOU ARE A SAFE DISTANCE AWAY, YOU REALIZE HOW DELICIOUS THE SANDWICH SMELLS. YOU'RE ALMOST BACK HOME, BUT ALSO FEELING QUITE PECKISH AFTER ALL THAT RUNNING. TO TAKE A BIG BITE OF THE ALIEN'S SANDWICH, TURN TO PAGE 297. TO ABSTAIN AND HEAD BACK HOME, TURN TO PAGE 367.

CONSENT

Ask nicely. Keep your hands to yourself. No means no. Content Warning: this show contains scenes of domestic violence and strobe lights. Please note: participants are welcome to opt out of this experience at any time. "Please dress warmly and wear sensible shoes."[1]

What is consent? Consent is ongoing, enthusiastic, and informed.

When doing pretty much anything with another person, asking for consent is necessary for good RELATIONS. In pre-school lessons on sharing, asking for consent is one of the earliest ways we teach children to be good friends. As adults, we're taught that healthy pleasure and INTIMACY require asking for and receiving a certain kind of robust consent. As adults (and as children, in different ways), having control over our body and our surroundings is necessary to our human experience. Once, Jenn told me her favourite thing about being an adult is saying no to things she doesn't want to do. Giving and receiving consent can be liberating and clarifying for both parties in a relational EXCHANGE because in order to achieve consent, both parties must mutually agree to a given action. As a legal concept, informed consent entered the vernacular in the mid-twentieth century[2] and it is really only in the last decade

---

1   bluemouth inc., "Please Dress Warmly and Wear Sensible Shoes," *Canadian Theatre Review* 126 (Spring 2006): 16–22.

2   In her article "The Disappearing Fourth Wall: Law, Ethics, and Experiential Theatre," Mary LaFrance, a law professor at UNLV, considers ethical and legal issues raised by immersive and participatory performances. She notes that, although the theatre label appears to give permission to behave in ways that might be "illegal, offensive or actionable in a different setting," simply calling an event "theatre" does not render it exempt from liability for physical and emotional harms that might arise (516). The bar, however, for a tort claim of emotional distress is quite high, applying to a person who "'engages in extreme and outrageous conduct' that intentionally or recklessly causes severe emotional distress to another. [. . . The] victim's distress must be 'so severe that no reasonable person could be expected to endure it'" (537–38). She recognizes that theatre has a long history of making audiences uncomfortable and that, moreover, participatory audiences are often willing to be emotionally vulnerable with the expectation that this is in service of their main goal, which is to be entertained. Ultimately, LaFrance recommends a four-point scheme for risk-reduction: 1) screening and disclosures prior to the performance; 2) care in selecting venues, focusing on physical safety, e.g., uneven floors, getting lost, low lighting, crowds, etc.; 3) supervision by people trained to notice and deal with patrons in distress and to identify people who pose risks to self or others; and 4)

that major theatres in Canada have adopted policies around content warnings that provide additional information about what to expect with regard to potentially disturbing subject matter or depictions, sometimes including a plot synopsis or a list of support resources. When content warnings are made visible to audiences in advance, they offer an implicit invitation to OPT OUT of the experience. When audiences are more knowledgeable, consent is more robust. We now have information and that allows for choices to attend or not attend.

This may well be sufficient when the primary mode of engagement in typical BOURGEOIS THEATRE is watching, and the audience is safely separated from the fictional world by a fourth wall. However, what happens when participatory dramaturgies move beyond the engagement of our eyes and ears with a fictional plot? What happens when creators are asking audience-players to provide intimate, AUTOBIOGRAPHICAL details as creative input or to place our bodies into proximity with others? (see SWEATING, FOOT WASHING, and HANDS)

Consent is informed. To be fully informed, however, runs counter to the essential quality of drama that unfolds in linear time as if it is spontaneous. A key part of the experience is bearing witness in real time to each fresh unexpected moment. An emphasis on linear Aristotelian dramaturgy suggests that knowing exactly what's ahead can undermine an experience. While being surprised through the enacted revelations of a dramatic plot can be moving, informed consent requires participants to know what's in store. In David Ball's prescriptive guide to dramaturgy *Backwards and Forwards*, he insists upon discovery as a core dramaturgical principle. For Ball, "Dramatic tension requires that the audience desire to find out what is coming up."[3] How can asking for informed consent in participatory dramaturgies still centre the audience's experience of discovery?

Two shows, David Gagnon Walker's *This is the Story of the Child Ruled by Fear* and Radix Theatre's *TBD*, use theatrical REHEARSAL embedded in the performance structure as a dramaturgical strategy to provide audience-participants with a kind of preview as a foundation for informed consent. In *TBD*, participants are asked to embark on a three-week-long experience, meditating on death, transformation, and rebirth, beginning with the

---

content regulation, including recognition that some content is simply inappropriate and using talkbacks or other transition activities to acclimatize participants back to the real world after an emotionally heightened experience (*Vanderbilt Journal of Entertainment and Technology* 15, no. 3 (2013): 506–82).

3   David Ball, *Backwards and Forwards: A Technical Manual for Reading Plays* (Southern Illinois UP, 1983), 59.

moment of their own (fictional) demise. Besides the heavy content, the participatory activities staged in *TBD* are notably invasive. For example, during the experience, actors put up missing-person signs with your face on them in your neighbourhood. On one day, an actor in a featureless morph suit enters your house with an offer to help you with a household task. Participants are (with their permission) geotracked through their phone for the duration of the experience. To achieve informed consent, Radix Theatre is explicit as to what the performance will entail. First, participants fill out a waiver

MISSING

CAN YOU HEAR US?
LET US KNOW WHERE YOU ARE
AND HOW YOU ARE DOING.

before they start. Participants must acknowledge that "*TBD* will bring up notions of death or dying and that I am mentally and emotionally stable enough for this to occur." The waiver also asks comprehensive questions about participants' life circumstances: "Do you live alone? If you live with others, will they be comfortable with a *TBD* performer visiting your home a couple of times?" Second, before the performance begins in earnest (before you "die"), there is an "intake day," which functions much like a meet and greet. Participants meet each other and the acting company. A schedule is passed around. Radix Theatre lays out the tasks and scenes associated with each day of the experience in great detail, giving participants an arena to ask any questions they have. This reveal is not too revealing because the point of the show is an experiential exploration of death. (see MINDFULNESS) The surprising future discovery of what will happen to you isn't the point, but rather what you think about what happens to you in the moment as it's happening to you.

There is a pre-show moment in David Gagnon Walker's *This is the Story of the Child Ruled by Fear* that offers an invitation with similar intentions. In this piece, participants are asked to recite from a script with other audience members. The script itself, an autobiographical story written by Walker, is about fears and facing them. Depending on where the audience is sitting in the room, they are each cast in a role and given characters to play (including a chorus). Participants are asked to read aloud with strangers, an anxiety-inducing experience for some. Participants are informed of what they are reading through the script in their lap. While the participants gain confidence in their collective reading, Walker's "child" faces fears of their own. Formally, Walker models a kind of bravery through his invitation to participation, while his characters inside the play display their own small acts of bravery. In the first moments of the play, Walker asks two of his participants to read a scene and he gives them some directorial coaching. Readers are given an opportunity outside of the frame, before the formal "reading" begins, to warm up their voices, to understand what is being asked of them, and to see what it might feel like. Because this piece is about being anxious, the participants' comfort is of the utmost importance. Using a "cold read" as a recognizable rehearsal technique to hold onto, Walker invites participants to play "theatre" together.

In his essay, "Notes on the Elimination of the Audience," Allan Kaprow, writing about Happenings,[4] makes the point that it is a "mark of mutual respect" if the participants have a clear idea what they are to do, and that full disclosure does not reduce impact. He writes that for participants "knowledge of the schema is necessary, professional talent is not."[5] In order to experience the full transformative potential of both the shows described here, participants need to feel safe. Participants feel safer when they are given the opportunity to give their informed consent. In the case of these shows, the experience isn't about the suspense of what happens next as it unfolds, but rather a personal and lived experience of the work as it happens. Being told about that in advance doesn't spoil it, because it can't be spoiled.

---

4   It is Kaprow who coined the term "Happenings" circa 1959. Michael Kirby in his anthology of Happenings published in 1965 attempts a definition, describing these performance events as "a purposefully composed form of theatre in which diverse alogical elements, including nonmatrixed performing, are organized in a compartmented structure" (*Happenings: An Illustrated Anthology, Scripts and Productions by Jim Dine, Red Grooms, Allan Kaprow, Claes Oldenburg, Robert Whitman* (E. P. Dutton & Co., 1965), 21). Basically, Happenings were things that happened, were generally non-representational and participatory, invoking collaboration between performers and the audience. Happenings flourished as a genre in North America in the 1960s and early 1970s.

5   Allan Kaprow, "Notes on the Elimination of the Audience," in *Participation*, edited by Claire Bishop (MIT P, 2006), 103. He elaborates, "Then, on a human plane, to assemble people unprepared for an event and say that they are 'participating' if apples are thrown at them or they are herded about is to ask very little of the whole notion of participation. Most of the time the response of such an audience is half-hearted or even reluctant, and sometimes the reaction is vicious and therefore destructive to the work (though I suspect that in numerous instances of violent reaction to such treatment it was caused by the latent sadism in the action, which they quite rightly resented)."

CRAFTS

When I walk by the elementary school on the way to the university, I have a full view of what looks like a kindergarten class on the corner. I see the newest set of craft projects plastered to the windows in a charming, tiny art gallery. On this day in February, there are about a dozen portraits of penguins. Although all the penguins are made with precisely the same ingredients (the same two colours of orange and black PAINT and white paper) and with the same prompt (paint half the penguin and then fold in half to make a symmetrical print), because of the individual INTERPRETATION by the students and the ranging level of their skills, the final results present a weird (but very cute) display of creative multiplicities. Sometimes the penguin's beak is as big as its head, or its feet are where its knees should be, and it makes me smile. At least one of the penguins looks quite a lot like a pumpkin.

Crafting has long been a creative space where popular participation is an active ingredient.[1] Besides little kids in little classrooms, crafts can, of course, send powerful political messages. I'm thinking of AIDS quilts[2] or civic architecture encased by anonymous crocheting yarn-bombers. The key features of crafting include some (usually fairly mundane) materials to be manipulated, a set of instructions or a RECIPE, and the LABOUR of a group of people working on some sort of more-or-less predetermined creative output. (see TOGETHER ALONE) Although there are debates about the contemporary paradigm shift of binarizing art from

---

1   Because of their humble DIY quality, crafts serve as a flattener, an accessible approach to creative input. Professor of Women and Gender studies at Carleton, Ann Cvetkovich argues that crafts are reparative, they represent the human desire and "attempt to make things, to be creative, to do something" (161). In her book *Depression: A Public Feeling*, Cvetkovich opposes academic work with craft. She is optimistic about crafting's UTOPIAN potential when she argues that "crafting conveys a DIY conviction that creativity and even art is available for everyone and that the result had not be special to be meaningful hence it challenges perfectionism and hierarchies demanded and fostered by academic work" ((Duke UP, 2012), 190).

2   The NAMES Project AIDS Memorial Quilt, known as AIDS Quilt, is a memorial quilt dedicated to people who lost their lives to AIDS-related causes. Started in 1985 by AIDS activist Cleve Jones when rampant homophobia meant that many folks who died of AIDS went without funerals, panels of the quilt were made by individuals, organizations, or in community quilting bees and stitched together in celebration and in mourning ("NAMES Project Aids Memorial Quilt," *Wikipedia*, en.wikipedia.org /wiki/NAMES_Project_AIDS_Memorial_Quilt).

craft and artist from ORDINARY PEOPLE with creative hobbies, thinking about crafting as a participatory dramaturgy is productive. What is it that audience-makers are doing by and with crafts? One way to think about this is that crafting is creative but within limits. Not just anything goes. As Katie Salen and Eric Zimmerman note, a defining characteristic of play is freedom within prescribed limits.[3] This same tension manifests in crafting. In this way, crafting is a material manifestation of fill-in-the-blanks as a strategy of participatory performance creation. Consider also *Embrace* as a participatory cooking show. Making food is also a kind of crafting. (see MAD LIBS)

In her doctoral thesis "Stitches, Bitches, and Bodies: Textiles and the Twenty-First Century 'Female' Body," theatre practitioner and scholar Thea Fitz-James argues for thinking about crafts "themselves as performers."[4] These craft-THINGS act as co-creators of meaning in performance. They are our scene partners. Fitz-James engages with the debates on categorizing craft. Her work wants to "better understand the complexities of everyday life" and explore "craft not as a socialist antidote to capitalism, or as opposition to either art or machinery, but rather as a set of cultural texts, or in this case, cultural performances."[5] She situates crafting "as a verb (and not only a noun) . . . [outlining] the performance of craft, but also [pointing] to the messiness of making, and the physical and bodily performer behind the object."[6] Crafts join participants as active participants in the meaning-making, even challenging the binaries of assumed roles between performer and object, participant and artist. As objects with particular and sometimes non-cooperative physical properties, crafts have a mind of their own. Sometimes they resist our easy manipulation. They are, as Jane Bennett asserts, if not actually animate, then vibrant.[7] They manipulate us as much as we manipulate them.

Adrienne Wong's *SmartSmart* uses crafting as a dramaturgy to explore this ambiguous relationship. Which one of us is the subject and which the object? Who is leading and who is following? Actor or audience? When we entered the workshop space in the basement of Vancouver's Russian Hall at the 2023 PushOFF festival, we were met with long tables

---

3   Katie Salen and Eric Zimmerman, *Rules of Play: Game Design Fundamentals* (MIT P, 2004), 304.

4   Charlotte Anthea Fitz-James, "Stitches, Bitches, and Bodies: Textiles and the Twenty-First Century 'Female' Body" (York U, September 2020), 3.

5   Fitz-James, 9–10.

6   Fitz-James, 15.

7   Jane Bennett, *Vibrant Matter: A Political Ecology of Things* (Duke UP, 2010).

CRAFTS

covered with fabric and ribbons. We were given scissors and sticky tape and told that our task was to create theatregoing outfits for our personal smartphones using the materials in front of us. We worked away, quiet and focused, dressing our phones up for a night out. After we were finished, we were asked to turn them on to record video and place them in a tiered phone rack that served as their "seats." A curtain between us closed and then reopened a moment later, signalling the start of the "show." We were bathed in colourful lights. Boisterous dance music started, and we took this as an INVITATION to dance as our phones in their crafted get-ups watched us. (It was weird and awesome. I laughed.)

See TYRANNY

CREW

Michael Kirby, in his article "On Acting and Not-Acting," notes the contributions of stage attendants "such as the Kurombo and Kōken of Kabuki ... these attendants move props into position and remove them, help with on-stage costume changes and even serve tea to the actors. Their dress distinguishes them from the actors, and they are not included in the informational structure of the narrative. Even if the spectator ignores them as people, however, they are not invisible. They do not act, and yet they are part of the visual presentation."[1] On Kirby's proposed spectrum between not-acting and acting, this kind of stage behaviour is designated as nonmatrixed. These stage attendants "perform" in a postdramatic sense. (Writing in 1972, however, Kirby doesn't yet have that term to hand.) They are not embedded in the representational situation. Accomplices to the fiction, they remain, instead, outside its BOUNDARIES. (see THE MATRIX)

Sitting at the table for the play/dinner party *Long Distance Relationships for Mythical Times*, I hold the warm TEACUP in my hands, savouring the heat and breathing the scented steam. Ten of us have gathered down the sides of the table for stories and food. At the head of the table, performer Gloria Mok uses small objects as puppets to weave together her tales in three different registers—the mythical past of legend, her parents' youthful courtship, and her own current relationship with her "apart-ner." At a couple of intervals between stories, she asks two of us audience-guests to reach in front of us, and prepare to gently spin two cānzhuō zhuànpán, (circular tabletop trays) holding the teapots. "Three, two, one, go," she instructs. The spinning action is mesmerizing, and with musical underscoring, it effectively denotes the scene change, moving us from one time period to another.

Illuminations: Human/Nature, created by the Montréal multimedia company Moment Factory with artist Sarah Fuller, could not be more different. After being bused to a site in either Banff National Park or alternatively Rouge National Park, our group was given a multimedia tool kit consisting of a lantern, a backpack containing an audio speaker, flashlights, and a portable handheld projector slightly larger than a box of Timbits. At intervals during our night hike, accompanied by our personal mobile soundtrack, we used the projector to overlay animations

---

1   Michael Kirby, "On Acting and Not-Acting," *The Drama Review: TDR* 16, no. 1 (March 1972): 3.

on the landscape. We revealed a turtle crawling across the land. A long-gone settlement appeared to float on the surface of the lake. Atop a rock outcropping, a wolf of light raised its head to howl.

In both shows, our function as participants is to be stagehands, lighting technicians, and sound technicians. Basically, we are the crew. After we give the tea a spin, we serve it to our table companions. We are helpers to the artists; we make the show happen in a very practical way. And significantly we do this from outside the frame. We do actions, but we do not ACT insofar as we do not become characters.

In a general sense, our LABOUR has meaning since we are more than happy to help and to feel useful. These small contributions activate embodied understanding through our HANDS; learning flows through a different modality of touch and movement, not just through the distanced sensory impressions of our eyes and ears. Being a part of the doing of the dramatic workings opens an alternate way of knowing. In a specific sense, in the case of *Long Distance Relationships*, being the ones who activate the spinning tea trays connects us (and our bodies) to the cyclical patterns of those eternally repeated stories of separated lovers. The mythical past, the recent past, and Gloria's own present are linked by this recurring trope. The same tale spins around again. In this very small way, we assume some AGENCY; we are helping not just the performance, but also the lovers' stories go round again. Something similar happens in *Illuminations* when we use the audio and visual overlays to reveal old traces on the landscape of today.

Michi Saagiig Nishnaabeg scholar, writer, and artist Leanne Betasamosake Simpson tells the story of her work doing a re-mapping project with a group of Indigenous Elders from the Anishinaabeg reserve community of Long Lake #58. As part of a project to make a "land-use atlas," Simpson and her colleagues in anthropology interviewed the Elders, overlaying their knowledge and experiences of the land on another map, created and used by the state to show physical and topographical features. She says: "We marked down all of their traplines, and the ones before that and the ones before that. We marked down hunting ground and fishing sites, berry patches, ricing camps and medicine spots. We marked down birthplaces and graves. We marked down places where stories happened. We marked down ceremonial sites, places where they lived, places where life happened . . . We marked down travel routes, spring water spots, songs and prayers. Places where feet touched the earth for the first time. Places where promises were made."[2]

---

2   Leanne Betasamosake Simpson, *As We Have Always Done: Indigenous Freedom through Radical Resistance* (U of Minnesota P, 2017), 14.

Simpson positions these "complex, interconnected cycling processes that make up a nonlinear, overlapping emergent and responsive network of relationships of deep reciprocity, intimate and global interconnection and interdependence, that spirals across time and space"[3] as an ethical framework. The linking function that we perform is akin to the "re" part of resurgence. She continues: "The idea of my arms embracing my grandchildren, and their arms embracing their grandchildren is communication in the Nishnaabeg word 'kobade.' According to elder Edna Manitowabi, kobade is a word we use to refer to our great-grandparents and our great-grandchildren. It means a link in a chain—a link in the chain between generations, between nations, between states of being, between individuals. I am a link in a chain. We are all links in a chain."[4]

In both plays, the actions we undertake as crew actively inscribe a kind of cross-temporality, bringing the past into the present. The past is not far away. It is not gone. It is here and we are linked to it.

See LAND and THINGS

---

3   Simpson, *As We Have Always Done*, 24.
4   Simpson, *As We Have Always Done*, 8.

CRISIS

In his book *Simming: Participatory Performance and the Making of Meaning*, Scott Magelssen devotes two chapters to immersive simulations, so-called "SIMS," where the ostensible goal is to give us a taste of a future—some of these futures being more likely than others. One of his chapter examples concerns a mass emergency preparedness drill for anthrax contamination[1]—hopefully unlikely. The other chapter describes a more intimate experience of wearing various kinds of prosthetics, an "old" suit, meant to mimic an experience of aging, with diminished mobility, vision, and hearing[2]—almost certain to happen if I live into my seventh, eighth, or even ninth decade. Future-oriented sims have a strong pedagogical component. In Augusto Boal's terms, they REHEARSE us for real life.[3] These are what Magelssen calls "invocational simmings." Counterintuitively, these narratives of catastrophe and collapse "are by nature optimistic in that they imagine positive change as an achievable possibility through performance . . . A completed scenario results in the reversal of the current status quo, deemed unsatisfying by the participants."[4] Through present imagined adversity, we can effect a better future. Despite the claims of offering hope, you would think that in the summer of 2020, during the early waves of the COVID pandemic, the last thing we need is to play-act at coping with life-disrupting crisis.

This particular (faux) crisis began with a man in what looked like a hazmat suit standing across the street from my house. I could see him from the front window. He was holding a walkie-talkie. I picked up the matching one that had been left for me on the front step. He asked me questions: If the power went out, what would I have for dinner? What about two weeks from now? Did I have people that I could go to? Who are my people? This is the prequel to the show *Revelations* presented by

---

1   Scott Magelssen, "Preempting Trauma," in *Simming: Participatory Performance and the Making of Meaning* (U of Michigan P, 2014), 115–37.

2   Scott Magelssen, "Senior Moments," in *Simming: Participatory Performance and the Making of Meaning* (U of Michigan P, 2014), 138–54.

3   From Boal's definition of forum theatre, which he famously parses as "rehearsal for the revolution" (Augusto Boal, *Theatre of the Oppressed*, translated by Charles A. McBride and Maria-Odilia Leal McBride (THEATRE COMMUNICATIONS GROUP, 1985), 141; cited in Scott Magelssen, *Simming: Participatory Performance and the Making of Meaning* (U of Michigan P, 2014), 5).

4   Magelssen, *Simming*, 13.

Toronto-based theatre creators Anahita Dehbonehie, Griffin McInnes, and Aidan Morishita-Miki. At the designated showtime on the following evening, I gathered in my backyard (outdoors and two metres distant, as so many of us did that summer) with a small group of friends who were my fellow audience-participants and teammates. (see US) This time we used the walkie-talkie to talk to other groups located in other nearby backyards. In the face of (faux) nuclear fallout, we were tasked with formulating an escape plan. The crux of the game is a version of the prisoner's dilemma.[5] We needed to negotiate our choice of escape route to collectively make use of limited options. Some options were better for whoever gets there first, but some were good (but not best) for everyone, but only if we could trust each other and agree. The walkie-talkies created some unexpected narrative complications when our research assistant Charlotte's team forgot that when the channel is live the other team could hear them, and they ended up spilling their nefarious plans to the competition. Complete failure at being SNEAKY. Getting their just desserts, their team did not survive the apocalypse. The second part of *Revelations* involved everyone travelling to a nearby park and converging on a meeting spot that was decorated with festive twinkle lights. It was here that the choices and their consequences would be revealed. Revelations! Some people survived, some did not. Everyone ate cupcakes.

Even if we died by failing to cooperate or by being just plain unlucky, we were nevertheless rewarded with, what was at that time, a precious and particularly delightful social experience. Seeing other people—some friends and some strangers—in three dimensions, from head-to-toe, live and in-person was a remarkable treat. (And cupcakes!) (see FRIENDSHIP) *Revelations* also matches the characteristics of what Magelssen calls an effigy sim. These "environments stage worlds that, through a degree of remove, surrogate or stand in for other ones."[6] In this case, the COVID lesson is inescapable. COVID revealed to many of us for the first time that we are not actually fully autonomous operators. The idea that we live in a collective with reciprocal responsibility for others became concrete. This particular crisis was shaped in fundamental ways by the pathology of person-to-person virus transmission. Staying home, staying apart, wearing a mask, and getting vaccinated—these individual actions of ours are linked to the well-being of us all.

---

5   The prisoner's dilemma is a well-recognized predicament in game theory. In moments of crisis, do you act in your own self-interest and betray the group and possibly receive a high-value reward, or do you act with the group's best interest in mind and receive a guaranteed reward of lower value?

6   Magelssen, *Simming*, 18.

COVID was (and is) a profoundly participatory crisis. Ameliorative impact on the spread of the virus and, by extension, the protection of the vulnerable among us was achieved by direct collective action.[7] (see ANTS)

This call to reciprocity and taking responsibility through individual actions for the well-being of others is also a key theme of the climate crisis. By naming the current geological era the Anthropocene, we acknowledge the transformative effects of human actions on our[8] planet. (see TEACUPS) We are called to leverage the power of collective action, making changes (even sacrifices) at an individual level for the good of the whole. In a 2013 conversation between Naomi Klein and Leanne Betasamosake Simpson, Klein asks, "If extractivism is a mindset, a way of looking at the world, what is the alternative?" Simpson replies, "Responsibility. Because I think when people extract things, they're taking and they're running and they're using it for just their own good. What's missing is the responsibility. If you're not developing relationships with the people, you're not giving back, you're not sticking around to see the impact of the extraction. You're moving to someplace else. The alternative is deep reciprocity. It's respect, it's relationship, it's responsibility, and it's local. If you're forced to stay in your 50-mile radius, then you very much are going to experience the impacts of extractivist behavior. The only way you can shield yourself from that is when you get your food from around the world or from someplace else. So the more distance and the more globalization then the more shielded I am from the negative impacts of extractivist behavior."[9]

Klein, in her book, *This Changes Everything: Capitalism vs. The Climate*, situates this thinking as networked collective action, calling for mass

---

7   To read more about the ways collective action can be enacted and co-opted, read Keren Zaiontz, "Participatory Political Violence: The Sensorial Toll of the Trucker's Convoy," *Canadian Theatre Review* 197 (Winter 2024): 25–31.

8   In Robyn Maynard and Leanne Betasamosake Simpson's *Rehearsals for Living*, Maynard complicates who exactly is implicated when talking about "our" planet's destruction in the Anthropocene. In a letter to Simpson, Maynard points to Kathryn Yussof's *A Billion Black Anthropocenes or None*, rightfully mentioning that the "we" that ruined the planet is not *everyone* on the planet, but more specifically those who participate and benefit from white supremacy and racial capitalism. On page 19 of *Rehearsals for Living* she says, "It's perhaps the final insult that you and I, our respective communities, only enter, exceedingly belatedly, and only abstractly and contingently, into the universal 'we' once it is time to identify the architects of the climate disaster, only to disappear from it again in the next headline, thought, etc." (Alfred A. Knopf, 2022).

9   Naomi Klein, "Dancing the World into Being: A Conversation with Idle No More's Leanne Simpson," *Yes!*, 6 March 2013, yesmagazine.org/social-justice/2013/03/06 /dancing-the-world-into-being-a-conversation-with-idle-no-more-leanne-simpson.

social movement to instigate economic change. She notes that many prior social movements like the US civil rights movement, although successful with respect to unseating institutional discrimination, did not manage to recast the economic LANDSCAPE: "Sharing legal status is one thing; sharing resources is quite another."[10] For the kind of change she imagines, Klein finds possible precedents in movements for the abolition of slavery and for countries in the Global South to experience independence from colonial powers. "Both of these transformative movements forced ruling elites to relinquish practices that were still extraordinarily profitable, much as fossil fuel extraction is today."[11] Like the survival performance-game *Revelations* and the survival not-a-game of daily life during the pre-vaccine COVID era, we are called to make choices that certainly will have detrimental (or at the very least unappealing) effects on us as individuals as we cast our lot for the collective good. As Klein writes, "For any of this to change, a worldview will need to rise to the fore that sees nature, other nations, and our own neighbors not as adversaries, but as partners in a grant project of mutual reinvention."[12]

See ABYDOS, SHEEP, and SEEDS

WHAT ARE 5 THINGS THAT YOU WOULD PACK IN A GO-BAG IN CASE OF AN EMERGENCY? WRITE OR DRAW THEM BELOW.

---

10   Naomi Klein, *This Changes Everything: Capitalism vs. The Climate* (Alfred A. Knopf Canada, 2014), 454.

11   Klein, *This Changes Everything*, 455.

12   Klein, *This Changes Everything*, 23.

CROWDSOURCE

See ANTS

DEMOCRACY

One of the seemingly desirable properties claimed for theatrical participation is that it is democratic. Let's test that proposition.[1] The central point of attraction that pulls audience participation into correspondence with democratic citizenship on the political stage is that word "participation."[2] If we put these two spheres into conversation, we might ask how a participatory work of art is or is not an egalitarian society founded on rights and obligations. Political participation, manifested primarily as engagement with the electoral system, either through voting or by standing for election as a representative (and by myriad ways of supporting these two functions), is the lifeblood of democratic society.[3] Are audience-participants voters? Yes, we are, actually; insofar as we make choices about where to stand and what to look at. (see CHOOSE YOUR OWN ADVENTURE)[4]

---

1 Patrick Blenkarn, "If Not Democratic?" *Canadian Theatre Review* 197 (Winter 2024): 36–41.

2 As Anna Wilson and others note, "democracy" is applied to participatory works of art to suggest that they are more "civilized and progressive," that participation in and of itself can render an artwork "good." The use of this adjective "all too often engenders the work of art with a sense of importance by sheer virtue of its form alone" ("Punchdrunk, Participation and the Political Democratisation Within *Masque of the Red Death*," *Studies in Theatre and Performance* 36, no. 2 (2016): 159–76). Markus Miessen identifies this perception broadly across the first decade of the twenty-first century, noting "an almost fundamentalist willingness toward inclusion that goes hand in hand with a grotesquely uncritical mode of setting up structures and frameworks for this so-called participation to take place, be it on the scale of national politics, local government, projects in the art world and so forth" (*The Nightmare of Participation: Crossbench Praxis as a Mode of Criticality* (Sternberg P, 2010), 45).

3 The core principle behind participatory democracy is that having more people involved makes for not just more legitimate decisions, but actually makes for better decisions, period. There is more diversity of input, which generates more equitable and accountable outcomes. Participatory democracy makes the world better for more people. Jacques Rancière ties democracy directly to participation, thinking about who gets to "take part": "Democracy is the power of those who have no specific qualification for ruling, except the fact of having no qualification. As I interpret it, the *demos*—the political subject as such—has to be identified with the totality made by those who have no 'qualification.' I call it the count of the uncounted—or the part of those who have no part" (*Dissensus: On Politics and Aesthetics* (Bloomsbury, 2010), 78).

4 See also James Frieze, "Beyond the Zero-Sum Game: Participation and the Optics of Opting," *Contemporary Theatre Review* 25, no. 2 (2015): 216–29.

But this role is almost entirely reactive. We choose from a slate of pre-determined options.

Voting is a democratic function, true. But the essence of democracy is that it is a framework for organizing decision-making power for our group, whether that group is a nation, a city, or an assemblage of people gathered for an aesthetic experience. Power is held by politicians and by artists; they are makers and givers, the initiators of policies and ideas that shape experience, whereas citizens and audiences are, in general, receivers. Where audiences diverge from democratic citizens is in the transferability of that power. Audiences do not stand as representatives. There is no mechanism for audiences to assume the mantle of power. In this respect, politicians are in a fundamental way interchangeable with citizens. A foundational principle of democracy is that anyone can become a representative of the people. (Now obviously there are persistent systemic barriers to this being true in practice, but nevertheless the principle holds.) An elected representative is just that: a representative, a placeholder for the community at large, selected through direct exercise of political franchise. Setting aside the fact that artists are not elected, the important part is that they are not representatives. They are not just like us; they are not PROXIES. The power of the elected leader is contingent, held in trust, whereas the "power" of the artist is innate to being an artist and is not transferable in the same way. Artists, arguably, have special skills in creating and communicating messages and experiences. Being responsible for the vision behind that creation is what makes an artist an artist. The work of the artist is given to the audience, not done on their behalf. CLAIRE BISHOP makes this point in the conclusion to *Artificial Hells*, her book about the politics of audience participation. She writes, "The artist relies on the participants' creative exploitation of the situation he/she offers—just as the participants require the artists' cue and direction. The relationship between the artist/participant is a continual play of mutual tension, recognition, and dependency [. . .] or even the collectively negotiated dynamic of stand-up comedy."[5]

If the work of the artist is entirely displaced by the work of the audience, is it still a work of art? (This question arises out of the insertion of the audience as co-maker, generating a creative tension between control and randomness.) (see RECIPE and ALEA) Arguably there is an upper limit where theatre ceases to be theatre. Everyone can be a representative. Can everyone be an artist?[6] With this question in mind, I want to turn

---

5   Claire Bishop, *Artificial Hells: Participatory Art and the Politics of Spectatorship* (Verso, 2012), 279.

6   See RITUAL.

to a production where participation by audience-citizens in the making of art-society is the theme. The play is asking how we navigate what we give and what we get when it comes to making space or limiting space for free speech. This is the policy question of what is good for Canadian society at large. But also, the play examines its own processes in how the verbatim makers also make space or limit space for the curated speech they have previously collected and for spontaneous "raw" audience speech.

The Assembly: Montreal is the creation of Porte Parole, and playwrights Annabel Soutar, Alex Ivanovici, and Brett Watson. Building on the company's past practice in verbatim performance, to develop the script *The Assembly* creators brought together four ORDINARY Canadians from diverse ideological perspectives for a conversation. That conversation was then curated, recorded, and edited by the playwrights for re-performance by four actors. Intentionally seeded with strong personalities with diametrically opposed points of view, the ensuing conversation was heated and hostile, both originally and in its verbatim replication. About three-quarters of the way through the performance, this verbatim-style restating of the debate is interrupted. The actors step out of their roles and cede the table to the audience. They exit and the house lights come up. For the next twenty minutes, self-selected members of the audience approach the table, sit, and speak. Inspired by Lois Weaver's Long Table practice,[7] everyone is welcome, and one chair must remain empty so that anyone can join at any time. This scene plays out differently every night, creating something both ephemeral and unique, but something interesting happened in the version captured by the archival video that I watched.

"Listen to the people that are angry, but also listen to us speaking calmly. 'Cause it takes a lot of energy to speak calmly even though I'm furious. And I have a lot of things to be furious about. But I'm not taking up too much space. And I don't want to." The second-last audience-citizen representative of the Long Table is an Indigenous man. He places a firm and repeated emphasis on the value of distinguishing the emotion of the content (anger) and the emotion of the style of speech (calm). Connecting to Bishop's criteria, he first exhorts us to listen as an act of recognition, to recognize the speaker, "the people who are angry," and also to recognize how they are speaking—"listen to us speaking calmly." Listening, the way he frames it, is founded on recognition, literally re-cognition, knowing again and with intention in that act. It seems deceptively passive but is not. He identifies a productive tension between calmness and anger, between the rightful source of anger and

---

7   "Long Table," *Split Britches*, split-britches.com/long-table. Long table refers to a structured dinner party where conversation is the main course.

the respect to be given to the control of calmness. Also, he marks the tension between talking, taking up space, and listening, ceding space to others. He points to the essential need for that balance in tension. Recognition and tension are Bishop's first two characteristics of participation that I am linking to audience-citizenship.

"Our problem really is can we listen to each other? . . . Even if they are really angry and it's not the right way to project how we are feeling, I think we should still listen to them, understand what they are saying . . . Try to adapt our words to other people's ears." The final audience speaker who shares these words begins by introducing herself. "My name is Alicia. And I'm thirteen." Alicia speaks to Bishop's second two characteristics—dependency and NEGOTIATION. She picks up the previous thread about listening and acknowledges the essential relationality of listening. She notes that a person becomes angry because people aren't listening to them and, in our anger, we don't listen to others. She recognizes this conflict and calls it a "contradiction." Contradiction is a perfectly apt word choice being from its roots—"against" plus "speaking." Alicia's contribution articulates precisely the participatory EXCHANGE model of citizenship; we give so we can get. We adapt our ears to other people's words, so even if what they are saying is hard to hear, we need to try to listen. The move to listening shifts the focus away from a conflictual mode of trying to change people's minds and instead turns to the connective tissue of coexistence, acknowledging our mutual dependency in the theatre and in the polis. This again points to the meta-objective of participation, improving the methods by which we go about improving the world.[8] As Jen Harvie writes in *Fair Play*, "We need to learn from and about each other, to be able to rely on and support each other and to negotiate our similarities and differences if not always, if ever, to resolve them. We need some 'fellow feeling,' some social sympathy, to check unreserved self-interest. We also need social engagement to sustain democracy, people's shared exercise of power."[9]

Of course, the majority of the citizens in the miniature society of the theatre are listeners, and not usually speakers. "Audience" means listeners, from the Latin *audire*. In this general state, audiences and citizens are similar. In the specific scene of the Long Table, audiences of *The Assembly* manifest citizenship in another way as they are potential speakers, and that potential is important as it connects to the principle of interchangeable representation. Perhaps then it is not so remarkable that when these audience-citizens come to speak as representatives, they talk about how to listen.

---

8   Jenn Stephenson, "Assembling the Audience-Citizen (Or, Should Each Person be Responsible for Their Own Paté?)," *Performance Matters* 5, no. 2 (2019): 163–68.

9   Jen Harvie, *Fair Play: Art, Performance and Neoliberalism* (Palgrave Macmillan, 2013), 2.

DISSENSUS

An announcement from Central disrupts the seasonal harvesting work of the Northeast Division. Our territorial expansion has impinged on an Indigenous population. We are told that our actions have made it difficult for them to continue living in traditional ways. They ask that we halt our harvesting activities in this area and cease advancement on this LAND. Central says we must decide on a course of action and presents us with three equally problematic options.

This is *New Societies*, a conversational tabletop role-playing game augmented by live actors to create a participatory theatre experience.[1] The audience of up to forty-eight players is divided into eight divisions and prompted to create their UTOPIAN society on this resource-rich, ostensibly uninhabited world. In many respects, it is a quintessential game of colonial exploitation with built-in neoliberal capitalist expectations of "growth" and "advancement" en route to "WINNING." And yet, things are not as they seem. On one hand, *New Societies* follows typical game paradigms with a set framework for game play, apparently structured by set rules and outcomes. On the other hand, *New Societies* is a drama with actor-characters who perform a predetermined narrative arc.

When you arrive at *New Societies* you are assigned to a team representing one of eight divisions, according to eight compass points. The first time I played, I was in the "East" division. Each division has a facilitator who instructs the players on how to play the game, GUIDING us through various phases of action like harvesting or spending credits on improvements. At frequent intervals during *New Societies*, the regular seasonal game-action of "harvesting" resources from a territory of land is interrupted by an announcement from Central. Your division is then presented with a problem to solve and a slate of solutions: "There has been an outbreak of an unknown disease. Will you resolve to: annihilate the infected area, eliminating all trace of life in that section; quarantine and support potentially infected citizens while they focus on creating a vaccination; or send a crew to relocate the infected bodies into another division." There are no easy answers.

---

1   *New Societies* premiered for in-person play 11–14 September 2019 at the SFU Goldcorp Center for the Arts (Vancouver). The version that I am referring to here was produced for online audience-players by Rumble Theatre, Vancouver, for two nights in December 2021 and two more nights in January 2022.

And this is where you first get the inkling that *New Societies* is not really a civilization SIM. Given that *New Societies* is strictly time-limited at two hours, it is noteworthy that significant time is "wasted" in these debates. Compounding the delay of the resource-acquisition of the harvest, the material benefits of making effective decisions in terms of gaining "points" are completely obscured. It is never clear to us what impact our decisions will have. In fact, when directly asked about this, the response of the facilitator is deliberately vague. And yet, I would argue that these debates are actually the point of *New Societies*. What should this new society value? How do we govern in a way that is consistent with those values, and that produces our desired outcomes? How do we deal with disagreements? It is literally dialogic, aligned with Grant Kester's ideas of conversation as a principal mode of interactivity in socially turned art works.[2] (see STRUMPET) *New Societies* as an event is intended to create space outside of our ordinary lives where we are gathered to have some challenging political conversations with strangers, literally about how the polis should operate. And so, what happens is that, because the game framework is very weak at this point—we have no "game" information to guide our decisions—we fall back on our real-world knowledge and values.

Here are a few illustrative examples of actual conversations from one performance-game: the South division is trying to decide whether or not to go over capacity in harvesting. Player X says, "It's just not clear what kind of results this will cause, right . . . We keep exceeding our capacity." Player T says, "But we could get more land." Sarcastically, X responds, "Because we know gentrification is good." They all laugh. And T says, "It makes better coffee." In later game play, the South division takes the land from the West division, offering to pay for it after they have already taken it. Player N from the West notes ironically, "The colonial legacy of Canada." The West decides to send this message back to the South: "We do not believe in private ownership of property. Your choices are re-enacting the colonial genocide of Canadian history. We encourage you to reconsider your choices."[3]

In every case, none of the proffered solutions is without its drawbacks. After grappling with these options and finding all of them unpalatable for different reasons, a division will typically muse about alternatives or grumble and wish for something not on the list. Initially, in game play, audience-players make these offers jokingly or without expectation of

---

2   Grant Kester, *Conversation Pieces: Community and Communication in Modern Art*, updated edition (U of California P, 2013).

3   *New Societies* archival video, 7 January 2022.

uptake. Then someone might ask the facilitator, "Can we do that?" or the facilitator might hint that their creative proposals are not entirely impossible. When this behaviour emerges, it marks a significant change in how that division engages with *New Societies*. I want to underscore that this tactic is not "in the rules" and until it happens is nowhere suggested as possible. And yet, it happens spontaneously with some frequency and when it happens, it is embraced by the facilitators. The game becomes iteratively responsive to the act of creative resistance, becoming an assertion of AGENCY. (see EMERGENCE)

To take another actual example,[4] the West division is not happy with the options presented in a motion that asserts either "this society provides for those who can articulate a need or for anyone, regardless of need." Player K says, "Well yes, because none of these things are very good. By themselves, none of them are good." Player M responds, "I don't think we'll get the opportunity to write a detailed human rights ..." The facilitator then says, "Is there something more specific you'd like to come up with yourself? Because that could be done." At that point the group has a fairly lengthy discussion about the concept of universal basic income. They assert a need to support people with disabilities. In the end, the facilitator records their customized response to the motion. Later in the game, the facilitator reports that "because of UBI, people are happier. Communal health has increased by one and your arts has also increased as people have that funding for what they need to do. So, congratulations. Your UBI appears to be paying off." Faced with civil unrest due to competing claims of land ownership, Player H of the West division[5] says, "I'd love to get away from land ownership as a concept." Player J says, "Can we deny private property of wealth?" The group decides on a new motion to "deny private ownership of property" in their division.

At about two-thirds of the way through their game, a player from the Northwest says, "I'm starting to realize that maybe playing this like a game is not the best."

The participatory dramaturgy at work here through these improvisations where players not only imagine new ways of world-making but also in the process crack open the game itself is an example of what Jacques Rancière calls dissensus. In the opening essay of his book *Dissensus*, "Ten Theses on Politics," Thesis 8 declares, "The essential work of politics is the configuration of its own space. It is to make the world of its subjects and its operations seen. The essence of politics is

---

4   *New Societies* archival video, 11 December 2021.
5   *New Societies* archival video, 7 January 2022.

the manifestation of dissensus as the presence of two worlds in one."[6] Significantly, "dissensus is not a confrontation between interests or opinions."[7] Rancière says this exact thing at least three different times in the book. The key operation of dissensus is a kind of refiguring of space, reimagining and creating new capacities for what can be done, seen, and named. "It is the instituting of a dispute over the distribution of the sensible."[8] For Rancière, "the distribution" or "the partition of the sensible" is a way of dividing the world and the people in it. It is a double action that both separates or excludes and also "allows participation."[9] Basically how I understand this is that this partition reconfigures what can be sensed; that is, what is part of common experience and what is excluded. "Politics, before all else, is an intervention in the visible and the sayable."[10] For the audience-player-colonists of *New Societies*, by resisting the predetermined paths and forging new options, they are bringing things, previously invisible and silent, into the realm of what can be sensed. They are carving out a different arrangement of the political space.

See NEGOTIATION and KILLJOY

---

6 Jacques Rancière, *Dissensus: On Politics and Aesthetics* (Bloomsbury, 2010), 45.

7 Rancière, *Dissensus*, 46.

8 Rancière, *Dissensus*, 45.

9 Rancière, *Dissensus*, 44.

10 Rancière, *Dissensus*, 45.

DRIFT

"Let's enter the city and start walking. Take this street until something pulls you in a different direction. For the purpose of this exercise, drop whatever your usual motives are for walking about this place. Allow yourself to simply drift. Obey your instincts. Follow the most inviting path."[1] Walking in the city of Whitehorse, I feel myself pulled towards the river. It is wide and flat. The buildings are at my back. In my aural headspace, through the earbuds, though, is another location altogether. Sounds of a much busier, noisier cityscape. My eyes are in Whitehorse, but my ears are in Ottawa. This is *Landline*, created by Adrienne Wong and Dustin Harvey—an audiowalk, shared by two people in synchronous time, connected by texting but physically in different cities.

Landline is, at its foundation, a drift—or what founding member of the Situationist movement Guy Debord alternately calls a "dérive." In *Theory of the Dérive*, Debord writes, the dérive is "a mode of experiential behaviour linked to the conditions of urban society: a technique of rapid passage through varied ambiances."[2] The main goal of a dérive is to engage in MINDFUL consideration of the city. By deliberately abandoning our usual purposes for moving and looking, we are pushed to move differently and to look differently. Drifting, we become open to serendipity. (see ALEA) When I participated in *Landline* in Kitchener (linked to Vancouver), I noticed during my stroll some metal racks for locking up bicycles that were cleverly shaped like bicycles. I then walked past a bicycle store and remarked my visual pleasure in the window display. When a man rode past me on a bicycle carrying (somehow) a full sheet of plywood, I was astonished. Coincidences had become aesthetic coherence. My altered attentiveness was making patterns. A paranoiac conspiracy of bicycles? (see Q) We create what Debord calls "constructed situations" that engage and activate us, standing in opposition to the specular bind of capitalism. Drifting without direction, without navigational intent can also be disorienting—and like serendipity this can be a dramaturgical feature. (see BEING LOST)

Drift is a counterpoint to SEEKING; we are not goal-driven, or at least our goal-purpose is muted. Drift is not passive, however. As Debord insists,

---

1   Adrienne Wong and Dustin Harvey, "*LANDLINE:* Halifax to Vancouver," *Canadian Theatre Review* 159 (Summer 2014): 70.

2   Guy Debord, "Définitions," *Internationale Situationniste* 1 (June 1958).

"The role of the 'public' . . . must ever diminish, while the share of those who cannot be called actors but, in a new meaning of the term 'livers' will increase."[3] (Can't say that I am fond of the term "livers" to denote engaged participation in life. It sounds like internal organs. But I get where Debord— or his translator?—is coming from.) A Situationist[4] drifter performs "the practice of a passionate uprooting through the hurried change of environments."[5] Participation manifests as disengaged but curious movement that, combined with an alert gaze, shapes an experience and opens the drifter to potential (but as yet undetermined) meaning.[6]

How does drift feature as a dramaturgical strategy for participation in *Landline* specifically? The first thing to notice is perhaps how *Landline* as a drift leans into a sense that, as an urban walker, we are no one in particular, unremarkable, almost invisible in the city. Our attention is strongly directed outward. "Observe the city as if you were seeing it for the first time."[7] We are mobile eyes; looking, but not being looked at. This sense of being a GHOST is underscored by our two similarly invisible, ethereal companions. The voice in our ears, Adrienne as the audiowalk narrator and guide, is as close as she can be. We carry her in the space between our ears and behind our eyes. Similarly, our intercity scene partner is also close but unseen. TEXT MESSAGING creates a particularly ambivalent intimacy as we are invited to share our thoughts and impressions with a faceless stranger. This dynamic is liberating and creates an unexpectedly warm ENCOUNTER. At one point we were asked to wave to our new friend and scene partner, thousands of kilometres distant. Wait! Did someone just see me wave to no one? (see SECRET WEIRDOS) While on the one hand we drift anonymously in the city, on the other hand *Landline*

---

3   Tom McDonough, editor, *Guy Debord and the Situationist International: Texts and Documents* (MIT P, 2002), 47.

4   Situationism is a mid-twentieth century movement of avant-garde and anti-capitalist artists, thinkers, and political theorists. Situationism addresses a concern that because people are governed more by their external worlds than internal ones, capitalism is eroding humans and human relationships.

5   McDonough, *Guy Debord*, 46.

6   Liesbeth Groot Nibbelink introduces the concept of "nomadic theatre," drawing on the work of Deleuze and Guattari, to describe audiences with a mobile perspective. Nomadism is not about "wandering without aim . . . [rather, it] emerges when norms or standards are disturbed or deviated from . . . The nomadic is intrinsically connected to the 'undoing' and distribution of territories, and hence, to processes of deterritorialisation and reterritorialisation" ("Bordering and Shattering the Stage: Mobile Audiences as Compositional Forces" in *Staging Spectators in Immersive Performances: Commit Yourself!* edited by Doris Kolesch, Theresa Schütz, and Sophie Nikoleit (Routledge, 2019), 59–60). See also LAND.

7   Wong and Harvey, "*LANDLINE*," 71.

invites us to also consider that we might be performers. Adrienne tells us a story about living in her high-rise apartment. "Sometimes, at night, I like to turn on the lights and leave the blinds open . . . And as I go about my business, I wonder what they think of my actions, the pajamas I've chosen, the state of my kitchen, how I can get my heels right down to the floor in downward dog." But then she concludes, "When I look out my window I see there is no one looking . . . My neighbours are so accustomed to our proximity that averting the gaze is second nature for them. Either that or I'm not very interesting."[8]

The same applies to the cityscape. Either we are so accustomed that we cease to see it and/or it is not very interesting. Just as we are caught between invisibility as an audience-watcher and visibility as a performer,[9] the city is ambiguously constructed as both a set and a setting. "You may want to think of this moment as a scene change. Look around. You may want to think of the other people you see on the streets as the technicians, moving scenery and props around backstage, or as other actors getting ready for their next cue."[10] This ONTOLOGICAL DUALITY imposed on the city is precisely the same as that generated by the theatrical frame, or indeed any aesthetic frame. We become acutely attuned to OSTRANENIE and see the world both in that specially heightened way as a work of art and we also see the frame, drawing attention to the act of aestheticization—to the perceptual attitude that makes an object into a work of art.

Ultimately, the puzzle of ambiguous ontology, of being inside/outside, feeds my self-consciousness as a participant-audience-performer and increases my sense of being in the world. By making strange the nature of how the world is and how I am in it, my attention is focused squarely on the BOUNDARY of myself in the world; on the surface of my skin as it were. The gaze of the dérive is self-reflexive, inviting consideration not just the beauty and intrigue of the world as world, but on my unique place in the world, on the interface of spatially engaged, embedded participation as an act of world-making.

---

8   Wong and Harvey, "LANDLINE," 71.

9   Narrator Adrienne invites us, "You may want to think of this moment as blocking" (Wong and Harvey, "LANDLINE," 72). Of course, blocking is what actors do. Real people just walk.

10   Wong and Harvey, "LANDLINE," 74.

ELBOWS

In "The Distribution of the Sensible," French political theorist Jacques Rancière makes the point that proximity is spatial but also ideological. He is thinking about how "a distribution of spaces, times, and forms of activity [. . .] determines the very manner in which something in common lends itself to participation and in what way various individuals have a part in this distribution."[1] In this way it is possible to talk about how specific aesthetic practices contribute to the shaping of community, speaking to "ways of doing and making" as well as relationship and visibility within those communities. "Politics plays itself out in the theatrical paradigm as the relationship between the stage and the audience, as meaning produced by the actor's body, as games of proximity or distance."[2] In the context of participatory performance events, we might extend the relations of proximity from just between stage and audience to include also proximity between and among audience members.[3]

Presented in a black box studio space, *Café Sarajevo* by bluemouth inc. is framed as a live podcast. We listen on headphones to the audio narration, with two hosts interviewing company members Lucy Simic and Stephen O'Connell about their visit to Sarajevo in 2016, twenty years after the end of the civil war that held the city under lethal years-long siege by snipers. The standing audience of about forty people is entirely mobile. For each "scene" of the podcast, roughly recreating Lucy and Stephen's travels, we flow to organically arrange ourselves. Some people stand or lean on the walls, some sit on the floor closest to the actors. There are a few portable plastic stools.

---

1   Jacques Rancière, "The Distribution of the Sensible: Politics and Aesthetics," in *The Politics of Aesthetics: The Distribution of the Sensible*, translated by Gabriel Rockhill (Continuum, 2004), 12.

2   Rancière, "The Distribution of the Sensible," 17.

3   *Performing Proximity: Curious Intimacies* (Palgrave Macmillan, 2014) by Leslie Hill and Helen Paris similarly focuses on physical distance between actors and audience members, examining affective and communicative potential in live encounters at an intimate range. They ask, "How does it feel? How long can it last? How close is too close?" They draw on the groundbreaking work in the science of proxemics by Edward T. Hall. I estimate that the typical spacing of audience to audience in *Café Sarajevo* fell within what Hall characterizes as the "personal zone" (50 to 120 centimetres). My recollection is that even as we tried to maintain an appropriate "social" distance from other strangers, the environment of the show and our competing desire to be close enough to see and hear pressed us together.

Then in the off-air breaks between scenes, we are hastily herded into a new configuration elsewhere in the space. For each scene, we need to navigate and NEGOTIATE to find a space and a view. In addition to the live action, we are also given objects called "cardboards." These are hand-held personal virtual-reality viewers; little boxes with screens that we hold up to our faces. Inside are 360° videos of Lucy and Stephen on their trip—on the steps of their apartment in Brooklyn, at Lucy's mother's house in Porec, driving down the road to Sarajevo, sitting in a café. We tilt our heads up and down. We turn around. Elbows akimbo, we blindly bump, apologizing, into our neighbours. It strikes me that this exploratory combination of the ASYMMETRY of our point-of-view positioning, in relation to the actors and the accidental, but oh-so-polite incursions we make on each other as we continually shift, shapes my understanding of *Café Sarajevo*.

The podcast-within-the-play overtly presents its key question: "What causes people to divide? Are these divisions part of our nature? Or is it something else?" Set in the early days of the Trump administration in the US, through Lucy and Stephen's travels, we are invited to "tackle the question of why that sense of togetherness feels necessary, even urgent." In a telling scene, Lucy is discomfited when ordering coffee in a Sarajevo café: she calls it "Turkish coffee" while the guide, Dino, calls it "Bosnian coffee." Lucy is unsure if she is presenting as simply naive or whether she has revealed some kind of unintended political bias and Dino is now judging her. Something similar happens in a conversation with a local named Samara who deflects Lucy's questions about Muslim tourists in Sarajevo. Samara says, "It is no longer appropriate to ask a Sarajevan what religion they observe. Or our nationality. If someone asks us, we just smile and say we are Sarajevan." In the closing moments of the play, we return to a video from the beginning—a televised debate from 1971 between Noam Chomsky and Michel Foucault. In this clip, Chomsky makes the point that power doesn't imply justice or correctness and therefore it may be necessary to stage acts of civil disobedience to prevent the state from perpetrating criminal acts. Specifically in the context of the Vietnam War, his point is that illegal acts in support of anti-war views are right and proper. What, therefore, would constitute civil disobedience in the context of the Sarajevan civil war narrowly or more generally in the current divisive moment in US politics? How does civil disobedience counter sectarianism? The answer, the play suggests, lies in eschewing revenge and blame, and embracing a kind of radical forgiveness; offering forgiveness even for the unforgivable.

And this is where the participatory dramaturgy of *Café Sarajevo* neatly underscores this point, bringing the play's understanding into our bodies.

In a different essay by Rancière ("Problems and Transformations in Critical Art"), he responds to the priority that relational art puts on the ENCOUNTER, noting the stakes in using art to generate those encounters: "The loss of the 'social bond,' and the duty incumbent on artists to work to repair it, are the words on the agenda. But an acknowledgement of this loss can be more ambitious. It's not only the forms of civility that we will have lost, but the very sense of the co-presence of beings and things that constitutes a world."[4] I appreciate his challenge that encounter is the foundation of the co-presence and the collective work of world constitution, but I am also very taken by the idea of losing simple but basic "forms of civility" and what the potentially deadly outcomes of that might be. The embodied experience of the mobile, closely packed, bumper-car audience of *Café Sarajevo*, isolated by our headphones and (at times) our VR viewers, is constantly engaged in negotiation for sight lines. We are far from sectarian violence to be sure, but in this very gentle way, through proximal and social INTIMACY, we are reminded that we are in this together and need to find ways to share the space and accommodate everyone.[5] "When we fathom another person or creature, or when we experience the form of things in our everyday world . . . we let our own surface sensitivities come to the fore. In so doing, we open ourselves to fathoming the density of another living being or thing . . . We open ourselves to new possibilities of attunement."[6] Maybe even building a world together. Engaged in participatory co-creation, we are all *Café Sarajevans*.

See DISSENSUS

---

4   Jacques Rancière, "Problems and Transformations in Critical Art," in *Participation: Documents of Contemporary Art*, edited and translated by Claire Bishop (MIT P, 2006), 90.
5   Gareth White in "The Promise of Participation Revisited: Affective Strategies of Participation" sweetly recalls a participatory performance premised on the sharing of hopes. He writes, "My own reluctant offerings are drawn into the rhythm and mesh of a performance-as-assembly, a being together with others whose hopes may not be identical, but who can be persuaded to yearn together" (159). He knits together assemblages in physical proximity with assemblages of intersubjectivities where he enacts "hungry mind reading" to imagine what others nearby are thinking. Present but fundamentally unknowable, these other embodied minds are provocations. I want to know what moves them. Ultimately, he concludes that "by staging spectators, people, and bodies, [performance] stages and restages an affective politics where bodies are channels for political energies rather than their instantiations of identities" (*Staging Spectators in Immersive Performances: Commit Yourself!* edited by Doris Kolesch, Theresa Schütz, and Sophie Nikoleit (Routledge, 2019), 168).
6   Maxine Sheets-Johnstone, *The Corporeal Turn: An Interdisciplinary Reader* (Imprint Academic, 2009), 144.

EMBODIMENT

See ELBOWS and SWEATING

BELOW IS A NONOGRAM. THE DIGITS ABOVE AND TO THE
LEFT OF THE GRAPH INDICATE HOW MANY SPACES IN THAT
ROW OR COLUMN ARE COLOURED IN. WHERE TWO DIGITS
APPEAR, IT MEANS THAT THERE IS A BREAK BETWEEN TWO
SECTIONS. USE LOGIC TO PINPOINT EXACTLY WHICH SPACES
ARE COLOURED IN, AND ONCE ALL OF THE DIGITS ARE SATISFIED,
YOU WILL BE LEFT WITH AN ANSWER!

(HINT: X = the number of times Lucy is mentioned in ELBOWS,
Y = the number of footnotes in ELBOWS)

	0	1	y+4	y+4	2 2 1	2 2	2 2	2	2	3
X+1										
8										
2 1										
2										
5										
5										
2										
2										
2										
4										

ANSWER:

EMERGENCE

Is participatory theatre a phenomenon of emergence? As described by Steven Johnson in his book *Emergence: The Connected Lives of Ants, Brains, Cities and Software*, emergence is "a mathematical model wherein simple AGENTS following simple rules could generate amazingly complex structures . . . In these systems, agents residing on one scale start producing behaviour that lies one scale above them: ants create colonies, urbanites create neighbourhoods, simple pattern recognition software learns how to recommend new books."[1] Is this what is happening when audience-players play performance-games in very flexible open space, creating new and unexpected outcomes and experiences? (see PLAYGROUNDS) I think the answer is both "no" and "yes." Narrowly defined, participatory theatre, even though it ticks a number of boxes, matching some key characteristics of emergent phenomena, doesn't fulfill others. Johnson articulates four key elements necessary for the emergence of complexity: indirect control, pattern recognition, neighbour interaction, and feedback.

Indirect control means that complex behaviours emerge not because they were planned from the beginning by a higher-order creator (in the theatrical context, an artist) but because a slate of simple rules combine with each other and with environment conditions to produce something novel. It is essentially a decentralized, "bottom-up" phenomenon. Flocking birds in flight follow three simple general rules: avoid collision with immediate neighbours, be proximally attracted to others of your same kind, and move in the same direction.[2] The whole system is in motion as each bird follows these algorithms, reacting in real time to changing conditions. And so complex patterns emerge from combinations of simple rules.

Often things that audience-players do in participatory contexts do arise spontaneously, out of the grassroots as it were. Participatory works structured around RECIPES of audience tasks offer very loose guidelines

1   Steven Johnson, *Emergence: The Connected Lives of Ants, Brains, Cities and Software* (Scribner, 2001), 15 and 18.
2   Peter Friederici, "How a Flock of Birds Can Fly and Move Together," *Audubon Magazine* (March–April 2009), audubon.org/magazine/march-april-2009/how-flock-birds-can-fly-and-move-together#:~:text=It%20turns%20out%20that%20only,the%20rest%20of%20the%20group.

that encourage unpredictable creative contributions. In *Future Perfect*, for example, the text of civic bylaws has been chopped up into single-word fragments. Participants are invited to reassemble these now random words to create new sentences and envision rules for a different kind of city with new social interactions and expectations. Out of these novel combinations, the permutations are endless. Activities like playing blindfolded guessing games, nighttime hide-and-seek, and PAINTING the walls in *The Stranger 2.0: Above* are similarly unprescribed and extremely variable. Meaning emerges through responsive individual audience behaviour. So, yes, in this respect the artistic work arises through indirect control. The artist establishes few parameters and those parameters are very broad, open to an almost infinite potential field of inputs.

Game designer Warren Spector defines emergence as "engines of perpetual novelty." He exhorts other designers to share the spotlight with players, inviting them to be co-creators. "Embrace the idea that your job is to bound the player experience, to put a sort of creative box around it—but you don't determine the player experience. It's not about 'here's where every player does X.' . . . Embrace this idea that the most interesting games are those that let players devise personally meaningful goals, formulate and execute plans to achieve their goals," says Spector.[3] To keep the game sufficiently open he recommends the creation of global rules rather than specific ones, "build[ing] interlocking systems that are predictable and consistent . . . but not predetermined."[4] Spector gives this example: "some objects are flammable, some guards are light-sensitive, the player has torches."[5] Through this kind of indirect, second-order game design, players can learn how certain objects behave and apply those properties in a variety of ways.

In Espen J. Aarseth's taxonomy of user functions in literary cybertexts, "textonic" is the most dynamic and ergodic (that is, the most "work involved"). The work of a textonic reader of a cybertext involves the actual creation of new "textons"—new chunks of narrative.[6] A participatory audience-player might do something similar, albeit generating new pathways of action or creating new scenes (or finding a newfangled

3   Leigh Alexander, "Spector: Go Emergent—Game Design is Not All About You," *Game Developer*, 16 November 2013, gamedeveloper.com/design/spector -go-emergent---game-design-is-not-all-about-you.

4   Alexander, "Spector."

5   Alexander, "Spector."

6   Espen J. Aarseth, *Cybertext: Perspectives on Ergodic Literature* (Johns Hopkins UP, 1997), 62–64.

makeshift use for a torch), rather than literally writing paragraphs of new words. In Outside the March's 90s video-store themed escape room-play *Love Without Late Fees*, participants generate new pathways in precisely this way when their actions determine the next events of a new couple's love story. Depending on both the movies they choose to rent and the order, participants see an entirely different relationship journey and outcome. In *Through My Lens*, the content of the show is generated spontaneously in response to a series of photographs. In conversation with the photographer Amy Amantea (an artist with a lived experience of blindness), a sighted audience-participant verbalizes a description of their impression of the image. In both cases, the performance arises organically out of logical, but not narrowly predetermined, interactions between agents and the environment, as Spector envisions. So, if we are looking for a more theatrically apt term to replace Aarseth's concept of the textonic, and are thinking about this in accordance with this more relaxed definition of "emergent play," then "emergence" might be a good candidate.

But on the other hand, there is a critical difference. Unlike flocking birds, audience reactions do not follow precise algorithms. New ideas do emerge as an experience of the play-game parameters, but they do not become "complex" in the same way that thousands of birds become a wheeling flock. This speaks to the second and third characteristics of pattern recognition and neighbour interaction. Birds become a flock through the myriad continual RELATIONAL adjustments by rule-fol-lowing birds. Human neighbourhoods emerge in cities of millions of people similarly as each individual identifies and reacts to particular geo-social conditions of their environment and then locates them-selves accordingly. (see DRIFT) Although audience-players do undertake actions that incorporate interpersonal and environmental stimuli, their choices are more nuanced and more variable. But more significantly, in theatre there just aren't enough of these interactions with either the environment or with our immediate neighbours to generate large-scale patterns of complexity. (see NEGOTIATION) There aren't enough par-ticipants and/or there aren't enough repetitive iterations over time. Participatory performance doesn't (in Jeremy Campbell's phrase) "jump the complexity barrier."[7]

Where participatory performance is most closely aligned with models of emergence is with regard to the fourth criterion: feedback. AUTOPOIESIS describes a responsive feedback loop in a closed system.

7 Jeremy Campbell, *Grammatical Man: Information, Entropy, Language and Life* (Simon and Schuster, 1982), 99–111.

From a plain language definition, emergence captures the process of something coming into view or coming into being.[8] This notion of something new emerging out of previous conditions aptly describes the synthesis at work when audience members become creative contributors to the flow of a performance event and to its incipient meaning. The recombinatory properties of this kind of work connect to properties of "interoperability" in emergent systems. *Wikipedia* gives the example of what happens when a rider and a bicycle converge. The act of rolling down the street under human-powered locomotion is something that was not there previously. Interoperability can also produce effects that were unexpected or that are entirely novel. Thinking about the game of poker, Katie Salen and Eric Zimmerman suggest that "bluffing" is an emergent strategy, unforeseen by the game's designers.[9] (see GOING ROGUE) Game play as an emergent phenomenon arises as the product of context-dependent interactions. "The behaviour of the overall system *cannot* be obtained by *summing* the behaviours of its constituent parts. We can no more truly understand strategies in a board game by compiling statistics of the movements of the pieces than we can understand the behaviour of an ANT colony in terms of averages. Under these conditions the whole is indeed more than the sum of its parts."[10]

One more thought: A frequent factor driving instances of emergence is "phase transition." Phase transition is an abrupt change in the basic conditions. So, for example, when the temperature drops below zero degrees Celsius, water molecules behave differently to align in a lattice forming ice, or when the ground drops away beneath a procession of ants, they use their bodies to form a bridge. This invites the question: Does the MAGIC CIRCLE that contains theatre and games instigate a phase transition that changes human behaviour to create new possible structures or patterns?[11]

See SEEDS and DISSENSUS

---

8   "Emergence," *Oxford Dictionary*, oed.com/search/dictionary/?scope=Entries &q=emergence.

9   Katie Salen and Eric Zimmerman, *Rules of Play: Game Design Fundamentals* (MIT P, 2004), 164.

10   John Holland, *Emergence: From Chaos to Order* (Perseus, 1998), 122.

11   John Rennie, "How Complex Wholes Emerge From Simple Parts," *Quanta Magazine*, 20 December 2018, quantamagazine.org/emergence-how-complex -wholes-emerge-from-simple-parts-20181220/.

ENCOUNTER

"Art is a state of encounter," says Nicolas Bourriaud in his book *Relational Aesthetics*.[1] There, Bourriaud advocates for a new RELATION between the human viewer and the art object—a trend in the field of visual art that he sees developing since the early 1990s.[2] "Artistic practice is now focused upon the sphere of inter-human relations . . . So the artist sets his sights more and more clearly on the relations that his work will create among his public, and on the invention of models of sociability."[3] Work in this mode is temporal rather than spatial. Bourriaud likens it to a rendezvous. These ephemeral moments of sociability arise to engender "dialogue, discussion, and that form of inter-human negotiation that Marcel Duchamp called the 'coefficient of art.'"[4]

A prime example of this genre is the work of German "theatre-label" Rimini Protokoll[5] (including the *100% City* series, *Cargo X*,[6] and *Cross-Word Pit Stop*[7]) that invites "experts of the everyday" to perform as themselves, and to function as creative collaborators. (see ORDINARY PEOPLE) Bringing various kinds of "strangers" to the stage, whether they be a hundred statistically representative occupants of your city,[8] two Romanian logistics truck drivers, or four octogenarian women who train to become Formula 1 drivers, dialogic work in this mode activates a profound sense of being in relation to these ordinary yet remarkable lives, but also consideration of what it means to be in relation broadly to all the others who constitute our social spheres.

---

1   Nicolas Bourriaud, *Relational Aesthetics*, translated by Simon Pleasance and Fronza Woods (Les presses du réel, 2002), 18.
2   Claire Bishop, "The Social Turn: Collaboration and Its Discontents," *Artforum International* 44, no. 6 (February 2006): 178–83.
3   Bourriaud, *Relational Aesthetics*, 28.
4   Bourriaud, *Relational Aesthetics*, 41.
5   Founded in 2000, Rimini Protokoll are Helgard Haug, Stefan Kaegi, and Daniel Wetzel.
6   "Cargo X," *Rimini Protokoll*, rimini-protokoll.de/website/en/projects/cargo.
7   "Cross-Word Pit Stop," *Rimini Protokoll*, rimini-protokoll.de/website/en/project /kreuzwortraetsel-boxenstopp.
8   "City as Stage," *Rimini Protokoll*, rimini-protokoll.de/website/en/project /city-as-stage. See also Jenn Stephenson, "Real People Part 2: Insecurity and Ethical Failure in the Encounter with Strangers—*100% Vancouver*, RARE, and *Polyglotte*," in *Insecurity: Perils and Products of Theatres of the Real* (U of Toronto P, 2019), 48–90.

Participatory art, for Bourriaud, is principally a vehicle for tightening social bonds. Relational encounter fills a critical contemporary need for social exchange as opportunities for interpersonal interaction are diminishing, Bourriaud argues. Interchanges that "once represented so many opportunities for exchanges, pleasure and squabbling"[9] are being increasingly mechanized and automated. In particular, Bourriaud is not fond of bank machines. To that exemplar, I might add bagging your own groceries, pay at the pump gas stations, food vending machines, and wake-up robocalls. The tellers, gas station attendants, restaurant servers, and hotel desk clerks with whom we formerly shared even these most superficial human contacts have vanished. Bishop summarizes Bourriaud's attitude: "The creative energy of participatory practices rehumanizes—or at least de-alienates—a society rendered numb and fragmented by the repressive instrumentality of capitalism."[10]

With the shift to participation, however, I become a collaborator, part of a bidirectional partnership towards the creation of a more dynamic encounter.[11] In the introduction to their edited collection on performance and participation, Anna Harpin and Helen Nicholson offer the following provocation: "Participation is, then, less an action than an encounter and a perception."[12] *Human Library* is perhaps the quintessential example of this in a pure form. The *Human Library* project literally manifests this notion of the encounter with a stranger. The subtitle for the project is "Unjudge someone" with the tag line, "We publish people as open books." The way this works is that each "book" is a person, representing "a stigmatized group in the community"[13] who meets a "reader." The encounter between the "reader" and the "book" takes the form of a question-and-answer EXCHANGE to expand mutual understanding through difficult conversations.

---

9   Bourriaud, *Relational Aesthetics*, 17.

10   Claire Bishop, "The Social Turn," 180. Also see Claire Bishop, *Artificial Hells: Participatory Art and the Politics of Spectatorship* (Verso, 2012).

11   Adam Alston, *Beyond Immersive Theatre, Aesthetics, Politics, and Productive Participation* (Palgrave Macmillan, 2016); Gareth White, *Audience Participation in Theatre: Aesthetics of the Invitation* (Palgrave Macmillan, 2013); and Keren Zaiontz, "Narcissistic Spectatorship in Immersive and One-on-One Performance" *Theatre Journal* 66, no. 3 (2014): 405–25.

12   Anna Harpin and Helen Nicholson, "Performance and Participation," in *Performance and Participation: Practices, Audiences, Politics*, edited by Anna Harpin and Helen Nicholson (Palgrave Macmillan, 2017), 6.

13   "Human Library Book FAQ," *Human Library*, humanlibrary.org/meet-our-human -books/the-human-library-book-faq/.

The mundane social situations described above—the bank teller, the wake-up call service, my neighbour in the library—point precisely to the scope and scale of the field of Bourriaud's attention. These are relationships in what I would describe as a socially proximate middle range. These are the quotidian, casual interactions with people who are essentially strangers, but they are familiar strangers. They are the people you meet walking the dog or while paying for groceries or getting on and off the bus. If you see the same person more than once, we might go so far as to characterize them as an acquaintance. Maybe you know their name, maybe you only know the dog's name. We are all always surrounded by this loose knit, comforting (?) fabric of humanity. Socially turned works on this scale, then, are "microscopic attempts . . . to [revisit] spaces of conviviality and crucibles where heterogeneous modes of sociability can be worked out . . . Inventing new relations with our neighbours seems to be a matter of much greater urgency than 'making tomorrows sing.' That is all, but it is still a lot,"[14] says Bourriaud.

That said, an artwork intended to remediate a lost sociality between parent and child does not seem to be what Bourriaud has in mind. And, of course, you can see why this is so. Within this smallest circle of relationship, there is, in theory, no need to establish kinship; we are already kin. If the idea of the socially turned, aesthetic encounter is that manufactured situations of interpersonal social connection in those ad hoc communities of casual acquaintances, or even among strangers, are restorative, what is to be gained in the aesthetic construction of an encounter between those who are already ineffably known to each other? This is the dramaturgical puzzle offered by *Soon, Tomorrow Maybe* written by Marie Ayotte and presented by Théâtre Déchaînés.

The play begins when the phone rings. An alto voice says, "Hello? Jenn?" She stammers, " . . . Oh, hi. I . . . I was afraid you wouldn't pick up. That . . . that . . . that you wouldn't . . . (*She trails off.*) But you did. I'm glad. [Why wouldn't I pick up? Why is this person worried/flustered?] It's . . . hmm . . . I'm happy to talk to you. It's strange to hear your voice."[15] I'm confused. This is the natural state of any audience member at the beginning of the show. I'm working to piece together the logic of this world. Who is this character? What are the parameters of their lived context? My first clue is that they seem to know me from when I was very young. "It, um, reminds me of when you used

---

14 Bourriaud, *Relational Aesthetics*, 44.
15 I experienced *Soon, Tomorrow Maybe* on 30 September 2021. The quotations I am using here are drawn from a copy of the script dated 14 July 2021, which was generously provided to me by the playwright.

to create all kind of these imaginary worlds . . . You must have been five or six. Maybe seven?" Eventually, I clue into the idea that this woman is my mother. The dramaturgical qualities of a dominantly aural theatre create a pervasive alternate world that operates in the interstices of my normal world, and where I can provisionally accept this relationship. (see PHONES)

Once inside the fictional world, however, I have a different problem to solve. Why doesn't my mother know me? In the beginning of the conversation, my mother asks about my day. Okay. That seems like a reasonable question. But then she asks what kind of job I have. That's odd. Finally, she asks if I have kids and wants to know details about them. So, if my mother doesn't know that I have kids, where has she been for the last twenty-two years? Evidently, going back to the question of the narrow social sphere of kinship, there has been some kind of estrangement, which goes some way to explaining how the dramaturgy of relational encounter plays out here. This mother is, indeed, at least partially a stranger. Moreover, this relationship is further complicated by the fact that the actor with whom I am having this conversation, and with whom I am collaboratively crafting this fictional relationship, this theatre event experience, is also a stranger. The actor in this context is not dissimilar to Bourriaud's early morning call service; our relationship shaped by our efforts towards a neutrally polite, frictionless interaction.

Soon, Tomorrow Maybe subsumes this formal problem of encounter as its main theme. While I am indeed detached but polite—mostly caused by the combination of being a nice audience member and a tentatively warm but confused daughter—my mother is distressed. For her, this phone call is a moment of pivotal confession. It emerges that she was a reluctant mother. She didn't really want kids, didn't really want me. Then, after my birth, she was still unhappy. She didn't feel the infinite love that she thought was expected. She felt trapped. "Holding you in my arms . . . didn't feel . . . that special to me. Not any more than a lot of other things, at least. Talking about your weight and development stages with other moms bored me . . . But every passing day with this impression that I would never make it, that I wasn't the mother you needed, that we didn't bond in the way we were supposed to . . . Well the doubt crept in. What if . . . What if it weren't temporary?" It occurs to me that postpartum depression, at least as experienced by "my" mother, is a malady of encounter. The expectation is that mother and child connect; this first encounter ought to be instant and profound. Yet, the child is a stranger that remains strange.

In this dialogue, she seeks my approbation, confirmation that she wasn't a bad mother, that she isn't crazy or abnormal, that her feelings are valid, that I know she did her best. I step strongly into my role, and my participatory action is to reassure her. I tell her: No, she isn't a bad mother. No, she isn't crazy or abnormal. Yes, her feelings are valid. Yes, I know she did her best. Perhaps it is too late. Perhaps the relationships— all the relationships, not just those of kinship—we idealize can never be realized, and yet the attempt seems worthwhile. We try. Our continual participation in theatre performances like these and in the exchanges of everyday life is REHEARSAL for the next time and the next time.

EXCHANGE

In the relational ENCOUNTER, exchange is what is promised and what is desired, and yet the nature of exchange is precisely the problem with a performance encounter, both in reception and in response. "The degree of participation required of the onlooker by the artist . . . gives rise to a specific 'arena of exchange,'"[1] says Nicolas Bourriaud.

In his book *Stage Fright, Animals, and Other Theatrical Problems*, Nicholas Ridout devotes a chapter to the embarrassment experienced by an audience subjected to direct address.[2] Questions arise about the ontology of the looker. Am I being seen by the actor or by the character? And beyond that, who am I in this encounter? A fellow fictional character? Out of this insecure ontology, one relationship persists. In his analysis, Ridout identifies the root of my embarrassment in the commercial exchange at the heart of the theatre event where I pay to consume someone else's labour as my leisure. (see INSTRUMENTALITY) He writes, "For in the theatre of capitalism, the reverse gaze must always acknowledge, however tacitly, an intimate economic relation: I paid to have this man look at me, and he is paid to look. Our INTIMACY is always already alienated. It is a difficult intimacy."[3] This is the problem of reception. I am embarrassed by what I am taking from this exchange.

But conversely, I am also discomfited by the problem of response and what I am compelled to give (beyond money) to this exchange. In theatre settings influenced by nineteenth-century realism and the proscenium stage, I am asked for very little, beyond my quiet presence and my cognitive and emotional engagement. In participatory theatre, the cost of exchange is higher; I am given more, but more is expected in return.

---

1   Nicolas Bourriaud, *Relational Aesthetics*, translated by Simon Pleasance and Fronza Woods (Les presses du réel, 2002), 17.

2   In her dissertation "Intercultural Relations: Direct Audience Address in Contemporary Theatre in Canada," Signy Lynch makes the case that direct address can be conceptualized as a participatory phenomenon. Pushing beyond Ridout's assertion that being seen by the actors is embarrassing for the audience, she argues that "direct address functions as a specific invitation to these spectators, one which once accepted begins a participatory relationship" (12) and that through the lens of participation, direct address can be understood as an intercultural bridge (York U, 2021).

3   Nicholas Ridout, *Stage Fright, Animals, and Other Theatrical Problems* (Cambridge UP, 2006), 80.

In a multivocal reflection, three UK theatre scholars—Deirdre Heddon, Helen Iball, and Rachel Zerihan—examine their own encounters as the recipients of performative care in immersive theatre works to make visible the awkwardness that manifests from the guilty self-conscious pressure in wanting (but failing) to be a good sport. Or in Zerihan's words, "My role as a dutiful spectator . . . was led by my desire to please . . . [my] desire to 'give good audience.'"[4]

A common trope of one-on-one performance is the expression of CARE for the audience member. Affection, intimacy, even love. But since these goods are offered in the context of an artificial, that is, staged encounter with a stranger, affects of care are invariably tainted by awareness of the conditions, or what participatory theatre-artist Sarah Conn refers to as the "criteria of coexistence"[5] of the participants in the exchange itself. Zerihan doesn't want to rudely reject the hated strawberries she is indulgently gifted within a romantic one-on-one performance. A feverish Heddon gamely accepts being tucked into bed with a performer, even though the bed she craves is her own. Even beyond a distaste for strawberries and an incipient flu, the acceptance of gestures of care from a stranger is inevitably fraught.

Created by Christine Quintana and the Good Things To Do Collective, *Good Things To Do* cleverly sidesteps this problem of commodified encounter by presenting an entirely virtual partner. For the entirety of the performance, I am perfectly alone, cozy in my camping tent. Manifesting only as black TEXT on the white screen of the tent-laptop, my "dream-friend" cannot be seen or heard, and it is through this lack of physicality that we are able to connect without activating either the problem of reception or the problem of response. My partner is no one in particular and simultaneously is anyone. The result is that this anonymous noncorporeality doesn't trigger either the obligation to reciprocal performance or the cringe-inducing sense of accepting intimacy from an obvious stranger. (see PHONES)

The real-world artist-makers of *Good Things To Do* are present, but they are also invisible. Assuredly, the mechanics are apparent to us. Someone plays the violin and walks near while I am sleep-dreaming. The music is potently live, and I can sense their shadow on my tent-fort. Someone (or several someones) writes the words on the paper boats and

---

4   Deirdre Heddon, Helen Iball, and Rachel Zerihan, "Come Closer: Confessions of Intimate Spectators in One to One Performance," *Contemporary Theatre Review* 22, no. 1 (2012): 123–24.

5   Sarah Conn, "Experiments in Care as a Reciprocal Act," *Canadian Theatre Review* 197 (Winter 2024): 64–70.

sets them afloat unseen. I know they are there, and I know what they are doing to make the magic happen. And yet, in the haze of the caring affect of the performance, I can allow myself to believe in the magic too. Surreal, as if music and paper boats were conjured somehow.

Popcorn Galaxies's *The Dead Letter Office* sets the stage for participants to send personal letters to willing but incorrect recipients. "Inspired by the phenomenon of lost, undeliverable, and misdirected mail that finds its way into the postal service's office [as] "dead letters,"[6] *The Dead Letter Office* is an asynchronous participatory mail exchange. In an extensive sign-up form, participants first must CONSENT to both sending and receiving anonymous letters from other participants about meaningful, personal matters. After consenting to this facilitated correspondence, participants write and mail a letter to Popcorn Galaxies's June Fukumura and Keely O'Brien, addressed to someone from their own life. A letter that they dream of writing but which they would never actually send to that person—an ex that caused significant emotional pain, an old friend that slipped away. June and Keely then forward this letter to another participant in the project, anonymously connecting the pair and inviting them to respond to one another. While June and Keely have invested some thought in the pairings, for the most part they are not involved after the connection is made. The correspondence can stay anonymous or the pen pals can get to know each other in more depth.

In both *Good Things To Do* and *The Dead Letter Office*, the artists facilitating the exchange are not visible participants in the exchange. Different than the immediate (and awkward) relationships that may emerge from staged face-to-face encounters, these distanced, mediated exchanges provide an alternate (less imposing?) conduit while still delivering a reciprocal feeling of that give and get.

---

6   "The Dead Letter Office," *Popcorn Galaxies*, popcorngalaxies.ca/the-dead-letter
-office.html.

WRITE OUT A LIST OF AT LEAST 10 GOOD THINGS TO DO
AND FOLD IT INTO A BOAT!

MAKING AN ORIGAMI BOAT

1. FIND A SQUARE PIECE OF PAPER

2. FOLD IT IN HALF

3. FOLD THAT AGAIN INTO A SMALLER SQUARE

4. PEEL DOWN THE LOOSE CORNER AND FOLD IT THERE

5. TURN IT AROUND

6. FOLD THAT INTO A TRIANGLE

7. PUSH THE TOP CORNERS TOGETHER, MAKING A DIAMOND WITH A LINE DOWN THE MIDDLE

8. FLIP IT UPSIDE DOWN

9. PULL OPEN THE SIDES TO FORM THE BOAT

10. FOLD AND SHAPE!

EXTRAORDINARY

Jane's Walks,[1] guerrilla gardening, urban foraging, Situationist dérives,[2] yarn bombing, parkour, ghost bikes. Responsive to specific urban locations, these participatory performance-actions assert community. Invariably, the socially engaged artists of these works offer only the *thinnest* frame around everyday life, like a clear glass container to carry play. Creators in this mode, like the Fluxus artists of the 1960s, and contemporary Canadian creators Mia Rushton and Eric Moschopedis (Mia + Eric) rely upon their participants fully as collaborators, both "creative and resistive."[3] These artistic practices function like a magnifying glass to marvel at the everyday as art in itself. In line with Nicolas Bourriaud's *Relational Aesthetics*, these artists use participation to reframe everyday places and experiences for participants through peer-to-peer RELATIONAL encounter, often in concert with a third element of civic space. From the perspective of participants in this work, this kind of social art aims to facilitate "sociopathic relationships," remapping everyday life into a kind of community-imagined UTOPIA.[4] Different from the purely aesthetic illumination that happens with OSTRANENIE, this kind of relational encounter has a strong focus on materiality and community. There is no show. The process is the show. This work is firmly rooted in conditions already achieved by the everyday world, its magic harkening back to the simple interaction at the place where it happens to be. These artists build PLAYGROUNDS and offer RECIPES, and then attempt to erase themselves from the narrative construction of the work, allowing the participants to take the lead.

Eric Moschopedis and Laura Leif as co-leaders of *Imaginary Ordinary* inhabited an empty storefront in downtown Calgary to hold space for a month-long local gathering. The storefront space offered a very loose frame for activity, but participants were expected to populate it with their ideas. In his review, Andy Houston describes the space as having "a fun and funky décor . . . Wall space was devoted to the display of

---

1 Jane Jacobs was an American Canadian urban geographer who, after her death, inspired Jane's Walks, free public walking tours in urban city centres.
2 See DRIFT.
3 Eric Moschopedis, "Public Dreaming and the Transgression of Neo-Liberal Borders," *Public* 23, no. 45 (June 2012): 192–99.
4 Peter Mark Keays and Eric Moschopedis, editors, *Imaginary Ordinary*, 2010.

various projects; there was a collection of comfortable chairs and a large table for gathering, and even a modest kitchen space so tea and other refreshments could be served."[5] The space served as a hub for "connecting and reconnecting," providing a container for participants to fill with whatever story they felt like telling.[6] Houston continues, "There were excursions, some in groups, such as the psycho-geography inspired Urban Wander nights, and some were set up for exploration solo or in pairs, where participants were invited to borrow 'do it yourself' kits that offered guidance and the equipment for unique journeys, from bird watching in the nearby parks to a romantic drink for two in a destination to be discovered. There were also all manner of events organized in the Centre Street location, from collective cooking projects based on locally purchased foods, to quirky themed craft events, dances, and tributes to local community members."[7]

The framework encouraged participants to take over the community hub, to feel ownership over the community centre and whatever activities were inside. Participants in *Imaginary Ordinary* referred to it as a "mapping process, a reconfiguration" as the artist-leaders drew up the coordinates, but community participants did the surveying, plotting foliage, and imagining places for growth.

Created in collaboration between Mia + Eric and UK-based performance duo Action Hero (Gemma Paintin and James Stenhouse), *Future Perfect: New Bylaws for Civic Spaces*, is another act of public and participatory community art. In *Future Perfect*'s Toronto iteration at the SummerWorks Festival in 2022, participants were invited to rewrite Toronto's bylaws, by reorganizing words from existing bylaws that were literally cut up word by word before being glued onto new pages in new orders. "Meticulously rearranged into a new set of rules for a transitioning world," these new bylaws were then posted publicly on Twitter, and selected transformed bylaws were pasted on billboards in the city. The results were poetic and playful: Engage a tree or it expires.[8] A park

---

5   Andrew Houston, "The Experience of *Imaginary Ordinary*," *Canadian Theatre Review* 148 (Fall 2011): 95.

6   Keays and Moschopedis, *Imaginary Ordinary*.

7   Houston, "The Experience of *Imaginary Ordinary*," 95.

8   @FP_new_rules, "engage a tree or it expires," *Twitter*, 16 August 22, twitter.com /FP_new_rules/status/1559696601899323393.

is established by committee.[9] Any weeds.[10] Toronto is a personal playground of corporate council.[11] Animal advertising is under suspension.[12]

Hunter, Gatherer, Purveyor (2012) is another collaborative community artwork hosted by Mia + Eric. Dressed as hybrid vendors/park wardens and performing as urban foragers, the pair led local group walks and "collected and dehydrated roots, barks, fruits, grasses, moss, berries, weeds, and other plant life that [they] found on front lawns, hanging over fences, along boulevards, in back lanes, or in empty lots with the intention of making community-specific edible art objects that [they] could feed to residents—popsicles!"[13] Over time, they not only discovered and shared the taste of different neighbourhoods, Mia + Eric also report that the plant life "welcomed them in," opening avenues for conversations with residents, neighbours, and passersby. "We were so close you could taste it."[14]

In each case, these participatory works activate real civic space both in its geographic materiality but also on a social level. The ordinary becomes extraordinary, but also the extraordinary quality of these curated performance events reignites our appreciation for and engagement with the ordinary.

9   @FP_new_rules, "a park is established by a committee," *Twitter*, 12 August 22, twitter.com/FP_new_rules/status/1558139850171219969.

10   @FP_new_rules, "any weeds," *Twitter*, 11 August 22, twitter.com/FP_new_rules /status/1557830311236476929.

11   @FP_new_rules, "Toronto is a personal playground of corporate council," *Twitter*, 13 August 22, twitter.com/FP_new_rules/status/1558507466853437442.

12   @FP_new_rules, "animal advertising is under suspension," *Twitter*, 10 August 22, twitter.com/FP_new_rules/status/1557449329912193024.

13   Eric Moschopedis and Mia Rushton, "Digesting *Hunter, Gatherer, Purveyor*," *Canadian Theatre Review* 163 (Summer 2015): 31.

14   Moschopedis and Rushton, "Digesting," 32.

USE ONLY THE WORDS BELOW TO MAKE A SENTENCE OR POEM IN THE SPACE PROVIDED.

GUERRILLA   MARVEL   THROUGH   IT

ARTIST   A   EVERYDAY   PROCESS

AT   CONSTRUCT   GROWTH   IN

LIFE   SPACE   IS   PARTICIPATE

BORROW   COMMUNITY   WORLD

BUT   EXTRAORDINARY   MAKE   S

HYBRID   THE   NEW   ACTIVATE

PLANT   SOCIAL   LEVEL   ENGAGEMENT

- - - - - - - - - - - - - - -

FASCISM

If not the first of its kind, *Tamara* is certainly one the very earliest exemplars of the contemporary genre of environmental performance for an exploratory audience,[1] or what we are calling here CHOOSE YOUR OWN ADVENTURE. Premiering in Toronto's Strachan House in Trinity Bellwoods park in 1981, *Tamara* was written by John Krizanc, directed by Richard Rose, and produced by Rose's company Necessary Angel. The eponymous Tamara is art deco painter and muse Tamara de Lempicka who has been invited as a house guest to Il Vittoriale, the villa of poet Gabriele d'Annunzio. Like Tamara, we are also guests. Upon arrival, audience-spectators relinquish their passport tickets to Aldo Finzi, a black-uniformed, Fascist policeman who issues a set of very strict prohibitions on our behaviour: "If you wish to enjoy your stay here, you must obey our laws." When another character suggests, "Laws are meant to be broken," Finzi counters, "No, Signore, men are meant to be broken."[2] Thus cowed, we receive further instructions: "You must move quickly and quietly . . . And speak only when spoken to. Capisce?" "Do not open a closed door." "Do not get in the way, and do not stand in front of a doorway. You never know who is going to kick it down."[3] You are only able to change paths when two characters meet, switching to follow the other one. "Anyone found wandering around on their own will be deported."[4] Ostensibly, these are the safety rules for a free-range audience unaccustomed to this novel format. But these restrictions in the

---

1   Part of the fame of *Tamara* is that the show was refinanced by media mogul Moses Znaimer, who subsequently moved the show to the Hollywood American Legion Hall in Los Angeles in 1984, where it ran for nine years, and to the Park Avenue Armoury, New York, in 1987, where it ran for five years. Ticket prices, once $20, were now as high as $130 and included a champagne cocktail and lavish intermezzo buffet. Celebrities flocked to be part of the party that was *Tamara*. Not surprisingly the politics of the show changed substantially in this new context. Ric Knowles documents this transformation in his article "Reading Material: Transfers, Remounts, and the Production of Meaning in Contemporary Toronto Drama and Theatre," *Essays on Canadian Writing* 51/52 (Winter 93/Spring 94): 258–95.

2   John Krizanc, *Tamara: The Story You Experience From Room to Room* (Stoddart, 1989), 21.

3   Krizanc, *Tamara*, 24–25.

4   Krizanc, *Tamara*, 24.

context of our relative mobile freedom constitute the central paradox of dramaturgies of participation in *Tamara*.

For writer Krizanc, the AGENCY afforded the audience to follow any character and to compose their own unique narrative, combining between two and ten simultaneous scenes divided into twenty-one sequential acts, spoke directly to his goals for the work. In an interview with the playwright, Ric Knowles summarizes his thoughts: "The play was designed by Krizanc to be 'a critique of Fascism' and an interrogation of the artist's responsibility to society. Krizanc felt that because 'one of the problems with theatre is that you're subjected to the particular politics of the authors or the directors,' not to mention the TYRANNY of traditional wisdoms about blocking and focus on the proscenium stage, 'the best way to write a critique of Fascism was to give people more DEMOCRATIC freedom than they've ever had in the theatre.'"[5] In his forward to the published version of the play, Alberto Manguel underscores this understanding. "Never before had a theatre-going audience had this kind of freedom."[6] He calls *Tamara* "the first democratic play."[7] Manguel concludes, this free play is "the exact antithesis of fascism, because it condemns the audience to the unbearable freedom of a concerned and active WITNESS."[8] (see PLAYGROUNDS)

However, coloured by our subjection to the policing of Finzi in the fictional world and the play's strict behavioural codes that keep us contained in the actual world, we are not as free as all that. As Viviana Comensoli notes in her review of the published script, "Thus what appears initially to be a radical and liberating theatrical experience is undermined by a tyrannical superstructure."[9] Knowles makes a similar point, observing that "any real audience participation is precluded because the cast does not acknowledge its existence. The audience has no influence on the outcome of the plots, and the script is carefully constructed in order to provide the 'essential' information for each member no matter what plot or character he or she chooses to follow."[10] (see GHOSTS) It is true that we do have some choices, but ultimately *Tamara* is a closed world. The audience is impotent and invisible; our apparent

---

5   Knowles, "Reading Material," 267. Original Krizanc quotes are pulled from "Interview: John Krizanc," *Books In Canada* (March 1988): 34.

6   Alberto Manguel, "Foreword," *Tamara: The Story You Experience From Room to Room* by John Krizanc (Stoddart, 1989), 7.

7   Manguel, "Foreword," 7.

8   Manguel, "Foreword," 9.

9   Viviana Comensoli, "Environmental Theatre," *Canadian Literature* 128 (Spring 1991): 153.

10   Knowles, "Reading Material," 272.

choices reduced to a PHONY MULTIPLICITY. "The spectator creates his/her art within what is at root a manipulated set of circumstances, a state of artistic 'fascism' where the choices are dependent upon conventions set up by the production."[11] The metatheatrical tension between freedom and constraint complicates this pioneering work.

See COMPLICITY and SHOPPING

---

11   Richard Plant, "The Deconstruction of Pleasure: John Krizanc's *Tamara*, Richard Rose and the Necessary Angel Theatre Company," unpublished essay, subsequently translated and published as "Die dekonstruktion des vergnugens: John Krizanc's *Tamara*, Richard Rose, und die Necessary Angel Theatre Company," *Das Englisch-Kanadische Drama*, edited by Albert-Rainer Glaap (Schwann, 1992): 257–68. Cited in Knowles, "Reading Material."

FIRST-PERSON SHOOTER

One of our fundamental delineating characteristics for defining participatory theatre is that the audience arrives as audience. Their purpose is to be SPECTATORS of an aesthetic experience, consumers of a work of art. It is only after that initial position has been established that the audience may change their orientation to the work and accept the INVITATION to become active co-creators. (This is why although we do talk about some adjacent examples like pop-up performances by ORDINARY PEOPLE—flash mobs and zombie walks—as well as amateur theatre works arising out of community-engaged or applied theatre praxis, we have excluded them from our more narrow scope for participatory theatre.) The what and the how and the why of that invitation and its acceptance shape the transposition of the audience attendee into an audience-participant or audience-player. The nature of this shift is that a singular set of perspectives and associated tasks and actions splits into two. I am now both a contributor to the aesthetic experience (perhaps even a character) and I retain my original role as the watcher/consumer of that experience.[1]

I am the watcher from behind my own eyeballs. The proscenium, instead of being somewhere over there, is the front of my face—the bridge of my nose, the ridges of my eyebrows, the frame of my glasses. It is not simply that I have stepped through the frame or that the frame has disappeared. The theatrical frame remains (as it must) but it has moved. (see MAGIC CIRCLE)

The phrase "first-person shooter" comes from video games when, in 1992, *Wolfenstein 3D* pioneered gameplay that depicted an immersive environment and a first-person point of view.[2] The degree of change

---

1   Liesbeth Groot Nibbelink makes a related point when she articulates her resistance to calling immersive and/or participatory audiences "performers" or, following Boal, "spect-actors." She writes, "I find those qualifications a little problematic," and I agree ("Bordering and Shattering the Stage: Mobile Audiences as Compositional Forces," in *Staging Spectators in Immersive Performances: Commit Yourself!* edited by Doris Kolesch, Theresa Schütz, and Sophie Nikoleit (Routledge, 2019), 62). Her key point of contention is that these participatory audiences do not rehearse; they feel uneasy, and are not sure what to do. (see GUIDES)

2   "First Person Shooter," *Wikipedia*, en.wikipedia.org/wiki/First-person_shooter. Although *Wolfenstein 3D* is credited with being the first video game to launch this style of play, games of this kind are popularly known as *Doom* clones, in reference

brought about by this innovation is significant as the relation between the player and their fictionally immersed avatar is reconfigured. In two-dimensional (2D) games, I look from a distanced position (often above) onto the field of play where my personal game token or MEEPLE performs my represented actions—consider *Monopoly* where I am the shoe, or *PacMan* where I am a yellow circle with a triangular mouth.[3] In three-dimensional (3D) games, as the player, I am representationally embodied, looking through the eyes of my avatar.

Of course, I live my whole life this way. Humans exist in first person, perceiving the world through our forward-facing eyes fixed at approximately one and a half metres above the ground. I can see my hands but not the back of my neck. So mundane and familiar, this experiential situation is unremarkable to us. As philosopher Maurice Merleau-Ponty writes in *The Phenomenology of Perception*, "When I transfer my gaze from one object to another, I have no consciousness of my eye as an object, as a globe suspended in its socket, of its shifting or of its rest in objective space, nor of what results upon the retina."[4] It is Merleau-Ponty who, in his conception of the entanglement of the mind with the body, coins the immensely apt (and clever) term "eye/I." Moreover, as recounted in an anecdote in the book, about a pair of scissors, Merleau-Ponty notes that unlike the search for scissors, a subject "has no need to look for his hand or his fingers, for they are not objects to be found in objective space."[5]

As uninteresting as our facticity of being-in-the-world is, when addressed in art, it becomes a dramaturgical vehicle for meaning. Self-referential play concerning this condition of our ONTOLOGICAL DUALITY as both spectator and participant, both outside and inside the theatrical-game frame renders it interesting. Édouard Manet's painting *Bar at the Folies-Bergère* (1882) depicts a young woman working as a bartender, with the wall behind her an immense mirror that reflects the action of the night club. What intrigues people about the painting is the

---

to the highly popular *Doom* (1993), which is "often considered the most influential game in this genre."

3   The analogy to theatre doesn't quite map because the one-to-one connection of player to avatar doesn't manifest in theatre. Spectators do observe the actions of fictional characters from a distance. The key is that in BOURGEOIS THEATRE the audience is ontologically singular. We might associate with the characters through catharsis or through empathy with characters that we relate to, but they are not directly our representative extensions.

4   Maurice Merleau-Ponty, *The Phenomenology of Perception*, translated by Donald A. Landes (Routledge, 2012), 291.

5   Merleau-Ponty, *The Phenomenology of Perception*, 108.

inclusion in the mirror of a man in a hat who stands close to the bar and appears to be in conversation with the woman. Whereas she appears twice in the painting—we see her from the front directly and we see her back in the mirror—he only appears once. The trick of the perspective implies that we are the man. Observing the painting, I stand precisely where he would be.[6] Delightfully, I am both myself in the actual world and simultaneously my outward features have been transformed into the man and I am transported into the fictional world.

One way that this duality is rendered meaningful in participatory performance works is by thematizing the specific relation of the "eye" to the "I," between my gaze and my ability to move my consciousness through space. I am a camera. I choose what to look at. This is where the main action of the audience-player is SEEKING or DRIFT. Dramaturgical meaning attaches to the choices that I make of how I combine looking with moving. Sometimes meaning also arises out of the novelty of my renewed self-awareness that I am indeed a camera. (Look! I'm looking! So cool.)

Another way that this duality of being both a distanced watcher and an immersed participant manifests as a thematic feature is when these two positions are mismatched. The separation of the audience-self and the player/character-self can create an ethical dilemma if these different positions require or expect different actions and impute different culpability for the consequences of those actions. I am always and inescapably me and actual-world Jenn may feel some responsibility for the choices made by a fictional-world Jenn who has different priorities.[7] (see COMPLICITY, FASCISM, and FUTILITY) Conversely, actual-world Jenn might decide to do something to make the performance-game more "fun," like pressing the giant red button that says, "Don't press this," but that choice might negatively impact fictional-Jenn who gets

---

6   Malcolm Park, "Manet's *Bar at the Folies-Bergère*: One Scholar's Perspective," *Getty Museum*, getty.edu/art/exhibitions/manet_bar/looking_glass.html.

7   In their chapter in *Immersive Gameplay*, Nordic larp theorists Markus Montola and Jussi Holopainen call this "first person audience" and make note of a feature called "bleed" or "bleed games." Neither positive nor negative, bleed refers to situations when the player feels strong emotions in the real world generated by events in the fictional world. The border between my success or failure and my character's success or failure can be quite thin (Markus Montola and Jussi Holopainen, "First Person Audience and the Art of Painful Role-Playing," *Immersive Gameplay: Essays on Participatory Media and Role-Playing*, edited by Evan Torner and William J. White (McFarland and Company, 2012), 13–30). See also Sarah Lynne Bowman, "Bleed: The Spillover Between Player and Character," *Nordic Larp*, 2 March 2015, nordiclarp.org /2015/03/02/bleed-the-spillover-between-player-and-character/.

eaten by zombies. (see GOING ROGUE) When immersed into a fictional world that is very different from our usual context, there is an inevitable dissonance. There may be benefits to that aphorism that enjoins us to walk a mile in someone else's shoes; however, in the end, those cannot be my shoes. And at the end of a sweaty uncomfortable walk, unlike the original wearer, I get to take off the shoes, go home and have a shower. (see WITNESS) Natalie Alvarez in her book *Immersions in Cultural Difference: Tourism, War, Performance*, considers the impacts and the ethics of "dark tourism," sites that are "designed as transient experiences for visitors who only temporarily occupy them . . . consensual acts of contained transgression organized around a set of desired pedagogical effects."[8] Her examples include a simulated migrant Mexico-US border run—called the *caminata nocturna* or "night walk"—and a military-use training installation of a mock Afghan village in Alberta. For Alvarez, "These sites reveal how empathy becomes instrumentalized in a way that leads to very misleading intimacies with the cultural others they often imaginatively totalize." But she notes, while some of her examples uphold these tendencies, others co-opt and reframe immersive practices in sophisticated ways "to offer a useful counterpoint that troubles this perspective."[9] (see UTOPIA)

8   Natalie Alvarez, *Immersions in Cultural Difference: Tourism, War, Performance* (U of Michigan P, 2018), 1.

9   Alvarez, *Immersions in Cultural Difference*, 3. Scott Magelssen examines another instance of a similarly fraught intercultural immersive simulation called *Follow the North Star*, where participants at Conner Prairie, a living history museum in Indiana, re-enact the journey of escaped African American slaves in the late-nineteenth century US south (*Simming: Participatory Performance and the Making of Meaning* (U of Michigan P, 2014), 29–47). See also Ruth Laurion Bowman, "Troubling Bodies in *Follow the North Star*," in *Reframing Immersive Theatre: The Politics and Pragmatics of Participatory Performance*, edited by James Frieze (Palgrave Macmillan, 2016), 63–76.

SPOT THE DIFFERENCES BETWEEN THESE TWO IMAGES. THE NUMBER OF DIFFERENCES WILL BE YOUR ANSWER, SO LOOK CAREFULLY!

ANSWER:

FOOT WASHING

Here's a question: What is the least that we can do and still consider our action to be participation? When attending a formally traditional performance of quietly-sit-very-still-in-the-dark BOURGEOIS THEATRE, there is no doubt that I am doing something. It is not the action of my body, but it is the action of my mind. I am absorbing phenomenological and semiotic inputs of various kinds and doing the creative work of meaning-making. (see INTERPRETATION) Another sort of cognitive activity arises in works that are meditative in nature. Setting up contemplative conditions, these are works that invite MINDFULNESS.[1] Reducing our scope even more, the least active verbs are verbs of ontology, simple beingness—I am; you are; she is. Perhaps I might expand simple existence slightly to encompass presence. I am here. That is, I am co-located with the work of art. (Philosophical digression: Of course, what constitutes "here" is flexible in our virtually augmented world. And for theatre, I would add that I also need to be in a shared "now"; otherwise, this is TV. Sidestepping a long dissertation on co-presence,[2] I will however insist that there needs to be a "conduit" between the work and the audience-participant. There needs to be a channel for AUTOPOIESIS.)

When an artwork asks me to simply be, attention on simply being is thematized. What is it like to be? To be here? To be now? To be me here and now? The interface between me and my encompassing phenomenological context is where the art happens. And this is precisely the experiential driver of immersive theatre. In immersive theatre, the

---

1   I'm thinking of something like *What Happens to You Happens to Me* by Susanna Fournier, a "participatory storytelling experience." It is described as "a letter, a questionnaire, a thought-experiment, a mindfulness exercise that takes the listener on a journey through grief and loneliness." The work that the audience-participant is asked to do begins with interpretive sense-making but moves to an activity of self-reflection. "*What Happens to You Happens to Me,*" *Susanna Fournier,* susannafournier.com /what-happens-to-you-happens-to-me.

2   Cormac Power, *Presence in Play: A Critique of Theories of Presence in the Theatre* (Rodopi, 2008).

environment (distinct from my usual immersion in the actual world)[3] and my sensory, haptic engagement with it is the "where" of meaning.[4]

Is immersive theatre participatory?[5] Yes? No? Adam Alston asserts that from a foundational perspective audiencing is always attuned to its sensory interface with the world. "Once spectatorship is acknowledged as an embodied and potentially affective activity, all theatre and performance is, or at least has the potential to be an immersive activity."[6] This is participation on a similar level to that of interpretation where my entanglement with a specific physical context generates meaningful sensory experience. (That context might be a traditional theatre space. Or not.)

It is Josephine Machon who asserts with confidence that "immersive theatres are always interdisciplinary and participatory . . . Immersive work establishes a unique exchange that prioritises embodied engagement within the proceedings and any subsequent contemplation of the

---

3   I'm leaning into the idea here that we are always already immersed—in the air, in the physics of our usual reality. It is the change of medium—being newly immersed in water, for example—that activates our critical attention and is the carrier of aesthetic meaning in immersive art works.

4   I want to mention here an article by Matthew Reason, "Participatory Audiencing and the Committed Return" in *Staging Spectators in Immersive Performances: Commit Yourself!* edited by Doris Kolesch, Theresa Schütz, and Sophie Nikoleit (Routledge, 2019), 88–101. Reason tells a story about a participatory experience where his main action was to "commit," to go along with it. He was led blindfolded through a richly sensory environment. Afterwards, he felt something lacking. Reason describes this feeling eloquently as being kissed but not kissing back. Rather than having had an experience, he asserts that "an experience had me." (Wow! What a great turn of phrase.) Basically, the audience-participant had no opportunity to speak back to the work. Reason quotes Grant Kester's opinion that "the possibility of a dialogical relationship that breaks down the conventional distinction between artist, artwork and audience—a relationship that allows the viewer to 'speak back' to the artist in certain ways, and in which this reply becomes in effect a part of the 'work' itself" ("Dialogical Aesthetics: A Critical Framework for Littoral Art" *Variant* 9 (Winter 1999/2000), variant.org.uk/9texts/KesterSupplement.html). Reason concludes with a reference to Rancière, remarking that not all spectatorship experiences are emancipated. "Spectatorship can become dulled, controlled, manipulatory, passive" (93).

5   Considering the converse case, I will point out that participatory theatre is not always immersive. It is not uncommon for participation in performance to unfold in a postdramatic mode. Audience-participants do actions. We perform, but not within or in the service of a fictional cosmos. Our active contributions remain stubbornly part of the actual world. If there is a frame, it is the very thin frame of "performance" or "play" rather than fiction.

6   Adam Alston, "Audience Participation and Neoliberal Value," *Performance Research* 18, no. 2 (2013): 129.

work. Immersive theatres attune the audience-participant to respond in a holistic fashion, charged by a *felt* quality in the event that uncovers—indeed, requires—a corporeal appreciation of the artwork."[7] Immersive theatre leverages attention on environmental difference to produce a visceral response. Participation arises then in the interplay or fusion between the audience and their sensory engagement, between the felt and the understood, generating a reflexive sense of their own beingness.[8] (see SWEATING and HANDS)

Machon, writing about her experience of Adrian Howells's performance piece *The Pleasure of Being: Washing, Feeding, Holding*,[9] identifies the locus of her co-authorship of the work in touch, specifically how her body becomes "the source and the site of the performance."[10] Eschewing the position of agential subject, audience-participants become objects. In this role, we are (mostly passive) recipients of the performance's verbs. We are not doing things so much as having things done to us. Using my body as a sensory canvas involves me differently than when I am used as PAINT. In a work like *100% Vancouver*, if I am one of the chosen hundred, there is a curated display and arrangement of my physical characteristics or my specific history of lived experience to constitute the building blocks of meaning in the performance. I am the material of the work, usually for the apprehension of a secondary audience—basically, paint. Immersive work positions the audience-object differently. Aesthetic meaning is generated not as an output of my body, but instead through the interplay of stimulus inputs on and in my body. As Machon says, it arises out of a kind of sensory fusion, or synaesthesia; the audience-participant is concurrently the source and site of the performance.

One way that participatory immersive performances activate my body in this fused dual mode is through touch. I am touched and the nerve endings in my skin generate sensation. As theatre theorist Erika Fischer-Lichte notes, there is a long-standing and deeply held opposition to the

---

7   Josephine Machon, "On Being Immersed: The Pleasure of Being, Washing, Feeding, Holding," *Reframing Immersive Theatre: The Politics and Pragmatics of Participatory Performance*, edited by James Frieze (Palgrave Macmillan, 2016), 30.

8   Machon, "On Being Immersed," 33.

9   The collected works of UK artist Adrian Howells are foundational to this genre of performance practice that involves caring, intimate physical encounter between the audience-participant and Howells in one-on-one encounters that variously involve being washed, being fed, and being held. See *It's All Allowed: Performances of Adrian Howells*, edited by Deirdre Heddon and Dominic Johnson (Live Art Development Agency, 2016). Howells presents a first-person document of his work *Foot Washing for the Sole* in *Performance Research* 17, no. 2 (2012): 128–31.

10   Machon, "On Being Immersed," 41.

inclusion of touch in performance between audience and actors. She notes two possible reasons for this. First, "theatre represents a public medium, while physical contact belongs to the sphere of intimacy."[11] And second, arising from the priorities of eighteenth-century European illusionistic theatre, there is a strict opposition between seeing and touching. Reaching into the distanced illusion, physical contact "[performs] the invasion of the real into fiction."[12]

In participatory performance, the issue around the blurring of the fictional and the actual is somewhat ameliorated as the audience is welcomed into the fictional space as a co-creator, becoming a pseudo-character. (see ACTING and THE MATRIX) However, from another perspective I, the audience-participant, do still remain fixedly in the actual world, a consumer of an aesthetic experience. (see FIRST-PERSON SHOOTER) And it is this positionality that makes what is being done to me still inescapably actual and public. This is why I feel self-conscious. The ENCOUNTER of touch asks too much of me. Even with deeply thoughtful care practices, I still feel a curdling awareness of an embarrassing transactionality ever-present below the surface.[13] If this is not the desired outcome (and perhaps in some cases it could well be), then how is this kind of emotional spoilage to be avoided?

The only Canadian entry in Nato Thompson's book/catalogue *Living as Form: Socially Engaged Art from 1991–2011* is *Haircuts by Children*, created by Darren O'Donnell and his company Mammalian Diving Reflex. Client-participants arrive at a salon run by preteens and entrust their hair (and their vanity) to these unexpected stylists and their scissors. Premiering in Toronto in 2006, the show has been presented dozens of times across four continents. It is billed as "an event that will test your courage and faith in the future. Let them cut your fears away as they prove themselves creative leaders, capable and responsible citizens and dedicated coiffures."[14] Although my body constitutes the canvas of

---

11   Erika Fischer-Lichte, *The Transformative Power of Performance: A New Aesthetics*, translated by Saskya Iris Jain (Routledge, 2008), 60.

12   Fischer-Lichte, *The Transformative Power of Performance*, 60.

13   Nicholas Ridout, "Embarrassment: The Predicament of the Audience," *Stage Fright, Animals and Other Theatrical Problems* (Cambridge UP, 2006). Ridout parses out the reasons for the acute embarrassment of the audience hailed by direct address, located in the realization of the mutual actuality of me and the actor, but he also recognizes that there is pleasure in this embarrassment and that it is perhaps not forgone: "If self-recognition is the pleasure that we gain, then some degree of self-disclosure is the price to be paid for it" (79).

14   Darren O'Donnell, *Haircuts by Children and Other Evidence for a New Social Contract* (Coach House, 2018).

Haircuts by Children and, like other touch-based works, the show evokes the experience of receiving a personal service,[15] the understanding of the work really pivots on the gap of expectations in capacity between children and adults. My hair is simply the vehicle for this disjunctive experience. An experience that is heightened by our high-stakes investment of self-esteem in one's appearance and the actually low-stakes of the enterprise. (It's just hair.)

Shows with such an intense somatic focus are relatively rare in the contemporary Canadian scene, so it is interesting that our other principal exemplar is also a hair show. *Higher Hair*, presented at SummerWorks 2022 invites the audience-participant to "enter a super-natural spa that practices time as non-linear, wellness as CARE, community and reciprocity, beauty as becoming, hair stylists as healers, and hair as sacred technology of archival and antennae."[16] The show is experienced in pairs as "Community Cosmetic Healers" Hima Batavia and Nikola Steer (aka her burlesque moniker Coco Framboise) offer an "encounter of somatic activation" that involves consensual hair play. After a CEREMONIAL induction, I am invited to recline on a chaise, accompanied by peaceful, dim lighting and a meditative audio track. As my hair is lightly stroked and carefully arranged and rearranged, I am prompted to consider its/my genealogy and social influences. How is my hair and my relationship to it shaped by politics? Do I face censure for having hair that is too short? Too coarse and curly? Too thin or sparse? Inappropriately covered? Or inappropriately uncovered? I consider my persistent daily efforts to straighten out my Ashkenazi frizziness. I also contemplate hair expectations connected to aging. Is my hair too long for a woman my age? (Is this a bizarre question?) What about those incipient greys? Shifting generations from my genetic inheritance to my legacy. I wonder what cultural biases am I imposing on my children as standards of "tidiness" but really are performances of gender norming.

Despite our physical closeness, the "healers" of *Higher Hair* are not claiming a relationship; they position themselves and the work clearly

---

15   A recognizable trope in intimate participatory performance is the replication of actions of personal services. These are activities where we commonly accept touching by strangers. The frame of "service" renders my body neutral, a thing that needs to be fixed or maintained, and posits the service provider as a skilled professional—for a medical or dental check-up; aesthetic services like manicure or facial; therapeutic interventions like physio or massage treatment. This is why sex work can be complicated, because the implied romantic connection is absent. I suppose the opposite is also true when a mundane service like feeding a child or elderly parent or giving a manicure to a partner becomes an act of love.

16   "Higher Hair," *SummerWorks 2022*, summerworks.ca/show/higher-hair/.

in the realm of a service—a spiritual service rather than an aesthetic one, but a service, nonetheless. This demarcation of distance is freeing. The service is impersonally personal. The performance is not figured as an ENCOUNTER between myself and Hima or Nikola. This is in no way an erotic tryst. Rather, dressed in white satiny robe-dresses, with spangles on their skin, and ensconced in a kind of temple of mirrors, candles, and flowing fabrics, they are the handmaidens (hairmaidens?) of a private assignation between me and my hair. It is indeed intimate.

See INTIMACY and TEXT MESSAGING

·DRAW THEM ALL A NEW HAIRCUT.

FRIENDSHIP

Some participatory work, especially participatory work made amid the COVID-19 pandemic, celebrates the pleasures of affection found in embodied relationality. A prime example is Cellar Door Project's *To You*. Performed during the early lockdown phase of the pandemic, *To You* is a pop-up porch play I created with Kay Kenney and Laura Chaignon. After we were told to physically isolate ourselves in our homes in March 2020, I was feeling depressed, and profoundly disconnected from my community. I missed my people. I missed my family. It's hard to remember now, but by May 2020, I had spent six full weeks in an apartment of just eighty square metres with only one other person and a little white cat. Streets and stores were empty. People went months and months without seeing their mothers, their children, their partners—anyone at all.

In honour of my twenty-seventh birthday, over the course of two days in May 2020, Laura, Kay and I travelled around Kingston, landing at the front doors, steps, and driveways of pre-selected friends or family to stage a fake surprise birthday party. For person after person, it became their birthday. In May. Surprise! After the fanfare that accompanied our arrival, each porch party would start with me recounting the first time I had met my audience-participant. When I performed this for Jenn, I told the story of the first day of DRAM100 in my undergrad at Queen's. I sat near the front, an obvious keener. Jenn, who was the professor, made a real effort to learn all of our names and I remembered feeling very seen, like I was in exactly the place I was supposed to be. This book is written more than ten years after that day, and we are still in meaningful relation with one another. Together, we reminisced about our shared history of friendship. I then asked the participant to share a story about their most memorable birthday party and I told stories of my own. We clumsily tried (and failed) to share a cupcake while maintaining the mandated two metres of social distance. For the grand finale, Whitney Houston's "I Just Wanna Dance with Somebody (Who Loves Me)" blasted out of our car stereo, while Kay taught the participant some easy-to-follow choreography and we performed it triumphantly together on the street. We shared a wink acknowledging the upsurge of public silliness we all shared. (see SECRET WEIRDOS) As we drove away, I felt the pang of separation again; the experience was bittersweet.

To You was born out of a real desire to reconnect with our loved ones. We certainly hadn't knocked on each other's doors or shared a meal or danced together for weeks and weeks before this. We were missing the material intimacy of our friendship, but were also missing the more abstract threads that tied us together. We were friends, but friends estranged by circumstances and in need of remediative CARE. *To You* strengthened the bonds of our pre-established relationships through both nostalgic reminiscence and a fun, new shared experience in the present. The renewal of this relationship is both historical, rooted in memory, as well as oriented towards our future. I was reminded that, beyond dancing in public and sharing stories, I was committed to care for these people in my lives. Even if I wasn't nearby, I'd always be there.

Six months after *To You*, I started a Ph.D. and I took a course on prison abolition. Grappling with abolition[1] asked me to consider caring so *deeply* about people, strangers, that I would be committed to address harm-doing without causing more harm. Among other things, abolition is the choice to move through the world, holding the belief that everyone matters, everyone deserves freedom, and everyone deserves care. Importantly, upholding abolition's inherent principles of care extend beyond our personal networks, reaching through bars to hold space for complete strangers.

Activist, scholar, and former poet laureate of Halifax, El Jones writes her most recent book, *Abolitionist Intimacies*, about the "movement to abolish prisons through the Black feminist principles of care and collectivity."[2] In this collection of essays and poems, she looks closely at her own personal practices of relational intimacy with friends inside and how these practices act as an integral part of the complex world-building project that is prison abolition. She recounts countless visits to the Burnside Jail in Dartmouth, Nova Scotia, bringing books and notes to loved ones. She tells stories of phone calls on Christmas and shopping trips for clothes for folks who have been recently released. For Jones, "Abolition is not only a political movement to end prisons; it is also an intimate one deeply motivated by commitment and love."[3] Through her own abolitionist experiences undertaking these myriad small acts of friendship and care, Jones argues that through intimate connection

---

[1]   Abolition means the destruction of a reliance on racial and carceral capitalism in the name of "justice" in favour of the (re)creation of different ways to reduce and address harm. See REMOTE CONTROL and my upcoming Ph.D. dissertation.

[2]   El Jones, *Abolitionist Intimacies* (Fernwood Publishing, 2022), back cover.

[3]   Jones, *Abolitionist Intimacies*, back cover.

and relationship, we are performing tiny vignettes of a new world that does not rely on carceral violence and racial capitalism within which we relate to each other only in conflict. As a method, INTIMACY in this context insists on abolition not (only) as a conceptual exercise, but as a material one. While she does conceptual policy work, like writing public opinion pieces and lobbying the Nova Scotia government for better conditions inside, Jones materializes abolition through showing up actively for her friends inside. For Jones, abolitionist intimacies are intensely participatory. "At the heart of the exploration of intimacy throughout this work is the ongoing, loving sharing of our lives and experiences between those inside and me on the outside. I name this method abolitionist intimacies. Intimacy is both my subject and my research method."[4]

In this context, deep and meaningful interpersonal friendships with material ramifications, different from one-off ENCOUNTERS, accomplish key steps within the abolitionist process. For Jones, by changing the way we relate to one another through showing up for each other with love, even in the face of conflict and harm, we are living abolition. In a conversation between artist and abolitionist Syrus Marcus Ware and Giselle Dias (Niigaanii Zhaawshko Giizhigokwe) in *Until We are Free: Reflections on Black Lives Matter*, Ware says that for him "abolition would only come through a revolutionary process where everything would change . . . abolition is, yes, the closing and ending of our reliance on the prison-industrial complex as a way of handling our conflict, but it's also an entirely new way of being and relating to each other in the world."[5]

El Jones's *Abolitionist Intimacies* insists that the prison industrial complex enacts its carceral violence by restricting human intimacy, by severing relations from loved ones inside, but also with other people at large. Beyond captivity, by limiting phone calls and insisting on "no touching" in visitations, the prison industrial complex punishes through intimacy restriction. The reliance on carceral violence as a method of addressing harm is a major CRISIS of the twenty-first century and some participatory dramaturgies offer participants a rehearsal in other ways of responding to the crisis.[6] (see TOGETHER ALONE) Abolition

---

4   Jones, *Abolitionist Intimacies*, 4–5.
5   Rodney Diverlus, Sandy Hudson, and Syrus Marcus Ware. *Until We Are Free: Reflections on Black Lives Matter in Canada* (U of Regina P, 2020), 33.
6   Richard Lam's *The Candlemaker's Game* is a conflict-management SIM, using transformative justice frameworks and techniques from cognitive behavioural therapy to give participants a chance to analyze a major conflict from their lives.

asserts that the violence of carceral isolation is not an appropriate response to harm. Jones argues that abolition can exist in her reassertion of friendship and love on either side of the prison walls. Abolition is fundamentally a participatory act.

See LAND

FUTILITY

Written and performed by Cliff Cardinal, *Huff* literally needs the audience to act to start the play and save Cardinal as the character Wind from suicide by anoxia. The protective frame between the fiction and actual danger here is unspeakably thin. The risk presents itself as distressingly real. *"Wind enters. He has a plastic bag over his head. It's duct-taped around his throat to create an airtight seal."* His hands are locked in handcuffs behind his back. "Turn off your fucking cellphone. Put the remote down. This is an interruption of your regularly scheduled program. Don't worry though. Your normal show will be on again soon. This isn't life or death. Not for you."[1] For a couple of minutes that feel like eternity, Wind continues this monologue. He tells us about anoxia, and how he will die. "This is a suicide attempt. I say 'attempt' but it's looking pretty good. I should know. I've done this before."[2] Struggling to remove the bag, he falls to the floor. Then he turns to an audience member, leaning forward into their face, he asks them to get the bag off. The demand is urgent. "Seriously. This isn't a metaphor. If you don't help me I'll suffocate right here."[3] The next stage direction is telling. *"If the audience member says anything aside from 'yes,' Wind goes to someone else."*[4] An audience member must act. Someone needs to intervene to remove the bag and unlock the handcuffs. The ONTOLOGICAL DUALITY of Wind, Cardinal, and the play *Huff* itself collapse into singularity. Unless the audience-player does as commanded, all three will cease to exist. Wind will end. Cardinal will end and the play will end. This is not the cool detachment of a puzzle-solving detective.

Grabbed and shaken hard like this at the very start of the play, the audience is "in deep" in terms of our responsibility. And of course, this is the point. Once freed from the bag and the handcuffs, *"Wind thrusts the plastic bag back into the audience member's hands . . .* Hold on to this for me. And don't give it back no matter what I say. Okay? I need you."[5] We understand the stakes of keeping hold of the bag, and the tendency of audiences to be generally obedient to dramatic instruction supports

1   Cliff Cardinal, *Huff*, in *Huff & Stitch* (Playwrights Canada, 2017), 5.
2   Cardinal, *Huff*, 6.
3   Cardinal, *Huff*, 6.
4   Cardinal, *Huff*, 6–7.
5   Cardinal, *Huff*, 7.

undertaking this action as "good." By following directions, we are good players of the game—we didn't break the play—and we get positive feedback as moral humans. These two participatory actions align. At the end, however, the play pulls the rug out from under us, and flips this equation. Wind again approaches that same audience member and demands the return of the plastic bag. His intentions seem clear. What to do? What kind of "good" should we be? Who is asking for the bag? The suicidal character? Or the actor? (see BAD FAITH)

The play accounts for a branching action and closes off possibilities. If the audience member offers the bag, Wind refuses it. Either way, without the plastic bag, Wind returns to the stage. *"He takes another plastic bag out of his pocket. He puts it on his head. He duct tapes a seal around his throat.* But no matter how many times you try and save me you can still find me here . . . Six minutes under. See? I told you."[6] The moment is deeply unsettling to say the least. Our culpability extends not just to our participation here, and how we answer the call to action in the theatre, but also to the built-in dead ends of society at large and we are called to consider how, by our actions and by our not-actions, we participate in the systemic oppression that brought Wind here in this moment.

See COMPLICITY and OR ELSE

6   Cardinal, *Huff*, 53–54.

GAME OVER. PLAY AGAIN?

Dramatic works end when they reach the end of the plotted narrative arc. Under an Aristotelian dramaturgical model, that means that the intrusion that disrupted the initial stasis has been resolved and we return to a new stasis.[1] Games, on the other hand, end when they end. Now, some games are quite Aristotelian in this respect, and they follow a similar line of thinking, guided by a sort of narrative arc. They end when you WIN. You complete the set task, the storyline is complete, and the game ends. By contrast, for some games the story never ends. I end. Games like this always end with my death. Every time. "Game Over." The game world is theoretically infinite, and you play and play until you die (that is, until your avatar runs out of "lives" or other essential life-giving resources). Then it loops around, and I am asked cheerfully, "Play again?" Given these disparate logics of how games and dramas end, it is valuable to consider how play ends in the hybrid intersection of the two genres.

In an escape room, time is dominant. The game is over after sixty minutes, no matter what. Wherever you are in the story or however close you are to escaping, if time runs out, you are done. Instantly. When I did *Escape From the Tower* (Secret City Adventures), time ran out, and we all "died" in an air raid that we failed to prevent. The group was so close; the actors then showed us the solution to the last puzzle. (see SLACK) Technically we were brought to the end of the story, but it was told to us, we didn't "live" it. The story was resolved for us as exposition outside the fictional frame of the game play.

The trio of plays that make up *Tape Escape*, produced by Outside the March, each enact a different ending strategy, but all three productively grapple with the tension between a rule-determined game end and a narrative-driven dramatic end. In an interview with co-creator Mitchell Cushman, he affirmed this tension between narrative impulses and win conditions as one of the major challenges of creation.[2] Set in a 90s video store, (staged in the actual now-defunct 90s video store, Queen Video, on Toronto's Bloor Street West) *Tape Escape* presents three different hour-long puzzle-based experiences.

---

1   David Ball, *Backwards and Forwards: A Technical Manual for Reading Plays* (Southern Illinois UP, 1983).

2   Mitchell Cushman and Julie Tepperman, personal interview, 8 April 2020.

Yesterday's Heroes adheres the most tightly to a time-based dramaturgy. It is the most lyrical of the three with two parallel plots. One plot features a fairytale-like animated story of a dancing girl who seems to be trapped in a tree; our task (perhaps) is to rescue her. The other plot bends time into the future of the video store to the night of a staff party when five young employees will die when the store burns to the ground. Like an escape room, *Yesterday's Heroes* only ends one way—you solve the puzzle, escape and win, or you run out of time and you don't. Once you enter the final room, thick with low-lying fog and smelling of smoke, surrounded by five birch tree trunks, you have only a short time remaining to solve it, if you fail (which we both did on separate occasions), the story ends. Immediately and without resolution. Here, there is a case to be made that there is a thematic justification. Failure feeds the melancholy of not saving the ghost girl and is also somehow connected to the mood of the fire that destroys the store and kills five employees, which we could not prevent. Failure specifically means not being a hero. (see BAD FAITH)

In the second *Tape Escape* installment, a romantic comedy titled *Love Without Late Fees*, the outcomes of each puzzle (win or lose) determine which video Sarah and Matt will rent. The video as determined by our play shapes the twists and turns of their relationship. If they rent *Jurassic Park*, Matt proposes marriage just five weeks into the relationship. If they rent *Scream*, Sarah gets cold feet and calls off the wedding. Each puzzle play shapes the forking narrative. (see CHOOSE YOUR OWN ADVENTURE) The relationship of the dating couple evolves to an end point no matter what we do, but the specific ending is one of thirty-two different permutations. At each fork, we are aware that there were other paths that existed but did not come to pass. At the end, we are elegantly made aware of Sarah and Matt's other futures through a video-wall collage depicting the multiverse of all their endings. Again, thematically this resonates. Love feels like that. Relationships are an accretion of serendipity, shaped by myriad small insignificant choices like what video we should rent on a Saturday date night.

For the last escape-room play of this trio, the connection to how the game play ends is tied to our sensory experience of solving the puzzles themselves. *A Grown Up's Guide to Flying* begins as a Peter Pan-themed scavenger hunt created by video store employee Gene for his kid sister Kelly on her eighth birthday. As the play progresses, we learn that Kelly is gradually losing her eyesight. In formal parallel to this plot line, the puzzles shift from being initially sight driven—we are asked to sort colours into a rainbow and use a uv flashlight to read secret symbols—to sorting vials by smell and listening to an audio recording of a call-sign code. In the end, the players solve the final puzzles as if we are ourselves visually impaired.[3]

Do you want to play again? Reviewing our experiences of *Tape Escape*, I think no. (But Mariah thought yes. Maybe there is confetti if you win?) (see JUICINESS) These divergent takes relate (we think) to whether this is at heart a game or a drama. It depends perhaps on where variability, and thus replayability, enters the equation. In BOURGEOIS (read "rehearsed") THEATRE, variability in a single production is limited by intent. Ideally, the performance is the same night after night. It isn't quite, of course, but replication is an overt goal. A pure game, however, is replayable. You can play soccer over and over with unending variability. A corollary to variability versus fixity through REHEARSAL is the pre-scripted nature of the dramatic text. The ending of a drama may be uncertain to a first-time spectator, but the ending is known. It is known to the artists, and the audience knows that they know. Drama is planned and its determined aesthetic choices drive the meaning. Conversely, play is an "uncertain activity. Doubt must remain until the end, and hinges on the denouement . . . An outcome known in advance, with no possibility of error or surprise, clearly leading to an inescapable result, is incompatible with the nature of play."[4] A puzzle game, though, is like a drama, having perhaps more limited replay value.[5] Once solved, the answer is known. Where does the locus of interest lie, then, in these drama-game hybrids?

---

3   Much of the story for this episode of *Tape Escape* was inspired by Devon Healy, the Blindness and Performance Consultant for *A Grown-Up's Guide to Flying*, and their experiences living with Stargardt's Disease. The script for this show is published in *Canadian Theatre Review* 197 (Winter 2024): 71–76.

4   Roger Caillois, *Man, Play and Games*, translated by Meyer Barash (U of Illinois P, 1961), 7.

5   Taking a slightly different tack, Mariah notes that, in ambulatory immersive works, the replay value lies in "collectability." It is often not possible to fully explore the entire space and all the performed scenes in one visit to something like *Brantwood*. With its close to a dozen concurrent scenes, getting even a fraction of the whole experience is impossible. For *Tamara*, collectability through repetition was encouraged through discounted tickets for return attendees. This collectability is emphasized in fan communities, where player-participants will attend a show multiple times to experience it all. For more, read Jen Harvie's writing on Punchdrunk's *Sleep No More* in *Fair Play: Art, Performance and Neoliberalism* (Palgrave Macmillan, 2013).

THE ALIEN THANKS YOU FOR WARNING THEM ABOUT THE CHEESE SANDWICH;
WHAT A DISASTER THAT COULD HAVE BEEN! THEY DECIDE TO GIVE YOU A
GOLDEN SHEEP AS THANKS. IT PRODUCES GOLDEN MILK. TURN TO PAGE 198
TO FIND OUT WHAT HAPPENS WHEN YOU TAKE THIS PRIZE BACK HOME.

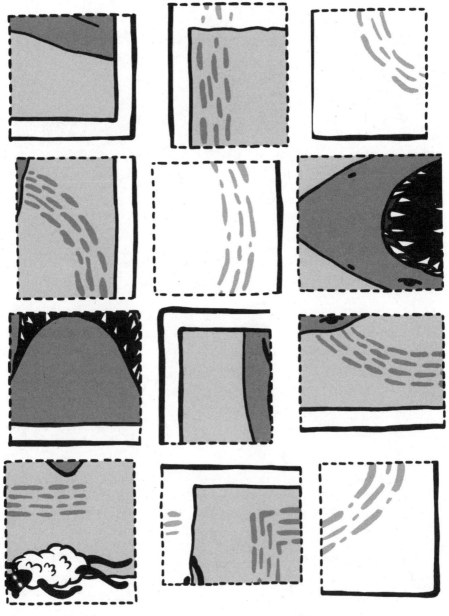

ANSWER:

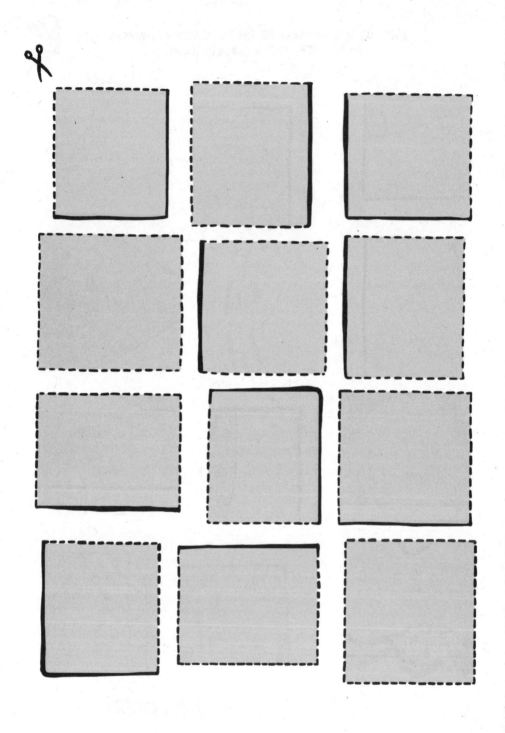

GHOSTS

Created by Julie Tepperman and Mitchell Cushman, the immersive, site-specific musical *Brantwood* is an epic example of the CHOOSE YOUR OWN ADVENTURE genre of audience-player participation. The event begins when the audience is assigned a locker, given a blue academic gown, and invited to board a yellow school bus that will take us to our alma mater, Brantwood, for our high school reunion. We are also marking the graduation of the final class under the shadow of the imminent closing of the school, before it is turned into the Chalkboard Loft condos. When we arrive at the school, Principal Headley is determined to open a time capsule prematurely against the dictates of its creators and the exhortations of class valedictorian Tiffany Fisher. In that moment, there is a "cosmic explosion," and we are hurtled back into Brantwood's past. The play presents eleven concurrent plots, one for each decade of the school's history, from stories about "racism and gender politics in the 1930s and 1940s; sexual awakenings and deviances in the 1970s; drug culture in the 1980s; transgender issues in the 1990s,"[1] even looking into the future where a couple living in their loft condo are haunted by ghosts of Brantwood's past. The last scene brings everyone together in the gym for the finale "Heaven is a High School Dance."

Key to the dramaturgy of *Brantwood* is the exploratory ASYMMETRY of the audience, which is assigned an ambiguous state of existence. Although we begin as alumni, cast as materially present and with an equivalent ontology as the other characters in the opening frame, once we are catapulted into the decades past, who we are and our capacity for action is not as clear. (see AGENCY) In an article written for *Canadian Theatre Review*, Tepperman and Cushman explain the power of this liminal characterization of the audience-players. Because the audience is now mobile and in close proximity to the characters, our relationship to them changes. As the creators write, "It is a strange sensation to stand next to someone who is in pain (even if you know they are an actor portraying a character) and to not do something, not step in and help. The dilemma of 'should I intervene, or will I ruin the scene?' is palpable, not dissimilar to the way a passive bystander might feel in a real-life scenario

---

1   Julie Tepperman and Mitchell Cushman, "BRANTWOOD: Canada's Largest Experiment in Immersive Theatre," *Canadian Theatre Review* 173 (Winter 2018): 11.

as they question whether or not they should intervene."[2] And whether we do or not, the quality of our engagement is markedly different than that of the seated, static audience of BOURGEOIS THEATRE. We are caught, tangled in the veil of the theatrical frame, present both in their time and ours.

In *Tamara*, the audience, although mobile and empowered to choose our own adventure, is still purposely contained. There, we are unacknowledged and thus relegated to bearing witness, COMPLICIT by our compelled silence. In *Brantwood*, the situation is more nuanced. The audience roam the halls for the most part invisible, or at least semi-present but still mostly passive as an undifferentiated mass of students, filling hallways and sitting in classroom desks.

Writing about his play *Living Rooms*, set in a house in the St. Kilda neighbourhood of Melbourne, Australia, and performed circa 1986, Paul Davies states that "in an intercalation of heterochronies that results from these spatial and temporal instabilities, one room's past effectively becomes another's future and vice versa."[3] This is exactly what is happening in *Brantwood*. Davies calls it "heterochronic permeability."[4] The audience begins as alumni. And as alumni we are already out of our own time as we return to high school no longer the teens we once were. After the cosmic explosion, we are time-travelling ghosts. This experience of displacement in time is central to the understanding of *Brantwood* where cross temporal currents are deeply meaningful. We are able to see how the different decades of Brantwood loop and intertwine.

In one such heterochronic moment, plot lines from 1937 and 1986 leak into each other. Jonathan, a student in the 1980s, delivers a presentation on FASCIST-sympathetic youth clubs in Canada in the 1930s. As part of his slide show, he includes an archival image of three Brantwood students assaulting a Jewish classmate whom they have tied to a pole on the basketball court. One of the students looks exactly like him and as we watch, Jonathan strips off his jacket to reveal a Hitler Youth uniform and he transforms into Karl. The projection screen/window blind is raised, and moving the window to look out, we see history come to life on the basketball court below. Some audience members follow Jonathan/Karl as he enters the outdoor scene. Some remain in the classroom, watching from the window. Still others WITNESS the anti-Semitic beating in 1937, unaware of the 1986 redux.

---

2   Tepperman and Cushman, "BRANTWOOD," 12.

3   Paul Davies, "Full Houses: Staging Drama in an Historic Mansion," *Popular Entertainment Studies* 2, no. 1 (2011): 87.

4   Davies, "Full Houses," 89.

The dramaturgical choice of this participatory format of wandering exploration, casting us as heterochronic ghosts, potently underscores *Brantwood*'s thematic preoccupation with a shared ambivalent emotional relationship to graduation. It captures the liminality of the RITUAL transition of youth to adulthood. We want to stay, but we can't. Teenagers grow up, but they don't. The students sing, "I hurry to class. I love learning but I'm not gonna pass / Cause returning to school each day is all I need, just let me stay forever. Forever young. Forever together. Forever the best years of our lives." As adults from the future, we are able to connect the dots across time. Ghosts, displaced in time and embedded in this synchronous but multiple narrative, we see the repetitions. We stand both inside the seemingly eternal and unchanging experience of being a teenager and outside our own lived past from which we have been exiled. The melancholy (or for some the JOY) of a high school reunion is that you can't really return. You will never be eighteen again. And yet the state of being eighteen is forever, with the same thrills and disappointments, triumphs and tragedies enacted on eternal repeat.

See SURROGATION

GOING ROGUE

According to Katie Salen and Eric Zimmerman's neat taxonomy, a CHEATER is a player who only pretends to possess the lusory attitude (meaning, an agreement to follow the arbitrary rules of the game),[1] yet they have an "excessive zeal" for their prelusory goal, that is, they really want to WIN and damn the rules.[2] The opposite of a cheater is not the "standard player" who follows the rules but also wants to win, but is rather the "trifler" who follows the rules in a sociable lackadaisical manner, but couldn't care less about winning. (This is, of course, totally maddening in its own way as any younger sibling knows.) Bernard Suits (*The Grasshopper*) describes this as a "deficiency of zeal."[3] Filling in the fourth quadrant is the player who neither wants to win nor do they make any effort to follow the rules. This is the one who tips over the chessboard, scattering the pieces on the floor, or who peeks into the *Clue* envelope and prematurely announces the identity of the murderer. The spoilsport is a destructive force who "shatters the play-world itself. By withdrawing from the game, he reveals the relativity and fragility of the play-world in which he had temporarily shut himself."[4]

This description of the spoilsport by Johan Huizinga (*Homo Ludens: A Study of the Play Element in Culture*) points to several noteworthy observations about degenerate play. The first is the collaborative nature of the MAGIC CIRCLE, which is both its strength and a critical vulnerability. There are some basic things that we all need to agree about in order to play. One of those things is that this is indeed (merely) a game and that its arbitrary fictions are worth sustaining. (So, for example, in soccer, we need to agree that you can't touch the ball with your hands. This is what Bernard Suits means by "lusory attitude." And we need to agree that scoring the most goals, although important, is not *that* important. This is the prelusory goal.) If just one player refuses, the game-world circle will not be sustained. Next, is the obvious but also provocative point that the spoilsport was, before their rejection,

---

1   Katie Salen and Eric Zimmerman, *Rules of Play: Game Design Fundamentals* (MIT P, 2004), 274–75.

2   Bernard Suits, *The Grasshopper: Games, Life and Utopia* (U of Toronto P, 1978), 46.

3   Suits, *The Grasshopper*, 46.

4   Johan Huizinga, *Homo Ludens: A Study of the Play-Element in Culture* (Routledge & Kegan Paul, 1955), 11.

a member of the play collective. He chose, at least initially, to "shut himself" inside the circle. This is the source of his power to break the world. It is meaningful in this respect that it is the understanding of those players on the inside that matters; no one cares what anyone outside the circle thinks. (see SECRET WEIRDOS) Finally, note the very specific characteristic of the spoilsport, which is that when this player decides that for whatever reason they are "done" (usually boredom or frustration, but see also KILLJOY), they choose obliteration rather than creative adaptation. And this is the reason why hackers and those who "go rogue" are, frankly, way more interesting than a sulky destroyer. The game as it stands is not meeting their needs, but they remain inside the circle, exercising playful stealth to reshape the experience. (see SNEAKY NINJAS)

Essentially, rogues have alternate prelusory goals. They are neither "excessive" nor "deficient"; they are simply doing something else entirely. Take for example, the playground game known as grounders. Usually played by slightly older children, perhaps ages eight to twelve, grounders makes use of those ubiquitous climber structures in parks that incorporate slides, poles, ladders, or horizontal monkey bars. (You know the ones.) Grounders is basically a game of tag, except the person who is "it" has to keep their eyes closed, and you can't get caught touching the ground. (Is this dangerous? Probably.) What intrigues me about grounders is how older children who are bored with the space as-is have "hacked" the PLAYGROUND. They have added levels of challenge and complexity to repurpose the existing space. Moreover, they play in and around the younger ones who are using the space in more conventional ways. (Did I say this was dangerous? Feel free to ignore my opinions on this subject. My kids do.) This kind of innovative roguery is creative, taking something old to make something new and possibly better.

Anyway . . . whereas cheaters and spoilsports are somewhat rare in participatory theatre, rogues are more common; they are frequently accommodated and even encouraged. One way that this kind of interstitial, alternate play is fostered is in participatory contexts where the rules are few and the goals expansive. When the space of play is broad, then there is plenty of room for rogues. *Walk Walk Dance*, an outdoor interactive art installation, created by Montréal's Daily tous les jours is a prime example. Consisting of a teal carpet approximately two metres wide and thirty metres long, and marked at intervals with thin orange stripes, this runway invites us to roll, jump, step, and dance along its length. The lines are movement responsive and crossing over them activates musical sounds from nearby speakers. The goal of *Walk Walk*

Dance is so open and flexible, you can't go wrong. Anything goes. Either everyone is a rogue or no one is.

Rogues are walking the line between control and randomness. Randomness is, as CLAIRE BISHOP notes, an aesthetic benefit to the work as its input can be enriching. Yet often some guardrails of control are needed so that we can all play together and the game-performance proceeds.[5] In performances where the goals of the participants are a little more defined, more directed towards a specific type or limited number of ends, it can be a challenge to channel roguishness.[6] Andy Thompson, in an article for the *Canadian Theatre Review* special issue on gaming, shares his strategies for managing an overly exuberant audience in *The Zombie Syndrome*. Billed as a "site-specific, smartphone-enabled theatre adventure series," *The Zombie Syndrome* tasked teams of collaborative audience-players to save the world from imminent zombie apocalypse.[7] In his reflection, Thompson recognizes a built-in tension between what he describes as "theatrical values" versus "gaming values." He points out that, "indeed, the 'correct choice' . . . while deemed intellectually superior, was not nearly as theatrically rewarding as making the 'stupid choice' and unleashing a horde of zombies to chase tormented audiences across Granville Island."[8] Thompson also concedes that the outcome of the "wrong choice," i.e., pushing the button labelled "Do Not Touch"

---

5 In a discussion about their durational participatory dance-improv, creators Aurélie Pedron and Kathy Casey talk about the necessity for a structured invitation in the face of a work with lots of room for audience freedom. Aurélie says, "Yes. To allow for this kind of freedom, we need a structure that is almost invisible but very solid." Read more in Aurélie Pedron and Kathy Casey's "Freedom in the Invitation: Lilith & Cie's *Invisible*," *Canadian Theatre Review* 197 (Winter 2024), 82–89.

6 In an interview with Liam Karry of Single Thread Theatre Company, he noted that participatory audiences can sometimes become engaged in pushing the boundaries of an environment (physical or virtual), testing the limits of what they are able to do and where they are able to go. Karry and his co-creators have nicknamed that type of audience-player "That Guy." Participants who become "That Guy" are often very experienced in immersive interactive play. I have heard this also characterized as a "gamer" attitude (which involves touching everything and pushing all the buttons), in contrast to an "audience" attitude (which involves a more detached wait-and-see spectatorship). Liam Karry and Alex Dault, personal interview, 14 July 2021.

7 Andy Thompson, "The Virtual Stage's *Zombie Syndrome*: Interactive Gaming on the Mean Streets of Vancouver," *Canadian Theatre Review* 178 (Spring 2019): 21. One of the performances in this series, *Alien Contagion: The Rise of the Zombie Syndrome*, is published in *Long Live the New Flesh: Six Plays from the Digital Frontier*, edited by David Owen (Playwrights Canada, 2021), 1–42.

8 Thompson, "The Virtual Stage's *Zombie Syndrome*," 24.

was "unquestionably awesome."[9] Agree 100 per cent. "Losing" and getting eaten by zombies is way more fun than "winning" and not getting eaten by zombies. Obviously. In this case for Thompson and his creative team, the part of their dramaturgical solution to manage rogues involved adding a points system that rewarded both smart choices and also "fun" choices.

Occasionally, the alignment between our real-world goals as audience-players and our fictional goals as character-players is neutral or indifferent. In *Love Without Late Fees*, the success or failure of my group's "escape room" puzzle-solving did not correspond to either a positive or negative outcome for our fictional protagonists. The actions of the escape room players did determine which branch of the forked-narrative the story followed, but it was not baked-in that winning the game would engender happiness for the lovers Matt and Sarah. We were basically just randomness generators. (see ALEA) On the other hand, in *Foreign Radical*, these two sets of goals are inversely aligned as the players' motivation to do something fun (or really to do anything) is censured by the fictional world. The play purposely sets us up as participatory audiences to participate and then, when we cross that line, shames us for behaving unethically. (see COMPLICITY)

DO NOT PUSH

9   Thompson, "The Virtual Stage's *Zombie Syndrome*," 24.

GUIDES

I'm sitting in a theatre auditorium facing the stage. The pre-show music fades and so do the lights. I'm sitting in the dark. And I know exactly what to do next. I don't know what will happen in the fictional world of the play, but I do know what I'm doing to contribute to the performance as a real-world event. I should remain seated, keep my limbs still, keep my eyes open, listen attentively, and remain (mostly) silent.[1] I also know what to do to contribute to the performance, to determine meaning and bring the fiction into existence, assessing my phenomenological impressions and applying my semiotic skills. I am actively engaged as an audience member and my role is INTERPRETIVE. Long experience in this style of BOURGEOIS THEATRE breeds familiarity; I've got this. Participatory theatre, though, not so much.

When audiences become players, other things are expected from me in addition to SPECTATORSHIP. But the tricky bit is that I don't know what those other things might be, since each participatory theatre experience builds its own set of user functions and worlding conventions almost from scratch. In addition to being a co-creator of the theatre event, I might also have some role to play in a fiction. In both of these realms, broadly, I want to avoid failure. Janet H. Murray, in her fantastically prescient book *Hamlet on the Holodeck*, includes a section titled "Giving Shape to Anxiety" in which she recognizes the underlying panic of being dropped into an entirely foreign immersive fictional world as innate to the form.[2] There is a built-in tension between tightly gated, simple, forward-only, virtual journeys, which are unthreatening and actually kind of boring, and vast rhizome structures, which can be overwhelming in their infinitude. The task for creators of digital

---

1   I continue to be fascinated by pre-show announcements to turn off cellphones. Initially I chalked this up to the novelty of cellphone ownership and the need to educate audiences regarding the new etiquette. Sometimes this message is paired with a humorous reminder to unwrap noisy candies prior to the start of the performance in preparation for mid-performance consumption. (Who are these candy suckers? Who does this?!) Decades later, these announcements persist. Why do we still need to be instructed on this particular aspect of participation as spectators?

2   I (Jenn) expand on Murray's insight that anxiety is endemic to immersive experience in a chapter in *Insecurity: Perils and Products of Theatres of the Real*, "Real Bodies Part 2: Narcissistic Spectatorship in Theatrical 'Haunted Houses' of Solo Immersive Performance—*Everyman*" (U of Toronto P, 2019), 210–25.

narratives, she writes, lies in "arousing and regulating the anxiety intrinsic to the form by harnessing it to the act of navigation. Suspense, fear of abandonment, fear of lurking attackers, and fear of loss of self in the undifferentiated mass are part of the emotional landscape of the shimmering web."[3] Supplementing Murray's focus on how to navigate the space and not get lost, (see BEING LOST) I have more questions. What are my goals? Is there a desired outcome or experience? I might need to know how to "win." What should I do or not do? And how do I do it? This is about the mechanics of how to participate, but also about the natural laws and social rules of the world. Finally, I want to know if I am "doing it right." Hopefully, there will be some recursive input to let me know I'm on the right track. This could be quantitative, perhaps in the form of game points, or qualitative, where upon success, another scene is revealed and the story progresses.

To successfully manage these expectations, audience-players of participatory theatre need guides.[4] And so, beyond the facilitation of the INVITATION to transform into a participant, we need performance-specific instructions and support in how to participate appropriately, successfully, safely, and happily.

It is important to note that each of these to-be-determined aspects of audience-player knowledge span both my actual-world situation in creating and sustaining an artwork and my fictional-world situation in creating and sustaining a representational story-world. For example, in Jordan Tannahill's immersive VR work *Draw Me Close*, the question of navigation and how to move operates on two channels. Audience-player movement pertains both to gaining some preliminary technical competence in looking around and walking with a VR headset, as well as negotiating the fictional geography of my/Jordan's childhood home, intuiting that I should now open the door or cross to the window. Guides both teach us the rules of how to play this game and at the same time help us to manage the uncertainty of learning a new game form on the fly. Guides lead us through putting our portion of the procedural RECIPE of the participatory work into practice. Guides might be people, or they might not. (see TEACUPS)

3   Janet H. Murray, *Hamlet on the Holodeck: The Future of Narrative in Cyberspace*, updated edition (MIT P, 2017), 168.
4   I want to acknowledge the work of Derek Manderson who originally articulated this concept of the "guide" in participatory theatre in specific relation to the theories of Sławomir Świontek and Alexander García Düttman as part of an undergraduate summer research fellowship under my supervision at Queen's University.

I think it is because audience-players have this synchronous yet paradoxical dual commitment to the sustainment of both real-world and fictional-world functions (see BAD FAITH), our guides also need to have dual ontological status and be able to operate in both realms. In parallel with audience expectations, the guide is likewise concerned with both form and content, and so this goes beyond instructions that are exclusive to the actual world, beyond a pre-show email or the show program. The guide is more than an usher, stage manager, or security—although they may also encompass some or all of these roles.[5] In his discussion of the invitation, Gareth White acknowledges a potential role for performers as facilitators: "they can give further instruction, advice, and encouragement to participants after they have become involved."[6] He notes that they are inside the frame, but are also observing it, not from the outside, but with an outsider's eye.[7]

Murray suggests that one way to smooth the awkwardness of a reader-player who comes to the immersive game-world as an almost blank slate is to cast them as a visitor.[8] The visit trope cleverly carries with it an essential and plausibly justified ignorance. A visitor can be confused. A visitor can also ask questions. Some parallel examples of audience casting in this vein include *It Comes in Waves* (we are party guests), *Ambrose* (we are detectives), *The Archive of Missing Things* (we are visitors to the museum-archive), and *Saving Wonderland* (we are Alice). Sometimes we are no one in particular or our particular identity remains undefined, but when we are given a role, it can establish just a sliver of frame and give latitude for needed uncertainty and/or nosiness.

This leads to the question: If we are cast as visitors (or similar) to excuse our lack of knowledge, who are the guides? What fictional roles can be aptly applied to guides in alignment with their "guide" functions?

One common role that fits the general mandate of being a guide is that of a teacher or coach. Carmen Aguirre's play *Broken Tailbone*

---

5   So, for example, in the context of tabletop role playing, a Dungeon Master isn't a guide in this way, because the DM doesn't enter into the fiction. A DM does not exist inside the world. Managing the game mechanic, they are an omnipotent narrator or even god-like. Their ontology is very different from that of the character-players. An escape-room administrator is sort of like this. They are available to provide puzzle hints or assistance in an emergency, but they do not have status within the world.

6   Gareth White, *Audience Participation in Theatre: Aesthetics of the Invitation* (Palgrave Macmillan, 2013), 49.

7   Gareth White, *Audience Participation in Theatre*, 49. White gives an example from applied theatre practice, referencing the Joker in Augusto Boal's forum theatre, who serves as a kind of master of ceremonies or moderator to the dramatic exercise.

8   Janet H. Murray, *Hamlet on the Holodeck*, 132–36.

is literally a salsa lesson and Aguirre is my teacher. Step-by-step, she provides beginner dance instruction. Live music and the rhythmic undulation of the assembled audience underscore her monologues. Set in a theatre turned into a basketball court, our guides in *Monday Nights* are the referee and the four team captains. At the outset, each audience-player chooses one of four colour teams. Between our captain and the referee, the audience-players understand the rules of the various basketball drills we will perform. The referee's whistle tells us when each drill will start and stop, how the points will be apportioned and what constitutes a "win." The captains provide some skills instruction to novices and lots of encouragement. In the *Tape Escape* trilogy, our guide is a video store employee; not quite a teacher or coach, but their job is to help us. This is what retail workers do. In each of these cases, the fictional frame of expert assistance is dominant—learn to dance, play basketball, find the video to rent; the real-world context doesn't disappear, but the mechanics of how to do the play event are tightly aligned with navigating the fictional activity. If we are able to participate sufficiently in our fictional roles, success in sustaining the performance follows.

Another common role is that of a host or dealer. *4inXchange* works this way. The four audience-players sit at a table with the two performers. Dressed in white suits, white wigs, white sunglasses, they appear to be somewhat surreal venture capitalists. (What does a venture capitalist look like?) As part of a "business meeting," they propose questions to be answered and lead us in interactive mini-games about money. The host in *Foreign Radical* occupies the same role as a kind of game master; and this version of the guide reminds me that being nice to us is not a requirement. Here the questioning is aggressive and vaguely threatening, the games disconcertingly not fun, and the outcomes of "winning" ambiguous in their desirability. (But of course, in a play about government surveillance and the policing of potential homegrown terrorists, this is a legible dramaturgical choice.) The guided blindfolded meditation of *SensoryBox* also operates like this as we are told which items to pick up and how to handle them. What is evident in this construction of the guide role is that with a "thinner" fictional world, simple game play is prioritized. In essence, these are postdramas, in that they eschew mimesis, the actions performed are not representational.[9] They

---

9   Hans-Thies Lehmann, *Postdramatic Theatre*, translated by Karen Jürs-Munby (Routledge, 2006). The term postdrama attempts to capture a new formalist aesthetic of theatre performance that is not so much "post" in the sense of being "after" but rather as "beyond" drama. Postdramatic theatre works set aside representation

are task-oriented, almost ceremonial. The performance activity is a real-world game-event, and our task is simply (well, sometimes not so simply) to enact instructions. If we do this in support of the event, the fiction (minimal to almost non-existent) follows.[10]

Still in the postdramatic mode, a subgenre of the guide as dealer is the leader. *You Are Here*, created and performed by Shari Kasman, is literally a TOUR. The absurd premise of the work being a tour of inside jokes, rather than facts about Bloordale Village in Toronto. The audience-player task is to perform the role of attentive tourist, where most often they are actually knowing neighbour, co-creating the content with guide Kasman and weighing in on their decaying public infrastructure. Leader guides can also be silent, relying on gestures to direct our corresponding actions. In *b side*, our guides lead us down an alley simply by walking/dancing ahead of us. As they go, the audience is pulled along as if on an invisible tether. (Back to Murray's anxieties, no one wants to get left behind.) A parallel technique to "follow me" is "copy me." Having synchronized the private music in our earbuds, our guide in the *Stranger 2.0: Above* dances with us. Together we flap our arms and groove down the sidewalk. (see SECRET WEIRDOS) It is worth noting that the geography of the alley and the sidewalk also act as nonhuman guides that keep us, literally, on track.

Both coaches and dealers are leaders; they stand above us, elevated by their knowledge and separated from us by the role-structure of the activity. Sometimes instead of being led from in front, we can be guided from the side, by characters who possess extra knowledge and are attuned to the goals of the event but play "with" us. In *Necessary Dream*, one of our co-dreamers is Jessie Rainbow.[11] The collaborative performance task is to "make a dream" and, of course, we have no idea how to do that, and so we need help. Jessie Rainbow is not a deceptive "plant" however; we recognize her as being "of the game" and not an audience member. In

---

and do not attempt to establish a closed fictional cosmos (Lehmann, *Postdramatic Theatre*, 99). Lehmann claims that postdramatic theatre is the "first to turn the level of the real explicitly into a 'co-player'" (Lehmann, *Postdramatic Theatre*, 100). Postdrama aestheticizes the real spatio-temporal material situation of the performance event.

10   Another subtle variation on the dealer is the interviewer. The guide is leading our action but does this exclusively through dialogic question and answer. The first section of *Lost Together*, in which creator/performers Shira and Michaela ask us questions about the thing that we have lost, is a prime example of the guide as interviewer.

11   Presented online at rEvolver Festival in Vancouver, BC May–June 2021. Game design by Jackson Tegu.

this capacity, she acts as a slightly more expert peer. Perhaps we might think of her in role-playing game terms as an NPC (non-player character). Controlled by the computer or dungeon master, NPCs are typically supporting characters or extras in the fictional world with "a predetermined set of behaviours"; they can be allies, bystanders, or dependents and "often serve as in-game support for new players."[12]

. As a rule, the play doesn't want us to get lost, or be embarrassed, confused about what to do, or anxious about attacks from marauding orcs. (Except, of course, when it does.) Human guide characters are an elegant dual-ontology, dramaturgical strategy to manage our immersion in strange new worlds. In the absence of a human guide, however, all is not lost. Just as we would in a novel real-life situation, we can look to other nonhuman contextual elements of the fictional environment for assistance and for those face-saving directive social cues. (see THE MATRIX)

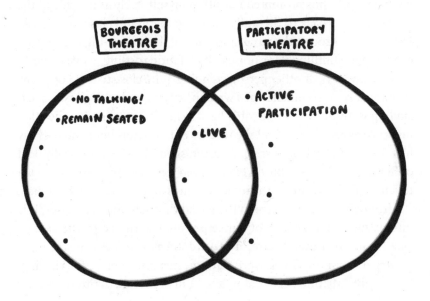

IN WHAT WAYS ARE BOURGEOIS THEATRE AND PARTICIPATORY THEATRE SIMILAR? IN WHAT WAYS ARE THEY DIFFERENT?

BOURGEOIS THEATRE

PARTICIPATORY THEATRE

• NO TALKING!
• REMAIN SEATED

• ACTIVE PARTICIPATION

• LIVE

HANDS

I am handed an envelope that literally says "INVITATION" on the front. I open it and inside are instructions. It is suggested that I explore the studio space of the show with my ears. (see PHONES) Find a spot and close my eyes and experience the performance space through sound alone. This is the pre-show activity of *Polymorphic Microbe Bodies*, a dance piece created by Hanna Sybille Müller and Erin Robinsong, and staged in Montréal as part of OFFTA 2023. The promotional blurb on the festival website points out that, "Like planets, our bodies are composed of ecosystems, inhabitants and RELATIONSHIPS. More than half the cells in our bodies are not human; bacteria, viruses, archaea, and fungi together form 'our' body." We are invited to consider, "What does it mean to be a multispecies community? How do we feel our multiplicity? This multisensory dance work invites audiences on a somatic journey into their own bodies. Guided by sound, smell, touch, language, and taste, we travel the microbial worlds inside our mouths, guts, and imaginaries." Thus prompted I position myself safely at the side of the room, with my back to the wall of black drapery, and close my eyes. As I am sorting through the aural landscape of the room—high ceiling, no echoes, soft shuffling floor noises, thick fabric rustling, whispering—I become aware of another person standing quite close to me. I open my eyes and discover a middle-aged woman, greying and with glasses; she is smiling softly at me. I smile softly back to her. To my surprise, she takes my smile as acceptance, and she reaches out and runs her hand over my hair. I am not upset, but I am quite astonished.[1] This is very socially bold of her. I guess her invitation encouraged her to explore the room via touch—and I'm a thing in the room, and my hair has attracted her touch.

Although we may engage in the world through our five senses, it is interesting to note which of our senses are prioritized by the experiences that constitute "theatre." The word "theatre" comes from the Latin *theatrum*, from the Greek word θέατρον, meaning a place for viewing. Contrarily, Aristotle (who is also Greek), in his *Poetics* (written circa 335

---

1   Here is an instance where positionality is central to the participatory experience. Feeling an openness to a stranger touching your hair is not experienced by all participators. In 2016, Solange Knowles released her song "Don't Touch My Hair," an ode to the discomfort Black women may feel regarding the exploitation of their hair.

BCE), discounts the visual of drama, listing spectacle as the sixth and last of his elements of drama. (The other five, if you must know, ranked in order are plot, character, thought, diction, and song.) Playwright Ben Jonson, Shakespeare's friend, grappled throughout his career to describe what he believed to be the right function of the audience in the exercise of their senses. In the opening to his play *The Staple of News* (performed in 1625), the Prologue declares on behalf of the playwright,

> For your own sakes, not his, he bade me say,
> Would you were come to hear, not see a Play.
> Though we his Actors must provide for those,
> Who are our guests, here, in the way of shows
> The maker hath not so; he'd have you wise
> Much rather by your ears, than by your eyes.

Jonson hopes we are here to hear the play and not to see it. For Jonson, audiences are the preferred discerning playgoers over spectators.

The debate in emphasis between hearing and seeing is interesting for sure, especially as it directs the parameters of our participatory engagement, but what about the other senses? What if we were to smell or taste a play? (see TEA) What about touching a play? Theatre scholar Erika Fischer-Lichte remarks on the persistent opposition to touch between playgoers and performers in theatre, which she attributes to two factors. In brief, firstly, touch is a feature of the private sphere, whereas performance is public. And second, she argues that modern realism is threatened by touch which compromises the distant security of representational illusion.[2] (see FOOT WASHING) That said, participatory theatre tends to put audience-players inside the MAGIC CIRCLE, inside the illusion (or sometimes embraces postdrama, eschewing illusion entirely) and participatory theatre also not infrequently ignores that nice distinction between public and private behaviours. There is lots of touching in participatory theatre. (It's terrifying.) Beyond tactile interaction with the performers, as participants, as part of our interactive function, we are often asked to do THINGS with things. (see LABOUR)

Sometimes things come in boxes. In September 2020, I bought a ticket to a live theatre performance. (A pretty exciting event in my pre-vaccine lockdown life.) And about a week before the scheduled day and time, I received in the MAIL a largish box wrapped in shiny silver paper. I am told via email instructions very strictly not to open it. And so, it sits in

2   Erika Fischer-Lichte, *The Transformative Power of Performance*, translated by Saskya Iris Jain (Routledge, 2008), 60–67.

my kitchen, waiting. It is a very ostentatious object. At the appointed moment for the performance, I log on from home to a video livestream and I am connected to an in-person, live performance, happening for a very small, socially distanced audience in West Village Theatre in Calgary. This is *SensoryBox*, created by Eric Rose and Christopher Duthie of Edmonton's Ghost River Theatre.[3] Both audiences are greeted by solo performer Mike Tan. On his instruction, each of us is told to open the envelope attached to the top of our box. In my envelope, I find a "Scientifically Designed Immersion Device" (also known as a blindfold) to focus my attention on my senses as I explore this show.

Each section of the show centres on our sensory engagement with one of the objects in the box. There's a butterscotch hard candy, a whistle, a container of Playdough, a tiny fluffy pompom, a marble, and a balloon. At one point, we are prompted to "reach into your box and find a little square with a rough texture. It's an itty-bitty gritty square." I find a piece of sandpaper. My hands roam over the rough side, the smooth side, the edges. I hear Mike Tan say, "Are you holding your square of sandpaper? Great. We won't spend very long here . . . this one's mainly for me. The day everything shut down in March, I was working on a show with a woman named Sandra. She was the last person whose hand I shook when shaking hands felt normal. I wanted to honour that in some way so just go with me on this: Touch your sandpaper with your fingers. (*Wait.*) Say: 'Hello, Sandra.' (*Wait.*) Say: 'Nice to meet you, Sandra.' (*Wait.*) Say: 'Whoa, Sandra, your hands are pretty rough. Have you thought about moisturizing? It's so dry in Alberta.' Ok, ok, thanks for humouring me, folks. Now with that in mind . . . Whose hand did you last shake? (*Wait.*) Feel their hand in yours now."

Demetria. I remember Demetria. She was a new acquaintance, and I shook her hand. On the last day of the before times, I was on Mykonos, which was just as sharply blue and windy as it can be in March. I thanked Demetria for a lovely day hosting us on her farm and giving us a TOUR of the island by bicycle. Her hand in mine. So nice to meet you. Thank you. (That evening the world changed and we scuttled our March Break holiday travels and hurried home to be sequestered in a two-week strict quarantine. I still joke about the time I flew to Greece for the weekend. A privileged absurdity to be sure.) Fast forward more than two years to the writing of this entry and my world is back to "normal." The emotional wave of remembering that last handshake, immersed in the moment

---

3   Excerpts from the script for Ghost River Theatre's *SensoryBox* are published in *Canadian Theatre Review* 188 (Fall 2021): 78–80.

when we didn't know if there would ever be a vaccine or when we would be able to shake hands again if ever, seems so very far away now.

Senses are, of course, powerful activators of emotions. Both from our memories and in our lived interactions with the world around us, we are continually registering a lot of sensory information. And this information can tell stories. Touch, smell, and taste could be the language of performance arts just like seeing and hearing. Up close as participants, instead of being spectators or audiences, we could be tactillians (?!), olfacerers, or gustatores.

Back in Montréal at *Polymorphic Microbe Bodies*, I am on the floor, a comfy blue blanket over my head, pretending along with a room full of other participants to be gut microbiota. In addition to the dancers and a percussionist, there is, right beside me, a performer who is peeling fruit, hanging the rinds from an umbrella skeleton, like a tropical mobile. She is squishing the fibrous pulp near a microphone. I'm so close I get splashed a bit. She waves herbs like a fan, before ripping them into tiny pieces. Wet organic citrus smells. Cucumbers too. These are the sounds of my innards. Towards the end of the performance, she smiles softly at me. I smile softly back at her. She offers me a small cup of JUICE. It smells fresh and tastes even better.

ALTER A PAGE IN THIS BOOK SO THAT SOMEONE CAN ENGAGE WITH IT USING A SENSE OTHER THAN SIGHT (eg. DYE IT WITH A TEA BAG, SPRAY IT WITH PERFUME, CUT HOLES IN IT).

ILINX

Game theorist Roger Caillois's fourth category of play (after agôn, ALEA, and mimicry) is ilinx. Following in his accustomed, ostentatiously erudite style, Caillois borrows the deliberately obscure but deliciously pretentious term "ilinx" from the Greek word for "whirlpool." In the context of play, actions of ilinx are "based on the pursuit of vertigo and . . . consist of an attempt to momentarily destroy the stability of perception and inflict a kind of voluptuous panic upon an otherwise lucid mind."[1] This is the feeling of spinning in circles until you fall down. This is the feeling of a roller coaster. This is the feeling of purposely knocking over a giant tower of blocks.

How do you trigger this feeling and activate it as a generative dramaturgy in participatory performance? Intense time pressure will activate ilinx. In the waning seconds of an escape room with a countdown timer, players experience that flustered panic, a pleasurable swirling as we try to move our hands faster or just try to think faster. Win or lose, there is a visceral rush in the crush and release of that end moment. Connected to WINNING, ilinx is an emotional intensifier. Intense physical activity, especially if combined with self-conscious foolishness, will activate ilinx.[2] (see SECRET WEIRDOS) The section in *The Stranger 2.0: Above* where we are asked to dance like birds, flapping our arms and skipping along the side of the road to the private music in our earbuds does this. Looking like idiots and getting honked at by passing cars is a thrill. (Trust me. It is.) I think the "looking like idiots" is an important part of this dramaturgy. It adds the same spicy complexity as losing (or almost losing) an escape room. More than just SWEATING, our joy in ilinx is tempered with being losers, being outsiders, with mistakes or aberrations. Our JOY in ilinx comes from the adrenaline present when you have to both play and work really hard to squeak out a win. (Not sure I'm explaining this well.) Along those lines, destroying things will also activate ilinx. When I take a hammer to my chosen ceramic TEACUP or cut my chosen teddy bear to ribbons, stuffing everywhere, I experience that vertiginous joyful

---

1   Roger Caillois, *Man, Play and Games*, translated by Meyer Barash (U of Illinois P, 1961), 23.

2   Positionality matters in participation. And so it is important to note that many of these tactics for activating ilinx are potentially inaccessible to audience members depending on their physical, mental, and emotional needs.

thrill mixed with the darkness of transgressive destruction.[3] Considering Mammalian Diving Reflex's *Haircuts by Children*, I think there is also a hint of ilinx, when I am the object of disorder rather than the active agent. Getting my hair cut by an unrestrained eight-year-old with aesthetic ambitions has the same mood of unhinged giddiness. This could be fun? (see FOOT WASHING)

Ilinx is basically physical pleasure in disorder. As a dramaturgical strategy, we can see how it opens up various related understandings pertaining to the joyful freedom of being outside the rules, of being a vulnerable fool, of destroying something so we can start again. Ilinx shows us that the things we thought mattered maybe don't. You don't need to be so serious all the time.

See AROUSAL

RIP OUT A PAGE OF THIS BOOK IN A PUBLIC SPACE AND PUT IT IN YOUR MOUTH. WRITE WHAT HAPPENED AND HOW IT MADE YOU FEEL.

---

3 Created by New Zealand artist Kate McIntosh, *Worktable* first asks us to make a choice from a shelf of mundane domestic objects—a radio, glasses, an apple, a book, a lamp. Then we enter a private workspace equipped with tools of all kinds and a sign on the wall instructing us to take apart the object. We can do this meticulously or carelessly. This show was presented in Montréal, Canada, in June 2021.

INSTRUMENTALITY

See OR ELSE

FILL IN THE BINGO CARD BELOW USING WORDS FROM THE NEXT 3 ENTRIES (see INTERPRETATION, INTIMACY, AND INVITATION). AFTER DABBING ALL OF THE WORDS THAT APPEAR IN THESE ENTRIES, YOUR ANSWER WILL APPEAR.

B	I	N	G	O
RANCIÈRE	ROGER CAILLOIS	NEW SOCIETIES	CHER	SUSAN BENNETT
ALANIS MORISSETTE	FREUD	RACHEL FENSHAM	NEW AGE ATTITUDES	BRECHT
INTIMATE KARAOKE	STETHO-SCOPE	FREE	POST-IT NOTES	SEE REFUSAL
ESPEN J. AARSETH	SCISSORS	CHOIR! CHOIR! CHOIR!	IBSEN	POPCORN GALAXIES
UTERINE CONCERT HALL	AMANDA SUM	UTOPIA	BRICK THROWING	LOST TOGETHER

ANSWER:

INTERPRETATION

In his effort to define ergodic literature, Espen J. Aarseth (*Cybertext*) engages with this question by considering its opposite: "If ergodic literature is to make sense as a concept, there must also be nonergodic literature."[1] Aarseth coins the term "ergodic" by marrying the Greek *ergon* meaning "work" to *hodos* meaning "path." From this formulation, we can divine that his interest is not only in the labour of readers (also audience), but specifically in their efforts towards the exploration and/or construction of the path, that is, the experience of the literary work as a map or as a journey through a landscape. (see CHOOSE YOUR OWN ADVENTURE and MAD LIBS) Continuing to define the nonergodic, he asserts that, in this case, "the effort to traverse the text is trivial, with no extranoematic responsibilities placed on the reader except (for example) eye movement and the periodic or arbitrary turning of pages."[2] (The word "extranoematic" is Aarseth being decorative. "Noematic" is a word from phenomenology—credited to Edmund Husserl who is building upon the ideas of René Descartes—that describes how phenomena of our environment are given to our senses. Through the cognitively embodied act of noesis, we create the world.) As much as I value Aarseth's commitment to carving out a space for a more interactive genre, his audacity in asserting that typical readers merely move their eyes and turn the pages is astonishing. (Eeep! Hello reader! I can only imagine the cage match between Aarseth and Jacques Rancière. See more below.) In his taxonomy of reader user-functions, interpretation is nonergodic. To be fair, Aarseth does modify his understanding somewhat in the pages that follow as he makes a more nuanced distinction between the ergodic LABOUR of navigating a forking hypertext and the work done through active interpretation of semantic ambiguity. His point is that interpretation is still labour, but of a different quality. With this distinction in hand, I want to pause here to examine how interpretation operates a mode of participation.

Susan Bennett, in her influential book *Theatre Audiences*, asserts the centrality of the audience in creating performance. She writes, "Audiences clearly play a role in the theatre but what kind of role? . . . In

---

1   Espen J. Aarseth, *Cybertext: Perspectives on Ergodic Literature* (Johns Hopkins UP, 1997), 17.

2   Aarseth, 1–2.

a self-conscious communication-oriented theatre (such as Schechner's TPG or the Living Theater of Beck and Malina), the audience's role (although not its social construction) is, at least in some ways, visible. But in theatre demanding the (theoretically) more or less total passivity of the audience, how can its relationship to the self-contained dramatic world be described?"[3] Bennett, drawing on the influence of Bertolt Brecht and reader-response theorists Stanley Fish, Wolfgang Iser, and Hans Robert Jauss, turns attention to how audiences are readied to cooperate in their role as receiver and assembler of closed text with a (more or less) predetermined aesthetic message. For Brecht, the self-aware hard-working audience is formulated as a critical bridge between the fictional world of the play and the way in which the live event is embedded in its real-world political context. Bennett quotes Stephen Heath who writes, regarding the effect of Brechtian alienation, "[It] is not that the spectator is held separate to the action of the play, and from there effectively placed in a relation of identification to the hero as totalising consciousness, but rather the spectator is himself included in the movement from ideology to real, from illusion to objective truth (the political analysis of forms of representation in the their determinations, the activity of the play.)"[4] For Brecht, the participation of the spectator is activated politically through their interpretive efforts, as the exposure of the theatrical apparatus displays its constructedness and, from there, exposes the constructedness of the real-world social apparatus. If theatre can be dismantled, so can ideology. (see A AND B)

Taking another tack, reader-response theory recognizes the cognitive activity of readers (again also audience) as they apply different pre-existing frames and strategies to the determination of meaning. Iser, for example, models a collaborative triad between the text, the reader, and their interaction, whereby "textual structures are transmuted through ideational activities into personal experiences."[5] This approach "leads to syntheses which are neither manifested in the printed text, nor produced solely by the reader's imagination, and the project of which they consist are themselves of a dual nature: they emerge from the reader, but they are also GUIDED by signals which 'project' themselves into

3   Susan Bennett, *Theatre Audiences: A Theory of Production and Reception*, 2nd edition (Routledge, 1997), 17.

4   Stephen Heath, "Lessons from Brecht," *Screen* 15 (1974): 116. Quoted in Bennett, *Theatre Audiences*, 29.

5   Wolfgang Iser, *The Act of Reading: A Theory of Aesthetic Response* (Johns Hopkins UP, 1978), 38. Quoted in Bennett, *Theatre Audiences*, 43.

him."[6] It is Marcel Duchamp who writes, "All in all, the creative act is not performed by the artist alone; the spectator brings the work into contact with the external world by deciphering and interpreting its inner qualifications and thus adds his contribution to the creative act."[7]

Jacques Rancière is another who stakes a claim for interpretation as participation. In "The Emancipated Spectator," he begins by outlining what he sees as the critique of spectators, before presenting a rebuttal. "According to the accusers, being a spectator is a bad thing for two reasons. First, viewing is the opposite of knowing: the spectator is held before an appearance in a state of ignorance about the process of production of this appearance and about the reality it conceals. Second, it is the opposite of acting; the spectator remains immobile in her seat, passive."[8] And then he says famously, by way of a summary, "To be a spectator is to be separated from both the capacity to know and the power to act."[9]

The remedy, then, is to restore to this audience role knowledge—specifically of how the work is made; of the process of its creation, free from illusion; and action—to become active, perhaps in body, perhaps in mind. "Emancipation begins when we challenge the opposition between viewing and ACTING . . . The spectator also acts."[10] And this action is the work of observation, but also selection, comparison, and interpretation. The spectator is an autonomous meaning-maker. "She composes her own poem with the elements of the poem before her. She participates in the performance by refashioning it in her own way—by drawing back, for example, from the vital energy that it is supposed to transmit in order to make a pure image and associate this image with a story which she has read or dreamt, experienced or invented . . . This is a crucial point: spectators see, feel and understand something in as much as they compose their own poem, as, in their way, do actors or playwrights, directors, dancers or performers."[11] Each of these theoretical framings of readers and spectators speaks to the necessary participatory work that audiences always do. The key difference is that, although the interpretive audience is an active receiver and an assembler of meaning,

---

6   Wolfgang Iser, *The Act of Reading: A Theory of Aesthetic Response* (Johns Hopkins UP, 1978), 135. Quoted in Bennett, *Theatre Audiences*, 43–44.

7   Marcel Duchamp, "The Creative Act," *Salt Seller: The Writings of Marcel Duchamp*, edited by Michael Sanouillet and Elmer Paterson (Oxford UP, 1973), 140.

8   Jacques Rancière, *The Emancipated Spectator*, translated by Gregory Elliot (Verso 2009), 2.

9   Rancière, *The Emancipated Spectator*, 2.

10   Rancière, *The Emancipated Spectator*, 13.

11   Rancière, *The Emancipated Spectator*, 13.

they do not generate novel input. (There was a plan to insert here a historical overview of audience interventions that shape the performance, beginning with conventional responses like clapping or booing,[12] continuing to purposeful disruptions like heckling and unexpected disruptions like fire or medical emergency, escalating in impact through to full-scale rioting. But that is another story.) And so, even as the recent shift to participatory work that asks for more—work that locates the SPECTATOR and their participation as the subject of the work—the critical work of interpretation is not to be dismissed or minimized.

---

12 "Of course all audiences are participatory. Without participation performance would be nothing but action happening in the presence of other people. Audiences laugh, clap, cry, fidget and occasionally heckle; they pay for tickets, they turn up at the theatre, they stay to the end of the performance or they walk out. They are affected emotionally, cognitively and physically by the action they witness" (Gareth White, *Audience Participation in Theatre: Aesthetics of the Invitation* (Palgrave Macmillan, 2013), 3).

INTIMACY

Ten participants stand in a circle, holding HANDS and looking into one another's eyes. A group of five audience members take turns spinning a tray that holds a blue-and-white teapot while sharing a beautiful meal. I text back and forth with a stranger at 3 a.m.

Participatory theatre is necessarily intimate. Through the RELATIONALITY that participatory theatre invites, the interpersonal connection between the participants to one another as well as between artists and participants inevitably deepens. Inviting thematic reflection on the nature of the ENCOUNTER, participatory theatre collapses the distance between artist and participant in different ways to different ends. In some cases, the usual conventional physical distances contract, calling the participant up out of their seat and into close proximity with the artist and with other participants. (see ELBOWS) Caring touch also elicits feelings of intimacy. (see FOOT WASHING) In other cases, it is social distance that is condensed. Sometimes, as in shows like *Lost Together* or *The Dead Letter Office*, the participants share AUTOBIOGRAPHICAL confessions with ostensible strangers. Tanya Marquardt's *Some Must Watch While Some Must Sleep* fosters a kind of friendship through an extended two-week exchange of TEXT MESSAGES about dreams that turn out to be nightmares. The dancers of Lilith & Cie's *Invisible* cohabit the dance studio with the audience over the course of seventy-two hours, NEGOTIATING a soundtrack to "render collective intelligence visible."[1]

If you've done it yourself, you know that singing karaoke is definitely an exercise in vulnerability. Amateur singers put themselves into the (hopefully) generous hands of an audience of friends and strangers in a dimly lit bar. They reveal their secret selves through their song selections, inexperienced dance moves, and occasional off-kilter pitch. (My go-to karaoke song is definitely Alanis Morissette's "You Oughta Know." Jenn avoids karaoke at all costs but has been known (once, under duress) to perform ABBA's "Mamma Mia.") In the karaoke club, mutual JOY rests in the intimacy that this shared risk and vulnerability brings. Everyone's a little bit bad, but we're all bad together!

---

1   "Invisible," *Lilith & Cie*, lilithetcie.com/portfolio/invisible-en/.

Dayna McLeod's *Intimate Karaoke* ratchets up the usual performative vulnerability by using a unique concert "venue" for both singer and listener.[2] Subtitled *Live at Uterine Concert Hall*, McLeod invites participants to don a pair of headphones and sing their karaoke song aloud in a room full of strangers (!) without backup instrumentals. (!!) Just so I'm clear, this means that if you chose to embrace your inner Celine Dion in *Intimate Karaoke*, your audience is hearing only your voice, without hearing the instrumental accompaniment, at full volume. This is only the first performance venue in *Intimate Karaoke*. The singer's microphone cord is also run into another room and connected to a speaker that has been inserted inside McLeod's vaginal canal. The vocal stylings of these audience-singers is emitted into the "uterine" concert hall.[3] One by one, participants go see McLeod and, using a stethoscope, these listeners access the full audio experience, the live karaoke vocals now heard with fully-scored backing tracks.

The singer's vulnerability is matched (or overcome?) by McLeod's. She challenges the singers to be comfortable with singing in silence when by comparison she is splayed open on a table. "Intimacy as a method of connecting with an audience is central to my performance practice," says McLeod.[4] You sing aloud and a cappella in public; she inserts that performance into her body. Her body becomes the venue, and she invites us inside. When offering one's body as the site of performance, intimacy becomes a site of dialogue. McLeod positions the vulnerability of her co-creators alongside her own spread legs. I'll do it, if you do. Intimacy isn't always physical, sometimes it can manifest in other displays of vulnerability and connection.

I remember asking McLeod, "Do you have any requests of what songs we can sing that will feel nice in your body?" "I prefer if people sing punchier songs, like rock and roll or metal," she responded. So, I sang Alanis Morissette.

Apart from the charming mess that is karaoke, how else does participation foster intimacy? Can strangers become friends? This question is the basis for *Perfect Strangers*. Created by the Popcorn Galaxies duo of June Fukumura and Keely O'Brien, the performance is part audio-tour,

---

2   Dayna McLeod, "Uterine Concert Hall," *Danya McLeod*, 18 September 2021, daynarama.com/uterine-concert-hall/. See also Dayna McLeod, "This is What it Sounds Like: *Intimate Karaoke: Live at Uterine Concert Hall*," *Canadian Theatre Review* 184 (Fall 2020): 33–38.

3   Alanna Thain, "From Specular to Speculative: Intimate Encounters @ Uterine Concert Hall," *FADO*, 2018, performanceart.ca/book/golden-book-5/.

4   McLeod, "Uterine Concert Hall."

part friendship-ritual, pairing audience-participants who have never met to go on a guided walking TOUR of a given neighbourhood together. The conversation prompts are scaffolded, from easy-to-answer questions about day-to-day life to deeper, more personal questions about hopes and dreams for the future. While they walk and talk, the pairs are given Post-it Notes and markers, encouraged to leave traces of their conversation in the form of sticky paper squares along their route. On their website, Fukumura and O'Brien describe each Post-it-Note trail as "a miniature guerilla art-installation for other passers-by . . . animating the landscape with a fleeting archive of transforming relationships."[5]

At the beginning of the performance, each participant is asked to draw their new stranger-friend on a Post-it. While maintaining eye contact without looking at the Post-it, each partner makes a portrait sketch. The results are often clumsy and quirky doodles with disarming charm and honesty.[6] Because participants aren't looking at what they are drawing, this observational CRAFT has both high and low stakes. While sustained eye contact with a stranger is intense, the doodle is not *supposed* to be good. At the end of the journey, the partners are again asked to draw each other on the flip side of the same Post-it. This time, participants are asked to look at their canvas and try again to capture their stranger-friend's likeness. The new drawings are always more elaborate, capturing details about their partner's face and mood. Before, after. Strangers, friends.

In both shows, intimacy is not catalyzed through touch or even physical closeness. Instead, it is a cognitive effect born out of mutual vulnerability. Taking that step into the unknown makes us emotionally open, and the other person, equally open, slips in.

5   "Perfect Strangers," *Popcorn Galaxies*, 2023, popcorngalaxies.ca/perfect-strangers.html.
6   Popcorn Galaxies features a gallery of the "before" and "after" sides of each Post-it Note from *Perfect Strangers* on their website, popcorngalaxies.ca /perfect-strangers-collection.html.

DRAW A PORTRAIT OF SOMEONE WITHOUT TAKING YOUR PEN OFF THE PAGE.

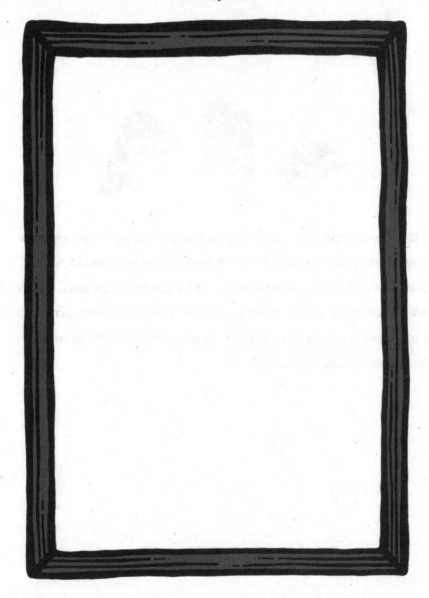

YOUR COMRADES ARE DIVIDED UPON SEEING THE ALIEN-GIVEN GIFT. SOME BELIEVE THAT ANYTHING COMING FROM AN ALIEN IS CURSED, WHILE OTHERS BELIEVE THAT DRINKING THE SHEEP'S GOLDEN MILK WILL GRANT ONE EXTRATERRESTRIAL POWERS. TO DECRY ANY DEALINGS WITH WICKED ALIENS AND THEIR CURSED OBJECTS, TURN TO PAGE 303. TO DRINK THE GOLDEN MILK, TURN TO PAGE 297.

INVITATION

See REFUSAL

JOY

Nineteenth-century French philosopher Émile Durkheim asserts that although society is made up of many singular people, society cannot be studied only through the psychology or biology of indivduals. Establishing sociology as its own autonomous discipline, Durkheim claims that there are certain "'social facts' [or] elements of collective life that exist independently of and are able to exert and influence on the individual,"[1] and so those collective features are worthy of study. Durkheim insists on the transformative power of the collective in the human experience. In his study of religion and CEREMONY, he identifies "collective effervescence" as one of the core social processes of people in organized groups. Often activated by unified mass speaking, singing, or dancing, collective effervescence is that ineffable, beyond-words feeling when you are almost outside your own body. It feels like a fizzy kind of floating; being part of something that is bigger and more profound than a single person. It is a social expression with an energetic power. Durkheim asserts that "a religion comes into being and is legitimated" through this collective effervescence, referring to moments in social life when "individuals come into close contact with one another and when they are assembled in such a fashion, a certain 'electricity' is created and released, leading participants to a high degree of collective emotional excitement or delirium."[2] (see ILINX)

British cultural anthropologist Victor Turner was also interested in this electricity in collectivity through RITUAL, specifically ritual's capability for transformation. Importantly for Turner, this collective magic is active and powerful. What Turner calls "communitas" is a renewing and revitalizing collective experience that counters both individualism and the control, discipline, and ultimately alienation that comes with the institutional structure of society.[3] Turner's communitas fills up our tanks, restoring our relational fuel that is emptied from the individual pursuit within institutionalized discipline. Most importantly, this

---

1   "Émile Durkheim (1858–1917)," *Internet Encyclopedia of Philosophy: A Peer-Reviewed Academic Resource*, iep.utm.edu/emile-durkheim/.

2   "Émile Durkheim."

3   Tim Olaveson, "Collective Effervescence and Communitas: Processual Models of Ritual and Society in Emile Durkheim and Victor Turner," *Dialectical Anthropology* 26, no. 2 (2001): 89–12.

interdependent "extra-individual force, which is a core element of religion, transports the individuals into a new, ideal realm, lifts them up outside of themselves, and makes them feel as if they are in contact with an extraordinary energy."[4] Collective effervescence and communitas are energizing, renewing our capacities as social creatures. (see TOGETHER ALONE and UTOPIA) How does collective effervescence function as a participatory dramaturgy?

"Grilled cheese, sandwich time, pull a radish from the sun, pull a radish from the sun, I'm a snake, a snake, in local honey." Using evocative and surreal prompts, Alyssa Martin (Rock Bottom Movement) coaches a group of novice dancers (most of whom are children under five). Live music is provided by Jacob Vanderham (Telehorn) as we move in synchronicity. It's easy to follow this everyday image-based choreography and, actually, we look great. We are SWEATY and people strolling through the farmer's market are staring at us, but we feel great. Invited by SummerWorks curators in August 2023 to "activate the market," *The Lettuce Head Experience* popped up during the performance festival at three markets across Toronto. Part of the pleasure resides in just moving my body, getting my blood flowing, and being silly in public. But another part of it is in the coordination, in the group feeling of being in unison movement. I love that I know what I'm doing and that we all match.

In Nightswimming's *Why We Are Here!* singing is the vehicle for that sense of matched togetherness. Created by Martin Julien and Brian Quirt, drop-in choir participants are coached in curated repertoire by guest conductors at various site-specific locations. We learn songs in multiple parts and even a little choreography, and our sound activates these somewhat unexpected public spaces—the Toronto city council chambers, a ferry, a greenhouse, and the lobby of the Aga Khan Museum, among others. Collective effervescence is activated not merely by physical proximity, but also in getting close to others sonically. Although I control my voice alone, I NEGOTIATE harmonic and dissonant notes and tempo with those around me to craft something bigger. I adjust my volume or my pitch if I notice it rubs up against someone else's volume or pitch. (see ELBOWS) It feels good to achieve harmony and balance in this negotiation. I feel the hair on my neck stand up when my voice blends just right with another's. I'll admit that as a singer and a musician, I am a bit biased. Nearly every time I hit a juicy harmony with others, my arms fill with goosebumps, and I feel the intense desire to cry. Where I feel community recognition or negotiated collectivity though, others may be fearful, worried about being judged.

---

4   "Émile Durkheim."

In an opinion piece in *The New York Times* in summer 2021, titled "There's a Specific Kind of Joy We've Been Missing," organizational psychologist Adam Grant argues that the pandemic contributed to a widespread loss of happiness in a very specific way. Grant reiterates Durkheim's principle as "the sense of energy and harmony people feel when they come together in a group around a shared purpose."[5] He points out that, although in a choir, the shared purpose really is musical harmony, collective effervescence can explain the "synchrony you feel when you slide into rhythm with strangers on a dance floor, colleagues in a brainstorming session, cousins at a religious service or teammates on a soccer field."[6] In his article, Grant argues that the restrictive public health measures of the COVID-19 CRISIS have largely prevented this specific kind of joy in togetherness from radiating as social distancing affects our happiness because "peak happiness lies mostly in collective activity."[7]

Following the onset of the COVID-19 pandemic in spring 2020, fu-GEN Asian-Canadian Theatre Company offered collective joy-inducing activities through *Online Joy Edit*.[8] In a series of one-on-one interactions over Zoom and other chat platforms, eight artist-creators led participants through short interactions ignited by a deep desire for "one thing in short supply these days: JOY."[9] Featuring Maddie Bautista, Natalie Tin Yin Gan, Vienna Hehir, Luigi Ceccon, Aaron Jan, Ming-Bo Lam, Janice Jo Lee, Adrienne Wong, Miquelon Rodriguez, and André Dae Kim, *Online Joy Edit* reminded us that, although smaller and glitchier than a large, live, in-person gathering, two people meeting on Zoom can also invite collective effervescence. Each artist (or pair of artists) shaped their ENCOUNTER differently. Vienna Hehir and Luigi Ceccon asked

5   Adam Grant, "There's a Specific Kind of Joy We've Been Missing," *The New York Times*, 13 July 2021, nytimes.com/2021/07/10/opinion/sunday/covid-group-emotions-happiness.html.

6   Grant, "There's a Specific Kind of Joy."

7   Grant, "There's a Specific Kind of Joy."

8   It is notable that this work arises in the specific context of a period when the Asian community in Canada and around the world experienced a spike in anti-Asian racism at the onset of the COVID-19 pandemic due to racist characterizations of the virus. Read more by Izumi Sakamoto, Kennes Lin, Jessie Tang, Hogan Lam, Bernie Yeung, Amy Nhkum, Evelyn Cheung, Kedi Zhao, and Patricia Quan, "2020 in Hindsight: Intergenerational Conversations on Anti-Asian Racism During the COVID-19 Pandemic," *Chinese Canadian National Council Toronto Chapter (CCNCTO) and Factor-Inwentash Faculty of Social Work*, 14 March 2023, socialwork.utoronto.ca/wp-content/uploads/2023/03/2020-in-Hindsight-English.pdf.

9   "Projects," *fu-GEN*, 2023, fu-gen.org/past-projects.

participants to recall a joyful time and then, as the participant re-experienced joy in the memory, they snapped a sneaky portrait photo. Natalie Tin Yin Gan offered "dramatic readings by candlelight of [her youthful] cringe-worthy online blog posts."[10] Maddie Bautista guided her participants through a (possibly equally cringe-worthy) singing of Queen's "Bohemian Rhapsody." Although the pandemic prevented us from gathering in groups of more than five or ten (or whatever the current social bubble restrictions were), *Online Joy Edit*, at the very least, connected "me and you." These performance pairs emphasized Grant's notion that, although "you can feel depressed and anxious alone . . . it's rare to laugh alone or love alone. Joy shared is joy sustained."[11]

See MOB

---

10 "Online Joy Edit," *fu-GEN*, 2020, fu-gen.org/online.
11 Grant, "There's a Specific Kind of Joy."

JUICINESS

I win at Solitaire on my phone and the nicely piled cards spring off their stacks, bouncing in a colourful cascade, flipping and flying off the bottom of my SCREEN. I made this happen. This is juicy. Juiciness is a calculated effect of video games that makes them feel truly responsive through immediate pleasurable feedback.[1] (see AUTOPOIESIS) How are participatory theatre-game hybrids juicy? (How is this book on participatory theatre-games juicy?) If the aim of juiciness is to make digitally programmed games feel live, then actual living co-present actors are very juicy. There is no need for an improvisation of faux LIVENESS; they are alive. Nikola and Hima, my GUIDES in *Higher Hair* make eye contact. They smile as they escort me to my chaise lounge. Their affect radiates personal attention, and these cues are rich compensation for my participation. Jordan and Maddie, corporate executives as emotional bankers (*4inXchange*), with their synchronized movements and cool white wigs and matching white suits, exhibit a more muted affect, but compared to a video game, still juicy. The game show host in *Foreign Radical* is cool to the point of hostility. He is live and responsive, but the feeling is not pleasurable. The feedback loop is disjunctive, and outcomes of my actions seem bureaucratic and arbitrary. Not juicy? Or maybe juicy, but sour instead of sweet? Even though it is actually live, contemporary BOURGEOIS THEATRE is not juicy at all. No doubt, there are other pleasures of the silent and dark auditorium, but they do not stem from mutual responsiveness, generating direct feedback to audience action.

Good Things To Do (which, being mostly a preset digital text, does express definite characteristics of a video game) generates this feeling of juiciness through intervals of live chat, which lend to the whole recorded text a thin illusion of spontaneity. But it also supplements that effect through the magical delivery of gifts, like hot TEA and an origami paper boat inscribed with our personal CROWDSOURCED list of "good things to do." In combination, these tactics both make the digital character persona feel present and make our contributions meaningful, as our actions directly drive outcomes. (see AGENCY) As seen here, technology as a performance partner can also create juiciness. Responding to the voices of spontaneous public speaker-participants,

---

[1]   Jesper Juul, *A Casual Revolution: Reinventing Video Games and Their Players* (MIT P, 2010), 45.

Mégaphone (created by Moment Factory) projects an evolving word-frequency cloud and soundwave visualizations of the speakers' voices on the neighbouring, multi-storey building of the Université du Québec à Montréal. If something I do creates a reaction that is custom and direct, a reflection of my participation at this moment, I have an effect. I feel JOY and wonder at my power. This is an entirely different result than, say, a lightshow or fireworks, which—although spectacular—are fixed.

Juiciness is about being given something for my participation. I am still contributing. I have not escaped the seemingly inevitable neoliberal INSTRUMENTALITY of my do-it-yourself labour. And yet there is this gift. Even beyond reciprocation, it transcends the reward of a beautiful special effect or the souvenir of the origami boat; these juicy responses are personal, and I feel seen. I matter.

Not all participation is by definition juicy. Placing lemons in the alleyway in *b side*, ironically, isn't juicy. It is introspective, even sly, but there is no responsive feedback and so, not juicy. Our reward comes a bit later. Leaving the lemons, when we reach the end of the alleyway, we find ourselves in a parkette. There we are gifted with a lemonade social—and that is definitely juicy.

KILLJOY

As Sara Ahmed writes on her blog, *Feminist Killjoys*, women are taught that those who lead with a positive outlook are praised and celebrated, while those who question unfair systems and practices are silenced, ignored, shamed, or villainized. Killjoys are contained and nullified, being branded as "nags," "complainers," or "bitches."[1]

Ahmed's figure of the feminist killjoy is a very specific kind of complainer. She writes: "The word 'dissidence' . . . derives from the Latin *dis*-'apart' + *sedere* 'to sit.' The dissident is the one who sits apart. Or the dissident is the one who would be unseated by taking up a place at the table: your seat is the site of disagreement . . . To be unseated at the table of happiness might be to threaten not simply that table, but what gathers around it, what gathers on it. When you are unseated you can even get in the way of those who are seated, those who want more than anything to keep their seats. To threaten the loss of the seat can be to kill the joy of the seated."[2] The killjoy possesses the courage to challenge abusive or unjust situations. By calling out systemic inequities, abuse and harassment, racism, sexism, and any and all other kinds of unethical social discrimination,[3] the killjoy interrupts the flow of action. The killjoy says, "Stop!" and audaciously REFUSES to just "go along with it." This interruption is peremptory; it is impolite; it is "out of line"; and it is awkward. And, with a certainty, it is upsetting to others who are seated happily at the table, who were, up to this point, just going along. (see TYRANNY)

As spaces of sociality, governed by systems of rules (some explicit and some implicit), game-theatre hybrids can also invite, even necessitate, the intervention of a killjoy. While the need for a killjoy might arise in any number of participatory scenarios, *New Societies*, created by

---

1   Major parts of this entry were originally conceptualized and written by Mary Tooley as part of her independent study project in the autumn of 2021 under Jenn's supervision. This version is published here with her permission.

2   Sara Ahmed, "Feminist Killjoys (And Other Willful Subjects)," *The Scholar and Feminist Online* 8, no. 3 (Summer 2010), sfonline.barnard.edu/polyphonic /print_ahmed.htm.

3   It is important to flag that both of the killjoys mentioned here, Mariah and Mary, are white women. Killjoys who do not benefit from such a close proximity to whiteness have a different kind of engagement with the inequities they are calling out.

Brian Postalian and Re:Current theatre arguably locates the killjoy as its primary game mechanic. Superficially framed as a colonization sim (see SHEEP), *New Societies* subtly encourages the audience-players to refuse the game that they are being offered and to improvise alternative decolonial ways of being.

Through what is billed as a "mega-game of collaboration, competition, and potential Utopia,"[4] *New Societies* divides participatory audiences into "divisions" of up to six players. Each division takes its name from one of the eight compass points. The first time I played I was in the "East" division. Each division is tasked with harvesting resources. At the end of each round, divisions decide how they want to invest those harvested resources in political infrastructure and, when catastrophe strikes (over-population, drought, civil war), players need to decide how they want to navigate the ethical implications of their actions. When your division is torn apart by violence associated with land claims, players are asked how they want to share the LAND between warring groups. When a pandemic hits (woof, I know), players are asked if they want to quarantine the entire population while they pursue the development of a global vaccine, or deport infected individuals to another division, or eradicate all life in the affected area. A critical part of the game mechanic of *New Societies* is not just that the questions strike uncomfortably close to home, but also that we are not given any objective rule structures to incentivize a particular strategy. The outcome of our choices is entirely opaque. Without access to a strategic logic of the fictional world, we end up relying on our real-world understanding for context.[5] (see DISSENSUS)

Out of this tension between game and not-game, I had a very strong reaction the first time I played *New Societies*. It was obvious that I was practicing utopia building with a group of people who had a very different understanding of utopia than I did. More importantly, they had a different understanding of the game than I did. I constantly fought with my group about the ramifications of choices we made in the game.

---

4   "New Societies," *Re:Current Theatre*, 2022, recurrenttheatre.com/projects/new-societies/.

5   For example, in another blatantly settler-colonial game, *Settlers of Catan*, accumulating enough "soldiers" to attain the achievement of "Largest Army" is worth pursuing since, by doing so, I will acquire two points towards the ten I need to win. The game rules communicate a built-in value system. In *New Societies*, the advantages versus costs of any choice are not laid out for the divisions, and so the player-societies lapse into discussions of the ethics of militarism, the morality of peacekeeping, and the corrupt economics of the military-industrial complex. (This, I believe, is the point of *New Societies*. The game-performance event is designed to foster conversations about high-stakes problems with strangers.)

I found myself up against players who kept minimizing my ideas around mirrored real-world implications and reminding me, "It's only a game." I was grumpy, because I felt like I wasn't being heard. It reminded me of being an angry young feminist at my family table as a kid, arguing with my dad about our different politics. (Shout out to my dad for eating dinner with this feminist killjoy for all these years. He's now working through the reading list of my Ph.D. coursework!) In the case of *New Societies*, if I actually wanted to build a utopia in the way I imagined it, I would have to be a stick in the mud, call out hypocrisy, and ruin the fun of the game. The second time I played *New Societies*, I put this plan into action. Enter the killjoy.

The killjoy, who on a superficial level may enact an annoying buzz kill, acts to foster inclusion. Despite their destructive tactics, they are an optimistic refuser. Their actions are rooted in calling out injustice and inequities that will eventually lead to positive change—even though it might end not only in losing the game, but perhaps also in destroying the game entirely. But from the killjoy's point of view, the game was unjust to begin with. A killjoy says the unsayable, bringing politics into an apolitical space. Though we are made uncomfortable by it, this state of discomfort is crucial in provoking change. Naturally, most people wish to avoid discomfort, so this interruption forces us to become aware, to engage with the issues at hand, and (hopefully) to make decisions that will alter the present situation. The role of the killjoy is less selfish than GOING ROGUE and more abrasive than OPTING OUT. (I say this as a proud killjoy. Sometimes sandpaper is rough.)

In the case of *New Societies*, our killjoy tendencies are encouraged, since playing the game to "win" forces players to take some uncomfortable positions, making choices that are expedient or cheap but also play out as callous at best and amoral at worst. For example, as more groups decide to overharvest resources to meet their division's needs, the health of the entire system goes down, and society begins to decline. If divisions ignore cries from their citizens in favour of expediency, riots break out. As I discovered, the site of contention is the MAGIC CIRCLE itself. Both as a game and as theatre, *New Societies* is set apart from real-world consequences; and yet the thinness of the frame combined with the interpersonal sociality of my postdramatic performance as myself makes it difficult to agree that this is just a game, just a play. The killjoy of *New Societies* speaks an unpleasant truth and asserts that this cannot be just a game. If our tabletop UTOPIA is to be won only through the strategies of colonialism, we might need to be okay with losing this game.[6] *New Societies* invites us to enact an alternate play strategy where we can practise speaking those dreams aloud in a collective that may not (yet) share the shape of those dreams. We are challenged to agree together to make difficult decisions against the baked-in racism and casual extractivism of colonial capitalism, but also against the WIN-conditions of *New Societies* that, at least initially, seem to reward that system.[7]

See WITNESS

---

6   For a more extensive discussion of how actual audience-players of *New Societies* grapple with colonialism through game play, see Jenn Stephenson and Mariah Horner, "Decolonial Improvisations in Hybrid Theatre-Game Play in Re:Current Theatre's *New Societies*," conference paper presented at *Canadian Game Studies Association*, May 2022. Listen to audio of that presentation via the downloadable link here: drive.google.com/file/d/1xRL705OzQTNMMAQd87Q8BhlZ1bz3-30A/view.
7   Every iteration of *New Societies* ends in global collapse due to resource depletion and environmental degradation. This is where we are reminded that *New Societies* is not (only) a game. It lacks that quality of games whereby the outcome is directly premised on our play actions. *New Societies* is also a drama with a predetermined denouement, aligned to its thematic understanding. (see GAME OVER. PLAY AGAIN?)

LABOUR

The actual doing of something is a key quality of participatory theatre. We do work when we participate. When trying to parse out exactly what we mean by participation, the nature of the audience action comes to the fore. Now, without question, audiences are always doing something. Even BOURGEOIS THEATRE audiences attending conventional fourth-wall realism are not inert; they are INTERPRETING. But what about all those other verbs? It is Shannon Steen, writing about the neoliberal impulses of certain kinds of non-fiction theatre, who remarks on the sheer "verbiness"[1] of theatre that calls us to "perform."[2] So many verbs. What about the actions of running, dancing, singing, storytelling, eating, building, or making? The list goes on.

Adam Alston ("Audience Participation and Neoliberal Value") connects immersive theatre to neoliberalism through its promoted values "such as entrepreneurialism, as well as the valorization of risk, agency and responsibility."[3] (For more about entrepreneurialism, see SHOPPING. For more about risk, see AROUSAL.) A slight digression here: Alston folds participation into immersive theatre when he writes, "The demands made of audiences to do something in an immersive theatre event are stretched and magnified" in ways that he characterizes as "both manifold and significant."[4] And yet there is an important conceptual gap between these two terms; they are not fully synonymous. An event can be participatory without being immersive; consider postdramatic performance activities that do not instigate a fictional world, like the conversational games of *Lost Together* or *Through My Lens*. Conversely, an event can be immersive without being participatory; consider the recent trend in commercial, touristic, immersive art exhibits—immersive Van Gogh, immersive Klimt,[5] or the

---

1 Shannon Steen, "Neoliberal Scandals: Foxconn, Mike Daisey, and the Turn Toward Nonfiction Drama," *Theatre Journal* 66, no. 1 (March 2014): 17.
2 She doesn't directly identify it as "participatory." In becoming people who perform, we participate. There is, however, a meaningful but subtle distinction between these two terms.
3 Adam Alston, "Audience Participation and Neoliberal Value: Risk, Agency, and Responsibility in Immersive Theatre," *Performance Research* 18, no. 2 (2013): 128.
4 Alston, "Audience Participation and Neoliberal Value," 129.
5 "Immersive VanGogh Exhibit Toronto," *Immersive VanGogh Exhibit*, 2023, vangoghexhibit.ca; "Immersive Klimt Revolution," *Immersive Klimt Revolution*, immersiveklimt.com/.

planetariums of my childhood. Nevertheless, much immersive theatre does lean into participation, especially participation figured as navigation of an immersive geography. This is where Alston sets up camp. He highlights the implied boldness of the immersed participatory audience as an explorer, recognizing the drive to seize the opportunity for oneself by putting yourself forward, by stepping up, by reaching out and grabbing, by enacting what he calls "a persistent reaching towards a maximization of experience."[6] Like Keren Zaiontz ("Narcissistic Spectatorship"), Alston notes the alignment between entrepreneurial SEEKING and striving and self-indulgence.[7] The individual audience member is the locus of the experience in a unique way. The show is "by me" created by my talents and special efforts, but it is also "about me," as the site of being active in this way is also pleasurable. "The point is that pleasurable or challenging experience is not just a fortunate by-product of the theatre event, but is, in many respects, immersive [participatory] theatre's raison d'être."[8] Audience action when framed as creative, innovative, or activist feels empowering for sure. It also feels good. The agential glow-up of my action makes me feel that I am a positive force, making the world a better place.

Stripped of the veneer of entrepreneurialism however, sometimes work is just work. Rather than creators, sometimes we are just labourers. Jen Harvie, in her book *Fair Play: Art, Performance and Neoliberalism*, was one of the first to identify this phenomenon where our leisure is subverted into labour. Audiences become ad hoc amateur performers; and, in some cases, the professional performers actually vanish from the space entirely. It is a matter of debate whether audiences are passively exploited or, as Alston argues, the audiences themselves actively exploit opportunities to be expressive, to be empowered, to claim agency in the making of art and performance. "Whatever one's position in these arguments, they indicate, first, that labour is circulating widely across makers and audiences in contemporary art and performance, and second, that this circulation of labour is important and demands scrutiny because it articulates and significantly affects social power relations."[9] Audiences are one part of this labour ecosystem. Precarity marks not only the travails of the art-preneur mired in gig culture, but also the outsourcing and the downloading of labour to audiences who are deskilled—obviously we are not trained, let alone rehearsed (although sometimes this is the

6   Alston, "Audience Participation and Neoliberal Value," 130.

7   Keren Zaiontz, "Narcissistic Spectatorship in Immersive and One-on-One Performance," *Theatre Journal* 66, no. 3 (2014): 405–25.

8   Alston, "Audience Participation and Neoliberal Value," 130.

9   Jen Harvie, *Fair Play: Art, Performance and Neoliberalism* (Palgrave, 2013), 28–29.

root of our charm; see PAINT)—and disposable—there will be more new audience-performers tomorrow. As Harvie asserts, "These audiences become the epitome of the underemployed theatre worker."[10]

In one corner of the stage space, two audience members assembled sandwiches. While in the centre, several other people sorted mismatched socks, fresh from the laundry, into pairs. Still others used a manual air pump to inflate a mattress. One audience member above on the gallery level changed a flat tire on a bicycle. Another offered kind words to a melancholy cast member lying on the floor. The house lights never dimmed and even those of us who chose not to leave our seats were invited to contribute our labour as documentarians and publicists, taking photos or videos of the proceedings and posting them to social media. This first "act" of *Ça a l'air synthétique bonjour hi*, created by Francophone artists Burcu Emeç, Michael Martini, Nien Tzu Weng, and Roxa Hy, asks, "What if an audience was paid for contributing to an artwork?" In exchange for our engagement with these completely ordinary and seemingly meaningless tasks, audience labourers are offered actual, real cash money. We are told from the outset that the budget for the evening is $264. Once we have completed a task, we are invited to walk over to a corner table and negotiate our fee. We could invent new tasks to increase our fee. Mariah garnered $12 for making the sandwiches. Our research assistant Derek earned $5 for being one of the mattress inflators. At one performance, Jenn was awarded the last dollar as a "consulting fee" for recommending that the show not go into debt against the next night's budget, and so ended the first act.

In this explicit association of audience participation with paid labour, *Ça a l'air synthétique bonjour hi* presents a pointed critique of the INSTRUMENTALITY of neoliberalism. As capitalist efficiency collides with our desire for authenticity, personalization, and the do-it-yourself ethos, audience members become the performers of our own performance that we paid for. As discussed above, on the one hand, I am delighted at being invited into the playing space and to demonstrate my AGENCY in customizing my own aesthetic experience. While on the other hand, the same invitation to enter the stage space, where I bought a ticket, for the purpose of doing work there for free, requires me to (twice) pay to play, while simultaneously decommodifying the work of the artist. *Ça a l'air synthétique bonjour hi* plays on this delight—audience members joyfully perform their chosen, absurdly mundane tasks—while turning the tables to re-commodify our labour

10   Harvie, *Fair Play*, 47.

by actually paying us. Of course, all participatory theatre is subject to this uncomfortable condition. In this, the play is wickedly subversive in its self-reflexivity. *Ça a l'air synthétique bonjour hi* uses this genre to critique the genre.[11]

MAKE AT LEAST 5 DOODLES OF THINGS MENTIONED IN THIS ENTRY.

NO, YOU WILL NOT BE COMPENSATED.

---

[11] The video-game-theatre performance *asses.masses* by Patrick Blenkarn and Milton Lim also takes labour as its central theme. In this show, an interactive video game is played by whichever audience members step forward to claim the controller, while the rest of us watch and contribute advice. (see POLITICS OF THE BASEMENT and MOB) The show recounts the adventures of a herd of digital donkeys—Bad Ass, Lazy Ass, and others—on a quest for enlightenment and labour revolution. Creator Lim's website describes the show as "*Animal Farm* meets *Aesop's Fables* retold by Franz Kafka, Karl Marx, and Sonic the Hedgehog" (*Milton Lim*, miltonlim.com/assesmasses).

LAND

Relational art emphasizes the interconnectedness of human life. This is not only an exercise in artistic metaphor. For Nicolas Bourriaud, "the role of artworks is no longer to form imaginary and utopian realities, but to actually be ways of living and models of action within the existing real."[1] The generative function of relational art iterates beyond the frame, it's REHEARSAL at world building through an actual tending to our relationships with the social creatures (friends and strangers) in our lives. In his book *Relational Aesthetics*, Bourriaud asks us to look beyond the artwork itself and towards "a set of artistic practices which take as their theoretical and practical point of departure, the whole of human relations and their social context, rather than an independent and private space."[2] What are the "whole of human relations"? Who, or what, sits in that pantheon, and when, or where, can we find them?

Beyond the interhuman connections of FRIENDSHIP, many Indigenous knowledge practices around relationality presuppose a broader understanding, extending those relations: in the present to include the land, the flora and fauna; in the past to include our ancestors and the ancestors of those to whom we as settlers have caused violence; and in the future to generations of our children beyond us. (see CREW) Indigenous notions of relation expand our community across time, space, and species in the face of settler colonialism that has sought to sever those relations. In talking about the state-sponsored destruction of Indigenous forms of social kinship in favour of heteronormative nuclear families, Leanne Betasamosake Simpson says "Michi Saagiig Nishnaabeg nationhood is at its core relational, and all of our political practices stem from the establishment and maintenance of good relations."[3]

To be clear, this relationality isn't sprawling forever to everything that has existed and ever will exist. There is a specific anchoring to the land, to its geography. In her discussion of Indigenous relationality between nations, Simpson stresses the concept of "grounded normativity," or a deeply nation-specific approach to Indigenous knowledge systems that

---

1   Nicolas Bourriaud, *Relational Aesthetics*, translated by Simon Pleasance and Fronza Woods (Les presses du réel, 2002), 13.

2   Bourriaud, *Relational Aesthetics*, 113.

3   Leanne Betasamosake Simpson, *As We Have Always Done: Indigenous Freedom through Radical Resistance* (U of Minnesota P, 2017), 110.

"generates nations as networks of complex, layered, multidimensional, intimate relationships with human and nonhuman beings."[4] These relations extend beyond the collective of social creatures in Bourriaud's relational art to nonhuman members of our network. Further, this relationality is not just about knowing and reconnecting with life in your present, but also recognizing a *responsibility* to that larger temporal network. That responsibility to one's relations starts with an awareness of your own positionality as a being in relation to other beings. In a piece in *Canadian Theatre Review* about the complexities of land acknowledgements, Kanonhsyonne Janice C. Hill, a Mohawk Turtle Clan grandmother says, "It is customary and respectful that before I address a group I place myself in relation to who I am within my family, clan, and Nation."[5]

Joe Osawabine, a member of the Debajehmujig Storytellers collective based on Wikwemikong Uncededed Territory (Manitoulin Island), asserts that in his performance practice "[the] one thing I cannot change or would not change is the knowledge and responsibility that I have been gifted these stories from my elders . . . the responsibility that we have to share them to benefit the future lives of all our descendants. My grandchildren. Your grandchildren."[6] In their TOURING show, *The Global Savages*, Debajehmujig members travel to selected cities around the world[7] to tell "the 18,000-year animated oral history of the Indigenous peoples of North America also known as Turtle Island in ninety minutes or less."[8] Before they can begin this daunting task, the performers of *The Global Savages* must prepare. A week before the public performance, the four characters—Sky Woman (Jessica Wilde-Peltier); Chibiabos, the musician (Bruce Naokwegijig), Debajehmud, the storyteller (Joe Osawabine), and Mudjeekawis, the record keeper (Josh Peltier)— enter the city on foot at sunrise and walk, travelling along a culturally

4 Leanne Betasamosake Simpson, "Indigenous Resurgence and Co-Resistance," *Critical Ethnic Studies* 2, no. 2 (Fall 2016): 23.

5 Dylan Robinson, Kanonhsyonne Janice C. Hill, Armand Garnet Ruffo, Selena Couture, and Lisa Cooke Ravensbergen, "Rethinking the Practice and Performance of Indigenous Land Acknowledgement," *Canadian Theatre Review* 177 (Winter 2019), 23.

6 Debajehmujig Storytellers, "*The Global Savages* Pitch," *YouTube*, 28 January 2013, youtube.com/watch?v=SMOpZfyI16w&ab_channel=DebajehmujigStorytellers.

7 Between 2011 and 2013, Debajehmujig brought *The Global Savages* to Canadian cities Brantford and Waterloo in Ontario, Halifax, Vancouver, and cities in France, Scotland, Belgium, and the Netherlands.

8 Ron Berti and Barry Freeman, "A Journey through Time and Place in Debajehmujig's *The Global Savages*: A Slideshow," *Canadian Theatre Review* 157 (Winter 2014): ctr.utpjournals.press/doi/pdf/10.3138/ctr.157.001b.

significant route selected by someone from the community or identified through their own research.[9] They bring gifts to the cultural hosts they meet along the way. As they perform this walking RITUAL, they share meals and make efforts to learn more about their host community by sharing stories of their own. In their packs, they carry a large map of the world, "indicating all land and water, but no borders, no names, no titles."[10] Through conversation, they collaborate with strangers to locate each other on the borderless map. On the final day, the performers invite participants to a "gathering place," a circle around a large fire under an open sky.

Relationality asks you to be a WITNESS to your relations, exercising care through an obligation to the human and nonhuman characters in our networks. Relation comes with an obligation not just to *know* your neighbours but also to care for them.[11] In her book *As We Have Always Done*, Simpson shares the teaching of "*Kina Gchi Nishnaabeg-ogamig*" or a "connectivity based on the sanctity of the land, the love we have for our families, or language, our way of life. It is relationships based on deep reciprocity, respect, noninterference, self-determination, and freedom . . . It is a nationhood based on a series of radiating responsibilities."[12]

Created by settler artist-gardeners Yarrow Collective, *POLLINATORS* is a participatory gardening installation series that playfully invites urban humans to participate in building an ecosystem by planting a garden. During the SKAMpede performance festival in July 2021, Yarrow Collective tended to interactive gardens at four locations around downtown Victoria. Through interactive workshops with professional artists, performance activists, backyard gardeners, and a certified bee steward, participants learned about flora and fauna native to their location. Participants made seed balls and planted them in public gardens. *POLLINATORS* participants literally get their hands dirty digging into and

---

9   Debajehmujig Storytellers, "*The Global Savages* Pitch."

10   Berti and Freeman, "A Journey through Time and Place."

11   In his keynote at the 2021 Canadian Association for Theatre Research (CATR) conference, Kevin Loring, artistic director of the National Arts Centre Indigenous Theatre, was insistent that it is integral that theatres, as "publicly funded enterprises, must be obligated" to nurture the relations around them. In the summer of July 2020 when wildfires destroyed Loring's community of Lytton, BC, he divested funds from the NAC to mutual aid efforts out west. If participatory art can amplify relations within the frame, Indigenous ways of knowing remind us of the responsibility of the WITNESS beyond the frame. Kevin Loring, "Re-turning the Page: How Theatre Practice Must Bravely Return Into a Post-Pandemic, De-Colonial, Anti-Racist World," *YouTube*, 8 July 2021, youtube.com/watch?v=935_BXxCbCQ&t=4s.

12   Simpson, *As We Have Always Done,* 8~9.

excavating the interconnected relationality between the present, the land itself, and the ancestors that inhabit that land.[13]

Yarrow Collective is deeply invested in a complex awareness of relationality that includes the social creatures of our daily life and the land. Yarrow Collective asserts that for settlers like us, in "learning to be good visitors on this land, we seek to disrupt colonial, extractive assumptions around what 'gardening' is and imagine what it can be."[14] They honour these relations by paying their "respects to the traditional keepers of this land, the ləkʷəŋən-speaking people, now known as the Esquimalt and Songhees Nations. The loss of bee and plant habitat in this territory are a direct result of colonization and stolen land."[15] Through the participatory act of gardening, Yarrow Collective leverages relationality to become an act of reconciliation, an attempted remediation. The work tends to roots, nurtures sustainment, and yields fruits for the future.

See SEEDS and MINDFULNESS

13   Laurel Green and Sammi Gough, "Seeding the Future (This is Not a Metaphor)," *Canadian Theatre Review* 197 (Winter 2024): 14–20.

14   "Voices in Nature 2022," *Pacific Opera*, 18–19 June 2022, pacificopera.ca/event /voices-in-nature-2/.

15   "Voices in Nature," *Pacific Opera*, 23–26 June 2022, pacificopera.ca/event /voices-in-nature/.

WRITE A LAND ACKNOWLEDGEMENT FOR WHERE YOU ARE.

LIVENESS

Considering the relationship of liveness in the context of the twentieth-century advent of broadcast media, Philip Auslander writes, "The live is actually an effect of mediatization, not the other way around. It was the development of recording technologies that made it possible to perceive existing representations as 'live.' Prior to the advent of those technologies (e.g., sound recording and motion pictures), there was no such thing as 'live' performance, for that category has meaning only in relation to an opposing possibility."[1] It is a provocative idea, to be sure. Everything was "live"—so obviously and unequivocally that we didn't need a word for that—until it wasn't. For categorizing different conceptualizations of liveness, Steve Wurtzler offers a useful template, dividing modes of technologically mediated and non-mediated co-presence into four quadrants: here and now; here but not now; now but not here; and not here and not now.[2]

In a participatory theatre work where audience-players co-occupy physical space with the actor-creators, we are all both here and now. We are together in a mutual space, engaged in a contemporaneously unfolding activity. And so, it doesn't occur to us to ask, "Is it live?" Short of the actors being very convincing holographic projections, we can be very confident that the experience is "live." That is, it is happening in a shared now and a shared here.

But, if we are not physically sharing immediate co-adjacent space, how can I know if you are with me, that we are co-present somehow? What if we are now, but not here? In order to participate, we need to be somehow "with" as a precondition to interaction. We can be with people, or with THINGS, or with an environment (see BEING LOST and DRIFT), but there needs to be some kind of RELATIONALITY. And relation needs a conduit of togetherness.[3] But that conduit need not be

---

1 Philip Auslander, *Liveness: Performance in a Mediatized Culture*, 2nd edition (Routledge, 2008), 56.

2 Steve Wurtzler, "She Sang Live, But the Microphone Was Off: The Live, the Recorded, and the Subject of Representation," in *Sound Theory Sound Practise*, edited by Rick Altman (Routledge, 1992), 87–103.

3 See Kelsey Jacobson's work on this topic, "The Pervasive Real: Virtual Co-Presence in Jordan Tannahill's YouTube Play *rihannaboi95*," *Contemporary Theatre Review* 32, vol. 2 (2022): 191–205; and her research blog *Being Together*, kelseyjacobson.ca /being-together-blog.

immediate—that is, unmediated—in order for us to be together. A relational connection can be established via PHONE or TEXT MESSAGE. These synchronous conduits establish, if not a shared physical space, then at least a shared virtual or imagined space where we are linked by technology. During COVID, many of us became conversant (too much so for some) with video links, participating in "live" interactions via Zoom.

Where things get interesting is that, for video calling, it can be ambiguous as to whether or not the performance is live. How can I confirm if the actions that I am SPECTATOR to are unfolding now? Perhaps they have been previously recorded. In the case of recorded media, say the streaming of an archival of a play, we are neither here nor now. As viewers, we are separated by both time and space from the moment of performance. Reception and production are divorced. And in that chasm of divorce, it is difficult to say that we are participating. We lack open channels of connection among ourselves in the audience and between the audience and the artists.[4] I might argue that, if we were gathered together in a movie theatre, then there might be a sense of parallel participation in a common event, engendered by the audience doing a thing together. But I would also argue that the movie itself is secondary to that feeling. There is coordinated engagement in a shared activity that is coincidentally within the movie theatre space. Nevertheless, we cannot cross through the screen.

Several COVID-era theatre productions, where it was very clear that we were not mutually here, flipped this script, correlating liveness to participation and using participation as the bonafides of liveness in a shared now.[5] Created and performed by Daveed Goldman and Nobu Adilman and running off and on since 2011, *Choir! Choir! Choir!* stages

---

4   One mode of recorded connection that spans time (not now) and space (not here) that does allow this crossover is MAIL. Exchanging postcards or playing chess by letter is a mutual endeavour of participation that is both distanced and asynchronous, but it is slow. Very slow.

5   Wurtzler's fourth category, "here but not now," which is needed of course for the symmetry of the model, is perhaps the least relevant to the challenge of participation when being here together is exactly what a pandemic does not allow. The example that Wurtzler gives is stadium Jumbotron replay. The broadcast and the original event share the identical "here" but are asynchronous. That said, perhaps I am being too hasty in dismissing this quadrant. I can imagine a performance game that involves being in the same place but at different times. A scavenger hunt where each participant or group of participants serially checks in at the same stations, for example. Geocaching works this way. The hider and the seeker never meet. Our feeling of live connectivity, the feeling of co-participation, arises from the awareness that someone stood exactly on this spot before me. Museums also express a frisson of liveness in the same way. The aura of the object stretches across millennia.

weekly drop-in choirs at bars and theatres worldwide, inviting strangers to sing harmonies together with no pressure. Their online rendition of *C!C!C!* was the very first show that I participated in after the first COVID lockdown sent me home in mid-March 2020. Through social media, Nobu and Daveed invited their fans to sing with them from their living rooms, calling the event an "Epic Love Song Social Distansing-along!" They posted lyrics to *C!C!C!* classics online and over eight thousand singers participated. Using Facebook Live, two technologies were combined, with video broadcast going "out" and chat for content coming "in." Daveed and Nobu were able to read the chat to know that we were present, singing our hearts out, even though they couldn't hear us. They responded to the chat, bantering in this slightly syncopated, asynchronous way with the audience.[6]

Saving Wonderland, powered by Gamiotics, interlaces alternating episodes of recorded scenes with live, interactive (This is how we know those were live) collaborative group games. Part online escape room, part CHOOSE YOUR OWN ADVENTURE story, the audience members who are communally cast as "Alice" are tasked with (obviously) saving Wonderland, which is under threat of digital degradation by the Jabberwock. Different choices lead to differing sequences and ultimately to different outcomes. Chunks of exposition leading up to our game tasks are clearly pre-recorded. Interestingly, the solo live "performer" is the invisible stage manager who presses "play" for each scene and then cues up the next scene as appropriate, in response to the results of our game play.

Leslie Ting's *Speculation* is a live-streamed film-theatre hybrid that asserts its liveness through a call-in portion where audiences participate in a collaborative staging of John Cage's "4'33"", a work of music scored for silence, where the intention is for any usually ignored background noise to come to awareness. Playing at the fully remote version of the Festival of Live Digital Art (FOLDA) in the summer of 2021, *Speculation* is part violin concert and part monologue about Ting supporting her mother through vision loss. While the violin concert is pre-recorded, in the final moments of the show, Ting and her team go live to invite participation by encouraging audience members to phone into a collective

---

6 The cooking show *Embrace* has a similar bivalent structure. The show could be recorded, but we know that it is live when the performer in their kitchen reads our messages from the Zoom chat and responds to us in our kitchens. These responses do not have any direct effect on the performance; we lack AGENCY to make meaningful change. They do, however, serve to communicate liveness and to reinforce our connection as a community. (see TOGETHER ALONE)

conference call that would be streamed online. Delightfully glitchy, this conference call absorbs and repeats sounds from all of the simultaneous phone-ins in looping layers. In an interview with Ting, she recounted a charming moment in one of the performances at FOLDA when "early in the phone-call section someone said, 'Are you serious?' and it just started looping over and over again. I'm sure someone was caught off guard about listening and being heard," Ting said. [7]

Confession: That was me. I was that someone. I was watching the live-streamed show seated on a picnic bench in my backyard when I picked up the phone to call in. I was so shocked by the sudden assertion of liveness and the simplicity of the technique that I spoke aloud! I was a bit embarrassed to hear my own exclamation on repeat, but it certainly firmly rooted me in the live experience.

7   Leslie Ting, personal interview, 14 February 2023.

MAD LIBS

Upon entering the _____ (noun), the audience-players are given a _____ (adjective) _____ (noun). Holding this with our _____ (plural body part), we are then encouraged by _____ (name of a celebrity) to form a _____ (geometric shape) and _____ (present tense verb) in perfect unison.

The name Mad Libs for this ridiculous fill-in-the-blank game (or what *Wikipedia* calls a "phrasal word template game"[1]) dates from the 1950s and blends the phrase "ad libs" with the mood of madcap silliness. Of course, its informal history goes back further than that, finding parallels with parlour games like Consequences and the surrealist art game Exquisite Corpse.[2] Here, we are using Mad Libs as a shorthand for a genre of participation where we are asked to do exactly this and fill in blanks in a preset performance text. These audience-player contributions take a number of forms.

In shows like *100% Vancouver* or *Le Grand Continental*, there is a predetermined choreographic framework that specifies a need for a certain number of ORDINARY PEOPLE to occupy those spaces with our bodies. The thematic understanding of the show is premised entirely on how these non-professional actors or dancers come to visibility on the stage, carrying meaning in their very ordinariness. These two examples also draw on a dramaturgy of mass assembly. Performing *100% Vancouver* requires exactly one hundred inhabitants of Vancouver. *Le Grand Continental* does not specify location, but it also foregrounds the performance of a large group, as evidenced by the word "grand" in its name and its promotional boasts that there are hundreds of dancers in each iteration. In 2017, *Le super méga continental* featured 375 dancers in honour of the 375th anniversary of Montréal's founding.[3]

Another type of audience-player fill-in-the-blanks is a conversational ENCOUNTER. Shows like *Lost Together* and *4inXchange* are premised on some form of question and answer. Often these questions go beyond our personal participation to seek AUTOBIOGRAPHICAL information. This dramaturgical move shifts the content of the show from being

---

1   "Mad Libs," *Wikipedia*, en.wikipedia.org/wiki/Mad_Libs.

2   "Mad Libs," *Wikipedia*.

3   "*Le super mega continental*," *Festival TransAmériques*, 2017, fta.ca/en/archive/le-super-mega-continental/.

"by me" to being both "by me" and "about me." Depending on how the performance collects, processes, and responds to our inputs, the shape and meaning of the show will vary. Substituting tasks for words, other performances invite gestural contributions. In *It Comes in Waves*, we paddle a canoe on Lake Ontario to the island where we set up benches and tables, and hang decorations for a party. In *Counting Sheep*, we build a protest barricade, crouch down to avoid being hit by police bullets (represented by ominous black paper airplanes), and return the attack, throwing (foam) bricks. In *La Rivoluzione Siamo Noi—The Change Maker*, we participate in a kind of acting class, given instructions such as "walk around the room and make eye contact with other participants," or "stand in a circle and hold hands." The list goes on. In every case, the act of putting ourselves into spaces, blanks opened by the performance RECIPE, has significant impact on our experience and understanding.

In his four-part taxonomy of user functions in interactive literature, Espen J. Aarseth describes, as the third category, texts where the work is "constructive," the other categories being interpretive, explorative (see SEEKING), and the fourth category that he calls "textonic." (see EMERGENCE) As with the exploratory function, construction is also ergodic (meaning "requiring nontrivial effort"[4]), but the LABOUR of the reader in the manipulation of textons and scriptons is different.

Textons are strings of information as they appear in the text. These could be words or phrases, sentences. In the case of performance, these could be lines of dialogue or scenes. Scriptons are also strings of information. Scriptons are assembled from textons, arranged in the order they appear to the reader. (Please do forgive Aarseth's computing jargon.) Basically, if the reader is exploring a text (see CHOOSE YOUR OWN ADVENTURE) then all the textons already exist and the reader navigates from one to another along a forking path. A unique scripton presents itself as the resulting singular narrative. It is a hypertextual journey across a static landscape. By contrast, if the reader-function is configurative, the reader creates new scriptons "by rearranging textons or changing the variables." This renders the work cybertextual, in a dynamic, evolving, and responsive landscape. Texts that lend themselves to configuration are by definition user-oriented and indeterminate.[5] In terms of participatory performance, the work of configuration is dominated by exactly this strategy of "changing the variables," as different audience-players invited to fill in the gaps are likely to do so

---

4   Espen J. Aarseth, *Cybertext: Perspectives on Ergodic Literature* (Johns Hopkins UP, 1997), 1.

5   Aarseth, *Cybertext*, 62–75.

differently. And as a result of these new inputs, the work responds to varying degrees, generating new meanings and experiences.

This conception of participatory readers (audiences) as gap-fillers has led a number of scholars engaged with interactive fictions to identify an affiliation with the reader-response theory of Wolfgang Iser.[6] To this view, readers are always active in their interpretation of literature, entering into a continual process of creating and revising meaning. Blanks (or *leerstellen*) "invoke familiar or determinate elements only to cancel them out. What is canceled, however, remains in view, and thus brings about modifications in the reader's attitude toward what is familiar or determinate—in other words he is guided to adopt a position *in relation* to the text."[7] This semantic NEGOTIATION with the literary work, shaped by both conventional repertoires as well as by the reader's own expectations, combines in a synthesis which is "neither manifested in the printed text, nor produced solely by the reader's imagination, and the project of which they consist are themselves of a dual nature: they emerge from the reader, but are also GUIDED by signals which 'project' themselves into him."[8] Aarseth documents this take, but then suggests why the gap-filling LABOUR described by Iser is quite different from the constructive work done by ergodic readers of cybertexts. He points out that the nature of the gap and our interaction with it is very different. The work done by a participatory audience is not filling aesthetic gaps—it is not INTERPRETIVE or at least not only interpretive.

The core question is basically how big are the blanks? First, how much flexibility do we have with our inputs? Are there "right" answers or does anything go? Second, how much do these inputs affect the work? Is this meaningful play? Do we have AGENCY? Ine Therese Berg notes, "The players might not influence the dramaturgical structure, but the energy and relationships that occur in the performance depend on them."[9]

Sometimes the gaps we are asked to fill are spatialized. The task is a simple one: Place an object in a location of your choosing. Our act will not alter the narrative of the performance, however; play continues just the same, regardless of what we do. These blanks are very small. Meaning arises out of that process of choosing. My participation in

---

6   Aarseth, *Cybertext*, 110–11.

7   Wolfgang Iser, *The Act of Reading: A Theory of Aesthetic Response* (Johns Hopkins UP, 1978), 169.

8   Iser, *The Act of Reading*, 135; Susan Bennett, *Theatre Audiences: A Theory of Production and Reception*, 2nd edition (Routledge, 1997), 43–44.

9   Ine Therese Berg, "Participation to the People!: Locating the Popular in Rimini Protokoll's *Home Visit Europe*," *Nordic Theatre Studies* 29, no. 2 (2017): 175.

Citation begins with me being given a stone. It is grey and round and fits in my palm. I carry it, warm in my hand, as the group moves off on our walk. These sites are familiar to me—the grounds of Queen's University, the city of Kingston, the pathway that cuts across City Park. Led by the voice of Lisa Cooke Ravensbergen in my ears, this audiowalk upends my experience. I am disoriented. An Indigenous graduate student, mother of a young son, and an artist-storyteller, Lisa reveals her lived experience of this deeply colonized space. With her words in my ears, I see differently. How long has that graffiti of Louis Riel, tucked away on the hidden face of a low concrete plinth, been there? I notice the honorific names of the buildings, the austere limestone architecture. As we cross the park, following the red cloths tied to a progression of lamp posts, I get a sinking feeling. I know where we are going. I know what we are going to find at the end of this path. And then there we are, standing at the base of an immense statue of the city's most famous son—Sir John A. Macdonald—Canada's first prime minister and architect of Indigenous cultural genocide.[10] Ravensbergen's recasting of this space and her calling out my relation to the land on which I am standing feels like a punch in the stomach. I knew some of this. But I also didn't. I was willfully ignorant. Before ending, her voice on the audio track in my ears charges me to decide what to do with the stone. Where should I place it? Where does it belong? What will my choice purport? How can I make the stone speak? (In *b side*, the task is to place lemons and the feeling is entirely different.) In terms of participation, my physical act is a small one of limited scope. The narrative is not affected by my action, but my relation to it is profoundly reshaped.

Sometimes the gaps we are asked to fill are verbal, such that our contributions constitute almost the entire text. The RECIPE carves out and reserves this space for us. *Mégaphone*, produced in Montréal during the autumn months of 2013, is a work of this kind.[11] A co-production between Moment Factory and the National Film Board of Canada, *Mégaphone* was a public participatory installation in three zones. The

---

10　When *Citation* premiered at the 2018 Festival of Live Digital Art in Kingston, Ontario, the statue of Sir John A. Macdonald still stood, stoic and menacing in City Park where it had stood since 1885. In the summer of 2021, after nearly a year of active civic protest against memorializing violent characters of Canadian history, Sir John A. Macdonald was removed from City Park and placed in Cataraqui Cemetery, where he was buried. I was there when he was covered with a red cloth and hoisted off his pedestal with heavy machinery. We danced and laughed with the ghosts of the stones from *Citation*.

11　Other works with a similar structure, inviting expansive speech, include *The Assembly*, *Lost Together*, and the role of the visual describers in *Through My Lens*.

first zone featured a promenade gallery, displaying profiles of seven key local figures "who have shaped public space in Montréal with their words."[12] The second zone formed a public square with a large seating area facing a stage. On the stage, the only visual element was a large red megaphone, its horn well above head height. People were invited to approach the megaphone, take hold of the attached microphone, and speak. Any and all thoughts were welcome. A slogan on the shipping container side walls proclaimed: "Lance une idée sur ta ville. Light the city up with your idea." These speeches were then transposed using voice recognition software to the third zone—the nearby multi-storey facade of one of the buildings at Université du Québec à Montréal. The facade formed an immense projection screen where the speeches were visualized as live sound waves and also an evolving word cloud. Although seemingly random, *Mégaphone* transcends the nonsense of the Mad Libs game to stage in the aggregate a meaningful collation of words. The result is a durational work that brings attention both to individual speech and to the collective political power of a vibrant culture of public discourse.[13]

---

12   "Mégaphone: A Voice Recognition Urban Art Installation," *Moment Factory*, 2013, momentfactory.com/work/shows/all/megaphone.
13   The show *Seiji's Perfect Day* by Popcorn Galaxies is an actual literal Mad Lib. Participants are prompted to phone a hotline with an answering machine where they can record themselves reading their story. Other audience members could listen to the recordings on the show's website.

THIS MAD LIB IS FROM *SEIJI'S PERFECT DAY*, A PERFORMANCE CREATED BY THE POPCORN GALAXIES DUO JUNE FUKUMURA AND KEELY O'BRIEN, REPRINTED WITH PERMISSION. TRY IT OUT!

IF YOU COULD GIVE THE PERFECT DAY TO SOMEONE YOU LOVE, WITHOUT ANY RESTRICTIONS, WHAT WOULD THAT DAY LOOK LIKE?

ON _____'S PERFECT DAY, HE/SHE/THEY ATE _____ FOR BREAKFAST. THEY SPENT THE MORNING _____. THE WEATHER WAS _____. A MYSTERIOUS GIFT ARRIVED ON THE DOORSTEP, IT WAS A _____. IN THE AFTERNOON, THEY _____. IT MADE THEM REMEMBER THE TIME _____. MIRACULOUSLY, _____. THAT NIGHT, THEY _____ WITH _____. AT THE END OF THE DAY, THEY THOUGHT TO THEMSELF, "_____."

MAGIC CIRCLE

Without the theatrical frame that carves out space from the actual world to bring a new fictional world into being, there can be no theatre. The same is true of the magic circle. Games become possible through this essential act of division. Both dramatic play and game play are premised in a foundational way on being distinct from ordinary life.

Johan Huizinga (*Homo Ludens*) writes, "The turf, the tennis-court, the chessboard, and pavement-hopscotch cannot be formally distinguished from the temple or the magic circle."[1] Here, the magic circle gestures towards a kind of RITUAL space. Huizinga forges the link between that sacred division and similar, but mundane, game boundaries. It is Katie Salen and Eric Zimmerman (*Rules of Play*) who fully articulate "magic circle" as the core delimiter that inscribes the cognitive field of play.[2] The magic circle may often also manifest physically. Sometimes it is the turf, the tennis court, the chessboard, or the pavement hopscotch described by Huizinga. Sometimes it is indeed a circle, like a cricket pitch or crokinole board, or simply a loose gathering of players. Likewise, the theatrical frame can be literally a proscenium frame, gold-painted and baroque.

What are other ways that the magic circle and theatrical frame are either similar or different? As elements of division or separation, both the circle and the frame are by nature exclusionary. What do they exclude? Distinct from the ordinary world, different rules apply inside the magic circle and the theatrical frame. The most significant of these differences is the idea that certain real-world principles are rendered invalid or don't "count" within the borders of the game or the drama. (see KILLJOY) Roger Caillois (*Man, Play and Games*) provocatively asserts that at the end of the game "nothing has been harvested or manufactured, no masterpiece has been created, no capital has accrued. Play is an occasion of pure waste: waste of time, energy, ingenuity, skill, and often money."[3] Games are in this way entirely non-instrumental. The things

---

1 Johan Huizinga, *Homo Ludens: A Study of the Play-Element in Culture* (Routledge & Kegan Paul, 1955), 20.

2 Katie Salen and Eric Zimmerman, *Rules of Play: Game Design Fundamentals* (MIT P, 2004), 93–99.

3 Roger Caillois, *Man, Play and Games*, translated by Meyer Barash (U of Illinois P, 1961), 5–6.

that the players do only matter to the goals of the game. Once those goals are reached (or not), you WIN (or lose). And so what? Drama as art does not fully escape the draw of INSTRUMENTALITY. In theatre, a masterpiece may well have been created. However, within the frame, actions taken as part of the fictional world do not have real-world effects. In his book, *How to Do Things with Words*, linguist J. L. Austin explicitly declares speech acts, like promising, naming, or cursing, to be "*in a peculiar way* hollow or void if said by an actor on the stage, . . . Language in such circumstances is in special ways—intelligibly—used not seriously, but in many ways *parasitic* upon its normal use—ways which fall under the doctrine of the *etiolations* of language."[4] What this means, in effect, is that stage actions are non-binding. The performed wedding of two characters does not similarly bind the actors in legal matrimony.

Another thing that the circle and the frame exclude (or at least restrict) is risk. Michael J. Apter writes, "In the play-state, you experience a *protective frame* which stands between you and the 'real' world and its problems, creating an enchanted zone in which . . . you are confident that no harm can come."[5] Safe inside, dying is not "for real." In games as well as in drama, we play out scenarios without real-world consequences. Players are not entirely free from physical risk; obviously accidental injuries happen. The key is that the actions done as "pretend" do not carry real-world consequences. This delimitation of risk applies not only to the AROUSAL of physical danger but also to social dangers. Inside the circle and the frame, players—game or dramatic—are not held to the same standards of normal behaviour. For example, two characters kiss. (Ask me about the time I kissed a clown in Rebecca Northan's *Queer Blind Date*.) Even though the actor bodies are not romantic partners, this action carries no real-world stigma. Similarly, a game of Twister directs players into peculiarly intimate body postures, which under non-game circumstances would draw censure. Bending the parameters of what is acceptable and engaging in winkingly risqué acts is, in fact, the point of the game. The circle and frame exclude judgment to free the players from social restraints. It is okay to be sexy or silly.

What else do these framing structures allow or generate? The theatre frame creates a provisionally real, alternative fictional world. The frame generates the field of mimesis, the space where the players generate performances "as if" they were real. The magic circle also allows players to

---

4   J. L. Austin, *How to Do Things with Words* (Oxford UP, 1962), 22.

5   Michael J. Apter, "A Structural Phenomenology of Play," in *Adult Play: A Reversal Theory Approach*, edited by John H. Kerr and Michael J. Apter (Swets and Zeitlinger, 1991), 15.

behave differently. Inside the circle, players participate in what Bernard Suits (*The Grasshopper: Games, Life and Utopia*) calls the "lusory attitude."[6] A player with this correct ludic or playful attitude agrees to strive for the game's goals by taking the long way around, as it were. We agree to only touch the ball with our feet or with a particular kind of stick. We agree to stay within bounds. We agree to take turns. There are more efficient ways to achieve the basic goals of the game by picking up the ball with our hands or by not allowing other players time for their dice rolls, but it is more fun this way. Fiction engenders a fully distinct ONTOLOGICAL DUALITY. The lusory attitude also allows players to be "other," but they do not change the nature of their being, and so the difference is behavioural rather than ontological. (see MEEPLES)

As mentioned at the outset, the magic circle and theatre frame are both created through collective agreement to establish the perceptual difference between inside and outside. The main work is cognitive. As such these boundaries require continual maintenance and can be quite fragile. Physical demarcation assists this work. Likewise, RITUALS for starting and ending the game or drama, like blowing a whistle or dimming the lights, also mark the frames and assert their power. Resistance to these ritualistic or conventional procedures is a threat to the frame. Unlike CHEATERS or hackers who target specific rules with an eye to facilitating their winning, spoilsports REFUSE the core premise of the magic circle or the theatre frame, aiming to effect the dissolution of the game or drama in its entirety. As Caillois notes, "The game is ruined by the nihilist who denounces the rules as absurd and conventional, who refuses to play because the game is meaningless."[7] (see GOING ROGUE)

More pernicious than the direct threat of nihilism to play frames is persistent uncertainty. What happens when we are unable to determine if a frame is present and if so, what kind of frame it is? Being able to concretely discern and perform within frame norms is a life skill. And failure to adhere to frame expectations, not playing the game "correctly," leads to stigma. One of the great strengths of performative play frames is that they can be flexible, adapting to new social collective understandings. Fluidity of framing, allowing society to think new thoughts about what kind of identity performances "count," has been a potent force in the socially progressive movements of the last century. Persistent uncertainty is part of the forces of change. But sometimes ambivalent

---

6   Bernard Suits, *The Grasshopper: Games, Life and Utopia* (U of Toronto P, 1978), 36–40.

7   Caillois, *Man, Play and Games*, 7.

framing leaves us uncertain about how to interpret a situation as valid. (see WITNESS)

TBD by Radix Theatre is a twenty-one day pervasive experience inspired by the *Bardo Thodol* (*Tibetan Book of the Dead*). To create space for a profoundly affecting meditation on the value of your life, the play straddles the ontological boundary of the magic circle, generating a productive blurring. The play begins with your "death" and so, from the outset, you are both dead and not. Andrew Laurenson, a member of Radix Theatre, observes that the ambiguous frame allows for the participant's entire life to feel touched by the performance. "The in-between and the during changes constantly," Laurenson says. "Performers aren't 'presenting' but rather 'framing.'"[8] For example, on day five, posters appear overnight in your neighbourhood that address you by name. The posters exhort you to "let us know where you are and how you are doing," and provide a *TBD* hotline phone number.[9] Am I missing? I didn't think so. But maybe I am? And perhaps my neighbours think so too? Given this unstable framing, what is their appropriate reaction?

And then, looking beyond the specific way that dramaturgies manipulate the magic circle, creating meaning in performances, we can see how insecurity about this kind of framing of what is real or true can have serious consquences in the political and social spheres. When people are fearful, all kinds of conspiracies thrive and experts are distrusted. Is this vaccine safe? Says who? (see Q) Our experiences with play frames—the magic circle and the performative theatre frame—can give us a context for practice and foster increased sophistication in building and preserving social frames that manifest our collective values for what "counts."[10]

See BOUNDARY VIOLATIONS and FIRST-PERSON SHOOTER

---

8   Andrew Laurenson, personal interview, 19 January 2022.

9   The Radix Collective, *TBD*, *Canadian Theatre Review* 197 (Winter 2024): 94–103.

10   For a more detailed discussion of this phenomenon and the role theatres of the real play in creating and combatting insecurity, see Jenn Stephenson, "Coda: Theatres of the Real in the Age of Post-Reality," in *Insecurity: Perils and Products of Theatres of the Real* (U of Toronto P, 2019), 226–34.

RUN THE HOPSCOTCH COURSE WITH YOUR FINGERS.

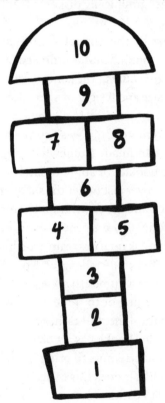

MAIL

When the COVID-19 pandemic temporarily put a pause on embodied theatre-going in 2020, participatory theatre-makers looking for other venues and other ways to connect with co-creative audiences, rediscovered mail art, using the public postal service as a conduit for that connection. Of course, unlike the synchronous co-presence of shared time and space with immediate felt impacts, theatre by mail is geographically dispersed and asynchronous. This is slow theatre.

Produced as part of the virtual 2021 PushOFF Festival (usually Vancouver), Amanda Sum's *New Age Attitudes: Live in Concert* is one such work. Subtitled "*A Lo-Fi Listen,*" the concert arrives in the mail—a brown envelope about the size and weight of a CD. (Before I opened it, I actually thought it was a CD. This seemed to me to be an obvious way to present a concert of music remotely. My, was I surprised!) Inside the envelope was not a CD but a handmade (somewhat roughly assembled) brown construction paper booklet of approximately a dozen pages. The first instruction is on the cover just under the show title: "Open at 8:00 p.m." Again, I am perplexed and my expectations confounded: 8 p.m. on what day? In what time zone? (My brain moves slowly sometimes.) It takes me a while to realize there is no livestream scheduled. The show happens whenever I begin. (That could indeed be 8 p.m. Or not.)

Participatory theatre assumes that we participate in RELATION to someone or to some thing or to some place. As we've said elsewhere, you cannot participate alone. But rather than lean into the interactive relation of myself to the booklet as art object, *New Age Attitudes* enacts a neat magic trick and attempts to bring Amanda and me into a close mutual ENCOUNTER. It does this by leaning into the dramaturgical properties of Canada Post to create a meaningful bridge when we are not both "now" and we are not both "here." (see LIVENESS)

First, as already mentioned, mail is asynchronous. Even at its quickest, the time delay between sender and receiver is substantial, extending over several days. Each person at either end of this conduit acts independently from the other. Writing and reading are never simultaneous; first one, then a delay, then the other. Notably, neither partner bears WITNESS to the moment of the other's action. Second, mail also means that our connection has no face. The receiver is not engaged by the eye contact of a gaze, nor (unless they have met before) are they privy to knowing the sender's face or body or age or gender performance, and so on. (see PHONES) And relatedly, there is no voice. The text of a letter may have a tone, or a mood, conveyed by the arrangement of words (or even the style of handwriting), but there is no sound, no aurality. Finally, mail is a tangible object. It moves across geography, travelling through the postal service from there to here. (This is what mail is.) The thing that was touched by the sender is later also touched by the receiver. It could be handcrafted—but not necessarily. Also, the object exists before I open it. There is an anticipation in arrival and then a kind of pleasure in the unwrapping or unboxing. And as a correlative, it exists afterwards. There are remains; perhaps a souvenir. (Sometimes the object acts as a gift that persists afterwards, embodying a marker of ongoing care or commitment.) (see SEEDS) It is worth noting that all of these characteristics are meaningfully heightened, first, in relation to how they do or do not align with live participatory theatre practice—for example, consider the dynamics both thrilling and awkward of looking at and being looked at by an actual person, a stranger, who is now a scene partner. And second, in relation to life under the work-from-home, remote-schooling, and online-shopping phase of the pandemic. Consider the intense focus at that time of isolation on the ordering and arrival of things that were delivered.

Back to *New Age Attitudes* and creator Amanda Sum. Before the concert proper, the booklet invites me to sign a "contract between parties" where Amanda is "Amanda" (she has already signed) and I am "audient." I add my signature beside the X, agreeing that we will "share this night, and this time and this space with each other."

The concert is composed of six "songs" interspersed with some banter and direct-address mini-essays. The "songs" are a mixture of listening instructions ("Close your eyes. Count from 1 to 60."), one-sided banter from Amanda ("Let's sit in this minute together, shall we?" "Can you hear me? I'm singing to you."), and verbal descriptions of the music ("Echoey, atmospheric synth in an F major chord. Clear and warm.") paired with the printed lyrics. Notice the scenographic markers of live performance in Amanda's illustrations: the iconic red curtain, the spotlight, even the corded microphone.[1]

---

1   In September 2022, *New Age Attitudes* was released as an actual album, written and performed by Amanda Sum. The music video for "Different Than Before" by Mayumi Yoshida was nominated for a Juno Award in 2023. At PushOFF in January 2023, a performance of *New Age Attitudes* combined our experience of reading and interacting with the booklet with an actual peformance with actual music by actual Amanda.

What emerges over the course of the concert is what I would describe as a two-part theme. One part develops a sustained meditation on being alone. Being alone is characterized as being lonely, but also as strength and a comfortable independence: "I get to be my own, / I'll do it by myself, [. . .] I can whisper when I walk / Tell the trails all my secrets / Don't gotta worry if they'll tattle or they'll keep it." This, of course, maps nicely onto my reading-and-imagining-as-listening context: "Maybe, like, how you are. In your room. Right now." This kind of solitary experience is what mail is—private, silent, intimate. Just like the forest walk Amanda describes, a letter is a place to store a secret. The reading and writing of letters are close-kept activities, not just solitary but also manifesting in a fairly small, circumscribed spatiality. In our hands. In another song, Amanda figures her solitary body as fashioned from paper: "A small house. A clean room. A dead space. A cocoon. Cut me out, it's lonely. Then take my limbs and hold me. Closer. Pick the pieces when they fall, put together, and make a human catalogue of my body. Shape me." And, of course, she is made of paper here. Amanda is only paper. Paper that we are not only reading but handling. You can see since the eighteenth century, marking the beginnings of a universal codified postal system, why letters carry certain cultural meanings, having been associated with political subversion, illicit sexual liaisons (see also Valentine's Day as a postal festival), even occult practice. And then beyond that, this kind of solitary, introspective, close-up experience is what (for many) pandemic isolation has been. (Digression: During the stay-at-home phase of pandemic, I would continually misplace my glasses. Being only for distance, I never needed them, since my whole world was never more than a few feet distant in any direction, and all my attention was directed no further than the tips of my fingers.) Amanda-as-mail puts herself into that contained circle of close proximity. As she notes on the land acknowledgement page of her concert booklet: "This was made on the unceded territories of the Musqueam, Squamish, and Tseil-Waututh Nations, also known as Vancouver, and it will be performed in your hands, wherever you may be."

For the second part of the theme, the song lyrics and Amanda's asides emphasize that we are not only alone, that we are also tethered in a meaningful way to Amanda. There is a section between songs of what Amanda terms "awkward banter." She writes, "Tell me about yourself, so that I am not the only one performing awkward banter." This INVITATION explicitly links me to Amanda: "Tell me." But also, we are connected by the suggestion that we are both doing the same thing. The next page features two prompts with three blank lines under each for us to fill in. "Your simple pleasures: (i.e., the smell of a new book, unintentional matching outfits, fresh sheets)" and "Your simple pains: (i.e., glasses fog in the fucking rain)." It is not quite an exchange but, in that stretched imagined space-time between past-Amanda and future-Jenn, there is a relational bridge.

The same song about telling my secrets to the trails as I walk concludes with, "So I'll turn to you when the timing is right / The trails are only nice in the summertime. [. . .] All I really know is / You were wearing green and I was wearing paisley." This pairing of ideas filters through the whole concert. Amanda will say, "I like being here and spending time with you" followed by a song about saying, doing, and knowing something that "nobody knows / So put it away and lock it down, lock it light, lock it low." And then the next verse: something you want, something you wish, something you wear, "nobody cares." So we get this oscillation between being alone (Which sometimes is invisibility or isolation, but sometimes is empowered autonomy. Sometimes it is both simultaneously.) and being in relation to others, specifically Amanda.

What fascinates me is that this doubled theme made manifest in the content/experience of *New Age Attitudes* is repeated in the formal dramaturgical characteristics of mail. The writing and reading of mail is an autonomous creation; the player-performer is perhaps not always literally alone (but could be), but is alone insofar as they are entirely both audience and performer, separated from the artist-procedural author. Mail, by definition, is transmissible across time and space. And yet, the asynchronous and distanced enactment of this performance by mail is not entirely autonomous. The instructions of the event score itself constitute a bridge back to the author, activating a bilateral relationality. Amanda speaks to me via the concert booklet. My performance responds to Amanda. We cannot see or hear each other. Alone and yet together. It is a kind of relational interaction, running once in each direction, but it does not loop. Amanda is aware of me somewhere in her future. I am aware of Amanda somewhere in my past. We might coincidentally occupy synchronous time, but we can't know that. And the performance does not expect it.

Beyond this, Amanda recognizes the possibility that I didn't even play the game. Maybe I OPTED OUT of this performance RECIPE. But mostly she is hopeful. "Maybe you flipped through this in a couple of minutes, or maybe you accepted the invite to indulge in time together." She points to the tangible form of the booklet itself as something that might persist beyond the performance moment. She seems to suggest that, even dormant, "even after time is exhausted and retires for the night," the mail-performance carries our shared experience, holding memory but also a series of potentialities for other alternate and ongoing exchanges. "Maybe we do eat, we do drink, we do entertain, or maybe we simply listen. Because as much as you are my audient, or audience (or what have you), I am yours."[2]

DEAR READER,

I HOPE THIS FINDS YOU WELL. I'VE HAD TO RUSH OUT TO CATCH A PERFORMANCE AND DIDN'T HAVE TIME TO DO THE GARDENING— WOULD YOU MIND PITCHING IN? PLEASE COMPLETE THE FOLLOWING:

1. HARVEST THE RADISHES AND PUT THEM IN THE RADISH BINS
2. PICK THE LAST APPLE AND PUT IT IN THE BASKET
3. COMPOST THE REST OF THE FOOD WASTE

BE SURE TO CUT OUT THE IMAGE BEFORE FOLDING, AND FOLD DIRECTLY ON THE DASHED LINES.

THERE MIGHT BE AN ANSWER IN IT FOR YOU...

BEST,
—M.S.

---

2   Another example of participatory performance by mail is *The Dead Letter Office* curated by Popcorn Galaxies (June Fukumura and Keely O'Brien). Participants are invited to write the letter that you never sent—a secret unrequited-love letter or a suppressed angry screed. Write it and send it in to Popcorn Galaxies. They will forward the letters to other audience-writers. If you write a letter, you receive a letter. As one audience-writer reports, "It's like finding a hole in a tree and telling your secrets into it. And then you also get to be the tree and receive somebody's secrets."

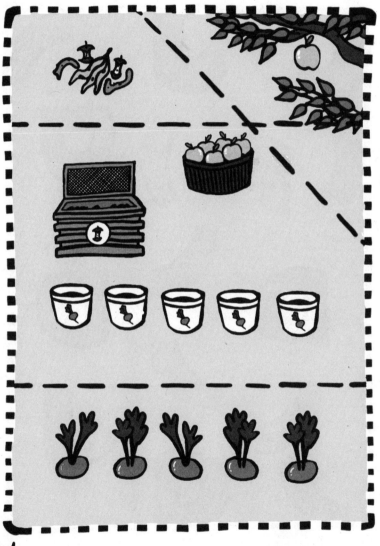

ANSWER:

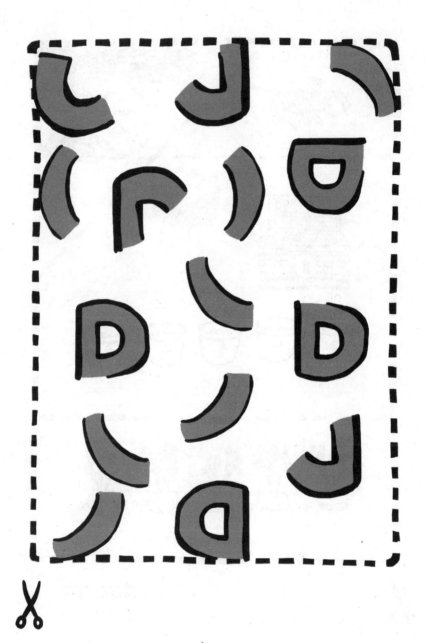

MEEPLES

In *How Games Move Us*, Katherine Isbister observes that customization of your video game character increases identification and connection.[1] In many games, I am invited to select not only the surface appearance of my avatar, but also capabilities, values, social traits, favourite items, and even a lifetime wish.[2] These avatars are what Isbister calls "inhabitable protagonists." Through actions and experience, as well as observation, players "project themselves into the character on four levels: visceral, cognitive, social and fantasy."[3] Part of my emotional attachment to my avatar lies simply in the ability to make these choices, another part lies in the narcisstic pleasure of making the avatar as like me as possible. Denis Diderot in his treatise on playwriting "Conversations on *The Natural Son*" (1757) makes a similar point when he argues that characters should be shaped by their social station, and that their social station should align with that of the audience for maximum impact. He writes, "A character need only be slightly exaggerated for the spectator to be able to say to himself, 'I'm not like that.' But he cannot deceive himself in this way when it is his social function that is being portrayed before him; he cannot fail to recognize his duties. He is compelled to apply what he hears to himself."[4]

For both Isbister and Diderot, the thinking is that a similarity of association across worlds creates a kind of empathetic bridge of relatability. However, in the context of mimetic BOURGEOIS THEATRE, the connection between audience and character is distanced across the theatrical frame. An audience member seated in the actual world

---

1   Katherine Isbister, *How Games Move Us: Emotion by Design* (MIT P, 2017), 32. See also Katherine Isbister, *Better Game Characters By Design: A Psychological Approach* (Taylor and Francis, 2006). On the other hand, as Isbister notes, quoting Scott McCloud (*Understanding Comics*), "A more abstract and stylized rendition of a character allows viewers to project more of themselves onto the characters, without getting distracted by specific personal qualities and mannerisms" (*How Games Move Us*, 36). Perhaps we might understand this as a version of the phenomenon of the uncanny valley. Avatars with definite personal similarities are appealing but a too close, too detailed simulacrum becomes cringy and off-putting.

2   Isbister, *How Games Move Us*, 33.

3   Isbister, *How Games Move Us*, 11.

4   Denis Diderot, "Conversations on *The Natural Son*" (1757), in *Theatre/Theory/Theatre: The Major Critical Texts from Aristotle and Zeami to Soyinka and Havel*, edited by Daniel Gerould (Applause, 2000), 196.

perceives a reflexive alignment with the actions and emotions of a character in the fictional world, an alignment that is parallel but separate. Audience belief activates the fiction in perception, but we remain bodily actual. (see ONTOLOGICAL DUALITY) The fiction is "over there." The audience does not enter into the fiction; we are not characters. There are two worlds and they do not cross or combine. By contrast, when we become "players," then we do enter into the MAGIC CIRCLE. In a game situation, the avatar living their best life in the game world is not just like me, it *is* me. "I" am able to exist in two worlds, embodied as a representation of self in the fictional world.

Another of Roger Caillois's (*Man, Play and Games*) four categories of play (along with ALEA, agôn, and ILINX) is mimicry.[5] Theatrical representation is an expression of pure mimicry. Mimicry arises as a style of play in games like children's pretend make-believe. But even games without an explicit dramatic frame express that same "as if" as a metaphor. Chess is "as if" war. (So are most sports. "Deeeeeefense!"[6]) *Settlers of Catan* is "as if" colonization. The board is a kind of fictional LAND in miniature and the tokens represent the players' cities, settlements, roads, and so on. Representational meeples—me as a game token—allow me to cross over and become embodied as a character in the fiction, while my audience body remains in the actual world.[7] The game metaphors create a "split" case where players are divided into two spaces with a bridged identity, being both in and out. In the actual world, I hold the cards. I roll the dice. And I plan strategy. As a meeple, alternate me runs around the board and buys properties or solves

5   Roger Caillois, *Man, Play and Games*, translated by Meyer Barash (U of Illinois P, 1961),19–22.

6   In basketball, for example, the other team is the enemy. The game alternates between castle siege and defence. The ball is precious. Putting it in the opposite basket is an attack. Defend the breach of your own territory. Raptors do war with Warriors, Wizards, Hornets, and so on. It is "underdeveloped" as a fictional world, but it is still a world apart with a certain value system that shapes victory or defeat, shaped by the rules.

7   Note that this is similar but meaningfully different to how an actor experiences these two worlds. Actors in a drama exist in both the actual world and in the fictional world with one body—so they do not make use of meeples. More importantly, they do not participate in the fictional world as representatives of themselves. They play assigned roles, but they are not "personally" invested in the character's actions. The character is not an extension of themselves. In addition, their training and their understanding that this is a job (ideally) buffers them from too closely associating with the character. The character is a role, but it is not a version of themselves (usually). (Obviously this is complicated for autobiographical performance, and also for acting methods that rely directly on foundations of personal experience.)

murders. I build cities and I wage war. I am "red." (Always red.) I am the shoe. Even the line at the tip of pencil in a paper maze puzzle is me.

Immersive theatre turns us into life-size meeples. I am my own avatar. And now I am in the fiction and the role is inside my own body. But who am I now? This is a critical question: not just "who is the audience?" but "how does it make sense that I am here?" Sophie Nield, in her article "The Rise of the Character Named Spectator," recognizes that this is a tricky and fragile moment. In our audience role, we don't belong here, and we are embarrassed to make eye contact with characters across worlds. We are in the actor's nightmare, compelled to perform a role that we have not rehearsed. She continues, "Perhaps the tension and the melancholy of it comes from the fact that we all know that if one of us tells [the actor] to fuck off, we break some kind of spell, and the whole experience suffers. So, we feel the thinness of his performance, not the thinness of our civility."[8] Becoming a meeple acts as a kind of costume or ontological overlay that helps me to fit in (or at least provides a plausible cover and prevents rudeness).

Even in works where the fiction is very thin (I'm thinking of postdramatic works that stage events or actions rather than give birth to developed dramatic worlds.), there is still a distinction of my role from the actual world. In this case, I am mostly myself but a plus plus version of myself—braver, nicer, more candid—according to the INVITATION offered by the work. There are always two of me (or at least one divided in two). I cannot be merely singular: that would be neither performance nor a game, that would just be life—just me dancing, skating, or going for a run. Fun to do, for sure, but not performance. Even in a postdramatic work like *b side*, where my role involves strolling down an urban alleyway, tasked with mindfully placing three lemons along the route, I am still Jenn but now I have a mission with a secondary identity. I am "Jenn, placer of lemons." The lemons take on an "as if," as important as putting a basketball in the net. Meaning is heightened well beyond the actual mechanics of the act.

Isbister writes, "A reader or filmgoer [or playgoer] may feel many emotions when presented with horrific fictional acts on the page or screen, but responsibility and guilt are generally not among them. At most, they may feel a sense of uneasy collusion. Conversely, a film viewer might feel joyful when the protagonist wins, but is not likely to feel a sense of personal responsibility and pride."[9] Sometimes this duality between me and my meeple causes fruitful tension. When we are in alignment,

8   Sophie Nield, "The Rise of the Character Named Spectator," *Contemporary Theatre Review* 18, no. 4 (2008): 534.
9   Isbister, *How Games Move Us*, 8–9.

the emotions generated by this connection between inside "me" and outside "me" can cross over and I am gratified by our joint accomplishments. Good game play or good performance can be matched by fictional successes—like having more money or land. (see WINNING) I feel for the character, but I can also feel the feelings of the character. When we are not in alignment, I can experience guilt for actions undertaken by my meeple that are unethical, at odds with real-world personal values. Inside-me and outside-me can have different priorities, incentives, goals. (see COMPLICITY, FUTILITY, and FASCISM)

Ultimately, the audience's representational role is directly aligned with the play's understanding. What kind of meeple am I? What are my powers? Our capacity to act in a meaningful way (or not) informs what participation means in this particular world/work. Are we GHOSTS who can see but not act? Is our role to observe and attest as WITNESSES? Are we gods or the embodiment of fate who can have effects, but are ontologically aloof from the consequences of our decisions? Or are we actually characters empowered to influence our world? And if we are empowered to act, what consequence do we bear? What is the scope of our AGENCY? Can we change the ending? (see GAME OVER. PLAY AGAIN?) When participation is always about participation, how the audience-player is cast provides critical clues about what the performance-game is saying about the political and ethical implications of participation.

See FIRST-PERSON SHOOTER and REMOTE CONTROL

DRAW YOURSELF IN CARTOON VERSION HERE.

MINDFULNESS

Sitting or standing perfectly still, attentive yet relaxed. My eyes are resting closed. Outwardly there is silence. Inside, the voice in my head (in my earbuds) is suggesting that this is "something we do together." With no motion and no noise, on the surface of it, this doesn't look much like participation. What is it that we might do together? What is the nature of my participation? Then, the invitation: "I wonder if you could take some time (however long you want) and go on a bit of a journey together. Some might call it a questionnaire. Others, a story. Maybe it's a thought experiment or a chance to let your imagination take you somewhere you need or want to go. Can I have your attention? (I promise I'll give it back afterwards.) There's a lot going on *out there* in the world and there's also a lot going on *in there*, you know, in the feelings . . . " Written by Susanna Fournier and voiced by Kristen Thomson, *What Happens to You, Happens to Me*[1] is a participatory, asynchronous audio experience where my work as audience-participant is to imagine, to engage my thoughts in response to the prompts in this ostensibly one-sided conversation. What I'm doing here is different from INTERPRETATION, although it is that too. I'm actively making meaning from this story-artwork. How I answer the questionnaire (see MAD LIBS) and the private images that I paint are entirely unique to me, each choice determining the shape, colour, and texture of my experience. And although it is arguably not AUTOPOIETIC—there is no feedback loop that changes the instigating text—my choices shape the meaning. I have agency over my own mental constructions and as a result I am a fully collaborative co-author.[2] (see PHONY MULTIPLICITY)

Being asked questions necessarily interpellates me as an "answerer." I am brought into dialogue and am hailed as an ontological equal; we are in the same world and have the same status of being. Addressed as

---

1   Produced by Canadian Stage in July 2020 and directed by ted witzel, *What Happens to You, Happens to Me* confronted our collective grief in pandemic isolation, inviting thoughtfulness about our innate need for connections with others.

2   It is Allan Kaprow who writes, "A Happening may be scored for *just watching*. Persons will do nothing else. They will watch things, possibly each other, possibly actions not performed by themselves, such as a bus stopping to pick up commuters. This would not take place in a theater or arena, but anywhere else. It could be an extremely meditative occupation when done devotedly; just 'cute' when done indifferently" (*Assemblage, Environments & Happenings* (Harry N. Abrams, 1966), 197).

"you" by the other, who is "I," we enter into RELATION. Who the other persona is and how we have connected remains uncertain, but somehow we meet. As the other asserts, "This isn't a podcast." It is collaborative; they wonder, maybe this is a voice memo, or the cinematic voiceover of a letter read out loud, "Maybe I'm the wind."

Instead of an ENCOUNTER with another person, *Biidaaban*, created by Lisa Cooke Ravensbergen with audio collaborator Mishelle Cuttler, fosters an introspective connection to the land (wherever you may be). With the eight-minute-thirty-second audio track cued up, we are instructed that "this performance-CEREMONY is to be done at dawn. Please find a safe place to be by yourself outside, ideally on the land. As close to water as you can be."[3] The title *Biidaaban*, meaning dawn or the first light of day in Anishinaabemowin, is paired with the subtitle *"A Sonic Call to the Future."* The soundscape itself is an entrancing flow of low rumbling submerged deep water sounds, whale calls, heartbeats, the beat of waves shifting to running water in a stream. There are also voices, whispering and singing, sometimes solo sometimes in concert with another. Many of the words I don't recognize or can't quite hear. One word that I do discern is *"biskaabiiyang." Biskaabiiyang* refers to "a decolonizing theory based in Anishinabek thought [that] fights colonial erasure. *Biskaabiiyang* is a returning to one's self, a verb meaning to look back and to reinterpret Anishinabek teachings in our contemporary context in ways that 'bring meaning to our practices and illuminate our lifeways' today."[4] Despite how introspective and outwardly static my participation is, I comprehend *Biidaaban* as a call to action, and the first action is to make myself present at dawn, on the LAND, and to listen. A third example of guided meditation as a framework for participatory theatre is *The Candlemaker's Game*, which invites us to

---

3   For Jenn this meant a fifteen-minute trek to the edge of Lake Ontario, in February, looking across the nearly, but not entirely, frozen water, to the giant windmills of Wolfe Island, the Tett Centre arts complex at my back. I walked six blocks from my house in the Skeleton Park neighbourhood to the frozen marsh at Doug Fluhrer Park. In my cumbersome winter jacket, I sat on a rock on the shore with my feet dangling close to the snow-covered water. Under the audio track through my headphones, I could hear the sound of cars driving over the LaSalle Causeway. Because each car brings a different pitch and timbre, it reminded me of whales, crying to each other under water from afar. I tried to sit still, contemplative and quiet, but the harsh February air froze my bones if I didn't keep moving. Instead, I paced along the crunchy shoreline, listening.

4   Damien Lee, "Re-Envisioning Reconciliation," *Briarpatch*, 1 January 2012, briarpatchmagazine.com/articles/view/re-envisioning-reconciliation.

"Enter. Cast. Breathe. Navigate. Escape."[5] First presented as part of a festival of verbatim theatre, the performance deviates from the usual verbatim formula for personal testimony that is collected, edited, and revoiced. Instead, the testimony here is yours and, in lieu of being passed on to the ventriloquism of a verbatim actor, it is whispered by you to yourself. Billed as a blend of "conflict management, divination, and tabletop gaming,"[6] *The Candlemaker's Game* uses a tarot-like deck of question cards that prompt you to recall and reflect on a conflict from your actual life-history. Each person's experience is entirely private. (see TOGETHER ALONE)

When you arrive before entering the performance space, you are asked to choose from your own life an interpersonal conflict to consider. You've been warned about this in advance and are advised not to choose something too painful or fresh. After you've chosen the conflict, you are given an apron and then guided to a cauldron of molten wax to create a wax figure and a six-sided die. Because the figures are molded at the beginning of each experience, they stay warm and soft in your hands while you play. Next, you are guided into a dimly-lit, warm makerspace. In an interview with creator Richard Lam, he described this space as a "very reverent space with a lot of spiritual power."[7] In the centre of the room is a workspace for an experienced craftsperson—The Candlemaker, pouring and manipulating hot wax in silence. The Candlemaker is encircled by nine stations for the audience-players, spread out with plenty of room in between. At each station there is a notebook, a deck of cards, and a candle. These cards, divided into suits, correspond with questions in the notebook that prompt players to reflect on the conflict they have chosen. The prompts start with subjective prompts about the players in the conflict. "What is their name?" "What is your relationship to them?" As participants progress, the questions become more nuanced. "What might have been going on with the other person that had nothing to do with you? Did you do something in this conflict that had a different effect than you intended? Do they think they carry any harm today?"[8] The first suit prepares you to describe facts about the conflict, the second focuses on process, the third suit is for feeling, and the fourth suit probes

5   "Proximity Lab Presents: *The Candlemaker's Game*," *Happening Next*, March 2022, happeningnext.com/event/proximity-lab-presents-the-candlemakers-game -eid4snvɪrndjpɪ.

6   "Proximity Lab Presents: *The Candlemaker's Game*."

7   Richard Lam, personal interview, 30 June 2022.

8   "*The Candlemaker's Game* Guidebook," email correspondence, 18 May 2023.

into the future. Like *Biidaaban*, the final card is a call to action: Do you want to reach out to this person or not?

All three participatory meditations place value on the power of story. Meditation becomes a kind of playwriting, an act of self-transformation. Richard Lam says his acting skills in navigating desires and action were entirely transferable to conflict management strategies within transformative justice frameworks. I understand *biskaabiiyang* to be about putting stories and traditional teachings into action. Fournier's narrator asserts: "You can't really escape story. / You make stories, you reject them, you run away from them, you run right back into them. A storyteller I know recently said, 'When we know what story we're in, we know what kind of ending we can hope for.' / Another storyteller I know (and I know quite a few) said, 'Everyone alive right now has the potential to create a story we haven't seen before.' / And then another storyteller I know said, 'Stories repeat until they get the ending they want.' / But what do you think? / I mean, what kind of story are we in? / Is it new? Is it repeating itself?"

MOB

Rachel Fensham, in her article "Postdramatic Spectatorship: Participate or Else," describes characteristics of the postdramatic SPECTATOR.[1] Having coined the term postdramatic theatre to describe a certain kind of performance avant-garde prevalent in late-twentieth century Europe, Hans-Thies Lehmann's conception of postdrama is more of a collation of associated dramaturgical practices than a singular prescriptive genre model. One of the principal features of postdrama that can be distilled from his observations is that works in this mode fail to manifest a separate fictional world. Performance happens, and actions carry aesthetic meaning, but it happens in the same world that the audience also inhabits. There is no MAGIC CIRCLE. (see BOUNDARY VIOLATIONS) Fensham, then, proposes that because of this altered dramatic ontology, a new kind of spectator comes into being. (Fensham's article title notwithstanding, I would argue that not all postdramatic works are necessarily participatory, but once you erase the frame that divides the realm of the characters from the realm of the audience, participation is that much easier. Since we are all now in the same time and space, we can make contact.)

Fensham lists four characteristics of what she dubs "an 'ideal' spectator [emerging] in the postdramatic paradigm": one, the spectator is "an actor, who is co-present in the situation of events taking place around them" (see ACTING and THE MATRIX); two, "a sensory being whose immediate experience produces self-reflection, and heightened awareness" (see OSTRANENIE, HANDS, and SWEATING); three, "an initiate who follows the simultaneity of multiple activities and the shared space of a ritualized staging" (see RITUAL and INTIMACY); and four, "a molecular body in the collective contagion of the audience." (In our post-COVID world, I find this last one particularly provocative.)

Let us consider this last characteristic. What meanings emerge from the dramaturgy of the audience when we are cast as a collective? As a contagion? The constrained, sitting silently in the dark audience of BOURGEOIS THEATRE is a collective. With large purpose-built theatre venues (many, many rows of good looking, but not so comfortable chairs),

---

1   Rachel Fensham, "Postdramatic Spectatorship: Participate or Else," *Critical Stages* 7 (December 2012): critical-stages.org/7/postdramatic-spectatorship-participate -or-else/.

this type of theatre expects attendance en masse. But how are we a mass? How do we relate to one another? Well, mostly we don't. The mix of geography and Victorian-era behaviour conventions means that our interactions are restricted. Each audience member engages in parallel with the performance (see INTERPRETATION) but not peer to peer. (In fact, when we do become aware of our peers in the house—ringing cellphones, coming in late, whispering loudly, or Heaven forfend, coughing—we are upset, since they are disrupting my perfect communion with the stage.) We do laugh or gasp, and we applaud (when appropriate); we are together, yes, but not fully in community.

Just as postdramatic theatre is not always participatory theatre, I would say that participatory theatre does not always activate a meaningful experience of collectivity. (Sometimes but not always. Lots of participatory dramaturgies are solos.) Nevertheless, once you turn up the lights and INVITE audience-players to move and make sounds, they become features of the performance event.[2] As I can see them, they become mise en scène. Then, as they do stuff, they become actors that I watch. I audience them and they audience me.

That said, if we are forced into proximity, then we need to NEGOTIATE. *A Grimm Night* (Transcen|Dance), which features danced fairytales for a masked, mobile audience, works this way. So does *Café Sarajevo* (bluemouth inc.), where I (politely) jostle for a good viewing spot, mindful of my ELBOWS. The core dramaturgy here is to manage (even optimize) my own audience experience while not being an asshole. (It is probably not a coincidence that *Café Sarajevo* is about civil war in a very small country.) Participatory choirs like *Choir! Choir! Choir!* and *Why We Are Here!* as well as other mass vocal experiences like choral speaking in *This is the Story of the Child Ruled by Fear* and solstice screaming (exactly what it says it is by Radix Theatre) activate the negotiation of proximity through sound only, as we blend our voices to create something more. It is a very different experience singing, speaking, or screaming by yourself. The collectivity of these activities is meaningful. Being camouflaged by the group lessens my self-consciousness and empowers me to make noises and behave in ways that I would never if

---

2   It behooves us to ask, "Who is powerful in participatory audiences?" Who exactly are the ones who step forward to accept the invitation? There is a hard-to-shake tendency to think of audience participation as homogenous, but of course it is not, just as audiences are not. The power that spawns participatory boldness lies in all kinds of social capital, which is not equitably distributed, rooted in specialized insider knowledge, physical ability, youth, normative gender performance, masculinity, and so on.

alone. The erosion of social boundaries caused by my membership in a group is liberating. (Perhaps too much so.) This is the power of the CROWD, of the mob,[3] of the herd.[4]

It is 10 p.m. I have already been in the theatre for six hours and we are nowhere near done yet. The studio space is noisy. Some audience-participants are sprawled on the floor, others are taking up two or three chairs with their feet up and their shoes off. There are half-eaten fruit trays and a plate of cookie crumbs. I have an unfinished beer at my feet. The audience is chanting "ORB! ORB! ORB! ORB!" in solidarity with our PROXY player Derek, who was navigating a difficult level in this live, group video-game-performance. Appearing on the big screen as a donkey avatar, Derek needed to float his "ass" around four cosmic puzzles that involved matching coloured orbs. He was patient, but he seemed to be at a bit of a loss on the right answer to the puzzle. The right answer didn't seem to matter much though; silly hour had begun. The vibe in the room reminded me of a kids' sleepover, when the adrenaline of staying up late with your friends slowly dissolves polite behaviour into loopy chaos. (see ILINX) This is not how *asses.masses* started hours earlier.

Created by Patrick Blenkarn and Milton Lim, *asses.masses* is an epic tale featuring a herd of unemployed donkeys who are seeking a better future. Structured in ten episodes, the story unfolds through a video game where audience-players take turns with the PlayStation controller to make choices and complete various tasks. Each player assumes the role of the episode's protagonist, a rotating cast of donkey avatars with sassy names like Trusty Ass, Kick Ass, and Bad Ass. Those of us who are not holding the controller, who are not the asses, we are the masses. (see POLITICS OF THE BASEMENT)

---

3   In the immersive simulation *Counting Sheep* (see SHEEP) we are literally a mob engaged in anti-government protest. That is our character role. As such, there is some collaborative behaviour, passing benches and tires along the line, hand to hand, to form the barricade. We all do the same thing—we all throw bricks; we all dance. We are a gestural choir. We are doing the same things together, but not "to" or "with" each other.

4   In his consideration of the TYRANNY of participation in the context of global development studies, Bill Cooke ("The Social Psychological Limits of Participation") catalogues all the ways that participatory groups are actually terrible decision makers. Among the pitfalls groups are prone to encounter are: making excessively risky choices; the Abilene Paradox in which we make a choice that no one wants because we falsely believe that it will make others happy; group think; and coercive persuasion. He writes, "Unless well-documented limitations of participation are acknowledged, it will continue to contain within it the seeds of its own destruction, and, worse, harm those it would claim to help" (in *Participation: The New Tyranny?*, edited by Bill Cooke and Uma Kothari (Zed, 2001), 102).

What fascinates me about *asses.masses* with regard to the audience role as herd is that we are given no instructions whatsoever. And yet, the time that I participated over the course of the seven-and-a-half-hour performance-game, a kind of community developed. During an early episode, a lonely bag of chips wandered up and down the rows. It didn't seem to matter who it belonged to and people helped themselves before passing it on. We also decided that it was fun to chant, "Ass Power!" So we did. We created our own mini-games. Prior to the start of the last episode, one audience member announced that they were taking bets as to when the show would end. Many people contributed guesses. (My guess of 11:37 p.m. was the winner!) These are just some of the kinds of spontaneous collective behaviours that emerged out of the durational collapsing formality of audience etiquette.

This herd mentality playing out in the interstices of the show also fed into the show itself, enabling our successes. One of the game-puzzles was a complex version of a memory tile-matching game. The audience quickly and collectively developed a strategy whereby different people memorized different pairs and then shouted them out to the solo player who clicked on them. This happened with almost no coordinating discussion. Near the end, we got a bit stuck and couldn't figure out how to turn the assembled donkeys into a chorus. Somehow, we got the wacky idea that we should all sing (or bray). So we did. (It was spectacularly foolish—and also not the right answer.) The solution in the end required enough fingers from four players to all press the buttons of the controller simultaneously and make all the donkeys glow. And then, as exhausted and punchy as we were, when tasked with drafting a manifesto of the asses' final demands, our group of about twenty-five people undertook a serious discussion about decolonization, labour rights, equity of opportunity, fair compensation for work, the right to leisure, self-determination, and resource sustainability. There was no rush and we cared to take the time to hear everyone's point of view and to get it right. As Katherine Isbister writes in *How Games Move Us*, "The game worlds they create may be imaginary, but the social dynamics are not."[5] This might all be about digital asses, but our herd is real.

As Deborah Pollard writes, the time-based dramaturgy of long durational works generates an experience that is "sprawling, unruly, and avoids tidy conclusions. It is visceral, visual, and physical. And it is political in the challenges it poses to the ethical potential of the perceptions it invites and the traditions it strategically seeks to interrupt."[6] In the same

---

5   Katherine Isbister, *How Games Move Us: Emotion by Design* (MIT P, 2017), 53.
6   Deborah Pollard, "Entanglements with Time: Staging Duration and Repetition in the Theatre," *Australasian Drama Studies* 76 (April 2020): 338.

article, she quotes Tim Etchells (Forced Entertainment) who asserts that "engaging with the timeframe knocks you into a different kind of relationship to the world."[7] It is interesting to note that in the durational works that Pollard and Etchells are creating and writing about, as with other recent Canadian examples that I can think of—Lilith & C[ie]'s seventy-two-hour dance performance *Invisible* (see NEGOTIATION) or *The Godot Cycle* performed in the Honest Ed's parking garage[8] over fifty-four hours—it is the actors who are running this marathon. This is not to say that audiences to "marathon theatre"[9] are not deeply affected, we are. But we get to sit down, close our eyes, even leave and come back again. The show *asses.masses* affords us a very rare opportunity to push ourselves as audience-players through an extended effort.

Describing the audience experience of the Toronto *Godot Cycle*, Lawrence Switzky writes, "The unusual duration of the piece allowed them to tear down and then rebuild collective feelings."[10] Our lived experience of duration has the power to create and to destroy. (Duration in this way is fundamentally abolitionist. My Ph.D. research is specifically interested in theatre's dramaturgical capacities for creation and destruction. If a herd can start a revolution, can they also abolish the prison-industrial complex?) In the case of *asses.masses*, it took time (much more time than a play is normally allotted) for the audience to remake itself, to become a herd. Time seems to be a critical ingredient for the development of an affective community relationship among audience-participants. I cannot begin to imagine what we would have been like after seventy-two hours, let alone another eight. Close to midnight, after an elegant and moving epilogue bonus episode, we stumbled out of the theatre and into the parking lot, to haul our asses off to bed.[11]

---

7   Pollard, "Staging Duration and Repetition," 337.
8   Presented in July 2011 at the Toronto Fringe Festival, Samuel Beckett's play *Waiting for Godot* was performed twenty-three times in a continuous loop by Eric Craig (Vladimir) and David Christo (Estragon). Guest actors took turns playing Lucky, Pozzo, and The Boy. David Yee, who wrote about the show for *Canadian Theatre Review*, calls it "the most honest fucking thing I've seen in a very long time" ("I Feel Like We've Been Here Before: A Review of *The Godot Cycle*," *Canadian Theatre Review* 152 (Fall 2012): 69).
9   Marathon theatre is defined by Jonathan Kalb as a performance longer than four hours. *Great Lengths: Seven Works of Marathon Theater* (U of Michigan P, 2011), 18–22.
10   Lawrence Switzky, "Marathon Theatre as Affective Labour: Productive Exhaustion in *The Godot Cycle* and *Life and Times*," *Canadian Theatre Review* 162 (Spring 2015): 26–30.
11   Jenn Stephenson and Derek Manderson, "Herd Dramaturgies: Participatory Audience as Proto-Society in *asses.masses*," *Theater* 55, no. 3 (forthcoming October 2024).

GAME ON! USE THE CLUES BELOW TO DETERMINE WHICH ASSES.MASSES PLAYER ATE THE LAST OF THE COMMUNAL POTATO CHIPS. ONCE YOU HAVE DISCOVERED THIS, THE ANSWER WILL BE THE FIRST LETTER OF THEIR NAME.

CLUES: THIS PLAYER IS NOT WEARING HAIRCLIPS.

THIS PLAYER IS NOT WEARING A TOQUE.

THIS PLAYER IS WEARING DARK PANTS.

THIS PLAYER DOES NOT HAVE FRECKLES.

THIS PLAYER IS SITTING NEXT TO SOMEONE IN A COLLARED SHIRT.

THIS PLAYER IS WEARING STRIPES.

THIS PLAYER IS WEARING A PIECE OF JEWELLERY.

WHO IS IT?

ANSWER:

NEGOTIATION

Picture this. Four friends, a little drunk on Kingston's Howe Island, sanitizing HANDS and tossing copies of new Canadian scripts over a bonfire. We haven't seen each other in nearly six months due to social isolation measures to prevent the spread of COVID-19. As we sit around our campfire, we try to settle on casting for our cold read. Three of us are artists and the fourth, a soft-spoken cattle farmer, was feeling a little hesitant. "Tim should play the character Bb because the script says it should be the 'kindest, gentlest person' among us." Tim's not sure but he agrees, to appease us. Tracey and Laura take up the two characters with the most lines, and I decide to listen because there are only three characters. "Should we start now?" "Wait, how do you think I should read this character?" "Should I sit next to you or across from you?" "Should someone read the stage directions?" "Are we ready? Let's start."

These new Canadian scripts are a part of *Plays2Perform@Home*, created by Vancouver-based Boca del Lupo as a response to the social distancing recommendations that followed the onset of the pandemic. Sold as a "boutique box set" of scripts, each collection of P2P@H features four new works by Canadian playwrights, divided into separate booklets by character, and mailed directly to your home. (see ACTING) The creators ask the audience to become actors and to speak the roles. The ensemble consists of your close friends and family, whoever was in your "bubble" at the time. With the forced "intermission" from live performance due to the pandemic, this box set is exciting for theatre people and more than minimally tolerable for their bubble-mates who have been dragged into the exercise.[1] In P2P@H, there is no director or instigating artist present to guide us. The work has been freed from the usual team of director, producer, designers, actors, stage managers, and CREW to be staged autonomously by the audience-participants. We need to decide as a group if, and when, and where, and how we are going to make theatre happen.

Part of the west coast bundle of P2P@H, Hiro Kanagawa's play, (actually called) *Negotiations* (See what we did there?) asks participants to

---

[1]   Some of the P2P@H make intentional space for these reluctant actors. In Tara Beagan's *Super* in the west coast set of plays, a character description reads, "Symm is a powerful presence because of their silence. This might be the person who least wants to read" (*Super*, in *Plays2Perform@Home* (Boca del Lupo, 2021), 1).

replicate in a series of formal mediations the realities of the pandemic. Playing characters that may or may not be ourselves, we have to figure out whether or not we will take our masks off. Yes or no? To get a bit closer? Shall we? And eventually to (maybe?) touch. Ideally, the readers perform these negotiations live as themselves but, as Kanagawa acknowledges, "It is also possible, especially if there is an audience, that the stage directions are read out loud and then performed. Or you might choose to just read the stage directions out loud and not perform them at all. In that sense, the reading of the play is itself a negotiation, not only between the two actors reading it, but between the actors and the playwright."[2] This play invites readers to fully put the script down and *actually* negotiate these boundaries as co-creative participants.

Where *Negotiations* allows us to practice negotiations in our bubbles, Lilith & Cie's *Invisible* asks participants to negotiate with a larger community of strangers on a larger scale. Through participation and response, the aim of *Invisible* is to "make the intelligence of the collective visible." In July 2022 at OFFTA[3] in Montréal, participants were invited to share a studio theatre for three days with ten dancers and a dog. Over a full seventy-two hours, we could come and go as we pleased. During the performance, we were invited to participate in tasks like opening studio windows, operating the lights, reconfiguring the carpets and furniture in the space. We were instructed to play music through overhead speakers by plugging into aux cords hanging from the ceiling. The participants negotiated with each other, subtly sharing the cords and taking turns while the dancers improvised to our inputs.

We met a GUIDE at the beginning of the experience, but we were not led with a heavy hand during the performance and the sandbox was relatively open.[4] (see PLAYGROUNDS) Instead, participants had to rely on each other in the room, moving slowly and sharing the floor, without a script to tell us what was next. When I entered the room for the first time, I opened the door to the performance space as five dancers moved to ambient tones while audience members cozied up on chairs around the perimeter. I was way too nervous to play music during this

---

2   Hiro Kanagawa, *Negotiations*, in *Plays2Perform@Home* (Boca del Lupo, 2021), 1.
3   OFFTA is an annual festival on the fringes of Festival TransAmérique. The festival work tends to be Canadian (but not exclusively) and often experimental.
4   When we're learning the rules, a guide invites us to play a tabletop game that mirrors the geography of the performance space. With a deck of cards, he offers suggestions for participation. "Silence is a possibility." "Do nothing, receive." "Now might be a good time to play your music." "Lay down in the centre of the space." "Go look out the window." "Read a performer's notebook." All of the tasks have an effect both on the dancers and also the other folks in the room.

first visit. I wanted to learn how to play from the way the other players were playing. A woman played some 70s Joe Cocker, then someone else followed it up with Elvis Presley's "Can't Help Falling in Love with You." A third person played the audio of the famous "Wiiiiiilson!" scene from the movie *Castaway* through the overhead speakers. Someone else played a funky French song and we all bopped our heads.

As *Invisible*'s dancers continued their sustained exploration of collective intelligence, I left the theatre and walked fifteen thousand steps through Montréal, thinking about what song I'd play. I felt an immense pressure to honour the aux cord and play something the room would enjoy! When I returned to the theatre at 2 a.m., the dog was sleeping deeply on a pillow and the dancers were vibrating in the centre of the room. There was a couple, making out, that dominated the cord with the heavy beats of intense EDM. Creator Aurélie Pedron then hit a gong to play Lee Perry's "Having a Party," completely changing the vibe. On the last morning, having run through many scenarios in my head, I sat near an aux cord as a dancer approached. "Have you played music yet? It's fun, you'll like it." I worked up the courage and played "Bad Girls" by Donna Summer. My neighbours started swaying and I was satisfied with my relational contribution. I honoured the aux cord. One of the dancers offered me some chocolate. A reward.

Jill Dolan says, "Utopian performatives, in their doings, make palpable an affective vision of how the world might be better."[5] *Invisible* makes the world better through relation, observation, negotiation, collaboration, and intimacy. (see ELBOWS) *Invisible* insists that we can reveal the collective intelligence by being patient, being here and now together, negotiating our actions in a collective. In the case of *Invisible*, we are afforded time to craft those negotiations. In a similar way that EMERGENCE needs scale to perform many, many iterations and achieve phase change, the collective needs time. Time is the collective's embrace, not physical touch.

In *Invisible*, there is no plot and there are no characters beyond the participants and the dancers inhabiting the room, existing and exhausted, inescapably present. The durational time strengthens the connection, and the performance space provides the container within which participants negotiate our participatory inputs. Who should play the music next? What will happen if I get close to you while you're dancing? *Invisible* offers time as a compositional tool to stitch together an intimate community, a micro-UTOPIA. In *Negotiations*, the plot is

---

5   Jill Dolan, *Utopia in Performance: Finding Hope at the Theater* (U of Michigan P, 2005), 6.

us. Kanagawa is offering us a chance to rehearse the kind of real negotiation that we would eventually have to undergo when we re-entered the world beyond our COVID bubbles. (see CRISIS) Because we had been apart, both *Negotiations* and *Invisible* offered a space to relearn ways to work through complexity in collectives. In both of these occasions, the negotiations are happening not only between the participants and the work of art but also amongst participants. In a way, both *P2P@H* and *Invisible* invite their participants to renegotiate closeness in the wake of pandemic social distance.

NOISE

"Is that a clue?" "Is this a clue?" A scavenger hunt featuring the solving of riddles is a familiar participatory motif that invites audiences to explore their environment with heightened senses. We are invited to be SEEKERS, to accumulate information that will reveal or unlock the next stage of our experience.

Before they started the countdown clock on the *Escape from the Tower* escape room at Casa Loma in Toronto, our team was told by our game hosts to ignore any graffiti that we might see etched into the brick walls. The graffiti was old, and therefore protected as historically precious; it was part of history, just not part of the historical-fiction world of our wwii puzzle adventure. One advantage of getting out of the theatre and into actual-world sites is having a set that is fully realized, three-dimensional, and richly detailed; what literary theorist Roman Ingarden, in his phenomenology of reader experience, would call "determinate" (as opposed to literary or dramatic artworks, which are necessarily "indeterminate").[1] There is no backstage if the world is your stage. The disadvantage of a fully determinate world, however, is that it is cognitively noisy. Theatres are quiet.

As purpose-built spaces for communication, theatres have strategies for controlling and shaping that communication for clarity. In the BOURGEOIS THEATRE, information is intentionally limited and tightly managed. A darkened auditorium, artificially muted, with its climate-controlled comfort, is hermetically isolated from the importunities of the world at large. It focuses our attention on the brightly lit stage area and prevents interest in our fellow audience members, the ceiling and walls of the room, and even our own bodies. (I am noisy. In an immersive production, where my body has not been "dimmed and immobilized," my body is noisy. That is, my body is emitting information frequently at odds with the fictional world I am trying to comprehend and navigate. This is why theatre scholar and immersed audience-participant Sophie Nield is so concerned about how her "not-mediaeval bright green handbag" is understood by the monk Abelard.[2] (see THE MATRIX) This is why, I suspect, that immersive works often cast the roaming audience

---

1   Roman Ingarden, *The Literary Work of Art* (Northwestern UP, 1973), 246–47.
2   Sophie Nield, "The Rise of the Character Named Spectator," *Contemporary Theatre Review* 18, no. 4 (2008): 531.

as GHOSTS.) For what cannot be painted black, dimmed, or muted, there are conventions that tell us what we should pay no mind—the gilded proscenium painted with dancing Greek goddesses, the tall man's head in the row in front of me, the obvious microphone worn by the musical theatre lead, the glowing conductor in the orchestra pit. The list goes on. We become well trained.[3]

In the lingo of information theory, information does not equal meaning. Information is the "portion of a signal or message which conveys meaning"[4]; the rest is noise. Claude Shannon, who coined the term "information theory," teasingly asserted, "The 'meaning' of a message is generally irrelevant." The provocation that Shannon offered was instrumental in focusing thinking on the properties of information, separate from its precise conveyed content, to articulate some foundational principles. One of these principles is that "information is closely associated with uncertainty."[5] Uncertainty is a measure of the number of possible messages. If there is only one message, there is no uncertainty. A second principle asserts that "some messages may be likelier than others, and information implies surprise."[6] Yet another principle tells us what seems obvious, though it is profound in its simplicity: "What is significant is the difficulty in transmitting the message from one point to another."[7] This is where noise comes in.

Noise is "interference in the signal that enters into a channel of transmission. In affecting the transmission process, noise affects the amount of information in a message."[8] Invariably, the goal is to reduce or eliminate noise. Most of the time we want our message to be delivered accurately and efficiently. However, when the lusory attitude is activated, efficiency goes out the window. Bernard Suits (*The Grasshopper:*

---

3   In their book on remediation, Jay David Bolter and Richard Grusin call this phenomenon "transparent mediation." This is when the user interface becomes cognitively invisible. For example, for an experienced reader of print media, the actual materiality of paper and its ink imprints are rendered transparent and we are easily immersed in the meaning and experience of the ideas conveyed. We have "learned to overlook, or 'look through' the conventions" (*Remediation: Understanding New Media* (MIT P, 1999), 72–73).

4   "Information," *Wikipedia*, en.wikipedia.org/wiki/Information.

5   James Gleick, *The Information: A History, A Theory, A Flood* (Vintage, 2012), 219; Shannon's original essay *A Mathematical Theory of Communication* says, "With equally likely events there is more choice, or uncertainty, when there are more possible events."

6   Gleick, *The Information*, 219.

7   Gleick, *The Information*, 219.

8   Katie Salen and Eric Zimmerman, *Rules of Play: Game Design Fundamentals* (MIT P, 2004), 196.

Games, Life and Utopia) vividly captures the lusory attitude when he points out that if we were not voluntarily partaking in the pleasures of playing a game, it would be much more efficient to simply pick up the golf ball with our hands and drop it into the cup, than trying to hit it with a rather thin stick.[9] The lusory attitude is critical to playfulness. And as Katie Salen and Eric Zimmerman (*Rules of Play*) point out, the introduction and even augmentation of signal noise in contradiction to direct and simple communication can be the entire point of the lusory attitude in certain games. Consider the classic parlour games Charades and Broken Telephone.[10]

Created by Zuppa Theatre Co., in 2018, *This Is Nowhere* is a sprawling, "app-guided quest in downtown Halifax," with live performances that unfolded in twelve secret locations.[11] To lead participants to each of those twelve performance stations, the app provided a series of clues. Some of these are trivia questions where the answer factoids offer illumination. Others invite you to search out significant visual elements in your surroundings. The app also includes a kind of hotter-colder guidance using symbols; more stars mean you are getting closer; exclamation points mean you've passed your destination or are going the wrong way. The effect of this allusive and slippery GUIDE is that audience-players wander with their heads up through the city, attentively scanning for possible relevance. Being staged in the interstices of a fully determinate actual world, *This Is Nowhere* is a performance with a lot of noise. In fact, the reflexive experience of sifting through excess noise is, I think, part of the point. (see SNEAKY NINJAS) The key participatory dramaturgy at work is the sifting and sorting of noise from signal. As the app-narrator notes at one point, "You may observe several things happening at this site. Some of it is meant for you."

Instructions for finding the first performance station, with the theme "Love," begin with a general location, telling me to position myself "between Citadel Hill and Spring Garden Road." Next, I am told, "Look for orange and silver. And bubbles. They exist in a couple of places, but you'll have to find the right one." I start to wander and sixty seconds later the app tells

---

9   Bernard Suits, *The Grasshopper: Games, Life and Utopia* (U of Toronto P, 1978), 23–24.

10   Charades is an acting out and guessing kind of party game. In Charades, groups decipher pantomimed clues for words they assemble into a phrase. In Broken Telephone, a message is whispered person-to-person along the line, inevitably heard and misheard, and then misspoken, creating an intentional kind of noisy test of communication.

11   Each search has a theme such as love, belief, authority, inclusion, memory, age, and so on.

me, "Some doors are not easily opened. Some doors are never opened. Should they be?" (Later, when I reach my destination, my feeling of success is affirmed when I connect the "orange and silver. And bubbles" to the apartment building logo. The door is indeed locked, but I am provided with a passcode to enter the lobby where I am met by a greeter-character.) "A woman is heartbroken in her apartment." "At least she doesn't have to go far to get some breathing space." The phrase "breathing space" is another latent clue. It is only after I arrive that I get a little thrill in clocking the Breathing Space hair salon across the street from my final destination. Parcelled out phrase-by-phrase with sixty or ninety seconds delay between each one, the clues keep coming. The next app-text gives me a bit of fictional history: "In 1968, the secretive Nowhere Collective often met in this neighbourhood. New apartment buildings have replaced the old homes that once occupied these streets." (I think I'm looking for an apartment building.) "One of the members lived on a street named after a British industrial city." "They were known for their expertise in the fine arts." And then a clue based in real history: "'Will we be extremists for hate or for love?' Martin Luther King wrote these words from a jail in Alabama." Putting these two sets of clues together, I get Birmingham—both an industrial city and the textual source of the famous "Letter from Birmingham Jail."[12] Aha! This game moment is built on a rapid shift from the puzzlement of aporia to the epiphany of knowing. Standing on Birmingham Street and getting warmer, the app prompts: "There is a Latin word that refers to knowledge in the fine arts." "It starts with 'V.'" An assist from Google gives me *virtu*. Finally, if I'm not quite there yet, the app takes pity on me and says: "Find the main entrance of the Vertu Suites." And then ninety seconds later it pinpoints an address: "It is at 1530 Birmingham St."

In a pervasive performance like *This Is Nowhere*, there arise problems (well, not exactly *problems*) with basic ONTOLOGICAL DUALITY. Even in theatre with a strong perceptual frame, some objects remain stubbornly actual. This is the problem identified by Bert O. States (*Great Reckonings in Little Rooms*) concerning dogs on stage. Some objects such as dogs and ticking clocks have a high degree of, what States calls, "*en soi*," that is, they don't slide easily into the fictional world; their realness is just too interesting.[13] I have written about this phenomenon elsewhere,

---

12   The way to counter signal noise is through redundancy. Sending multiple copies of relevant information increases the likelihood of comprehension. This is what *This Is Nowhere* is doing by layering in clues in different registers that, in combination, lead me to a singular location—it's a dramaturgy of redundancy.

13   Jenn Stephenson, "Singular Impressions: Meta-Theatre on Renaissance Celebrities and Corpses," *Studies in Theatre and Performance* 27, no. 2 (2007): 137–53.

adding to States's list things like celebrities, babies, fire, water, food, and actors pretending to be dead. #BertStatesFanGirl. Pervasive performance, especially where our attention is deliberately drawn to the real world as a fictional canvas, invites us to see everything as connected, though only a small portion has been curated as part of the fiction.[14] One meaning that we could derive from this worlding abundance of signal (information plus noise) is that everything I need is in the world already. I don't need to build it; I just need to find it.

Coined by Stephen Covey in his bestseller *The Seven Habits of Highly Effective People*, the concept of the abundance mindset points to a perspective in which a person believes "that there is plenty out there and enough to spare for everybody."[15] The abundance mindset stands in opposition to the scarcity mindset, which believes that life is a zero-sum game. Executive leadership coach Katia Verresen lists six practical tools for cultivating an abundance mindset and number one on her list is noticing. "Abundance is really your ability to see more in your life: More options, more choices, more resources. And that starts with noticing more," says Verresen.[16] "You never have the full story. If you're in a meeting, there are as many realities as there are people in the room. There's always a different way to see something." Noticing as we lean into abundance thinking is a skill that can be developed through practice.

The dramaturgy of abundance melds nicely with the modality of the real-world scavenger hunt and also with some of the overarching themes of *This Is Nowhere*. The basic premise of the show is that fifty years ago, in 1968, the Nowhere Collective envisioned a blueprint for the city of Halifax, for its future; then they and all traces of their work suddenly vanished. "Some people barely noticed. Something had been there, and then wasn't. They went about their business. That's just how a city is. Things come and go, some you notice, some you don't. It's not possible to mark every passing. But other people were heartbroken. These strange messages of love and hope and new days had vanished, leaving a blank

---

14   This is paranoia. "Have you ever had a sudden sense that your surroundings are casting up messages written in code, pieces that you need to gather into a whole?" (see Q) "Thomas Pynchon had [this] in mind when he defined 'paranoia' as 'the realization that *everything is connected*, everything in the Creation—not yet blindingly one, but at least connected . . .'" (*Gravity's Rainbow*, 820, quoted by Stuart Moulthrop, "You Say You Want a Revolution? Hypertext and the Laws of Media," *Postmodern Culture* 1, no. 3 (May 1991)).

15   Stephen R. Covey, *The Seven Habits of Highly Effective People: Powerful Lessons in Personal Change* (Simon & Schuster, 1989), 220.

16   Katia Verresen, "The Remarkable Advantage of Abundant Thinking," *First Round Review*, review.firstround.com/the-remarkable-advantage-of-abundant-thinking.

space. Fifty years have passed. Now we are writing a New Blueprint and you can be one of its authors." *This Is Nowhere* wants its audience-participants to get to know the city of today, to get people to think about what is and to really take notice, with the goal of getting people to think about what might be instead. If we look hard at the ambivalently real/ fictional world of Halifax/Nowhere in 1968/2018, we might be able to look through and then beyond. As the app promises, "The future always seems elusive, but glimpses of it are everywhere."

ONTOLOGICAL DUALITY

The coexistence of two worlds—actual and fictional—is a defining feature of theatricality. It is essential to our comprehension of art as art that it is both an event in the actual world (the play starts at 8 p.m. at the Theatre Centre on Queen Street) comprised of actual material (real actor bodies occupy real theatre space and wear clothes and interact with set and props) *and* that bodies forth a fictional world (Prince Hamlet in Elsinore). These ontologically distinct worlds—one actual and one fictional—are equally co-present to our understanding, despite their different status of beingness. Josette Féral's theory of theatricality pinpoints the cognitive act of carving out space from the mundane world as central to the creation of dramatic fiction: "Thus, theatricality as alterity emerges through a cleft in quotidian space. The cleft can be the result of an actor's seizing control of the quotidian and turning it into theatrical space; it can also be the result of a spectator's gaze constituting the space as theatrical."[1] The cleft border—its creation and maintenance—is key. (see BOUNDARY VIOLATIONS)

A key quality of play is its essential not-seriousness. Things that happen inside the MAGIC CIRCLE of a game do not "count" in the actual world. This distinction between what counts and what does not count is a manifestation of the border that makes both fiction and play possible. Fictional acts have a similar discounted non-serious value. J. L. Austin in *How to do Things with Words*, demonstrates that when performative statement, such as the words used in getting married or making a promise, are enacted in the actual world, they are powerful; however, those same words spoken inside a dramatic world are invalid or, as he says, they are "infelicitous."[2] They do not cross the frame and therefore are not in force in the world. The playing of game has a similar duality to theatre. The actions and objects of game play are ontologically doubled. From the perspective of the actual world, the black knight crosses the chessboard and lands on a square occupied by a white pawn. The white pawn is removed from the board and set aside. Inside the fictional world, the cavalry of the black army has successfully defeated an infantry platoon of the white army, and occupies new territory, advancing

1   Josette Féral, "Theatricality: The Specificity of Theatrical Language," translated by Ronald P. Bermingham, *SubStance* 31, no. 2 and 3 (2002): 97.

2   J. L. Austin, *How to Do Things with Words* (Oxford UP, 1962), 16.

across the field of battle. Games like chess are premised on a metaphor of war that establishes the fictional context for the game action. Even games with a "thin" metaphor still exhibit this core duality. Basketball (*Monday Nights*) is still, at heart, a game of territorial war, with each offensive press aimed at attacking the "castle" of the "enemy."

In the complete absence of a fictional scenario, a different kind of non-seriousness manifests through the lusory attitude. As defined by Bernard Suits, the lusory attitude asserts a kind of playful irrationality, where players pursue their game goals in a purposely arbitrary and often roundabout way.[3] Acquiescing to the ludic illogic of the MAGIC CIRCLE, we become SECRET WEIRDOS. Even though the shortest route to "home" from first base is to run back the way we came, the lusory attitude of the rules of play require a baseball player to go the long way around, touching second and third bases and then the home plate in order, in order to score a run. In the alternate parallel world of games, real-world efficiency and logic do not operate.

Pervasive performances that blend the usually distinct duality of the real world and the fictional game-world are ripe for "Garfinkeling" as the border between these two worlds becomes quite thin. An eponymous term associated with UCLA sociologist Harold Garfinkel to describe "breaching experiments" that break or reveal social order, Garfinkeling occurs "when a researcher knowingly violates a social norm while interacting with other people to reveal how commonly accepted social knowledge is left unquestioned in everyday life."[4] Examples include ignoring a queue and barging to the front of the line, or haggling for the price of a meal in a restaurant. As the audience-players move through real environments, our duality activates the Garfinkeling; we follow logics and goal-value systems that are different than everyday life. Take *Landline* as an example. Guided by the narrative voice in my earbuds, I walk through the city, as I do every day. But the game instructions Garfinkel the conventions of walking. I am asked to follow a stranger. This is odd. (see SNEAKY NINJAS) And in the breach, I become (self)-conscious of the appropriate speed and proximity of my walking. In performances where the participatory act is conversational or confessional, the work encourages us to breach social boundaries regarding what are appropriate things to share with people who are essentially strangers, be they fellow audience-players or the artist-game-makers. Is the effect liberating and therapeutic? (as in *Perfect Strangers*) Or

3   Bernard Suits, *The Grasshopper: Games, Life and Utopia* (U of Toronto P, 1978).
4   Thomas S. Wright, "Garfinkeling," in *The SAGE Encyclopedia of Communication Research Methods*, edited by Mike Allen (SAGE, 2017), doi.org/10.4135/9781483381411.n216.

intrusive and uncomfortable? (as in *Foreign Radical*) Or some combination of both? (as in *WorryWarts*)

4inXchange by xLq problematizes this essential ontological duality of the worlds of play to invite participants to engage playfully and Garfinkel with the nature of money. To begin, four audience-players enter the boardroom and encounter $1,000 in cash, in various colourful denominations arrayed on the table. Money, especially paper money, which has no intrinsic value, possesses as a central quality this same key dual ontology. A single object is simultaneously both just paper and carries a socially agreed upon but essentially arbitrary value or meaning. This green (or blue, or purple, or red, or brown) rectangular piece of paper with its detailed images, numbers, and words becomes valuable at a certain relative rate only because we all agree that it is so. This is exactly the question that *4inXchange* is concerned with. What is valuable to you and why? Through a series of interactive quizzes, competitive team tasks, and mini-games that use the money as a prop object, the work playfully turns our perceptions of money topsy-turvy. Sometimes the game is about what this money will (or won't) buy. "How much would you spend on the perfect outfit?" Sometimes the game is about colour matching or manipulating the money according to its rigidity or strength as a building material: "Use all the cash on the table to make an image inspired by a story one of the four shared." At the very end, we are invited to take home with us as much or as little of the money on the table as we wish. And suddenly, in that moment, the prop escapes the play-world and becomes money again.

The test of ontological duality as a core characteristic of both theatre and games helps to delineate the fringes of these genres. There are activities that are playful but are not, I would argue, play. For example, Brian Sutton-Smith (*The Ambiguity of Play*) includes hobbies like baking, playing an instrument, and word play in his taxonomy of play.[5] These are diversions of leisure and are properly distinguished from "work," but are not dualistic play. Baking cookies, although pleasant, is only one thing—I am a single ontological entity that is doing a singular activity in the actual world. I am not a MEEPLE making cookies. The cookies are nothing other than cookies.

---

5   Brian Sutton-Smith, *The Ambiguity of Play* (Harvard UP, 1997), 4–5.

BREAK THE FOLLOWING DOLLAR AMOUNTS DOWN TO THE LEAST
AMOUNT OF BILLS AND COINS AS POSSIBLE. FOR EXAMPLE, TRY $288:

$288 = [100] + [100] + [50] + [20] + [10] + [5] + ② + ①

YOU MAY HAVE TO DO SOME INVESTIGATING TO GET EACH DOLLAR AMOUNT. THE
ANSWER WILL BE THE NUMBER OF [100] BILLS DIVIDED BY THE NUMBER
OF ① COINS.

$ _365_ = ▢ + ▢ + ▢ + ▢ + ▢ + ▢
(Page number of the last page of SHOPPING)

$____ = ▢ + ▢ + O + O
(Page number of the first page of DISSENSUS)

$____ = ▢ + ▢ + ▢ + ▢ + ▢ + ▢ + O
(Page number of the first page of UTOPIA)

$____ = ▢ + ▢ + ▢ + O + O
(Page number of the first page of BOURGEOIS THEATRE)

$____ = ▢ + ▢ + ▢ + ▢ + ▢ + O + O
(Page number of the Second page of REMOTE CONTROL)

$____ = ▢ + ▢ + ▢ + ▢ + ▢ + O + O
(Page number of the first page of JOY, minus 2)

$____ = ▢ + ▢ + O
(Page number of the Second page of ASYMMETRY)

ANSWER:

OPT OUT

CONSENT is informed, requiring advance knowledge of what I am agreeing to so that I can make a good choice. My agreement then is full and authentic. Consent is also ongoing. Just saying "yes" once at the commencement of my experience is now understood to be insufficient. The voluntary purchase of a ticket cannot be read as a contract that conveys my assent to anything that happens next. I need to be able to say "yes." (see YES, LET'S!) I also need to be able to say "no" at the beginning and then at any future point along the way. Consent, then, is also ongoing.

Frequently, I have had the experience where—as part of the pre-show orientation, when I perhaps take off my shoes, or am given headphones, or am about to be led blindfolded into the performance space—I am told explicitly that, if I want my participation to end, all I have to do is say "stop!" I've also been told that it is okay to stand up and walk away; no words are necessary and the performers will not be offended. (Nevertheless, there are strong pressures on audiences to be nice, to play along, and to "give good audience."[1] I don't want to be seen as rude, even amidst a moment of my own discomfort or distress.) In other performance contexts, there are sometimes options that allow for a more or less intense experience. In *Broken Tailbone*, there are benches around the perimeter of the room and if I wish to take a break from the salsa dance lesson, I can. Or I could choose to sit and watch right from the outset. When we eat together in Gloria Mok's *Long Distance Relationships for Mythical Times*, I was offered jasmine tea; but if I didn't want tea, there was also hot water, and also cold water. For each course of the shared meal, I could decline outright or be provided with alternatives for various dietary needs and preferences. (In that case, the opt-out options came via an advance day-before Google form.)

Another way to make opting out easy in the live performance moment is to offer a named and dedicated space for it. In Rebecca Northan's improv show *Blind Date*, there is, near the front edge of the stage close to the audience, a large square taped out on the floor. As Mimi the Clown explains to her audience-date, who is also her co-improviser (and also to

---

1   Deirdre Heddon, Helen Iball, and Rachel Zerihan, "Come Closer: Confessions of Intimate Spectators in One to One Performance," *Contemporary Theatre Review* 22, no. 1 (2021): 120–33.

us), this is a time-out zone, accessible either to her or to the participant at any time during the show. The square offers a safe space outside the MAGIC CIRCLE, a haven of the actual world where both performers can step out of their fictional roles. It is a way to press "pause." From there they can discuss something that is not working, something that is making them feel uncomfortable; they can talk through what needs to change and what might happen next. It is a deliberate opportunity for re-establishing the contract of consent necessary before once again pressing "play" and returning to the game play of improvisation. This is not a true REFUSAL, but it is a reinforcement of consent. It is a time out rather than an opt out. The show creates a space for a specific pattern of pause-negotiate-restart. The audience-date can opt out of their role if they choose. That option is provided to them. However, when that happens (very, very rarely), they are replaced by a new audience-date, and the show resumes. Their involvement ends, but the mechanism allows the show to continue unscathed.[2]

The square in *Blind Date* is a space of mutual CARE; it is here that the participant can reflect on their interactions inside the first-person fiction and recognize that what they are doing is indeed risky. The time-out square empowers the audience member; it evens the playing field somewhat between the audience-novice who is finding their way and the actor-clown Mimi who has done this before. The AROUSAL of risk is part of the thrill. But significantly, from the audience's perspective, the existence of the time-out square, whether or not it is used in the particular performance we attend, and our understanding of its purpose, reassures us that both Mimi and her date are in recognizance of the limits of their comfort. In one performance I witnessed, "time out!" was called by a woman in the audience who was the wife of the blind date, and Mimi and the woman's husband went to stand in the square. It seemed to be mostly a playful joke. Nothing was wrong, but it was charming to see this couple take a moment to reaffirm their consent to continue to play this edgy game.

This strategy reminds me of a note written by playwright Jennifer Haley in the dramatis personae for *The Nether*, a play that debates

---

2   In a production of *Queer Blind Date*, Mimi called "time out" because it really seemed like her audience-date was having a terrible time on stage, bored and fidgety. Uncomfortable. An on-stage kiss was coming up next and because of the moment's vulnerable intimacy, Mimi asked for a check-in. Her date, having just asked if she could vape on stage, decided in the time-out square that she wanted to opt out of the kiss. Mimi employed another strategy for seeking consent and invited a "stand-in" to replace her date, just for a few minutes. I was the stunt double. I kissed the clown.

(among other things) the ethics of pedophilia in virtual worlds enacted by avatars. She specifies that the actor playing the child, Iris, must in fact be a child of the correct age. She argues in an explanatory note that if the actor Iris is clearly a child, then the audience will feel confident that we will not at any point have to bear witness to any staged acts of child abuse. We are expected to understand that the child-actor will be kept safe. In *Blind Date*, the presence of the time-out square reassures me that the action on stage will not harm either Mimi nor her date (or me by extension), that no one will be pressed beyond their comfort zone because anyone could halt the action before it crossed that line. In both plays, it is the awareness of the real-world frame, that the characters are actors who are also participatory bodies, that helps to manage the fiction.

OR ELSE

Participation by audience-players is always to some extent compelled. Invitations by their nature expect a response. And as we have written elsewhere, there is strong encouragement to say yes. It is polite. Also, refusal is hard. (see COMPLICITY) Beyond this, participatory engagement is usually why I'm here in the first place. I bought a ticket for a participatory show. I want to do the thing. On the surface, this is not a problem. I've been invited and I'm willing. But it is worth digging a little deeper into how my desire to participate has been shaped by contemporary political and economic forces and, by extension, how the consequences of REFUSAL are correspondingly heightened.

Although it may be couched in different phrasing, gestures, or in non-verbal suggestive affordances (see TEACUPS), the essence of the INVITATION to participate is an imperative: "Do it." This makes me think about the marketing powerhouse of the Nike slogan "Just Do It" with the dynamic swoosh. That's me swooshing and I love it. But as much as I do indeed love it, it behooves us to ask, "Why not just don't do it?" How might we resist the imperative to do anything?

Shannon Steen considers this question in her *Theatre Journal* article "Neoliberal Scandals: Foxconn, Mike Daisey, and the Turn Toward Nonfiction Drama." She begins with a summary of key ideas from the book *Perform or Else* by Jon McKenzie. Identifying this trend in corporate thinking, McKenzie exposes how perniciously pervasive the drive for performance is. The actions of our LABOUR, of doing things, have been reframed as performance, and we are being measured. We now not only have performance evaluations at work, but there are performance metrics of how efficiently we are getting things done. We talk about salespeople who are top performers and athletes who are high-performance entities. Perform is what we must do. As Steen writes, "The phrase 'perform or else' orders and delimits the sense of personal behaviour and choice available to the addressee."[1]

Steen then contextualizes the impulse to perform or else as not just a coincidental feature of the neoliberal era, but in fact locates performance as a constitutive mechanic of neoliberalism. (Arguably, this is the controlling political ethos of our times, characterized by free choice,

---

  1   Shannon Steen, "Neoliberal Scandals: Foxconn, Mike Daisey, and the Turn Toward Nonfiction Drama," *Theatre Journal* 66, no. 1 (March 2014): 2.

entrepreneurship, and self-determination.) "Neoliberalism depends on what we might call a performative imperative, an urgent call to act on a set of possibilities that are positioned to seem essential, obvious, and inevitable."[2] One of the modes of what she calls "neoliberalism's theatrical life" is seduction. Performance—"just doing it"—is empowering. I feel strong and capable. I embrace my own choices as desirable self-determination. What I have done is by me and for me, and that feels good. This is the core appeal of DIY. When I'm SHOPPING, I like that I have bagged my own groceries in exactly the way that I like them organized. But wait . . . this is a trick. The grocery store has removed a service and I am replacing someone else's labour. This bait-and-switch is precisely how we are stickily imbricated in neoliberal downloading. We have blissfully come to assume responsibility for things that were previously done for us. And this is not always a good thing.

The reorganization of the traditional relations of the public and private spheres is a core strategy of neoliberalism—reorganization not for our pleasure, but because it is efficient. Trust is placed in the free market to find these efficiencies and make the best decisions about how to deliver not only commercial goods, but now also public services. As social services like hospitals, roads, and education are privatized, "needs formerly met by public agencies on the principle of citizen rights or through personal relationships in communities or families are now to be met by companies selling services in a market."[3] We need to recall that there are major impacts of this kind of forced independence on people who for all kinds of reasons—disability, age, small children under foot— do not find self-checkout delightful. Steen points out that "the austerity regimes of the post-financial meltdown period (which have been used across the developed world to justify the dismantling of public infrastructural projects from education, to health care, to safety, to transport and communications) are saturated with metaphors of performance like these, which are then used to entice the addressee to accept a set of conditions (extreme work hours or the conversion of state services to private, fee-based ones) to which they might otherwise object."[4]

---

2   Steen, "Neoliberal Scandals," 2. For more, see Maurya Wickstrom, *Performance in the Blockades of Neoliberalism: Thinking the Political Anew* (Palgrave Macmillan, 2012) and Jen Harvie, *Fair Play: Art, Performance and Neoliberalism* (Palgrave Macmillan, 2013).

3   Raewyn Connell, "Understanding Neoliberalism," in *Neoliberalism and Everyday Life*, edited by Meg Luxton and Susan Braedley (McGill-Queen's UP, 2010), 23.

4   Steen, "Neoliberal Scandals," 3.

This is precisely what is happening in participatory theatre. In fact, I would argue that it is this paradigm of pleasurable neoliberal downloading that is the foundation of twenty-first century participatory theatre. And is one of the distinguishing features of this contemporary mode of artistic audience-participation from its early-twentieth and mid-twentieth century predecessors. (see CLAIRE BISHOP) In these interactive works, I pay for a ticket to get an experience. And to get that experience, I do a substantial part of the work. Basically, I pay twice. Moreover, my donated labour provides the raw material for the artists who, in the end, walk away with the cultural capital. (see PAINT) Now, don't get me wrong. There is no finger pointing of wrongdoing or blame to be apportioned here. I am not being abused. I am a willing and happy participant. Right? I want this. It's fun to make art and to be enabled in this way. And yet...

In addition to seduction, another mode of neoliberalism's theatrical life identified by Steen is how it fosters new forms of protest. The very disturbing example that Steen presents is the 2010 Foxconn worker suicides at the factories in Shenzhen, China. A dozen workers died and twenty more made attempts on their lives in response to untenable working conditions, before company executives intervened.[5] Steen is careful not to simply categorize suicide as a protest performance. What she concludes is "if, however, we understand neoliberalism to be fundamentally dependent on the language of performance, then it does seem that the suicides stage a preemptive exposure of the false choice between death by overwork or the economic death implied by 'perform or else.'"[6]

Part of the construction of neoliberal performance is that in fact there is no alternative. I want to shift gears here. I am mindful that Steen's account of the deaths of oppressed workers in Shenzhen is devastating. Without trivializing the real tragedy of the Foxconn workers, I want to consider what that impossible alternative looks like in metaphorical terms in relation to participatory performance. What does this level of radical refusal look like? What happens when, instead of choosing "perform," you choose the "or else"?

Two things happen when you, as an audience-player, decline to perform. Essentially, you "or else" yourself out of the system. One, you kill the event. No participant, no show. Of course, one's individual power of refusal is directly proportional to the number of audience-players. In a one-on-one participatory performance, all it takes is for that one person to opt not to perform to make the show cease to exist. Two, and

---

5   Steen, "Neoliberal Scandals," 5.
6   Steen, "Neoliberal Scandals," 7.

this is a bit more nuanced, but also consider that if the audience-player declines to perform, then they also cease to exist. If they don't perform themselves into being, then that performative self does not materialize. The "Jenn" who is the protagonist of any particular participatory fictional world is either not born from the outset or dies at the moment of my non-performance. It is, then, a kind of performative suicide.

From seduction to protest, Steen connects the dots linking the Foxconn tragedy to the first celebrated and then derided documentary monologist Mike Daisey and his show about deplorable labour abuses, *The Agony and the Ecstasy of Steve Jobs*. From there, her argument dilates to consider how a rise in the popularity of non-fiction forms is yet another one of neoliberalism's theatrical manifestations. Testimonial and documentary theatre is often positioned as having a utility beyond that of fictional art forms. These more journalistic forms make claims to practical applications as activism. Unlike a production of *Hamlet*, they are actually doing something. Embedded at least partially in the real world through the postdramatic realness of the audience-players, participatory theatre also falls prey to this kind of self-aggrandizement. Utility quickly slides into instrumentality and the question becomes, "Useful to whom?"

Having worked through Steen's argument and viewing participatory performance this way through the neoliberal lens, "or else" starts to look like a pretty good option.

ORDINARY PEOPLE

What distinguishes participatory theatre from other drama practices that involve "ordinary people" in the theatre-making process? Drama in the applied theatre tradition is participatory in that it invites people who might ordinarily be members of the audience to take part in the work of theatrical creation. An overarching term that describes a genre of practice that involves "self-conscious attempts to influence political reality," applied theatre, sometimes called grassroots theatre or social theatre, engages community members in its storytelling.[1] Popular theatre, documentary theatre, theatre in education, theatre of the oppressed, prison theatre, and community-based theatre all fall under this categorical umbrella. Although the principal point of action in the name "applied theatre" points to the overarching methodology that features "facilitated intervention from the outside with communities for whom theatricality is not intrinsic," the participatory aspects direct attention to who constitutes those communities and how they are engaged.[2] Work that falls under the broad categories of applied theatre or community-engaged theatre speaks to some of the same preoccupying concerns of participatory theatre—concerns about the nature of the invitation to step out of the audience and participate, concerns about managing physical risk and social risk, concerns about the ethical distribution of social and dramatic power among contributors with diverse theatrical skills and investments, and so on. Participation by not-the-usual suspects in the act of theatre-making—and the various implications of bringing in these voices and bodies—is central to both practices. And yet, I want to sketch a distinction while also recognizing this territory of overlap.

Example 1: A community group containing both professional and non-professional theater-makers gathers to develop a dramatic performance consisting of AUTOBIOGRAPHICAL stories, pertaining to a shared experience. Example 2: Verbatim testimony of an acutely pertinent issue is collected, selected, and ventriloquized by professional

---

1   Bill McDonnell, "Theatre, Resistance and Community—Some Reflections on 'Hard' Interventionary Theatre," in *Drama as Social Intervention*, edited by Michael Balfour and John W. Somers (Captus, 2006), 2.
2   Monica Prendergast and Juliana Saxton, "Theories and Histories of Applied Theatre," in *Applied Theatre: International Case Studies and Challenges for Practice*, edited by Monica Prendergast and Juliana Saxton (Intellect, 2009), 12.

actors for a cohort audience that contains members of the source community. Both of these scenarios are familiar applied theatre models. However, I would exclude them from counting as participatory performance. In both cases, these are ordinary people who become actors or even characters and perform for an audience. They are not themselves *of* the audience. A defining characteristic of participatory theatre that I am attempting to carve out here is that participants arrive first and primarily as audience members. As such, their goals are those of an audience—to access an aesthetic experience. (see SHOPPING) In the end, they depart as audience members. Even if during the performance they had become actors or characters, they still concurrently retain their audience awareness and positionality. (see FIRST-PERSON SHOOTER)

Works like *100% Vancouver* and *Le Grand Continental* are performed by ordinary people who step in to fill gaps in a performance RECIPE. Their bodies, their capacities, and their life experiences are the artistic medium, the PAINT on the participatory canvas. The fact of their ordinariness marks them as akin to the audience and this is an essential vehicle for our understanding of these works. The understanding of the artwork pivots on our delighted recognition of that bond of similarity. "You're just like me!" The percentiles of *100% Vancouver* represent me as an inhabitant of Vancouver, I am one of them. Likewise, the amateur dance enthusiasts of *Le Grand Continental* are also me (or could be me if I had taken the publicly offered opportunity to join them months previous and learn their choreography). I am thrilled by their skill; this thrill is inflected particularly as I identify as holding the same potential as any one of them. Flash mobs are like this too.[3] At the height of their popularity, I witnessed a flash mob in the library at Queen's University when one by one, and then in small groups, formerly busy and unremarkable students stood up from their study carrels, dropped their books, and burst into song and dance. Stauffer Library had been transformed into the set of a spontaneous musical. The critical distinction is that ordinary people participate, but the audience does not participate. In each of these examples, there is a separate audience with a separate role

---

3   Coined by Bill Wasik of *Harper's Magazine*, a "flashmob" refers to a group of people who suddenly gather in a public place, perform briefly, and then disappear. Sometimes participants freeze, or clap, or perform well-rehearsed choreography. While flashmobs can function as community expression and good old-fashioned performance, they are also commonly used as marketing campaigns. While a flashmob occurring at a Macy's department store in 2003 claims to be the first of its kind, mass choreographed actions of ordinary people also have ties to political performance art movements from the 1960s onwards. "Flash Mob," *Wikipedia*, en.wikipedia.org /wiki/Flash_mob.

from the ordinary-people performers without potential for crossover. The plays affirm and thematize the ordinariness of the performers, but theatricality makes them not like us. They have entered the frame.

Example 3: A forum theatre performance presents a particular social conundrum, outlining the scenario and stopping at the point of decision. What should the protagonist do? An audience member steps in and assumes the role of the protagonist enacting next steps towards a potential solution. Conceived and popularized by Augusto Boal, forum theatre invites ordinary people into the MAGIC CIRCLE, to enter a prospective scenario and to perform a contingent futurity. What might happen next? Speculative dramatic role-playing presents "a vision of the world in transformation and therefore is inevitably political insofar as it shows the means of carrying out that transformation or of delaying it."[4] For Boal, the active engagement of forum theatre leans into the belief that "theatre is change and not a simple presentation of what exists: it is becoming and not being."[5] Boal's approach resonates with both Antonin Artaud and Bertolt Brecht (see A AND B), locating theatre's power as a liberatory and transformative art form in the action of the audience. Famously, Boal asserted that "perhaps the theater is not revolutionary in itself, but it is surely a REHEARSAL for the revolution."[6] This is another recognizable applied theatre mode. In this case, I would say yes, this is participatory theatre. Critical to the theoretical framework we are offering here, the participant-protagonist comes out of the audience and, even though they step in as an actor, their audience position and awareness persists. That dual position and awareness is actually essential to their participation.

The interstitial long-table scene of *The Assembly: Montreal*, created by verbatim theatre company Porte Parole, works this way. To create the show, *The Assembly* invited four ordinary Canadians with diverse opinions to discuss politics. This conversation was recorded, collected, and modified for re-performance by four actors. As the group was intentionally curated to have opposing points of view, the ensuing conversation was animated and intense, both in its original context with its original inhabitants and in its verbatim repetition with the actors from Porte Parole. As mentioned above, verbatim theatre does make use of ordinary people, but also as mentioned above it is arguably not participatory. About three-quarters of the way through the performance,

---

4   Augusto Boal, *Theatre of the Oppressed*, translated by Charles A. McBride and Maria-Odilia Leal McBride (Theatre Communications Group, 1985), xiii.

5   Boal, *Theatre of the Oppressed*, 28.

6   Boal, *Theatre of the Oppressed*, 122.

this verbatim-style restating of the debate is interrupted and the actors step out of their roles to cede the table to the audience. The actors exit, the house lights come up, and the floor is open. For the next twenty minutes, self-selected members of the audience approach the table, sit, and speak. Inspired by Lois Weaver's Long Table practice, everyone is welcome, and one chair must remain empty so that anyone can join at any time. This shift creates a bridge where the ordinary people of the audience can offer a kind of asynchronous response to the "ordinary" people that they've been watching. It feels like another level of theatrical framing has been stripped away and our feeling of realness of the audience-speakers is bolstered by comparison with the previous reality claims of the ventriloquized verbatim testifiers. Their credentials as being audience-members just seconds before makes their ordinariness more potent.[7]

See SHEEP

---

7   As a side observation, it is interesting to note that in the archival version of *The Assembly: Montreal* that I viewed, the audience members don't want to talk about the hot-button issues directly but instead offer insights into the nature of productive listening. (see DEMOCRACY)

OSTRANENIE

I find myself on a hot summer day standing in an urban laneway, a narrow strip of pavement running between two parallel rows of garages and back fences. In common with the other twenty people or so, I am clutching a lemon. The yellow skin is a bright (almost startling) pop of colour in the sun-washed concrete and faded asphalt of the back alley. I pay close attention to the lemon's dimples, the slightly pointed ends, its weight and firm density. I close my eyes and hold it to my nose. Accompanied by music and intermittent dance-movement performances, my task is to stroll forward and place this first of three lemons somewhere in the lane. Is it best positioned at the intersection of two cracks on the ground or is it better balanced on the handle of the garage door? These aesthetic lemon dilemmas are consuming. (I like "lemon dilemmas.") Upon reaching the far end of this slow journey, I am rewarded with a tangy cold cup of lemonade. (see JUICINESS) The tactile yellow enigmas transformed to juice feels like a revelation. Wow, lemonade! An everyday magic trick. This is *b side*, created by Molly Johnson and Meredith Thompson.

The central dramaturgy of *b side* is the overt framing of everyday objects and experiences to shift them from mundane to remarkable. (Literally remark-able.) This effect of making the lemons lemony is what the literary theorist of Russian formalism Viktor Shklovsky calls "ostranenie." He argues that this is the entire point of art: "art exists that one may recover the sensation of life; it exists to make one feel things, to make the stone *stony*."[1] Shklovsky suggests that art does this by placing everyday life at perceptual distance—defamiliarizing it—so that it becomes freshly re-visible to us. This is what poetry does as a technique of art, for example. The reformulation of life in stylized language creates a certain cognitive friction that returns the sensation of life to us. Our perception is made more acute through our LABOUR. We are more open to what the object or experience conveys.

In lieu of poetry as the catalyzing friction, I would argue that in *b side* participation is the chosen technique of ostranenie, of aesthetic defamiliarization. Through my bodily actions and my directing consciousness towards the given task, I become responsively engaged not only with the

---

1   Viktor Shklovsky, "Art as Technique," in *Russian Formalist Criticism: Four Essays*, edited by Lee T. Lemon and Marion J. Reis (U of Nebraska P, 1965), 12.

lemons, but that attention also rebounds onto the alleyway, the other participants, and myself. Grant Kester (*Conversation Pieces*) in his writing about dialogic art, acknowledges the relation of dialogic art to Russian formalism but with a twist. He writes, "The assigned role of art, then, is to awaken the viewer through the administration of a therapeutic cognitive disruption."[2] The twist is that the disruption does not manifest in a singular moment, but is durational, founded in co-responsive interaction. Dialogic works "build on this [Russian formalist] tradition through their interest in challenging fixed identities and perceptions of difference not simply as an instantaneous, prediscursive flash of insight, but as a decentering, a movement outside self (and self-interest) through dialogue extended over time."[3] It is a conversation. For Kester, it is the "process of open-ended dialogical interaction that is itself the 'work' of art."[4]

Marvin Carlson in his introduction to Erika Fischer-Lichte's *Transformative Power of Performance* makes a similar connection and modification. He notes that Fischer-Lichte's concept of "enchantment" has resonance with defamiliarization. He repeats the Shklovsky quote about making the stone stony and underscores the point that "art is a way of experiencing the artfulness of an object; the object is not important."[5] A central tenet of Fischer-Lichte's theory of transformation is that performance is a process wherein "the commonplace appears transfigured and becomes conspicuous."[6] (An excellent definition of ostranenie.) But Carlson continues, and says it would be a mistake to assume Fischer-Lichte's ideas are merely updated Russian formalism. He highlights her contribution that rests in the critical shift from the materiality of the art object to an event-experience of dynamic being in the world. To this view, art changes from a noun into a verb. It is not something we look at or listen to, but something that we do. (see STRUMPET) As Kester does, Fischer-Lichte construes this process as a durational and dialogic feedback loop. (see AUTOPOIESIS)

The play *b side* is about ostranenie. It is difficult to attribute a meaning to *b side* beyond the pure experience of heightened noticing and the

---

2   Grant Kester, *Conversation Pieces: Community and Communication in Modern Art*, updated edition (U of California P, 2013), xvi.

3   Kester, *Conversation Pieces*, 84–85.

4   Kester, *Conversation Pieces*, 87.

5   Marvin Carlson, "Introduction," in *The Transformative Power of Performance: A New Aesthetics* by Erika Fischer-Lichte, translated by Saskya Iris Jain (Routledge, 2008), 6–7.

6   Carlson, "Introduction," 7.

associated pleasure of that noticing. (see NOISE) This is its JOY. *Manual* too is dominantly a play about ostranenie.

Manual, created by Christopher Willes and Adam Kinner is set in a library. The show is an entirely silent duet for two. The performance begins with me and Christopher looking at a notebook in Christopher's hand. There are pre-written, pencilled messages on a palm-sized, spiral-bound flip notebook, such as, "Is this thing on?" I follow Christopher silently through the library, trailing a metre behind. Initially I am attuned with heightened attention to the library-ness of the library. Look, books! (Cool.) We play follow-the-leader through the stacks. When Christopher pauses to inspect the bookshelf, so do I. He points to a book title on a spine. (I can't remember exactly what he picked, but it amused me.) I choose a similarly quirky book title and touch it. He picks another one. So do I. Is that what was supposed to happen? Dunno. It is a silent improvisation. Throw the ball. Catch it. Throw it back. This is a very satisfying kind of co-creative partnership. A tiny game for two.

A couple of things that are not happening here. *Manual* is not exploratory. It is not CHOOSE YOUR OWN ADVENTURE or even a DRIFT. We are not set loose in the library to choose an autonomous path. The other quality to notice about *Manual*, specifically in my relationship to Christopher, is that this is not an ENCOUNTER. The intent of the experience is not for us to meet each other. The focus of the work is not AUTOBIOGRAPHICAL. Just as it is not about Christopher, it is not about me as me. In addition to remaining almost completely silent, which restricts verbal interaction, there is no mutual gaze; Christopher doesn't look at me. He is either ahead of me or he seems to hover just behind my shoulder. We look at things together, but we do not look at each other. Just as I am not "me"; Christopher is also not "Christopher." *Manual* is not about confessing or sharing secrets. (Which is, to be honest, a relief sometimes.) But we are engaged in a kind of INTIMACY. We are playing a private game in a public space. We are making secrets. (see SECRET WEIRDOS)

Why is the play called *Manual*? Always a good question. Certainly, the show is manual, that is, it is tactile with your HANDS in a way that much theatre is not. Christopher's hands are a prominent element. He flips the pages of his instructional notebook. In another extended scene, he also performs a kind of hand-choreography when he opens for me a series of books, deliberately turning to pre-bookmarked pages, and slides sheets of cardboard to hide and reveal portions of the chosen pages. I did consciously remark Christopher's hands—the skin, the nails, their texture and shade. A manual is also a book of instructions. Thinking specifically through the lens of participation, a manual is a "how to do stuff." And of course, participation is all about doing stuff. Usually things that we have not done before in places we have not been before. And as we've noted elsewhere, participatory audiences need instructions. (see THE MATRIX and RECIPE) The contents of a library—fiction and non-fiction—are manuals for everything in our existence, I suppose. The show itself then perhaps is a manual to the manual, an experience in how to "library." This is how you search—first you walk. This is how you choose books—try pointing. This is how you look—really look. This is how you read—let's read together. Concentrate. This is how you put the books back—notice how they wait so patiently. It is a complete lifetime of libraries in miniature.

And what is not to love about really looking at a library. You will have to excuse my sentimentality, but as an academic who spends a lot of mundane time in libraries, the experience of aesthetic defamiliarization blossoms into affection and I am reminded by *Manual* that a library truly is an everyday miracle in action.

Even when not explicitly thematized as part of the core understanding of the artwork, the ostranenie of participation places the audience-player inside the frame, while at the same time drawing attention to that framing. In response to the INVITATION to cross over the border and transform from being a singular audience member to an active player-participant, we still retain our original point of view as spectators. It is like those FIRST-PERSON SHOOTER games where we witness our own performance through the proscenium of our eyes. Of course, life is always perceived in this way through the phenomenological eye/I. It is the performative frame of deliberate participation that sets the self and its actions and perceptions at a distance for aesthetic consideration. (Look at me being me. Me? Me!) And so we can see in these strong cases of the ostranenie of participation that this, in a weak way, is always the case.

WHILE FOLLOWING CHRISTOPHER THROUGH THE LIBRARY, YOU NOTICE THAT HE HAS DROPPED SOME BOOKS ALONG THE WAY. AFTER NAVIGATING THE MAZE BELOW FROM START TO FINISH, COUNT THE NUMBER OF BOOKS (📚) THAT LIE ALONG THE CORRECT PATHWAY. THIS NUMBER WILL BE YOUR ANSWER.

START

FINISH

ANSWER:

PAINT

In their starter definitions of participation, both Gareth White (*Audience Participation*) and Claire Bishop (*Artificial Hells*) propose that an essential characteristic in this genre is that actual-world people are its constitutive material. Not those sparkly, special people—actors—who are trained to become fictional beings. Actual, ORDINARY PEOPLE, non-trained, off-the-street people, people just like us. If a participatory work of art were a painting, we would be the paint. This is the nature of our participation. Bishop organizes her book "around a definition of participation in which people constitute the central artistic medium and material, in the manner of theatre and performance."[1] White concurs, "These processes make the audience member into material that is used to compose the performance: an artistic medium."[2]

Is that what participatory audiences are? Paint? Really?

For certain performance works, including some of the ones that Bishop and White write about, the answer to this question is firmly, "Yes." There is a category of artworks where the principal focus is deliberately and meaningfully placed on the mundane human as material. This is what Bishop and others call "delegated performance"[3] which she defines as "the act of hiring non-professionals or specialists in other fields to undertake the job of being present and performing at a particular time and a particular place on behalf of the artist, and following his/her instructions."[4] This is different from simply hiring people as actors because the artists "tend to hire people to perform their own socio-economic category, be this on the basis of gender, class, ethnicity, age, disability, or (more rarely) a profession."[5] The reason they are recruited is simply the ordinary realness of themselves as themselves. They are not just mundane humans. It is their specific mundanity that is of interest. Their appeal lies in the fact that they are not actors; their value is

---

1   Claire Bishop, *Artificial Hells: Participatory Art and the Politics of Spectatorship* (Verso, 2012), 2.
2   Gareth White, *Audience Participation in Theatre: Aesthetics of the Invitation* (Palgrave Macmillan 2013), 9.
3   Bishop, *Artificial Hells*, 219; Shannon Jackson, *Social Works: Performing Art, Supporting Publics* (Routledge, 2011).
4   Bishop, *Artificial Hells*, 219.
5   Bishop, *Artificial Hells*, 219.

that they are strangers to the stage.[6] Germany-based collective Rimini Protokoll calls these delegated performers "experts of the everyday." The Rimini Protokoll franchise *100% Vancouver* is a prime example.

Our aesthetic interest in the one hundred Vancouverites arrayed on the stage lies in how they physically manifest the demographics of the city of Vancouver, each representing a percentile, proportionally mapped according to their mix of gender, age, marital status, ethnicity, and neighbourhood.[7] Participation is solicited using a "statistical chain reaction" with each person inviting the next person to fill in the blanks and collect a precisely representative sample of Vancouverites, bringing one hundred people to the stage in correspondence with recent census data. The show is structured as a series of questions to which the participants respond by physically arranging themselves on the circular stage, turning into human pie charts and infographics. Their participation is shaped by how these unique humans fill in the generic data blanks. (see MAD LIBS) So, for example, they are asked to line up by age from youngest to oldest. In this tension between the general and the specific, a central concern of *100% Vancouver* is how the participants successfully map themselves onto the census data (or not). Revealing frictions emerge when the bodies don't match the data. How do we represent those identity markers who constitute less than one per cent of the city? How do we represent "other"? What about those things the census doesn't ask about, like non-binary genders? The participants are also asked additional autobiographical questions like "who owns their own home?" or "who has children?" But then these expand to encompass less formal questions about their histories, and their values. "Who has broken the law?" "Who grows their own food?" "Who is in love?" Oscillating between their role as percentiles, standing in for 6,463 other Vancouver residents and presenting themselves as unique individuals, these one hundred people are raised to our attention. The kaleidoscope of their intersecting identities is offered for our contemplation as a reflection of our city. Watching the patterns resolve and dissolve, we

---

6   Jenn Stephenson, "Real People Part 2: Insecurity and Ethical Failure in the Encounter with Strangers—*100% Vancouver*, RARE, and *Polyglotte*," in *Insecurity: Perils and Products of Theatres of the Real* (U of Toronto P, 2019), 48–90.

7   For more about *100% City* in Canada, see Tim Carlson, "Matter of Protokoll," *Rimini Protokoll*, 21 January 2011, rimini-protokoll.de/website/en/text/matter-of -protokoll; Richard C. Windeyer, "Petri Dish Deceptions: A Search for 100% Veracity in Rimini Protokoll's Statistical Portrait of Montreal," *Canadian Theatre Review* 175 (Summer 2018), 29–34; and Keren Zaiontz, "Performing Visions of Governmentality: Care and Capital in *100% Vancouver*," *Theatre Research International* 39, no. 2 (2014): 101–19.

ask, "Is that me?" and "Is this a Vancouver that I recognize?" There is a potent thrill in the ENCOUNTER with this hundred and their very present realness. And I don't want to devalue that. But, apart from the show's particular value as a work of art, the participants themselves are essentially widgets. This is further underscored by the context of the work as an episode of the *100% City* series, whether in Vancouver or Barcelona or Berlin. The work is made of them as components. The work is about them and yet it is not theirs.

One small, somewhat digressive difference between delegated performance and our other examples of participatory theatre is the situation of the audience. For delegated performance, the human material is incorporated prior to the performance moment. They are subsumed wholly into the work, which then other non-participatory audiences come to witness. Flashmobbers rehearse their choreo ahead of time, performing it as a surprise for onlookers. For the participatory audience, they significantly arrive to the work as audience and are then transformed (or not; see REFUSAL) into participants. This shift is critical to their concurrent, split perspective on themselves as both performers and audience. This duality is captured in the identifier "audience-player." (Or perhaps better "player-audience"? For more about this, see FIRST-PERSON SHOOTER and MEEPLES.)

Participatory audiences are co-creators of the work. So perhaps a fruitful strategy is to unpick what we understand about being a creator versus being a medium. What is the difference between holding the paintbrush and being brushed? Can you be a blend of both? What does it mean to be co-creative? Can the medium of an artwork be sensibly thought of as a co-creator? This is a provocation to think about what participants bring to their engagement—and who or what their collaborators might be. (see THINGS)

First, we have presence. Both still and in movement, we exist. We have bodies. *Le Grand Continental* trades on the effect of the mass gathering of diverse bodies in choreographed synchronicity. The show revels in the tension between our acute awareness of these bodies as ordinary and our pleasure in their demonstrated expertise (or, if not in their expertise at least in their brave enthusiasm). Next, as bodies exist in time and space, they accrue histories. They have positionalities. Like *Le Grand Continental*, *100% Vancouver* relies on the productive binocular effect of seeing the single and the mass. For *100% Vancouver*, bodies are framed by identities and lived experience, oscillating between being an individual and a representative in the collective. But even with a scattering of some unique stories, the dominant understanding depends on seeing each person's individuality in the context of the whole, marked by the five census categories. Still widgets (mostly).

If we keep going in this direction, we might start to see much of a participant's contributions as paint. Participants share stories and answer questions. My AUTOBIOGRAPHY becomes paint. My creative input becomes paint. Participants choose directions to explore (see CHOOSE YOUR OWN ADVENTURE), and my choices shape narrative outcomes. The effect of my agency becomes paint. Ultimately, I think this circles back around to a key observation repeated elsewhere that participatory performance is marked by a narcissism where the work is not only *for* me and *by* me, but also *about* me. And digging deeper along this line of thinking, we could add that it is *of* me. It is me. And then, of course, this opens up questions about ethics and compensation. (see CONSENT, INSTRUMENTALITY, and LABOUR)

In the end, I think that participation as medium is weak sauce. It points to something useful and it is worth remarking the self as a material element of participation, but it also reveals itself as a definition to be profoundly lacking once we look beyond delegated performance. Consideration of the participatory audience-player must encompass more than a creatively passive act of solicited contribution. It is gratifying to be a kind of patron. It is flattering to have one's portrait painted. It is fun to be an amateur actor. In case after case, however, we see that the fundamental appeal of participation is to be a maker, to make a meaningful impact on the work at hand.[8] I want to be a player. I don't want to be paint, or at least not only.

See AGENCY and ORDINARY PEOPLE

---

8   See discussion of "meaningful play" in Katie Salen and Eric Zimmerman, *Rules of Play: Game Design Fundamentals* (MIT P, 2004), 31–36.

PHONES

In his book *Conversation Pieces*, Grant Kester documents the early history of the social turn in visual art, tracing a shift from object art (paintings, prints, sculpture, and the like) to a more relational, durational, process-based approach.[1] This is art that feels more like theatre. (see STRUMPET) This more social art, where the aesthetic experience is developed in the here and now, replaces what he calls the "banking" style of art, in which the artist deposits work to be withdrawn by a viewer later and possibly elsewhere.[2] Emphasis is placed on the co-presence in time and space of the artist and viewer in the moment of artistic creation. "This catalyzation of the viewer, the movement toward direct interaction, decisively shifts the locus of aesthetic meaning from the moment of creative plenitude in the solitary act of making to a social and discursive realm of shared experience, dialogue, and physical movement."[3] For Kester, the essence of this kind of participatory work rests in the improvisatory give-and-take of a conversation, of a dialogue.

In the wake of the recent pandemic that forced a spatial separation between artists and audiences, I witnessed, for the first time in my several decades as a theatregoer, theatre by phone.[4] Instead of an 8 p.m. dimming of the house lights followed by the raising of the curtain, my phone rings. I answer it and become a character and co-creator. In this medium, these plays are literally dialogic art. Although phone plays do share some similarities with audiowalks (also known as podplays)—both being intimate aural experiences—whereas audiowalks are monologues, phone plays are participatory dialogues. Also, where audiowalks tend to direct a primary aesthetic focus on the immersed experience of a given location or environment, (see

---

1   Grant Kester, *Conversation Pieces: Community and Communication in Modern Art*, updated edition (U of California P, 2013).
2   Kester, *Conversation Pieces*, 10.
3   Kester, *Conversation Pieces*, 54.
4   First demonstrated in 1881 and commercialized in 1890, the théâtrophone enabled subscribers to listen to live opera and theatre broadcasts in Europe (*Wikipedia*, en.wikipedia.org/wiki/Théâtrophone). Theatre by phone also shares some characteristics with audiowalks or podplays (especially now that phones are no longer attached to the wall). Other additional examples of phone-based participatory plays not discussed in this entry are *The Corona Variations* by Julie Tepperman, Olivier Choinière's *Les secours arriveront bientôt*, and of course the *Red Phone* play series curated by Boca del Lupo.

OSTRANENIE and DRIFT) for these phone plays my spatiality is irrelevant, or at best secondary, being typically my familiar domestic setting.[5]

The medium of the phone generates some unique dramaturgical qualities. First of all, this is a theatrical ENCOUNTER without a face and without a gaze. There is no actor looking at me with expectation, and I am not being looked at. (see EXCHANGE) I am invisible and so are they. And as a result, I would argue we are more open to INTIMACY. Further, phone calls are by nature intimate and private, occurring in the aural headspace in my ears and behind my eyes. Even if I don't use earbuds, the phone is pressed close against my face. Group phone calls outside of work settings are rare; more common is a one-to-one connection. Moreover, phone calls are private spaces; what I say can be heard by someone nearby perhaps, but what I hear is for my ears only.[6]

In *The Ministry of Mundane Mysteries*, our shared invisibility combined with the intimate privacy of a phone call is liberatory, enabling me (usually pretty serious and shy) to be playful. Silly, even. By contrast, in *Soon, Tomorrow Maybe* the same qualities amplify the emotional stakes, setting the stage for secrets, confessions, and ultimately forgiveness. It is perhaps not entirely coincidental that both plays are fundamentally mysterious. *Mundane Mysteries* is literally a whodunit, while in *Soon, Tomorrow Maybe* the mystery is existential as we work to untangle our comprehension of how we are in relation to this caller who, claiming an intimate connection, knows so much about us and yet altogether too little.

Produced by Outside the March in the earliest weeks of Canada's pandemic quarantine, *The Ministry of Mundane Mysteries* created a series of personalized dramatic dialogues for an audience of one. After signing up and registering your mundane mystery with the Ministry (Mine was the "Mystery of the Door that Won't Stay Closed." Mariah's was the "Mystery of the Missing Cake Pan."), each seeker receives one ten-minute phone call at a set time, each day for six days in a row. This extended serial structure also aligns smartly with the qualities of phone calls. I may very well phone someone daily; conversely, it is unlikely that I would return to the theatre six days in a row. Beginning with my first call, a case intake

---

5   This focus on the domestic setting became particularly meaningful during the lockdown phases of the pandemic, during which many people were isolated at home, apart from daily neighbourhood walks.

6   Phone calls also have a built-in social script. We know how to answer the phone and how to take turns talking and how to say goodbye. Like other transplanted everyday-behaviour frames, our repertoire of telephone etiquette grants an unrehearsed audience-participant insight into what might be expected of us and provides a modicum of security in what is otherwise a journey into unknown territory. (see THE MATRIX)

interview by Inspector Doyle, the archly goofy narrative was built on the details of my personal mystery. Each radically improvisational phone call evolved as an extended game of "YES, LET'S!" in which whatever is said is, without question, taken as true. Speaking to one character-caller at a time, the audience is a truly dialogic partner as we are cast as the protagonist-client. The give-and-take of a shared fiction was buoyantly amusing. And the expectation of wondering who might call tomorrow (I interacted with four different characters over the six days) and what might happen next added to the durational charm.

As part of the AUTOPOIETIC feedback loop of question and answer, the play became, I will argue, a form of augmented reality (AR). AR refers to a tech intervention when something digital is overlaid onto an image or experience of the real world. (Think Pokémon GO!) In this case, the phone was the technological instrument. Each day the personal details I offered were embroidered and returned to the story in an expanded form. It became clear that between episodes the actor/playwrights were doing a bit of local research, layering real-world details that thickened the plot. In my mystery, my dog Paulina became a character and that, combined with a love of Shakespeare, led to an episode in which I was phoned from a (faux) secret stakeout at the local Grand Theatre. In Mariah's mystery, her roommate became a character and Northside, her favourite coffee shop, a set. By episode two, her inspector was knowledgeable about the Kingston coffee scene, the menu at Northside, and the Australian owners who were fingered as suspects in the cake pan theft. The effect of this AUTOBIOGRAPHICAL enrichment is that the bespoke fictional world of Mundane Mysteries lives in the gaps of my actual-world life. These absurd things that are happening could be real. Why not? I think that the medium of theatre-by-phone encourages this blending. Because the fictional reality augmentations are created only aurally and overlaid on the visuality of my own living space, and because my contributions as co-creator lean into my actual life circumstances, the zany narrative of these inspectors of the small intrigues of everyday life slips into the interstices of my life with ease. As a result, my life is just a little more colourful, a little more goofy. And I am given a refreshed appreciation of the mysteriousness of the mundane.

Soon, Tomorrow Maybe, written by Marie Ayotte and presented by Théâtre Déchaînés, attempts to perform a similar slippage into one's real life. The hour-long phone call is somewhat more monologic than *Mundane Mysteries*, but it still enacts a dialogue and anchors itself in your life through the sharing of personal details. When I answer the phone, it's a woman's voice and she is excited but nervous. "I was afraid you wouldn't pick up . . . But you did. I'm glad." About ten minutes of the play have elapsed when she says, "I thought about you the other day. Well, I think about you every day, but ..." and shares a reminiscence about the garden and how much I liked the orange day lilies, concluding with "those were the flowers your dad brought me the day after I told him I was pregnant with you." Puzzlement turns to illumination. Ah wow! This is my mother. And then again puzzlement. This is my mother? Obviously, this is not my mother. Not only did we not have a garden with orange day lilies, but the voice is all wrong. And yet, the dramaturgical properties of a phone call help this faux narrative insinuate itself into my life as a playful possibility. (see ENCOUNTER)

Visually, the scenography of this play-world is my own house. Far from being incongruous, the visual and haptic qualities of the house and my body within it are successfully absorbed. Where on the one hand, the fully determinate environment of the house supports the persuasive possibility of the pervasive fiction, by contrast, it is the indeterminate quality of the mother that makes her similarly plausible. Because the mother is invisible, there are fewer points of friction in my audience belief stance. She does not have a face or a body that I can see. The voice is still not her voice, and some recounted details are not true of my memories, but through this partial manifestation, because there is less detail, there is less work to erase the inevitable inconsistency. Overall, the bivalent auditory indeterminacy of the character combined with a pervasive visual and haptic determinacy of the space innate to this characteristic mediated connection of a phone call fosters intimacy in the encounter. The actor becomes a possible, or at least provisionally acceptable, version of my mother.

The intimacy of this faceless narrative slips past my defences. As I listen and insert responses, my thoughts are consumed by my own mother and myself as a mother. The story of *Soon, Tomorrow Maybe* is one of deep ambivalence about motherhood, about regrets, and about struggling and failing to live up to social expectations that take the unconditional joy of being a mother as a given. Towards the end of the performance, there is an ontological curveball, which I will not reveal here, but which profoundly reframes my relationship to this speaker who is (not) my mother. In the final line of the play, she tearfully asks, "Can you ever forgive me?" There is no other answer I can give but "yes."

WHAT MUNDANE MYSTERY WOULD YOU GIVE TO YOUR INSPECTOR?
"THE MYSTERY OF THE _____"

PHONY MULTIPLICITY

Audience-participants are agents. How that agency is initiated and then progressively shaped is a central dramaturgy of participation. (Do I dare to argue that it is the primary, or even the only, dramaturgy?) Every aspect of participation comes down to choices. Will I or won't I? What will I? How will I? The framing of those choices in the interests of a desired aesthetic or experiential effect is the main task of the artist-curators of participatory works. Astrid Breel in her spectatorship study of audience-participants asserts that "the manipulation of agency becomes aesthetic in this moment because the artist has carefully considered how to frame the agency of the participant, through the invitation, in order to create a particular experience."[1] So, not only do individual acts of audience agency shape meaning in performance, but the consciously composed experience of exercising agency (or not) also carries aesthetic meaning.

Game design theorists Katie Salen and Eric Zimmerman (*Rules of Play*) introduce the concept of "meaningful play." They begin with the premise that meaningful play is the goal of all play creation. Meaningful play "emerges from the relationship between player action and system outcome; it is the process by which a player takes action within the designed system of a game and the system responds to the action."[2] More specifically, the causality between action and outcome needs to be "discernible"—that is, the results of action are communicated to the player—and "integrated"—impact is not simply immediate, but affects future possible actions and outcomes.[3]

Presented with the opportunity to be an agent, I am sometimes suspicious. Is meaningful play available here? Do my actions have consequences? Really? Astrid Breel is suspicious too. She asks, "Is the agency on offer completely genuine?" and "Can a work really offer agency to a participant?" before leading to her research question: "How important

---

1   Astrid Breel, "Audience Agency in Participatory Performance: A Methodology for Examining Aesthetic Experience," *Participations: Journal of Audience and Reception Studies* 12, no. 1 (May 2015): 381.

2   Katie Salen and Eric Zimmerman, *Rules of Play: Game Design Fundamentals* (MIT P, 2004), 34.

3   Salen and Zimmerman, *Rules of Play*, 34–35.

is a sense of agency in how audiences respond to the experience?"[4] A corollary to the question about the authenticity of offers of agency pertains to phony multiplicity. Frequently in the context of consumer culture, we are presented with myriad choices. Too many choices. And then in that abundance (or excess) we realize that in fact these choices, though plentiful, are entirely superficial. (I'm put in mind of that Bruce Springsteen song "57 Channels (And Nothin' On.)" Only fifty-seven channels, how quaint. Consider that it was 1992.) Paradoxically nearly infinite consumer choice serves as a kind of a pacifier, papering over a lack of meaningful political choices. Breel asks, "How important is a sense of agency in how audiences respond to the experience?" I'd like to shape my question differently to ask, "How does our sense of agency (or lack thereof) constitute a dramaturgical structure that informs our understanding of the experience?" Basically, I'm asking, "What kind of stories can agency tell?"

Red Phone—a series of plays produced by Boca del Lupo—works in a similar way to other PHONE plays and to other works that give the audience-actor a script to read. I'm standing in a phone booth, and the performance begins when the phone rings and I pick it up. It is a sturdy retro red handset attached to the wall of the booth. Above the phone's body is a SCREEN, right at eye-level. My script appears on the screen in text chunks. Changing every twenty or thirty seconds, the text keeps pace with my recitation. My job is to read. I am an actor delivering my lines. I make a serious attempt to give the lines some colour. (see ACTING) Unlike other phone plays *Soon, Tomorrow Maybe* and *Ministry of Mundane Mysteries*, I am not "me." My responses are entirely fixed by the provided script. And unlike other scripted plays *This is the Story of the Child Ruled by Fear* and *Plays2Perform@Home* (also by Boca del Lupo), I don't have the whole script in advance. (see CONSENT) It is this particular intersection of dramaturgies that shapes my relationship to agency in *Red Phone*.

The agency of the audience-participant here is narrowly constrained, but this constraint operates differently than say *Tamara* (FASCISM) or *Huff* (FUTILITY) or *Foreign Radical* (COMPLICITY). In each of those plays, restrictions on the actions available to the audience operate to shape a dilemma where we are "caught" either by our inaction or by being compelled into performing an action inside the fictional world that is at odds with our real-world values. Participation is leveraged to shape an experience of participation that then becomes meaningful

---

4   Breel, "Audience Agency," 370.

to our understanding. In *Red Phone*, we really only have one choice to make: start or stop. Once we accept the INVITATION and pick up the phone, we are on a kind of conveyor belt. Perhaps more accurately, it is like being strapped into a roller coaster or other amusement park ride. Making it stop, by REFUSING to continue, is a pretty big ask. I can say from my own experience there is a bit of adrenaline—in a good way—from working to keep up, to keep speaking the lines, in staying wholly present. (see AROUSAL) I definitely found it to be a flow experience, as defined by Mihály Csíkszentmihályi, riding that sweet zone, matching the skill level of the participant to the challenge level of the task.[5]

There is also a thrill because you don't know what's coming next for you as the actor nor for you as the character. This is another aspect of the constraints of the phone booth script track. You are not only "on rails" in terms of the action of the play, you are also locked into the character. The audience-actor is a puppet or, more accurately, we are the ventriloquist's dummy. (And I mean that in the nicest way.)

The script I participated in at the Vancouver Granville Island installation of *Red Phone* was Hiro Kanagawa's *Out of the Blue*. I was "A." Beginning on a phone call *in media res*, I don't know who I am or who I'm talking to. When B asks me point-blank, "Do you believe in God?" I find myself saying things like: "Um . . . I feel I'm spiritual. But . . . I wouldn't consider myself an actual follower of anything. And I don't believe I know or possess some absolute truth. I don't believe anybody does." B presses me. "So, agnostic then? Anti-theist? Anti-religious?" I explain: "Well . . . probably. But, really, I resist being labeled at all, being reduced to a word, a concept, because isn't that the problem? I mean, 'agnostic,' okay, it might be generally true, but it might imply something to you that isn't true about me." This scripted speech places me on the defensive, defending a deeply personal perspective, on a topic not usually lightly undertaken with casual acquaintances whose views are unknown. I feel cornered. It is simultaneously liberating and sort of appalling to have these words coming out of my mouth. It isn't me, and yet it is me. That's my voice, but these are not my thoughts. And I can't stop. There's no time to think or self-censor—and we don't or won't.

Normally actors are somewhat shielded from their characters by virtue of their training, their role as "actors," and also sometimes by rehearsal. Although the aim is to simulate spontaneity, theatre speeches are rehearsed and crafted. In *Red Phone*, the script simply unfurls. Even

---

5   Jeanne Nakamura and Mihály Csíkszentmihályi, "The Concept of Flow," in *Handbook of Positive Psychology*, edited by C. R. Snyder and Shane J. Lopez (Oxford UP, 2002), 90.

as an unexpected neophyte actor, I am sort of "protected" or distanced from my character, but it's a fragile relationship, not bolstered by either technique or preparation. I am flying an airplane by reading an instruction manual and I don't have a parachute. But at least I'm metaphorically dressed in a pilot's uniform. All I do—all I can do—is keep going and try to look like I know what I'm doing and hopefully land safely.

Dragged by the script, I get into an argument with B and accuse them of being judgmental. In an effort to make peace, I suggest that "we do something as simple as I'll donate 25 dollars to a charity or cause of your choice and you vice versa? Could we do that?" B seems amenable. "Possibly. I mean, we might each have our reasons why we might object to a certain organization or cause suggested by the other. Or object to charitable giving on principle. We don't really know the first thing about each other." And then a metatheatrical twist causes even the plane to vanish. Surreally, I hear myself saying, "Yes, I'm an unknown person in a phone booth. Not even a real phone booth. And so are you. And everything we've said to one another is scripted. An artifice.[6] (OMG! What?!) But still . . . let's not be cynical. Can we at least pledge to one another that we'll . . . perform some random act of kindness, say? Can we at least do that?" B responds gamely, "Transcend the artifice and limitations of this situation?" Who we are now as characters who seem to have broken out of the frame is a mystery. Versions of ourselves playing at being actors in a pretend phone booth, I suppose. Inexorably, I keep talking. I say, "What will we do when we finally meet? Shake hands? Hug? Search each other's eyes for some spark of recognition?" B recites their line, reading from the teleprompter: "Without a script we're free to do as we choose. We have free will." Phony multiplicity indeed.

See TYRANNY

---

6   Other *Red Phone* scripts do not display this kind of self-aware metatheatricality. (Being a metatheatre nerd, I was amazingly fortunate when my scene partner chose *Out of the Blue*.) There are more than a dozen other specially commissioned scripts for two people and a phone booth in the *Red Phone* canon. All are conversations of some kind—not all necessarily in a phone booth, or even on the phone—for which the two characters are not present in the same space and cannot see each other. We are voice only.

YOU TURN INTO GOOEY, RADIOACTIVE CHEESE!

YOUR STORY IS FOREVER TOLD AS A CAUTIONARY TALE.

THE END.

PLAYGROUNDS

In his chapter on playgrounds and the kind of meaningful play that is generated from their geography, game theorist and author of *Play Matters* Miguel Sicart makes an important distinction between *play* spaces and *game* spaces. Sicart explains that "a play space is a location specifically created to accommodate play but does not impose any particular type of play, set of activities, purpose, or goal or reward structure."[1] Play spaces are flexible, like a playground, a kindergarten classroom, a splash pad, or an open field. There is really no way to get it wrong when playing in a play space. Like a handle on a TEACUP, there are invitations and affordances that offer gestural clues for play, but there is plenty of freedom for players GOING ROGUE. Play spaces rely on imagination and creativity.

Game spaces are not as free. Katie Salen and Eric Zimmerman acknowledge the tension between freedom and restriction in games. They write, "Play is free movement within a more rigid structure . . . Play exists *because* of more rigid structures but also exists somehow in *opposition* to them."[2] They make a distinction between playing games and simply being playful. In games, the intended activity is firmly attached to the specific physical geography and design of a space. Sports fields and game boards are good examples of game spaces; the activities of the game are tied to the cartography of the space. There is an obvious way to move through *Snakes and Ladders* or the *Game of Life*. If players were to wear something on their feet other than skates in a hockey arena, it would be nearly impossible to use the ice rink. Game spaces also have props that nod explicitly to the intended activity. Like most categorical comparisons, game spaces and play spaces exist on a spectrum and are not a binary pair. Some game spaces have quite a lot of flexibility for embroidery, and some spaces of free play are repurposed game spaces. One can play both basketball and 21 at a basketball court, but it would be difficult to play anything other than *Monopoly* on a *Monopoly* board.[3]

---

1   Miguel Sicart, *Play Matters* (MIT P, 2014), 51.

2   Katie Salen and Eric Zimmerman, *Rules of Play: Game Design Fundamentals* (MIT P, 2004), 304.

3   Short for modification, "mods" involve altering an existing thing to change its appearance or functionality. Mods are popularly applied to video games like *Minecraft* to customize the coding to change what is possible within these creative worlds. Broadly, mods are the equivalent of "house rules" or other kinds of hacks

When talking about the difference between game spaces and play spaces, Sicart explains "how materiality and activity are joined together in the selected spaces of play. Playgrounds as metaphors also allow us to escape from game spaces, which are designed for the purpose of playing games but do not always allow the exploration of the creative and appropriative capacities of play."[4] Playgrounds use physical affordances to offer an INVITATION while not restricting the potentials of play. Playgrounds exist within a kind of "tension between appropriation and resistance: how a space offers itself to be appropriated by play, but how that space resists some forms of play, specifically those not allowed for political, legal, moral, or cultural reasons. Play relates to space through the ways of appropriation and the constant dance between resistance and surrender."[5] Playgrounds can act as "an invitation for the child (and the parents) to appropriate that space through play, to turn it into a play space."[6]

How does this dichotomy between play spaces and game spaces manifest as a participatory dramaturgy? One familiar pattern is that the tension between game spaces and play spaces aligns with CLAIRE BISHOP's recognition of choices participatory artist-creators make between randomness and control. Game spaces and play spaces are the geographical and spatial manifestations of this balance. Experiences with low randomness and high control, like escape rooms, are game spaces; there are specific puzzles to complete that constitute the design. If you decide to play some other game of your own invention in an escape room, you will likely not escape. By contrast, exploratory performance environments like *The Archive of Missing Things* or a mirror maze installation invite randomness through play spaces where participants are welcome to roam around and experience the narrative as they happen upon it. Milton Lim and Patrick Blenkarn's *asses.masses* takes place in a digital game space, a video game world populated by donkeys looking to mobilize a workers' revolution. In one way, *asses. masses* looks like a play space with open-ended opportunities

---

to make slightly different use of the same play components. For example, Greg Loring-Albright took the bestselling board game *Settlers of Catan* and reimagined the game play to present instead a decolonial narrative. The new game *First Nations of Catan* uses the same board but adds some additional pieces and changes some of the key rules and game mechanics. "The First Nations of Catan: Practices in Critical Modification," *Analog Game Studies*, 9 November 2015, analoggamestudies.org /2015/11/the-first-nations-of-catan-practices-in-critical-modification/.

4   Sicart, *Play Matters*, 59.
5   Sicart, *Play Matters*, 52.
6   Sicart, *Play Matters*, 51.

for wandering navigation, but there are limits. The virtual space is not infinite and players bump into invisible "walls" (sometimes actually visible walls or dead ends) in the video game world that herd them towards the only way out. For example, to complete the first level at the end of Episode 1, the donkey avatar must jump down a well.

Created and designed by Esmaa Mohamoud, *Double Dribble* was presented as part of the Playing in Public exhibition at the Bentway in Toronto. An exploration of the accessibility of public spaces through a surreal basketball court with nets of varying height and diameter, *Double Dribble* is a play space with activist intentions. Anchored in the game of basketball, *Double Dribble* "pushes the public to reinvent play and even dismantle the rules to play,"[7] inviting them to use their imagination and AGENCY to celebrate the variabilities of play. What does it mean if the hoop is impossibly small or way above my head? Conversely, what does it mean if the hoop is at knee height or if it is large enough to accommodate the diameter of several basketballs? *Double Dribble* doesn't offer answers, only asks us questions. *Double Dribble* is a political provocation. This play space under the Bentway left plenty of room for the randomness of audience-player input, (see ALEA) ultimately asking players to engage spatial obstacles and build new worlds. We are primed to extend that thinking to all the other arbitrary systems that shape our daily existence. What other games can I play within and around those structures, and what other ways might we live?

Although like *Double Dribble*, *Monday Nights* also takes place on a basketball court, 6th Man Collective manifests the court geography as a game space rather than a play space. *Monday Nights* focuses on teamwork *within* the rules and restrictions of basketball without asking participants to use play to innovate and reconfigure the space or its use. (It is perhaps notable in this context that one of the characters in *Monday Nights* is a referee, played by the ubiquitous Colin Doyle.) Where *Double Dribble* asks us to recalibrate our social structures through meaningful play, *Monday Nights* is about men finding their way through the (sometimes restrictive) social structures that already exist. What does it mean to be a husband? A father? A friend? How do I meet my own expectations and the expectations of others? What does "winning" look like under these parameters? Where *Double Dribble* is about innovating to move beyond constraints, *Monday Nights* is about finding ways to survive (and hopefully thrive) within them.

See HANDS, CHOOSE YOUR OWN ADVENTURE, and LABOUR

---

7   "Playing in Public: Double Dribble," *The Bentway*, play.thebentway.ca/experience /double-dribble/.

POLITICS OF THE BASEMENT

The interactive video-game play *asses.masses*, created by Patrick Blenkarn and Milton Lim, exemplifies a certain kind of collaborative ASYMMETRICAL participation where a few people, usually taking turns one by one, are doing the actual playing while the others watch. Via heckling, shouting warnings or encouragement,or contributing answers or advice, the watchers are figured here as also a type of engaged participants. We might call them "back-seat drivers." It is a familiar domestic arrangement: one or two people are on their feet in front of the screen playing Wii Sports, with a handful of others sprawled behind them on the couch, watching players as well as their avatars. When the round is over, perhaps they switch roles. Blenkarn poetically refers to this as the "politics of the basement."[1]

The first episode of *asses.masses* begins in a darkened theatre. There is a large screen at the front and a dramatically spot-lit plinth at the top of the aisle. On the plinth is a single PlayStation controller. The screen lights up and declares, "Avatar required." We wait. And we wait. No further instructions are provided. We wait some more. Finally, one intrepid audience member takes up the INVITATION and grabs the REMOTE CONTROLLER. Lim compares this to the apocryphal moment when Thespis stepped out of the Athenian chorus and spoke, becoming the first actor.[2] The first act of *asses.masses* is a trivia game; the first set of questions are about labour and political organization: Do you think of yourself as a political animal? Do you have an experience of doing manual labour every day for an extended period of time? Have you ever gone on a labour strike due to unfair or dangerous working conditions? The next set of questions is about asses (i.e., donkeys, not the other kind) in literature, history, philosophy, politics, and economics. Players get immediate feedback with flourishes or buzzers to indicate correct and incorrect answers. The second act is designed in the style of a two-dimensional 1980s video game. You are a donkey called "Trusty Ass" and your purpose is to "unite the workers" against the oppressors. When

1   Patrick dropped this beautiful phrase in our laps at the Arts, Culture, and Digital Transformation Summit at the Banff Centre for Arts and Creativity in November 2019.
2   Milton Lim, "Level UP Symposium Artists Q&A," *Level Up: The Dramaturgy of Digital Performance and Design*, Associated Designers of Canada, 15 February 2021, youtube.com/watch?v=hsbdRfKVWSM.

you encounter other donkeys (who have marvelously childish names like "Nice Ass" or "Smart Ass." My personal favourite was "Kick Ass"), you can recruit them to your revolutionary cause. They then follow you as you explore the simple, sparse landscape, dotted with rocks. Sometimes, using typed dialogue, the animated asses debate revolutionary strategy. Comrade Bad Ass, for example, slams peaceful braying and protesting and asks if the herd is prepared to "burn down the city and kill hundreds of innocent people." Although serious about labour issues, the cheeky brisk dialogue and simplistic visuals give this first episode an absurd feel. (At one point, the Ghost of Old Ass reminds the leader, "Less daydreaming and more uprising!") Episode 1 concludes when (after arriving to find the city already burning and hundreds of innocent people already dead. "Did the revolution start without us?") our avatar, Trusty Ass, seeking water to put out the fires, falls down a well and dies. Trusty Ass follows the light through a digital tunnel, is rendered again, and emerges in three-dimensions to frolic in an endless cinematic field of red flowers. The final screen declares, "To be continued . . . "

By framing a performance work about LABOUR in the context of a participatory play-game hybrid, *asses.masses* looks directly at the implications of how our audience-player labour is recruited, employed, and rewarded. (see INSTRUMENTALITY) In a play about a worker revolution, how can we shake free from becoming material instruments of the game? I think the play itself expresses some self-awareness of this oppressive dilemma, at least initially in the first episode, through its intentionally primitive visual style and very tight, gated structure.[3] (There is ultimately only one path and one ending to Episode 1. The well is the final boss and you die every time.) Moreover, there is the inescapable juxtaposition of how we share the load of the revolution with how the politics of the basement influences how we share (or don't share) the load of participation. I think the play's silence on how this leader is chosen, and how the controller might (or might not) be passed to another hero-participant is a meaningful dramaturgical choice, regarding these self-organizing politics. The game has a single hero-participant, self-selected by their boldness in seizing the controller. I wonder, what does this say about a patriarchal value system that values the bold, solitary leader? Is their boldness really a reward? Is this invitation to be bold telling us something else about how leaders are selected? How does

---

3   Ultimately, *asses.masses* expanded to include ten episodes incorporating a vast array of visual styles and game-play modes. Episodes feature tributes to classic, beloved video games like *Pong, Pokémon, Dance Dance Revolution, Final Fantasy, The Legend of Zelda, Super Mario Bros.*, and many more. Here we are only considering Episode 1.

this happen each time? Likewise, the scope for engagement (heckling, shouting warnings or encouragement, and contributing answers or advice) by the remaining watcher-participants is likewise fertile as an unstructured possibility. Do we want to be one of the asses or are we relegated to the masses? How does this polity of donkeys play the game and/or enact revolution together?[4]

See MOB

GASP! THE ALIEN HAS BEEN STANDING BEHIND YOU THE WHOLE TIME AND THEY HEARD EVERYTHING! BEFORE YOU HAVE TIME TO TRY AND EXPLAIN YOURSELF, THEY PULL OUT A LASER GUN AND ZAP YOU. TURN TO PAGE **297** TO FIND OUT YOUR FATE.

---

4   For a longer discussion of this exact question, see Jenn Stephenson and Derek Manderson, "Herd Dramaturgies: Participatory Audience as Proto-Society in *asses. masses*," *Theater* 55, no. 3 (forthcoming October 2024).

PROXIES

When we think of audience participation,
a scenario that commonly leaps to mind is
the request for a volunteer from the audience to come up on the stage.
This is a popular gimmick in a magic show where the magician seeks an
ORDINARY PERSON, chosen for their non-magical abilities and lack
of connection to the onstage trickery, to pick a card or select a number.
Of course, sometimes there is trickery within trickery and this seemingly
ordinary person is in fact a "plant," and not an audience member at all.
The suspicious can never be sure. The person might also use their senses
to inspect paraphernalia used in the trick to vouch for it really being as
it appears. They affirm for those of us at a distance that this egg is really
an egg, that this hat is really just a hat, that this metal ring is entirely
solid, that this box has no obvious secret compartments or trapdoors. I
was once witness to a magic show where a very young audience-assistant
dropped the egg on their shoes—oops!—where it splattered very authen-
tically, if messily. In these tasks of verification, the one audience member
stands in for the rest of us. Although they step forward to interact with
the performers and assist in the execution of the play, (see CREW) their
position remains firmly that of audience representative.

Beyond the practical function of being an up-close version of our eyes (or
HANDS), this audience-in-extension also carries our affinity. This person is
one of us and we want them to be successful and not be embarrassed. We
root for them. They are a hero. Rebecca Northan capitalizes on precisely
this baked-in dramaturgy of the heroic audience-avatar in her immensely
popular improv show, *Blind Date*. When Mimi the Clown's dinner date fails
to show up, she recruits a member of the audience to stand in. The entire
show then consists of Mimi and her audience date collaboratively enacting
scenes from their evening out—a romantic meal at a restaurant, the drive
home where they get pulled over by the police, canoodling on the sofa in
Mimi's apartment. Throughout, the actor playing Mimi encourages their
audience-ACTING partner. She works hard to make them look good. The
audience invariably finds this person charming in their ordinariness and we
view them with affection for the bravery of their ad hoc performance. This
same setup is heightened in another Northan improv piece, *Legend Has It*,
where the audience-player is cast literally as a sword-wielding hero tasked
with saving a fantasy land from a villainous oppressor. (see THE MATRIX)

In the magic show, or in a participatory improv like *Legend Has It*, there are two audiences with different but linked perspectives—one that is up close, hands-on and singular, and the other that is distanced, bearing WITNESS to the action and collective. The notion of the proxy acts as a bridge between the two. For those of us who are not chosen, we remain situated dominantly in the BOURGEOIS THEATRE context, primed to watch events unfold, and exercise our INTERPRETIVE meaning-making function. But a small part of us stretches over that proxy bridge to locate ourselves in the action by analogy. The volunteer-hero is me.[1] Conversely, even with the special insider status and more active role, the proxy player remains always in their original position as a ticket-buying audience member, partly what they consume now, however, is their own performance. (see FIRST-PERSON SHOOTER and SHOPPING)

Which brings me to *Café Sarajevo*. Created by the bluemouth inc. collective, *Café Sarajevo* is framed as a live podcast, recounting a visit to Sarajevo, twenty years after the end of the civil war, by two of the play's creators, Lucy Simic and Stephen O'Connell. The cast and all audience members wear Bluetooth headphones for the entire show through which we hear the amplified dialogue as well as background scoring and other sound effects. Gloria, the stage manager, cues the beginning of each scene broadcast, counting down the beats until we are "on air" by saying "four, three," and then switching to silent hand gestures for "*two*" and "*one*." The trope of the podcast centres narrative storytelling and alleviates any need or expectation for realistic scenography, or indeed for any scenography at all. Freed from visual mimesis, space is created for audience members to be recruited as unrehearsed voice actors. About eight audience members (chosen during the pre-show) have been given lanyards with name tags. At intervals, they read from scripts on music stands, performing dialogue in partnership with the members of the company. One is the announcer who reads the sponsorship credits at the top of the podcast. Others are locals met in Sarajevo—including guides Dino, Samara, and Jasmin. Through this collaboration, audience members populate Lucy's story, bringing it into our bodies. In this case, the effect of these proxies is a heightened empathy. We relate to them both

---

[1]   It is important to note that sometimes, the proxy doesn't feel like me. In other words, the positionalities of some audience members are not (and cannot be) represented accurately by the delegated proxy. Rebecca Northan responded to this in her creation of *Queer Blind Date*, another version of the show that features "dates" across the gender and sexuality spectrum.

as representatives of our audience-selves and as Sarajevans. Importantly, we feel through them and with them differently than we do the actors.

Something similar happens when four audience members become soccer players representing England and Croatia in the FIFA World Cup. The rest of us, standing shoulder to shoulder, our toes outlining a large white rectangle taped on the floor, are both the watching crowd and the game boundary. We use our feet to keep the ball in play, tapping it if it rolls near. The enthusiasm of the players is infectious, and the audience group becomes energized. (see MOB) When the ensuing fireworks cause the cast members (and with them the audience soccer players who mimic them) to drop to the floor covering and cowering as if sheltering from explosions, we are immediately sobered. The abrupt plummet from our adrenaline high is stunning. It is a powerful effect born out of our proxy participation, as the usual distance between actor-characters and audience is reduced when our audience-representatives become those actor-characters.

The dramaturgical function of the proxy is a literal manifestation of empathy's call to put yourself in another person's shoes. The audience, tethered to our proxy participant selves, has access via this bridge to the stakes of participation where we bear WITNESS, but our position is cushioned by distance and by remaining essentially invisible in the collective of the herd. We benefit from this RELATION, but the associated risks are mitigated.

See ELBOWS

Q

It is reminiscent of a joke told by a six-year-old. But instead of "How is an elephant like a loaf of bread?" I'm asking, "How is QAnon like *Ratatouille: The TikTok Musical?*" (Bear with me. I promise this is going somewhere.) In addition to their shared context, both phenomena rising to mass consciousness in the late days of the Trump presidency and in the shadow of pre-vaccine pandemic lockdowns, both QAnon and *Ratatouille: The Musical* are manifestations of participatory and emergent behaviours, made possible by Web 2.0 collaborative interactivity. But whereas the amateur artists of *Ratatouille: The Musical* created, well, a musical; the adherents of Q who elaborate the intricacies of the QAnon orthodoxy created an entire alternate reality.

QAnon is an apparently widespread American conspiracy theory, born in the dark corners of the web, that believes, among other things, that Donald Trump has been chosen to save America from a deep-state cabal of Satan-worshipping Democrats, who are also pedophiles.[1] *Ratatouille: The Musical*, on the other hand, was born on TikTok and is an assemblage of lyrics, music, dialogue, choreography, and set and costume design sketches, that reimagine the animated Disney/Pixar movie *Ratatouille* as a Broadway-style musical.[2] In early January 2021, both QAnon and *Ratatouille: The Musical* seeped out of the virtual realm and into the material one. Over a weekend in January 2021, a production featuring a cast of well-known Broadway performers, streamed on TodayTix. The event raised $1.9 million for the Actors Fund.[3] On 6 January, 2021, the day of the certification of the results of the 2020 election, a crowd comprised of right-wing "militias" and QAnon supporters who believed that the election had been "stolen," stormed the US Capitol building with

1   Kevin Roose, "What Is QAnon, the Viral Pro-Trump Conspiracy Theory?" *New York Times*, 3 September 2021, nytimes.com/article/what-is-qanon.html.

2   Rebecca Alter, "Broadway Is Closed but *Ratatouille* the Musical is Cooking on TikTok," *Vulture*, 19 November 2020, vulture.com/2020/11/ratatouille-musical-tiktok.html.

3   The official playbill for *Ratatouille: The TikTok Musical* can be found at playbill.com/article/presenting-the-official-fake-ratatouille-playbill; Alyssa Bereznak, "Anyone Can Cook: The Oral History of *Ratatouille: The Musical,*" *The Ringer*, 31 December 2020, theringer.com/movies/2020/12/31/22206943/ratatouille-musical-oral-history-tiktok-trend-making-of.

the aim of disrupting those proceedings. Five people including Capitol police and protestors died.[4]

Ratatouille: The Musical is at its heart a crowdsourced work. Beginning with an a cappella rendition of an ode to the main character, Remy the rat, posted by TikTok user Em Jaccs (Emily Jacobsen), other TikTok denizens augmented this initial song; Daniel Mertzlufft added orchestral scoring. Others constructed a set model, wrote and performed more songs, invented choreography, and even puppets. Not only is it participatory, but the iterative recycling and reimagining marks this as a potentially EMERGENT phenomenon. There is no director, no producer, no playwright or composer. Apart from the inspiration of the original movie, there is no controlling animus at all. There is no gatekeeping. Every contribution is valid—even potentially contradictory or exclusive elements become enfolded into the sprawling motley whole. One notable characteristic that distinguishes the *Ratatouille* project from myriad other similar collective works is that there is a knowing wink, a sly pretense that this could in fact be—*is*, in fact—real. Rebecca Alter makes this observation in her history of the musical's development on Vulture.com. She writes, "The specific appeal of the *Ratatouille* musical is the alternate reality of it all: It is not inconceivable that there is a timeline where *Ratatouille: The Musical* was announced as a big-budget, family-friendly production alongside the likes of *Aladdin*, *The Lion King*, and *The Little Mermaid*."[5] Additional creative elements that project that reality include a (faux) Broadway-style yellow-header Playbill and video from a high-school cast party at Denny's. This is where *Ratatouille: The Musical* tips into performance—using mimetic representation to create (probably) alternate fictional worlds.

Pervasive games, or alternative reality games (ARG) invite players to participate in covert activities in a hidden universe existing in parallel with the usual mundane one. (see SNEAKY NINJAS) One of the simplest pervasive games is perhaps *Assassins*, where a group of friends or co-workers are each given the name of another person in the group to "kill." The kill, depending on the agreed rules, is accomplished with a coloured dot sticker, water pistol, or simple touch tag. If you successfully assassinate your target, you take the name of their target and move on to your next mission. The winner is the last person still alive. The pervasive nature of *Assassins* arises from the extended duration and expansive boundary of

---

4   Jack Healy, "These Are the 5 People Who Died in the Capitol Riot," *New York Times*, 11 January 2021, nytimes.com/2021/01/11/us/who-died-in-capitol-building-attack.html.

5   Alter, "Broadway is Closed."

the game that takes place in the interstices of everyday life over the course of days or even weeks. There is also a critical element of being SECRET WEIRDOS, as your kills cannot be witnessed by anyone else, especially non-participant bystanders. The foundational book on this subject is *Pervasive Games: Theory and Design* by Markus Montola, Jaakko Stenros, and Annika Waern. [6] They begin with *Assassins* and trace the proliferation of the genre through fictional-game-events like *The Beast*,[7] *Shelby Logan's Run*,[8] and *Uncle Roy All Around You*,[9] linking at the end to the global TV phenomenon of *The Amazing Race*. These game-performance hybrids necessitate the imaginative invention of a separate world for the in-group of players within the MAGIC CIRCLE.

By this logic, QANON is a massive pervasive game. With its focus on discovering and decoding secret messages, the active logic of QANON's search for the ultimate truth is the same. In a September 2020 article in *WIRED Magazine*, writer Clive Thompson documents the insights of game designer Adrian Hon, who makes exactly this observation: "ARGS are designed to be clue-cracking, multiplatform scavenger hunts . . . To belong to the QANON pack is to be part of a massive crowdsourcing project that sees itself cracking a mystery."[10] There is real pleasure in solving these perceived puzzles.[11] The distinction, however, between the QANON alternate-reality narrative and that of something like aforementioned pervasive

<hr />

6   Markus Montola, Jaakko Stenros, and Annika Waern, *Pervasive Games: Theory and Design* (CRC, 2009).

7   *The Beast* is one of the earliest known mass ARG. It was developed as a promotional event in support of the movie *AI: Artificial Intelligence*. It ran approximately five months beginning in March 2001 and reached upwards of five thousand players worldwide ("*The Beast* (Game)," *Wikipedia*, wikipedia.org/wiki/The_Beast_(game)).

8   *Shelby Logan's Run* is the October 2002 Las Vegas iteration of a regular game, treasure/puzzle hunt, road rally called the Game occurring annually on the US west coast ("The Game (treasure hunt)," *Wikipedia*, wikipedia.org/wiki/The_Game_(treasure_hunt)).

9   *Uncle Roy All Around You* was a combined online and in-the-street mixed-reality game produced by Blast Theory in June 2003 in London, UK (blasttheory.co.uk/projects/uncle-roy-all-around-you/).

10   Clive Thompson, "QANON Is Like a Game—a Most Dangerous Game," *WIRED Magazine*, 22 September 2020, wired.com/story/qanon-most-dangerous-multiplatform-game/.

11   Kevin Roose, "A QANON 'Digital Soldier' Marches On, Undeterred by Theory's Unraveling," *New York Times*, 17 January 2021, nytimes.com/2021/01/17/technology/qanon-meme-queen.html. From a *New York Times* profile of a QANON "meme queen," the author writes, "What attracts Ms. Gilbert and many other people to QANON isn't just the content of the conspiracy theory itself. It's the community and sense of mission it provides. New QANON believers are invited to chat rooms and group texts, and their posts are showered with likes and retweets. They make friends, and are told that they are not lonely Facebook addicts squinting at zoomed-in paparazzi photos, but patriots gathering 'intel' for a righteous revolution."

game *The Beast* is that in the case of *The Beast*, it was a commercial, fictional creation of Microsoft/Warner Bros. to support the promotion of the film AI: *Artificial Intelligence*. There was an intelligence behind the game scenario. For QAnon, the hidden narrative that they seek to reveal is non-existent. There is no secret plan for global domination. There is no wizard behind the curtain. The truth is not out there. (Really.) Rather the "truth" is being created iteratively out of nothing by the SEEKERS.

What's fascinating about this, then, is how it illustrates emergence in action. Emergence is a participatory phenomenon. Emergence doesn't need a leader or a coherent narrative to get started, coherence arrives as a dumb product of the game mechanic, of the controlling algorithm. It is Internet-based social media platforms that provide the accelerator. Emergence algorithms require thousands, if not millions, of reactive local responses. Think flocking birds or colony-building ANTS. Conspiracy theories are not, in and of themselves, participatory. They are the result, however, of a participatory emergent algorithm that produces the standard genre characteristics of a conspiracy theory (or a murmuration of starlings or insect architecture).

Participation in conspiracy theories seems to align with feelings of powerlessness, perceptions of lack of control. It is not coincidental that paranoid conspiracy narratives tend to foster themes of control by elite "others." (Sometimes radical socialist Democrats and Zionist globalist Jews, but also aliens and lizard people.) The musical-theatre creators of *Ratatouille: The Musical* are also, within the realm of professional musical development, powerless. Their pretense that their *Ratatouille* musical is legitimized as really existing in a real Broadway theatre is a gesture of defiance that recognizes their outsider status.

RECIPE

"And what does it mean for the artist to surrender the security of self-expression for the risk of intersubjective engagement?"[1] By asking this question, Grant Kester (*Conversation Pieces*) digs at a kind of lurking insecurity that dogs participatory art, pitting control by the artist in opposition to randomness[2] introduced by interactive audiences. Frankly, I think this is kind of a red herring (and I think Kester is doing this on purpose—since it is, after all, a book about dialogic interactions). First, any performed artwork, manifesting not only in space, but also in time, is subject to the variability innate to performance. One pianist's performance of a Beethoven sonata will be necessarily different from another's. Likewise, centuries of Hamlets. Second, beyond putting a work into the hands of a unique artist-performer, intersubjective engagement is the province of every listener or spectator. It is a commonplace understanding that a work of art is only fully (and flexibly) made manifest via the active INTERPRETATION by an audience. The work done by a participatory co-creative audience combines both of these roles, being both durational performer and interpretive meaning-maker. All art exists on this continuum between control and randomness, and various placements on this line are not unfamiliar. BOURGEOIS THEATRE, which tends to value authored scripts, rigorous rehearsal to ensure near perfect repeatability, and a closed border between actors and audience, manifests high control with low randomness. By contrast, art movements like Fluxus event scores manifest low control with high randomness.

My favourite Fluxus[3] event score is *#2 Proposition* (1962) by Alison Knowles.[4] Mariah's favourite event score is *Snow Piece* by Yoko Ono,

---

1   Grant Kester, *Conversation Pieces: Community and Communication in Modern Art*, updated edition (U of California P, 2013), 8.

2   See Claire Bishop, "Introduction: Viewers as Producers," in *Participation* (MIT P, 2006), 12.

3   "Fluxus was an international, interdisciplinary community of artists, composers, designers, and poets during the 1960s and 1970s who engaged in experimental art performances that emphasized the artistic process over the finished product . . . They produced performance 'events,' which included enactments of scores, 'Neo-Dada' noise music, and time-based works . . . Many Fluxus artists share anti-commercial and anti-art sensibilities" ("Fluxus," *Wikipedia*, en.wikipedia.org/wiki/Fluxus).

4   See Ono's biography page on *FluxusMuseum* for a summary of her involvement and influence in the Fluxus movement: fluxusmuseum.org/holding-page-for-yoko-ono/.

which appears in her collection *Grapefruit*. **Knowles's work, which pre-miered at the Institute of Contemporary Arts in London, simply states: "Make a salad."**[5] **Although the best-known performances of this work in recent decades have featured very large-scale salad assembly, this is not required. In an April 2012 interview Knowles says, "I think the salad fits in anywhere . . . I think it fits into a romantic two-person dinner. I think it fits into Earth Day. You know, I was sitting in the Presidential dining room a while ago, and they served a salad . . . They didn't realize they were doing my piece."**[6] **I need to say here that Alison Knowles is a genius and her conception of the piece that every salad anywhere is a performance of her artwork makes my heart sing!** (And has changed salad for me forever.) **This is peak randomness.**

Food notwithstanding, an event score is a recipe. Hannah Higgins (who happens to be Knowles's daughter as well as an art historian) **writes in her book *Fluxus Experience* that it was George Brecht who first used the term event scores to describe these works. Yoko Ono, one of the original core members of the Fluxus movement, calls them "instructional poems." Knowles defines an event score as "a one or two line recipe for action."**[7] **"Event Scores, involve simple actions, ideas, and objects from everyday life recontextualized as performance. Event Scores are texts that can be seen as proposal pieces or instructions for actions. The idea of the score suggests musicality. Like a musical score, Event Scores can be realized by artists other than the original creator and are open to variation and interpretation."**[8] **Event scores basically say, "Do this."**

"Do this" is a core dramaturgical strategy for participatory theatre. When called upon to participate, we need to be told what to do (and where and when and how. And what not to do). **The originator of the recipe is what Janet Murray calls the "procedural author." In her work on digital narratives and games, Murray recognizes this need for a different kind of guidance for interactive readers and players. So, not only does the text need an author in the usual sense, but the world-specific rules of engagement also need to be authored. Murray**

---

5 "Event Scores," *Alison Knowles*, aknowles.com/eventscore.html.

6 Betsy Morais, "Salad as Performance Art," *The New Yorker*, 26 April 2012, newyorker.com/culture/culture-desk/salad-as-performance-art.

7 Sonnie Solomon, "How Alison Knowles's 'Event Scores' Offer Recipes for Action," *Carnegie Museum of Art Storyboard*, 11 October 2016, web.archive.org/web/20230208001131 /storyboard.cmoa.org/2016/10/how-alison-knowless-event-scores-act-as-recipes-for -action/.

8 "Event Scores."

writes, "Procedural authorship means writing the rules by which the texts appear as well as writing the texts themselves. It means writing the rules for the interactor's involvement, that is, the conditions under which things will happen in response to the participant's actions. It means establishing the properties of the objects and potential objects in the virtual world and the formulas for how they will relate to one another. The procedural author creates not just a set of scenes but a work of narrative possibilities."[9] Recontextualizing Murray's definition to live theatre performance, Gareth White notes not only the need for a controlling framework, but also a corresponding need to provide and articulate the spaces of participation. As he points out, "A significant part of the work of an interactive work consists of creating the structure within which particular gaps appear, and the work of the interactive performer consists of repeating this structure and allowing the participants to fill the gaps in different ways in each fresh iteration of the work."[10] In this way, the recipe addresses both of these aspects of participation. The event comes into existence both from the structure and from how the gaps are filled.

If the recipe is the foundational description of the participatory world-event framework, somehow that framework needs to be communicated to us. We are newbies in each new world and in desperate need of instruction. (If our role were to sit back and observe and interpret, then we don't need much, if any, direction. Our capacity for "breaking" the world, or "breaking" the performance event, is extremely limited. If we are to be participants however . . .) One communication strategy is for the content of the recipe to be delivered inside the fiction via the character type of the GUIDE. Another strategy does not require assigning a character role; instead the actions (or non-actions) expected by the recipe are silently implied by the built physical environment or other contextual factors. (see TEACUPS) Sometimes, as with an event-score performance prompt, we are simply handed the recipe directly and left to our own devices.

In the case of *La Rivoluzione Siamo Noi—The Change Maker* by DLT, the actor-creators do not seem to be present to lead us. The performance begins with an envelope that reads, Open me. When we do, we find a sheet of typed instructions. We are prompted to choose a leader. Our designated leader then reads the next instructions aloud. More generally,

9   Janet H Murray, *Hamlet on the Holodeck: The Future of Narrative in Cyberspace*, updated edition (MIT P, 2017), 187.
10   Gareth White, *Audience Participation in Theatre: Aesthetics of the Invitation* (Palgrave Macmillan, 2013), 30.

audience-participation is (gently?) dictated by dramaturgies built around usually implied imperative verb conjugations like, "Fill in the blanks!" (see MAD LIBS), "Follow me!" (see SWEATING and SEEKING), or "Make a choice!" (see CHOOSE YOUR OWN ADVENTURE) (For a discussion of what happens when we refuse the imperative and just "not," see OR ELSE.)

Given the guided directives of procedural authorship, we should not be surprised when the performance takes the shape of an actual recipe—complete with food. *Embrace* by Hazel Venzon and Sawa Theatre, written by Qudus Abusaleh, is a cooking show for an online audience, using food to bridge intercultural differences between audience members living in Canada and new arrivants to the country. In the hands-on version, audience-cooks receive a meal-kit parcel with all the measured ingredients, a recipe card, and a Zoom link.[11] Under the tutelage of three amateur chefs who are also recent immigrants— Yousef Almbaidin (*mulukhiya* cooked into a thick broth and served with rice), Suzan Palani (vegetable dolma), and Ameen Alnaser (*kunafah* pastry. His version features sweet cheese topped with pistachios and drizzled with attar, served with tea)—we learn to make all the parts of a Middle Eastern three-course meal from scratch. Accompanied by a musician in their kitchen-set who plays the daff and the tar, each chef-performer intersperses their cooking instructions with personal stories about what this food means to them. Ameen coaches us with those familiar imperatives: "Let's divide [the dough] in half. Put the second half aside and let's work on the other half. Let's cut it down to small pieces and then we'll start shredding it and chopping it into fine small pieces." Later, he urges us, "Don't waste any cheese, guys! Put as much as you can in the kunafah." While he grates, chops, stirs, and waits for the pie to bake, he tells us a series of stories from his childhood in Daraa, Syria, through his flight from the civil war to a UNHCR camp in Jordan, university studies, and finally immigration to Canada. (He sees a poster on a bulletin board asking if he wants to come to Canada. And he thinks, "Why not?") Ameen banters with the Zoom chefs, reading their chat messages. At one point he breaks off in the middle of a story with a new thought: "If there is one thing, guys, that I can share with you, that I hope would stick is that you always,

---

11   *Embrace* also allows for a third track. The DIY track involves parallel live cooking but with your own bought ingredients and a downloadable recipe card. *Embrace* was live-streamed in June 2021 from "the ancestral lands of the Oji-Cree, Dakota, and Dene Nations, and on the heartland of the Red River Metis"; a territory also known by its colonial name as Winnipeg, Manitoba.

always you should try the meals as a family. Don't eat alone. When we finish making this together today, invite everyone to the table. If you live alone, then today we will eat together as a family." Still dispensing imperatives, ("*Don't* eat alone. *Invite* everyone to the table.") Ameen has given us a recipe to combat isolation, to be in community, as best we can.

WRITE IN YOUR GO-TO RECIPE.

REFUSAL

No. No, I don't want to. No, thank you. (*Silence.*) Under no circumstances. No fucking way. Actually, if you don't mind, I'd rather not. (*Walking away. Walking out.*)

What does it mean when we talk about non-participation? The subtitle to Gareth White's book *Audience Participation in the Theatre* is "*Aesthetics of the Invitation.*" There, he considers the nature of the critical moment of the invitation, when those who began as only audience alter their roles and their behaviour to participate in the action of a performance.[1] He also considers the nature of that invitation—it could be overt or covert, implicit, or even accidental. He notes that there are sometimes allowances for uninvited participation.[2] Unsurprisingly given the scope of the book, White's focus is directed to the question assumed by the invitation, "Will you?" But it behooves us to also consider the answer to that question, because the answer to "will you?" is not always a simple and enthusiastic "yes." (see CONSENT and YES, LET'S!)

To begin with, I think it is important to recognize that in some cases, non-participation doesn't mean "won't" but is more like "can't." Sometimes the invitation is not expansive enough to include me or to permit my participation. Sometimes I am UNWELCOME. Sometimes the environmental or social parameters of the "ask" render me unable. It is valuable in this regard to follow the thinking embedded in the social model of disability. This model first introduced in 1983 by Mike Oliver (*Social Work with Disabled People*) separates impairment from disability. The model recognizes that there are environmental or systemic barriers in the world that render me unable to do certain things and that the removal of those barriers can reduce or eliminate obstacles to my participation. For example, using glasses can improve acuity for visual impairment or replacing stairs with ramps assists accessibility. In the theatre, this can also mean expanding modes of performative communication (like using ASL or visual description) or relaxing strict

---

1   Gareth White, *Audience Participation in Theatre: Aesthetics of the Invitation* (Palgrave Macmillan, 2013), 4.

2   White, *Audience Participation in Theatre*, 40–44.

behavioural rules of audience etiquette (like leaving the house lights on or not censuring talking and noise-making in the audience).[3]

Participatory theatre often makes an ask that is more demanding than typical BOURGEOIS THEATRE as in cases where audience-participants are asked to move (walk over rough terrain, climb stairs, run, dance, paddle a canoe), touch and be touched, eat or drink, answer intimate confessional questions. The list goes on. Often this expanded audience-ask is part of the thrill of participatory theatre, (see AROUSAL) but participatory theatre also expands the range of potential things that I cannot do. (Or cannot do today. Or cannot do here. Or cannot do under these circumstances.)

Leaving "can't" aside for the moment, I'd like to turn to "won't." What is communicated when, having been issued an invitation to participate, I refuse it?

One message that refusal communicates is: "I feel unsafe." The corollary of an invitation is a request for a contribution. When I am welcomed as a participant, I am being given an opportunity to join in. But on the flip side, being a participant asks something from me. I need to *do* something. Often that something is pretty low stakes, something fun or easy, something I would ordinarily have no qualms about saying yes to. But sometimes that something is too much. And of course, the line of "too much" varies from person to person. The most common situations where I have refused arise when I feel too exposed. Either I am being asked for something too intimate ("When was the last time you cried?"[4] My silent refusal translates as: "That is none of your business!") or that my contribution necessitates a possibly embarrassing leap into the unknown ("What is the sound of oblivion?"

---

3   The pre-show for *Access Me*, created by the Boys in Chairs collective, makes this social model of disability explicit when attendants offer to grab chairs for able-bodied participants who did not bring their own wheelchairs to meet *their* access needs and be able to sit down (*Access Me*, in *Interdependent Magic*, edited by Jessica Watkin (Playwrights Canada, 2022), 71).

4   An entire scene in *Ça a l'air synthétique bonjour hi* mocks this kind of confessional interrogation, when one of the actors interviews (and then seduces) a potted shrub. (see STRUMPET)

My silent refusal translates as: "WTF? Are you kidding?!"[5]) **Refusal is protective.**[6]

Refusal can shift in meaning from the personal to the political. Distinct from indicating that the game has gone too far, choosing not to participate can also send the message that the whole game is suspect. Refusal in this mode not only resists the rules but also challenges the source of authority for the rules. The game itself is called out as invalid. We notice the powerful politics of refusal most vibrantly through Indigenous assertions of sovereignty from the colonial state. Michi Saagiig Nishnaabeg scholar Leanne Betasamosake Simpson articulates this view in relation to the historically pervasive systems of colonial oppression and extractivism in Canada. She writes, "Participation, respect for individuals' autonomy, and diversity are values that are common amongst many Aboriginal peoples, although they must be viewed within our cultural contexts. In the face of colonialism, non-participation has also proven to be an effective form of resistance. Refusing to participate in co-management agreements, EIAs, treaty negotiations, natural resource management agreements, research projects and the Euro-Canadian educational system are effective ways of resisting the dominance of Euro-Canadian society, and its assimilative tendencies. By not participating, Aboriginal peoples send the message that the *process* is unacceptable to them. That the process or framework itself negates power sharing, traditional values, Indigenous knowledge and *meaningful* negotiation by Aboriginal peoples."[7]

Audra Simpson, a Mohawk woman of Kahnawà:ke, in her article, "Consent's Revenge" locates refusal as a forceful strategy for

---

5   In Single Thread Theatre Company's production of *Ambrose*, I was invited to step into a spotlight and sing a song of my choosing out into the darkened and empty auditorium of the seven-hundred-seat Grand Theatre. In retrospect, I wish I had really gone for it with a Broadway musical showstopper or operatic aria instead of cheeping out a pathetic "Twinkle Twinkle Little Star." But then that would be another Jenn who is not me.

6   Posing questions that challenge audience-participants to reveal themselves for our consumption in ways that make them vulnerable is in my opinion a cheap and careless way to evoke a thrill of realness. Conversely, I have witnessed numerous performance interviews in which the asking of a more ordinary and accessible question can generate the same charming sense of authenticity. I also believe that with good care practices and some scaffolding of expectations, audience-players can be supported in taking significant risks. Being a tiny bit brave and then being praised for your bravery can even be the entire point of the performance. (see OPT OUT)

7   Leanne Betasamosake Simpson, "Aboriginal Peoples and Knowledge: Decolonizing Our Processes," *Canadian Journal of Native Studies* 2, no. 1 (2001): 144.

interrogating and upending land treaties that were made under false faces. She writes, "Refusal holds on to a truth, structures this truth as stance through time, as its own structure a comingling with the force of presumed and inevitable disappearance and operates as the revenge of consent—the consent to these conditions, to the interpretation that this was fair, and the ongoing sense that this is all over with."[8] Although these Indigenous scholars and activists are writing about sovereignty and not participatory theatre, calls for Indigenous sovereignty teach us about the generative power of refusal.

"No" is powerful. "No" is also really hard to say. The foundational conditions of being an audience-player actively curtail refusal. From wanting to get value for money to not wanting to break the show or hurt the feelings of the artists and performers to not wanting to draw undue attention to ourselves, participants have many reasons to go along placidly, continuing their participation even through discomfort. Not infrequently, any potential feeling of being empowered to refuse is compromised by the power dynamics inherent in our positionality in relation to the person who issues the invitation. Rachel Zerihan beautifully captures this feeling in all its awful awkwardness in her reflection on her experience in Adrian Howells's *Garden of Adrian* where she was offered strawberries. "I don't like strawberries. 'I don't like strawberries' was all I needed to say. He asks me if I like them and I lie, 'yes,' though my eyes plead 'no.' Why lie? [. . .] My role as dutiful spectator in Howells' garden was led by my desire to please even though he had explicitly told me that I would not have to do anything I felt uncomfortable with shortly after the hug that marked my entrance to the garden space. The sensation of tasting the strawberry, quite clearly, was intended to be a pleasurable one and I remember trying to fake enjoyment. Like receiving an unwelcome lover, I feigned delight and satisfaction."[9] Uma Kothari notes in *Participation: The New Tyranny?* (see TYRANNY), "There is an implicit notion of deviancy for those who choose not to participate . . . there is no positive opposite or counter to participation—it is implicitly good, constructive, and productive."[10] (see KILLJOY)

---

8   Audra Simpson, "Consent's Revenge," *Cultural Anthropology* 31, no. 3 (2016): 330.

9   Deirdre Heddon, Helen Iball, and Rachel Zerihan, "Come Closer: Confessions of Intimate Spectators in One to One Performance," *Contemporary Theatre Review* 22, no. 1 (2012): 123.

10   Uma Kothari, "Power, Knowledge and Social Control in Participatory Development," in *Participation: The New Tyranny?*, edited by Bill Cooke and Uma Kothari (Zed, 2001), 148.

I think it is important to view the contexts and conventions of the invitation that encourage unthinking participation with some suspicion. Audience-participants need not always be "good" and participation qua participation might not always be "good" either. There is creative energy in subversion, in not following the rules, or in making up your own rules.[11] What happens if I GO ROGUE and instead of placing the lemon artfully in the alley as instructed (*b side*), I put it in my pocket? Or roll it down the length of the pavement? Or (*gasp!*) eat it?[12]

---

11 As exciting as this is to consider in the abstract, it almost never happens. I can think of only a tiny handful of examples where audience-participants did not follow expectations. The most common refusal being blinking silence, which is absorbed by the show as a kind of "pass" and far from hostile.

12 Karoline Gritzner notes that relational form is "not something predetermined or pre-conceived; it is not a self-positing organizing principle but something contingent and performative, entirely dependent on the situation and time of its taking place and shape, always in the making and therefore proximate to failure. Relational form, in other words, is 'formless.' It is possible that the relational art event does not materialize. If the participants fail or refuse to take part in an event which is essentially about their actions and reactions . . . the event might not take place and its potential might remain unexplored, its form unrealized." Gritzner places this observation in tension with the notion that participatory art can sometimes be "entirely predictable [since] the artists have constructed a game with a set of rules for us to follow." Refusal, thus, can be constructive when taken up in dialogue with the thing refused, as we argue here. But failure to take up the invitation can also mean that the work never comes into existence in the first place, rendering the meaning of refusal potentially null. "Form and Formlessness: Participation at the Limit," *Performance Research* 16, no. 4 (2011): 110. (see OR ELSE)

REHEARSAL

When I arrived at the performance of *Access Me*, created by Boys in Chairs Collective, I didn't bring my own chair. As the audience enters the theatre, we are welcomed and directed to choose a location around the perimeter of the space. If the audience member is arriving already seated, the attendant-greeter invites them to pick a spot. For those who arrived not seated, the attendant provides them with a chair and also offers to carry the chair to wherever they wish it to be if they are unable to carry it themselves. As the published script notes, "The audience will have to adjust to accommodate each other as more people arrive, collaborating to create access for everyone. In this spirit, one at a time, the audience creates the seating area together. The atmosphere is intimate, adaptive, and a bit chaotic."[1] With this calculated opening, *Access Me* flips the script on typical theatre architecture, and by doing so, draws attention to the diversity of how we participate. Did you bring your own chair or not? Does your chair have wheels or not? And through a choreography of needs negotiation, all are made welcome.[2]

To begin the show itself, audience members read aloud from question cards that we have been given upon entry; the questions focus on Queer and Disabled experiences of sex and dating: How do you have sex? What's your type? What do you wish you could experience in bed? How do I flirt with you? If I date you, will I have to be your attendant?[3] The dialogue fostered by the questions forms the basis for how performers Frank, Ken, and Andrew—all three are wheelchair users—introduce themselves as they respond by describing their own physical attributes and revealing their fetishes and turn-ons. Sometimes the audience members balk, and resist speaking the script they have been assigned, protesting that the questions are unkind or too personally invasive.

---

1   Boys in Chairs Collective, *Access Me*, in *Interdependent Magic: Disability Performance in Canada*, edited by Jessica Watkin (Playwrights Canada, 2022), 71.

2   It should be noted that participatory theatre as a genre can be appallingly inaccessible. Yes, there are pre-show emails, often with extensive warnings, explanations, and advice. Nevertheless, there are instances where I am simply unable to participate because of my limitations. Barriers include uneven terrain or stairs, information that is either exclusively visual or exclusively aural, being asked to ingest food or drink with unknown ingredients, being compelled to go "fast" or be skilled in some particular way, or just being expected to "bravely" embrace the unknown. Of course, many plays are created with thoughtful attention to audience access needs, but many are not.

3   Boys in Chairs, *Access Me*, 116.

When that happens, the three remind them that they have certainly heard these questions before. Frank, Ken, and Andrew answer these questions with grace. Our ENCOUNTER is structured by the questions. And instead of the more usual pattern, in which the audience is the AUTOBIOGRAPHICAL protagonist, we interview the performers.

Later, Andrew asks an audience member to pretend to be his care worker and lift him into a mobility device. "A lot of you might not have any experience of this kind of thing, but what if I gave you some?"[4] By the end of the play, an audience member is cast as Andrew's ultimate crush, "Ginger Beef," for a re-enactment of a first date. Andrew asks Ginger Beef, "I'm wondering if you would like to take off my shirt for me?"[5] If the participant ACTING in the role of Ginger Beef agrees, Andrew coaches him, "What you're going to do is lean me forward a little bit, and you're going to pull the shirt up over my head. Take my shoulders and pull. You're doing great . . . nearly there . . . pull harder!"[6] After Andrew challenges Ginger Beef to throw the shirt across the room passionately, Andrew asks if Ginger Beef would like to take off his own shirt as well. If he CONSENTS, both men go behind a curtain for the last sexy reveal of the evening—Andrew in a leather harness and Ginger Beef in a shirt that reads, *Disabled People Are Sexy*.

Access Me is a rehearsal for the disability justice revolution. By inviting audiences to participate in CARE actions, Boys in Chairs stages a chance for participants to try out the kinds of gestural relation needed to build interdependent networks of care. If a person in the audience has no previous experience in offering care to a Disabled person or feels uncomfortable or afraid doing so, the Boys in Chairs collective offers a low-stakes rehearsal. In her book *Care Work: Dreaming Disability Justice*, disability justice scholar Leah Lakshmi Piepzna-Samarasinha reminds us of the necessity of thinking about care not only as a place for interdependent survival, but also a place for JOY. We can see how the use of rehearsal as a participatory dramaturgy serves to break away from "traditional formats of 'access as service begrudgingly offered to disabled people by non-disabled people who feel grumpy about it' to 'access as a collective joy and offering we can give to each other.'"[7] Piepzna-Samarasinha goes on to ask, "What does it mean to shift our ideas of access and care (whether it's disability, child care, economic access, or many more) from an individual chore, an unfortunate cost of having an

4   Boys in Chairs, *Access Me*, 77.
5   Boys in Chairs, *Access Me*, 111.
6   Boys in Chairs, *Access Me*, 111.
7   Leah Lakshmi Piepzna-Samarasinha, *Care Work: Dreaming Disability Justice* (Arsenal Pulp, 2018), 17.

unfortunate body, to a collective responsibility that's maybe even deeply joyful?"[8] Or sexy? (see INTIMACY)

This rehearsal is also a preemptive gift. A practical SIM for the future. Piepzna-Samarasinha calls us to heed her warning about the necessity of practising disability justice: "realize you are or will be us."[9] Although disability justice activists work to unravel the ableism associated with the fear of becoming Disabled, in another breath Piepzna-Samarasinha warns that aging affects non-Disabled folks with vision loss, hearing loss, mobility loss, or memory loss. Able-bodied folks are not practised in the kinds of adaptations that may be needed to live a (sexy) Disabled life in a world designed for able-bodied folks. Rehearsal, in this context, links the present to the future. It invites us to think with our bodies about what we might do for others if not today then someday, and what we ourselves might need, if not today then someday. These skills require "a set of innovative, virtuosic skills" that is well-practised by many Disabled folks.[10] When mutual aid networks sprawled to encourage the establishment of care webs in the COVID-19 pandemic, Disabled people already had practices in place. Piepzna-Samarasinha cites Vancouver's Radical Access Mapping Project and says "if you don't know how to do access, ask disabled people. We've been doing it for a long time, usually on no money, and we're really good at it."[11] The implied message, of course, is, "And with practice you could be too."

See ABYDOS, SHEEP, and SWEATING

---

8   Piepzna-Samarasinha, *Care Work*, 33.

9   Piepzna-Samarasinha, *Care Work*, 129.

10 Piepzna-Samarasinha, *Care Work*, 126.

11 *Radical Access Mapping Project*, radicalaccessiblecommunities.wordpress.com/, quoted by Piepzna-Samarasinha, *Care Work*, 16–17.

FILL IN THE EVENT SPACE BELOW SO THAT IT FITS
6 CHAIRS, 10 WHEELCHAIRS, AND AN ACCESSIBLE
LANEWAY FOR THE PERFORMERS.

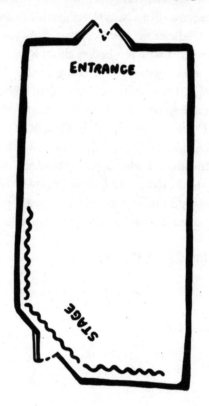

CONNECT THE DOTS BELOW AND ON THE BACK OF THIS PAGE TO FORM TWO SETS OF SHAPES. NUMBER AND LETTER DOTS DO NOT CONNECT. UPON COMPLETING BOTH SIDES, YOU MAY NEED SOME LIGHT TO "SEE THROUGH" TO THIS PUZZLE'S ANSWER.

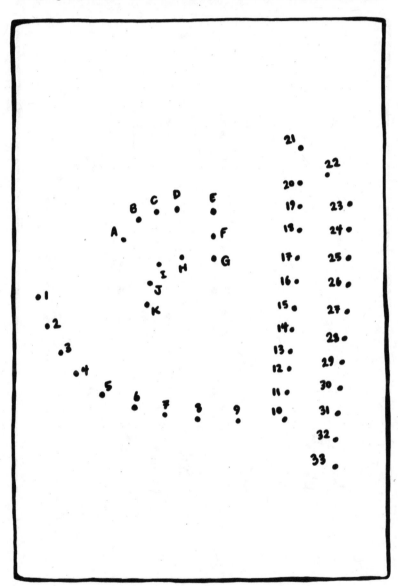

ANSWER:

RELATION

See FRIENDSHIP and LAND

REMOTE CONTROL

> In using people as a medium, participatory art has always had a double ONTOLOGICAL status: it is both an event in the world, and at one remove from it. As such, it has the capacity to communicate on two levels—to participants and to spectators—the paradoxes that are repressed in everyday discourse, and to elicit perverse, disturbing and pleasurable experiences that enlarge our capacity to imagine the world and our relations anew. —Claire Bishop, *Artificial Hells*, 284.

As the four audience-players log in to the familiar pandemic-era theatre arena that is Zoom, we are met with a screen-shared visual of a black-and-white sketched video of the waiting room of the "Sleep Institute." We are about to embark on the live narrative-based game created by Sébastien Heins called *The Itinerary: Playtest.* And we are in control. A clock ticks away. There are magazines and an empty leather chair on the perimeter of the room. A bird flies by the window. A lab technician rushes past, hurrying us to the "Sleep Chamber." Although the lab tech's tone is light, it's rushed. It's clear the players have an important job to do. We are needed.

While we're being "configured" in the Sleep Chamber, we are told to close our eyes and rest our hands on our phones, which are opened to an interactive multiple choice-type app designed by artist and programmer Jacob Niedzwiecki. We are told to breathe deeply, then we are told to open our eyes. "In the next room over from me, there is a person sleeping. We are connecting you with them. We need you to communicate to them that—" The lab tech is cut off. "The . . . is in your hands." The Sleep Chamber visual goes black and when the feed returns, we see a live video of a man in a room alone.

We meet Calvin, played by Heins, sleeping soundly on a bed in a sparsely furnished cell-like room. It is not clear if he is a captive but when a command suddenly appears on the app: "Wake Up," it seems that he is somehow, for some reason, under our command. Players are instructed to each take their turn prescribing actions to Calvin through the app. One of the players selects Wake Up and Calvin immediately rises in response, as if actually operated by a remote controller. The four players take turns using the app to select actions from a dropdown menu to prescribe to Calvin. Brush teeth. Eat breakfast. Meditate. Write a song. Pray aloud. Play trashketball. The immediacy is as remarkable as it is unnerving. Calvin is our avatar and we, as a collective, are taking turns "playing" his life like a character in a video game. After a few turns of passing the figurative controller, when it's my turn, a message appears to me. "At 0600 the next morning, this person is to die. We leave it to you to tell them or not."[1] I unmute myself when directed and read my line, telling Calvin he will die tomorrow. As Calvin—and the players—grapple with what's next, new options appear on the app. "Attempt escape." "Call for help." "Psych yourself up." "Promise organs."[2] More time passes, and our choices determine what Calvin will do with his final hours. After Calvin completes this final task, he opens the door and exits the room. This is the end. Although we did not cause Calvin's death—we don't know why his life is to be terminated—nevertheless we hold his final hours literally in our hands. Did we do a good job? (see COMPLICITY) And are we actually culpable somehow?

Unlike a character in a video game, *The Itinerary*'s Calvin is a live avatar embodied by a live actor. Everything the players select for Calvin, Sébastien has to *actually* do. If his players select "play trashketball" over and over again, Sébastien will start SWEATING. If players continue to select "do pushups," Sébastien's arms will inevitably get sore. As a real-life avatar, his physical body is subject to actually being tired, injured, embarrassed, or bored. It's true that all characters, within the participatory context or not, are embodied by real actors. Actor bodies remain visible and hardworking under the veil of their characters. The difference between the actors embodying characters in these works of BOURGEOIS THEATRE and *The Itinerary: Playtest* is about who is wielding control. In theatre behind the fourth wall, the actors' bodies are most often controlled by the script or by the director.[3] In *The Itinerary*, the

---

1   Sébastien Heins, *The Itinerary: Playtest, Canadian Theatre Review* 188 (Fall 2021): 70.

2   Heins, *The Itinerary*, 70.

3   One example of this kind of control by a director is in the casting process. Normally, actors are contracted knowing what roles they have been assigned; however, repertory companies like the Stratford Festival have a long-standing practice of offering "As Cast" contracts that allow actors to be cast later on in miscellaneous smaller parts. As part of the Stratford Festival social media takeover by Black artists in June 2020, actor E. B. Smith called out these "As Cast" contracts, tweeting that this practice "amounts to the forfeiture of all agency for actors" (Karen Fricker and Carly Maga, "The Stratford Festival Admitted Its Own Systemic Racism and Gave Black Artists a Chance to Speak Out,"

audience-participants are controlling the actions of Sébastien. While both *asses.masses* and *Ça a l'air synthétique bonjour hi* take the distribution of audience LABOUR as a core theme, in *The Itinerary: Playtest*, the players are forced to reckon with the specific cost of Sébastien's labour and our ethical obligation to treat his body fairly.

Who we are or why we hold power over him is not entirely clear. He wears a uniform and his blank room is equipped only with basic necessities. There is no explicit reason why he is slated to die at dawn. Is he being punished for a crime? Should I understand this as a judicial execution by my own government? One thematic understanding that seems to present itself for this relationship of control between us and Calvin/Sébastien is a metaphor of the carceral state. Although we are told this is a sleep clinic, Calvin/Sébastien appears to be an inmate of some kind. The tangled control that we exert over both Calvin the character and Sébastien the actor collapses aesthetic distance. The character's life is no longer an analogy but has tangible real-world effects for which I am responsible.

In June 2023, three years after the workshop "playtest" of *The Itinerary*, Heins returned with a new iteration of the show, now called *No Save Points*. Here, the thread of control between the audience-players and Sébastien was even more direct and the metaphor of control quite different. Sébastien was rigged up with electrical buzzers on the skin of his torso. Linked to Game Boy–style controllers, the buzzers would deliver small shocks corresponding to the left, right, up, down buttons of the device. In addition, Sébastien was no longer the fictional Calvin but an autobiographical version of himself. As autobiographical performance, the meaning of control came into focus as a metaphor for Huntington's Disease (HD). Huntington's Disease is a genetic neurodegenerative disorder with physical, emotional, and cognitive symptoms.[4] Among the physical symptoms are involuntary movements like fidgeting or twitching. The various episodes of *No Save Points* deliver stories about Sébastien's mother's lived experience of this illness as well as his own coming to terms with his knowledge that he is a carrier of the HD gene. Being subject to external control by the audience-players depicts both the physical diminishment of embodied control of HD and also

Toronto Star, 10 June 2020, thestar.com/entertainment/stage/the-stratford-festival-admitted-its-own-systemic-racism-and-gave-black-artists-a-chance-to/article_c25a6eaa-5667-5e54-9bdf-d8a8f14a6c26.html). See also #CastingByConsent on Twitter.

4 "What is Huntington Disease?" *Huntington Society of Canada*, huntingtonsociety.ca/learn-about-hd/what-is-huntingtons/.

the existential lack of control in knowing something about your own genetic future. Despite the serious implications of this story, Heins in *No Save Points* carries the performance with remarkable grace.

Participatory works that emphasize agency and EMERGENCE can push beyond mere fictional implications and have real-world effects. The seeds that players plant in Laurel Green and Sarah Conn's *Remixed* can produce actual, edible microgreens. Jenn's pothos plant, given to her as a gift in *To You* continues to sprawl across her windowsill. Pen pals that are connected through letters sent in *The Dead Letter Office* can stay in touch long after the show is over. The remote control in both *The Itinerary: Playtest* and *No Save Points* acts as a similar fulcrum between my choices and their outcomes on Sébastien's actual body. These doubled relationships that cross over the BOUNDARY between the actual and the fictional elicit the "perverse, disturbing" experiences imagined by CLAIRE BISHOP, offering us the ability to "enlarge our capacity to imagine the world and our relations anew."[5]

See FRIENDSHIP, MEEPLES, and BOUNDARY VIOLATIONS

---

5   Claire Bishop, *Artificial Hells: Participatory Art and the Politics of Spectatorship* (Verso, 2012), 284.

RITUAL

Just as game mechanics and behaviours are applied to provide dramaturgical structures for participation in theatre-game hybrids, so too are the mechanics and behaviours of rituals applied, creating theatre-ritual hybrids. But where games are circumscribed by the boundary of the MAGIC CIRCLE, which carves out a non-serious space that both prohibits and protects from real-world consequences, rituals strive to transfer their semi-fictional activities into meaningful efficacy. The essential nature of ritual is founded in a belief that the "as if" can become manifest. Real-world implication is key. Or at the very least there is a kind of productive ambiguity between fictional or metaphorical action and actual effects. Catholic communion invites the ingestion of a wafer and wine—transubstantiated into the body and blood of Christ—to confer blessing on the worshippers. Growing a "playoff beard" and ceasing to shave facial hair—keeping things resolutely the same—ensures the continuation of a WINNING streak en route to the Stanley Cup. Formal or informal, religious or profane, rituals are GUIDES, rituals are scripts that shape behaviour and lead to expected outcomes. (see ACTING)

American director Richard Schechner, known for both his controversial staging of participatory Happening *Dionysus in '69*[1] and his (now-contested) anthropological writing on ritual and performance, positions theatre and ritual as fundamentally related, but as binary opposites.[2] In

---

1   As Arnold Aronson notes in his historical account of the Performance Group's production of *Dionysus in '69*, the premise of the work was that audience members and actors were equals in a democratic enterprise. Without the formal cues to comprehend the event as theatre and their role as audience, "Some spectators assumed that the Performance Group was a kind of cult and wanted to join. Occasionally, the audience participation crossed acceptable boundaries as some male spectators took advantage of ritual-like scenes to join the action and fondle the female performers. The performers demanded that [director Richard] Schechner restructure these scenes more rigidly so that clear-cut and appropriate boundaries would be established" (Aronson, *American Avant-garde Theatre: A History* (Routledge, 2000), 100). I cite this example to point out not only that norms of social behaviour were breached resulting in sexual assault, but also that the source of these breaches was a confusion about the necessary division between performers and audience members, even in radically democratic participatory artworks.

2   Richard Schechner, "From Ritual to Theatre and Back," in *Ritual, Play, and Performance: Readings in the Social Sciences/Theatre*, edited by Richard Schechner and Mady Schuman (Seabury, 1976), 207.

his 1976 book *Ritual, Play, and Performance*, Schechner says the critical difference between the theatre and ritual comes down to their function; what are they trying to do? Where ritual aims at real-world effects and transformation, Schechner's theatre slides into something more trivial, what he labels "entertainment." Schechner argues that the performance of ritual "both symbolizes and actualizes the change in status . . . This convergence of symbolic and actual event is missing from esthetic theatre."[3] Ritual performs metaphorical rites of change and through those enacted patterns also attempts to make those changes actually manifest. By contrast, change in theatre is more representative; we are changed (*if* we are changed) by analogy. According to Schechner's list of characteristics, ritual seeks "results, links to an absent Other, abolishes time/symbolic time, brings [the] Other here, [the] performer [is] possessed [or] in trance, [the] *audience participates*, audience believes, criticism is forbidden, [there is] collective creativity"[4] (emphasis added is mine). His entertainment category, where he slots BOURGEOIS THEATRE, is characterized as "fun, for those here now . . . [The] performer displays learned skills. [The] audience watches; [the] audience appreciates. Criticism is encouraged."[5] While Schechner positions theatre and ritual as opposites on a continuum, participatory theatre occupies a kind of blended intermediate position, being both efficacious as well as manifesting qualities of traditional entertainment modes. Because the interactive audience straddles the boundary between actual and fictional worlds, it is a kind of both/and. (see BOUNDARY VIOLATIONS and FIRST-PERSON SHOOTER)

Participatory performance *Holy Moly* created by Vancouver-based Jarin Schexnider playfully borrows ritual patterns to tell an AUTOBIOGRAPHICAL story. And like the lives of other spiritual leaders, meaning is drawn from the events of that life lived to provide inspiration for those who follow. *Holy Moly* is founded in Jarin's middle-class upbringing in Louisiana in the 1980s to shape our participation as congregants in the "Church of Jarin" where we find and become our "best selves." Bestseller *Chicken Soup for the Soul* is her Bible. The altar at the front holds childhood treasures from that pivotal decade in Jarin's life, including a soccer ball, stuffed animals, and an egg cup. (?!) For the sermon, each audience-congregant is given headphones and a personal cassette-tape player. Buoyed by the soundtrack

---

3   Schechner, "From Ritual to Theatre," 205.
4   Schechner, "From Ritual to Theatre," 206–07.
5   Schechner, "From Ritual to Theatre," 206–07.

of 80s pop music and Jarin's own personal testimony, I was encouraged to celebrate myself, tasked by the voice in my head to applaud my accomplishments. When I did, I was greeted by smatterings of applause around the room as other people reached the same point on their own audio tracks. (see TOGETHER ALONE) Communion was a meringue. In a memorable moment, Jarin offered each audience-congregant their personal blessing. Holding a jellyfish Beanie Baby called Goochy, (If you are a person of a certain age, who had a 1980s childhood, you know what this is. Yes, you do.) Jarin shook the stuffed animal in an arc beside my legs, torso, over my head, and then down the other side the same way while she explained that I was receiving the blessing of Goochy. The echo of the sprinkling of holy water on the congregation during Easter Catholic ceremonies is clear.[6] "Sprinkling" by Goochy is silly and entirely fabricated, but I get it. Familiar ritual patterns are activated, and I am indeed blessed.[7]

Our priestess GUIDES for Horizon Factory's *Deep Gazing* were each dressed entirely in royal blue: sleeveless shirts, jogging pants with two white stripes down the outside leg, and a small bonnet tied under the chin with stripes to match the pants. As we sat on blankets at the water's edge, the "Sisters of Nephology" danced with immense blue plastic tarp-bags, catching the wind and rendering it into concrete shapes. We were then invited to form a circle and take our places around the edge of a "dewdrop" (actually one of those multicoloured, fabric parachutes). Holding the edges, we marched in a circle, changing directions several times and stopping to float it upwards, pulling it down before marching again. Like we did in my elementary-school memories of gym class, we were instructed to sit down on the inside edge of the inflated parachute, enclosing us all under its saturated dome. The priestesses presented a mini-lecture about the different types of clouds we might see as we looked up. They then handed out square mirrors the size of my two palms to each audience member and encouraged us to lie on our backs and move the mirrors so as to capture a section of the sky. We were instructed to use the mirror cloud-images to scry, or locate some

---

6   As part of *asperges*, the rite of sprinkling, holy water is sprinkled upon the whole congregation at once with a brush or silver ball on a stick, a symbolic reminder of the more individual ceremony of baptism.

7   This account of *Holy Moly* is based on the experiences of our research assistant Charlotte Dorey. Major parts of this entry were originally conceptualized and written by Charlotte as part of her independent study project in fall 2022 under Jenn's supervision. This version is published here with her permission.

meaning gifted to us from above. After some time, they encouraged us to discuss our findings with the folks around us. This lesson in looking is useful in everyday life. *Deep Gazing* asked you to "let the clouds direct you in ways of seeing, slowing, being in-relation, and reimagining possible futures."[8] *Deep Gazing* reminds us that we are not alone; quiet help from above is always there for those who seek it.

Rituals provide patterns for participation and knowing those patterns guides the audience not just in our actions—knowing what to do—but also in what to feel. Focusing on cosmic transformation within the constraints of our everyday life is both mystical and practical. Sometimes my usual tangible mundane supports are not enough to get me through or to lift me up. I need a little extra boost. And why not look to the supernatural for help? I feel a little less overwhelmed in my struggles, a promise that I am not alone in an uncaring universe. Messages of hope are there in the cumulus clouds overhead. And protection comes from an old and trusted-from-childhood (stuffed) companion.

See CEREMONY

FILL THIS ALTAR WITH THINGS THAT ARE IMPORTANT TO YOU.

8   "Deep Gazing," *SummerWorks*, summerworks.ca/show/deep-gazing/.

SCREENS

Screens here refer not to a computer screen or a movie screen but rather screen in the sense of a shield or sheltering barrier. In an 1899 paper, Sigmund Freud introduced the term "screen memories" to describe the subjective memorializing of an event with such brightness it is "ultra-clear"; this exceptional luminosity is paradoxically intended to disguise rather than reveal something that has been subconsciously repressed.[1] One key feature of screen memories in relation to strategic conceal-ment is that while important elements were omitted, as part of the camouflage, trivial elements were retained, even highlighted.[2] This is a screen sort of like a defensive basketball screen, but also like a magic trick—look over here at this shiny object while I hide the other thing in my pocket. Métis visual artist, curator, and critical arts writer David Garneau writes about strategies of resistance to cultural appropriation and assimilation, and adapts Freud's idea, shifting from screen memories to screen objects to describe a parallel defensive technique. He asserts, "Indigenous cultures have since contact devised ingenious ways to pro-tect their sacred things from appropriation through the use of screen objects."[3] Screen objects, then, are constructed fakes that appear superfi-cially to be authentic cultural objects but are rendered non-functional in a fundamental way, having their meaningful context held back. Garneau gives the example of Haida ceremonial pipe carvers who made souvenir facsimiles for tourists that were blocked inside; the holes of the bowl and stem did not line up, and so the purpose of these pipes was delib-erately (and secretly) defeated. Garneau wittily calls these "artifakes."[4]

The power of these screen objects lies in their declaration of meanings, feelings, and understandings that are too precious to be debased by shar-ing with the undeserving, with those who lack proper understanding,

---

1   Eugene J. Mahon, "Screen Memories: A Neglected Freudian Discovery?" *The Psychoanalytic Quarterly* 85, no. 1 (2016): 61.

2   Mahon, "Screen Memories," 65.

3   David Garneau, "Imaginary Spaces of Conciliation and Reconciliation: Art, Curation, and Healing," in *Arts of Engagement: Taking Aesthetic Action In and Beyond the Truth and Reconciliation Commission of Canada*, edited by Dylan Robinson and Keavy Martin (Wilfrid Laurier UP, 2016), 26.

4   Garneau, "Imaginary Spaces," 26. Garneau acknowledges the source of this example from Carol Sheehan's exhibition *Pipes That Won't Smoke, Coal That Won't Burn*, 1983.

(INSPIRED BY FIRSTARTS.CA, "HISTORICAL ARGILLITE ART OF THE HAIDA")

and so are strategically rendered as off limits. It is a subtle, slantwise act of resistance by deflection. "The primary sites of Indigenous resistance, then, are not the rare open battles between the colonized and the dominant but the everyday active refusals of complete engagement with agents of assimilation. This includes speaking with one's own in one's own way, refusing translation and full explanations, creating trade goods that imitate core culture without violating it, and refusing to be a Native informant."[5] Refusal to facilitate accessibility is an act of UNWELCOME and resistance.

Although the stakes are very different, there are circumstances in the context of participatory artworks where a request is founded on a false sense of relationship, and a similar REFUSAL of complete engagement may be called for. It is common for the experiential impact of a participatory performance to be premised on a manufactured INTIMACY either between the performer and the audience-participant or between participant peers. Striving to quickly attain this intimacy, sometimes performances will leverage the innate power imbalance between the artist-creator and the audience-participant to exert social pressure[6] on the participant to reveal AUTOBIOGRAPHICAL information or personal opinions that feel uncomfortably invasive. In this way the artist-creator, although well-intentioned, oversteps and becomes impudent; they have not earned my secrets. In a participatory show, I once found myself on a conference call with a group of anonymous audience members. When the artist asked each participant in the group to share their biggest secret with these strangers, I lied. The screen was a protective measure, a response to a trespassing question that I didn't feel safe answering. In cases like this, this tactic of offering the verbal equivalent of a screen as a protective facade can be applied. Another time I was paired with a fellow audience member who should have been a stranger, but actually turned out to be someone I knew slightly. The remote structure of the show kept us from making visual contact. I remained invisible and kept my anonymity by using a false name. (Don't judge me. Doesn't everyone have a Starbucks name, anyway?[7])

---

5   Garneau, "Imaginary Spaces," 23.

6   This social pressure to be accommodating and play along with the demands of the performance so as not to upset the performer or "break" the theatre event is what Deirdre Heddon, Helen Iball, and Rachel Zerihan refer to as the desire to "give good audience" ("Come Closer: Confessions of Intimate Spectators in One to One Performance," *Contemporary Theatre Review* 22, no. 1 (2012): 120–33).

7   Stina Chang, "What Is a Starbucks Name, And Why Is It Useful?" *Study Breaks*, 9 September 2019, studybreaks.com/thoughts/starbucks-name/.

The imbalance between the performance and participants functions as a kind of TYRANNY; these partners are not equal. When questions are asked, responses—honest authentic responses—are implicitly expected. For the most part, this interrogation is intended to be benevolent and provide the audience with an experience as agreed; however, good intentions are not sufficient to frame awareness of appropriate borders of intimate revelation (which are of course unique to each participant). "What is your greatest fear?" "How do you cope with things that make you feel worried?" "Who here considers themselves an atheist?" Sometimes the exposure of such secrets is a thrill, designed and accepted as part of the risk AROUSAL of the experience. Sometimes such a request is met with resistance. (And accompanied by eye-blinking astonishment at such presumption! You are asking me to tell you what?!) The needed context of earned trust has not been established—and perhaps in some cases can never be established within the truncated artificial situation of a performance event. As with the reporting of childhood dreams and traumas in psychoanalysis and with acquisition of Indigenous artifacts by tourists, there is an implicit expectation of authenticity and truth, and yet, there are no guarantees. Secret substitution of an object or anecdote stripped of value responds to the request on a surface level. It does not disrupt the relationship of EXCHANGE, but the act of withholding meaningfully redistributes control, returning power to the giver.

Of course, in the context of a theatre performance, this strategy is further legitimated (and complicated) by the usual ONTOLOGICAL DUALITY of theatrical frame. Just as the real objects of actor and stage set become characters and settings, leaving aside their actual-world selves and stepping into the fictional world, so too the audience-player can make a similar move. It need not be actually "me" answering these personal questions; I can become a somewhat fictional version of myself, and offer screen answers from that alternate positionality. Indeed, the frame comes into play whether I explicitly hold it up or not. I can still choose to tell "truth" if I wish, but it is a naive audience-player or artist-performer who doesn't appreciate the potential for the protective camouflage of ambiguity and obfuscation.[8]

---

8   I admit that I have been that naive audience-player on more than one occasion. The lure of truth-telling is powerful and the superficial sense that through participation I have established a relationship with the performer is also compelling. In those cases, I walk away with a sense of self-betrayal that I have given away too much where those revelations have not been earned. Ultimately, of course, I am (or expect myself to be) a sophisticated theatregoer who should know better. (see AUTOBIOGRAPHY)

SECRET WEIRDOS

"This is for *us*, not for the 'others.' What the 'others' do 'outside' is no concern of ours at the moment. Inside the circle of the game the laws and customs of ordinary life no longer count. We are different and do things differently."[1] Johan Huizinga (*Homo Ludens*) claims that an essential component of the core definition of playing a game is that it "promotes the formation of social groups which tend to surround themselves with secrecy and to stress their difference from the common world by disguise or other means."[2] Upon entering the MAGIC CIRCLE, play is separate, secluded from the world. Game play is circumscribed in both time and space. Play begins and play ends. It is a special time; it is not always. Play is spatially restricted to being "in bounds." "[Playgrounds are] forbidden spots, isolated, hedged round, hallowed within which special rules obtain. [Places of play are] temporary worlds within the ordinary world, dedicated to the performance of an act apart."[3]

Roger Caillois (*Man, Play and Games*) takes exception to Huizinga's assertion that play is secretive. "It is meritorious and fruitful," he writes, "to have grasped the affinity which exists between play and the secret or mysterious, but this relationship cannot be part of the definition of play, which is nearly always spectacular or ostentatious." He continues, asserting that the transformation of the mysterious into play is "necessarily to the detriment of the secret and mysterious, which play exposes, publishes and somehow *expends*."[4] Caillois seems to be arguing that the seriousness that underpins the efficacy of rituals, "mysteries" understood in the religious sense, is undermined by play. The playfulness of play—the structuring of play as a fiction, as an alternate world—renders the investment of the realness of a mystery moot. When ritual becomes play, "the mystery may no longer be awesome."[5] I recognize Caillois's point that recognizing the fictive nature of play is at odds

1   Johan Huizinga, *Homo Ludens: A Study of the Play-Element in Culture* (Routledge & Kegan Paul, 1955), 12.
2   Huizinga, *Homo Ludens*, 13.
3   Huizinga, *Homo Ludens*, 10.
4   Roger Caillois, *Man, Play and Games*, translated by Meyer Barash (U of Illinois P, 1961), 4.
5   Caillois, *Man, Play and Games*, 4–5.

with the serious investment of belief in mystery; but I think Huizinga is pointing to something more mundane.

Those inside the circle become players. Our secrecy is not actual disguise or camouflage, but the entering into a parallel but separate ontological state. Our apartness is a feature of adopting what Bernard Suits calls the "lusory attitude." The playful attitude means that we do things for reasons that are not obvious or efficient, but because the game presents us with arbitrarily indirect paths to achieve the game's goals. As Suits writes, the lusory attitude compels us to (cheerfully) "adopt rules which require one to employ worse rather than better means for reaching an end . . . In anything but a game the gratuitous introduction of unnecessary obstacles to the achievement of an end is regarded as a decidedly irrational thing to do, whereas in a game it appears to be an absolutely essential thing to do."[6] It is the lusory attitude that says we can't touch the chalk lines when we hop from one end of the pavement to the other. It is the lusory attitude that says that a golf ball must be batted with a thin metal stick to get it into the hole. The irrationality of play makes us look foolish. And so, as players we end up doing some awkward weird thing that can't be explained to outsiders.

Doing the weird thing we are doing bonds us together like a kind of STICKINESS against the world. We do not become invisible. Caillois is quite correct; we are ostentatious. Our oddly alternate actions become a curious spectacle for bystanders. It could be as simple as walking with a lusory attitude, strolling without direction, noticing the alienated environment. (see DRIFT) The audiowalk *Landline* brands us as walking weirdos, as each player is pinned with a large tag, declaring, "Can't talk. I'm in a show." Wandering in Whitehorse, I exchanged a knowing eye-contact smile with a stranger as we crossed the street going in opposite directions. Their coat tag identified them as another person who was "in" the secret.[7] This sense that we are "in," and other people who are "out" may be staring at "US," is particularly acute in pervasive performance-games that occupy an ontologically blended public environment. The intersecting solo walk of *Landline* activated this feeling of being oddly apart in secret. Group walking in public as in *Citation* also does this. Simply gathering a dozen people in a public library who are all wearing bulky headphones and using matching iPads (*The Archive of Missing Things*) will also activate the circle of weird secrecy. We are not blending in. And even if perhaps we do pass unnoticed, our lusory attitude sets us apart and makes us self-conscious. More

---

6   Bernard Suits, *The Grasshopper: Games, Life and Utopia* (U of Toronto P, 1978), 38–39.

7   It is perhaps not a coincidence that the company belonging to one of the two creators of *Landline*, Dustin Harvey, is called xoSecret Theatre.

eccentric actions, like dancing exuberantly to silent (secret) pod music (*The Stranger 2.0: Above*) or chasing zombies through the streets of Vancouver (*The Zombie Syndrome*), will brand a group of players as secret weirdos. In *b side* a group of audience-players was invited to place with intention three lemons at meaningful locations of their choice as they progressed along an urban laneway, accompanied by live music. Each afternoon and evening that August when the show was running, local residents gathered to watch this odd invasion from their back decks and over their fences.

In that case, being observed (and also judged) was an explicit feature of the dramaturgy. Actors are watched. Audience members are not. Players are also not essentially either spectacle or spectators. Do there need to be outsiders or non-players to make us feel like insiders? No, I don't think so. Separation from the world is the catalyst and our self-conscious awareness of that separation does the rest. I watch myself watching myself. We can be both players and witnesses simultaneously watching the action, like a FIRST-PERSON SHOOTER game, unfold from behind my own eyes. Inside the magic circle, we become a collective, bonded by our strangeness. The show *b side* culminated in a lemonade social in a nearby park. Who knows what happened to the dozens of artful lemons? Is a lost lemon also a residual secret weirdo?

A story. Sometimes being a weirdo is not so amusing. One recent show we participated in featured a small group of four audience members following an actor through streets and alleys in downtown Toronto in the St. Lawrence Market area at night. The actor in character was behaving erratically; they ran, stopped, ran, stopped, stared with great intensity at a maintenance hole cover, and fell to the ground writhing from an apparent seizure. Appropriate perhaps for one who would be our guide into Hell, shouting, "Abandon hope all ye who enter here," but certainly alarming for ordinary public observation. We became self-consciously aware of urban passersby who were indeed judging us for our distanced posture. We were clearly "with" the actor, and yet we took no action to remedy their distress. This moment, for me, invites consideration of the ethical obligation not only to audience-players but also perhaps for inadvertent bystanders who peer into an uncertain fictional frame.

CALL A FRIEND AND READ AN ENTRY TO THEM, OR ALTERNATE READING PARAGRAPHS WITH SOMEONE NEARBY.

SEEDS

In the early days of the COVID pandemic in May 2020, my co-creator Laura Chaignon made twenty muffins while I gingerly snipped off twenty cuttings of a sprawling pothos plant. In the pop-up pandemic porch show we were creating with dancer Kay Kenney, called *To You*, the muffin was a reminder that, while we can offer gifts to those outside our home, we can't share a meal within two metres of one another. In this performance, which was also a mock surprise birthday party, we offered our beloved participants a plant, a gift that could only stay alive and be carried into the future with their tender loving care (manifesting as regular watering). The plant was a gift, but it was also a clock—a marker of friendship that sustains over time, celebrating our past but also reaching into the future. This live plant cutting, like theatre, like the march towards UTOPIA, acknowledges co-presence by virtue of its continued existence; it requires a mutual WITNESSING and responsive tending in order to survive.

Remixed, created by the artists who brought us *Trophy*, similarly invites the future-extended act of gardening as an expression of mutually responsive co-presence. The artists blend the materiality of receiving a gift-to-grow in the mail with an app-based personal questionnaire. Beyond the immediacy of the encounter, the performance stretches our time together, inviting interactive participation before, during, and after the time we share at the show. The creators, Laurel Green and Sarah Conn, are thoughtful practitioners of CARE, moving audiences softly through use of both stories and music. This care also has an activist component; they give us something to care for, to care about. In the middle of the experience, participants are invited to plant a package of radish seeds and tend to them after the show is over. Through a personal playlist, *Remixed* offers stories from people who experienced great change, and then provides the tools to plant change (a seed that will become a radish plant) and watch it grow. The point of *Remixed* was to soothe us through all of the confusing and extreme change we had experienced since March 2020 with a physical reminder of resilience. The plant functions like a contract—I'll take care of the plant, like the show took care of me.[1] Nurturing change through emergence is the participatory dramaturgy at work INVITING us to tend to living things.

---

1   Sarah Conn, "Experiments in Care as a Reciprocal Act," *Canadian Theatre Review* 197 (Winter 2024): 64–70.

Both *Remixed* and adrienne maree brown's *Emergent Strategy* are inspired by novelist Octavia Butler's works of science fiction that investigate how humans relate to change. (Butler's perhaps most repeated quotation states, "All that you touch / You Change. / All that you Change / Changes you. / The only lasting truth / Is Change. / God / Is Change."[2]) For brown, the concept of EMERGENCE "emphasizes critical connections over critical mass, building authentic relationships, listening with all the senses of the body and the mind."[3] Emergence is a particularly ripe concept when thinking about participatory dramaturgies, and more specifically, the call of *Remixed* to listen closely to stories of transformation and then transform yourself. brown looks to the natural world to REHEARSE the "ways we create the next world."[4] Through listening to the testimony (potentially transforming ourselves) and planting a seed (potentially transforming it too), our small acts assemble the show but also reassemble ourselves, sending us off into the world with a sense of our own potential. *Remixed* is a gift made uniquely and specifically for me.

BOURGEOIS THEATRE doesn't typically leave us with tangible souvenirs of our experience. What does it mean for artists to give audiences a gift that is really a living thing that persists? What changes about the relationship between art and audience if I have to continue tending to the work for months after the show?[5] I now have an obligation to a living entity. It's not just remembrance, not just an intended gesture, but a commitment to ongoing action in concrete form. If we ascribe to director and playwright Kevin Loring's (Nlaka'pamux from the Lytton First Nation in BC) view that theatre-makers post-pandemic have a renewed responsibility to *tend* to the relations around them,[6] shows like *Remixed* and *To You* stage a tiny REHEARSAL of that process. For the artists involved in *Remixed, To You*, and for Kevin Loring, the metaphoric tending that happens inside the fictional frame is not enough. A plant that requires tending or an actual donation from a theatre to a community in need leaps beyond the frame and into the world. All three examples teach us to participate in active nurturing by inviting the dramaturgy of

2   Octavia E. Butler, *Parable of the Sower* (Grand Central, 2019), 3.

3   adrienne maree brown, *Emergent Strategy: Shaping Change, Changing Worlds* (AK, 2017), 3.

4   brown, *Emergent Strategy*, 4.

5   Jenn still has her pothos cutting from *To You*, but I'm sad to report that the radish from *Remixed* died.

6   Kevin Loring. "Re-turning the Page: How Theatre Practice Must Bravely Return Into a Post-Pandemic, De-Colonial, Anti-Racist World," *YouTube*, 8 July 2021, youtube.com/watch?v=935_BXxCbCQ&t=4s.

gardening, an ongoing and relational kind of care pointed towards resilience, Indigenous survivance,[7] and growth. As adrienne maree brown states, one principle of her emergent strategy is the notion that "what you pay attention to grows."[8]

The compelled future contract of care for a plant initiates a much more RELATIONAL and ongoing experience. Much like the implications of the Anthropocene, (see CRISIS) growing a garden reminds us that we have both a history of actions with effects and a participatory obligation to the future. Also, brown's insistence on the fact that "small is good, small is all," reminds us that even tiny moments of nurturing are contributing to the wild future that is imagined.[9] Like anthropocentric awareness, we got ourselves into this mess and we are being challenged to get ourselves out of it. Ongoing post-performance plant care reminds me of a durational manifestation of my effect on my relations. I say relations in the same way that Indigenous scholars and thinkers acknowledge plants and the natural world as relations, not just objects. Both *Emergent Strategy* and *Remixed* rehearse "ways for humans to practice being in right relationship to our home and each other, to practice complexity, and grow a compelling future together through relatively simple interactions."[10] (see LAND)

What else does gardening do? For brown, the elements of an emergent strategy are: "Fractal" or the awareness of the "Relationship between Small and Large"; "Adaptive," or an awareness of "How we Change"; "Interdependence and Decentralization"; "Non-linear and Iterative"; "Resilient and Transformative"; and are involved in the process of "Creating More Possibilities."[11]

If we can conceptualize the dramaturgy of gardening as an emergent strategy, *Remixed* reminds us that participation and theatrical practice more generally are dependent on change. Much like CRAFTING, gardening is an anticapitalist endeavour that requires imagination and resilience for transformation. In the abundance of life present in the garden and the theatre, we find both growth and entropy. Through this

---

7   The term survivance in its contemporary context was first employed by Anishinaabe cultural theorist Gerald Vizenor, in his book *Manifest Manners: Narratives on Postindian Survivance*: "Survivance is an active sense of presence, the continuance of native stories, not a mere reaction, or a survivable name. Native survivance stories are renunciations of dominance, tragedy and victimry" ((U of Nebraska P, 1999), vii). "Survivance," *Wikipedia*, en.wikipedia.org/wiki/Survivance.

8   brown, *Emergent Strategy*, 42.

9   brown, *Emergent Strategy*, 41.

10   brown, *Emergent Strategy*, 24.

11   brown, *Emergent Strategy*, 50.

process, we can embrace emergence, or the sometimes random and iter-
ating potential that is alive in the natural world. The mushrooms invite
a kind of beetle that eats my radishes. Everything survives.

DRAW THE GROWTH OF A PLANT IN FOUR STAGES.

SEEKING

James Frieze, in his work on the nature of the "forensic turn" in theatre performance, argues that "contemporary theatre, like all of contemporary culture, is obsessed with the detection, verification, and display of information . . . In both the new museum and the story-trail immersive, the sensation of access to evidence afforded to the viewer-turned-participant is heightened by hands-on, interactive, multimedia design features. Through these features, which bring 'dead' objects and texts back to life, the promise of the archive is itself resurrected."[1] The combination of immersion and mobility with the prompt to actively participate generates this forensic desire to uncover truth, to solve puzzles, to get to the heart of things. Shaped by the exploration of the unknown and driven by the invitation to participate, my user function is that of a detective. This formal curiosity stimulated by branching narratives or free-range environments often aligns with the fictional content and I become a detective in the fiction too. (It is perhaps not surprising then that early commercial role-playing party games were murder mysteries circa 1985.[2])

When the next item that I encounter in the archive is a toy train I know I am on the right track (no pun intended), and I am getting closer to the heart—the heart of *The Archive of Missing Things*. Created by Zuppa Theatre Co. of Halifax, Nova Scotia, *The Archive* is a single-player, site-generic game performance that combines three concurrent elements: a hypertextual maze, an audio track, and live actors in a public library.[3] As player-searchers, we are given an iPad, headphones, an "archivist's notebook," and instructions to listen to directions and to follow our nose. Invited to sit in a corner of the library, we wait for an audio track to play. We are then introduced to our audio GUIDE, the voice of a child introducing us to the expectations of the performance

1   James Frieze, "One Step Forward, One Step Back: Resisting the Forensic Turn," in *Performance and Participation: Practices, Audiences, Politics*," edited by Anna Harpin and Helen Nicholson (Palgrave Macmillan, 2017), 191–92.

2   "The History of the Murder Mystery Game: From Poe to Zoom!" *Dainty Dames Events*, 17 November 2020, daintydamesevents.com/daily-dames/the-history-of-the-murder-mystery-game-from-poe-to-zoom.

3   Dawn Tracey Brandes, "Navigating the Digital and the Real in Zuppa Theatre Co.'s *The Archive of Missing Things*," *Canadian Theatre Review* 174 (Spring 2018): 79–82.

and to the fictive narrative of Ezekiel Mason and his daughter Beatrice Mason's archive of missing and lost objects. We explore the archive by tapping on different choices on the iPad. To begin, we are told that there are four items on display in the entrance exhibit, one of which conceals a stairwell that will take us deeper into the collection. I choose the wooden dodo bird. The virtual archive is immense, spanning seven floors, with, I estimate, at least a hundred unique objects with stories that span thousands of individual lexia.[4] After reading the history of the bird that served as a doorstop in a family house and then was poignantly misplaced, I am told, "Imagine you are standing at a door." The door leads to a stairwell and I descend to the second floor and the Nostalgia Exhibit, where I am asked to choose between "River," "Bread End," "Travel Journal," and "Fur Choker." In this archive of mundane but lost things everything might be meaningful. And as we are told, "These objects must be given stories. An object without a story is a form of garbage. Garbage is the scourge of our age."

In a parallel track to our virtual explorations, microperformances swirl around us. Three seemingly ordinary library patrons—two friends and a stranger—browse the books, make a birthday card for a friend, look for a lost pendant, and perhaps not-so-ordinarily sing a song. They are walking clues. Snooping on their ostensibly private conversations, we glean the keywords that shape our navigation choices inside the virtual archive on the iPad. If we hear a story about an uncle in Nepal, we are cued to choose the display of Nepalese shoes inside the digital scavenger hunt. Likewise, the archival toy train is echoed by a wooden toy train revealed on the library shelves. Everything might be a clue—the dialogue, the clothes they wear (especially if they change), the books and other objects they carry as they peruse the stacks and make small talk.

There is a tension in the audience's experience of the work between being a seeker and being a wanderer. *The Archive* wills us to be both. Artistic Director Alex McLean envisions his work in a canon of "theatre that privileges acts of collective contemplation over emotional catharsis."[5] Collective contemplation manifests through our virtual wandering as we review the archive's quirky and eclectic but melancholic exhibits. In parallel to this drift, audience-players in *The Archive of Missing Things* are also cast as detectives looking for the heart of the archive. We are

4   Roland Barthes, *S/Z: An Essay*, translated by Richard Miller (Farrar, Straus and Giroux, 1975), 13.

5   Alex McLean, Kate Cayley, and Stewart Legere, "Approaching Ambient Drama: Reflections on Two Immersive Experiments," *Canadian Theatre Review* 173 (Winter 2018): 21.

eager to make connections between the live play and the archival exhibits. We get a thrill when we know the right one to choose. (The dodo bird was the right answer because I remembered seeing one just like it on the box-office table.) And yet as I am chasing the heart, I become inadvertently but inescapably involved in a lengthy—elegant and engaging, but lengthy—digression on nineteenth-century ladies' fans and their (apparently faux) secret language. Caught between "DRIFT" and "seek," audience-players experience *The Archive of Missing Things* as a combination of a timed corn maze and an art gallery. We are seekers, charged with attaining the secret heart. Something must be found. And yet, what if we ourselves are lost? (see BEING LOST)

Navigation is one of our key tasks. I spend a lot of energy in the archive trying not to get lost. I need to find the way. This is a classic CHOOSE YOUR OWN ADVENTURE narrative structure. One of the additional specific dramaturgies of *The Archive* is that you cannot go in reverse; you cannot turn around. And so, if you make a "wrong" choice that does not move you towards the heart, you need to go through the same exhibit again, making a different choice when you get back to the fork. *The Archive* instructs us, "You may find yourself going in circles. That too is part of our story."

Descending through all seven floors and entering into the heart of the archive is our navigational goal, spatialized through the floors, doors, and staircases, but we also have a goal as a player-detective. Not just, "Where is the heart?" but, "What is the heart?" "What is the secret?" The archive contains a number of mysteries and secrets. "Do you believe that something you've lost will some-day be returned to you, possibly in a way that no one could have predicted?" (see SURROGATION) What is this thing that was lost and might return? There is a little boy—the train is his. Who is he? Is he the child that is lost? There is more than one. What is the significance of particular objects, especially those catalogued with low numbers, like the train, which is Item 10, that seem to have been in the archive the longest? Are they connected to the heart? Here two of Espen J. Aarseth's ergodic user-functions combine—exploration intersects with INTERPRETATION.[6] Our action is aligned with meaning-making. The dramaturgical action of seeking and puzzle-solving operates in support of the play's thematic concerns. As Beatrice says of her father, who started the collection of missing things: "I believe he felt that by

---

6   Espen J. Aarseth, *Cybertext: Perspectives on Ergodic Literature* (Johns Hopkins UP, 1997), 64.

piecing all of them together one could solve the mystery of loss itself." This is our journey too.

The play asks, "What does it feel to lose something?" In the exhibits we ENCOUNTER things that are extinct. Things that are obsolete. Things that have been destroyed. Things that have been lost through violence or through carelessness or through sheer mishap. In the end, (I can tell you without spoiling the mystery) we are given permission to release ourselves from being bound (as Beatrice is) by loss. We are told to "act as I wished her [Beatrice] to do . . . Go outside as though the past were not so heavy. But keep it close. Walk through the streets as though the particular life you bear were more particular that you know it to be." Cherish and be MINDFUL of the past, but do not dwell there, waiting for lost things to return. Find your own heart.

See SHOPPING

HIDDEN IN THESE LETTERS ARE SEVEN OBJECTS MENTIONED IN *THE ARCHIVE OF MISSING THINGS* (HINT: see SEEKING). USE THE IMAGES BELOW TO IDENTIFY THEM AND CROSS THE WORDS OUT. THE RESULTING LETTERS WILL LEAD YOU TO YOUR ANSWER.

```
N  R  I  V  E  R  U  M  B  B  R  E
A  D  E  N  D  E  R  O  T  R  A  V
E  L  J  O  U  R  N  A  L  F  BI  F
U  R  C  H  O  K  E  R  R  D  N  E
P  A  L  E  S  E  S  H  O  E  S  S
B  E  L  D  O  D  O  BI  R  D  O  W
```

ANSWER:

SELF-CARE

I am cozily established inside the tent (replete with twinkle lights and soft blankets) when the persona on my laptop again addresses me via TEXT MESSAGE. It is not a neutral voice, but someone who is eager, almost nervous: "I can't believe that you're here." But then, surprisingly, they claim a connection: "It was the rain that reminded me of you." Accompanied by live violin music from outside the tent, the text on the laptop unfolds screen by screen with the story of my intangible friend's recurring dream. A dream and I am in it. It begins with my friend alone playing in a field of daisies, barefoot.

The text scrolls and I read along. My friend describes a shadow that blots out the sky and a loud noise—a roar of sound like screaming or construction or alarms. In a panic, they run to the edge of a lake in the moonlight and then under the lake, being chased by the noise. Underwater it is icy, painfully cold. Then "it's someone else's hand in mine, so warm, like a breath into mittens on a freezing day. The hand is pulling me up . . . It's you." And just like that I am the saviour of the text persona, my dream friend.

What follows is a narrative montage of joyful images. We are floating on the lake, perched on a glowing cardboard city—a "paper empire." Somehow I am the leader and I know how to fly and so we do. And then we land in my town. We pass the library and smell the books. The breakfast place down the street. We go to my house where we jump on the bed. At this peak, the story takes a turn and the mood turns sombre. We get down off the bed and the dream journey retraces its steps in reverse back to the field of daisies. Next time, when the shadow comes again, before the sound can do harm, my friend remembers "the purr of the books, the smell of hot coffee, the ding of the coins . . . That's when I woke up."

The story in the tent doesn't end there. I am told that for a while the nightmare stopped. But over time my friend starts to forget "my magic," and when the shadow returns yet again, they run to the lake and are again submerged, but this time no one comes to pull them out. Surreal and evocative in its icy beauty, we are offered this haunting image of lonely despair. A soul in need, unable to connect. "I keep waiting for your hand to appear. For you to pull me out and set me on my way." "Teach me how to save myself."

This is the participatory moment of AUTOPOIESIS. The screen prompts me, "Let's make a list of good things to do." A cursor appears in a text box at the bottom of the screen and I understand that it is my turn to type. "Go for walks," I type. My words appear on the screen in an orange text bubble. Then more words appear in a red bubble, in a blue bubble, in a green bubble: "Dance in the kitchen." "Eat chocolate." "Phone a friend." I realize with some surprise and delight that these other coloured bubbles are coming from the other invisible audience members whom I imagine ensconced nearby in other tents like mine. (see TOGETHER ALONE) As the CROWDSOURCED list of "good things to do" grows, it becomes clear to me that the dream of shadow and the NOISE and the image of being stuck under the water of the cold lake present an analogy for depression, but could easily apply to loneliness or to those times life is just too difficult to be lived. So initially my friend is trapped, and I pull them up. We give tips for how the friend can pull themselves up. Then there is a twist: my friend says, "And one day I'll make it to the surface of the water. You will too." Now the implication is that we also need to be pulled up and we have reminded ourselves how to do this.

Having described *Good Things To Do* in some detail, I want to ask, "Who cares?" How do these performances of care exhibit and interrogate the LABOUR of caring? How does performance both enact and undermine neoliberal ideas about how we care for each other as individuals, as local community clusters, and as a society under governmental and institutional systems? In certain unintentional but inevitable ways, the dramaturgical choices of *Good Things To Do* align with neoliberal ideologies.[1]

In general, the actions undertaken by audience-participants in the creation of participatory artworks operate as a kind of neoliberal downloading. Instead of being the recipient of an experience (as audiences to BOURGEOIS THEATRE mostly are), I contribute my LABOUR—sometimes physical, sometimes affective—to make the experience for myself. (see OR ELSE) In *Good Things To Do*, neoliberal downloading manifests here specifically with respect to routines of attention and caregiving. Although we are asked to contribute to the list of good things to do,

---

1   This argument here is reproduced from a more extended piece of writing: Jenn Stephenson, "'Who Cares?': The Neoliberal Problem of Performing Care in Immersive and Participatory Play," *Contemporary Theatre Review* 32, no. 1 (2022): 91–100. In that article, I also consider how elements of metatheatrical play in *Good Things To Do* help the work to slip away and escape this neoliberal imbrication. But for the moment here, I want to focus on self-care as a participatory dramaturgy.

to share our magic with our virtual friend, that list is for us. Thinking about what is good to do, what we can do to combat our own shadows of paralyzing stress, depression, and anxiety generates a list that is a compendium of self-care techniques.

Self-care rose to prominence as a trend in 2016. As a social practice, self-care affirms that you are enough as you are, that you should do whatever is best for you, and that in itself isn't selfish. Inevitably this idea of self-care has been commodified as beauty routines, spa packages, daily planners, meditation apps, wellness foods like teas and dark chocolate, and even a Twitter @selfcare_bot. At its origins, the trend draws inspiration from the words of poet Audre Lorde, who writes in *A Burst of Light and Other Essays*, "Caring for myself is not self-indulgence, it is self-preservation, and that is an act of political warfare."[2] "In this formulation, self-care was no longer a litmus test for social equality; it was a way [for Black women] to insist to a violent and oppressive culture that you mattered, that you were worthy of care."[3] Self-care transcends simple pampering by being tied to an assertion of the value of every individual. This is all good to a point. The complication of self-care, apart from its mass commercialization, is that by asserting the value of the individual it participates in an individualism that we might find uncomfortable. Laurie Penny writes, "The risk of promoting individual self-care as a solution to existential anxiety or oppression is that victims will become isolated in a futile struggle to solve their own problems rather than collectively change the systems causing them harm."[4] Self-care encourages us to retreat into our own small personal worlds. Thus, self-care performs as a tool of neoliberalism. Self-carers are bearing the burdens of a value system that prioritizes the individual over the collective, promoting independence and DIYism. In essence, when I am in need, I should not expect assistance. I alone am responsible for my own care and well-being.

Turning to the interpersonal connection between me and my virtual friend, another typical pattern of behaviour under neoliberalism becomes apparent. Neoliberal governments shift responsibility to individuals for their own well-being through the reduction of social services, and when we are no longer able to care for ourselves, individuals in need look to their family and friend networks to fill that gap. Leah Lakshmi Piepzna-Samarasinha, in her book *Care Work: Dreaming Disability Justice*,

2   Audre Lorde, *A Burst of Light and Other Essays* (AK, 2017), 130.
3   Jordan Kisner, "The Politics of Conspicuous Displays of Self-Care," *The New Yorker*, 14 March 2017, newyorker.com/culture/culture-desk/the-politics-of-selfcare.
4   Kisner, "The Politics of Conspicuous Displays of Self-Care."

fiercely advocates for community-based mutual aid "care webs," but also recognizes the complexity of these interdependent entanglements. She presses us to "find ways to keep each other alive when the state is fucked, and community can be fucked and inadequate too . . . [She thinks about her friend's statement that she shouldn't have to rely on being liked or loved to get care] . . . I want us to dream mutual aid in our postapocalyptic revolutionary societies where everyone gets to access many kinds of care—from friends and internet strangers, from disabled community centres, and from some kind of non-fucked-up non-state state that would pay caregivers well and give them health benefits and time off and enshrine sick and disabled autonomy and choice."[5] (see REHEARSAL) I think actually in a small way *Good Things To Do* does this. If I lean into the ambiguity of who needs help and reframe the list as not for me but for others, then our little network of tents is a care web. We are giving help anonymously to invisible others. Just like I do for my virtual friend. EXCHANGE is not possible or expected. And so we resist the neoliberal bootstrap hellscape.

When I exit my tent, I find a large bowl of water with an origami paper boat floating on the surface. A replica in miniature of the dream-image of the paper city skimming the dark lake. There is one bowl for each of us. I pick up the boat and discover that the list of good things to do we just generated is written on the paper. I take the boat. The curtains to the Isabel Bader Centre rehearsal hall are now open, exposing a full wall of windows. From the lakeside venue, I look out across the water, past the sailboats on this June day, and out to the gently turning windmills of Wolfe Island.

And this is the thing about *Good Things To Do*. For sure it is implicated in the instrumentality of self-care, and for sure in my participation I am a handmaiden of neoliberalism. But, at this moment, I don't care. The show feels like a gift. True, I have given my affective labour to make for myself a list of things to do when I feel low. But the show has given me much more—a slowly unfolding MINDFUL experience, the surreal affection of my text friend, the aesthetic pleasure of the dream narrative, and the cozy solitary restfulness of the tent. From these small gifts, the frayed edges of my tired soul are soothed.

See FOOT WASHING and INSTRUMENTALITY

---

5   Leah Lakshmi Piepzna-Samarasinha, *Care Work: Dreaming Disability Justice* (Arsenal Pulp, 2018), 63, 65.

SHEEP

Performance scholar Rebecca Schneider (*Performing Remains*) notes that among the compelling features of historical re-enactment are the "curious inadequacies of the copy."[1] No matter how persistent or meticulous we may be in our efforts at authentic replication, of say a War of 1812 battlefield or late-nineteenth-century rural schoolroom, perfect repetition is impossible. But then, this is part of the appeal. This is the slippery beauty in the collision of theatricality and time. She writes, "Any time-based art encounters its most interesting aspect in the fold: the double, the second, the clone, the uncanny, the *againness* of (re) enactment."[2] Scott Magelssen identifies the locus of this bent perception in the "consciousness of doubleness."[3] It is not only that there is a difference, but that we are acutely—and aesthetically—aware of that difference. Magelssen invites us when considering such SIMS to note the "ways in which they create new experiences that draw on, play with, wink at, or otherwise comment on the events they reference."[4] We need to get close, but will never quite merge into singularity, and in that failure we make meaning.[5]

Counting Sheep is a guerrilla-folk musical created by Mark and Marichka Marczyk and their band Lemon Bucket Orkestra. Performed entirely in Ukrainian by the musicians wearing half-face sheep masks, the performance is an interactive recreation of the anti-government protests in Kyiv in winter 2013–2014. Termed the Euromaidan, or Maidan Uprising, citizens occupied Maidan Square for several months, where they built barricades and clashed with police.[6] Surrounding the audience on three sides are giant screens that display video footage from TV

---

1   Rebecca Schneider, *Performing Remains: Art and War in Times of Theatrical Reenactment* (Routledge, 2011), 6.

2   Schneider, *Performing Remains*, 6.

3   Richard Bauman, quoted in Scott Magelssen, *Simming: Participatory Performance and the Making of Meaning* (U of Michigan P, 2014), 10.

4   Magelssen, *Simming*, 10.

5   This argument and some of the text appears previously in Jenn Stephenson, "Real Bodies Part 1: The Traumatic Real in Immersive Performances of Political Crisis and Insecurity—*Counting Sheep* and *Foreign Radical*," in *Insecurity: Perils and Products of Theatres of the Real* (U of Toronto P, 2019), 185–95.

6   Ultimately the popular action was successful, and, in February 2014, pro-Russian president Viktor Yanukovych fled first to Donetsk and Crimea, and then to

broadcasts of the protests, complete with chyron channel logos across the bottom of the images. In performance, the sequence of our live action mimics that of the videos. First, the crowd gathers, eating and drinking, dancing, building a barricade, a wedding, more dancing. Our embodied (re)presentation follows the staging of increasingly violent confrontations with helmeted riot police-sheep, to the burning of the barricade, to a funeral. And finally to a concluding scene where we bear WITNESS to the Russian military invasion and local defence of the Crimea region. The immersive news videos create a kind of mimetic

vertigo about who is who. Are they real or are we real? Are they copying us or are we copying them? The screens sway ontologically and become windows. As they vanish, our horizon stretches and the two MOBS—one in the physical now and one of the image then—merge. It's a conundrum of LIVENESS. We seem to co-occupy space and time. We become extras in their world; or, are they in ours? I find myself wondering, "Is the Lemon Bucket Orkestra playing the music they are dancing to in Kyiv?" There is a TV cameraman-sheep who films it all. Is that us on the screen? (We never get "live" footage, and the link is imaginary, but still it seems almost possible.)

By the same token, the differences are palpable. The stylistic theatrical frame around *Counting Sheep* is thick. The bricks that we throw at the riot police are newspaper-wrapped foam blocks. The bullets they fire back at us are crisp black paper airplanes, which, although harmless, are scary. I can see the incomplete verisimilitude all around me and compare the wooden scaffold Christmas tree in Maidan Square, visible in the videos, to its smaller replica in the corner of the performance space. Also, as mentioned, the musicians are sheep, and they only sing in Ukrainian. But, most importantly, my audience-protestor body is stubbornly actual. No matter the attempts to become immersed in winter in

Kyiv, I'm stuck in a community hall/theatre in Toronto. It's June and I'm wearing shorts. Alison Griffiths, writing about immersivity in cinemas, museums, and cathedrals, remarks on the specific interstitial quality of being immersed: We are "neither fully lost in the experience, nor completely in the here and now . . . We are never fully 'there' because our bodies can never fully leave the 'here.'"[7] Our immersed presence works against immersion. Audiences guarantee the failure of a perfect totally

---

Russia. Although, of course, the longer effects of the conflict between Eurocentric and Russia-centric tensions in the region are still being experienced.

7   Alison Griffiths, *Shivers Down Your Spine: Cinema, Museums, and the Immersive View* (Columbia UP, 2008), 3, 285.

immersive environment.[8] Moving my body reminds me that indeed I have a body. I am a body. Not merely a cognitive eye/I, I experience theatrical immersion on different planes as adrenaline, as choreography, as an obstructed view, as tired feet. (see SWEATING) Food is really real and it is really entering my body. And like dancing or throwing bricks, it is a real thing that I am doing. These real actions intersect uncertainly with the more patently fictive elements of the performance.

Critically, it is in those gaps, in that failure, that meaning arises out of our experience. Schneider writes, "The effort at gestic cloning both succeeds . . . and completely fails as the problem of unruly details (call it gender difference, bodily difference, language difference, anachronism, or any number of inevitable errors) takes the stage with a palpable force in direct proportion to the technical accomplishment of reiterating the affects of the 'master's piece' faithfully."[9] This inescapable feature, being caught in an interstitial layer that is neither quite inside or outside the fictive environment, is a foundational experience of the immersed audience. It is a different kind of postdramatic indecidability than that described by Hans-Thies Lehmann.[10] It is not that I cannot ascertain whether I myself am actual or fictional as in Lehmann's model; it is that I am simultaneously both. I shimmer in my awareness of myself as the material actor in the creation of the work, improvising my way through an unknown script; in my mimetic role as a protestor performing for myself (see FIRST-PERSON SHOOTER) and also as part of the sceno-graphic field of others;[11] and finally in my imputed real-world existence occupied by concerns that are not performative but spectatorial.

In concert with the general feeling of situational displacement, particular moments in *Counting Sheep* apply this same effect of insecure or ambiguous ontology to open other meaningful gaps of representation. During a riot sequence where police fire on the crowd, several sheep are shot and killed. As one sheep lies prone on the floor, a cellphone rings. It is the standard factory setting "Opening (Default)" ringtone, sounding like jaunty marimbas. The first reaction is a kind of subdued panic accompanied by the patting of pockets as audience members search for

---

8   Adam Alston, *Beyond Immersive Theatre: Aesthetics, Political and Productive Participation* (Palgrave Macmillan, 2016), 61.

9   Schneider, *Performing Remains*, 112.

10   Hans-Thies Lehmann, *Postdramatic Theatre*, translated by Karen Jürs-Munby (Routledge, 2006).

11   For more about this concept of mimetic shimmering among different onto-logical poles, see Patrick Duggan, *Trauma-Tragedy: Symptoms of Contemporary Performance* (Manchester UP, 2015).

SHEEP

the culprit, worrying that it might be theirs. Once I have determined that it is not my phone, the second phase of my reaction is anger and (again subdued) annoyance at the profound rudeness of other people, marked by shuffling, sighing, and looking pointedly at other audience members. These first two reactions are decidedly grounded in the actual world as they speak to contraventions of the etiquette of the event as theatre. Then we identify the source of the sound. The cellphone is in the pocket of one of the dead sheep-protesters. Words are inadequate to describe the electricity of the revelation and magnitude of the perceptual recalibration that shakes the audience. This is what happens when young people die unexpectedly by violence. Their cellphones ring unanswered.

As Schneider writes so eloquently, it is through the "syncopated time of re-enactment [that] *then* and *now* puncture each other."[12] In the always failed, re-embodiment of historical simulation, we get caught. We stutter on time, getting caught in the threads. And in those catches and snags, we can touch the past.

See ACTING, ABYDOS, GUIDES, and TEACUPS

12 Schneider, *Performing Remains*, 2.

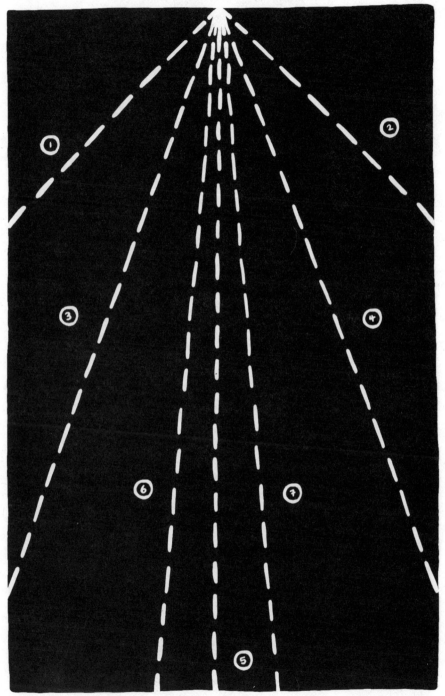

SHOPPING

In early 1990s New York, critic and scholar Elinor Fuchs encountered one of the earliest contemporary immersive theatre productions: *Tamara*. Initially performed at Strachan House in Toronto's Trinity Bellwoods Park, *Tamara* is a sprawling environmental work of over a hundred scenes stitched together in a CHOOSE YOUR OWN ADVENTURE format for a mobile audience. Premiering in 1981, the Mussolini-era drama, featuring early twentieth-century artist Tamara de Lempicka as the eponymous protagonist, is one of the first of its kind. (see FASCISM) From her writing in *The Death of Character: Perspectives on Theater After Modernism*, Fuchs is clearly engaged by what she recognizes as a new phenomenon, even as she is slightly repulsed by her own EMBODIED reaction to it. She writes, "In the conventional theater I am 'audience' or 'spectator,' all ears or all eyes, and otherwise cut off from the full response of my body. But *Tamara* wants my body. As a result, I bring a different kind of attention to this event. I must make choices, weigh my interests, and achieve them through actual physical pursuit, occasionally at a run. My attention is acute, looking for advantages—of place, storyline, and more material consumables in the form of food and drink. My zeal to possess is stimulated."[1] She describes this experience of consumption as a "mutual ingestus."[2] (see HANDS)

Beyond the environmental immersion of *Tamara*, there are other bodily pleasures. "The center of enjoyment at *Tamara* was unquestionably the food service: cocktails, buffet supper, dessert, coffee, 'champagne by Perrier Jouet.' Here the SPECTATORS fully 'take in' the spectacle. We are also in turn 'taken in by it . . . Consumption has worked its way down from eyes, ears, and emotions to the digestive organs of the theatregoer."[3] (see HANDS) Without an established term for what this is, Fuchs identifies the stimulation of acquisitive desire, particularly as it centres on the personal

---

1   Elinor Fuchs, *The Death of Character: Perspectives on Theater after Modernism* (Indiana UP, 1996), 132.

2   Fuchs, *The Death of Character*, 131.

3   Fuchs, *The Death of Character*, 131. One of the critiques of the play when it transferred to Los Angeles and New York turned on this point. The elevated opulence of the setting, and the consumer pleasures of haute food and drink, as remarked by Fuchs, served to distract audiences from the play's meditation on how their narrative choices of who to follow in this self-described "democratic" play live in contrast to their (necessarily) mute endorsement of Italian fascism.

"what I can get," as the key feature of this genre. She asks herself, where else does she experience this same feeling? Answer: shopping malls. It is not just that theatre experience is a commodity, but the branching and looping structure fosters self-gratifying, SEEKING behaviour as its main dramaturgical mechanic. Fuchs concludes, "Thus we may be seeing a new kind of theater that mimics in its underlying structures of presentation and reception the fundamental culture of contemporary capitalism."[4]

Keren Zaiontz takes this idea one step further, associating immersive exploratory theatre with INSTRUMENTAL neoliberalism. Like Fuchs, Zaiontz challenges herself as a critic to separate her immediate absorption in the experience from her cooler analysis. She reflects, "I am told what to do [in the performances], but in the days following the events I am prompted to ask myself what I have gained from proximity and co-presence with the performances. Works that challenge spectators to perform do not often grant this kind of reflection *during* performance, since the act of consuming yourself as theatre demands complete and continuous management of your own body within the theatrical space. You have to wait until you get off the ride to make sense of the experience."[5] And like Fuchs, Zaiontz frames the action of the audience-participant in immersive interactive performance as consumption, but for her the commodity offered for consumption is you. (see AUTOBIOGRAPHY) The critically delicious term that Zaiontz coins to describe this experience is "narcissistic spectatorship."[6] She goes on to identify a particular competitiveness in this self-absorbed participant qua subject-protagonist. If personal experience is the product, then how can it be optimized?[7] And so, not only are we the centre of the show, but we are primed in our acquisitiveness to make our experience the most unique and demonstrate how we are the best at participating.

In 1999, two American professors of business management named this consumer desire for intangibles the "experience economy." James H. Gilmore and B. Joseph Pine II propose in their book of the same name a timeline of changing focus from an economy driven by the extraction of resources (agrarian) to one driven by the making of goods (industrial) to one

---

4   Fuchs, *The Death of Character*, 129.

5   Keren Zaiontz, "Narcissistic Spectatorship in Immersive and One-on-One Performance," *Theatre Journal* 66, no. 3 (2014): 406–07.

6   Zaiontz, "Narcissistic Spectatorship," 407.

7   The negative corollary to this desire to collect experiences is captured in the millennial mindset of FOMO—Fear of Missing Out. Cultural currency is carried in the simple act of being present. You just had to be there. The ephemeral exclusivity of presence makes FOMO an acute symptom of the participatory zeitgeist.

driven by the offering of services and then, in the current moment, to one driven by the staging of experiences. The theatrical language of "staging" is notable. Gilmore and Pine write, "When a person buys a service, he purchases a set of intangible activities carried out on his behalf. But when he buys an experience, he pays to spend time enjoying a series of memorable events that a company stages—as in a theatrical play—to engage him in a personal way."[8] Restaurants like Rainforest Cafe, where food is merely the prop for an "eatertainment" experience, and stores like NikeTown that allow you to test out your new shoes on the in-store basketball court, constitute their foundational examples.[9] We are no longer choosing things—food or shoes—based on rational assessment of their objective qualities or features, but on how our interaction with these goods or services activate our feelings. It should surprise no one that their next book—*Authenticity: What Consumers Really Want*—looked into the secret heart of my craving for experience and gave advice on how to sell it to me. Twenty-first century participatory performance arises in concert with this zeitgeist.

Over time this trend moves from selling objects via gloss of experience in the late 1980s/1990s,[10] using experience to sell me things, to selling experience itself for its own sake in the 2000s to Millennials with FOMO. The commodity is the pleasurable, or at least stimulating, design of my time. (see AROUSAL) What is fascinating to me is how theatricality gets enfolded on itself. As Gilmore and Pine note, a theatrical performance is always already an experiential commodity. Then, theatre skills are used to elaborate experiences around objects. Storytelling and rich, immersive set design is used to cast me and my interaction with the object—the consumer and the commodity—as the joint protagonists of a memorable moment. And then this same application of intensely experiential theatricality is applied to theatre itself. (This is the same thing that happens when the theatrically inflected social turn that pushes visual art to focus on its durational relation to an audience migrates from art to theatre. It is a homecoming of sorts.) (see STRUMPET) Theatre and all ephemeral art (Thinking here also about tourism as a performance experience.) are only experiences and have ever been so. Of course life is just experience too—but now the "experience" is the point, amped up and crafted; it is the theme, not just merely the embodied emotional/intellectual passage

8   James H. Gilmore and B. Joseph Pine II, *The Experience Economy: Work is Theatre & Every Business is a Stage* (Harvard Business School P, 1999), 2.

9   Gilmore and Pine, *Experience Economy*, 3.

10   See Bernd H. Schmitt, *Experiential Marketing: How to Get Customers to Sense, Feel, Think, Act, Relate to Your Company and Brands* (Free Press, 1999); Maurya Wickstrom, *Performing Consumers: Global Capital and its Theatrical Seductions* (Routledge, 2006).

of time, but how you get the experience is meaningful. The experience is not being given to me; it is not dative. I am not the indirect object of the verb. I am a subject in the active voice. I take initiative and this generates a dramaturgy of acquisitiveness.[11] I activate my experience and then it is mine, mine, mine. And we are back to shopping.

For millennial audiences, acquisition of experience also requires documentation. If what I'm shopping for is ephemeral, I need receipts. ("Pics or it didn't happen.") This is what a selfie is. A selfie is the perfect vehicle as it carries its own verification. It says, "I was here," visually containing both "I" (my face in the foreground) and "here" (the environment or venue in the background) in one eminently shareable image.[12] Tracing yet another reflexive loop, the experience itself is made secondary to a new product that captures the experience. This phenomenon folds back on itself in the manifestation of what is variously described as an "Instagram space,"[13] "pop-up museum,"[14] or "interactive art maze."[15] These "snapworthy playgrounds"[16] typically consist of a series of rooms

---

11   Acquisitiveness at this expansive scale opens up the desire for completism. Taking action to acquire experience, I want all of it. In the case of *Tamara*, with multiple scenes running simultaneously, this is just not possible. A *New York Times* article from 1987 reports that twenty per cent of the show's nightly audience are returnees. ("'Tamara' From The Ground Floor Up," *The New York Times*, 29 November 1987, nytimes.com/1987/11/29/theater/tamara-from-the-ground-floor-up.html). *This Is Nowhere* by Zuppa Theatre Co. invokes a similar tension around the impossibility of completism. With twelve concurrent scenes scattered across Halifax, any given audience-participant might see four or five within the three-hour running time, but not all twelve. The failure to complete stimulates frustration perhaps, but also melancholy.

12   The SSHRC-funded research of Aimée Morrison (University of Waterloo) investigates the rhetoric of the selfie. In her own words, her research "aims to produce a mode of criticism suitable to extant and future online communication tools, attuned to notions of personal identity, and to the constructive role of technology in mediating these online. Basically, I'm trying to figure out how people decide how to represent themselves online, what motivates these decisions, and what effects they have" ("Aimée Morrison," *University of Waterloo*, uwaterloo.ca/english/people-profiles/aimee-morrison).

13   David Friend, "Selfie Shtick: Instagram-Friendly 'Happy Place' Comes to Toronto," CTV *News*, 1 November 2018, toronto.ctvnews.ca/selfie-shtick-instagram-friendly-happy-place-comes-to-toronto-1.4159502.

14   Jean Grant, "LIFEInside Eye Candy, Toronto's Newest Pop-Up Museum, With a Pizza Room and a Private Jet Booth," CTV *News*, 14 May 2019, torontolife.com/life/inside-eye-candy-torontos-newest-pop-museum-pizza-room-private-jet-booth/.

15   Raju Mudhar, "*The Funhouse* Wants to be More Than a Selfie Backdrop," *Toronto Star*, 1 June 2019, thestar.com/entertainment/2019/06/01/the-funhouse-wants-to-be-more-than-a-selfie-backdrop.html.

16   Friend, "Selfie Shtick."

designed for maximum visual stimulation where attendees can pose for and snap very desirable selfies. In a recent installation, one room is decked entirely in cherry blossoms, others feature floor-to-ceiling leopard print, or replicate the interior of a private jet.

Is a self-performance site entirely devoted to selecting, procuring, and then possessing the evidence of a fleeting but lux sensory moment the apotheosis of the experience economy? I can certainly imagine the 1980s celebrity LA audiences for *Tamara* or even the 1920s Tamara herself quite at home taking a selfie at Toronto's Happy Place in a room featuring a giant yellow slipper tub filled with yellow plastic ducks.

See LABOUR, OR ELSE, WINNING, and JUICINESS

TAKE A SELFIE WITH THIS BOOK!

SIM

See ABYDOS and SHEEP

WHEN YOU GET BACK TO YOUR COMRADES, YOU FIND THEM IN A STATE OF TURMOIL! AN ALIEN HAS ABDUCTED MINI SHEEP! YOUR COMRADES ARE UNDERSTANDABLY LOOKING FOR ANSWERS. THEY ASK WHERE YOU HAVE BEEN, AND WHAT'S WITH THE CHEESE SANDWICH? TO TELL THEM THE TRUTH ABOUT THE ALIEN AND THE STOLEN SANDWICH, TURN TO

PAGE 303. TO LIE AND SAY THAT YOU JUST PICKED IT UP FROM THE LOCAL DELI, TURN TO PAGE 378.

SLACK

The escape-room play *King of the Bootleggers*[1] is advertised (and so presumably designed) for twenty players. The afternoon I participated, there were only six in my group. Reflecting afterwards on the sequence of the puzzle tasks, I have a theory that the narrative progression of the escape room had been adjusted to compensate for the smaller number of players. In this story, with the criminal kingpin away for just sixty minutes, the players had to scramble to complete three initial tasks to take over as the new king of this Prohibition-era enterprise—find the moonshine recipe, the book of contacts, and the gold. We were divided in half, and while my group solved puzzles to assemble the moonshine recipe, the other group unlocked the book of contacts. After my group completed our task, we were taken to the speakeasy and played more mini-games to fill in blanks on a drink menu board. Soon the other group returned, and while we were making progress on this multi-part section of the game, they had been busy elsewhere and successfully found the gold. With time running out, I noticed that although the chalked menu board listed five drinks, with blank spaces to fill in missing words for each, three had already been written in when we started. This is when I first suspected that we had been given a "free pass," jumping us ahead in the plot. In the end, we didn't quite escape, but we were *so* close. When time ran out, we were grappling with the final puzzle and were caught red-handed, seconds away from success.

This ability to tailor the structure of the escape room ad hoc is a dramaturgical tool of participatory game-play hybrids that we are calling "slack." The effect of slack is to modify the pace of the player experience in response to the capabilities of the players. Escape rooms have a strict containing frame, typically built with a fixed time in which to "escape" and win. While the overt goal of the players is WINNING, escape rooms are about delivering a maximally "fun" experience. If we go too slow and don't get close to the end, then we feel that we have missed out on significant aspects of the game. Getting stuck early is frustrating and a lot less satisfying—not fun. Conversely, if we go too fast, the game is too easy and we finish early—also not fun. So, incorporating tasks that

---

1   Produced by Secret City Adventures, *King of the Bootleggers* is one of several escape rooms staged in Toronto's Casa Loma. These escape rooms are notable in that they feature live actors/characters in the puzzle scenarios with the audience-players.

can be skipped or added allows the creators to adjust on the fly for a given team's size or skill.

In a second show by the same company, *Escape from the Tower*[2]—a World War II counter-intelligence, code-breaking scenario, there was a moment near the end where something important was in a locked box and instead of presenting a puzzle to solve to procure the key, the GUIDE pulled it out of his pocket. I'm pretty sure that was a moment of slack because we needed to move faster. We were running out of time. In that attempt also we made it to within about a minute of "escaping." In this case, we all died, the tower destroyed by a German bombing raid that we failed to avert.

The Halifax-located scavenger hunt-esque show *This Is Nowhere*, created by Zuppa Theatre Co., uses its bespoke mobile phone app interface to manifest slack. The twelve performance stations scattered through the city core are not sequenced and it is not necessary or expected that every audience member will witness every scene at every station. Having completed one station, players are assigned their next destination by the app. The app takes into account how many people are already en route to each station and the audience capacity for each, which varies from one to twenty and adjusts accordingly. As the show approaches the culminating three-hour mark, all participants are directed by the app to the final station for a communal concluding scene. Fast-moving searchers will be able to reach more stations. Slower searchers will reach fewer. You could even stop for a coffee and snack before checking in for your next destination.

What is particularly invigorating about slack as a strategy of participatory dramaturgy is that neither theatre nor games manifest this flexible quality purposely to generate an optimal user experience (UX). In a theatre performance, the shape of the audience UX—our intellectual and emotional journey—is determined in advance and then fixed. Show after show, the "heat" always builds in the same way. Theatre is independent of time constraints; a dramatic performance is as long as it is. For games, UX is secondary to the prime objective of WINNING. Like theatre, games as part of their raison d'être generate heightened engagement. For both players and spectators, the product is an experience. But games are innately indifferent to the specific nature of that experience. A championship game tied 1–1 with one minute left to play has a different UX than one where the score is 12–0—especially if your team is losing. And again, like theatre, time is autonomous and fixed.

2　Also produced by Secret City Adventures at Casa Loma in Toronto.

Games don't care if you come close to winning. Escape rooms do seem to care. Almost escaping but not quite or escaping but just barely is the definition of an optimal escape-room experience. The ux is directly linked to time and so slack is a mechanism for recalibrating the "action" to time.

Video-game design has a similar function to slack called Dynamic Difficulty Adjustment (DDA), sort of like an artificially intelligent golf handicap. Katie Salen and Eric Zimmerman provide a short overview in their chapter on cybernetic games: (Notice their reference to participatory theatre as an analogous experience.) "DDA points to a different kind of game, a game that constantly anticipates the abilities of the player, reads the player's behavior, and makes adjustments accordingly. Playing a game becomes less like learning an expressive language and more like being the sole audience member for a participatory, improvisational performance, where the performers adjust their actions according to how you interact with them. Are you then playing the game, or is it playing you?"[3] Is slack CHEATING? It doesn't feel like cheating. (see BOUNDARY VIOLATIONS and GOING ROGUE) Perhaps part of the reason is that if it is well done, the introduction of the shortcut can be quite subtle. The players might proceed unaware. Or the players might not care. Unlike a game and more like a drama, escape-room rules and expectations of what is "fair play" in a narrative sense are not shared with us in advance. Getting help in a sport or game feels wrong; you can't change the size of the field or the number of players. You can't change the parameters of play, (like deciding in soccer that it is now okay to pick up the ball with your hands and throw it in the net) without breaching the lusory attitude.[4] In an escape room, the rules of play seem to evolve; the game world unfolds as you go, so there is no strict standard to adhere to. Slack is more like a plot twist than a hack. The irrelevance of cheating underscores the value placed on a maximally "fun" experience that takes precedence over winning.

---

3   Katie Salen and Eric Zimmerman, *Rules of Play: Game Design Fundamentals* (MIT P, 2004), 223. Matthew Reason identifies a similar feeling in an immersive work where he was the passive object of attention by the performers. He muses that perhaps rather than having had an experience, "an experience had me" ("Participatory Audiencing and the Committed Return," in *Staging Spectators in Immersive Performances: Commit Yourself!*, edited by Doris Kolesch, Theresa Schütz, and Sophie Nikoleit (Routledge, 2019), 88–101).

4   Bernard Suits points out that the definition of "playing a game is the voluntary attempt to overcome unnecessary obstacles." This is the lusory attitude. *The Grasshopper: Games, Life and Utopia* (U of Toronto P, 1978), 41. (see GOING ROGUE)

The escape-room experience is practically a textbook definition of being in "flow," characterized as "intense and focused concentration on what one is doing in the present moment, merging of action and awareness . . . a sense that one can control one's actions, that is, a sense that one can in principle deal with the situation because one knows how to respond to whatever happens next; distortion of temporal experience, experience of the activity as intrinsically rewarding."[5] Originally conceptualized by Mihály Csíkszentmihályi, flow is a relation of "optimal arousal" where perceived action opportunities (challenges) are positively correlated to perceived action capabilities.[6] If a task is too easy in relation to my skill level, then I am bored. If a task is too difficult in relation to my skill level, then I experience anxiety.[7] This relationship explains the benefit of an adaptable intervention like slack to keep players in the zone of flow in an autotelic activity where the experience itself is the product. Certainly, players of games and theatre audiences can and do experience flow in the intersection of their abilities and the physical and cognitive challenges presented. The difference is that slack adjusts immediately in real time where the typical dramaturgies of drama and games generally do not.

Slack is responsive. This responsiveness lays the foundation for EMERGENCE. Slack pays attention to player input and opens up the work to feedback. That said, slack is a very specific, limited kind of response. It is not fully dialogic. Slack is not an interactive conversation. Slack is a singular intervention that reshapes the narrative map; it is a pair of editing scissors.

See AUTOPOIESIS

---

5   Jeanne Nakamura and Mihály Csíkszentmihályi, "The Concept of Flow," in *Handbook of Positive Psychology*, edited by C. R. Snyder and Shane J. Lopez (Oxford UP, 2002), 90.

6   Nakamura and Csíkszentmihályi, "The Concept of Flow," 90.

7   Nakamura and Csíkszentmihályi, "The Concept of Flow," 94.

SNEAKY NINJAS

I went to the local game store with my son for something to do since we were taking a break from running errands downtown, and research happened. Among the murder-mystery dinner parties and escape-room-in-a-box games was a palm-sized black box marked *Sneaky Cards: Play It Forward*.[1] Designed by Gamewright, the box and many of the card faces feature a cartoon figure that looks like a young person dressed all in black with a partial face and head covering. (I think it is a pop-culture ninja?) Each of the fifty-five cards provides instructions for a specific task. "Make a speech in an elevator with more than three people you don't know." "Hold the door open for ten consecutive people." "Find a new favourite song." "Coin a new word or phrase." There are six broad categories of cards: Engage, Connect, Surprise, Care, Grow, Create. The card also invites you to pass it on once the task is complete—"slip this card into a pocket in a clothing store"—creating a chain of playing it forward as the next unwitting person takes up the task. Basically, these are a pack of ideas for acts of kindness/weirdness where the world is your PLAYGROUND.[2] The cards operate on the same principles of Fluxus-style event scores, providing a RECIPE for some kind of real-world performative action. The attitude of the cards blends self-improvement lite with caring social interactions. It is also a game that you are playing with no one watching, thus the sneaky part.[3] You are in the MAGIC CIRCLE, playing in the interstices of everyday existence. On the box, beside where it says this is a game for one and for people aged twelve years plus, it lists the estimated duration of the game as "your whole life."

---

1   "*Sneaky Cards: Play it Forward*," *Gamewright*, gamewright.com/product/Sneaky-Cards.

2   Games that happen in real-world spaces are well documented by Markus Montola, Jaakko Stenros, and Annika Waern in their book *Pervasive Games: Theory and Design* (Routledge, 2009). (see Q and SECRET WEIRDOS)

3   Zuppa Theatre Co.'s *This Is Nowhere* also taps into this sneakiness as we play private games in the actual world. We are instructed: "In the time that remains, follow clues to locations where unknown people await you. Be discreet. Don't draw too much attention to yourself. Pay attention to traffic and other passers-by. The city of the present won't stop just because you're looking towards the future. Good manners and the laws of traffic still apply. The present is the future arriving, and the only place you can actually live" ("Overture," *This Is Nowhere* app, September 2018).

In the case of *TBD*,[4] created by Radix Theatre (Vancouver) and based on the *Bardo Thodol—Tibetan Book of the Dead*—the time of the game is not your whole life, but rather your whole death and rebirth spun out over twenty-one consecutive days. The play-experience begins with the podcast narration of my death from a brain aneurysm and unfolds over three acts, one per week: Death, Becoming, and Rebirth. Through this journey, audience members interact daily with *TBD* performers who insert themselves into my regular routines via TEXT MESSAGES, videos, things that arrive in the MAIL, or are placed on my doorstep. Facilitated by an app that tracks my location in real time, there are also live encounters at random locations. Reviewer Colin Thomas describes being accosted in a parking garage by "spirit guides . . . their faces and clothing covered in ashes. They gave me a little bag that contained a cup of salt, which, they told me, was about how much salt my body had in it when I was alive. They suggested I carry the salt with me as a reminder."[5] On day eight, audience-deceased are invited to a nearby body of water. After walking for fifteen minutes, wearing noise-cancelling headphones, and carrying our personal salt, we arrive at the shore and are instructed to "look back the way you have come. Consider your journey to this point. Offer one pinch of salt to: all that you have done . . . all that you have seen . . . all whom you have loved . . . Place all the remaining salt in the palm of your hand. Consider what is possible? What is ready? What will be your first step? . . . Now release the rest of the salt to the sea, to dissolve and make new."[6]

Since this is a performance about my death, it makes sense that most of the scenes happen in the locations of my life, surreally interspersed with that now-past life in progress. The interstitial folding of time as I continue over three weeks to live my life, while also living my death, is profoundly unsettling. During the first week, posters are placed in my neighbourhood projecting me as a missing person. The somewhat elliptical text with my name at the top asks, "Can you hear us? Let us know where you are and how you are doing?" with a PHONE number to call and instructions to leave a message. On another day, an entirely black-clad, faceless silent performer arrives at my home with an offer to perform helpful household chores. (Another ninja?) Overall, the effect is

---

4 The script-recipe for this show appears in *Canadian Theatre Review* 197 (Winter 2024): 94–103.

5 Colin Thomas, "I was Dead for 17 Days and I Have Been Reborn for 2," *Mapping the Intuitive*, 13 November 2015, colinthomas.ca/2015/11/13/i-was-dead-for-17-days-and-i-have-been-reborn-for-2.

6 Radix Theatre, *TBD*, *Canadian Theatre Review* 197 (Winter 2024): 94–103.

one of OSTRANENIE—not just making the stone stony by putting an aesthetic frame around it, but bringing my entire existence into intense relief for my MINDFUL contemplation by inserting these performance events and activities into the very fabric of my life.

See DRIFT

CUT OUT AND COMPLETE THESE SNEAKY TASKS.

GIVE THIS
TO SOMEONE

WHO HAS A
CALMING
PRESENCE

DO SOMETHING
YOU HAVE BEEN
PUSHING OFF

THEN PASS THIS ON
TO SOMEONE ELSE

BUY SOMEONE
A LITTLE TREAT

THEN GIVE THEM
THIS CARD

GIVE THIS
TO SOMEONE

WHO HAS
GREAT STYLE

SPECTATOR

See INTERPRETATION and A AND B

YOUR COMRADES BELIEVE THE LIE, AND WITHOUT THINKING YOU
TAKE A TRIUMPHANT CHOMP OF THE ALIEN'S CHEESE SANDWICH.
IMMEDIATELY AFTER, YOUR STOMACH BEGINS TO GRUMBLE, AND YOU
FEEL STRANGE... TURN TO PAGE 297 TO FIND OUT YOUR FATE.

STICKINESS

There is an underlying assumption in participatory art-making that ENCOUNTERS really make a connection; an assumption that by eating together or solving puzzles together or being SECRET WEIRDOS together we are developing meaningful relationships that might transcend the immediate moment. Bojana Kunst, in her article "The Institution Between Precarization and Participation," suggests paradoxically that the vulnerability of institutional precarity prevents us from being affected in this way. She begins by citing Isabell Lorey to assert that precariousness has three dimensions.[1] One, socio-ontological life is always precarious. No person is ever completely autonomous and so we are always in need of help or protection. (see CRISIS) We are vulnerable to the precarity of life and health and also to a dependence on others in a social network for our continued well-being. Two, structural inequalities create social inequalities and as a result some lives are more precarious than others. The imbalance is a political structure layered onto the previous essential ontological characteristic of humanness. Third, in the contemporary neoliberal polity, we experience government precarization. The prioritization of independence, initiative, and entrepreneurship leads to the downloading of social services and a destabilization of integrated and interdependent ways of living. (see REHEARSAL) As Kunst observes, the result is a "production of a pertinent feeling of insecurity, which is always combined with the fear of insecurity itself."[2] To combat this fear of insecurity we are pushed into strategies of self-care, self-immunizing from everyone and everything. Ironically this protective retreat effectively separates us from those others who are necessary bulwarks against the precarity we fear. "'Self-immunization against all possible forms of precarity' which instead of opening the vulnerable life towards the other and towards the social, rehearses constant protection of one's own life toward other competing vulnerable and individual monads."[3]

So, although participatory play perhaps promises RELATIONAL connection and community, Kunst suggests that this is not what is

---

1   Isabell Lorey, *State of Insecurity: Government of the Precarious* (Verso, 2015).

2   Bojana Kunst, "The Institution Between Precarization and Participation," *Performance Research* 20, no. 4 (2015): 7.

3   Kunst, "The Institution Between Precarization and Participation," 10.

happening. Even though we share space, we do not affect each other. Mostly we engage in parallel play. (see TOGETHER ALONE) "The invitation to participation is actually a political and economic phantasm of a clean society of individuals who are doing things in common, however, and at the same time protecting their own interests in all of that."[4] The solution, she argues, is that we need to be sticky and messy, not smooth and clean. There needs to be real consequences, not more risk management. We need to eschew what she calls "floating clouds of experience" and embrace contamination through EMBODIED contact with others.

What does mess look like? Trying to answer this question leads me to actual mess, like being soaking wet in your clothes, being muddy and SWEATY, being so tired that you might cry. University student-orientation activities are tapping into this strategy to create close-knit groups of first years and an emotional bond to the university as alma mater. Even though much (much) tamer in recent years, orientation still features games played in pits of mud, shaving cream "fights," and wearing the same, now filthy "frosh" T-shirt for a week. I imagine at a more extreme intensity, military boot camp taps into the same principles. It is not just being messy, but being messy together. I have not (yet) experienced a theatrical play like this. This feels dangerous. (see AROUSAL)

Perhaps fear is messy? I believe that the adrenaline-fuelled fear inspired by the "haunted house" of Single Thread Theatre Company's solo-immersive production of the medieval drama *Everyman*, where I was cast as Everyman and compelled by Death to deliver a reckoning of my misspent life to God, made me vulnerable to what turned out to be a moving spiritual experience. More than ten years later I can still feel both the fear and the transcendence.[5] Perhaps sadness is messy? Telling the story of a long-ago friendship breakup to Shira Leuchter and Michaela Washburn in *Lost Together* brought the devastation I once felt into the present. No one had ever heard that story (Why would I share it?) and the experience of telling became truly meaningful. That AUTOBIOGRAPHICAL sharing is now layered into my loss and has coloured it differently. It is worth noting that both of these experiences of significant vulnerability were in shows where I was a solo audience. The connection, then, might be to the actors, but actually, I think upon consideration, the connection in contamination is to myself.

---

4   Kunst, "The Institution Between Precarization and Participation," 12.

5   Jenn Stephenson, "Real Bodies Part 2: Narcissistic Spectatorship in Theatrical 'Haunted Houses' of Solo Immersive Performance—*Everyman*," in *Insecurity: Perils and Products of Theatres of the Real* (U of Toronto P, 2019), 210–25.

Maybe the most we can expect is a polite but temporary rapport—a warm fellow feeling of connectedness in the moment that is not sustained. Maybe stickiness is impossible. Maybe the risk is too high?

See FOOT WASHING, INTIMACY, and TEXT MESSAGING

STRUMPET

In the second act of *Ça a l'air synthétique bonjour hi*, one of the actors approaches a potted conical evergreen shrub that is approximately her own height and size. The house lights dim and the stage lights create a dark and moody scene. She begins to question the plant: "Do you feel that people see the real you? Does this feel natural to you? Would you believe me if I told you I never felt so connected with somebody? Can I kiss you?" As this interaction unfolds, it becomes clear that this is a parody of the confessional questioning that audiences are often subject to in participatory performances. Where in the first act of *Ça a l'air synthétique bonjour hi* we contribute our physical LABOUR to make the performance work, in this second section, we bear witness to an absurdist take on participation as AUTOBIOGRAPHY. The shrub is clearly a stand-in for the audience-player. In this tangle of leisure and labour, the act of sharing personal details with a newly met stranger generates an innate tension between the pleasures of this kind of attention and a sense of invasive vulnerability of being asked to give more than is warranted or perhaps earned. Evoking this ambivalence, the scene in *Ça a l'air synthétique bonjour hi* reflects an unnatural forced INTIMACY. We watch as the performer embraces the shrub, stroking it and kissing it. She wraps her limbs around it erotically. Reaching some kind of climax, the actor collapses, catatonic. Another actor comes forward with a large roll of clear plastic wrapping, circling both the woman and the shrub, binding them together to "preserve the moment." With the help of an audience member, they are then hoisted onto a rolling dolly and carted off stage. That is the end of the scene.

From my analogous position in the role of the shrub, this (UNWELCOME?) seduction in the name of participation reminds me of Michael Fried's aggressive and aggrieved critique of the social turn in visual art in his notorious (in some circles) essay "Art and Objecthood." Fried is concerned with the insistent relationality in art that he names "literalist" work, specifically in contrast to modernist work. In Fried's characterization, a modernist work holds itself aloof from the viewer, confident in its autonomous objecthood. (Barnett Newman's imposing painting *Voice of Fire* with its three bold vertical stripes—blue, red, blue—does not care about you.[1]) On the other hand, literalist works are situational, encompassing not

---

1   Exhibited in the National Gallery of Canada (Ottawa) in the company of paintings by Jackson Pollock and Mark Rothko, the 5.4 metre by 2.4 metre canvas is a

only the surrounding space, but also the body of the beholder present in that space. (Consider how moving around a sculpture alters your perception of its composition. Taken to the extreme, participatory work is entirely dependent on the engagement of the viewer. If a participatory work falls in a forest, is it art?) To this view, literalist work is more theatrical, insofar as it a) requires the co-presence of the viewer to become manifest; and b) unfolds over the time period of that interaction. Maria Lind calls this shift towards aesthetic experiences residing in presence and duration rather than in an object the "dematerialization of the art object."[2] Fried, writing in 1967, doesn't identify this work as RELATIONAL (Nicolas Bourriaud's relational aesthetics dates from the 1990s) or indeed as participatory, but the identification of some art as interdependent with and responsive to its context is evident. Describing this interrelation, Fried characterizes the work of art as an unwelcome advance. He writes, "The things that are literalist works of art must somehow confront the beholder—they must, one might almost say, be placed not just in his space but in his way . . . In fact, being distanced by such objects is not, I suggest, entirely unlike being distanced, or crowded, by the silent presence of another person; the experience of coming upon literalist objects unexpectedly—for example, in somewhat darkened rooms—can be strongly, if momentarily, disquieting in just this way."[3] Fried describes the work in terms of its "obtrusiveness," its "aggressiveness," and the "special complicity that the work extorts from the beholder."[4]

Grant Kester in his book *Conversation Pieces* responds to Fried and revises the depiction of the needy situational artwork, characterizing it with sexual overtones that are not present in Fried. Kester writes, "Only by studiously ignoring the viewer's presence can the authentic work avoid the indignity of selling itself to the viewer like a cheap commodity."[5] It is "art that shamelessly importunes the viewer."[6] The efforts by

---

quintessential example of abstract modernism. Purchased in 1990 for a then-breathtaking $1.8 million, the acquisition "ignited a 'firestorm' of media attention and controversy . . . mostly centred on the question of whether the work was worthy of being called art" (John Geddes, "*Voice of Fire*: Are We Over This Yet?," *Maclean's*, 21 January 2010).

2   Maria Lind, "Returning on Bikes: Notes on Social Practice," in *Living as Form: Socially Engaged Art from 1991–2011*, edited by Nato Thompson (MIT P, 2017), 49.

3   Michael Fried, "Art and Objecthood (1967)," *Art and Objecthood: Essays and Reviews* (U of Chicago P, 1998), 154–55.

4   Fried, "Art and Objecthood," 155.

5   Grant Kester, *Conversation Pieces: Community and Communication in Modern Art*, updated edition (U of California P, 2013), 48.

6   Kester, *Conversation Pieces*, 49.

the work "to dramatize its own condition of being, actually constitutes a form of impoliteness—simultaneously distancing and coercing viewers, forcing them to become uncomfortably aware of the contingency of an aesthetic ENCOUNTER that they would prefer to simply enjoy."[7] I love this elaboration by Kester. The suggestion that participatory art coerces the engagement of the audience profoundly complicates the nature of the INVITATION and opens up consideration of all the ways that we would perhaps rather not participate. (see REFUSAL, KILLJOY, and GOING ROGUE) Participation is not always an unencumbered gift. First, our labour is not always entirely free as we often become entangled in the downloaded politics of neoliberal exchange, paying for our pleasure in complicated ways. And second, when the invitation is shaded by STICKY solicitation, we sometimes realize that, despite our desire, actually we would simply rather not.

An aside: it is interesting to consider Fried's condemnation of the theatricality of situational works of visual art as applied to works of theatrical and performance art, which are theatrical to begin with. Fried gestures towards this extension of his concerns as he sees theatre and theatricality as a threat not only to modernist painting but to art at large. He writes, "The success, even the survival, of the arts has come increasingly to depend on their ability to defeat theater."[8] To this view, increasing theatricality is a threat to modern theatre itself. Fried recognizes that even in theatre there is a mid-twentieth-century trend towards a more pervasive (invasive?) socially oriented theatricality. Explicitly mentioning Artaud and Brecht, Fried identifies in those theatres the same heightened desire of the artwork for meaningful interaction with its audience as in literalist visual art. Although Artaud and Brecht would not meet the terms of our working definition of participation as involving the meaningful play of audience-players as co-creators, nevertheless we can see how they are thinking about how audience engagement is central to the experience. (see A AND B) They both position a dynamic interdependent relationship between the audience and the artwork as the vehicle for realizing their particular aims. Ultimately, this extension by Fried underscores the notion that participatory theatre is an extreme example of the usual case. Theatre is always already a relational experience, arising out of presence and duration. (see INTERPRETATION)

---

7   Kester, *Conversation Pieces*, 56–57.
8   Fried, "Art and Objecthood," 163.

THE SEVEN WORDS BELOW HAVE BEEN ENCODED, WITH EACH LETTER STANDING IN FOR ANOTHER. USING THE CHART AND FIRST SOLVED WORD, UNCOVER THE REMAINING WORDS. THEN UNSCRAMBLE THE CIRCLED LETTERS TO OBTAIN THE ANSWER.

HINT: ALL WORDS CAN BE FOUND IN THE FIRST PARAGRAPH OF THE PREVIOUS ENTRY (see STRUMPET).

ENCODED	A	B	C	D	E	F	G	H	I	J	K	L	M
DECODED													

ENCODED	N	O	P	Q	R	S	T	U	V	W	X	Y	Z
DECODED												P	

YSHJXVXYSJTHO → P A R T I C I P A T O R Y

YTJJLR → _ _ _ _ _ _

VTGGLVJLR → _ Ⓞ _ _ _ _ _ _ _

ASKTIH → _ _ _ _ Ⓞ _

ALXUIHL → _ _ _ _ _ Ⓞ _

SKUIHRXUJ → _ _ _ _ _ _ _ _ _

YLHWTHDSGVL → _ _ _ Ⓞ _ _ _ _ _ _ _

ANSWER:

SURROGATION

A blurry Polaroid is my souvenir of the time that something I lost was returned to me. In the participatory EXCHANGE of *Lost Together*, my contributions are a personal story about a thing that I have lost and my melancholy and what I receive is (obviously) not the thing itself, but something arguably better, a sense of closure and a sense of lightness as the emotions associated with the thing lost are softened. *Lost Together*, created by Shira Leuchter, begins with the audience member being invited to share a memory about something that they have lost. Things like a bracelet or a jacket or a harmonica. Or they might not be things at all: an afternoon, or a friendship, or your memory. After about fifteen minutes of performer-hosts Shira with Michaela Washburn asking gentle questions—"Would you want that thing back again if you could?"—they retreat to a pair of fully stocked CRAFT tables, where they buzz away at making something I can't quite discern from my comfortable easy chair. I also can't hear their consultations and plans, since I am listening to audio recordings of other people's stories of loss—a lunchbox, a house, a grandmother's ring. Soon they return. They approach formally with a miniature object on a tray and present me with an interpretive recreation of my lost thing. I'm delighted, awed, and also a little charmed. I didn't think this exercise would make a difference, but it does.

My past loss becomes verbalized as AUTOBIOGRAPHY to Shira and Michaela. Autobiography then becomes materialized as craft. It undergoes an EMERGENT phase change, transmuting as if from gas to liquid to solid, essentially the same and yet distinct. The now of the show is another step in the journey of the lost item in time. The photo of the sculpture that I take away with me points backwards to the time of the show and carries the memory of the experience forwards into my future. A new experience has been added to the lived chain of this loss. This is what Mariah calls a "sense of since."[1] Like the centuries-old stone in the park that Mariah references, a new touchpoint in chronology is added by this performance. Now when I think about the thing I lost, I also think about *Lost Together*. This performative accretion has changed the original for me. This is not therapy, meant to make me feel better or "fix" me in some way, but through *Lost Together* loss has become performance and thus is augmented. In addition, loss becomes

---

1   Mariah Horner and Grahame Renyk, "Matter Matters: Performing *A Stone in the Woods*," *Canadian Theatre Review* 163 (Summer 2015): 59–63.

visible. Shared as a public artifact in the post-performance gallery, it is part of a constellation of loss. Many people have also lost "things." As Shira notes, "Loss doesn't have to be a solitary reckoning."[2] In the give-and-get of the transformation of AUTOPOIESIS, the feeling of the sculpture is returned. The empty space of loss is not filled exactly but reoccupied by this experience as a new stage in the living memory. (see BEING LOST)

Compagnie Marie Chouinard's responsive participatory dance piece *Une Plage de Temps/Time for Time* shares many of the same relational characteristics with *Lost Together*. Presented via Zoom, the work is comprised of a series of spontaneously improvised three-minute dance performances that draw "inspiration from a heartfelt wish that a member of the audience confides to a performer."[3] In each segment, a dancer who appeared to be alone in an all-white dance studio would approach the webcam, filling the screen with a close-up of their face. Then the view would shift to the audience member in their home describing their wish. The dancer would nod earnestly and retreat to begin their interpretive response. Chouinard describes this action as "incantatory dance, reminiscent of Pythia in Greece." Having completed their offering, the dancer-votary would again come forward to the webcam, eyes wide with a serious demeanour, ostensibly meeting the gaze of the audience-supplicant. In comparison to *Lost Together*, *Time for Time* enacts a similar autopoietic transformation of changing a personal story into an aesthetic object that both is and is not the original. Also, like *Lost Together*, there is a strong sense of recognition in RELATION; that is, you and your story are being seen and heard by another. Through that connection, the story is received and held with grace.[4]

I am going to argue that both the story of loss that becomes a sculpture and the heartfelt wish that turns into dance evoke cycles of surrogation. In

---

2   Shira Leuchter, personal interview, 23 January 2019.

3   "Compagnie Marie Chouinard: *Time for Time*," *Danse/Dance*, dansedanse.ca/en/compagnie-marie-chouinard-time-time.

4   Chris Dupuis, in his review of *Time for Time* in *Intermission Magazine*, questions the viability of this relationship, noting analogous connections via social media that are at heart superfluous. He writes, "What portends to be a genuine connection between two people is more often the *performance* of that connection, aimed at a wider audience as a form of entertainment or a way to increase social capital." He draws a link to the manufactured communities of social-media marketing. "I find myself wondering, is this connection to the work real? Or, like the connections we feel to an anonymous stranger online, is it all in our heads, fabricated by platforms that require our constant participation in order to generate data for their advertisers?" ("Review: Marie Chouinard's *Time for Time*," *Intermission Magazine*, 7 October 2020, intermissionmagazine.ca/reviews/review-marie-chouinards-time-for-time/).

his book *Cities of the Dead*, Joseph Roach encapsulates this performative technique of surrogation where ritualized re-enactments and re-embodiments both recognize loss and restore life. ("The King is Dead. Long live the King.")[5] The sculpture of a lost thing found certainly matches this description. Necessarily imperfect performative recreation "fills by means of surrogation a vacancy created by the absence of an original."[6] Roach writes, "Like performance, memory operates as both quotation and invention, an improvisation on borrowed themes, with claims on the future as well as the past."[7] Where I think this claim to surrogation gets a bit slippery is in the acknowledgement that unlike a thing lost, a wish is not a thing of the past, once in existence and now gone. It has no need of being brought forward into the present and revitalized. And yet it is perhaps not too much of a stretch to see a memory and a wish as correlates. Both the lost thing and the heartfelt wish are things that are by definition not here in the present, one no more and one yet to be. When both are materialized and embodied through performance, we are comforted, reassured the thing lost remains somehow, and also that the thing not yet may still come to pass. The surrogate works by "empowering the living through the performance of memory [or a wish]."[8]

At the end of *Lost Together* I am disappointed to realize that the sculpture presented to me must remain in the gallery of other lost-found sculptures. By the third hour of *Time for Time*, I have to admit with no little embarrassment that I have exhausted my stamina for contemporary non-narrative dance. In both cases, in spite of my lack of congeniality, it is important to the effect of surrogation that the length of the reiterative process is apparent. Surrogation links each past-present or present-future pair to the next one in a theoretically unending chain. Embedding each loss-sculpture and each wish-dance in an evident sequence of ritualized re-enactment situates each individual loss and each individual wish in a community of losses and wishes. I understand that loss is everywhere and so are wishes. I am unique but I am not alone.

See TOGETHER ALONE

---

5   This argument regarding surrogation in *Lost Together* is more fully developed in Jenn's article "Autobiography in the Audience: Emergent Dramaturgies of Loss in *Lost Together* and *Foreign Radical*," *Theatre Research in Canada* 43, no. 2 (November 2022): 81–95.

6   Joseph Roach, *Cities of the Dead: Circum-Atlantic Performance* (Columbia UP, 1996), 36.

7   Roach, *Cities of the Dead*, 33.

8   Roach, *Cities of the Dead*, 34.

SWEATING

Broken Tailbone is an interactive salsa dance lesson combined with first-person storytelling that unspools the history of Latinx revolutionary movements through social-justice songs. Created and performed by Carmen Aguirre with DJ Don Pedro, the show begins with the question "Do you want to know how I actually broke my tailbone?" Of course, we do want to know, but it is not until the very end of the show that we finally hear the racy, raw, and boldly candid story that responds to that question. Given this framed structure, I think reviewer Andrea Warner is absolutely correct when she asserts that "we, the audience, need to earn the story."[1] Welcoming salsa novices to the theatre transformed into a dance club, Aguirre instructs the standing audience: "Bend your knees and start to make a circle with your tailbone. That is very good. Make a circle with your tailbone. Do not think about fucking. Although quite often these dances lead to fucking, we're not going to think about that right now. No. We are going to think about making love to Mother Earth . . . Because it is harvest."[2] Moving my body in this sensuous way, while not thinking about fucking (which of course I am) is a reflexive experience in EMBODIMENT, a necessary sweaty journey through Aguirre's memoir.

It is now commonly understood and accepted that the cognitive function of the brain is not separate from the body. The Cartesian mind-body divide has been bridged by theories of embodied cognition,[3] which assert that "movement prefigures the lines of intentionality, gesture formulates the contours of social cognition, and in both the most general and most specific ways, embodiment shapes the mind."[4] Michelle Maiese (*Embodiment, Emotion, and Cognition*) writes, "The overall structure of conscious experience and patterns of engagement with my environment

1   Andrea Warner, "Carmen Aguirre's *Broken Tailbone* is a Visceral, Sensual Dance of Resistance," *The Georgia Straight*, 15 February 2018, straight.com/arts/1033336/carmen-aguirres-broken-tailbone-visceral-sensual-dance-resistance.

2   "*Broken Tailbone* trailer 5 min cut," *Vimeo*, vimeo.com/295662740?embedded=true&source=video_title&owner=25951710.

3   Key works of the embodied cognition approach include Antonio Damasio's *Descartes' Error: Emotion, Reason, and the Human Brain* (Putnam, 1994) and Fransciso J. Varela, Evan Thompson, and Eleanor Rosch's *The Embodied Mind: Cognitive Science and Human Experience* (MIT P, 1993).

4   Shaun Gallagher, *How the Body Shapes the Mind* (Clarendon P, 2005), 1.

are a function of my embodiment . . . Consciousness is not simply something that happens within our brains, but rather something that we *do* through our living animal bodies and our dynamic bodily engagement with the world."[5] Amy Cook and Rhonda Blair have done extensive work in this field connecting the neuroscience of embodied cognition to the theatrical experience of both actors and audience members.[6] Writing about the specific application of 4E cognition (embodied, embedded, extended, and enacted) to theatre, Cook underscores how this research supports a key dramaturgical belief which asserts that "the staging of the audience is critical to theatrical experience."[7] Although Cook tends to focus on the hermeneutic work of audiencing, she conceptualizes this INTERPRETATION in a broad flow of bodily feelings and situations. She thinks about fidgeting, leaning forward, laughing, etc. She also recognizes that there is a wider applicability to non-traditional audiencing contexts and audience actions, where "contemporary theatre that calls attention to the staging of the audience" (read immersive or participatory) can open new possibilities of meanings.

How might embodied cognition connect specifically to participatory audience bodies? I think the key lies in the fourth "E" from 4E cognition theory, which is "enacted." This means that cognition arises as a result of interaction between the self and the environment via AUTOPOIESIS. A vital idea behind this is that the nervous system is not merely computational, a collector and processor of input, but actually creates meaning. Taking that a step further, cognition is the "exercise of skillful knowhow; that is, cognitive structures emerge from sensorimotor patterns of perception and action."[8] Enactivism asserts that the world does not exist autonomously—through the active interrelation of an organism in and on its environment the world comes into being. Together, the environment and the organism "enact a world," making us, in fundamental ways, co-creators.[9] Essentially, my actions in relation to the stimuli of the environment bring meaning into existence, opening a feedback loop between myself and the world.

---

5   Michelle Maiese, *Embodiment, Emotion, and Cognition* (Palgrave Macmillan, 2011), 11.

6   Amy Cook and Rhonda Blair, *Theatre Cognition and Performance: Languages, Bodies, and Ecologies* (Bloomsbury Methuen Drama, 2016); Rhonda Blair, *The Actor, Image and Action: Acting and Cognitive Neuroscience* (Routledge, 2008).

7   Amy Cook, "4E Cognition in the Humanities," in *Oxford Handbook of 4E Cognition* (Oxford UP, 2018), 876.

8   Evan Thompson, "The Enactive Approach," *Mind in Life: Biology, Phenomenology and the Sciences of Mind* (Belknap, 2007), 11.

9   Thompson, "The Enactive Approach," 13–15.

This neurobiological focus on the body of the audience-player as an organism in communion with its environment finds resonance with the writing of Antonin Artaud and his rightly infamous Theatre of Cruelty. Artaud grouses that when we hear the word "cruelty" we too easily assume this to mean "blood," but he corrects us; this is not what he is saying. It is not the violence and cruelty that we might enact on one another, but rather an existential violence: "the much more terrible and necessary cruelty which THINGS can exercise against us. We are not free. And the sky can still fall on our heads."[10] Theatre, to him, is one of the unique places where this feeling can be experienced.[11] Bringing to bear extremes of light and sound, Artaud imagines the effects of a penetrating and encompassing viscerality. He describes the effect of musical vibrations felt through the skin flattened against the resonant ground. He writes, "If music affects snakes, it is not on account of the spiritual notions it offers them, but because snakes are long and coil themselves upon the earth . . . I propose to treat the spectators like the snakecharmer's subjects and conduct them by means of their organisms to an apprehension of the subtlest notions."[12] The audience of cruelty experiences a series of reverberations that "incites the organism . . . to take attitudes in harmony with the gesture."[13]

I want to suggest that this is what is happening to my body and my awareness in *Broken Tailbone*. My actions, enscripted in the participatory dramaturgy of the show where I circle my tailbone, rotating my hips in synchrony with the lusty music, where I dance in the close embrace of a complete stranger, where I get down on my hands and knees to hump the floor (more making love to Mother Earth), awaken and heat my eroticism along with my muscles. (see AROUSAL) What is happening here is not a SIM. I have not been cast in a role and am not engaging in the mimetic representation of a past or imagined event. (see SHEEP) It is true that the throwing of bricks and the building of a barricade in a show like *Counting Sheep* does infiltrate my body in the way I am describing here to some extent, but significantly in *Broken Tailbone* the framing scenario of a simulation doesn't fully come into focus. I am not

---

10 Antonin Artaud, "No More Masterpieces," *Theatre and Its Double*, translated by Mary Caroline Richards (Grove, 1958), 79.

11 Artaud writes, "The theater is the only place in the world, the last general means we still possess of directly affecting the organism and, in periods of neurosis and petty sensuality like the one in which we are immersed, of attacking this sensuality by physical means it cannot withstand" ("No More Masterpieces," 81).

12 Artaud, "No More Masterpieces," 81.

13 Artaud, "No More Masterpieces," 81.

immersed in empathetic imagination with Aguirre's personal experience or with the stories of her revolutionary compatriots. I am just sweating.

Kathleen Smith, another *Broken Tailbone* reviewer, writes, "There's something profound about the synergy between personal physicality and the political struggles that Aguirre's structured improv investigates. Moving the body to express everything from sexual agency to tenderness to political defiance is an important and time-honoured tradition."[14] Yes, I agree. I would however take this further in connection with my creative and generative embodied experience. I need to move through Aguirre's dramaturgy. I need to get her stories into my body through pulsing, gyrating, swaying, and sweating. I need to be tired, hot, and a bit dizzy. Only then am I ready to absorb her story, with my blood and not with my brain (or not only), ready to think with my tailbone. (Ready to not think about fucking.)

---

14 Kathleen Smith, "Carmen Aguirre's *Broken Tailbone* Serves Up Moving Stories . . . And Moves," *NOW Magazine*, 4 October 2019, nowtoronto.com/culture /carmen-aguirres-broken-tailbone-serves-up-moving-stories-and-moves/.

TEA

Gloria Mok's *Long Distance Relationships for Mythical Times*
begins with tea. The table where ten of us gather for food
and stories is anchored by two circular cānzhuō zhuànpán, each with
a blue-and-white ceramic teapot. Scene breaks are marked by spinning
the trays and refreshing our hot tea. (see CREW) Cozy in a private tent,
an audience-participant for *Good Things To Do*, I am instructed by my
disembodied text-friend that if I search in the corner under the blanket
I will find a gift. It's my favourite, I'm told. What it is feels like magic—a
jar of hot camomile tea. (see SELF-CARE)

I started thinking about the dramaturgy of tea when I met photographer and raconteur Amy Amantea, participating in her performance
Through My Lens. After being greeted by Amy and settling into a chair
in a square, screened space that combines a photography studio
with a lightbox gallery, she asks if I would like some tea. She asks
me what kind I prefer, and we joke about one of the tea types she
has on offer that is called Vancouver Waterfront. (This seems like
a marketing gaffe, if true. Almost certainly, I don't want to drink the
Vancouver waterfront.) I choose the vanilla rooibos. She asks me to select
a mug from her table by describing it to her. I say, "I'd like the white one
with the blue rim." Amy is a bit confused by this choice. I try to say more,
"More like ivory with a soft blue watercolour rim?" She says, "The one
with penguins?" Now I'm confused because I don't see any penguins.
Then we realize I can't see the penguins because that side of the mug is
turned away from me. And Amy hardly can see the mug at all because
she has a lived experience of blindness. Once we have this sorted out,
Amy picks up the kettle, selects a tea bag, and pours hot water into my
chosen cup until the digital liquid level indicator beeps to tell Amy the
cup is full. Amy hands me the cup and I warm my hands in the cold
studio. She introduces me to her camera (named Whisper) and she clicks
away, creating portraits while asking me about myself—who I am and
what I care about.

What are participatory shows doing with tea?

In a talkback after her show, someone asked some version of this
question and Amy offered a two-part answer. First, the ritual of offering and pouring tea establishes that Amy is visually impaired. A cup
is acquired. A tea bag is added. Water poured. The beeper beeps. Tea

is served. And through the audience-participant's observation of this choreography we learn something about Amy and her abilities. Amy asserts that this is intentional on her part. The sequence is crafted to show us before she tells us that she is in the "two per cent club," having no vision in one eye and only two per cent of "normal" vision in the other. Second, Amy says, offering tea positions our relationship as one of hospitality—we are settling in for chat. Tea is a shortcut to a kind of warm, personal EXCHANGE. It puts me at my ease. I want to take Amy's idea a bit further to note that in the context of participatory performance, tea is a specific (and familiar) kind of INVITATION. Tea "casts" me in the role as Amy's guest and potential friend. For a newly arrived audience-participant who is actively trying to figure out who and where I am and what I should or should not do, this ritual is a helpful and recognizable behaviour MATRIX. (see ACTING) Beyond the actual comforts of tea-drinking, the tea serves as a kind of GUIDE, sketching parameters for my participation.

It also occurs to me with regard to *Through My Lens* in particular that tea is a multisensory experience. (see HANDS) The liquid is hot, the cup warm. It tastes good and it smells better. It is a golden ruby colour in the white mug. My principal task as an audience-participant also engages with our senses' borders. At Amy's request, I attempt to use words to describe several photographs that she has taken.[1] Basically, I am turning a visual image into words and sounds.[2] Between me and Amy we are bridging worlds comparing our sensory reports—photographs and stories. *Through My Lens* is a heightened and defamiliarized exploration of transmigration of our sense experience. (see OSTRANENIE) At the end of the show, Amy offers me one more of these trans-sensory reconfigurations. She asks if I would like to see myself the way she sees me. She begins by revealing on a screen one of the photographs she has taken during our conversation at the beginning. I am stunned. Actually stunned. It is the most "me" picture I have ever seen.

---

1   I also end up waving my hands around when words fail me. At one point I vigorously rub my hands and snap my fingers to communicate a texture.

2   In June 2022, I had the privilege of attending an "alpha" version of *Through My Lens* presented by FOLDA (Festival of Live Digital Art). In that version, Amy appeared on the screen via Zoom to a dual audience with some of us in-person in a screening room and others elsewhere on Zoom. Whereas the 2023 version that I experienced is a one-on-one, in the earlier presentation Amy selected the describer from the audiences. One describer she selected was a Deaf artist and actor based here in Kingston. What followed was an even more profound journey of sensory transmigration as the image was described gesturally using ASL. An ASL interpreter then converted gestural language into aural English. I was mesmerized.

No one has ever presented me with a reflection of myself that feels so remarkably authentic. Amy then applies a digital overlay to the image that represents how she sees the world. Finally, Amy tells me what she sees in this portrait of me. She describes me back to myself. And this is the product of this show. I suspect that Amy forges this INTIMATE, affectionate relation with every audience-participant. I think it would be fair to attribute a large portion of this to Amy's charisma as a performer, but the reciprocal social RITUAL of offering and drinking tea literally warms us up.

MAKE YOURSELF A CUP OF TEA.

TEACUPS

As the audience waits in seats in the dimly lit studio, a large projection screen reads "press X to begin" as a spotlight shines brightly on a white podium with a single PlayStation controller. The invitation at the beginning of Milton Lim and Patrick Blenkarn's *asses.masses* is quiet but clear—someone from the audience needs to pick up the controller and play as player one. Although Milton and Patrick are not visible in the room, through both the staging and the props the INVITATION to participate is obvious. (There is something enticing but also forceful about the opening that reminds me of the commands in *Alice in Wonderland*'s first trip down the rabbit hole. Drink Me. Eat Me. It's the invitation as an imperative.)

When an audience-player finally does pick up the controller, its smooth edges fit perfectly in their hand. Each thumb rests on a crucial button. The buttons under their thumbs swivel intuitively, the springs perfectly reactive. The player's palm rests comfortably curled over the ergonomic corners of the plastic controller. Two index fingers extend to reach the left and right triggers. Like playing thumb war, the equipment requires nimble HANDS. The weight of the controller is balanced, heavy, and present but not cumbersome. This prop is a well-designed instrument for playing.

In order to avoid BEING LOST, participatory audiences arrive needing instruction. Because participants are asked to do something beyond INTERPRETATION, they need guidance. Whether the instructions arrive through a pre-show email, a set of written prompts like a script, or an actual person laying out the rules, participatory audiences learn both what is permissible and what is prohibited by the artists through some sort of information source. Sometimes these instructions are vague and sometimes they are specific. Very rarely participants are left to learn alone, but when we are, we can look to both the props and the geography to tell us what to do.

Although I may not know all of the rules of the video game universe in *asses.masses*, I instinctively know how to hold a video game controller. The design of the object teaches me how to interact with it. There is generally only one obvious way to hold the controller. My two hands naturally rest with my thumbs near the buttons. I know that the movable joysticks are useful for traversing and my right thumb most likely rests closest to the button that makes me "go." The shape of the controller is giving me a series of clues for how to use it. Like a handle on a teacup or the hip-height fits-perfectly-in-my-palm doorknob, the design and texture of this object is a guide for its use. In a way, these clues, or what psychologist James J. Gibson names "affordances," are GUIDES, offering implicit instructions or clues to the player on how to play. The affordances that are perceived from each object or spatial arrangement act as a set of instructions on how the object or space is to be used, structuring the intended participation. Escape rooms rely heavily on affordances to offer mute clues to players on how to solve the puzzle. If pianos are meant to be played, what happens when I play this note? If tapes are meant to be inserted into a VCR player, I wonder what will happen if I insert the tape into this here tape player. Once I played an escape room where players needed to set a dinner table to unlock the next set of clues. Empty place settings were invitation enough.

Humans engage with their THINGS through design choices that implicitly tell us how to interact. Many objects need no instructions, their inherent qualities instruction enough. A chair is obviously designed to sit in. Forks, pens, and flashlights are to be held in my hand the "right" way up for eating, writing, and illumination. Referring to both the environment and the human, affordances imply "the complementarity of the animal and the environment."[1]

At the end of DLT's show *Off Limits Zone*,[2] after the performer removed my blindfold, I was given a small paper bag and told to walk about a hundred metres down the abandoned rail tracks in Toronto's Port Lands towards a kind of porch attached to the decommissioned Hearn Generating Station. As I moved through the desolate landscape, I saw another person holding an identical bag walking towards me, towards the same destination. We met. The matching bags silently provided a complete set of instructions. We understood perfectly what to do. Open the bags. And so we did. Inside my bag were two drinks. Inside their bag were two snacks. (You know what happened next. Obviously.)

Although he spends most of the article talking about objects, Gibson says affordances are also visible in surfaces, layouts, places, and hiding places.[3] The long alleyway in Molly Johnson and Meredith Thompson's

---

1 James J. Gibson, "The Theory of Affordances (1979)," in *The People, Place and Space Reader*, edited by Jen Jack Gieseking, William Mangold, Cindi Katz, Setha Low, and Susan Saegert (Routledge, 2014), 56.

2 Dopo Lavoro Teatrale's *Off Limits Zone* premiered at the 2016 Luminato Festival in Toronto. *Off Limits Zone* was directed by Daniele Bartolini and featured performers Hasmig Tashdjian, Danya Buonastella, Rory de Brouwer, Raylene Turner, Daniel Carter, Joslyn Rogers, Neha Poduval, Maggie Hunter, Adam Bromley, Jordan Campbell, Maddie Bautista, Sohee Maeng, Gino Buenaventura, and Oriana Mambie.

3 Gibson, "The Theory of Affordances," 57–58.

b side beckons us to walk ahead in a straight line. Its geography says, "Forward. This way." In Single Thread Theatre Company's *Everyman*, participants are sitting in the dark in a theatre chair when a door cracks open and light spills into the room. We instinctively walk through the opening towards the light. Gareth White notes that the messages communicated by contextual affordances in both the built and social environments are sometimes so strong that "the body makes decisions 'before you know it.'"[4]

In performance, artist-creators leverage the communicative influence of spatial affordances to keep audiences on track. Our understanding blooms in response to the way objects and spaces have been constructed to accommodate the human. However, taken to its extreme, we see this same imprinting of the human on the landscape during what is being called, in geological terms, the Anthropocene Epoch. Writing in 1979, well before the term Anthropocene came into common usage, Gibson recognizes affordances as the tools of a radical endeavour to reshape the world to suit human needs and dimensions. He asks plaintively, "Why has man changed the shapes and substances of his environment? To change what it affords him. He has made more available what benefits him and less pressing what injures him."[5] Centring human AGENCY and its effects, the Anthropocene finds an uncomfortable parallel in participatory artworks that also privilege action and interaction as the locus of meaning generation.[6] For good or for ill, the power of people as individuals and in groups to make meaningful change is a central thematic driver of participatory performance.

---

4 Gareth White, *Audience Participation in Theatre: Aesthetics of the Invitation* (Palgrave Macmillan, 2013), 123.

5 Gibson, "The Theory of Affordances," 56.

6 It was at the Digital Arts Summit hosted by the Banff Centre for Arts and Creativity in November 2019 where Jenn and I heard a talk by Canadian interdisciplinary artist and scholar David Maggs titled "Sustainability in an Imaginary World" in which he sketched out this analogous relationship between the impacts of our past and potential future actions on the environment and the use of participatory performance to model or reveal that agency. I was struck at the time by how the revelation of this connection was profoundly underscored by my awareness of the incredible beauty and power of the natural landscape all around me, visible through the conference centre's window wall as Maggs spoke—the iconic Cascade Mountain looming right there, the forested valley with an early dusting of snow, the clouds, and the sky. I could suddenly see my own complicity in its potential destruction.

TEXT MESSAGES

> Maybe let's meet tonight. In the dreamtime. Go find our ears.
> Meet me by the river. I'll bring a basket.

> Love that idea.

> Have you ever dreamed with the dreamer before?

> I'll bring a blanket. Two times dreaming.
> I wonder what it's like to meet in a dream.
> How will I know it's you? How will you know it's me?

> I will know you by our crunch.

> Of course.

> And I will be the basket.

> I will be the river.

> See you tonight.
> I'll be the one with my feet in the water.

> See you tonight.
> I'll be the one holding the basket.[1]

Some Must Watch While Some Must Sleep by Tanya Marquardt is a one-to-one participatory performance that happens mainly over SMS.[2] Each evening for fourteen evenings in a row, you EXCHANGE text messages with "Tanya" and with their sleep persona named "X." As you answer questions, play word association games, and practise a kind of

---

1   Excerpt from *Some Must Watch While Some Must Sleep* text messages exchanged between X (on the left) and Jenn (on the right), 2 June 2021. The text-messaging script for this show is published in *Canadian Theatre Review 197* (Winter 2024): 42–55.
2   There are some parts of episodes that are delivered as audio files. Also, there are two sections that are videos where a figure (Tanya) in a red mask that covers their face leads the audience-participant through choreographed movements.

sleep meditation, the lines between dreaming and waking blur and an impressionistic, fragmented story starts to reveal itself. Sometimes the exchanges are nonsensical, sometimes flirtatious. Close as my fingertips, the performance feels INTIMATE, almost as if we are whispering to each other.

What are the dramaturgical properties of text messaging? How might the specific participatory qualities of this theatre-by-text shape my experience? One notable characteristic is that both of us are invisible. There is no body, no face. Age, gender, and race all slip away. Tanya and X only exist visually in my imagination. They don't even have a voice. No sound at all.[3] This indeterminacy is wonderfully freeing, as we meet with no assumptions about who I might be. Or who Tanya might be.[4] A corollary of this profoundly non-visual theatre is that there is no gaze. (see UTOPIA) Tanya is not looking at me. We aren't making awkward eye contact. (What a relief!) All that mutual looking and nodding and smiling is hard work. Stressful. With text messaging we don't need to do that.

Another dramaturgical feature of theatre-by-text-message is that while we are physically distant, we are digitally co-located as we both appear on the screen of my phone. Tanya/X are the grey bubbles on the left. I am the green bubbles on the right. (see MEEPLES) This is our scenography. Would it be accurate to assert that we are both "here"? Similarly, we are both sort of "now." Texting is synchronous, mostly. There are some nights where I arrive late and Tanya or X is waiting for me. There are also (I have to confess) a couple of nights where I failed to show up at all.[5] When we are both present, we are LIVE. I can see Tanya/X thinking and typing. Three flickering dots. Often our conversation gets out of sequence. I'm lagging, still typing a reply, and Tanya has skipped ahead. There are pauses and overlaps. This creates a kind of surreal poetry at times. I'm fascinated by the aesthetics of the glitch.

---

3 Although as mentioned in this particular show, there are audio segments that are spoken by a voice that introduces themselves as Tanya. Also, there are recordings of sleep talking and this voice is presumably X.

4 As Roland Barthes asserts, "Writing is the destruction of every voice, of every point of origin. Writing is that neutral, composite, oblique space where our subject slips away; the negative where all identity is lost, starting with the very identity of the body writing" ("Death of the Author," *Image—Music—Text*, translated by Stephen Heath (Fontana, 1977), 142). Barthes is positing the death of the author, but the same destructive effacement pertains to the performer in a live encounter and also to me as an audience-participant.

5 One night I had something come up unexpectedly that precluded my attendance, and one night I just plugged my phone in to charge and forgot about the performance entirely.

Texting is an invitation to play. It's like throwing a ball back and forth. Texting wants a response. (My teenage daughter tells me that it is very rude to leave someone "on read," opening the text and reading the message but not replying. Don't do that. Sending two unrelated thoughts in a row, "double texting," is too eager, especially for someone you don't know well yet. Don't text like it's an email. Long paragraphs are for Boomers.) And yet, you don't actually need to respond. You can just let the silence sit. You can respond later. Or never. The trajectory of the throw and catch connects us. Intimate and yet distanced. Texting is like writing letters but faster. MAIL is paradoxically distanced and yet intimate in the same way. It is also tactile—an object that is first touched by one and then by the other. It is a travelling secret. Consider the device in your hands. It is held, even cradled. We carry our devices with us. We keep them close. (Confession: I sleep with my phone under my pillow.) During the fourteen days of *Some Must Watch*, Tanya and X became quite close to me. It was a private time we spent together, playing secret games. (see SECRET WEIRDOS)

What eventually emerges in *Some Must Watch* is that there has been a traumatic event. Over the course of several text sessions spanning days ten through fourteen, we are led by dreams to a cabin in the woods. X is there waiting for us. X says, "'Meet me at the door to the cabin.' You meet them at the door to the cabin. There are jackets and shoes hanging on hooks. X points to the shoes and points to the jackets and says, 'Shoes are shoes and jackets are jackets, and you need both to have an adventure.' X gives you a pair of shoes and a jacket and pushes you out the door. They lock it and that's when you wake up. :)" In the next session, which is experienced as an audio monologue voiced by Tanya, your journey is narrated. You follow a path in the woods to a house under construction. Somehow in dream logic it is your house. You wander the house until you come to a room where the walls are painted in blood. Curled up in the corner of the room is a body also covered in blood. You pick up the body and carry it to the ocean. In the shallow surf, you wash the body, looking for the source of the blood, a wound. As you wash, you find nothing. Nothing. When you wash off the face, it's your face. The body is clean. And you see there is no cut. There is no wound. The audio ends there. My main thought after this nightmare/dream episode was, "I'm okay. Something terrible happened, but I'm okay." Distressing for sure, but also stabilizing. I felt like I was able to deal. I'd been through something, but I was safe and well.

Part of the source of this sense of safety was the RELATIONAL connection established in the early days of the performance. Conversely, our detachment also provides a kind of zone of safety. The asynchronicity of texting—slower and more disjunctive than a face-to-face narrative—creates space. There is a measured pace. It takes time to type, send, receive, and read. I am not being rushed, flooded by the story. I can take it in at my own pace. Read, think, absorb. It is easy to OPT OUT if necessary. The texts buffer emotion. There is also no pressure in the gaze. Tanya/X expects very little of me. I could do nothing—just let the text of the story flow by without any interaction. This is very different from the intense performative encounter of a typical in-person synchronous one-to-one theatre experience.

Texting also achieves the opposite of asynchronous slowness and detachment. Tanya asks me at intervals how I'm doing and seeks my CONSENT. Do I want to continue? Am I ready for another story? But even beyond these explicit care offerings, simply knowing that Tanya and I are co-present is a line between us. I'm not alone. I can reach out to them. They are right there nestled in my palms. As I work through the lived journey and subsequent understanding of the nightmare parable of myself as bloodied but unwounded, I feel secure that Tanya is holding me. Through almost two weeks of texting, of playing catch and return, of sharing dream memories, I trust them. It's easy over text messaging to accept Tanya's offer of friendship. They say, "I like you. Let's be friends. Let's be each other's sleep blankets." The idea that we meet in each other's dreams feels possible. No assumptions. We could be anyone. And so why not be FRIENDS?[6]

6   In the months since *Some Must Watch*, I've met Tanya, finally, in person. And we like each other a lot. A lot considering that we are still basically strangers. There is a pull of affection. Maybe that's a fabrication. But I feel it.

ANSWER MINI SHEEP'S RIDDLE.

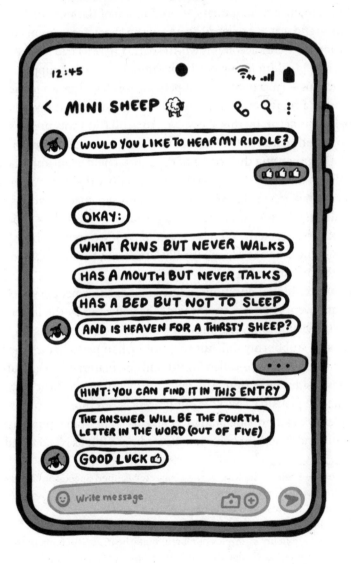

ANSWER:

THE MATRIX

Sophie Nield in her article "The Rise of the Character Named Spectator" describes a sort of surreal, out-of-body experience that she had while being audience to an immersive production of the story of Abelard and Heloise and was approached by one of the characters, a monk in need of assistance. Nield's account is worth sharing here: "I had a small moment of crisis. I had no idea what I was supposed to do. I suppose I did do something—I'm a polite sort of person, I probably gave a moue of sympathy or a rueful smile. But I really was not sure what I was needed to do, by this actor, by this show. Not to act back, I was pretty sure, not to pretend to be another monk, or a serving wench, or even a scholar."[1] Documenting this welter of thoughts, Nield beautifully captures a common dilemma for immersive participatory theatre: "And as I stood there in my not-mediaeval clothes with my not-mediaeval bright green handbag, it occurred to me—who on earth is this monk supposed to think I am?"[2] Exactly. Who is the audience if we are no longer "merely" an audience? As she says poetically later on in her article, "How else is this theatre dreaming us?"[3]

This existential question—who are all of these people watching the private events of a fictional world?—is deflected by the imposition of silent invisibility on the audience of BOURGEOIS THEATRE,[4] but becomes stubbornly difficult to ignore when participants themselves cross through that so-called fourth wall and materialize as agents themselves inside the fiction. The question "who are we?" is central. First, we need a plausible cover for our presence. But more than this, a sense of identity can provide guidance, give us some stable purchase in the fiction, and shape our behaviour accordingly. But as Nield wonders and

---

1   Sophie Nield, "The Rise of the Character Named Spectator," *Contemporary Theatre Review* 18, no. 4 (2008): 531.
2   Nield, "The Rise of the Character Named Spectator," 531.
3   Nield, "The Rise of the Character Named Spectator," 534.
4   There are many examples of playful metatheatricality that slip through the fourth wall to acknowledge the actual-world performance situation. My personal favourite is Helena in *A Midsummer Night's Dream* when she resists the idea that she risks her reputation being alone in the forest with Demetrius: "Nor doth this wood lack worlds of company, / For you in my respect are all the world: / Then how can it be said I am alone, / When all the world is here to look on me?" (2.1.223–26). In the contemporary Globe Theatre, certainly all the world is here to look on her.

worries, we are not "actors" in the full sense with rehearsed characterizations. We are something less than an actor-character and something more than a SPECTATOR.

Suspended between acting and not-acting, we might look to Michael Kirby for insight. Writing in 1972, Kirby is thinking about Happenings, and in trying to describe what he sees he makes the observation that not all performing is acting: "The performers in Happenings generally tended to 'be' nobody or nothing other than themselves; nor did they represent, or pretend to be in, a time or place different than that of the spectator. They walked, ran, said words, sang, washed dishes, swept, operated machines and stage devices, and so forth, but they did not feign or impersonate."[5] Developing this further, Kirby proposes a continuum of behaviours with acting at one end and not-acting at the other. He considers to what degree a performer is "embedded . . . in matrices of pretended or represented character, situation, place and time" and calls a performer who is aloof from this enmeshment as "nonmatrixed."[6] He then notes that costuming could contribute in a minor way to a performer becoming matrixed. Without intention and even without any overt action at all, a costume can act as a sign of the fictional world and the actor's role in it. Kirby calls this state, just one step away from not-acting, a "symbolized matrix."[7] Kirby is not thinking about audience-participants here; he is thinking about costumed stagehands or static supernumeraries. But I think the potential application to unrehearsed audience-players is fruitful. Even lacking costumes, immersed audiences can be matrixed by the setting. And then this contextual matrix becomes an implicit GUIDE. Having been given a role, or at least a not-awkward reason for our presence, we can shape our responses accordingly.

Erving Goffman describes how this works in real life through the concept of frame analysis. "We look at our experiences in different ways, bringing to them different assumptions about their meaning: we place them into frames that enable our understanding. As well as structuring our perceptions, frames allow us to manage the different episodes of life, and our behaviour in social life in particular . . . [Frames] describe our

---

5   Michael Kirby, "On Acting and Not-Acting," in *Acting (Re)Considered: A Theoretical and Practical Guide*, edited by Phillip B. Zarrilli (Routledge, 2002), 40. Basically, Kirby is describing what now might be called "postdrama."

6   Kirby, "On Acting and Not-Acting," 41.

7   Kirby, "On Acting and Not-Acting," 41.

functional understanding of interactions in everyday life."[8] One kind of frame is the theatre frame. This is the perceptual context that tells us that what is happening on stage within that frame is "non-serious." We are confident that there is no need to intervene and save Desdemona from her mimetic suffocation. Allan Kaprow (*Essays on the Blurring of Art and Life*) recognizes vernacular social frames that tell us how to participate in popular gatherings, citing "political rallies, demonstrations, holiday celebrations, and social dancing. Parts of the common culture, they are known and accepted; the moves individuals must make are familiar, and their goals or uses are assumed to be clear."[9] (see RITUAL)

Beyond vernacular performances that guide participation in the event in general—what I am distinguishing as skill-frames—there are also familiar narrative or situational frames that are productively borrowed, migrating from real life into the fiction. It is these frames that establish the fictional matrix. I'm thinking of a set-up like being a homicide detective. When the first character I encounter in a one-on-one "haunted house" asks me how my investigation is progressing into the disappearance of Ambrose Small, a millionaire theatre magnate who famously went missing in 1919, I know who I am (*Ambrose*).[10] Or a set-up like being part of a popular street demonstration. When I am passed a bench and directed to add it to the barricade and then someone presses a newspaper-wrapped (foam) brick into my hand as we face a line of masked riot police, I know who I am (*Counting Sheep*). An immersive set environment might serve the same function as being hailed by a character. If I walk into a Prohibition-era speakeasy (*King of the Bootleggers*) or an old-fashioned, red telephone booth on an urban street corner (*Red Phone*) I may not have any real-world experience of any of these implied scenarios and yet my accumulated experience of the news, TV shows, novels, etc., provides (probably) sufficient context for at least a small characterization.

Created by Rebecca Northan and Spontaneous Theatre, *Blind Date* exemplifies this use of a real-life matrix—a blind date—to provide the suddenly immersed audience-player with a script, or at least a known set of behavioural tropes. By the time the audience is settled in their seats for the start of the show, Mimi the Clown has been waiting at a

---

8   Gareth White, *Audience Participation in Theatre: Aesthetics of the Invitation* (Palgrave Macmillan, 2013), 34.

9   Allan Kaprow, "Participation Performance (1977)," in *Essays on the Blurring of Art and Life*, edited by Jeff Kelley (U of California P, 1993), 181.

10   Alex Dault and Liam Karry, "Second Person, Singular," *Canadian Theatre Review* 173 (Winter 2018): 75–78.

beautiful French café for a blind date for two hours. Fed up with waiting, she changes her plans and invites a man[11] from the audience to join her on stage as her blind date. Mimi and the man have dinner at a French restaurant, drive back to her place, canoodle a bit on her couch, and then fast forward five years into the future to see how they end up.

Understandably, the blind-date scenario is a vulnerable, anxious experience for the audience member, abruptly placed in the awkward situation of performing for a room of friends and strangers. But then again, blind dates in the real world can be awkward affairs too. This parallel of familiarity between real world and performed "blind date" narratives provides context and a clear container for expectations and behaviours of both parties. Even if this is outside of one's own lived experience, the episodes of the plot follow stereotyped heterosexual courting conventions, common to Hollywood romantic comedies. Via this dramaturgical strategy, Northan and her co-creators have cleverly given the audience-guest an implicit script that he can confidently follow. The show leans on recognizable tropes for the benefit of the blind date audience-player and for the success of the show. What should he say to a flirtatious woman in a restaurant? Should he pick up the cheque for dinner or propose they split the bill? Should they kiss on the first date or not? Organizing these improvised moments is an overall meta-narrative GUIDE for the audience-member who suddenly becomes an actor. If the player says, "YES, LET'S!" and is open to the game, the show is a success.

In the final scene, Mimi and her date are cuddled up in bed (Mimi having just given birth to their child—don't ask.) and she tells him, "All the things I love about you." She praises him for having a sense of play, a generous and open spirit, for being brave. This speech speaks both to the guest-as-date/husband in the fictional cosmos but also to the actual audience member who has very gamely gone through this experience. The qualities she lists are positive ones to find in a life partner, but also the qualities of someone who has been a very good sport and play partner through this somewhat compelled improv performance. And because the veneer of fiction is so thin in this performance, the audience at large (and the guest-date himself) clearly understands that this

THE MATRIX

THE MATRIX

---

11   There is another version of the show called *Queer Blind Date*, where the improvising pairs are diverse across the spectrums of gender and sexuality. The heteronormative dating cliché matrix is tossed out. Queerness is, by definition, rich in its alternatives and multiplicities, so a single matrix does not emerge in the same way. While some talking points are to be expected, like sharing autobiographical stories of "coming out" or detailing the specifics of how this particular pair has sex, "scripts" for the audience-date are much more variable.

is thanks for a performance job well done. Improvisational skills will stand you in good stead in life and in love. Ultimately, his real experience of the last ninety minutes—how to be brave, how to be generous, how to be open to surprises—is the theme of the show.[12] Understanding and working in relation to the anchoring conventions provide the safety net that makes this exploration possible.

As Kaprow notes, "Participation presupposes shared assumptions, interests, language, meanings, contexts, and uses. It cannot take place otherwise."[13] This necessary foundation is both a benefit and a liability. The benefit is that the fixity of its known parameters allows communal action to go forward and be broadly legible. The liability lies in the flip side of the same coin. Since "the frames of audience participation are always citational . . . At worst, it runs the risk of reproducing discourses that perpetuate oppression or discrimination, or fails to articulate any viewpoints except those of the dominant culture."[14] Certainly, *Blind Date* plays on conventions that might be perceived as myopically American, sexist, and/or heteronormative, but then that is part of the joke. Some portion of the audience's pleasure is premised on watching some very dated gender tropes play out, but also on setting up the opportunity for the possible resistance and reframing of those same tropes in full knowledge of their pervasive cultural power.

See SIM and ABYDOS

---

12 Jenn Stephenson, "How To Be a Gentleman," *Upsurges of the Real: A Performance Research Blog*, 22 July 2015, realtheatre.blog/2015/07/22/how-to-be-a-gentleman/.

13 Kaprow, "Participation Performance," 185.

14 White, *Audience Participation in Theatre*, 54.

THINGS

Some of my earliest writing in the realm of theatre of the real was on the active power and personality of things. In a piece I co-authored for *Canadian Theatre Review* with Grahame Renyk called "Matter Matters: Performing a Stone in the Woods," we traced the time-travelling power of a centuries-old observatory stone in Kingston.[1] We were interested in this stone as a continuous public WITNESS, sitting quiet in a park since the nineteenth century. We imagined the stone watching the city through roughly two hundred years of change, designating the stone as an active member of both the present and the past. The stone is a vital participant in a networked RELATION to me, to the place, to everyone ever who passes by. We noticed that through site-specific performance we could activate not only the present and the past but the space *between* then and now through a staging focused on the active materiality of the stone. Materializing what we called the "then, now, and since" of the enduring historical object, performing with the stone allowed for a privileging of the object's memory along with what Jane Bennett calls its "thing-power."

Bennett opens her book[2] *Vibrant Matter* by rooting her thoughts on thing-power in Michel Foucault's work on biopower. It is biopower that exposes "the various micropolitical and macropolitical techniques through which the human body was disciplined, normalized, sped up and slowed down, gendered, sexed, nationalized, globalized, rendered disposable, or otherwise composed."[3] For both Bennett and Foucault, among others, outside forces, whether they are living or not, have a

---

1   Mariah Horner and Grahame Renyk, "Matter Matters: Performing a Stone in the Woods," *Canadian Theatre Review* 163 (Summer 2015): 59–63.

2   It is important to acknowledge that before the prevalence of "new" materialism as a way of understanding the power and interconnectedness of objects, Indigenous traditions of knowledge were (and are) already recognizing nonhuman agency. Virginie Magnat critically explores the field in her piece "(K)new Materialisms: Honouring Indigenous Perspectives," *Theatre Research in Canada* 43, no. 1 (2022): 24–37. In the article, Magnat acknowledges the indebtedness of her research to her Indigenous colleagues, emphasizing the generative potential of how "this non-anthropocentric conception of agency may be said to offer a truly radical, if not 'new,' eco-critical approach to the crucial questions raised by new materialist and posthumanist scholars" (24).

3   Jane Bennett, *Vibrant Matter: A Political Ecology of Things* (Duke UP, 2010), 1.

material effect on the body. "The point was," she says, "that cultural forms are themselves powerful, material assemblages with *resistant force*."[4] Where Foucault applies this thinking famously to his genealogies on discipline and punishment, sex, and queerness, Bennett applies the thinking to things. Thinking about the AGENCY of material things, Bennett is specifically interested in how objects have the power to *make things happen*. When I sit in a chair, the chair is shaping my body to her curves. I am sitting this way because the chair's design guides me. The act of sitting becomes collaborative. Nonhuman partners can also be unruly, resistant to our plans and forcing us to make changes.[5] *Vibrant Matter* looks to "highlight the active role of *nonhuman* materials in public life." Bennett says, "In short, I will try to give voice to a thing-power."[6] In a story about garbage from early in the Introduction, she says she "caught a glimpse of an energetic vitality inside each of these things, things that I generally conceived as inert. In this assemblage, *objects* appeared as *things*, that is, as vivid entities not entirely reducible to the contexts in which (human) subjects set them, never entirely exhausted by their semiotics."[7] Thinking about objects as actants recognizes that "the capacity of these bodies was not restricted to a passive 'intractability' but also included the ability to make things happen, to produce effects."[8]

Later in the book, Bennett is struck by the ways in which American hyperconsumption has affected thing-power. "It hit me then in a visceral way how American materialism, which requires buying ever-increasing numbers of products purchased in ever-shorter cycles, is *antimateriality*."[9] Although things have the capacity to shape the world around them by countlessly producing objects and copies of objects, they conceal "the vitality of matter."[10] Thing-power is quieted by reducing things to their copy and then needing to junk them to buy the newest model. (see SHOPPING)

Theatre Replacement's *Best Life* accesses thing-power by casting household appliances as our actual scene partners. In this participatory

---

4   Bennett, *Vibrant Matter*, 1.

5   See Minty Donald, "Entided, Enwatered, Enwinded: Human/More-than-Human Agencies in Site-Specific Performance," in *Performing Objects and Theatrical Things*, edited by Marlis Schweitzer and Joanne Zerdy (Palgrave Macmillan, 2014), 118–31.

6   Bennett, *Vibrant Matter*, 2.

7   Bennett, *Vibrant Matter*, 5.

8   Bennett, *Vibrant Matter*, 5.

9   Bennett, *Vibrant Matter*, 5.

10   Bennett, *Vibrant Matter*, 5.

show about "the domestic machines you can't live without,"[11] participants are assigned an object and presented with an instruction manual. Although these machines vary in their uses, their typical users, and their era of use, they are all household appliances. They are all tools that make life "easier" but require human operation. From an Xbox controller and a washing machine, to a lawn mower, a rice cooker, and a TV, these objects are vibrant in the ways they beg me to use them.

As participants listen to AUTOBIOGRAPHICAL stories about memories associated with the objects, they follow the instructions in the manual and perform with their objects. The manual's instructions are stage directions (see RECIPE) and the object assigns and organizes my actions. (see TEACUPS) The washing machine manual asked its participants to sort laundry. The full load of clean clothes inside the basin begs me to sort the clothes by colour. The washer's flashing red light urgently says "action." I have to ask myself, "Who's in charge here?" These machines become active scene partners, co-creators of meaning and "holders of memories and caring companions to audience members."[12] Heeding the warning of Bennett's concern about hyper-materialism concealing the vitality of objects, *Best Life* re-establishes the object's livingness by reinforcing our true partnership.

Best Life also amplifies thing-power by voicing the memory of objects, instilling a witnessing eye behind the red power light on the TV or in the knobs of the washing machine. As we use the objects, they are watching us. There is a longevity to their existence. Grappling with how objects outlive the people who use them, *Best Life* is interested in the ways in which capitalism and materialism have created a series of vibrant objects that are, in essence, immortal. Like the observatory stone, the household appliances in *Best Life* act as vibrant witnesses to our lives, resilient survivors living as our ancestors before us and continuing in their material form after we're gone. In an interview with the online arts and culture publication *Stir*, creator Maiko Yamamoto says, "These machines will be on this planet for thousands of years because of the materiality of them."[13] Through tapping into these objects' thing-power by voicing their memory, the objects in *Best Life* live forever.

See CREW

11   Janet Smith, "Theatre Replacement's *Best Life* Explores Our Attachment to Domestic Machines," *Stir*, 28 October 2022, createastir.ca/articles/best-life-theatre-replacement-shadbolt-centre.
12   Smith, "Theatre Replacement's *Best Life*."
13   Smith, "Theatre Replacement's *Best Life*."

FILL IN THE CROSSWORD PUZZLE BELOW WITH ITEMS FOUND IN THE PREVIOUS ENTRY (see THINGS). EACH ITEM APPEARS IN THEATRE REPLACEMENT'S PERFORMANCE OF BEST LIFE. ONCE THE PUZZLE IS COMPLETE, UNSCRAMBLE THE CIRCLED LETTERS TO GET THE ANSWER.

ANSWER:

TOGETHER ALONE

The concept of being together alone, or what Jacques Rancière calls the "paradox of being together apart" is a specific kind of distanced RELATION.[1] It's different from FRIENDSHIP, which depends on a pre-existing fondness and awareness of one another. It's more like parallel play than collaborative play. Together alone is the feeling of doing independent work in a library or a coffee shop. You are surrounded by others, but you aren't necessarily engaging with others. At the library desk you could be buried in your work, wearing headphones to block out the distractions, but if you look up you see you are sharing space with many other people also living and working in their own little worlds. Together alone is also slightly different from a wider kind of relationality that describes an awareness of the interconnectedness of all things, human or nonhuman, on the earth. (see LAND) Being together alone speaks to a kind of shared time and space that requires co-presence without actual ENCOUNTER.

Thinking and writing about the busy Parisian suburbs in chapter three of *The Emancipated Spectator*, Rancière suggests that "constructing a place for solitude, an 'aesthetic place,' appears to be a task for committed art. The possibility of being apart appears to be precisely that dimension of social life which is rendered impossible by ordinary life in the Parisian suburbs."[2] Be it Paris or Toronto, metropoles are known for their buzzing busyness. In a cityscape, we are packed in tight with total strangers. Although I don't know my fellow urbanites, I'm rarely actually alone. For Rancière, the concept of being together and alone is nearly impossible but extremely desirable for populated urban city centres. Rancière believes we want to be both together and alone because "the link between the solitude of the artwork and human community is a matter of transformed 'sensation,'" and a step towards an awareness of the sensible public.[3]

1   Jacques Rancière, *The Emancipated Spectator*, translated by Gregory Elliot (Verso, 2009), 51.

2   Rancière, *The Emancipated Spectator*, 53–54.

3   Rancière, *The Emancipated Spectator*, 55–56. The word sensible is meaningful to Rancière as he describes the key function of political participation as the "distribution of the sensible"—that is, what can be sensed.

I recognize this desire. Although I am a social person, I love eating alone in a busy restaurant. When I was younger, I would sometimes wear headphones, bring a book, or entertain myself with TEXT MESSAGES, but now I love to quietly eat and watch people. I love noticing couples on first dates or families trying to soothe their crying children. I love the companionship and proximity that comes with being in a room full of people without the obligatory conversation that drains my social battery. To be clear, the desire to be together alone is different from a desire to be totally alone. Eating dinner in silence at home alone is a different sensation than eating dinner alone in a busy restaurant. Because I don't have a rich MINDFULNESS practice, I find being alone in a group of strangers to be relaxing for my busy brain. When I'm eating at a restaurant alone, I can relish the richness of other people's lives while being safe from confrontation and conversation at my table. Restaurants are public but not communal. Because I am sitting at a table when I eat alone, a marker of my personal space, I can be assured that I will remain alone. Like a kind of MAGIC CIRCLE, the table acts as a space to define my separation from the ensemble of eaters at the restaurant. When I am eating dinner alone, I am touched by Rancière's "poetic statement in four words, '*Séparés, on est ensemble.*'"[4]

Richard Lam's *The Candlemaker's Game* also relies on tables for one to assure private space in a public realm. In *The Candlemaker's Game*, participants are empowered to work through a personal conflict using Lam's tabletop transformative-justice game as a framework. When participants arrive, they are instructed by Lam to choose a conflict from their lives to work through. Participants are informed about this choice over email in advance and are advised to not choose something that is too painful or fresh. After participants have selected their conflict, they are given an apron and then guided to a cauldron of molten wax to cast their own wax figure and a die to play the game with. Because the hot wax is moulded at the beginning of each show, the figurines stay warm and soft in participants' hands while they play the tabletop game and move through their conflict. Like an act of companionship, the participants hold their wax close as they play. After they mould their MEEPLES, participants are guided as a group into the Candlemaker's workshop. A Candlemaker works in the centre of the room, surrounded by nine independent work stations with a notebook, a deck of cards, and a candle. The Candlemaker does not approach the participants for conversation but instead works silently alongside us as we move

4 Rancière, *The Emancipated Spectator*, 51.

through the instructions of the tabletop game. As all of us work on our craft in silence, we are comforted by each other's presence. In silence, we think about our conflict and consider the final invitation of the last card: "In resolving or softening this conflict, do you want to reach out to this person or not?"

All of the participant workspaces are distanced[5] from one another, facing inwards towards the Candlemaker. While participants are working through their inner conflict via the prompts on their cards, the room remains quiet. Participants are having an individual experience, collectively. Together and alone. For Lam it's important that "the content of your exploration is never available to anyone else. You're all doing the same thing together but you're doing it alone."[6] Because *The Candlemaker's Game* asks its participants to work through personal conflict, privacy is necessary. This is not therapy but rather an exercise in parallel play. Not everyone likes to disclose their problems as they move through them; however, like Rancière's poem, in *The Candlemaker's Game* I am reassured I am not alone in having conflict. Separate, but together. I am having a unique experience with my conflict that others are WITNESS to. I am kept accountable and on task in shaping my conflict like hot, mouldable wax, but I also feel a sense of solidarity in my conflict and grief. I am in relation with both the Candlemaker and with the other participants in the room. In Jean-Luc Nancy's book *Being Singular Plural*, he says there is solidarity in recognizing that we are singular plural beings "one with the other." "The ontology of being-with is an ontology of bodies, of every body, whether they be inanimate, animate, sentient, speaking, thinking, having weight, and so on."[7] Silent and thinking, all of the participants of *The Candlemaker's Game* can find solidarity in working through their individual conflicts with others following the same prompts.

Shira Leuchter and Michaela Washburn's *Lost Together* also skates between a solo and collective experience in service of soothing participant pain. Alone with Shira and Michaela, participants are asked to tell a story about something they have lost. Shira and Michaela then respond to this story with an offering, a CRAFT that is given to the participant

---

5   The initial prompt for Proximity Lab challenged artists to make "pandemic-proof" theatre. This formal requirement for distance shaped this show's content and design. "Proximity Lab: Developing Verbatim Theatre Presentation Models for a Post-Pandemic World," *Proximity Lab*, projecthumanity.ca/proximity-lab.

6   Richard Lam, personal interview, 30 June 2022.

7   Jean-Luc Nancy, *Being Singular Plural*, translated by Robert D. Richardson and Anne O'Byrne (Stanford UP, 2000), 84.

as a gift that represents the thing they have lost. (see SURROGATION) Although the show itself is a performance for one audience member at a time, during each run of *Lost Together* there is a physical gallery of lost objects that is hosted nearby. The crafted representation of my loss sits in a room with everyone else's loss-turned-craft. Our loss is both together and alone.

In terms of participatory dramaturgies, what does the "together" offer the "alone"? Togetherness offers solidarity and collective comfort. I am not alone in my conflict or in my grief. I am dealing with my personal heaviness, shoulder to shoulder with you dealing with yours. I can resolve conflict through both individual reflection and collective meditation. Theatre is a gathered act.

GO EAT DINNER IN A PUBLIC PLACE BY YOURSELF.

TOUR

A walking tour is a MATRIX, a set of implicit instructions that come set in a familiar framework that offers us a script for how to participate. Similar to borrowing the patterns of courtship in Rebecca Northan's *Blind Date* or the patterns of solving a crime in Outside the March's *The Ministry of Mundane Mysteries*, a tour matrix offers participants a kind of brief on behaviours they can expect from the experience. Tours are run by an expert who leads a group of non-experts. Tours are exploratory and ambulatory. Their structure is open and welcoming of questions and clarifications. Tours tend to happen in notable locations—in a museum or at a historical site or presenting a series of cultural landmarks, say in a city tour of New Orleans. Many notable urban geographers, like Jane Jacobs, use walking tours to complicate and enrich the urban experience beyond reading about a city's history and public policy through embodied and immersed praxis.[1] Andrew Houston elaborates on French philosopher Michel de Certeau's notion of walking as a kind of INTERPRETIVE world-making.[2] Houston says that walking is an "act of enunciation, to be perpetually working between the absence of what we imagine the space to be and the material evidence of its proper and present uses."[3]

On the surface, Shari Kasman's *You Are Here*[4] looks like the usual kind of walking tour, highlighting "the weird, wonderful, and whimsical" of Toronto's Bloordale Village.[5] Participants meet Kasman at the corner of Russet and Dufferin to see their first site. Pondering a pothole on Dufferin that has become filled with street water and garbage, Kasman

---

1   Jacobs inspired the practice of "Jane's Walks," which are volunteer-led neighbourhood walking tours, held in diverse locations annually since 2007 in the first weekend of May to honour Jacobs's birthday. "Jane's Walk," *Wikipedia*, en.wikipedia.org /wiki/Jane%27s_Walk.

2   Michel de Certeau, *The Practice of Everyday Life* (U of Minnesota P, 1998), 103.

3   Andrew Houston, "Introduction. The *Thirdspace* of Environmental and Site-Specific Theatre," in *Environmental and Site-specific Theatre*, edited by Andrew Houston (Playwrights Canada, 2007), vii.

4   Created and performed by Shari Kasman, presented at SummerWorks Festival, August 2022.

5   "You Are Here," *SummerWorks*, summerworks.ca/show/you-are-here/. The area known as Bloordale Village runs along Bloor Street between Dufferin and Lansdowne in Toronto's west end.

tells us this is the "Bloordale Pond," a natural phenomenon that boasts great biodiversity and significant curb appeal. She says it's a part of a pilot cultural project from the City of Toronto that serves to animate these ponds called "PondTO." We walk to Bloordale Beach, which is not a beach at all, but rather the fenced-in rubbled remains of a school that had been torn down and the resultant holes full of water. On a laminated printout, she shows us a picture of the old burned-out Shasta camper that served as the "lifeguard trailer." She flips to a "turtle sanctuary" complete with four or five plastic turtles. At one point, she rummages through her bag to find a few pieces of old terrazzo flooring that she claims washed up on the beach, but which are immediately recognizable as classic Canadian school flooring from the school's detritus in the background. When Kasman draws our attention to "Pigeon Corner," a chain-link fence that is home to dozens and dozens of birds, and asserts that it is a hot spot for pigeon dating and pigeon love, my suspicion is confirmed that this isn't an average walking tour.

You Are Here functions as a tour, but Kasman seems more sarcastic and ironic than informative. The "facts" she's giving us aren't actually facts, but inside jokes. She's a tour guide but isn't the kind of expert we recognize. Kasman isn't deceiving us but rather presenting us with an alternative reality, an underground truth that is recognizable by the people who know Bloordale Village. It's the stuff that people complain about to their neighbours. It's the inside joke or the Twitter meme that circulates among locals in a neighbourhood's hashtag. (Her jokes remind me of the time a raccoon died on Yonge Street, and City of Toronto animal services took so long to remove the body that people laid a vigil. The joke circulated on Twitter in 2015 as #DeadRaccoonTO and was eventually picked up by major news outlets.) My fellow participants' laughter in recognition is telling. In *You Are Here*, Kasman is reflecting back the community's own stories and jokes about the area as a productive display of urban disappointment. It's important to note that she isn't inventing new jokes; she isn't the architect of this comedy. Everyone in this neighbourhood seems to be in on it. Although I came from out of town, most of the other attendees either lived in Bloordale or were familiar with the existence of these comedic countersites. The other participants nodded in agreement at the existence of a "beach." As knowing insiders, they were able to play along with Kasman. They offered their cheeky insights and faux-memories of this community-built "beach." At one point a man carrying a six pack of beer emerged from Dufferin Mall and joined the tour. He shouted from the back of the tour, "Did you tell them about the lifeguard cabins?" When I checked, I found sixty-three

Google reviews on the "Bloordale Beach" geotag. In 2020, Bloordale Beach was the topic of a *blogTO* article,[6] a *Toronto Star* piece by urban geographer Shawn Micallef,[7] and was listed as number 203 of 651 "things to do in Toronto" on *Tripadvisor*.[8] Through CROWDSOURCED social media and recommender apps, they are community-building. Literally they are building their own defensive and biting—but loving—alternate version of Bloordale. Pointing out the problems can also be understood as community activism or productive citizen's critique. We're naming the problems, so we can laugh at them. And they're ours. Bloordale is a shithole, but it's our shithole.

There are other participatory negotiations in this co-created EMERGENT, alternate world. Kasman draws our attention to a man urinating on the fence in Pigeon Corner and attempts to fold him as a character into the ironic anti-tour. One member of the group speaks up to point out that there is a severe lack of public washrooms in Toronto, noting that we should be compassionate to people finding ways to meet their own needs. Abruptly the bitterly humorous facade that Kasman has created cracks and we remember this tour is really serving to draw our attention to actual failures in the civic infrastructure of Toronto. The communal work we have done in creating an imaginary alternative Bloordale that is quirkily chic and not at all a shithole and raising these critical civic issues up to public view might be the first step of what local participation might do. We've changed Bloordale in our collective imaginations, why not for real?

See ANTS and Q

---

6   Tanya Mok, "Bloordale Beach is Toronto's Only Beach Without a Body of Water Attached," *BlogTO*, 18 July 2020, blogto.com/city/2020/07/bloordale-beach-toronto/.
7   Shawn Micallef, "Watch for Sharks: Toronto's Newest Beach at Bloor and Dufferin Has Everything—Except Water," 9 August 2020, thestar.com/opinion /contributors/2020/08/09/watch-for-sharks-torontos-newest-beach-at-bloor-and -dufferin-has-everything-except-water.html.
8   "Bloordale Beach," *Tripadvisor*, tripadvisor.ca/Attraction_Review-g155019 -d21071614-Reviews-Bloordale_Beach-Toronto_Ontario.html.

MAKE A MAP OF WHERE YOU WOULD TAKE PEOPLE ON
A TOUR OF YOUR NEIGHBOURHOOD.

TYRANNY

Participation has a well-intentioned, virtuous glow around it. There is a perception that participation is by definition "a good thing." You can see why. Participation is inclusive. Participation is democratic.[1] Participation is empowering. Participation is a flat, non-hierarchical structure. And this is all true, except when it isn't. (Confession: Even this book sometimes falls prey to that uncritical value judgment that participatory theatre is to be preferred to say BOURGEOIS THEATRE, taking as given that the audience experience is just simply "better" when audiences become engaged co-creators.)

Participation as a tactic of social and political engagement arises out of a critique of top-down, externally imposed, and expert-oriented power structures that frequently exclude from the decision-making process those at the grassroots or local level who are likely to be the most affected by those decisions. Coming out of new ideas regarding local governance structures in the late 1960s, Sherry Arnstein's "Ladder of Participation" was a transformative idea in this regard. The ladder places modes of non-participation at the bottom of the ladder and slides upward through methods such as "informing," "consultation," and "placation" before arriving at "higher" modes of inclusive participation like "partnership" and "delegation," culminating in full "citizen control" on the top rung.[2] Similar thinking took deep root in the field of global development where the "recognition and support for greater involvement of 'local' people's perspectives, knowledge, priorities and skills presented an alternative to donor-driven and outsider-led development and was

---

1   It is Marvin Carlson in his book about realness, *Shattering Hamlet's Mirror*, who reminds me that Jean-Jacques Rousseau is one of the earliest proponents of a kind of participatory postdramatic theatre that shapes the demos, specifically his beloved Geneva. Like Plato, Rousseau is opposed to holding audiences "shut up in a gloomy cavern, there to sit for hours motionless, silent and inactive" but instead imagines communal spectacles "in the open air, in the face of heaven . . . What will there to be seen there? Nothing, if you will . . . the spectators themselves may be made actors" (Jean-Jacques Rousseau, "An Epistle from J.J. Rousseau, Citizen of Geneva to Mr. D'Alembert (1758)" in *Theatre Theory Theatre: The Major Critical Texts from Aristotle and Zeami to Soyinka and Havel*, edited by Daniel Gerould (Applause, 2002), 217.

2   Sherry R. Arnstein, "A Ladder of Citizen Participation," *Journal of the American Institute of Planners* 35, no. 4 (July 1969), 216–24. A visual of the complete ladder schema can be seen in that original article.   **421**

rapidly and widely adopted by individuals and organizations."[3] So far so good.

However, in the last two decades, there have been emerging calls for critical reassessment of the use of participation in development contexts. These critiques principally centre on questions of power, inviting a renewed understanding that participation (like everything else) is never exempt from pre-existing power structures and systems. (Thank you, Foucault.) We are reminded to examine the subtle applications of power to restrict inclusivity or to restrict the equal voicing of everyone's thoughts or to compel a false consensus. It is global development scholars Bill Cooke and Uma Kothari in their book *Participation: The New Tyranny?* who invoke the word "tyranny" to activate those questions about abuses of power to offer a bold (and by their own admission somewhat teasing) provocation to consider the implicit oppressions of participation.[4]

They identify three modes of tyranny regarding participation. And going through this list, we might here consider the applicability of their critiques to theatrical practice. One is tyranny of method. They ask, "Have participatory methods driven out others which have advantages that participation cannot provide?"[5] In the context of the Canadian performance ecosystem, I would argue that we are still far from a situation where participatory theatre has become the dominant mode to the exclusion of other performance modes. And yet, there is a feeling out there (I think) that participatory theatre is some kind of new cool, and as a result can sometimes be carelessly applied as an attractive gimmick.[6] However, it

---

3   Bill Cooke and Uma Kothari, "The Case for Participation as Tyranny," in *Participation: The New Tyranny?*, edited by Bill Cooke and Uma Kothari (Zed, 2001), 5.
4   Following the Cooke and Kothari collection of essays published in 2001, editors Sam Hickey and Giles Mohan responded in 2004 with another collection titled *Participation: From Tyranny to Transformation?* The homage, complete with colon and concluding question mark, is clear.
5   Cooke and Kothari, "The Case for Participation as Tyranny," 8.
6   *Globe and Mail* theatre critic J. Kelly Nestruck asserts that he is bored with immersive theatre that is banal or shallow ("Review: Why the 'Immersive' Theatre Trend Leads to Regressive Theatre like *Hogtown*," *Globe and Mail*, 24 July 2017, theglobeandmail.com/arts/theatre-and-performance/theatre-reviews/review-why-the-immersive-theatre-trend-leads-to-regressive-theatre-like-hogtown/article35786754/). *The Guardian*'s Charlotte Higgins makes the same observation as early as 2009 ("Immersive Theatre—Tired and Hackneyed Already?," *The Guardian*, 7 December 2009, theguardian.com/culture/charlottehigginsblog/2009/dec/07/theatre-punchdrunk). My favourite commentator who takes this view is Michael Billington, who condemns certain kinds of immersive theatre as "playground scarification" ("E is for Experiment," *The Guardian*, 10 January 2012, theguardian.com/stage/2012/jan/10/e-for-experiment-modern-drama).

behooves us to remember that participation is only one tool in a larger toolkit; like any tool, it has limitations, and there are better and worse contexts for its use and for the expenditure of our LABOUR in its service. It is necessary to consider (as we do throughout this book) how built-in dramaturgical properties of participation operate in support of communicating a particular understanding or generating a particular experience.

The second mode is tyranny of the group: Cooke and Kothari ask, "Do group dynamics lead to participatory decisions that reinforce the interests of the already powerful?"[7] (Yes.) (see MOB)

Third is tyranny of decision-making and control. For some purposes, participation might be a less-than-ideal mode of decision-making as it does not make space for expertise or curatorial oversight, or for intentional exclusion. Why does everyone need to be consulted? Do groups really make good decisions? And these concerns intersect with the issue above and the exercise of power within groups. How is the space for dissent protected? How are people subtly influenced to bend and agree or to hold back an unpalatable opinion?[8] (see KILLJOY) Reflecting on this question in the context of participatory theatre, we realized that there are actually very few cases where the audience action of participatory theatre is "make a single decision as a group." The exercise of agency through asserting a choice is certainly a core dramaturgical feature of participatory theatre; (see CHOOSE YOUR OWN ADVENTURE and PHONY MULTIPLICITY) however, those choices are almost always individual—either I am entirely alone in solo control of my actions or I am one of a mass of audience making autonomous decisions in parallel. In theatre-game hybrids, the need for absolute consensus is rare. (see DISSENSUS) Escape rooms invite and indeed expect a single decision, but how the group of players arrive at that decision is not mandated. Often the first, loudest, or luckiest person enters a choice on behalf of the rest. If the group decides informally to commit themselves to consensus, the game might be slowed to the point where we risk running out of time and losing the game. (see BAD FAITH)

Funny story: Once, when I was participating in an escape room, among the group of randomly assembled players, there was a posse of drunk women out for a night on the town. The escape room play stalled for about twenty minutes (!) when a (sober and competitive)

---

7   Cooke and Kothari, "The Case for Participation as Tyranny," 8.

8   In *Foreign Radical* maybe we don't speak our own personal truths when asked because our response might be embarrassing (watching porn) or illegal (smuggling across borders) or unpopular (opinions about genocide in Gaza). So, we suppress truth under social pressure.

audience-participant (me, actually) got into an argument with one of these margarita bachelorettes about which of us was more qualified to play the piano and attempt to solve the puzzle in a 1920s bootlegger gin joint. I have been playing piano since childhood. She had Fireball in her purse. I let her play and we ... lost.

Sarah C. White in her article "Depoliticising Development: The Uses and Abuses of Participation" smartly considers the alignment of the nature of participation with its functional goals in the context of development projects in the Global South. What I like about White's model is that she matches reasons why we participate with reasons why the opportunity to participate is activated in the first place. Both parties have goals. Sometimes they match. Of the four modes she lists—nominal, instrumental, representative, and transformative—the one that most commonly manifests in participatory theatre performance is instrumental participation. In this mode, the top-down reason for opening the work to participation is "efficiency" and the bottom-up reason for taking up that invitation to participate is the gains that result from the trade-off of my time and energy, or what she labels "cost." Participation in this mode both for artist-catalysts and for audience-players is about making the event-experience happen. Audience LABOUR is needed as input to make the thing go and audiences give their labour in EXCHANGE for their experience.

In her conclusion, White makes several recommendations that are transferable to the uses and abuses of participation as a theatrical mode. One, we need to recognize that participation is always political. What I understand her to be saying is that participation is always broadly about governance and the interpersonal web of rights and obligations that enable us to peacefully interact in society. Two, she calls us to analyze the interests represented. We need to ask who is not participating and why not. Third, it is imperative that we remember that participation and non-participation do not happen in an open arena. This is never a territory that can easily be assumed to be neutral and equitable. Participatory spaces enact the same "limitations on the process that derive from the power relations in wider society."[9]

Final thought: I would argue that the most potent source of tyranny in participatory theatre is actually the most fundamental and that is the pressure to participate in the first place. It is not so much the collective struggle of "what should we do?" but the omnipresent social coercion to simply "do." (see REFUSAL)

See CLAIRE BISHOP and DISSENSUS

---

9   Sarah C. White, "Depoliticising Development: The Uses and Abuses of Participation," *Development in Practice* 6, no. 1 (1996): 13.

UNWELCOME

Participation assumes an INVITATION. Something is happening some-place, and audience-players are welcomed with an invitation into the territory of the MAGIC CIRCLE of play. But what if we are not welcome? What if some are welcome participants but others are not? Normally, the value of universal access is invariably taken as given, and yet there are some contexts where a closed door is not only a valid option but is itself a powerful dramaturgical strategy that speaks in meaningful ways to the nature of an invitation and what or who authorizes that border crossing.

One specific example of being unwelcome manifests in Métis artist and thinker David Garneau's articulation of the necessity for what he calls "irreconcilable spaces of Aboriginality."[1] These are "gatherings, ceremony, nêhiyawak (Cree)-only discussions, kitchen-table conver-sations, email exchanges, et cetera, in which Blackfootness, Métisness, and so on, are performed without settler attendance. It is not a show for others."[2] The unwelcome of these irreconcilable spaces, first, asserts a private space, a convening—physical or virtual—that is closed to the gaze of outsiders. These are spaces of non-visibility that resist scopophilia. Second, Garneau says that beyond resistance to looking, these spaces also operate in resistance to resource extraction. There is a need to evade and resist colonial modes of engagement that are "characterized not only by scopophilia, a drive to look, but also by an urge to penetrate, to traverse, to know, to translate, to own and exploit. The attitude assumes that everything should be accessible to those with the means and will to access them; everything is ultimately comprehensible, a potential commodity, resource, or salvage."[3]

(What does this mean for my own Western-trained academic praxis? Read, collect, quote, cite, analyze, apply, synthesize, extend to new con-texts. This is what I do. I have become acutely aware that it is without doubt a deeply extractivist approach. I begin with the assumption that

---

1   David Garneau, "Imaginary Spaces of Conciliation and Reconciliation: Art, Curation and Healing," *Arts of Engagement: Taking Aesthetic Action In and Beyond the Truth and Reconciliation Commission of Canada*, edited by Dylan Robinson and Keavy Martin (Wilfrid Laurier UP, 2016), 27.

2   Garneau, "Imaginary Spaces," 27.

3   Garneau, "Imaginary Spaces," 23.

everything is available to be read, quoted, and repurposed. Surveying this page, quotation marks and parenthetical citation brackets now look to me like nothing so much as spoons for my hungry scholarship and the scoop-like jaws of a giant yellow bucket excavator. I feel ashamed of my familiar mode of operation, and at the same time am profoundly uncertain how to proceed. How to engage with knowledge from other sources with respect and reciprocity?)

Dylan Robinson, Stó:lō scholar and artist writing in his book *Hungry Listening*, takes the next logical step: "If Indigenous knowledge and culture is mined and extracted, then it would follow that another key intervention for disrupting the flow of extraction and consumption would be the blockade."[4] He then does exactly this and performs the exclusionary blockade surrounding an autonomous textual territory. On page twenty-five of the Introduction, he writes, "I ask you to affirm Indigenous sovereignty with the following injunction: If you are a non-Indigenous, settler, ally, or xwelítem reader, I ask that you stop reading at the end of this page ... The next section of the book, however, is written exclusively for Indigenous readers."[5] Writing stage directions for his own "paper theatre,"[6] he also provides an explicit invitation to rejoin the book later at the beginning of Chapter 1.

Among the modes of non-participation in participatory theatre, the strategy of the blockade, of being unwelcome, functions differently than other multilinear mappings that also close off possible paths. In a CHOOSE YOUR OWN ADVENTURE experience, multiple paths are available to you, but standing at the juncture you choose one over the others. You still remain ignorant; it is an experience that you will not have, but the key difference is that you had an open choice. And that awareness of the path not chosen, like the blockade, functions to create dramaturgical meaning. The path that is closed off not by choice but by the consequences of my action is also distinct from the blockade. In the basketball-themed play *Monday Nights*, each audience-player at the beginning needs to choose one of four teams—Red, Blue, Green, Black. Once we choose, we are seated in our designated quadrant with our new teammates. Our entire experience of the show is shaped by our affiliation, and we as we are afforded certain opportunities—for example, we can listen to private monologues by our own team captain—we are also

---

4   Dylan Robinson, *Hungry Listening: Resonant Theory for Indigenous Sound Studies* (U of Minnesota P, 2020), 23.

5   Robinson, *Hungry Listening*, 25.

6   Daniel Sack, "Introduction," in *Imagined Theatres: Writing for a Theoretical Stage* (Routledge, 2017), 1.

excluded from others. The closing of these alternate paths is entirely causal, tied directly to my actions; there are transparent consequences. I could have chosen another team. (Perhaps I might have been instead on the WINNING team.) It is a core dramaturgy of the show that any of the paths would be equally viable under other circumstances without prejudice.

What did I do at Robinson's injunction point? I stopped reading. My personal history is one that renders me unwelcome in this delimited space. I am the child of refugees. My parents arrived as children on Turtle Island to the city of Montréal by ship across the Atlantic in the years following World War II. All four of my grandparents were Holocaust survivors; their parents, most of their siblings, nieces, and nephews having been murdered by the Nazis. Being effectively stateless, Canada was a welcome haven. Clearly, I have no rights of welcome to asserted territory of Indigenous sovereignty, geographical or textual. However, my lifelong citizenship story is founded on the imaginary of being welcomed as a proud first-generation Canadian, and so it is a new thought for me to stop and think about who did that welcoming all those decades ago and what was their authority to do so? This is one of the effects of Robinson's performed blockade.

What does it feel like to be locked out? Surprise, certainly. What? I'm blocked?! That first hard stop is followed by a tingling pull of curiosity and FOMO.[7] What am I missing? No peeking. Really, no peeking. I feel like an outsider. This is, of course, the intention, and I must admit that this is not a common feeling for me. I am accustomed to being able to go where I want and feel welcome. I feel a bit bruised. Hmmph. Ultimately, my feeling is respect for the closed door; it is rude to go somewhere and force your way in when you are explicitly asked not to attend.

But this is exactly what I have done in life. (Even if not me, myself, directly as an immigrant. At the minimum I am the mute beneficiary of my unwitting ancestors' door crashing.) And so, the performance in *Hungry Listening* of a participatory blockade not only opens consideration of my personal imbrication in colonization and challenges me to figure out why I am unwelcome and what I can do in response, but on a general level engages the flip side of thinking about the invitation. Instead of focusing on how to make the transition to theatrical participation easy as Gareth White does,[8] by rendering that transition very difficult if not impossible as Robinson does, we now may be engaged with how and

---

7   FOMO or the "fear of missing out."
8   Gareth White, *Audience Participation in Theatre: Aesthetics of the Invitation* (Palgrave Macmillan, 2013).

why the border crossing of participation sometimes should be hard.[9] Who are the rightful holders of sovereign authority inside the circle, and what are the appropriate credentials to enter?

9   In *Take d Milk, Nah?* (Playwrights Canada, 2021), written and performed by Jivesh Parasram, Jiv stops the show and asks anyone who is unfamiliar with the feeling of being marginal, of "always watching from the sides" to leave the theatre. "I need you to go out there. I need you to go outside. For just five/ten minutes. I just need a space where I can talk to the folks who also have to live on the sides" (73). He is very insistent and gives audience members several chances to reassess their positionality and to really leave if they should. (Readers of the printed script who need to "leave" are encouraged to skip to page ninety-three.) When those who have left return, they find the remainder of the audience wearing party hats. (FOMO!) Jiv then explains why this act of exclusion was necessary: "So, for those of you who thought it was so you could go outside and really understand what it feels like to be a marginalized person . . . It's not that—you were outside for like five, seven minutes—it's not *quite* the same thing. It's just that part of the show was not made for you. And if that's troubling to you at all, then ask yourself how often you encounter spaces that *aren't* made for you?" (94).

US

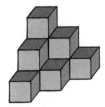

A very common point of focus in participatory theatre performances is on the singularity of the audience participant. I've written elsewhere that a recurring marker of certain types of participatory theatre is that it is not only created by me (through my participation) but also for me and about me.[1] The pull to AUTOBIOGRAPHY is strong. And you can see why. If the audience-participant is asked to do something or give something, all I have immediately at hand is myself—my physical LABOUR, my ideas, my opinions, my ability to solve puzzles, my personal history, etc. In a show like *The Ministry of Mundane Mysteries*, autobiographical play is crafted by and for a solo audience member out of the material of my mundane life. In *Perfect Strangers* created by Popcorn Galaxies, we share autobiographical details in an ambulatory peer-to-peer pairing of two. Even in larger audience groups, like TBD or *Intimate Karaoke*, although I might be surrounded by others, the focus of my experience still solidly lies on me as an individual. (see TOGETHER ALONE) My placement in relation to the participation of the others is sometimes serial and sometimes parallel, but in each of these examples we remain separate.

This, however, is not the case in *Saving Wonderland* and *This is the Story of the Child Ruled by Fear*. Instead of the personal focus of participation as autobiography, in these shows we are amalgamated, blended together, interchangeable; we are widgets; we are a collective. Our individuality is purposely effaced. My self as self is irrelevant. Of course, audiences are always already a mostly anonymous collective in this way. The difference in participatory performance situations is that the dramaturgical needs of the events compel our co-operation in certain ways. We need each other. In a very basic way, once we are out of our seats and standing in the light, audience-players rub together in novel, social ways that typically don't arise in BOURGEOIS THEATRE. We create space for each other. We might hold someone else's bag or coat, offer technical advice in online environments, or just pause to wait for the slowest among us. These are small acts of solidarity of an emerging community. (see ELBOWS)

---

1   See Jenn Stephenson, "Autobiography in the Audience: Emergent Dramaturgies of Loss in *Lost Together* and *Foreign Radical*," *Theatre Research in Canada* 43, no. 1 (2022): 81–95.

When I participated in *Foreign Radical*, the show was being presented in Quebec City. The show is performed in English and when it became apparent that some of our francophone audience comrades were struggling to fully comprehend the Host's demands, one audience member took initiative to act as a translator. Another entirely spontaneous peer-to-peer interaction happened when I saw *La Rivoluzione Siamo Noi—The Change Maker*. Upon arrival at the house where the show was happening, you would ring a buzzer for admittance and the front door would be unlocked for you. Eventually, those in the foyer who had already entered became self-appointed greeters and simply opened the door when the buzzer buzzed. These are small, perhaps ordinary acts of kindness, but it is notable that they happened autonomously of the artist-creators.

Presented online as part of the Next Stage Festival, *Saving Wonderland* blends dramatic storytelling with CHOOSE YOUR OWN ADVENTURE decision-making and escape room puzzle-solving. The show uses a range of tech platforms including live-action Zoom broadcast, audience chat, and an app for our PHONES. The premise of *Saving Wonderland* is that when Alice visited Wonderland previously, she broke it somehow— time is looping and the storyworld is disintegrating—and only Alice can fix it. What is central, however, is that all of us in the Zoom audience are collectively Alice. There is only one Alice, and it is us. The characters address us as Alice. This is similar in some respects to performances where one audience member is selected from the group to assume a role or perform a task. That one person, although detached from the mass, is still tethered to us in important ways. We see ourselves in their experience. They act as a kind of audience hero-representative within the fiction. (see PROXIES) What is different here is that we all become Alice. Many become one. And so we need to find ways to play together.

This collective play is managed via the custom game app that runs on our phones. When presented with a puzzle to solve or a choice to be made, we use the game app, which works like a poll. The majority vote determines our choices. Similarly, for the puzzles or other digital tasks, if most of the group gets the right answer, we are successful. Admittedly, it is entirely possible to do the show as a disparate assemblage of pure majority rule. On the other hand, on the night that I participated, a leader emerged in the chat and directed our voluntarily coordinated responses, saying, "Let's pick the Red Queen." Or, "I think the answer depends on a Fibonacci sequence." (I, for one, was happy to follow Jackson's lead. He always knew the right answers.) Either strategy is fine, but whether we remain aloof or choose to consult, the app operates to funnel our input into the oneness of Alice.[2] (The app game task where we each have to mash the on-screen button as fast as we can but without going "over" speaks especially strongly to our role in an invisible collective.)

Another show with a similar collective audience character and mode of participation is David Gagnon Walker's *This is the Story of the Child Ruled by Fear*. The play is a poetic fable of the eponymous child ruled by fear's journey. Here, a small number of audience-participants (perhaps six or eight people) sit at cabaret tables each equipped with a reading light and a script marked with highlighted section. (see CONSENT) When their turn comes, each of these participants joins in to read a character. The creator, Gagnon Walker, serves as the narrator. Audience-readers play a variety of different characters, but also significantly they all, at different times, give voice to the child. The rest of the audience is also invited when cued to become a chorus. (My favourite speech of the chorus is, "We are real. We are real. We are real.") Choral speaking is a low-stakes but highly effective way to bring us into participatory community, as we blend our individual contributions into something larger (and louder) than each of us alone. (see RITUAL) The audience literally speaks with one voice.[3] The effect of this collective reading is perfectly described by the show's promotional blurb, which describes the experience as "a playful leap of faith into the power of a roomful of people discovering a new story by creating it with each other." And so it is. The suggestion emerges that at some point in real life Gagnon Walker might be the child ruled by fear, but then through our dispersed and collective voicings so are we all. We all have fears and sometimes we can be brave and sometimes we can't. The play evades a simple answer. Nevertheless, the true outcome is that, in the end, together we have all created something that at the outset we couldn't have anticipated, and we journeyed together with generosity for the risk of participating. The result is a kind of vulnerable rough beauty.

See NEGOTIATION and MOB

---

2   Spoiler alert: the ending for my play-game experience (which was different from Mariah's) returned us all as Alice to a blue-sky morning on the riverbank in a time before we ever meet the White Rabbit and before the start of the events of the book *Alice in Wonderland*. We are told by the Cheshire Cat that the only way to really save Wonderland is for us not to enter in the first place. (see UNWELCOME) This is emotionally bittersweet but also astonishing in terms of game play and participation. Essentially, we are being told that the way to "win" is not to "play." (!!) We do not belong in Wonderland.

3   This dramaturgy manifests as group singing in drop-in choir performances like Nightswimming's *Why We Are Here!* and Daveed Goldman and Nobu Adilman's *Choir! Choir! Choir!*

UTOPIA

In her book *Utopia in Performance*, Jill Dolan writes about utopian performatives, not about utopian performances. Dolan emphasizes utopia not as a *place* but as a journey *towards*. It is a striving, not yet (perhaps never quite?) arriving. Utopia for Dolan is a hopeful feeling, sketched as "small but profound moments in which performance calls the attention of the audience in a way that lifts everyone slightly above the present."[1] Because of their transformative potential in the present, utopian performatives provide rich ground for practising or gesturing towards utopia in the gathered community we find at the theatre. Dolan articulates this hopeful quality of the theatre, looking to the warmth in community that arises from our co-present gathering, collective WITNESS to something. (see FRIENDSHIP and LAND) She says, "Utopian performatives, in their doings, make palpable an affective vision of how the world might be better."[2]

Each chapter of *Utopia in Performance* outlines a different one of her utopian dramaturgies. She recognizes utopian performatives in the repetition of rehearsals and in the power of changing personal narratives in AUTOBIOGRAPHICAL shows. She writes about the capacity for empathy-building through multi-vocal solo performances and finds hope in the performing public of a poetry jam. Dolan insists that "audiences are compelled to gather with others, to see people perform live, hoping, perhaps, for moments of transformation that might let them reconsider the world outside the theatre, from its micro to its macro arrangements."[3]

Participatory theatre could constitute another chapter of Dolan's book. The key here is the "micro and macro arrangements" that participation stages to bring together a group of people to negotiate and make decisions on a *small* scale. Participatory dramaturgies offer a space to practise, to grapple with world building up close, person to person. The work is intensely relational, and as Nicolas Bourriaud writes, "Social utopias and revolutionary hopes have given way to everyday micro-utopias

---

1   Jill Dolan, *Utopia in Performance: Finding Hope at the Theatre* (U of Michigan P, 2005), 165.

2   Dolan, *Utopia in Performance*, 6.

3   Dolan, *Utopia in Performance*, 36.

and imitative strategies."[4] In support of this proposal for effecting change through microgestures he quotes Félix Guattari, who concurs: "Just as I think it is illusory to aim at a step-by-step transformation of society, so I think that microscopic attempts, of the community and neighbourhood committee type, the organization of day-nurseries in the faculty, and the like, play an absolutely crucial role."[5] The key for Bourriaud is the creation of small moments of sociability. Moments where the artwork imitates or replicates those everyday interactions of life in the exchange of goods and services, in saying hello to a bus driver, or sharing pleasantries with a store clerk. Simple human contact among colleagues and clienteles. Abandoning faith in swift and radical social change, Bourriaud and Guattari, among others, propose changing the scale of their field of action. Political action at the microlevel does indeed become personal, shrunk to the very smallest unit of society—two people. You and another.

At the conclusion of *Gimme Shelter*, written and performed by Ravi Jain,[6] each audience member is directed to look across the alley stage to the ranks of our co-audience members seated on the other side. We are then instructed to make eye contact with the person directly across. Next, we are invited to come down off the seating bleachers and stand in rows on the stage. The gazing pairs approach each other, now less than half a metre apart. Prompted by the thematic context of a play about the global refugee CRISIS, the self-reflexive question arises: "What would you do for another human in need?" I admit that as the minutes ticked by, I was overtaken by an irrational attachment to my partner. In this tiny world of two people, not speaking and not touching, just looking, I was warmed by giving and receiving affectionate attention. My dominant thought was that I would do whatever was in my power to aid this person. It was love. (I comprehend that this makes no sense and is excessively sentimental. And yet ... Confession: one of my strengths—or weaknesses, actually—as an audience-participant is my lack of cynicism and my general willingness to go there.) INTIMATE participatory relational performances are micro-utopias with the potential to engender empathy and a sense of connection with a stranger.

---

4   Nicolas Bourriaud, *Relational Aesthetics*, translated by Simon Pleasance and Fronza Woods (Les presses du réel, 2002), 31.

5   Félix Guattari, *Molecular Revolution* (1984), quoted by Bourriaud, *Relational Aesthetics*, 31.

6   Presented as part of PANAMANIA, *Gimme Shelter* was staged at the Young Centre for the Arts in July 2015. The show was produced by Why Not Theatre, written and performed by Ravi Jain, and directed by Jenny Koons.

The night before *La Rivoluzione Siamo Noi—The Change Maker* by DLT, I was sent an email that cast me in the revolution with a group of strangers. The note connected me to two historical figures—controversial and influential Italian poet and filmmaker Pier Paolo Pasolini and socialist artist Joseph Beuys—and challenged me to consider what it would feel like to be a key player in a revolution. When I arrived at the Italian Cultural Institute of Toronto for the performance, I found myself part of a group of eight audience members who were invited into a small library surrounded by books in both Italian and English. The show began when a facilitator put an envelope on the table. "Open me," it said. We opened it and were instructed to look around at the books, select one that resonated with us, and flip through it. After looking through our books, we were prompted by another letter to get to know one another. "What is the most important thing that happened to you today?" Someone talked about their father's ninety-third birthday. Another talked about shovelling snow. Two people found similar experiences in having friends cancel their attendance to this very show. I talked about my five-year-old piano student reading music on the staff for the first time. The printed directions continued, "Pick something from your book and read it aloud."

My co-revolutionaries were an eclectic group. We varied in age, occupying a few generations between us. Our interesting and amazingly not-at-all awkward conversation was interrupted with an invitation to move into another room that looked like an acting studio—wood floors, white walls, an empty room. One of us read aloud instructions from yet another letter and led us all through a series of physical exercises of increasing mutual intimacy. Walk around the room. Make eye contact while you stroll. Start at the perimeter of the room with a finger outstretched and walk towards the centre until all your fingers touch. Stand with your backs to the group and back up until you are all touching. High five everyone! Fist bump everyone! Hold hands!

When we were told to "find a way to finish," the group struggled. What to do now? The two older Italian gentlemen in our group wanted to continue to discuss the problematic personal life of Pasolini. Two of the women wanted to know more about the writing of this very book on participatory dramaturgies. In the snowy dark, we stood outside the theatre chatting for thirty minutes after the show. In February. Our little community was keen to build deeper relationships and cast ourselves into the future together somehow. And so we decided to exchange emails. (To my amazement, I did actually receive emails from the group. Five people chimed in to affirm their warm interest in meeting again.

Even maybe travelling to Kingston to gather and be together again. And perhaps we will.)

And yet . . . Although they are powerful in their intimate and relational micro-utopian potential, utopian performatives are not enough. Is this our revolution? In the moment I can feel hopeful, wrapped in theatre's metaphor, but I cannot find the directions to utopia in a stranger's eyes. While hope is found at the theatre, refugees are still adrift and lost at sea. Utopia remains attached to its etymological roots, u-topos, no place.

See TYRANNY

WHAT IS THE MOST IMPORTANT THING THAT HAS HAPPENED TO YOU TODAY?

WINNING

See CHEATING

TAKE HEED! MARY HAS FOUND HERSELF IN A DUNGEON FILLED WITH FIRE-BREATHING DRAGONS AND STONE STAIRCASES. USING THE DICE ROLLS LAID OUT IN THE CHEATING ENTRY, MAP OUT HER JOURNEY. STEPPING ON THE TAIL OF A DRAGON SENDS MARY DOWN TO ITS MOUTH, WHILE STEPPING ON THE FIRST STEP OF A STAIRCASE WILL SEND HER TO ITS TOP. IF MARY MAKES IT TO LEVEL 100, THE ANSWER IS 1; IF NOT, THE ANSWER IS 0.

ANSWER:

WITNESS

As more than a thousand unmarked graves of children who were held captive at Canada's residential schools were unearthed in spring and summer 2021, Dr. Alan Lagimodiere, the new Indigenous Reconciliation and Northern Relations minister in Manitoba, spoke publicly for the first time in his new role.[1] In this speech, Lagimodiere says, "The residential school system was designed to take Indigenous children and give them the skills and abilities they would need to fit into society as it moved forward." At the time, many settlers in so-called Canada were finally unlearning this dangerous lie. Wab Kinew, the leader of Manitoba's NDP, interrupted Lagimodiere, approaching the podium saying, "I am an honorary witness to the Truth and Reconciliation Commission. I listened to stories of the survivors, and I cannot accept you saying what you just said about residential schools." More than listening to testimony, being an official Honorary Witness to the Truth and Reconciliation Commission (TRC) comes with an active commitment to tell the truth about colonial violence in so-called Canada. "Witnesses were asked to retain and care for the history they witness and, most importantly, to share it with their people when they return home."[2] Notably, the National Centre for Truth and Reconciliation asserts witnesses must *commit to participating* in a future where the genocide of Indigenous children is not forgotten or misunderstood. Kinew's active interruption and correction of Lagimodiere's narrative illustrates this commitment to participation that includes the destruction of false narratives.

Indigenous writer Samantha Nock unpacks the subtle differences between listening and witnessing. Nock insists that "too often we think that the act of listening is equal to the act of witnessing."[3] She describes listening as a passive endeavour. By contrast, she says that when we "witness a story we are not only present physically, but emotionally and

---

1 @elishadacey, "Here's the exchange between @WabKinew and Dr. Alan Lagimodiere, the new Indigenous Reconciliation and Northern Relations minister," *Twitter*, 15 July 2021, twitter.com/elishadacey/status/1415716784515305475.

2 "The NCTR Supports Honorary Witness and Invites Minister for Further Education," *The National Centre for Truth and Reconciliation*, 16 July 2021, https://nctr.ca /the-nctr-supports-honorary-witness-and-invites-minister-for-further-education/.

3 Samantha Nock, "Being a Witness: The Importance of Protecting Indigenous Women's Stories," *Rabble*, 4 September 2014, rabble.ca/blogs/bloggers/samantha-nock/2014/09 /being-witness-importance-protecting- indigenous-womens-stories.

spiritually, to hold this story in our hearts." When we witness a story, "that story becomes a part of us," and "you have entered a very specific and powerful relationship that exists between the storyteller and the witness."[4] Witnessing is an active and ongoing invitation to participate in relation; it's a contract between the witnessed and the witness, signed by the act of hearing testimony.

Our colleague Julie Salverson, a scholar of witnessing, writes, "To be a witness, I must find the resources to respond. It isn't only passing on a story that matters; I must let the story change me. This makes me vulnerable in the face of another's vulnerability. I participate in a relationship. But to be present in a relationship, I must have a self to offer. Tricky territory. Who, right now, has the nerve to reveal themselves?"[5] Salverson also asserts that "courageous happiness"[6] is a resource to activate witnessing. Where Nock names the agreement as "relational," Salverson says that "witnessing is a transaction that is personal, social and structural."[7]

Salverson cites the work of Roger Simon and Claudia Eppert who claim that witnessing "demands (but does not secure) acknowledgement, remembrance and consequence. Each aspect presents different obligations."[8] These three moments of witnessing—acknowledgement, remembrance, and consequence—are a map of activity from which participatory witnessing is charted. Acknowledgement is the awareness and confirmation of what is being witnessed. Remembrance "commits a person as an apprentice to testimony."[9] As an apprentice to testimony, the witness agrees to be employed by testimony; an apprentice signs a contract as a novice committed to work. Remembrance marks the changing of the witness. "The third term, 'consequence,' is about obligation, about what we do with the knowledge we perhaps wish we did not have."[10] Consequence marks the changing of the world. This is what Kinew does when he steps forward to speak.

This question of what I do with the knowledge that I perhaps wish I did not have is the central dramaturgical driver for Olivier Choinière's

---

4   Nock, "Being a Witness."

5   Julie Salverson and Bill Penner, "Loopings of Love and Rage: Sitting in the Trouble," *Canadian Theatre Review* 181 (Winter 2020): 37.

6   Julie Salverson, "Taking Liberties: A Theatre Class of Foolish Witnesses," *Research in Drama Education: The Journal of Applied Theatre and Performance* 13, no. 2 (June 2008): 246.

7   Salverson, "Taking Liberties," 246.

8   Salverson, "Taking Liberties," 247.

9   Salverson, "Taking Liberties," 247.

10   Salverson, "Taking Liberties," 248.

ascerbic public art piece *Les secours arriveront bientôt*. Montrealers strolling in the Quartier des spectacles were witness to surreal scenes of four superheros, identifiable by their authentic comic costumes, in severe distress—Superman lying prone on the concrete, unconscious and bleeding; Wonder Woman incoherent and covered in abrasions; Spider-Man panicking, tangled in his own web; and Batman frantic with his cape caught in a maintenance cover. Behind each scene of CRISIS a large billboard in comic-book font invited passersby to "appelez les secours!!" ("Call for help!!") and listed a phone number below. Each caller was connected to an intelligent automated attendant (actually a live actor pretending to be a virtual operator) who asked a series of questions, prompting audience members to repeat responses from a pre-set list of choices. The questions and the choices are however not entirely neutral. The first question invites audience-callers to identify their reason for calling: "Êtes-vous témoin d'un incident ou d'une catastrophe? Si vous êtes témoin d'un incident, dites: «Je suis témoin d'un incident», si vous êtes témoin d'une catastrophe, dites: «Je suis témoin d'une catastrophe.»"[11]

As the interview questions continue, the voice pushes the callers to make declarations about their own capacity to intervene and to actually take action. "Avez-vous confiance que les secours vont arriver? Ne serait-ce pas plus efficace et plus rapide d'intervenir vous-même? Si vous avez confiance que les secours vont arriver, dites: «Je fais confiance au secours», mais si vous jugez que vous pouvez intervenir vous-même, dites : «Je peux intervenir moi-même.»"[12] Ultimately, the performance leverages its innate ONTOLOGICAL DUALITY against us. What are we really witness to? And what are we really going to do about it? Wonder Woman is clearly in need of help, but she has supernatural powers—how can I, without any powers, do anything? As the automated operator says, "Si vous croyez au super-héros, pourquoi avez-vous appelé les secours?"[13] And also Wonder Woman is not real; it's a play. The sign says, "Call for help," but then what? Is a person coming to help? Is that person me? (see FUTILITY) "Si vous ne croyez pas au super-héros, en quoi croyez-vous?"[14] After repeating our response to this final question verbatim back

---

11 "Are you the witness to an incident or a disaster? If you are the witness to an incident, say: 'I am the witness to an incident,' if you are the witness to a disaster, say: 'I am the witness to a disaster.'"

12 "Do you trust that help will arrive? Wouldn't it be more efficient and faster to intervene yourself? If you have confidence that help will arrive, say: 'I am confident of help,' but if you feel that you can intervene yourself, say: 'I can intervene myself.'"

13 "If you believe in superheroes, why did you call for help?"

14 "If you don't believe in superheroes, what do you believe in?"

to us, the call comes to an abrupt (and unresolved) conclusion: "Merci. Comme témoin oculaire, votre point de vue est essentiel. Les secours arriveront bientôt. Au revoir."[15]

Witnessing is a core participatory dramaturgy. Bearing witness to crisis is a participatory dramaturgy that signs a deal to continue to participate beyond the show. As Salverson asserts, witnesses are not participants in "spectacle or escape, or passive avoidance, it is the deadly game of living with loss, living despite the humiliation of trying endlessly, living despite failure."[16] And so, in light of the example of Kinew's actions as a witness to the testimony of the Truth and Reconciliation Commission, I am inclined to read Choinière's *Les secours arriveront bientôt* as a commentary on my own wildly insufficient efforts towards decolonization, and my persistent feelings in light of that failure. I feel the same way about the radical complexities and human misery of homelessness in my city that I witness daily. I'm getting better at seeing and talking about what I am seeing, but actual, concrete change feels too expansive to be possible. But if not me, then who? I don't believe that help is on the way. I'm afraid I'm it.

---

15 "Thanks. As an eyewitness, your point of view is essential. Help will arrive soon. Bye."

16 Salverson, "Taking Liberties," 253.

YES, LET'S!

Improvisation is a core dramaturgy of participation. Part of the appeal of audience-participants
is that they are peak randomness generators (see ALEA) and
artists who are shaping works for interactivity with these audience-participants need to be flexible and responsive improvisers. (see
BETA) But audiences also rely on improvisation. Saying "yes" is the
inciting incident of participatory theatre. In order for audience-participants to play the game at all, we have to pick up the baton. We have to
accept the INVITATION. Arriving unrehearsed, audience-participants
are profoundly ignorant (perhaps calling them "innocent" would be a
nicer way to say that). We have no sense of where this is going. But what
we do bring, in that catalyzing word, "yes," is a willingness to enter the
world of play and not only discover it but create it as we go.

Best known for his contributions to the world of theatre sports, British
Canadian improviser Keith Johnstone created his improv system when
he was running actor development training at Royal Court Theatre's
educational department in the 1950s. He then moved to Calgary in
the 1970s and started Loose Moose Theatre, a company dedicated to
improvisational theatre.[1] Johnstone's work in improv aimed "to instill
in the participants of his workshops the creativity and spontaneity" to
encourage actors to follow their instincts and openly embrace whatever
comes to them.[2] Coined by Johnstone, the responsive phrase "yes, let's!"
is both a practical exercise and a core value of improv. To play "yes, let's!"
improvisers are instructed to begin by moving about a space naturally. A
member of the group then gives an offer: "Let's all walk backwards!" All
players then shout, "Yes, let's!"[3] and proceed to take up the offer—walking backwards—until someone hurls another suggestion into the room.
"Let's cluck like chickens!" "Yes, let's!" "Yes, let's" is about wholehearted
acceptance of the invitation. It is about saying yes and seeing where

---

1   "Keith Johnstone," *Wikipedia*, wikipedia.org/wiki/Keith_Johnstone.
2   James A. McLaughlin, "Why is Improv Funny? The Centrifugal Forces of
Johnstonian Improv," *Comedy Studies* 4, no. 1 (2013): 48.
3   Similarly, there is another classic improv game called "Yes, And" which is more
sequential in structure than simply affirmative. When one player makes an offer in
"Yes, And" the players must accept and accelerate, building upon and augmenting
what has come before.

it takes you. It is an echo that materializes the voice into gesture and asserts community. (Even before we decided on the title of this entry, I had this invitation to play tattooed on my right shoulder as a joyful reminder.) Elsewhere in this book, we have considered the negative, exploring various moods and meanings of saying "no." (see REFUSAL, KILLJOY, GOING ROGUE, and CHEATING) By contrast, "yes, let's!" is unabashedly positive, signalling acceptance of your collaborators' ideas and is the manifestation of a profoundly welcoming attitude to placing yourself into generative uncertainty. It is an acceptance of play and willingness to follow the lead of your partners, which might indeed involve clucking like chickens.

Or screaming.

In 2022, Radix Theatre (Vancouver) presented a free event, their *First Annual Silent Scream Solstice*. Participants were asked to join Radix on 21 December for a "walk in silence followed by a scream in darkness."[4] Taking inspiration from the Swedish screaming RITUAL of Elvavrålet, or the Flogsta scream, where students scream in unison to release stress,[5] Radix's event invited participants to release a guttural sound to free up the energy to face the rest of the long Canadian winter. The invitation was simple: meet at the gathering point, walk in silence, then scream.[6] Radix board member Cat Wong recorded the scream in what she called "ASSSSSMR (Autonomous Sensory Silent Scream Solstice Soundwalk Meridian Response)"[7] and uploaded it to SoundCloud,[8] capturing the event in shimmering detail. At the start of the recording, you can hear the group of screamers-in-waiting walking; the only sound is their boots trekking through the crunchy snow. At the three-minute mark a chorus of overlapping voices scream and yell and shout. After the initial scream fades into the winter darkness, there is an almost shy breath of silence before the voices start making whooping noises and howling

---

4   "Silent Scream Solstice," *Radix Theatre*, radixtheatre.org/.

5   Meg Van Huygen, "How Swedish Students Let Off Steam—By Screaming in Public," *Mental Floss*, 17 February 2017, mentalfloss.com/article/92357/how-swedish-students-let-steam-screaming-public.

6   If people needed a script, Radix Theatre provided one in multiple languages: "Aaaaaaaaaaaaaaaaaaaaaaaaaaaa! !!!!!!!!!!!!!!!!!!!! """"""""""""! आआआआआआआआआआआआआ! ××××××××××××××××××! आआआआआआआआआआआआआआआआआआआआआआ! !############## $%&'!((((((((((!)a)a)a)a)a)a)! ᎡᎡᎡᎡᎡᎡᎡᎡᎡᎡᎡᎡᎡᎡᎡᎡᎡᎡᎡᎡᎡᎡ!*+,,,,,,,,,,,,,,,,! ᎻᎻᎻᎻᎻᎻᎻᎻᎻᎻᎻᎻᎻᎻᎻᎻᎻ! Áaaaaaaaaaaaaaa! Ystyr geiriau: Aaaaaaaaaaaaa!" "Silent Scream Solstice," *Radix Theatre*, radixtheatre.org/.

7   "Silent Scream Solstice."

8   Radix Theatre, "Silent Scream Solstice Soundwalk," *SoundCloud*, soundcloud.com/radix-theatre/silent-scream-solstice-soundwalk.

like wolves. Then there's some laughing. The whole recording only lasts about five minutes, but we can imagine that the effects of this visceral release must last long into the winter night, echoing off the frozen snow around the screamers. Where solstice screaming is a community celebration, Anishinaabe artist Rebecca Belmore's iconic *Ayum-ee-aawach Oomama-mowan: Speaking to Their Mother* invites Indigenous voices to be raised, enacting a powerful act of ENCOUNTER and resistance. (see UNWELCOME) These voices are raised in what Belmore terms "political protest as poetic action."[9] Using a two-metre diameter wooden megaphone created by Belmore, *Ayum-ee-aawach Oomama-mowan* allows participants to speak directly to the LAND. Belmore, a member of the Lac Seul First Nation, initiated the performance as a response to the 1990 Oka Crisis, when the Canadian government sent an armed militia to violently confront the Kanien'kehá:ka in their resistance to Mohawk land at Kanesatake, south of Montréal, being developed into a golf course. In a CBC documentary, Belmore says that she initially "wanted to stage the ultimate protest on Parliament Hill," breaking "windows because they don't listen."[10] She eventually decided instead that this protest would manifest in a "megaphone, and instead of aiming it at the government I wanted to instead take it to Native people and turn it towards the land."[11] To that end, the work provides a stage for Indigenous folks to commune not with the Canadian state but rather with the land. Themselves.[12] *Ayum-ee-aawach Oomama-mowan* was "first used in 1991 in a meadow in Banff National Park where people's voices, spoken through the megaphone, would echo back nine times. The conversation bounced off the mountains beyond speakers. Again and again and again. Through an assertion of Indigenous harmony with the land, Belmore filled the air with reverberating sovereign voices. In 1992, Belmore toured the work across Canada to a number of sites where Indigenous land claims were being asserted and justice was being demanded."[13]

9 Rebecca Belmore, "Speaking to Their Mother," *Rebecca Belmore*, rebeccabelmore.com /exhibit/Speaking-to-Their-Mother.html.
10 "In the Making: Rebecca Belmore," CBC *Gem: Season 2, Episode 8*, 27 September 2019, gem.cbc.ca/in-the-making.
11 "In the Making: Rebecca Belmore."
12 "In the Making: Rebecca Belmore."
13 "Ayum-ee-aawach Oomama-mowan: Speaking to their Mother Gathering," *Art Museum at the University of Toronto*, 9 August 2014, artmuseum.utoronto.ca /program/ayum-ee-aawach-oomama-mowan-speaking-mother-gathering/.

Situated near the mouth of the wooden megaphone is "an electric handheld megaphone"[14] that amplifies the voice. Importantly, for Belmore, this amplification is not simply a means to be heard but rather an assertion of space specifically for Indigenous people to dialogue with the land. "Prioritizing the vibrational movement of the echo over the voice's amplification and turning the megaphone toward the land, as opposed to the Canadian government, enacts a refusal of settler state—defined politics of sovereignty."[15] Once the Indigenous participant says yes to Belmore's invitation, speaking into the microphone, the echoed voice becomes separate from the body, continuously asserting its sovereignty in conversation with the land.

Although it's the last alphabetical entry, "Yes, let's!" is the beginning and not the end. It is the most basic version of invitation that catalyzes all participatory work. Like an echo, saying "yes," screaming, or speaking sovereignty is a participatory dramaturgy that exists long after we're gone.

See AGENCY and US

---

14 Iris Sandjette Blake, "Decolonial Echoes: Voicing and Listening in Rebecca Belmore's Sound Performance," *Performance Matters* 6, no. 2 (2020): 13.

15 Blake, "Decolonial Echoes," 13.

Congratulations on making it to the final puzzle! Eight pieces of a mysterious QR code have been discovered and it is up to you to assemble them in order.

The first step is to cut out all eight QR code pieces on the following page. Try to cut directly on the dotted grey lines and not into the pieces of code, as this could affect the results.

Once you are finished, put the pieces aside and fill in the tables below with the answers to each puzzle. They are listed by entry, with the type of puzzle in parentheses.

Entry (Puzzle)	Answer	Symbol
Ants (Paint by Numbers)		🪶
Embodiment (Nonogram)		⚡
Game Over (Poster Puzzle)		🐂
Instrumentality (Bingo)		☕
Mail (Folding Puzzle)		📷
Mob (Guess the Character)		🕷
Relation (Connect the Dots)		🎮
Text Messages (Riddle)		📖

Being Lost (City Scramble)		🐂
First-Person Shooter (Spot the Differences)		☕
Ontological Duality (Bills and Coins)		🎮
Ostranenie (Maze)		🕷
Seeking (Word Crossout Puzzle)		🪶
Strumpet (Decoding Puzzle)		⚡
Things (Crossword)		📖
Winning (Dragons and Staircases)		📷

MATCH NUMBERS TO LETTERS USING THE SYMBOLS
THAT APPEARED NEXT TO EACH ANSWER IN THE PREVIOUS TABLES.

SYMBOL	NUMBER → LETTER		SYMBOL	NUMBER → LETTER
🪶	→		📟	→
⚡	→		🐜	→
🦇	→		🎮	→
☕	→		📖	→

THESE COMBINATIONS ARE THE COORDINATES FOR PLACING
THE QR CODE PIECES ONTO THE FINAL PUZZLE LEGEND. PLACE THE
PIECES SO THE NUMBERS ARE UPRIGHT, FACING AWAY FROM YOU.
IMAGINE THAT YOU ARE MAKING THE NUMBERS AND LETTERS TOUCH.

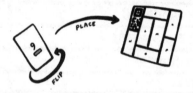

ONCE ALL OF THE PIECES ARE IN PLACE, YOU SHOULD HAVE A
COMPLETED QR CODE. IF THE ORDER IS CORRECT, THEN SCANNING
THE CODE WITH THE CAMERA OF A SMART DEVICE WILL SEND YOU
TO A SPECIAL ONLINE DESTINATION.

IF YOU ARE HAVING TROUBLE GETTING YOUR QR CODE TO WORK, TRY
ARRANGING THE PIECES ON A DARK SURFACE, ENSURING THAT THERE
ARE NO CRACKS BETWEEN THE CODE. REFER TO THE ANSWER KEY TO
MAKE SURE YOU HAVE THE RIGHT ANSWERS, AS WELL.

GOOD LUCK!

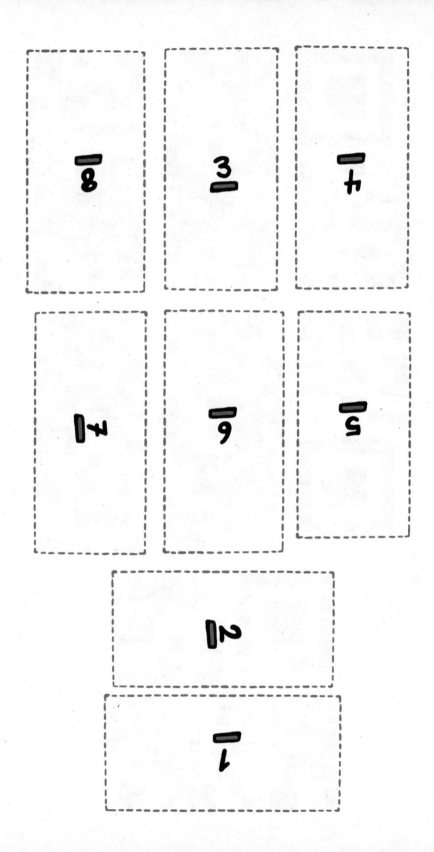

FINAL PUZZLE LEGEND

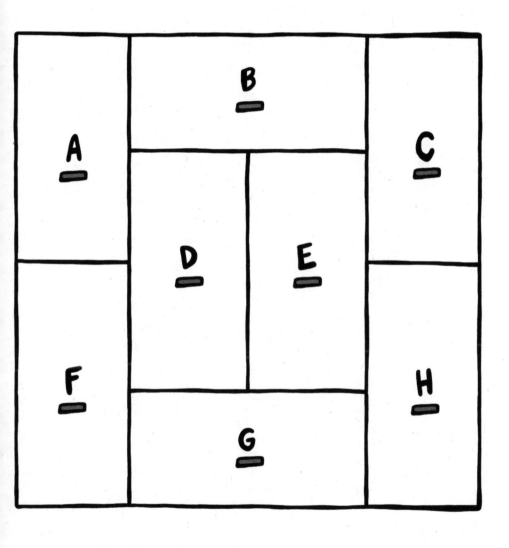

SELECTED PRODUCTION INDEX

100% VANCOUVER

One hundred "ordinary" Vancouverites are chosen to embody census data, with each person representing one percentile of the city. Answering autobiographical questions, they arrange themselves on stage in living data visualizations.

Directed by Amiel Gladstone. Casting director and dramaturge Tim Carlson. Part of the 100% City series conceptualized by Rimini Protokoll. Presented at PuSh International Performing Arts Festival (Vancouver, British Columbia), September 2011.

PAINT, FOOT WASHING, MAD LIBS, ORDINARY PEOPLE, ENCOUNTER

4INXCHANGE

Four audience members play games with a thousand dollars in actual cash to explore what they value most. How much would you pay for a meal? How much do you love your mother?

Created and performed by xLq (Jordan Campbell and Maddie Bautista) with Katherine Walker-Jones. Premiered at SummerWorks Festival (Toronto, Ontario), August 2018.

ONTOLOGICAL DUALITY, BETA, GUIDES, JUICINESS, MAD LIBS

ACCESS ME

An irreverent and sexy exploration of the experiences of three queer Disabled men. Audience-participants begin by asking candid questions about the sex lives of the performers, confronting taboo topics with humour and joy.

Presented by Boys in Chairs Collective. Featuring Andrew Gurza, Ken Harrower, and Frank Hull. Created and directed by Jonathan Senien. Associate director, creator, and producer Brian Postalian. Premiered at SummerWorks Festival (Toronto, Ontario), August 2017.

REHEARSAL

A GROWN UP'S GUIDE TO FLYING

(see TAPE ESCAPE)

GAME OVER. PLAY AGAIN?

AMBROSE

Cast as a detective, the solo audience member interviews suspects to discover what happened to Ambrose Small, who went missing in 1919 on the same day he sold his Ontario theatre empire for $1.7 million. An immersive, site-specific ghost story in Kingston's Grand Theatre.

Presented by Single Thread Theatre Company. Directed by Liam Karry. Written by Alex Dault, Liam Karry, and Daniele Bartolini. Premiered at the Kick & Push Festival (Kingston, Ontario), July–August 2015.

THE MATRIX, REFUSAL, GUIDES

THE ARCHIVE OF MISSING THINGS

A digital scavenger hunt where the covert audience seeks the heart of a maze-like archive. Set in a public library, audience-seekers are given headphones, a notebook, and an iPad. Live actors and audio narration provide navigational clues that guide our virtual explorations.

Created by Zuppa Theatre Co. with Kate Cayley. Directed by Alex McLean. Featuring Ursula Calder, Miranda Jones, and Stewart Legere. Narration by Gabriel Leblanc. Premiered at Stages Festival (Halifax, Nova Scotia), May 2017. We participated in August 2019 at the Sanderson Public Library, SummerWorks Festival (Toronto, Ontario).

SEEKING, CHOOSE YOUR OWN ADVENTURE, GUIDES, PLAYGROUNDS, SECRET WEIRDOS

THE ASSEMBLY–MONTRÉAL

A gathering of four people with very different views about democracy and free speech is transformed into a verbatim performance. Partway through, the performance is paused to allow audience members to take the stage and talk together about these issues.

Created by Annabel Soutar, Alex Ivanovici, and Brett Watson of Porte Parole. Directed by Chris Abraham. Featuring Jimmy Blais, Sean Colby, Alex Ivanovici, Tanja Jacobs, Ngozi Paul, and Brett Watson. Premiered at Streetcar Crowsnest (Toronto, Ontario), October–November 2018 and Théâtre ESPACE GO (Montréal, Quebec) November–December 2018.

DEMOCRACY, ORDINARY PEOPLE, MAD LIBS

ASSES.MASSES

A live video game about labour, revolution, and donkeys that takes roughly seven-and-a-half hours to play.

Created by Patrick Blenkarn and Milton Lim. Dramaturgy and co-writing by Laurel Green. Sound design and original compositions by David Mesiha. We participated in a beta-test version in November 2019 at the Banff Centre for the Arts (Banff, Alberta) and in the full ten-episode version in June 2023 at the Festival of Live Digital Art (Kingston, Ontario).

MOB, POLITICS OF THE BASEMENT, PLAYGROUNDS, LABOUR, TEACUPS

BEST LIFE

Audience-participants perform household tasks in concert with domestic appliances. These duets invite consideration of how these everyday things are collaborative partners and multigenerational witnesses to our lives.

Created by Maiko Yamamoto in collaboration with Antoine Bedard, Arthi Chandra, Itai Erdal, and Keely O'Brien. Presented by Theatre Replacement. Premiered at the Shadbolt Centre for the Arts (Burnaby, British Columbia), November 2022. We participated in January 2024 at HOLD ON LET GO (Vancouver, British Columbia).

THINGS

BIIDAABAN

Sub-titled "A Sonic Call to the Future," this audiowalk play invites listeners to approach the shores of wherever they may be on a February dawn.

Created by Lisa Cooke Ravensbergen with audio collaborator Mishelle Cuttler. Produced by Delinquent Theatre. Presented at PushOFF Festival and Talking Stick Festival (Vancouver, British Columbia), February 2021.

MINDFULNESS

[QUEER] BLIND DATE

Mimi the Clown has been stood up by her date for the evening. She picks a replacement date from the audience. Over the next ninety minutes, the two together improvise the story of their blind date.

Created and performed by Rebecca Northan. Premiered at Loose Moose (Calgary, Alberta) and Harbourfront's WorldStage (Toronto, Ontario) in 2010. The show subsequently toured internationally with presentations in New York City (2010) and London, UK (2013). We participated in January 2020 at the High Performance Rodeo (Calgary, Alberta).

THE MATRIX, OPT OUT, PROXIES, TOUR

BRANTWOOD

Audiences board a yellow school bus to return to Brantwood to attend their high-school reunion. Set in a decommissioned school building, scenes in this large-cast, immersive, site-specific musical span ten decades from 1920 to 2020.

Created, written, and directed by Mitchell Cushman and Julie Tepperman. Music and lyrics by Bram Gielen, Anika Johnson, and Britta Johnson. Presented with Sheridan College at Brantwood School (Oakville, Ontario), April 2015.

GHOSTS, CHOOSE YOUR OWN ADVENTURE, ACTING, GAME OVER. PLAY AGAIN?

BROKEN TAILBONE

A salsa dance lesson mixed with stories of dance-hall culture, sex, politics, and Aguirre's own autobiographical memories of her parents, her early adult years, and the story of how she broke her tailbone.

Written by Carmen Aguirre. Performed by Carmen Aguirre and DJ Don Pedro Chamale. Developed with Nightswimming Theatre. Premiered at the Uno Festival (Victoria, British Columbia), May 2017. We participated in October 2019 at Factory Theatre (Toronto, Ontario).

SWEATING, GUIDES, OPT OUT

B SIDE

Traversing a Queen West laneway, two performers and a strolling audience highlight what often goes unnoticed. Accompanied by music and dance, audience-participants with deliberation place three important lemons to mark this urban landscape. The play concludes with a lemonade social.

Created by Molly Johnson and Meredith Thomson. Presented at SummerWorks Festival (Toronto, Ontario), August 2018.

OSTRANENIE, GUIDES, JUICINESS, SECRET WEIRDOS, TEACUPS, BEING LOST, MAD LIBS

CAFÉ SARAJEVO

Using the frame of a live radio broadcast, the story follows actor Lucy Simic as she travels to her father's birthplace in Bosnia. Selected audience members perform roles of people she encountered in her journey.

Created and performed by bluemouth inc., who are Mariel Marshall, Peter Musante, Lucy Simic, and Stephen O'Connell. Creative Technologist Jacob Niedźwiecki. Presented at SummerWorks Festival (Toronto, Ontario), August 2019. We participated in February 2020 at the Theatre Centre (Toronto, Ontario).

ELBOWS, PROXIES

ÇA A L'AIR SYNTHÉTIQUE BONJOUR HI

Audience members are paid to perform banal tasks like folding socks or making sandwiches as the work questions the economics of participation. The second act shifts to an interrogation of affective labour as a performer conducts a confessional interview with a shrub.

Co-created and performed by Burcu Emeç, Michael Martini, Nien Tzu Weng, and Roxa Hy. Premiered at OFFTA Festival (Montréal, Quebec), May 2018. We participated in August 2019 at SummerWorks Festival (Toronto, Ontario).

LABOUR, STRUMPET, REFUSAL, REMOTE CONTROL

THE CANDLEMAKER'S GAME

Under the watchful eye of the Candlemaker, audiences are guided through a private card-based game that evokes a conflict-resolution process to reflect on an interpersonal issue from your real life.

Created by Richard Lam, Ruthie Luff, Scott Emerson Moyle, and Joe Pagnan, with the assistance of Susanna Fournier. The Candlemaker was played by Jillian Rees-Brown. Premiered at the Project Humanity Proximity Lab (Toronto, Ontario), March 2022.

TOGETHER ALONE, MINDFULNESS

CHOIR! CHOIR! CHOIR!

Arriving unrehearsed, the audience becomes a choir after they receive lyric sheets at the door and are taught their vocal parts. Unpreciousness motivates us as we perform popular songs with choral leaders DaBu.

Created and led by Daveed Goldman and Nobu Adilman. *Choir! Choir! Choir!* started in February 2011 as a weekly drop-in event. We participated in June 2019 at Festival of Live Digital Art (Kingston, Ontario).

JOY, LIVENESS, ANTS, ACTING, US

CITATION

Audiences carry a chosen stone in an audiowalk through colonial landmarks on the Queen's University campus and the city of Katarokwi-Kingston, including a statue of Sir John A. Macdonald in a public park. In an act of solidarity with Indigenous reclamation, each audience-walker decides what to do with the stone at the end.

Created and performed by Lisa Cooke Ravensbergen. Premiered at Festival of Live Digital Art (Kingston, Ontario), June 2018.

MAD LIBS, SECRET WEIRDOS

THE CORONA VARIATIONS

A cycle of six short phone plays set in the early days of the COVID-19 pandemic performed every half hour on one evening for one audience member (or household) at a time. One of the plays involved spontaneous improvisation by the audience-listener. Two others provided a script for the audience-player to assume a role.

Written and directed by Julie Tepperman. Presented by Convergence Theatre (Toronto, Ontario), April–May 2020.

ACTING, PHONES

COUNTING SHEEP: A GUERRILLA FOLK OPERA

Surrounded by video news footage of the Maidan Revolution in Kyiv in Winter 2014, immersed audience members re-enact key moments of the protest including eating, dancing, building a barricade, throwing bricks at riot police, and attending a funeral.

Created by Mark and Marichka Marczyk with collaborating directors Natalia Kaliada and Nicolai Khalezin (Belarus Free Theatre). Music performed by Lemon Bucket Orkestra. Premiered at SummerWorks Festival (Toronto, Ontario), May–June 2016.

SHEEP, ABYDOS, MAD LIBS, THE MATRIX, AUTOBIOGRAPHY, SWEATING

THE DEAD LETTER OFFICE

An interactive postal exchange where audiences both write and receive anonymous letters or postcards that they would never send in real life.

Created by Popcorn Galaxies, who are June Fukumura and Keely O'Brien. Presented at the Array Showcase hosted by Upintheair Theatre (Vancouver, British Columbia), December 2020.

EXCHANGE, MAIL, REMOTE CONTROL

DEEP GAZING

Inducted into the fictitious Order of Nephology (the study of clouds), audience members use scrying mirrors to look at the sky and prophesize. Performing in collaboration with the wind and the shore, two Sisters of the Order teach us to read the signs.

Created and performed by Erin Hill and Nina Vroemen (Horizon Factory). Presented at SummerWorks Festival (Toronto, Ontario), August 2022.

RITUAL

DRAW ME CLOSE

Cast as Jordan, the solo audience-participant enters into an animated virtual-reality environment where we co-perform an autobiographical story with an actor in a motion-capture suit who plays Jordan's (our) mother.

Written and directed by Jordan Tannahill. A National Film Board of Canada/National Theatre of Great Britain Production. Canadian premiere at the Young Centre for the Performing Arts (Toronto, Ontario), November 2021. Maggie Huculak and Caroline Gillis alternated in the role of the mother. Art by Teva Harrison.

ABYDOS, GUIDES, ACTING

EMBRACE

Following along with their own ingredients in their own home kitchens, audience-participants join an interactive Zoom cooking lesson. Over three separate episodes, Yousef, Suzan, and Ameen tell stories of their immigration to Canada while they teach you how to cook a three-course Middle Eastern meal from start to finish.

Created, directed, and produced by Hazel Venzon. Featuring Yousef Almbaidin, Suzan Palani, and Ameen Alnaser. Presented by U'ni Together and Sawa Theatre (Winnipeg, Manitoba), June 2021.

RECIPE, CRAFTS, LIVENESS

EVERYMAN

An adaptation of the medieval English morality play by the same name where the lone audience member is cast in the title role. Told by Death that they have been summoned to a final reckoning before God, the audience-Everyman journeys through a series of spiritual encounters with allegorical characters (Knowledge, Good Deeds, and others) before finally being placed into their grave.

Directed by Liam Karry. Presented by Single Thread Theatre Company (Kingston, Ontario), January–February 2007.

AROUSAL, STICKINESS, TEACUPS

FOREIGN RADICAL

Drawn into a series of confessional games by a malevolent host, mobile audience-players confess various illegal, controversial, or simply embarrassing views and past actions. We engage in spying on others and experience surveillance ourselves as we consider the governmental-judicial institutions that watch and control us.

Co-created by Tim Carlson, Jeremy Waller, David Mesiha, Kathleen Flaherty, Milton Lim, Aryo Khakpour, Florence Barrett, and Cande Andrade (Theatre Conspiracy). Directed by Jeremy P. Waller and Tim Carlson. Premiered at the Cultch (Vancouver, BC), April 2015. We participated in June 2017 at Carrefour International de Théâtre (Quebec City, Quebec).

COMPLICITY, ALEA, BOUNDARY VIOLATIONS, GOING ROGUE, GUIDES, JUICINESS, AUTOBIOGRAPHY, ONTOLOGICAL DUALITY, PHONY MULTIPLICITY

FUTURE PERFECT: NEW BYLAWS FOR CIVIC SPACES

Scissors in hand, participants are invited to cut up city bylaw documents that govern behaviour in public spaces to compose alternative statements. Published quickly on billboards and on Twitter these new rules help to perform a more "perfect" future.

Created by Mia Rushton and Eric Moschopedis (Mia + Eric) and Gemma Paintin and James Stenhouse (Action Hero UK). Premiered in Calgary, Alberta (August 2020). We participated in August 2022 at the SummerWorks Festival.

EXTRAORDINARY, EMERGENCE

THE GLOBAL SAVAGES

Four "global savages" travel the world to tell an eighteen-thousand-year-old history of Indigenous peoples in North America around a fire under the open sky. After immersing themselves in a new city and sharing meals with neighbours, their story is influenced by the community they are performing with.

Created by Debajehmujig Storytellers, featuring Joe Osawabine, Josh Peltier, Jessica Wilde-Peltier, and Bruce Naokwegijig. Artistic director Joe Osawabine. Artistic producer Ron Berti. Premiered at the Prismatic Festival (Halifax, Nova Scotia), October 2010.

LAND

GOOD THINGS TO DO

A show for one in a camping tent, in which the audience interacts via texting with a digital persona who claims friendship. A dreamscape narrative with live music offers a meditation on goodness, generosity, and gratitude.

Co-created by Christine Quintana (text and concept), Molly MacKinnon (sound design and composition), Sam MacKinnon (software design), and Mishelle Cutler (sound design and composition). Premiered at rEvolver Festival (Vancouver, British Columbia), May–June 2018. We participated in June 2018 at the Festival of Live Digital Art (Kingston, Ontario).

SELF-CARE, EXCHANGE, AROUSAL, JUICINESS

HAIRCUTS BY CHILDREN

An exercise in trust and in recalibrating expectations of what children are capable of, this show is exactly what it sounds like. Audience-participants put themselves and their hair into the hands of young hairstylists.

Conceived and directed by Darren O'Donnell (Mammalian Diving Reflex). Featuring local children from ages eight to twelve. Premiered at Harbourfront Centre (Toronto, Ontario), 2006. The show has toured extensively, being performed dozens of times on four continents.

FOOT WASHING, ILINX

HIGHER HAIR

In the hands of a "community cosmetic healer," audience members experience consensual hair play. Focused attention on its texture, length, and colour opens personal reflection on the intergenerational politics of hair.

Created by Hima Batavia. Performed by Hima Batavia and Nikola Steer (Coco Framboise). Premiered at Geary Art Crawl (Toronto, Ontario), October 2021. We participated in August 2022 at the SummerWorks Festival (Toronto, Ontario).

FOOT WASHING, JUICINESS

HOLY MOLY

Audience-congregants are immersed in semi-religious rituals inspired by pop culture icons of performer Jarin Schexnider's 1980s childhood to recover a sense of holiness.

Created and performed by Jarin Schexnider. Produced by Upintheair Theatre. Presented at rEvolver Festival (Vancouver, British Columbia), May–June 2022.

RITUAL

HUFF

Confronted by the character Wind, who is attempting suicide by anoxia, the audience is forced to consider what their culpability in this situation might be. Can Wind be saved?

Created and performed by Cliff Cardinal. Directed by Karin Randoja. Premiered at SummerWorks (Toronto, Ontario), August 2012. We participated in November 2019 at the Grand Theatre (Kingston, Ontario).

FUTILITY, BOUNDARY VIOLATIONS, PHONY MULTIPLICITY

ILLUMINATIONS: HUMAN/NATURE

Equipped with handheld video projectors and backpack audio speakers, audiences in small groups explore a national park. As they choose how to stage these sights and sounds, these multimedia stories reveal a tangled history of humans with the natural landscape.

Created by Sarah Fuller and Moment Factory (Montréal, Quebec). Presented in Rouge National Park (Ontario), 2017, and in Banff National Park (Alberta), 2017.

CREW, BEING LOST

INTIMATE KARAOKE, LIVE AT UTERINE CONCERT HALL

Audience-singers perform a cappella karaoke to a cabaret audience. In a nearby room, other audience-members can hear their vocals complete with backing instrumental score using a stethoscope to listen to a speaker located in the uterus of artist Dayna McLeod.

Created and performed by Danya McLeod. Uterine Concert Hall opened at the Foundrie Darling in Montréal in July 2016 with DJs Nik Forrest and Jackie Gallant. We participated in May 2019 at OFFTA (Montréal, Quebec).

INTIMACY, US

INVISIBLE

Invisible is an ode for ten dancers (and a dog), inviting audiences and performers to play, exchange, and connect. Over seventy-two hours, the spectator is called to experience the continuum of time and nourish the work's transformation through different interventions like choosing the soundtrack or reorganizing the space.

Artistic direction by Aurélie Pedron. Dramaturgy by Kathy Casey. Produced by Danse-Cité, Montréal Danse, and Lilith & Cie. Featuring Ariane Boulet, Charles Brécard, Rachel Harris, Emmanuel Jouthe, Luce Lainé, Abe Simon Mijnheer, Caroline Namts, Charlie Prince, Silvia Sanchez, and Zoë Vos. Presented at OFFTA (Montréal, Quebec), May 2022.

NEGOTIATION, INTIMACY

IT COMES IN WAVES

Audience-participants begin by canoeing to Toronto's Centre Island where, with the help of a guide, you prepare for a party.

Written by Jordan Tannahill, bluemouth inc., and Jennifer Tarver. Directed by Jennifer Tarver. Featuring Ciara Adams, Stephen O'Connell, Lucy Simic, and Dan Wild. Produced by Necessary Angel, bluemouth inc., and PANAMANIA at Gibraltar Artscape (Centre Island, Ontario), July 2015.

BEING LOST, MAD LIBS, GUIDES

THE ITINERARY: PLAYTEST

Using a custom app to dictate his actions, audience-players exert direct control over Sébastien, visible to us over Zoom. Eventually, we are told he has only hours left to live. What will we do with his remaining time?

Created and performed by Sébastien Heins. Directed by Mitchell Cushman and Sébastien Heins. Produced by Outside the March. Presented in development virtually at the Kick & Push Festival (Kingston, Ontario), August 2020. The final expanded version, called *No Save Points*, premiered at Lighthouse ArtSpace (Toronto, Ontario), June–July 2023.

REMOTE CONTROL, ASYMMETRY, BOUNDARY VIOLATIONS

LANDLINE

Two audience-players in two different cities are paired by text messaging as "scene partners." Accompanied by synchronized audio narration, the two drift in parallel through their respective cities.

Created by Adrienne Wong and Dustin Harvey. Between 2013 and 2018, the show has been performed in Victoria–Halifax, Whitehorse–Ottawa, Calgary–St. John's, Kitchener–Vancouver, Edinburgh–Reykjavik, and elsewhere. We participated in Kitchener (September 2015) and Whitehorse (June 2016).

DRIFT, SECRET WEIRDOS, ASYMMETRY, ONTOLOGICAL DUALITY

LA RIVOLUZIONE SIAMO NOI—THE CHANGE MAKER

Loosely framed through the artworks of Pier Paolo Pasolini and Joseph Beuys, audiences are recruited to social revolution as changemakers. There are no actors so the audience steps in, performing directed actions. In this microcommunity, each audience-player is a model for the others.

Concept and direction by Daniele Bartolini (DLT: Dopo Lavoro Teatrale). Written by Ada Aguilar, Daniele Bartolini, Marta Falugiani, Oana Parvan, and Stefania Vitulli. Presented at Istituto Italiano di Cultura Toronto (Toronto, Ontario), February 2023.

RECIPE, MAD LIBS, UTOPIA

LES SECOURS ARRIVERONT BIENTÔT

Superman, Wonder Woman, Batman, and Spider-Man are in distress. As a witness to this situation, what should you do? Audience-bystanders are provided with a phone number where they can report their observations and reply to prompts from an automated voice assistant. Help is on its way soon.

Text and direction by Olivier Choinière (L'ACTIVITÉ). Performed by Guillaume Chouinard, Emilie Gilbert, Jean-Sébastien Lavoie, and Philippe Racine. Voice assistants Andréanne Daigle, Rosalie Leblanc Houle, Audrey Perreault, and Gabrielle Poulin. Presented at Place des festivals (Montréal, Quebec), August–September 2020.

WITNESS

THE LETTUCE HEAD EXPERIENCE

An all-ages pop-up participatory dance event in a local farmer's market.

Choreography by Alyssa Martin (Rock Bottom Movement) and music by Jacob Vanderham (Telehorn). Presented at SummerWorks Festival (Toronto, Ontario), August 2023.

JOY

LONG DISTANCE RELATIONSHIPS FOR MYTHICAL TIMES

Three interwoven stories about love across distance accompany a dinner party for ten with tea and homemade food. At the end, audience-diners contribute their own relationship advice to a crowdsourced collection.

Created and conceived by Gloria Mok with Theatre du Poulet (Carmen Lee and Roland Chun Shing Au). Performed by Gloria Mok. Produced by 2b theatre company. Premiered at Halifax Central Library (Halifax, Nova Scotia), September 2021. We participated in August 2022 at the SummerWorks Festival (Toronto, Ontario).

CREW, OPT OUT

LOST TOGETHER

The story of something that I have lost is shared through a gentle solo interview with the two performers. Following these revelations, the two work together to craft an impressionistic, miniature sculpture of my loss, which is effectively returned to me.

Created by Shira Leuchter. Performed by Shira Leuchter and Michaela Washburn. Sound Design by Chris Hanratty. Premiered at SummerWorks Festival (Toronto, Ontario), August 2018. We participated in February 2019 at the Theatre Centre, Progress Festival (Toronto, Ontario).

SURROGATION, AUTOPOIESIS, TOGETHER ALONE, STICKINESS, AUTOBIOGRAPHY, MAD LIBS, US, GUIDES, LABOUR

LOVE WITHOUT LATE FEES

(see TAPE ESCAPE)

GAME OVER. PLAY AGAIN?, ALEA, GOING ROGUE, EMERGENCE

MANUAL

In this guided one-on-one exploration of a library, audiences play nearly silent games and whisper stories among the stacks. We point, we turn the pages of a picture book, we contemplate the past and the future of these books.

Created by Adam Kinner and Christopher Willes. Dramaturgy by Hanna Sybille Müller. Performed by Adam Kinner, Hanna Sybille Müller, Christopher Willes, Alexa Mardon, Chao-Ying Rao, and Denise Kenney. Premiered at OFFTA (Montréal, Quebec), June 2022.

OSTRANENIE

MÉGAPHONE

An outdoor, interactive, urban art installation featuring a microphone connected to a large red megaphone. Nightly, Montrealers speak and their speeches are amplified and turned into video projections and other responsive visual effects on the facade of a nearby building.

Created by Moment Factory. Directed by Étienne Paquette. Presented at Quartier des spectacles (Montréal, Quebec), September–November 2013.

MAD LIBS, JUICINESS

MINISTRY OF MUNDANE MYSTERIES

The personal mundane mysteries of audience-callers are investigated in a series of short daily episodes. Audiences co-improvise the dialogue over the phone with a rotating cast of characters.

Created by Nick Blais, Katherine Cullen, Mitchell Cushman, Anahita Dehbonehie, Colin Doyle, Sébastien Heins, Amy Keating, and Griffin McInnes. Produced by Outside the March (Toronto, Ontario). Premiered in March 2020.

PHONES, US, PHONY MULTIPLICITY, TOUR

MONDAY NIGHTS

Performed on a basketball court inside a theatre, the show invites audiences to join one of four teams. They participate in basketball drills and play 3-on-3 under the wise tutelage of their team captains.

Created and performed by Byron Abalos, Colin Doyle, Darrel Gamotin, Richard Lee, and Jeff Yung (6th Man Collective). Premiered at the Theatre Centre (Toronto, Ontario), September 2014. We participated in July 2017 at the Kick & Push Festival (Kingston, Ontario).

BAD FAITH, PLAYGROUNDS, ALEA, GUIDES, UNWELCOME, ONTOLOGICAL DUALITY

NEW AGE ATTITUDES: LIVE IN CONCERT

Subtitled "a lo-fi listen," the show arrives as a CD-size booklet in the mail. In combination with the pop-up book of lyrics and in-between-the-songs banter, the concert is a DIY experience since you have to imagine the music.

Created by Amanda Sum. Presented at PushOFF Festival (Vancouver, British Columbia), February 2021. Subsequently, New Age Attitudes was released as an album (with actual music) in September 2022. The video for "Better Than Before," directed by Mayumi Yoshida, was nominated for a Juno Award in 2023.

MAIL

NEW SOCIETIES

In teams of four to six people, audience-players are tasked with creating a utopia while overcoming various evolving catastrophes in this theatrical tabletop game. As the evening unfolds, there are opportunities for improvisation and for collaboration among the divisions.

Conceived and directed by Brian Postalian. Featuring Sena Cagla, Howard Dai, Alexa Fraser, Evan Medd, Hannah Meyers, Brian Postalian, Pascal Reiners, Amanda Sum, Meagan Woods, Montserrat Videla, Patrick Dodd, and Maria Escolan. Produced by Re:Current Theatre. Premiered at Simon Fraser University (Vancouver, British Columbia), September 2019. We participated in August 2020 via Zoom at the Kick & Push Festival (Kingston, Ontario).

DISSENSUS, KILLJOY

NO SAVE POINTS

Using sensors attached to the actor's body, the autobiographical protagonist becomes a literal puppet-avatar of the audience members who control his actions using a Game Boy interface to navigate live video-game challenges.

Created and performed by Sébastien Heins. Directed by Mitchell Cushman and Sébastien Heins. Produced by Outside the March. Premiered at the Lighthouse Artspace (Toronto, Ontario), June–July 2023.

REMOTE CONTROL

ONLINE JOY EDIT

A series of intimate duet activities for audience and performer—singing, dancing, poetry, *Animal Crossing*, photo portraiture—taking place online over various communications channels.

Created by fu-GEN theatre (Toronto, Ontario). Featuring Maddie Bautista, Natalie Tin Yin Gan, Vienna Hehir and Luigi Ceccon, Aaron Jan, Ming-Bo Lam, Janice Jo Lee, Miquelon Rodriguez, and André Dae Kim. Presented online in April 2020.

JOY

PERFECT STRANGERS

Audience members pair up to get to know each other through a guided questionnaire while walking the city. The two leave a trail of Post-it Notes behind them—a fleeting archive of their relationship.

Created by June Fukumura and Keely O'Brien (Popcorn Galaxies). Premiered at Richmond Culture Days (Richmond, British Columbia), September 2018.

US, INTIMACY, ONTOLOGICAL DUALITY

PLAYS2PERFORM@HOME

Four specially commissioned play-sets mailed to your door to be read aloud together in your pandemic "bubble."

Created by Boca del Lupo. The original set includes *Super* by Tara Beagan, *Negotiations* by Hiro Kanagawa, *Where does that blue come from? That robin's egg blue?* by Karen Hines, and *Pappadum* by Jovanni Sy. Published summer 2020.

ACTING, NEGOTIATION, ALEA, PHONY MULTIPLICITY

POLLINATORS

Guided by native species and the ecological process, audience-gardeners learn how to assemble seed balls, plant them, and contribute to their sustained presence on the land.

Produced by Yarrow Collective, who are lead gardener and co-producer Sammie Gough and dramaturg and co-producer Laurel Green. First presented as part of Theatre SKAM's SKAMpede (Victoria, British Columbia), July 2021.

LAND

POLYMORPHIC MICROBE BODIES

Swaddled in yellow-and-blue soft blankets, audience-microbes are immersed in a multisensory dance work.

Choreography and performance by Hanna Sybille Müller. Choreography, poetry, and sound by Erin Robinsong. Musician and sound designer Michel F. Côté. Featuring Lara Oundjian, Diego Gil, Emmanuel Jouthe, Rachel Harris, and Mathi Loslier-Pellerin. Presented at OFFTA (Montréal, Quebec), June 2023.

HANDS

RED PHONE

A series of five-minute scripted dialogues for two audience-actors set in two hand-crafted, fully enclosed phone booths outfitted with a vintage red phone and an integrated teleprompter.

Conceived by Sherry J. Yoon and designed by Jay Dodge with technology by Carey Dodge. Produced by Boca del Lupo. Premiered at the Fishbowl in collaboration with Vancouver Writers Fest, October 2016. We participated in January 2023 at Granville Island, Vancouver. Our script was *Out of the Blue* by Hiro Kanagawa.

PHONY MULTIPLICITY, ACTING, ALEA, THE MATRIX

REMIXED

A mixed-media listening party in which each audience member receives a personal playlist of true stories and music on the theme of change. Interspersed on the audio track are instructions guiding audiences to assemble a mini workspace and plant a radish seed.

Created by Trophy. Directed and produced by Sarah Conn. Dramaturg Laurel Green. Premiered at the In the Soil Arts Festival (St. Catharines, Ontario), June 2020. We participated in February 2021 at the undercurrents Festival (Ottawa, Ontario).

SEEDS, AUTOBIOGRAPHY, REMOTE CONTROL

REVELATIONS

Your household teams up (or competes) with other household-teams to develop a game strategy to survive the impending apocalypse. Some of you survive, some don't. Everyone gets cupcakes.

Created and directed by Anahita Dehbonehie, Griffin McInnes, and Aidan Morishita-Miki. Presented at the Kick & Push Festival (Kingston, Ontario), August–September 2020.

CRISIS

ROLL MODELS

The role-playing game *Dungeons & Dragons* is adapted into a live stage show. Four audience players create characters embodied by a cast of performer-avatars. Under the guidance of the dungeon master/emcee, the two groups work together to improvise a fantasy story.

Produced by the Art Folk Collective. Featuring Tyler Check, Sayer Roberts, Alicia Barban, Josh Blackstock, and Callum Lurie. Presented at the Kick & Push Festival (Kingston, Ontario), August 2021.

ALEA, CHEATING

SAVING WONDERLAND

Gathered online, the audience-collective interacts with characters from *Alice in Wonderland* and works together via a custom app to solve puzzles and save Wonderland from digital degradation by the Jabberwock.

Produced by David Carpenter and Gamiotics Studio. Written by David Andrew Laws, Kevin Hammonds, Attilio Rigotti, and Jacob Thompson. Directed by Attilio Rigotti. Presented at the Next Stage Theatre Festival (Toronto, Ontario), January 2022.

LIVENESS, US, ACTING, GUIDES

SEIJI'S PERFECT DAY

Using a Mad Libs–inspired template, audience members are invited to fill-in-the-blanks to describe the perfect day they've designed for a person they love. Afterwards, audience-writers are encouraged to phone a hotline and record their version of the story.

Produced by Popcorn Galaxies (June Fukumura and Keely O'Brien). Presented at the PushOFF Festival (Vancouver, British Columbia), February 2021.

MAD LIBS

SENSORYBOX

Guided by the voice of performer Mike Tan, blindfolded audience members uncover the mysterious contents of the box from the safety of their own home (or as one of a very limited audience of twenty in the theatre).

Directed and co-written by Eric Rose. Co-written by Christopher Duthie. Featuring Mike Tan. Premiered at Ghost River Theatre Workshop (Calgary, Alberta) and online, June 2020.

HANDS, GUIDES

SMARTSMART

Audience-participants craft fashionable outfits for their cellphones. Once dressed, the phones view a private theatre experience.

Written and performed by Adrienne Wong. Premiered at PushOFF (Vancouver, British Columbia), January 2023.

CRAFTS .

SOME MUST WATCH WHILE SOME MUST SLEEP

Through text messaging, audiences participate in word games and other question-and-answer improvisations with Tanya and with their "sleep persona," named X. Stretching over fourteen nights, the show is an intimate exploration of dreams and nightmares. And friendship.

Written and performed by Tanya Marquardt. Directed by Fay Nass. Music composed by Omar Zubair. Coding dramaturgy by Ainsley Ellia. Dramaturgy by Heidi Taylor. We participated in June 2021 at the Festival of Live Digital Art (Kingston, Ontario).

TEXT MESSAGES, INTIMACY, PHONES

SOON, TOMORROW MAYBE

The phone rings and the show begins. Over the course of a one-hour phone call, the audience converses with a woman who says she is your mother. A meditation on postpartum depression and the ambivalence of parenthood.

Created, written, and directed by Marie Ayotte. Presented by Théâtre Déchaînés (Montréal, Quebec), September–October 2021.

PHONES, ENCOUNTER

TAMARA

One of the earliest immersive, mobile audience theatreworks.

Written by John Krizanc. Directed by Richard Rose. Featuring Roger A. McKeen, Ian Black, Ramiro Puerta, Pátricia Nember, Frank Canino, Shelley Thompson, Denise Naples, Angelo Pedari, Maggie Huculak, and Mary Hawkins. Premiered at Strachan House (Toronto, Ontario), May 1981. The show subsequently toured for extended runs in both New York (1987–1992) and Los Angeles (1984–1993).

FASCISM, SHOPPING, BOUNDARY VIOLATIONS, COMPLICITY, GHOSTS, PHONY MULTIPLICITY, GAME OVER. PLAY AGAIN?

TAPE ESCAPE

Escape room meets immersive performance set in a 90s video store with three separate game-plays. The three "In-Store Rentals" are *Love Without Late Fees*, *A Grown-Up's Guide to Flying*, and *Yesterday's Heroes*.

Co-created by Vanessa Smythe, Mitchell Cushman, and Nick Bottomley. Presented by Outside the March in the former home of Queen Video (Toronto, Ontario), July 2019.

GAME OVER. PLAY AGAIN?, ALEA, GOING ROGUE, EMERGENCE, BAD FAITH

TBD

Beginning with your "death," this immersive, twenty-one-day performance infiltrates your life to offer a mediation on the nature of what meaning our life carries. Audience-participants attend special events solo and in groups, are met by strangers in their everyday lives, and receive packages and text messages.

Written and created by Jesse Garlick, Andreas Kahre, Andrew Laurenson, Billy Marchenski, Stefan Smulovitz, Emelia Symington Fedy, Paul Ternes, and Robyn Volk. Presented by Radix Theatre (Vancouver, British Columbia), October–November 2015.

SNEAKY NINJAS, CONSENT, ACTING, US

THE STRANGER 2.0: ABOVE & BELOW

Unfolding in two complementary halves, the show offers a playful experience for audience-friend pairs. We play hide-and-seek, dance down the sidewalk, paint walls, feel the vibrations of singing bowls massage therapy, and cross paths with other alt-universe audience-pairs.

Written and directed by Daniele Bartolini (DLT: Dopo Lavoro Teatrale) with a virtual-reality scene produced and developed by Toasterlab. We participated in September 2019 in Toronto, Ontario.

AROUSAL, BEING LOST, EMERGENCE, GUIDES, SECRET WEIRDOS

THIS IS NOWHERE

Wandering audiences are led on a city-wide scavenger hunt, led by a custom app that offered personal, timed puzzle clues. Scenes are discovered at twelve different stations where the Halifax of the past collides with the Halifax of the future.

Principal writer Kate Cayley. Conceived and directed by Alex McLean with Stewart Legere, Kathryn McCormack, Liliona Quarmyne, and Ben Stone. App developed by Andrew Burke. Presented by Zuppa Theatre Co. (Halifax, Nova Scotia), September 2018.

NOISE, SLACK, SHOPPING, SNEAKY NINJAS

THIS IS THE STORY OF THE CHILD RULED BY FEAR

Accompanying narrator and playwright David Gagnon Walker, self-selected audience-participants read roles in the show. Venturing into the unknown of the show-event, we all take turns reading the part of the Child and together work through our collective anxieties.

Written and performed by David Gagnon Walker. Directed by Christian Barry and Judy Wensel. Premiered at Found Festival (Edmonton, Alberta), July 2021. We participated in August 2022 at SummerWorks Festival (Toronto, Ontario).

CONSENT, US, ACTING, PHONY MULTIPLICITY

THROUGH MY LENS

Facing large, wall-sized images taken by photographer Amy Amantea, the solo audience-participant recounts what they see back to Amy, describing the photos which Amy, who has a lived experience of blindness, has not seen in the same way.

Written and performed by Amy Amantea. Written and directed by James Long. Premiered at Vines Festival (Vancouver, British Columbia), August 2021. We participated in June 2022 and June 2023 at the Festival of Live Digital Art (Kingston, Ontario).

TEA, EMERGENCE, LABOUR, MAD LIBS

TO YOU

A pop-up performance of your birthday celebration, staged on your own porch or driveway during the early lockdown phase of the COVID-19 pandemic.

Created by Laura Chaignon, Mariah Horner, and Kay Kenney. Presented by Cellar Door Project (Kingston, Ontario), May 2020.

SEEDS, FRIENDSHIP, ACTING, REMOTE CONTROL

WALK WALK DANCE

Participants walk, jump, roll, run, and dance on lines along the ground to create outdoor music in public spaces.

Created and produced by Daily tous les jours. Creative direction by Mouna Andraos and Melissa Mongiat. Presented in prototype form in June 2020 (Montréal, Quebec). Premiered at the Bentway (Toronto, Ontario), June–July 2021.

GOING ROGUE, CHOOSE YOUR OWN ADVENTURE

WHY WE ARE HERE

A site-specific drop-in choir where music is performed by the audience in venues that are normally not accessible for group singing like the Toronto Island Ferry, or city council chambers.

Created by Brian Quirt and Martin Julien. Produced by Nightswimming. Performed at various locations across Toronto, Ontario, in October– November 2012.

JOY, US, ACTING

WORRY WARTS

At the "Worry Depot" audience-participants anonymously share their worries through a series of activities including confessional dialogue with a "Keeper" and small-scale crafts like a paper chain of different colour-coded worry categories.

Conceived and directed by Julie Tepperman (Convergence Theatre). Designed by Anahita Dehbonehie. Featuring and co-created by Noah Beemer, Katherine Cullen, Colin A. Doyle, Sadie Epstein-Fine, Tal Katz, Jajube Mandiela, Faly Mevamanana, Natasha Ramondino, Tennille Read, Tymika Tafari, Julie Tepperman, Andy Trithardt, Margarita Valderrama, and Arielle Zamora. Presented at the SummerWorks Festival (Toronto, Ontario), August 2019.

AUTOBIOGRAPHY, ONTOLOGICAL DUALITY

YESTERDAY'S HEROES

(see TAPE ESCAPE)

GAME OVER. PLAY AGAIN?, BAD FAITH

THE ZOMBIE SYNDROME

Teams of audience-players, each with different "powers," work collaboratively with live actors in a large-scale, outdoors scavenger-hunt experience to prevent the zombie apocalypse.

Director, playwright, and producer Andy Thompson. Between 2012 and 2016, the show featured different episodes performed at different locations in and around Vancouver, British Columbia.

GOING ROGUE, SECRET WEIRDOS

INDEX

A

Aarseth, Espen J., 83–84, 126–27, 190, 224–25, 348

Abalos, Byron, 55, 473

abandonment, 41, 57, 177

abolition, 107, 158–60, 253

Abraham, Chris, 455

absurdity, 32, 184

abundance, 263, 294, 344

activists, 13, 34, 158, 211, 319, 342

adaptations, 173, 323, 463

Adilman, Nobu, 27, 35, 220–221, 431, 459

adrenaline, 37, 186, 251, 295, 306, 357

advertisers, 86, 387

affection, 135, 157, 283, 304, 402

Aga Khan Museum, 201

agôn, 29, 65, 186, 242

Aguirre, Carmen, 178–79, 389, 392, 458

Ahmed, Sara, 206

Alexander, Leigh, 126

algorithms, 125, 127, 310

Alice of Wonderland, 24, 178, 221, 396, 430–431, 478

aliens, 83, 310

Almbaidin, Yousef, 314

Alnaser, Ameen, 314–15, 462

alogical elements, 97

Alston, Adam, 130, 152, 210–211, 357

Altman, Rick, 219

Alvarez, Natalie, 149

Alvis, Cole, 74

Amantea, Amy, 63–64, 483

Amazing Race, The, 68, 309

ambiguity, 99, 169, 190, 267, 332, 338, 354

ambivalence, 292, 382, 479

American Sign Language (ASL), 316, 394

ancestors, 74, 214, 217, 314, 411, 427

anger, 111–12, 208, 358

Anishinaabe, 102, 246, 344, 444

announcements, 40, 113, 176

anoxia, 161, 466

Anthropocene Epoch, 6, 106, 344, 398

anthropology, 38, 102

anxiety, 24–25, 37, 39–40, 45–47, 57, 176–77, 353

apartments, 119, 121, 157, 262

apocalypse, 105, 174, 477, 485

applause, 241, 250, 334, 421

applications, 8, 261–62, 264, 328–29, 369, 372–73, 430, 469, 478, 482

Apter, Michael J., 37, 230

architects, 106, 226, 418

archives, 1–2, 6, 79, 84–85, 111, 155, 178, 196, 220, 223, 299, 340, 346–48, 455, 475

Aristotle, 163, 182, 241, 421

arms, 23, 39, 103, 132, 180, 186, 201

Arnstein, Sherry R., 421

Artaud, Antonin, 17–19, 278, 384, 391

Artificial Hells (Bishop), 88–90, 110, 130, 285, 328, 331

asymmetry, 41–43, 121, 169, 469

asynchronicity, 279, 402

attendance, 10, 88, 250, 400, 425, 434

"Audience Participation and Neoliberal Value" (Alston), 152, 210–211

Audience Participation in Theatre (White), 130, 178, 193, 285, 313, 316, 398, 406, 408, 427

audio, 25, 101–02, 117, 155, 165, 195, 209, 226, 245–46, 257, 290, 334, 346, 386, 399–401, 456, 477

audio narration, 120, 455, 469

audiowalks, 42, 117–18, 226, 289, 456, 460

Auslander, Philip, 219

Austin, J.L., 230, 265

authenticity, 21, 37, 212, 294, 318, 338, 363

authority, 78, 261, 318, 427–28

autonomy, 49, 105, 192, 237, 318, 354, 382, 443

avatars, 30, 32, 43, 57, 83, 147, 163, 241–43, 251, 271, 300–302, 329

Ayotte, Marie, 131, 291, 479

B

balance, 3, 32, 58, 64, 92, 112, 201, 299

Ball, David, 95, 163

Banff, AB, 12, 58, 101, 301, 398, 444, 456, 467

banter, 235, 473

barriers, 9, 77, 251, 316, 321, 355–56, 391, 406, 461

Barthes, Roland, 347, 400

Bartolini, Daniele, 397, 454, 470, 481

basketball, 9, 55–56, 170, 179, 242–43, 266, 298, 300, 363, 473

Batavia, Hima, 156, 204, 466

Bautista, Maddie, 63–64, 202–04, 397, 453

beaches, 11, 14, 59, 418–19

Beagan, Tara, 26, 475

beer, 251, 418

Belmore, Rebecca, 444–45

benches, 222, 224, 269, 406

Bennett, Jane, 99, 191–92, 409–11

Bennett, Susan, 190–191, 225

Bentway, The (Toronto), 86, 300, 483

Beuys, Joseph, 470

bicycles, 117, 128, 184, 212, 383

billboards, 140, 440, 464

birds, 39, 125, 127, 140, 186, 310, 328, 347, 418

blankets, 63, 185, 334, 351, 393, 399, 476

Blenkarn, Patrick, 109, 213, 251, 299, 301, 396, 456

blindness, 127, 165, 393, 483

blogs, 86, 206, 419, 438

blood, 39, 201, 332, 391–92, 401

Bloordale Village, 180, 417–19

Bloor Street, 417, 419

bluemouth inc., 58–59, 94, 120, 250, 305, 458, 468

Boal, Augusto, 104, 146, 178, 278

Boca del Lupo, 26, 255–56, 289, 294, 475

boldness, 67, 211, 250, 302

Bonnell, Yolanda, 74–76

borders, 9, 12, 91, 148–49, 216, 229, 265–66, 283, 311, 338, 394, 423, 425, 428

boredom, 79, 173

Bourriaud, Nicolas, 34, 88, 129–32, 134, 214–15, 383, 432–33

bowls, 46, 75, 336, 354

boxes, 26, 101, 121, 125–26, 183–84, 255, 304, 369, 372, 478

Braedley, Susan, 88, 273

brains, 44, 125, 234, 373, 389–90, 392, 414

branching narratives, 31, 42, 83, 162, 346, 362

bravery, 9, 11, 15, 38, 55–56, 96, 304, 318, 407–08, 431

Brecht, Bertolt, 17–19, 70, 191, 278, 384

Breel, Astrid, 293–94

bricks, 9, 14, 38, 224, 251, 356, 391, 406

bridges, 77, 128, 134, 146, 191, 234, 237, 241, 279, 305–06

Broadway, 62, 307–08, 318

Broken Telephone, 261

brown, adrienne maree, 34, 343–44

buses, 11, 24, 39, 131, 169, 245, 433, 457

buttons, 79, 148, 174, 252, 330, 396, 431

bylaws, 126, 140, 464

bystanders, 181, 309, 340–341

C

Caillois, Roger, 29, 65, 67, 78, 165, 186, 229, 231, 242, 339–40

Calgary, AB, 12, 42, 139, 184, 442, 457, 464, 469, 478

camouflage, 67, 81, 336, 338, 340

Campbell, Jordan, 63–64, 397, 453

Canadian Broadcasting Corporation (CBC), 74, 444

candies, 46, 176, 184

candles, 156, 203, 247, 414

canoes, 9, 59, 224, 317

canvases, 33, 153–54, 196

capital, 229, 286

  cultural, 274

  social, 250, 387

capitalism, 71, 75–77, 88, 99, 106–07, 117–18, 130, 134, 158, 209, 212, 344, 362, 411
  neoliberal, 44
  racial, 106, 159
Cardinal, Cliff, 67, 161, 466
Care Work (Piepzna-Samarasinha), 322–23, 353–54
Carlson, Marvin, 92, 281, 421
Carlson, Tim, 1, 91, 286, 453, 463
Casa Loma, 259, 369
Casey, Kathy, 64, 174, 468
cash, 63, 267, 453
catastrophe, 67, 104, 440, 474
categorization, 51, 219, 298
catharsis, 147, 347
Cayley, Kate, 347, 455
Ceccon, Luigi, 202, 475
celebrations, 9, 35, 81, 98, 157, 300, 334, 342
celebrities, 143, 223, 263, 365
chairs, 75, 80, 111, 140, 249, 251, 256, 279, 317, 321–22, 328, 386, 393, 397, 410
channels, 6, 21, 53, 105, 122, 151, 174, 177, 215, 220, 260, 294, 475
charm, 98, 195–96, 212, 222, 270, 291
chatting, 2, 202, 204, 221, 309, 394, 430
chess, 41, 172, 229, 242, 265–66
childhood, 46, 211, 302, 314, 333–34, 338, 424, 466
children, 10, 14, 46, 54, 80, 94, 131–32, 154–55, 157, 173, 271, 273, 346, 348, 407, 414, 427, 431, 438, 465
Choinière, Olivier, 289, 439, 441, 470
choirs, 27, 35–36, 202, 220, 250–251, 431, 459
Chomsky, Noam, 121
choreography, 157, 201, 277, 307–08, 321, 357, 394, 470, 476
cities, 35, 42, 117–20, 125–27, 129, 215, 226–27, 242–43, 261–64, 266, 286–87, 302, 369, 372, 388, 417, 419, 453, 460, 469
citizens, 109–10, 112–13, 154, 208, 273, 355, 421
cityscapes, 60, 117, 119, 413
civility, 109, 122, 243

climate, 7, 11, 13, 42, 106–07
clothes, 59, 92, 158, 347, 380, 404, 411
clowns, 230, 269–70, 304, 406, 457
clues, 10, 12, 24, 54, 131–32, 172, 244, 261–62, 298, 347, 372, 396–97, 455
coffee, 1, 10, 114, 121, 351, 361, 369, 413
collaboration, 34, 97, 129–30, 139–40, 172, 191, 207, 245, 251, 257, 287, 305, 443, 456, 461, 474, 476, 506
collages, 34–35, 164
collectivity, 158, 200–201, 250
colonialism, 74, 114, 208–09, 214, 217, 314, 318, 427, 438, 460
comedy, 26, 110, 164, 418, 442
comfort, 24–25, 38, 45, 59, 97, 131, 259, 270–271, 394, 416
commitment, 2, 56, 68, 78, 158, 190, 235, 343, 413, 438
commodities, 135, 362–63, 383, 425
communication, 52, 103, 114, 259–61, 273, 281, 289, 311, 313, 383, 398
communitas, 200–201
community, 86, 88–89, 120, 139–40, 155, 157, 214, 216, 250, 252, 256–57, 276–77, 309, 311, 354, 356, 387–88, 418–19, 432–34, 443–44
compensation, 204, 252, 288
competition, 29, 65, 105, 207, 362
confetti, 8, 56, 165
conflict, 112, 116, 159, 247–48, 356, 414–16
Conn, Sarah, 47, 135, 342, 477
connections, 51, 54, 76, 78, 131, 136, 155, 158, 220–221, 234, 241, 244–46, 290, 292, 343, 348, 351, 379–80, 387, 392
connectivity, 112, 216, 220
consciousness, 147–48, 191, 280, 355, 390
conspiracies, 232, 307, 309–10
constraints, 145, 294–95, 300, 335
consumers, 52, 89, 146, 154, 362–63
contact, 86, 89, 130, 154, 192, 200–201, 235, 249, 336–37, 368, 433
contamination, 104, 380
contemplation, 86, 152, 286, 347, 374
controllers, 43, 213, 251–52, 301–02, 328–29, 396
Convergence Theatre, 25, 45, 460

Conversation Pieces (Kester), 114, 281, 289, 311, 383–84
Cooke, Bill, 251, 319, 422–23
cookies, 251, 267
correspondence, 56, 109, 136, 247, 286
Costikyan, Greg, 30, 32, 62
COVID-19, 26, 86, 104–06, 202, 220–221, 258, 342
creativity, 6, 10, 98, 151, 298, 301, 333, 398, 442
crime, 18, 89, 330, 417
critiques, 7, 17, 19, 144, 151, 192, 212–13, 361, 382, 419, 421–22
crowds, 10, 59, 81, 94, 251, 306–07, 356–57
Csíkszentmihályi, Mihály, 295, 371
cues, 38, 110, 119, 181, 204, 221, 305, 332
culpability, 148, 162, 466
culture, 5, 7, 9, 34, 65, 71, 78, 169, 172, 227, 229, 337, 339, 346, 353, 362, 406, 408, 422, 426
cupcakes, 105, 157, 477
curiosity, 2, 21, 57, 120, 346, 427
Cushman, Mitchell, 163, 169–70, 457, 469, 472, 474, 480
customization, 44, 115, 212, 241
Cvetkovich, Ann, 98
Cybertext (Aarseth), 83–84, 126, 190, 224–25, 348

D

Dae Kim, André, 202, 475
Daisey, Mike, 44, 210, 272, 275
dance, 9, 18, 64, 67, 80, 100, 140, 157, 169, 173–74, 179–80, 186, 194, 202, 250–251, 277, 387–89, 391, 481, 483
Dance Dance Revolution, 302
danger, 30, 37–38, 161
Dault, Alex, 174, 406, 454
death, 33, 39, 95–96, 139, 161, 163, 232, 274, 373, 380, 400, 463, 481
Debajehmujig Storytellers, 215–16, 464
Debord, Guy, 88, 117–18
decolonization, 209, 216, 246, 252, 299, 318, 343, 441, 445
defamiliarization, 280–281
defences, 81, 242, 292, 336, 356

defiance, 77, 310, 392
Dehbonehie, Anahita, 472, 477, 484
delight, 32, 212, 319, 352
depression, 98, 132, 351–53, 479
design, 6, 13, 62, 126, 241, 252, 298–99, 301, 309, 363, 372, 396–97, 415, 465
designers, 33, 126, 128, 255, 311
destruction, 10, 106, 158, 172, 187, 214, 251, 253, 398, 400, 438
detachment, 65, 161, 402
detectives, 26, 178, 347
dialogue, 52–53, 129, 133, 195, 224, 245, 281, 289, 291, 302, 305, 307, 320–321, 347, 445, 472, 484
dice, 29–30, 32, 80, 231, 242
dictionaries, 9–10, 70, 128
Diderot, Denis, 69–70, 241
difference, 13, 41–42, 54, 112, 127, 229, 231, 281, 287, 299, 314, 329, 333, 339, 355–57, 371, 386, 429, 438
dilemmas, 105, 148, 169, 294, 302, 404
Dionysus, 332
direction, 8, 69, 79, 110, 117, 125, 236–37, 288, 313, 340, 470
directors, 96, 144, 192, 216, 255, 308, 329, 332, 343, 454, 485
disability, 115, 273, 285, 316–17, 321–23
discipline, 7, 29, 200, 410
disclosures, 94, 97
discomfort, 182, 208, 269, 319
disguises, 336, 339–40
disorientation, 58–60, 117
displacement, 170, 357
disruptions, 193, 250, 281, 308, 426
distance, 13, 17, 19, 67, 106, 120, 147, 156, 194, 236, 280, 283, 304, 306, 330, 341, 415, 471
distress, 94, 269, 341, 401, 440, 470
diversity, 11, 31, 109, 318, 321
Dodge, Jay, 26, 476
do-it-yourself (DIY), 37, 98, 140, 212
Dolan, Jill, 257, 432
donkeys, 213, 251–52, 299, 301–03, 456
doors, 42, 75, 85, 158, 262, 348
Doyle, Colin A., 45–47, 55, 300, 472–73, 484
dreams, 43, 135–36, 180, 194, 196, 209, 351–52, 354, 399–402, 404, 479

duality, 148, 181, 191, 225, 243, 265–66, 278, 287

Duchamp, Marcel, 129, 192

Dungeons & Dragons, 30, 79, 83, 477

Durkheim, Émile, 200–202

Duthie, Christopher, 184, 478

Düttman, Alexander García, 53, 177

E

ears, 1, 42, 95, 102, 112, 117–18, 182–83, 226, 290, 361, 399

economics, 107, 207, 272, 301, 322, 380, 459

ecosystems, 38, 182, 216, 390, 409

Edmonton, AB, 184, 482

education, 21, 89, 273, 276, 438, 442

elders, 76, 102–03, 215

Emancipated Spectator, The (Rancière), 18–19, 192, 413–14

emancipation, 43, 192

embarrassment, 68, 134, 154, 388

emotions, 44, 94, 111, 148, 154, 185–86, 202, 204, 241–44, 252, 361, 386, 389–90, 402

empathy, 147, 149, 305–06, 432–33

enactments, 22, 54, 79, 211, 237, 311, 355, 444

encouragement, 2, 178–79, 272, 301, 303

energy, 2, 19, 80, 111, 122, 130, 192, 201–02, 225, 229, 320, 348, 424, 443

entertainment, 8, 70, 88, 95, 238, 329, 333, 364, 387, 414

entropy, 127, 344

equality, 29, 353

errors, 2–3, 165, 357

escape rooms, 5, 10, 42, 54, 58, 68, 105, 163–64, 175, 178, 186, 259, 299, 368, 370–371, 397, 423, 430, 480

escaping, 12, 42, 105, 127, 163–64, 230, 247–48, 259, 299, 352, 368–70, 441

ethics, 57, 94, 129, 149, 207, 271, 286, 288

etiquette, 176, 358

Everyman, 39, 176, 380, 398, 463

exclusion, 89, 422–23, 428

experience economy, 362–63, 365

exploitation, 110, 113, 182

exploration, 57–58, 84, 96, 121, 140, 159, 190, 211, 257, 282, 299–300, 346, 348, 394, 408, 415, 417, 472, 479

exposition, 30, 163, 221

extraction, 106–07, 217, 362, 426

extractivism, 106, 209, 318, 425

eye contact, 196, 204, 224, 243, 433–34

F

failure, 32, 67, 148, 164, 175–76, 231, 320, 355–57, 364, 419, 441

fantasies, 19, 38, 241, 304

farmers' markets, 201, 470

fear, 11, 39, 57, 66, 68, 79, 95–96, 154, 177, 250, 294, 323, 362, 379–80, 427, 431, 482

feedback, 62, 125, 127, 162, 204–05, 301, 371

feedback loop, 49, 51, 127, 204, 245, 390

Feminist Killjoys (Ahmed), 206, 208

fences, 141, 280, 341, 418–19

Fensham, Rachel, 249

Festival of Live Digital Art (FOLDA), 35, 63, 221, 226, 394, 456, 459–60, 465, 479, 483

films, 7, 33, 35, 54, 84, 127, 220, 243, 257, 307–10, 356

fingers, 1, 147, 184, 236, 252, 274, 394, 396, 400, 434

Fischer-Lichte, Erika, 49–51, 69–70, 154, 183, 281

Fitz-James, Thea, 99

flash mobs, 9, 146, 277, 287

Fluxus Experience, 139, 311–12, 372

food, 14, 99, 101, 106, 140, 263, 312, 314, 321, 353, 357, 361, 363, 393, 471

forgiveness, 121, 290

Foucault, Michel, 60, 121, 409–10, 422

Fournier, Susanna, 151, 245, 248, 459

Foxconn, 44, 210, 272, 274–75

framework, 7, 11, 50, 74, 103, 109–10, 140, 159, 223, 246, 248, 278, 313, 318, 414, 417

freedom, 45, 64, 92, 99, 144–45, 158, 174, 216, 298

Freeman, Barry, 215–16

frictions, 32, 132, 280, 286, 292

INDEX

Fried, Michael, 382–84

Frieze, James, 17, 84, 109, 149, 153, 346

Fuchs, Elinor, 79, 361–62

fu-GEN Theatre, 202–03, 475

Fukumura, June, 136, 195–96, 238, 461, 475, 478

Fuller, Sarah, 101, 467

fun, 8, 78, 80, 139, 148, 158, 175, 179, 187, 208, 231, 243, 252, 257, 274, 288, 317, 333, 368, 370

funerals, 20, 98, 356, 461

G

galleries, 7, 85, 88, 196, 212, 227, 387–88, 393, 416

game behaviours, 65, 67

game design, 58, 78, 99, 126, 128, 172, 180, 229, 260, 288, 293, 298, 309, 370

game mechanics, 31–32, 178, 207, 299, 310, 332

Gamiotics Studio, 221, 478

Gamotin, Darrel, 55, 473

Gan, Natalie Tin Yin, 202–03, 475

gaps, 155, 210, 224–26, 277, 291, 313, 353, 357, 506

garages, 253, 280, 373

garbage, 347, 410, 417

gardens, 10, 42, 139, 216–17, 292, 342, 344

Garneau, David, 76, 336–37, 425

gates, 8, 32, 41, 58, 302

gaze, 19, 118–19, 134, 147–48, 235, 265, 282, 290, 387, 400, 402, 425, 433

gender, 98, 155, 235, 250, 285–86, 305, 357, 400, 407

generations, 6, 103, 214, 434

genocide, 11, 114, 226, 423, 438

geography, 11–12, 42, 180, 211, 214, 235, 250, 256, 298, 396, 398

Gerould, Daniel, 241, 421

gestures, 23, 69, 75, 90, 135, 180, 272, 305, 310, 343, 389, 391, 443

Gibson, James J., 397–98

gifts, 9, 204–05, 216, 235, 323, 331, 342–43, 354, 384, 393, 416

Gilmore, James H., 362–63

gimmicks, 90, 304, 422

glasses, 146, 182, 187, 236–37, 316

Gleick, James, 260

globalization, 106

Goldman, Daveed, 27, 35, 220–221, 431, 459

governments, 14, 31, 76, 89, 109, 179, 286, 330, 379, 421, 444

Grasshopper, The (Suits), 78, 172, 231, 260–261, 266, 340, 370

graves, 39, 102, 438, 463

Green, Laurel, 217, 331, 342, 456

Guattari, Félix, 118, 433

H

hair, 14, 154–56, 182, 187, 201, 332, 465–66

Halifax, NS, 117, 158, 215, 261, 263–64, 346, 364, 369, 455, 464, 469, 471, 482

Hamlet (Shakespeare), 52–54, 57–58, 71, 176–78, 265, 275, 311, 313

Hamlet on the Holodeck (Murray), 57, 177, 313

happiness, 89, 115, 175, 202, 206, 439

harm, 13, 37, 158–60, 230, 247, 251, 271, 351, 353

Harpin, Anna, 130, 346

Harris, Rachel, 468, 476

Harvey, Dustin, 64, 117–19, 340, 469

Harvie, Jen, 112, 165, 211, 273

health, 46, 88, 208, 273, 354, 379

Heath, Stephen, 191, 400

Heddon, Deirdre, 135, 153, 269, 319, 337

Heins, Sébastien, 42, 328–31, 469, 472, 474

High Performance Rodeo, 457

Hines, Karen, 26, 475

hobbies, 99, 267

honesty, 81, 196

host, 2, 6, 31, 91–92, 179, 184, 204, 430, 463

Houston, Andrew, 59, 139–40, 417

Howells, Adrian, 153, 319

Huculak, Maggie, 462, 480

hugging, 22–23, 296, 319

Huizinga, Johan, 78, 172, 229, 339–40

humans, 6, 14, 30, 58, 101, 115, 118, 147, 162, 216, 286, 343–44, 397, 410, 467

humour, 10, 21, 454
hypertext, 11, 83–84, 263, 346
hypocrisy, 45, 78, 208

I

identities, 64, 122, 172, 178, 191, 241–42,
    281, 286–87, 364, 383, 400, 404
ideology, 70–71, 120, 191
"Imaginary Spaces of Conciliation
    and Reconciliation" (Garneau), 76,
    336–37, 425
imagination, 9, 11, 191, 225, 245, 298,
    300, 344, 392, 400
Imagined Theatres (Sack, ed.), 9, 11, 426
immersion, 62, 66, 149, 152, 181, 259,
    346, 352, 356–57, 361
immersive environments, 22, 57, 84,
    146, 210, 357
immersive theatre, 39, 130, 151–53, 169,
    210–211, 243, 259, 357, 404, 422
immigration, 314, 427, 462
improvisation, 25, 30, 32, 79, 115, 204,
    207, 270, 282, 304, 357, 388, 392, 442,
    457, 460, 474, 477, 479
inclusivity, 109, 148, 154, 208, 261, 422
Indigenous knowledge, 102, 214–15,
    318–19, 336, 344, 409, 426, 444
Indigenous people, 74–77, 111, 113,
    214–16, 226, 409, 438, 444–45, 464
Indigenous performance, 74–77, 426
Indigenous sovereignty, 319, 426–27
individuality, 44, 200, 288, 353, 429
insecurity, 38–39, 42, 91, 129, 176, 232,
    286, 311, 355, 379–80, 504
*Insecurity: Perils and Products of
    Theatres of the Real* (Stephenson), 39,
    42, 91, 129, 176, 232, 286, 355, 380, 504
Instagram, 6, 9, 364, 506
instructions, 5, 10, 98, 177–80, 182–84,
    224, 234, 237, 252, 261, 282–83, 285,
    296, 301, 312–14, 372–73, 396–97, 411,
    415, 417
intelligence, 2, 256, 276, 310, 363
    collective, 194, 257
interactivity, 5, 79, 86, 114, 174, 216, 267,
    289, 301, 307, 312–13, 364, 442
introspection, 39, 205, 236, 246

invisibility, 119, 180, 237, 257, 290, 404
Iser, Wolfgang, 191–92, 225

J

Jacobs, Jane, 139, 417
Jan, Aaron, 202, 475
Johnson, Molly, 280, 397, 458
jokes, 180, 184, 270, 307, 393, 408, 418
Julien, Martin, 201, 484
Jürs-Munby, Karen, 70, 179, 357

K

Kanagawa, Hiro, 26–27, 255–56, 258,
    295, 475–76
Kaprow, Allan, 97, 245, 406, 408
karaoke, 194–95, 467
Karry, Liam, 174, 406, 454, 463
Kasman, Shari, 180, 417–19
Kester, Grant, 114, 152, 281, 289, 311, 383–84
Khakpour, Aryo, 91, 463
Kick & Push Festival, 454, 469, 473–
    74, 477
Kinew, Wab, 438–39, 441
King, Martin Luther, Jr., 262
Kingston, ON, 1, 12–13, 35, 76, 157, 226, 255,
    291, 394, 454, 456, 459–60, 463, 465–66,
    469, 473–74, 477, 479, 483, 505
Kinner, Adam, 282, 472
Kirby, Michael, 97, 101, 405
kissing, 152, 270, 382, 407
Kitchener, ON, 42, 117, 469
kitchens, 119, 140, 184, 221, 314, 352
Klein, Naomi, 106–07
Knowles, Ric, 143–44
Kolesch, Doris, 118, 122, 146, 152, 370
Kothari, Uma, 251, 319, 422–23
Krizanc, John, 143–44, 480

L

Lam, Ming-Bo, 202, 475
Lam, Richard, 159, 247–48, 414–15, 459
landscapes, 42, 57, 70, 102, 177, 182, 190,
    196, 224, 302, 397–98, 458, 467
language, 8, 127–28, 182, 185, 216, 230,
    274, 280, 357, 370, 390, 394, 408, 443

Laurenson, Andrew, 232, 481
Lauzon, Jani, 75–76
laws, 57, 65, 94, 143, 177, 263, 339, 372
leaders, 21, 110, 154, 180, 302, 310, 313, 333, 351, 430, 438
Lee, Richard, 55, 473
Legere, Stewart, 347, 455, 482
Lehmann, Hans-Thies, 70, 179–80, 249, 357
lemonade, 205, 280, 341, 458
Lemon Bucket Orkestra, 22, 355–56, 461
lemons, 9, 205, 226, 243, 280–281, 320, 341, 458
letters, 106, 136, 151, 220, 235–36, 238, 246, 331, 401, 434
Leuchter, Shira, 1, 50, 380, 386–87, 415, 471
liability, 38, 94, 408
libraries, 85, 131, 277, 282–83, 340, 346–47, 351, 413, 434, 455, 472
Lilith & Cie, 64, 174, 194, 253, 256, 468
Lim, Milton, 91, 213, 251, 299, 301, 396, 456, 463
limbs, 20, 176, 236, 382
limitations, 14, 84, 251, 296, 321, 423–24
listeners, 7, 112, 151, 195, 311, 456
listening, 63, 111–12, 165, 222, 235, 246, 279, 343, 386, 438, 445
liveness, 219–22, 234, 356, 459, 462, 478
logic, 13, 31, 131, 163, 207, 266, 309, 426
Long, James, 63–64, 483
Loring, Kevin, 216, 343
loss, 23, 25, 44, 51, 57, 65, 122, 177, 202, 206, 217, 221, 251, 323, 349, 380, 386–88, 416, 429, 441
Luminato Festival, 74, 86, 397
Luxton, Meg, 88, 273
Lynch, Signy, 2, 26, 134
lyrics, 35, 221, 235, 307, 457, 459, 473

M

machines, 10, 99, 130, 226–27, 405, 411
Machon, Josephine, 152–53
Magelssen, Scott, 21, 104–05, 149, 355
Magnat, Virginie, 409
Maidan Square, Kyiv, 22, 355–56
Maiese, Michelle, 389–90

maintenance, 2, 68, 214, 231, 265, 341, 440
manidoons collective, 74
manifestos, 59, 252
manipulation, 44, 57, 99, 152, 224, 293
maps, 2, 38, 43, 58–59, 78, 102, 147, 190, 216, 236, 286, 371, 439
Marczyk, Marichka, 22, 355, 461
Marquardt, Tanya, 47, 194, 399, 479
Martin, Alyssa, 201, 470
Martin, Keavy, 76, 336, 425
Martini, Michael, 212, 459
masks, 31, 105, 256, 355, 399
materiality, 139, 260, 281, 299, 342, 409–11
McInnes, Griffin, 105, 472, 477
McLean, Alex, 1, 347, 455, 482
McLeod, Dayna, 195, 467
media, 7, 74, 143, 219–20, 260, 263, 383
    social, 13, 212, 221, 329, 387
medicine, 74–77, 102
meditation, 40, 179, 232, 236, 245–46, 248, 353, 361, 416, 465, 479
megaphones, 227, 444–45, 472
melancholy, 23, 54, 164, 171, 243, 347, 364, 386
memory, 21, 23, 26, 42–43, 46, 50, 77, 158, 185, 203, 238, 245, 261, 292, 323, 334, 386–88, 402, 409, 411
Merleau-Ponty, Maurice, 147
Mesiha, David, 91, 456, 463
messiness, 92, 344, 380
metaphors, 161, 214, 217, 242, 266, 273–74, 299, 330, 332–33, 435
metatheatricality, 53, 262, 296, 352, 404
Métis, 74–75, 336, 425
microphones, 185, 219, 227, 235, 260, 445, 472
mimesis, 20, 70, 179, 230, 305, 357, 406
mimicry, 10, 31, 104, 186, 242, 306, 356, 362
Modernism, 79, 361
money, 46, 63, 70, 134, 179, 212, 229, 244, 267, 319, 323
monologues, 9, 55, 91, 161, 179, 221, 289, 426
Monopoly, 147, 298
Montola, Markus, 148, 309, 372

Montréal, QC, 101, 173, 182, 185, 187, 223, 226–27, 256–57, 278–79, 286, 440, 444, 455, 459, 467–68, 470, 472, 476, 479, 483

morality, 11, 29, 207, 463

Morishita-Miki, Aidan, 105, 477

Morrison, Aimée, 364

Moschopedis, Eric, 139–41, 464

mothers, 14, 22–23, 132–33, 157, 221, 226, 292, 444, 453, 462, 479

movement, 58, 75, 84, 102, 107, 118, 128, 158, 173, 191, 201, 204, 231, 281, 287, 289, 298, 330, 389, 399

Müller, Hanna Sybille, 182, 472, 476

multiplicity, 14, 41, 43, 98, 182, 407

Mumford, Meg, 69–70

mundanity, 26, 34, 98, 131, 147, 155, 187, 229, 280, 283, 285, 291, 308, 335, 340, 347, 429

Murray, Janet H., 57–58, 176, 178, 312

museums, 9, 21, 26, 88, 149, 178, 220, 346, 356, 364, 417

music, 80, 86, 135–36, 180, 186, 234–36, 256–57, 305, 307, 334, 341–42, 391, 400, 457–58, 461, 470, 473, 477, 479, 484

live, 179, 201, 257, 341, 351, 465, 483

musicians, 59, 201, 215, 314, 355–56, 476

mystery, 26–27, 39, 67, 290–291, 296, 309, 339–40, 348–49, 472

N

Naokwegijig, Bruce, 215, 464

"Narcissistic Spectatorship in Immersive and One-on-One Performance" (Zaiontz), 44, 79, 130, 211, 362

narratives, 30, 83, 86, 104, 113, 163, 177, 288, 292, 310, 312, 344, 348, 432, 438

narrators, 119, 178, 431, 482

National Centre for Truth and Reconciliation, 438

National Film Board, 22, 226, 462

National Theatre, 22, 462

navigation, 9, 58–59, 84–85, 111, 117, 121, 177, 179, 190, 207, 211, 247–48, 251, 259, 346, 348, 474

Necessary Angel Theatre Company, 145, 468

neighbourhoods, 58, 86, 96, 125, 127, 141, 196, 232, 262, 286, 290, 373, 417–18, 433

neighbours, 119, 121, 125, 127, 131, 141, 180, 216, 232, 257, 418, 464

neoliberalism, 44, 88, 112–13, 139, 165, 210–212, 272–74, 352–54

"Neoliberal Scandals" (Steen), 44, 210, 272–74

networks, 103, 158, 215–16, 322–23, 354, 379

New York City, NY, 143, 312, 353, 361, 457, 480

New York Times, 202, 307–09, 364

Niedzwiecki, Jacob, 41, 43, 328

Nield, Sophie, 243, 259, 404

nightmares, 194, 351, 401–02, 479

Nightswimming, 27, 75, 201, 431, 484

Nikoleit, Sophie, 118, 122, 146, 152, 370

Nock, Samantha, 438–39

noise, 41, 86, 182, 221, 245, 250–251, 259–61, 263, 282, 351–52, 443, 482

Nolan, Yvette, 27, 74–76

non-participation, 37, 69, 316, 318, 421, 424, 426

Nordic Larp, 7, 148

Northan, Rebecca, 230, 269, 304–05, 406–07, 417, 457

novels, 83, 406

novices, 30, 179, 389, 439

Nowhere Collective, 262–63

O

obligations, 53–54, 56, 109, 135, 216, 330, 341, 343, 424, 439

O'Brien, Keely, 136, 195–96, 238, 456, 461, 475, 478

observers, 17, 19, 92

O'Connell, Stephen, 58, 120, 305, 458, 468

O'Donnell, Darren, 154, 465

Ono, Yoko, 311–12

opposition, 29, 67, 70–71, 99, 117, 153–54, 183, 192, 263, 298, 311 oppression, 89, 162, 353, 408

organizations, 10, 98, 296, 301, 422, 433

Osawabine, Joe, 215, 464

Ottawa, ON, 12, 42, 117, 382, 469, 477

outsiders, 178, 186, 310, 340-341, 425, 427

ownership, 114-15, 140, 176

P

Paintin, Gemma, 140, 464

Palani, Suzan, 314, 462

pandemic, 12-13, 26, 35, 157, 202-03, 207, 220, 234-36, 245, 255-56, 258, 289-90, 307, 323, 460, 475, 483

panic, 15, 37, 176, 186, 351, 357

Parasram, Jivesh, 428

parents, 10, 14, 101, 131, 155, 299, 427, 458

parks, 105, 140-141, 173, 226, 341, 386, 409, 460, 467

parties, 9, 26, 59, 94, 143, 157, 164, 178, 224, 308, 342, 372, 407, 424, 428, 468, 477

partners, 35, 42, 107, 135, 155, 157, 196, 230, 234, 291, 304, 338, 407, 433, 443, 456

partnerships, 130, 282, 305, 411, 421

Pasolini, Pier Paolo, 434, 470

passivity, 17-18, 69, 92, 191

paths, 11, 30, 32, 42, 58-59, 83-84, 86, 116-17, 164, 190, 224, 226, 282, 302, 340, 401, 426-27, 481

patterns, 14, 34, 50, 58, 102, 125, 127, 322, 333, 335, 390

pauses, 15, 58, 76, 190, 234, 270, 400, 429

pavement, 229, 280, 320, 340

Pavis, Patrice, 70-71

Pedron, Aurélie, 64, 174, 257, 468

pen pals, 136, 331

perimeters, 46, 76, 256, 269, 321, 328, 434

permeability, 39, 170

permissions, 78, 94, 96, 206, 334, 349

personalization, 45, 212, 290

personas, 47, 64, 204, 246, 351, 465

phenomenology, 41, 147, 151, 190, 259, 283, 390

philosophy, 200, 301

pianos, 397, 424, 434

Piepzna-Samarasinha, Leah Lakshmi, 322-23, 353-54

Pine, Joseph, 362-63

podcasts, 120-121, 246, 289, 305, 373

poetry, 69, 83, 88, 158, 192, 280, 312, 432, 475-76

Pokémon, 33, 291, 302

politics, 84, 109-10, 115-16, 120-122, 130, 143-44, 149, 153, 155, 169, 208, 213, 301-02, 346, 353, 379, 384, 456, 458, 466

Pollard, Deborah, 252-53

Popcorn Galaxies, 136, 195-96, 227, 238, 429, 461, 475, 478

porches, 157, 342, 397, 483

Porte Parole, 111, 278, 455

portraits, 33, 55, 98, 288, 393, 395

positionalities, 14, 41, 76, 154, 182, 186, 215, 277, 287, 305, 319, 338, 428

Postalian, Brian, 64, 207, 454, 474

postdrama, 70, 179-80, 183, 210, 243, 249-50, 357, 405

posters, 34, 46-47, 232, 314, 373

Post-it Notes, 46-47, 196, 475

principles, 34, 65, 95, 110, 112, 158, 229, 260, 273, 296, 320, 344, 372, 380

Prismatic Festival, 464

privilege, 1, 6, 14, 19, 41, 63, 347, 394, 398, 409

protection, 106, 335, 379

protests, 224, 226, 251, 274-75, 302, 308, 321, 355-57, 444, 461

provocations, 2, 122, 130, 260, 287, 300, 422

proximities, 13, 37, 95, 119-20, 122, 131, 169, 194, 201, 206, 236, 250, 266, 362, 414

Proximity Lab, 247, 415

public spaces, 60, 86, 201, 227, 282, 300, 419, 464, 483

puppets, 101, 295, 308

PuSh International Performing Arts Festival, 43, 453

Pushoff Festival, 99, 234–35, 456, 473, 478–79

puzzles, 9–10, 14, 31, 42–43, 83, 85, 161, 163–65, 243, 251, 299, 309, 346, 348, 368–69, 379, 424, 429–30, 478, 482

Q

quarantines, 113, 184, 207

Queen's University, 1, 12, 177, 226, 277, 460, 504–05

Queen Video, 163, 480

queerness, 321, 407, 410, 454, 457

questionnaires, 151, 245, 342, 475

Quintana, Christine, 135, 465

Quirt, Brian, 201, 484

R

racism, 169, 202, 206, 209

radishes, 201, 342–43, 345, 477

Radix Theatre, 95–96, 232, 250, 373, 443, 481

Rancière, Jacques, 18–19, 43, 109, 115–16, 120, 122, 152, 190, 192, 413–15

randomness, 29–33, 43, 50, 62, 80, 110, 126, 174–75, 299–300, 311–12, 442

Ravensbergen, Lisa Cooke, 77, 215, 226, 246, 456, 460

realities, 63, 65–66, 76, 89, 91, 152, 192, 214, 256, 263, 276, 307–08, 418

realness, 262, 275, 279, 285, 287, 318, 339, 421

Reason, Matthew, 152, 370

Reddit, 33–34, 36

re-enactments, 20–21, 23, 114, 322, 355, 358

regrets, 30, 93, 292

Relational Aesthetics (Bourriaud), 34, 88, 129–31, 134, 214, 433

relationality, 35, 112, 157, 194, 214–17, 219, 237, 382, 413

remembrance, 60, 63, 343, 439

Renyk, Grahame, 386, 409

repetition, 165, 171, 252–53, 278, 355, 432

replayability, 43, 165

replicas, 20, 52, 111, 155, 165, 354–56

representation, 21, 51, 69–70, 112, 179, 183, 191, 219, 242, 308, 357, 391, 416

resistance, 67, 90, 115–16, 146, 231, 276, 299, 318, 336–38, 346, 389, 408, 425, 444

responsibility, 11, 38–39, 47, 105–06, 144, 148, 161, 210, 215–16, 243, 273, 323, 343

restaurants, 130, 266, 304, 363, 407, 414

restrictions, 143, 203, 294, 298, 300

revelations, 53, 95, 104–05, 107, 280, 338, 358, 398, 471, 477

revolutions, 70, 104, 159, 253, 263, 278, 299, 302–03, 309, 322, 392, 432, 434–35, 456, 470

rewards, 31, 105, 205, 209, 257, 298, 302

rhythms, 122, 179, 202

Ridout, Nicholas, 134, 154

Rimini Protokoll, 129, 225, 286, 453

Roach, Joseph, 388

Robinson, Dylan, 76, 215, 336, 425–27

Rodriguez, Miquelon, 202, 475

Rose, Eric, 184, 478

Rose, Richard, 143, 145, 480

Rouge National Urban Park, 58, 101, 467

Rushton, Mia, 141, 464

S

Sack, Daniel, 9, 11, 426

sacredness, 75–76

safety, 25, 40, 45, 49, 94, 143, 273, 401–02, 408, 478

Salen, Katie, 78, 99, 128, 172, 229, 260–261, 288, 293, 298, 370

Salverson, Julie, 439, 441

sandwiches, 201, 212, 459

scale, 6, 13, 109, 125, 131, 256–57, 364, 432–33

scenarios, 21, 25, 64, 80, 84, 169, 230, 257, 277–78, 304, 369, 406–07

Schechner, Richard, 191, 332–33

schedules, 3, 96, 161, 183

schemas, 97, 421

Schexnider, Jarin, 333–34, 466

Schneider, Rebecca, 23, 355, 357–58

Schütz, Theresa, 118, 122, 146, 152, 370

scissors, 100, 147, 154, 371, 464

scope, 12, 86, 128, 131, 146, 151, 226, 244, 303, 316

scores, 86, 266, 311–12, 369, 467

seats, 76, 92, 100, 192, 194, 206, 212, 396, 406, 429

secrets, 12, 14, 20, 164, 236–38, 261, 282, 290–291, 304, 310, 337–41, 348, 363, 401

security, 39–40, 45, 92, 178, 183, 290, 311

seduction, 273–75, 382

self-reflexivity, 25, 47, 119, 151, 213, 249

service, 31, 67, 90, 94, 131–32, 152, 155–56, 202, 273, 322, 353, 363, 379, 415, 423, 433

settlers, 75, 102, 207, 214, 217, 242, 426, 438, 445

Settlers of Catan, 207, 242, 299

sex, 155, 230, 321–23, 407, 410, 454, 458

Shakespeare, William, 66, 183, 291

Shannon, Claude, 260

Shklovsky, Viktor, 280–281

shoes, 5, 52, 55, 94, 147, 149, 243, 251, 269, 304, 306, 363, 401

Sicart, Miguel, 8, 298–99

signs, 5, 60, 96, 187, 235, 405, 439–41, 461

silence, 19, 67, 170, 195, 221, 245, 247, 255–56, 302, 316, 320, 401, 414–15, 443

Simic, Lucy, 305, 458, 468

Simming (Magelssen), 21, 104–05, 149, 355

Simpson, Leanne Betasamosake, 102–03, 106, 214–16, 318

simultaneity, 86, 222, 249

singing, 9, 27, 35, 75–76, 131, 195, 200–201, 203, 210, 221, 235, 246, 252, 318, 347, 356, 475

Single Thread Theatre Company, 174, 318, 380, 398, 454, 463

Situationism, 117–18, 139

sleep, 42–43, 47, 67, 135, 194, 328, 330, 399–402, 479

Small, Ambrose, 406, 454

snacks, 2, 369, 397

snakes, 201, 298, 391

snow, 22, 398, 434, 443–44

Snyder-Young, Dani, 14, 295, 371

soccer, 165, 172, 202, 370

sociability, 2, 129, 131, 433

society, 6, 9, 71, 88–89, 109, 112, 115, 117, 130, 144, 162, 200, 208, 231, 352, 380, 424, 433, 438

solidarity, 251, 415–16, 429, 460

songs, 35, 42–43, 85, 102, 182–83, 194–95, 201, 235–37, 257, 277, 308, 318, 328, 347, 389, 459

sound design, 27, 246, 305, 456, 465, 471

soundtracks, 101, 194, 334, 468

Soutar, Annabel, 111, 455

souvenirs, 205, 235, 336, 343, 386

sovereignty, 29, 318–19, 445

speeches, 25, 111, 226–27, 230, 372, 407, 438, 455, 472

spontaneity, 49, 204, 295, 406, 442

sports, 56, 242, 298, 370

Stanislavski, Konstantin, 69

Steen, Shannon, 44, 210, 272–75

Steer, Nikola, 155–56, 204, 466

Stenhouse, James, 140, 464

storytelling, 79, 210, 215, 248, 276, 305, 363, 389, 430, 439

Stratford Festival, 329

streets, 42, 104, 117, 119, 128, 157, 262, 340–341, 349, 351, 417

strolling, 117, 243, 280, 340, 434

Suits, Bernard, 78, 172, 231, 260–261, 266, 340

Sum, Amanda, 234–37, 473–74

summer, 26, 44, 53, 86, 91, 104–05, 117, 141, 202, 206, 216, 221, 226, 280, 286, 386, 409, 438, 475

SummerWorks Performance Festival, 140, 155, 201, 335, 417, 453–55, 458–59, 461, 464, 466, 470–471, 482, 484

superheroes, 440

surreality, 59, 91, 136, 179, 201, 223, 300, 351, 354, 400, 404

surveillance, 14, 31, 45, 92

Świontek, Slawomir, 52–53, 177

Switzky, Lawrence, 253

Sy, Jovanni, 26, 475

sympathy, 112, 404

synchronicity, 27, 117, 171, 178, 201–02, 220, 234, 237, 287, 391, 400

T

tables, 26–27, 45–46, 63, 92, 101–02, 111, 140, 179, 195, 206, 212, 224, 267, 279, 315, 386, 393, 414, 431, 434

tabletop gaming, 7, 43, 247

tactics, 47, 80, 115, 186, 204, 208, 337, 421

tactility, 22, 46, 183, 185, 280, 282, 401

Tannahill, Jordan, 22–24, 58, 177, 204, 219, 314, 462, 468

Tape Escape, 54, 58, 163–65, 179, 454, 471, 480, 484

Tarver, Jennifer, 58, 468

taxonomies, 172, 190, 224, 267

teams, 1, 3, 5, 30–31, 33, 41–42, 54–56, 105, 113, 174–75, 179, 221, 242, 255, 259, 369, 426–27, 473–74, 477, 485

technology, 22, 83, 86, 95, 155, 204, 219–21, 309, 364, 476

teenagers, 54–55, 170–171, 401

televisions, 151, 309, 355–56, 406, 411

tension, 12, 45, 53–54, 57, 67–68, 79, 93, 99, 110–112, 145, 163, 174, 176, 207, 243, 286–87, 298–99, 320, 347, 364

Tepperman, Julie, 25, 45, 163, 169–70, 289, 457, 460, 484

territory, 17, 38, 59, 84, 113, 118, 217, 236, 242, 265, 276, 290, 314, 424–27, 439

Theatre Replacement, 63, 410–411, 456

theatrical frame, 47, 66–67, 119, 146, 170, 229, 241, 279, 338, 356

theatricality, 66, 265, 276, 278, 355, 363, 384

themes, 31, 53–54, 56, 69–70, 85, 111, 132, 213, 236–37, 261, 263, 310, 330, 363, 388, 408, 477

therapy, 25, 159, 386, 415, 481

Thompson, Andy, 174–75, 390

Thompson, Meredith, 280, 397

Thompson, Nato, 154, 383

thrills, 11, 32, 37–39, 171, 186–87, 235, 262, 270, 277, 287, 295, 317–18, 338, 348

tickets, 11, 44, 79, 143, 165, 183, 193, 212, 269, 272, 274

TikTok, 5, 307–08

togetherness, 33, 121, 201–02, 219, 416

tools, 92, 187, 257, 263, 342, 353, 364, 368, 398, 411, 423

Toronto, ON, 70, 74, 86, 141, 201, 231–32, 253, 259, 261, 340–341, 355–56, 364, 369–70, 417–19, 453–55, 457–62, 465–66, 469–75, 478, 480–484

touch, 18, 23, 38, 102, 153–54, 159, 172, 174, 182–85, 194, 196, 231, 256–57, 282, 317, 331, 340, 343, 358

tourism, 91, 149, 336, 338, 363

tours, 2, 22, 180, 184, 196, 215, 417–19, 457, 472

transformations, 34, 50–51, 60, 95, 106, 122, 143, 200, 278, 281, 333, 335, 339, 343–44, 387, 422, 432–33, 468

Transformative Power of Performance, The (Fischer-Lichte), 49–51, 154, 183, 200, 281

transitions, 9, 95, 128, 427

tropes, 24, 102, 135, 155, 178, 305, 406–08

Trump, Donald, 121, 307

truth, 81, 191, 208, 295, 309–10, 319, 338, 343, 346, 418, 423, 438

Truth and Reconciliation Commission of Canada, 76, 336, 425, 438, 441

Twister, 46, 230

Twitter, 6, 140–141, 330, 353, 418, 438, 464

U

uncertainty, 25, 30, 32, 37–39, 57, 62, 177–78, 231, 260, 443

V

vaccines, 113, 185, 207, 232

Vanderham, Jacob, 201, 470

variability, 43, 62, 165, 224, 300, 311

ventriloquism, 247, 279, 295

Venzon, Hazel, 314, 462

verbs, 44, 99, 151, 153, 210, 223, 281, 364

video, 1, 22, 35, 54, 100, 114–15, 121, 163–64, 179, 212, 220–221, 308, 328, 356, 373, 389, 399, 473, 480

video games, 7, 43, 57, 146, 204, 213, 251, 298–302, 329, 370, 396, 456 viewers, 19, 31, 57, 74, 121, 129, 152, 220, 241, 281, 289, 311, 346, 382–84

violence, 18, 65, 94, 97, 122, 159–60, 207, 214, 349, 356, 358, 391

visual art, 7, 86, 88, 129, 289, 336, 363, 382, 384

visual description, 226, 316

vulnerability, 1, 172, 187, 194–96, 379–80, 382, 439

W

Waern, Annika, 309, 372

Walker, David Gagnon, 95–97, 431, 482

war, 18, 23, 120–121, 149, 207, 242–43, 250, 266, 305, 314, 355, 396

Ware, Syrus Marcus, 159

Washburn, Michaela, 50–51, 180, 380, 386, 415, 471

water, 27, 45, 59–60, 128, 152, 216, 246, 263, 269, 302, 334, 352, 354, 373, 393, 399, 418

Watkin, Jessica, 317, 321

waves, 45, 58–59, 104, 118, 178, 184–85, 224, 227, 246, 468

wax, 247, 414–15

weather, 5, 52

Whitehorse, Yukon, 12, 42, 117, 340, 469

Wickstrom, Maurya, 273, 363

Wikipedia, 6, 20, 33, 49, 98, 128, 146, 181, 223, 260, 277, 289, 309, 311, 344, 417, 442

Wilde-Peltier, Jessica, 215, 464

Willes, Christopher, 282, 472

Winnipeg, MB, 314, 462

winter, 22, 47, 63–64, 106, 109, 135, 143, 165, 169, 174, 215, 217, 342, 347, 355–56, 373, 399, 406, 439, 443–44

wizards, 54, 242, 310

Wolfe Island, ON, 246, 354

Wong, Adrienne, 42, 117–19, 202, 469, 479

workers, 13, 179, 224, 274, 299, 301

workshops, 216, 330, 442

worries, 9, 27, 35, 46, 55, 58, 60, 161, 236, 405, 484

Wurtzler, Steve, 219–20

Y

Yamamoto, Maiko, 456

Yarrow Collective, 216–17, 476

Yee, David, 253

Yoon, Sherry J., 26, 476

Z

Zaiontz, Keren, 44, 59, 79, 106, 130, 211, 286, 362

Zarrilli, Phillip B., 20–21, 405

Zerihan, Rachel, 135, 269, 319, 337

Zimmerman, Eric, 7–8, 78, 99, 128, 172, 229, 260–261, 288, 293, 298, 370

zombies, 146, 149, 174–75, 341

Zoom, 1, 12, 34–35, 202, 220–221, 314, 328, 346, 387, 394, 430, 469, 474

Zuppa Theatre Co, 79, 84, 261, 346, 364, 369, 372, 455, 482

ANSWER KEY

ANSWER KEY

ANTS

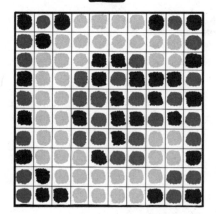

ANSWER: C

BEING LOST

AVJOASER ⓈA R A J E V O
OTRLMEAN M O N T R Ⓔ A L
IXAAFLH H A L I F A X
IYVK K Y I Ⓥ
OONOTTR T O R O N T O
HWIOTEHSRE W H I T Ⓔ H O R S E
ARADA D A R A A
VRVENCUOA V A Ⓝ C O U V E R

ANSWER: 7

EMBODIMENT

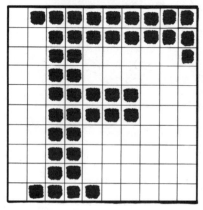

x=8 y=6   ANSWER: F

FIRST-PERSON SHOOTER

ANSWER: 3

ANSWER KEY

GAME OVER, PLAY AGAIN?

ANSWER: G

INSTRUMENTALITY

	ROGER CAILLOIS	NEW SOCIETIES	CHER	
	FREUD	RACHEL FENSHAM	NEW AGE ATTITUDES	
	SCISSORS	CHOIR! CHOIR! CHOIR!	IBSEN	
	AMANDA SUM	UTOPIA	BRICK THROWING	

ANSWER: H

MAIL

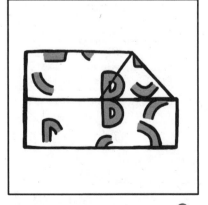

ANSWER: B

MOB

ANSWER: A

ANSWER KEY

ONTOLOGICAL DUALITY

$ 365 = [100] + [100] + [100] + [50] + [10] + [5]$

$ 113 = [100] + [10] + [1] + [1]$

$ 732 = [100] + [100] + [100] + [100] + [20] + [10] + [1]$

$ 69 = [50] + [10] + [5] + [1] + [1]$

$ 329 = [100] + [100] + [100] + [20] + [5] + [1] + [1]$

$ 198 = [100] + [50] + [20] + [10] + [5] + [1] + [1]$

$ 72 = [50] + [50] + [1]$

$[100] : 12 \qquad [1] : 2$

$12 \div 2 = 6$ ANSWER: 6

OSTRANENIE

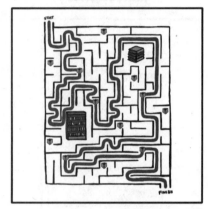

ANSWER: 5

RELATION

(WHEN HELD UP TO THE LIGHT)

ANSWER: D

SEEKING

"NUMBER OF BIRDS BELOW"

ANSWER: 2

ANSWER KEY

STRUMPET

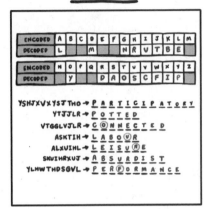

ENCODED	A	B	C	D	E	F	G	H	I	J	K	L	M
DECODED	L			M				N	R	V	T	B	E

ENCODED	N	O	P	Q	R	S	T	U	V	W	X	Y	Z
DECODED		Y			D	A	O	S	C	F	I	P	

YSHJXVXYSJ THO → P A R T I C I P A T O R Y
YTJJLR → P O T T E D
VTGGLVJLR → C O N N E C T E D
ASKTIH → L A B O U R
ALXVIHL → L E I S U R E
SKVIHRXVJ → A B S U R D I S T
YLMWTHDSGVL → P E R F O R M A N C E

ANSWER: 4

TEXT MESSAGES

"RIVER"   **ANSWER: E**

THINGS

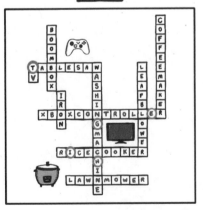

ANSWER: 8

WINNING

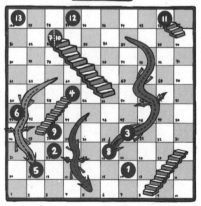

ANSWER: 1